# LUKE'S THRILLING GOSPEL

## BY THE SAME AUTHOR

# Luke's Thrilling Gospel

## Ivor Powell

**KREGEL PUBLICATIONS**
Grand Rapids, Michigan 49501

*Luke's Thrilling Gospel,* by Ivor Powell. © 1965 by Ivor
Powell. Published in 1984 by Kregel Publications, a division
of Kregel, Inc., P. O. Box 2607, Grand Rapids, Michigan
49501. All rights reserved.

**Library of Congress Cataloging-in-Publication Data**

Powell, Ivor, 1910-
    Luke's Thrilling Gospel.

    Reprint. Originally published: Grand Rapids, Mich.:
Zondervan Publishing House, c1965.
    Includes Index.
    1. Bible. N. T. Luke—Commentaries. 2. Bible. N. T.
Luke—Homiletical use. I. Title.
BS2595.3.P6      1984          226'.407          84-9637
                                                      CIP

ISBN 0-8254-3513-7

2 3 4 5 6 printing/year 94 93 92 91 90

# CONTENTS

# 8      Contents

# INTRODUCTION

Let me confess at the outset that this commentary has been written to help young ministers in the preparation of their sermons. During earlier years when I was the Pastor of a very busy church; when innumerable duties claimed my attention all the week, I often studied into the early hours of Sunday morning trying desperately to find something new for my long-suffering congregation. When my search seemed to fail my soul became a little alarmed. Again and again I turned to my commentaries only to discover they supplied all kinds of information which I did not need. *Oh, for a book to help me get a sermon!* As the evangelist of the Baptist Church I have travelled in many countries, but in them all I discovered other men acquainted with those frustrating searches for sermon material. Sometimes they were not able to remain in their studies as long as they would have desired; unfortunately they had to do the work of six men. To help these wonderful servants of God, this volume has been produced.

Readers will quickly discover that dates, references to ancient manuscripts, quotations from the early church fathers, and certain other material have been cut to a minimum. Wherever they were essential to the proper understanding of the text, they have been included. Yet my constant aim has been to make sermon preparation an increasing delight. If some of my readers desire additional scholastic details concerning the subject, I heartily recommend F. L. Godet's Commentary on the Gospel of Luke.*As far as I am aware he covers the widest field of scholastic research. The Rev. Norval Geldenhuys is one of the more recent authors, and his commentary now included in *The New International Commentary on the New Testament* represents the best in modern theological publications. Within this volume are several references to the works of these and other authors. Bishop Ryle and the Rev. William Barclay produced volumes on Luke's Gospel and their works provided much delight as they were used in study preparation for the production of this volume. Nevertheless nearly all the contents of this book came out of forty years of continuing study. What by God's grace I received and tried to proclaim, I now pass on to my younger brothers in the ministry.

At the outset I had to decide whether to use the text of the Authorized Version or that of a modern translation. Let it be candidly admitted

---

*Frederic L. Godet, *Commentary on Luke,* Kregel Publications, 1981

that some of the expressions used in the King James' version are archaic and difficult to understand. Some of the more recent translations are, to say the least, beautiful. Should I then use the script of a translation or stay with the old version? My own evangelistic meetings supplied the answer. I always invite my listeners to read responsively the Word of God, and having observed the results I know that the roots of the Authorized version go deep into the affections of millions of Christians. Throughout this commentary, therefore, I shall use the King James version of the Bible, but as readers will discover, there are many places where other translations are freely quoted and compared with the basic narrative. Students acquainted with the earlier commentary, *John's Wonderful Gospel* *will recognize the old pattern. Each verse is expounded; each chapter divided into convenient sections. At the end of each section, homilies are provided to help ministers in sermon preparation.

Finally I would pay sincere tribute to my publisher. It only remains to add that Luke's Gospel is indeed one of the most thrilling documents ever written. It is my sincere hope that this volume will contribute something to the understanding of this great section of the Word of God.

Santa Barbara,                                              IVOR POWELL
California.
1964.

---

*Ivor Powell, *John's Wonderful Gospel,* Kregel Publications, 1983.

# THE BELOVED PHYSICIAN

The entry of Luke into the sacred records of Scripture was so unannounced and unexpected that casual readers seldom noticed his arrival. Unlike John the Baptist whose coming was announced earlier by the angel; unlike Matthew, Mark, and John of whom much was written, Luke came from obscurity into the full glare of apostolic publicity. There was no fanfare of heralding trumpets; his arrival was revealed only by the appearance of a personal pronoun in a manuscript which he himself wrote.

"And a vision appeared unto Paul in the night; There stood a man of Macedonia, and prayed him saying, Come over into Macedonia and help us. And after he had seen the vision, immediately WE endeavoured to go into Macedonia, assuredly gathering that the Lord had called US for to preach the Gospel unto them" (Acts 15: 9–10).

From the beginning of the Christian era, two books, *Luke's Gospel*, and *The Acts of the Apostles*, have been credited to Luke, yet nowhere in these writings does the author's name appear. All the information concerning this gracious man is derived from seven brief passages of scripture. Colossians 4: 10–14; Philemon 24; 2 Timothy 4: 11; Luke 1: 1–4; Acts 16: 10–17; Acts 20: 5–21; Acts 27: 1–28: 16. Much speculation has been made regarding his nationality, but it remains extremely doubtful whether any man can write authoritatively on this subject. Some writers expressed the opinion that Luke was a Jew of Antioch, but others asserted he was a Syrian physician living in that same city. The preface to this volume explained why little mention will be made of endless dates and copious references to ancient manuscripts. An exception is made in this instance because certain passages from this Gospel will inevitably revive the subject of the Author's nationality and profession. There appears to be a great amount of support for the assertion that Luke was a Gentile physician. The Rev. Norval Geldenhuys in his commentary on Luke's Gospel (page 17), writes as follows:

"The anti-Marcionite Prologue to the Third Gospel (between A.D. 160 and 180), which survives in both Greek and Latin, gives the following account: 'Luke was an Antiochian of Syria, a physician by profession. He was a disciple of the apostles and later accompanied Paul until the latter's martyrdom. He served the Lord without distraction (or without blame), having neither wife nor children, and at the age of eighty-four he fell asleep in Boeota, full of the Holy Spirit. While there were

13

already Gospels previously in existence—that according to Matthew written in Judea, and that according to Mark written in Italy—Luke, moved by the Holy Spirit, composed the whole of his Gospel in the parts about Achaia. In his prologue he makes this very point clear, that other Gospels had been written before his, and that it was necessary to expound to the Gentile believers the accurate account of the (divine) dispensation, so that they should not be perverted by Jewish fables, nor be deceived by heretical and vain imaginations and thus err from the truth. And so right at the beginning he relates for us the nativity of John—a most essential matter, for John is the beginning of the Gospel, being our Lord's forerunner and companion both in the preparation of the Gospel, in the administration of baptism, and in the fellowship of the Spirit. This ministry (of John) had been mentioned by one of the Twelve Prophets (Malachi). And afterwards the same Luke wrote the Acts of the Apostles'."

At page 21 of the same volume, Geldenhuys further states, "The statement of the anti-Marcionite Prologue, which also occurs in Eusebius and Jerome, that Luke the author of the Gospel, was of Gentile descent and a former inhabitant of Antioch, also finds corroboration in the Gospel and Acts. With regard to the Gentile descent of the author, the books, e.g., show signs throughout that they were written for Gentiles by a person who himself was of Gentile descent. This is evident from such facts as that (a) the citations in Luke and Acts from the Old Testament are made from the Septuagint (Greek) translation and not from the Hebrew; (b) In the Gospel, the Lord is addressed not as 'Rabbi' but by the Greek titles *Didaskalos* (Teacher) and *Epistates* (Master); in other instances Hebrew names are avoided, or superseded by Greek names or paraphrases (e.g. 4: 2; 22: 40; 23: 33, and others); in the few cases where a Hebrew name is indeed retained, an explanation of the name is added (Acts 4: 36). (c) The author, unlike Matthew and Mark, never makes Jesus use Aramaic words, and only very occasionally the typically Jewish amen (verily); (d) The author is free from all Jewish particularism."[1]

From his own memoirs we glean the fact that Luke first met Paul in the thriving seaport town of Troas, the important gateway between the civilizations of West and East. Constantly ships were arriving there from the distant parts of the world, and almost daily along the trade routes of Asia, merchantmen brought their wares to this export center. There could hardly have been a more promising place for a young man to begin his medical career.

---

[1] *Commentary on the Gospel of Luke* by J. Norval Geldenhuys, London; Marshall, Morgan and Scott Ltd. *New London Commentary on the New Testament;* Grand Rapids, Michigan, U.S.A. Wm. B. Eerdmaus, *New International Commentary on the New Testament.*

It is not possible to be sure of the details of Luke's conversion and call to Christ's service, but the late Dr. F. B. Meyer expressed an opinion which, to say the least, deserves consideration. The revered doctor referred to Acts 15: 6–7, and emphasized the predicament which temporarily threatened the ruination of Paul's ministry. "Now when they had gone through Phrygia, and the region of Galatia, *and were forbidden of the Holy Spirit to preach the Word in Asia,* After they were come to Mysia, they assayed to go into Bithynia, but *the Spirit suffered them not.* And they passing by Mysia came down to Troas." These simple statements cannot be fully understood unless the reader takes time to examine a map of Paul's journeys. Had Paul been forbidden to preach in some specific city, he would have marched to a new center and possibly could have preached again within hours. To be forbidden to preach in a continent when he was still hundreds of miles from its borders meant an enforced silence that even Paul at that time could not have explained. We know now that a door was opening in Macedonia; we know also that open doors can suddenly close. To be present in time to take advantage of the new situation necessitated an enforced march. Had Paul stayed months in the market places of Asia, Europe might never have heard the Gospel from his lips. However, and this is most important, an exacting march of five, six, or more hundred miles over and through inhospitable territory would leave its mark upon God's servants. Dr. Meyer spoke of the rugged terrain and high plateaus through which the missionary party would be obliged to travel and suggested the possibility that when the journey was finished, Paul may have needed medical attention. When Timothy went in search of a doctor and found Luke, he made history.

We must not be surprised by Dr. Meyer's suggestion for there are times when God moves in mysterious ways, wonders to perform. There are occasions when God's miraculous power instantly banishes disease; at other times God prefers to work in different ways. Even Paul had to recognise this fact for on one notable occasion sickness deprived him of the services of a trusted co-worker. ". . . but Trophimus have I left at Miletum sick"—2 Timothy 4: 20. It should be remembered also that since Troas was still part of Asia, Paul's instructions forbade holding meetings in that busy city. How then could the physician hear the missionary's message? There is much to be said for Dr. Meyer's opinion; the great theologian might have been nearer to the truth than some people would admit.

If the young doctor came to visit the needy traveller, he would talk with the patient; and try to ascertain the case history of the man needing treatment. Possibly he returned several times, and it is not too much to believe that the impact of Paul's personality and the thrilling quality of his message brought the physician to Christ. Probably the doctor joyfully anticipated every encounter with the great preacher but when he heard Paul had been instructed to continue his journey, he became alarmed. Premonitions warned him that his new friend would still need help; that soon, a body already taxed to the limit, would be undergoing increased strain and hardship. The inviting frontiers of Europe were both thrilling and menacing. There was a prison in Philippi; and mobs in the city. What would this wonderful man do if his body and spirit were both broken? The more Dr. Luke considered these frightening possibilities, the more insistent became a whisper within his soul. Could there be a place for a doctor in that brave little band of Christian warriors? Could he preach with his hands whilst Paul preached with his voice? Would it be possible for him to visit the aged and the sick in the churches whilst his famous companion stood in the synagogues to proclaim the Master's message? We have no way of knowing how long these questions troubled the physician; we only know that when Paul and his companions walked to the quayside to board their ship, they were thrilled to see the young doctor, bag in hand, hurrying to join their party. Long afterward Luke wrote: "And after Paul had seen the vision, immediately *we* endeavoured to go into Macedonia, assuredly gathering that the Lord had called *us* to preach the Gospel unto them."

Let it be repeated once again that this is only a theory; an idea advanced by Dr. F. B. Meyer, but, to say the least, it seems logical, pleasant, commendable. Thereafter Luke was one of the most faithful of Paul's companions, remaining with the Apostle until the guillotine promoted the missionary to higher service. The New Testament reveals that Luke won for himself the cherished title, *the beloved physician.* Whilst Paul wrote his gospel in the minds of his audience, Luke engraved his image on their hearts. It is worthy of constant consideration that Luke's medical skill was never at variance with the miraculous powers of Paul's ministry. When Paul's touch brought relief to sufferers, the doctor praised the Lord for answered prayer; when Paul's ministry seemed to fall short of what was needed, Luke smiled, and thought, "I'm still needed." Perhaps while Paul preached by the hour in the synagogues and market places, Luke went looking for ailing Christians in the back streets of the great cities. Paul became accustomed to great crowds; Luke specialized in individuals. Both were fishers of men, but whereas Paul fished with a net; Luke used a line— his trophies were all hand picked! Often there was no need for Paul to heal for Luke had been there first, preventing disease. This was a greater ministry, for a fence on top of a cliff was better than an ambulance at the bottom!

Luke has often been compared with Mark, for both authors were greatly indebted to their companions for the inspiration which made

their Gospels possible. Mark was the emanuensis of Simon Peter; he
was the boy who made copious notes whenever the great Apostle
preached. When he finally marshalled his facts, and placed them in
chronological order, his book began to take shape. Ultimately the
whole church was thrilled by the appearance of what most scholars
agree was the first Gospel. Mark was its author, but in actual fact it
was the Gospel of Simon Peter. The same situation more or less existed
with Paul and Luke but the two cases were different. Luke certainly
profited by listening to Paul's exposition of the Word of God, but Paul
could not have supplied all the facts revealed in Luke's writings. With
the meticulous care of a doctor who recorded details in case histories,
this man went in search of facts and found them. There is reason to
believe that Luke was indebted to Paul, not for the facts he recorded,
but for the flaming evangelistic zeal which the apostle breathed into
the soul of the author. Simon Peter gave to Mark the letter of the
Word; Paul gave to Luke the spirit of it.

There were considerable periods of time when the itineraries of Paul
and his companions were halted. Thus, Luke had prolonged opportunities at Antioch, Jerusalem, and Rome to interview certain people
who had vital stories to tell in regard to the life and ministry of the
Lord. His medical qualifications removed the barriers of reluctant
shyness from the minds of certain famous women of the Church. Mary
would repeat the details of her pregnancy and reiterate the thrilling
account of those never-to-be-forgotten months when the creative power
of God worked in the hill country of Judea.

Thus as Luke gathered information, he realized he was in possession
of facts which had never been told; he held a priceless treasure. When
he shared his thoughts with Paul, the apostle would recognize the need
for an authentic record, and encourage his friend to produce the Gospel
in written form. It is almost certain that Matthew and Mark had by
this time published their Gospels, yet neither of these satisfied Luke's
analytical mind. His brethren had done a great job, but their story was
too circumscribed. Matthew had been absorbed with the fact that
Jesus had fulfilled the Messianic predictions; he saw only that the King
had come. Mark, that lovable boy, had been a true writer of all Peter
had preached. To him, as to his friend, it would ever be a source of
wonder that the King of Angels had made Himself of no reputation, and
had come down in the form of a servant, not to be ministered unto, but
to minister. Yet no mention had been made of those early days, for, after
all, who would be interested in the birth of a servant? Yes, Matthew
and Mark had done excellent jobs, but the irresistible urge within
Luke's heart reminded him of that other occasion when the same kind
of urge made him leave a promising practice in the city of Troas. Could
it be that the Lord wanted him to write a book? If so, he would write

a complete record. He would begin at the beginning, and would never finally put his pen aside until he had told everything. As a physician he had met innumerable patients; he had examined strong and weak bodies and had become acquainted with all kinds of people. Yet Jesus surpassed them all. His Master was perfection—absolute perfection; his Gospel would prove this point. The writings of Matthew, Mark, and Luke are known as *the synoptic gospels*—they belong to the same class of historical records, yet even a cursory glance enables the reader to know that only Luke's effort covered the entire range of those thirty-three thrilling years. In very deed and truth, this author began at the beginning and ended at the end. He commenced with the absorbing story of the Angel coming down from heaven to prepare the way for the incarnation of the Son of God; he terminated the account with the return of the same Son to the place whence He had come.

Finally, the opening statements of his gospel suggest that writing about Jesus had become a popular pastime among those who had anything to write. "Many" had produced manuscripts, and whilst some of these were destined to remain, less authentic accounts would soon be forgotten. Luke knew he had been given his greatest assignment, he was writing about his Lord. Perhaps at times his eyes grew moist but his pen moved on across the parchment. Somewhere between A.D. 67 and A.D. 80, his task was completed, and ultimately a few copies were made by the scribes of the church. Probably the aging physician hoped his book would last a long time; he could hardly have known it was to become immortal.

# The First Chapter of Luke

THEME: *Strange Events in Judah*

OUTLINE:
> I. A Doctor is Convinced. Verses 1–4
> II. A Priest is Amazed. Verses 5–25
> III. A Virgin is Thrilled. Verses 26–38
> IV. A Cousin is Excited. Verses 39–56
> V. A Father is Inspired. Verses 57–80

## SECTION ONE

*Expository Notes on Luke's Introduction to his Gospel*

Forasmuch as many have taken in hand to set forth in order a declaration of those things which are most surely believed among us, Even as they delivered them unto us, which from the beginning were eyewitnesses, and ministers of the word; It seemed good to me also, having had perfect understanding of all things from the very first, to write unto thee in order, most excellent Theophilus, That thou mightest know the certainty of those things, wherein thou wast instructed (vv. 1–4).

Writing of Luke's prologue, F. L. Godet has well said, "Not only is it written in the most classical Greek, but it reminds us by its contents of the similar preambles of the most illustrious Greek historians, especially those of Herodotus and Thucydides. The more thoroughly we examine it, the more we find of that delicacy of sentiment and refinement of mind which constitute the predominant traits of the Hellenic character ... The author does not put himself in the rank of the Christian authorities; he places himself modestly among men of the second order. He feels it necessary to excuse the boldness of his enterprize, by referring to the numerous analogous attempts that have preceded his own. He does not permit himself to undertake the work of writing a Gospel history until he has furnished himself with all the aids fitted to enable him to attain the lofty aim he sets before him. There is a striking contrast between his frank and modest attitude and that of a forger. It excludes even the ambitious part of a secretary of the apostle Paul, which tradition has not been slow to claim for the author of our Gospel." This style of introduction is unique in that its equivalent is not found anywhere else in the New Testament. Many readers hastily scan these opening verses apparently wishing to reach the more descriptive parts of Luke's story, but this is a mistake. Consideration of this prologue reveals much treasure, and promotes questions the answers to which must be intriguing. Here we have a masterly portrait of an author; here we see as nowhere else the greatness of the man through whom God gave the third Gospel. (See the homily at the end of this section.)

The New English Bible has rendered the passage thus: "Many writers have undertaken to draw up an account of the events that have happened among us, following the traditions handed down by the original eyewitnesses and servants of the Gospel. And so I in my turn, your Excellency, as one who has gone over the whole course of these events in detail, have decided to write a connected narrative for you, so as to give you authentic knowledge about the matters of which you have been informed." The *many writers* mentioned in the text suggest numerous people had commenced to write the things they knew of Jesus. It is generally conceded that both Matthew and Mark published their Gospels at an earlier date than Luke, but two men would hardly justify the use of the term "many writers." During the years which immediately followed the establishment of the church, the facts of the Gospel were handed down orally by those competent to speak. Yet it was obvious that sooner or later the need for written records would become urgent. A story often retold is apt to change; speakers are prone to interpret a message differently; and the original is thereby expanded. The *eyewitnesses* could not be expected to live for ever; what then would happen when they were promoted to higher service? Furthermore, even whilst they remained on earth, they could hardly be in several places at the same moment. The need increased therefore for an authentic record which could be faithfully copied and sent to the churches. It is the consensus of scholastic opinion that Mark's Gospel was speedily followed by Matthew's Gospel, but that there were other writings there can be no doubt. The first written accounts of the Lord's ministry were surely hailed with delight, and those responsible for the manuscripts suddenly found themselves covered with a glory they neither expected nor desired. There were other writers who probably for one reason or another coveted the same publicity, and at frequent intervals their manuscripts appeared. Some of these were forgeries; others may have been the work of sincere men whose enthusiasm exceeded their ability. It is not difficult to appreciate why Luke thought it necessary to write what he considered to be an authentic record. Furthermore, and in spite of the fact that he does

not include all the miracles and speeches of the Lord, this account is
the most complete of all the historical records. Matthew began his
account with a genealogy of the Messiah and followed this with a few
facts concerning the coming of the wise men to visit the new-born king.
Mark was content to begin with the appearance of John the Baptist.
Luke considered these records to be inadequate; he was in possession
of details, which were not only entrancingly beautiful, they were
essential to a complete chronological order of the events which God
had made possible in the hill country of Judah.

It should be noted that Luke did not attempt to write his Gospel
until he had become conversant with all the facts relevant to the story
he had to tell. There can be no doubt that he went out of his way to
obtain exclusive interviews with any person who could help; that he
spent much time eliciting information from the original eyewitnesses
of the miracles. With unending patience and meticulous care he sifted
the stories and wrote those which, in his opinion, were necessary to a
complete and accurate account of the ministry of the Master. His
reference to a "perfect understanding from the very first" suggests a
standard by which all material was either accepted or rejected.

There has been much discussion in regard to the identity of Theophilus. It is generally agreed that he was a person of exalted rank, and
probably one of considerable wealth and influence. See the homily at
the end of this section. Possibly he was a governor of some Roman
province, a man who later became a Christian. After comparing the
beginnings of the Gospel of Luke with the beginning of the Acts of
the Apostles and noting that in the latter instance Luke does not
address Theophilus as *Excellency,* Zahn and other commentators
advanced the theory that after receiving some instruction in the Christian faith, the dignitary embraced Christianity. Thus when Luke addressed his second book, or, as some think, the second half of the one
book, he addressed Theophilus as an equal. This may or may not be
true; to say the least, the thought is worthy of consideration.

Another aspect of truth must be considered. It was common practice
in the early centuries for an author to dedicate his work to some important personage in the hope the man would help to meet the cost of
reproducing the manuscript. Thus, Theophilus, whoever he might have
been, would more or less become responsible for the dissemination of
Luke's message. The Amplified New Testament renders verse 4: "My
purpose (in writing this message) is that you may know the full truth,
and understand with certainty and security against error, the accounts
(histories) and doctrines of the faith of which you have been informed
and in which you have been orally instructed." It becomes clear that
from some source this man had received tuition; that faith had been
engendered by that which he had heard. Yet faith which rests only

upon a man's testimony can hardly be as strong as necessity demands. Living faith must rest in the living word; either without the other is insufficient. Writing of this fact, Gerhard Kittel said, "The Jesus of History is valueless and unintelligible unless He be experienced and confessed by faith as the living Christ. But, if we would be true to the New Testament, we must at once reverse this judgment. The Christ of faith has no existence, is mere noise and smoke, apart from the reality of the Jesus of History. These two are utterly inseparable in the New Testament. They cannot even be thought of apart. There is no word about Christ which is not referred to Him who suffered under Pontius Pilate, and which is not at the same time intended as the Gospel applicable to all men of every time and in every place. Anyone who attempts first to separate the two, and then to describe only one of them has nothing in common with the New Testament." (*The Interpreter's Bible*, volume 8, page 29.) Hearing and acceptance of the spoken word may promote faith, but only acquaintance with the written word of Truth promotes the confidence necessary for the victorious continuance of the Christian. Luke rejoiced that his friend had heard the Gospel, but at the same time commended to his patron the record then coming into existence. We are therefore driven to the conclusion that what God has caused to be written is infinitely more important than anything any speaker may say about it.

## HOMILIES

### Study No. 1
#### PORTRAIT OF AN AUTHOR

The prologue to Luke's Gospel is unique not only in that the author explains the purpose of his writing, but also for the simple fact that nowhere else in the New Testament is this procedure repeated. In addition, although probably this was very far from the writer's mind, unwittingly he gave to the world the best pen-portrait of himself. We know from other sources that he was a physician; a companion of Paul; a trusted colleague, and a much beloved Christian. The first four verses of this Gospel contains small word-windows through which it is possible to see the author.

### His Scholarship
Mention has already been made in the expository notes that the introduction to the Gospel was written in the best classical Greek. Every commentator testifies that the man who penned those immortal words

was a man of education, breeding, and unusual talent. That the majority of the early church leaders were men of lesser brilliance became obvious when their enemies described them as *unlearned and ignorant men.* With the advent of Paul came the startling revelation that even men of learning could be attracted to the new faith. When Luke appeared on the scene this startling revelation became even more noticeable. The Gospel was not something reserved exclusively for the untutored and ignorant; it was for all men; none was too stupid to be loved; none too brilliant to be charmed.

### His Humility

Although his Gospel was destined to win the acclaim of a waiting world, never on any occasion did Luke add his own name to the record. He set out to make Christ the theme of his story and never for a single moment did he change his prearranged plans. He did not claim to be one of the original eyewitnesses, and never assumed greatness of any kind.

### His Perception

There is reason to believe that he had been able to peruse the manuscripts of Matthew and Mark; that whilst he appreciated their efforts, he nevertheless recognized they had omitted vital matters from their Gospels. Probably he was aware of the manuscripts forthcoming from other authors, and with keen perception foresaw the confusion which would result unless some authentic record could be placed in the hands of needy people. With the characteristics of a doctor, having recognized need, he proceeded to meet it.

### His Carefulness

It is very noteworthy that never once did he exhibit disapproval of what he had read in other manuscripts. Elsewhere in the New Testament, other authors vehemently denounced contemporary preachers. Luke never condemned nor criticized other writings and was content to explain, "It seemed good to me also, having had perfect understanding of all things from the very first, to write unto thee . . ." His choice of words under these circumstances revealed a quality of soul hard to find even among those destined to lead the church in her earliest crusades.

### His Willingness to Labour

It should not be forgotten that to produce this manuscript, Luke worked many hours. Probably he laboured when he might have been sleeping. His proximity to Paul would naturally mean work of varying kinds; his ministry in the churches would take much more of his time.

If it were necessary to make journeys to interview people important to his story, even more of his time would be used. Yet in addition to all this, the untiring doctor patiently assembled his facts, placed them in order and produced his book. Other less busy souls would have been too tired to look for a pen!

## His Foresight

This was revealed in two ways: (a) He gave great attention to detail. Aware of the fact that enemies of the faith might criticize his record, Luke made every effort to ascertain and thereafter reproduce only the truth. He *"had gone over the whole course in detail"* and *"had acquired a perfect understanding from the very first."* His record was therefore a safe foundation upon which his patron could rest his faith. (b) Doctors, even in those days, could be wealthy, but a physician who had forsaken all to follow Christ; a medical practitioner who had left his home to care for an itinerant preacher would hardly have the chance to accumulate wealth. How then would this manuscript be able to reach the people who needed its message? Somewhere along the journey, Dr. Luke had become acquainted with Theophilus, and with the eye of a seer perceived this man's dedication might furnish that which was necessary to meet the costs of copyists, scribes, and distributors. A stronger Theophilus would automatically mean a more useful Theophilus. Therefore Luke addressed his Gospel to this man of means, and by so doing revealed perception of the greatest degree.

## His Blessedness

Tradition says that God spared this author to reach the age of 84, and that then the beloved physician fell asleep. He succeeded in engraving his name upon the hearts of a vast host of fellow Christians, and even now after nineteen centuries, Luke remains one of the best loved of the Bible characters. He gave to the sacred records details unmentioned by other authors; he brought to the church a charm and grace second to none; he provided the pilgrims with an example of steadfastness hard to match. When others turned back, Luke continued to the glorious termination of his Christian pathway. Of him it could truly be said, "He hath done all things well." Such as he had, he gave, and whatsoever his hand found to do, he did it with all his might. It only remains for all to ask, What ought we to be doing for our Master?

### SECTION TWO

### A Necessary Introduction to the Study of Section Two

Much discussion has taken place about this, the real beginning of Luke's Gospel, because in language and style of writing, the script is very much different from that used in the prologue. Mention has already been made of the fact that in the first four verses of this book, the author used the best classical Greek and this has been cited as evidence that Luke was a Gentile. Here, however, the entire setting, changes abruptly to that of a Jewish community. Godet has said, "The first words of the narrative brings us back from the midst of Greece, whither we were transported by the prologue, into a completely Jewish world. The very style changes its character. From the fifth verse it is so saturated with Aramaisms that the contrast with the four preceding verses resulting from it obliges us to admit, either that the author artificially modifies his language in order to adapt it to his subject, and so produces an imitation . . . or that he is dealing with ancient documents, the Aramaic colouring of which he endeavours to preserve as faithfully as possible." (*Commentary on the Gospel of Luke*, F. L. Godet, page 69.)Published by Kregel Publications, Grand Rapids, Michigan

Throughout the Christian era other authors noticed this sudden and remarkable change and asserted the entire document was a fraud. Consequently a great deal of debate has been centred in this matter. It is not the purpose of this volume to cite again the lengthy arguments upon which other commentaries majored. Students in possession of any volume on Luke's Gospel can discover all the facts they wish to know. It is only necessary at this juncture to remember one or two details relevant to the subject.

It was the expressed intention of Luke to write the Gospel in its chronological order; to set down from the very first those things which had happened among the people. This explanation he provided in language essentially his own. Thereafter he recorded the facts of the beginning of the Gospel story. Why should he change what was given to him? Could there be any valid reason why he should change the speech, the mode of expression, the atmosphere of his surroundings when these things could be perfectly understood as they were? There are two possibilities in regard to the sources of his information. Probably Luke never had the privilege of interviewing Zacharias and Elizabeth for these saints were well advanced in years even before the birth of John the Baptist. Sixty or more years elapsed ere Luke joined the apostle Paul, and some years surely passed ere he began his search for facts to be included in his Gospel. Therefore he could not have conversed with the parents of the Wilderness Preacher. Whence then came the facts relating to the birth of John?

It must be remembered that Mary the mother of the Lord was a much younger woman; that she had spent months in the home of her cousin Elizabeth. These two godly women shared their secrets and in all probability repeated again and again their own intimate details of the immortal story. We do not know the date of Mary's death, but the

Scriptures record that she was present at the Cross; was afterward taken into the home of John, and later was present in the Upper Room at Pentecost (Acts 1: 14). At that time she might have been in her early fifties. It was completely possible then for her to have reached an age when Luke would have been able to speak with her of those early events in Judah. If, on the other hand, she was called to her eternal Home prior to Luke's arrival, it would at least have been possible for the Beloved Physician to converse with John in whose home Mary had lived. If Mary were the source of Luke's information, she would have described in detail the things which took place, and her speech would have been that of a Jewess. She would have mentioned for her Gentile visitor all that happened, and this would have been seen against a typically Hebrew setting. With the extreme care of a physician making notes, Luke would have written down all she said just as she said it. Why should it ever become necessary to change anything, especially since the account was beautiful, easily understood, and intensely thrilling? If, however, Mary had died, John would be able to tell Luke all he wished to know. It would be utterly fantastic to believe that the Apostle John could live so near to his "new mother," could love the Lord Jesus so much, and not exhibit interest in the manner by which God sent Him to be the Saviour of the world. There were scores of occasions when John heard Mary give her testimony, and finally her message must have been written on his heart. John was the last of the original eyewitnesses to be taken to Heaven, and therefore Luke had ample opportunity to see him and discover from his message all he wished to know.

Finally, since he himself admits that many writers had set in order the things believed among the Christians, there were in existence documents relating to the vital matters of their faith. Some think there was a master-document which comprised all that had even been written. This has been called the Q manuscript and some authors expressed the opinion that Luke gained much of his material from a careful reading of this record. There is no need whatsoever to reject this theory for if this were the case, it was also possible for Luke to check his information by direct conversation either with Mary or with John. Assuming for the moment that he had before him a manuscript outlining those memorable events in Judah, and assuming that its details were corroborated by Mary, John, or some other reliable witness, Luke would know that what he had was a true record—Why then should he change it? All that was necessary was to express this in his own language for his own people to read and understand. This has happened throughout the ages with every Bible translation, for the same verses have been expressed in many languages and only a small number of readers ever became aware of the difference of style existing between the first four and the following verses of Luke's narrative.

*Expository Notes on the Appearance of the Angel to Zacharias*

There was in the days of Herod, the king of Judea, a certain priest named Zacharias, of the course of Abia: and his wife was of the daughters of Aaron, and her name was Elizabeth. And they were both righteous before God, walking in all the commandments and ordinances of the Lord blameless. And they had no child, because that Elizabeth was barren, and they both were well stricken in years (vv 5–7).

The statement ". . . *in the days of Herod, the king of Judea*" sets the time of this visitation. According to the historian Josephus, Herod the Great died about the year 4 B.C., after having reigned for 36 years. By descent he was an Idumean but he had professed faith in the Jewish religion. He was called the King of Judea because the title had been given to him by the Roman Senate. It has been recorded that Antony and Octavius made the recommendation which was adopted by the ruling body. Thus this infamous man became the puppet ruler of Judea and his entire reign was marked by bloodshed. A measure of popularity was obtained through the ornate buildings which he erected and by the renovation and beautifying of the temple. Nevertheless when he died, everybody within the nation breathed a sigh of relief for he was unwanted by his family and hated by his people. Thus, the term "in the days of Herod, the King of Judea" refers to one of the darkest periods in Israel's history. The voice of God had not spoken through a prophet for four centuries; the spiritual life of the nation had gone into steep decline, and although certain nationalist leaders had endeavoured to lift their standard of defiance, their efforts had more or less been in vain. Yet when righteousness appeared to be a forgotten virtue, God began to work. It is well to remember that often the darkest hour is just before the dawn.

Luke recorded the fact that Zacharias belonged to the order of Abijah. The twenty-fourth chapter of the first book of Chronicles reveals that from the time of David the priestly family had been divided into twenty-four courses of which the order of Abijah was the eighth. These groups were responsible for eight days of duty (Sabbath to Sabbath) once every six months. The Babylonian captivity upset the usual order and many of the original groups failed to survive. Nevertheless as soon as it became possible, the remaining priests were divided again into the twenty-four orders each bearing the original name. When Zacharias married Elizabeth, a descendant of Aaron, his prestige was greatly enhanced. The name Zacharias means "The Lord remembers," that is: *God remembers His covenants with men*. The name

Elizabeth means "My God is an oath," and probably infers that God is always faithful to His promises. Was this one of the marriages solemnized in Heaven? "Both of them were upright and devout, blamelessly observing all the commandments and ordinances of the Lord. But they had no children, for Elizabeth was barren, and both were well-on in years." We are presented here with one of the strange anomalies of life which have challenged the righteous throughout the ages. It was the inherent right of women to bear children; it was the sincere prayer of every woman that she might give birth to the Messiah. Without the gift of a son, women were automatically barred from this possibility. Yet here were two people almost without equal in their day; they walked honourably and without blame before God only to see their virtue apparently passing unnoticed by the Lord. Other less virtuous people could have as many children as they desired; they prayed earnestly for a son, but their petitions remained unanswered. Did this test their faith? Did they ever have to resist bitterness of spirit? We may never know, but even if they did, these thoughts were quickly banished. We must remember that whilst God may appear to be slow, at least He is never blind. We should never interpret His withholding of blessing as a punishment; there are times when God has more patience than His people. He loves to do the right thing at the right time in the right place. Impetuosity has no part in the Divine programme.

And it came to pass that while he executed the priest's office before God in the order of his course, According to the custom of the priest's office, his lot was to burn incense when he went into the temple of the Lord. And the whole multitude of the people were praying without at the time of incense (vv. 8-10).

Exodus 30: 7-8 describes how God commanded the incense to be burned twice a day. "And Aaron shall burn thereon sweet incense every morning: when he dresseth the lamps, he shall burn incense upon it. And when Aaron lighteth the lamps at even, he shall burn incense upon it, a perpetual incense before the Lord throughout your generations." Thrice daily, public prayer was offered, and the third period began about three o'clock in the afternoon (Acts 10: 30). The first and final periods of prayer coincided with the offering of the incense (*Antiquities of Josephus*, xiv: 4, 3). As the priest went into the Holy Place to perform his act of service, the multitude of people stood outside ready to offer their supplications the moment the smoke of the incense began to ascend. It was considered a very great honour to burn the incense and because there were so many priests who coveted the privilege, the matter was settled by the casting of the lot. It was extremely doubtful whether any priest ever enjoyed the privilege twice in his lifetime. In view of the fact that at so many crucial points in this story every detail appears to fit into a master-plan, it is clear that God has more to do with the ordering of our lives than we would sometimes be willing to admit. Was it an accident that brought Zacharias to the temple at this time? Was it by mere chance that the lot fell on him to offer incense? He and his wife had been among the most faithful of the Lord's servants; their prayers had constantly indicated that faith was still existent on the earth. The *Talmud* says no priest was allowed to draw the lot the second time in one week. There are other writers who affirm that this privilege was known but once in a lifetime. Every man enabled to render the sacred service valued the privilege beyond words. He knew he was treading upon holy ground.

> And there appeared unto him an angel of the Lord standing on the right side of the altar of incense. And when Zacharias saw him, he was troubled and fear fell upon him. But the angel said unto him, Fear not, Zacharias; for thy prayer is heard; and thy wife Elizabeth shall bear thee a son, and thou shalt call his name John. And thou shalt have joy and gladness; and many shall rejoice at his birth. (New English Bible rendering: "Your heart will thrill with joy, and many will be glad that he was born) (vv. 11–14).

This section has been constantly criticized during the last century. For example, *The Interpreter's Bible* suggests, as do numerous other volumes, this story *may have been one of the many legends which circulated among the early church people.* Furthermore the same writers claim the account is not essential to the Gospel story. This, it may be added, is but a point of view with which many people would disagree. Is it so fantastic that God should send an angel to speak with the aged priest? The Bible has many stories of the coming of angels and of their subsequent service to the people of God. If we reject the one story, should we not reject them all? Are they all extracts from a great collection of legends, and if so, who is to draw the line of demarcation between the accurate and the legendary? 2 Kings 6: 17 suggests that there are occasions when we may be surrounded by angels. Daniel 10: 1–14 tells how "a shining one" came to Daniel with a very special message. Hebrews 1: 13–14 reads: "But to which of the angels said he at any time, Sit on my right hand, until I make thine enemies thy footstool? Are they not all ministering spirits sent forth to minister for them who shall be the heirs of salvation?" Furthermore since the Epistle to the Hebrews has many references to angels, if no such beings exist, the author must have been subject to continuing hallucinations.

The entrance to the temple faced the east, and on entering, the priest would have the golden altar straight ahead of him. This was so placed according to divine requirements; it stood at the end of the Holy Place and immediately in front of the Great Veil which separated the Holy Place from the Holy of Holies. On the one side stood *the table of shewbread* and on the other, the *great candelabrum*. The expression *the right side of the altar* probably should be decided from Zacharias' point of view. That would mean the angel would be standing between the altar and the table.

It was perfectly natural that the aged priest should be somewhat fearful when he became aware of the presence of another. This must not be interpreted as an indication of guilt, although who would not be a little apprehensive in the presence of a shining one? Such a visitation might be the harbinger of doom! This momentary feeling of dread was quickly dispelled by the angel's message. The visitor from heaven had come to announce glad tidings; prayer had prevailed, God was continuing to be gracious. It is not exactly easy to speak with assurance about the meaning of the text "for thy prayer is heard." Many commentators feel this was a reference to the nation-wide longing for the coming of the Messiah. They affirm that it would hardly be spiritual etiquette for a man in such a privileged position to seize the opportunity to make selfish requests. Possibly this would be the only time Zacharias would stand in that precise position. Would he not therefore, as the representative of his people, add his prayer to theirs with a sincere request that soon the Blessed One would come to help them? Furthermore, he would be aware that for his wife to bear children was now impossible. They had prayed for a son but hope had been abandoned. Why then should Zacharias be praying for the impossible?

However, F. L. Godet strongly disagrees with this explanation. He says, "The prayer of Zacharias to which the angel alludes would be, in the opinion of many, an entreaty for the advent of the Messiah. This, it is said, is the only solitude worthy of a priest in such a place and at such a time. But the preceding context (verse 7) is in no way favourable to this explanation, nor is that which follows (verse 13); for the sense of the *kai* is most certainly this: 'And *so* thy wife Elizabeth . . .' Further the two personal pronouns, *sou* and *soi*, 'thy wife shall bear *thee*,' as also the *soi*, 'thou shalt have' (verse 14) prove positively the entirely personal character of the prayer and its answer. The objection that, according to verse 7, he could no longer expect to have a child, and consequently could not pray with this design, exaggerates the meaning of this word" (*F. L. Godet on Luke*, page 77).

Whichever interpretation is correct, one thing is indisputable, the answer to this prayer had long been delayed. See the homily, Delayed Answers to Prayer, at the end of this section. The meaning of the name John is said to be "Jehovah shows grace" and such a name would be completely in keeping with all that was taking place at that time. The rendering as offered by the New English Bible is truly delightful, "Your heart will thrill with joy." There is no need to comment on this utterance; it is self-explanatory.

> For he shall be great in the sight of the Lord, and shall drink neither wine nor strong drink: and he shall be filled with the Holy Spirit, even from his mother's womb. And many of the children of Israel shall he turn to the Lord their God (vv. 15-16).

Perhaps preachers and teachers would like to consider this Scripture under four headings. (a) *The Unusual Privilege.* "For he shall be great in the sight of the Lord." There must always be a standard by which true greatness is measured. It was said of the Woman of Shunem that she was a great woman (II Kings 4: 8). There are various possibilities in regard to that particular text. She might have *been* (i) *great in physical strength;* (ii) *great in social position;* (iii) *great in spiritual power.* Men and women may seem great in their own eyes, or in the sight of their fellow citizen, but the supreme recommendation is to be great in the eyes of God. (b) *The Unusual Purity.* Prior to the birth of this child, God decreed he would resemble the Nazarites, for part of their ancient vow was complete abstinence from alcohol. Lange says, "By abstaining from all the comforts and conveniences of civilized life, such as wine, the bath, the cutting of the hair, and in this way approaching the state of nature, the Nazarite presented himself to the world as a man filled with a lofty thought, which absorbed all his interest, as a bearer of a word of God which was hidden in his heart." (c) *The Unusual Power.* During the Old Testament dispensations the Spirit of the Lord came upon men temporarily to give special power for a unique task. Yet in contrast to this state of affairs, John the Baptist would be permanently filled with the Holy Spirit from his mother's womb. Students might like to contrast this with Jeremiah 1: 4-5. "Then the word of the Lord came unto me saying, Before I formed thee in the inward parts I knew thee; and before thou camest forth out of the womb I sanctified thee, and I ordained thee a prophet unto the nations." The ways of the Lord are past finding out. (d) *The Unusual Preaching.* "And many of the children of Israel shall he turn unto the Lord their God." The inference here is that the children of Israel had turned away from their Lord. Sin had broken the relationship between God and His people. This great saint, filled with the Spirit, would be enabled by the Almighty to disturb the conscience of the nation. All preachers and theological institutions might be wise to reflect on the progressive nature of these details. There exists the danger today of educating a man's mind at the expense of his soul.

When spiritual passion is sacrificed on the altar of learning, even the most illustrious orator becomes a tinkling cymbal.

**And he shall go before him in the spirit and power of Elias, to turn the hearts of the fathers to the children, and the disobedient to the wisdom of the just; to make ready a people prepared for the Lord.** The New English Bible renders this passage as follows:

He will go before him as forerunner, possessed by the spirit and power of Elijah, to reconcile father and child, to convert the rebellious to the ways of the righteous, to prepare a people that shall be fit for the Lord (v. 17).

There appears to be particular significance attached to the opening sentence: *"And he shall go before him . . ."* It is generally interpreted that John the forerunner would go before the Messiah, but is this strictly in harmony with the text? The previous verse had spoken of "the Lord their God" and since this pregnant sentence follows immediately, good exegesis demands that the statements be taken together. The *him* of the text can only refer to the Lord their God of Whom mention has already been made. John shall go before the Lord God for He it is Who shall suddenly come to His temple. Naturally reference is made to the Coming Messiah but there are deeper depths of meaning in the verses. It will be the Lord God, Who in the Person of the Messiah will suddenly make His appearance. The coming One would therefore be infinitely more than the Messiah, the accepted king of Israel, he would be the Divine King—the King of the Ages.

The statement that John would come in the spirit and power of Elias must be considered in the closest harmony with other relevant verses. It is clear from Matthew 17: 10 that Israel believed the coming of the Messiah would be preceded by the reappearance of the prophet Elijah. This was based upon Malachi's prediction, "Behold, I will send Elijah the prophet before the coming of the great and dreadful day of the Lord" (Malachi 4: 5). Yet John himself was quick to deny the rumour that he was the reincarnation of the ancient prophet. "And this is the record of John, when the Jews sent priests and Levites from Jerusalem to ask him, Who art thou? . . . And they asked him . . . Art thou Elias? And he saith, I am not" (John 1: 19–21). Nevertheless at a later date, the disciples of Christ asked their Master, ". . . Why then say the scribes that Elias must first come? And Jesus answered and said unto them, Elias truly shall first come and restore all things. But I say unto you, That Elias is come already, and they knew him not, but have done unto him whatsoever they listed" (Matthew 17: 10–12). Malachi prophesied Elijah would make his appearance before *that great and dreadful day of the Lord.* There is only one logical interpretation of the Saviour's utterance. He asserted that John the Baptist had indeed come in the *spirit* of his famous predecessor; that in view of the current rejection both of the Baptist and of Jesus Himself, his coming had preceded a great and dreadful day, for Israel had rejected the Blessed One. They cried, "His blood be on us and on our children" and that startling request was destined to have serious repercussions throughout the ages. The Bible teaches that prior to the end of the Age, two great witnesses will make an appearance to declare the word of God and defy the powers of evil. For a little while they will appear to be invincible but eventually will be slain and remain unburied in the streets. Their ultimate resurrection and ascension to Heaven introduce strange events in the earth (Revelation 10: 3–13). Within certain evangelical circles this passage of scripture has given rise to unending debate. Romans 5: 12 states categorically that ". . . death passed upon all men." Some interpret this as *"the sentence of death passed upon all men."* This has not really been fulfilled for neither Elijah nor Enoch died. The one ascended to heaven, and the other "was not, for God took him." The teaching has been advanced that in the closing period of time, these men will be the two witnesses of whom mention has been made. Their subsequent death completes the circle of finality and thus vindicates the veracity of the Word of God. If this be true, then in a most literal sense, Malachi's prediction will be fulfilled.

And Zacharias said unto the angel, Whereby shall I know this? for I am an old man, and my wife well stricken in years. And the angel answering said unto him, I am Gabriel, that stand in the presence of God; and am sent to speak unto thee, and to shew thee these glad tidings. And, behold, thou shalt be dumb, and not able to speak, until the day that these things shall be performed, because thou believest not my words, which shall be fulfilled in their season (vv. 18–20).

Concerning the names of the angels, Geldenhuys has a very illuminating paragraph on page 67 of his book, *Commentary on the Gospel of Luke.* "Only two angels are mentioned by name in the canonical books of the Bible, Gabriel and Michael. Gabriel means 'Man of God'; and Michael, 'Who is like God?'" Critics here ask the sarcastic question whether Hebrew is spoken in heaven. These names are, however, symbolical in order to indicate what are the special functions of these celestial personalities. When we speak to anybody, we do it in such a way that he is able to understand us. So also when God reveals heavenly truths to man He does so in the language of human beings, in such a manner as is intelligible to them. Thus Gabriel, according to the name he bears, and his description as one who stands in the presence of God, is *the mighty messenger of God.* Therefore, throughout the Holy Scriptures, he appears as the one who brings good tidings from God to man (Daniel 8: 16 and 9: 21; Luke 1: 19–26). Michael, again, as his name indicates, is the destroyer of everyone who dares to aspire to equality with God or to resist Him (Daniel 10: 13 and 21; Daniel 12: 1; Jude 9; Revelation 12: 7). Thus Gabriel is the one who builds and Michael is the one that overthrows. In the case of Michael, the justice and judicial activity of God plays its part, while in Gabriel's case, the grace and redeeming activity of the Lord are in the foreground. In extra-Biblical Jewish writings and legends the exact opposite is the case, which proves that the Bible does not borrow from Jewish or other fables.

Perhaps it is easy to understand why Zacharias asked for a sign. *"WHEREBY* shall I know this?" Some of the patriarchs had similarly asked for a sign, but they did not have the illuminating radiance of successive revelations of the will and promises of God. Zacharias apparently should have known better than doubt the word of God's messenger, but let us not be too harsh in our judgment for there was an added reason why it was necessary to deprive the priest of his speech.

> And the people waited for Zacharias, and marvelled that he tarried so long in the temple. And when he came out, he could not speak unto them: and they perceived that he had seen a vision in the temple, for "he stood there making signs unto them and remained dumb" (vv. 21-22).

Had the aged priest been able to describe what had taken place, would the people have believed his testimony? Perhaps they might have listened with interest to his description of the angel who had stood at the right side of the altar, but what would have been their reactions when he announced his aged and barren wife was to become a mother? They might have said he was suffering from sunstroke! Probably after a few distortions this story would have become the best joke of the nation and would have been retold with varying adjustments in a thousand places. We know that the speechlessness of the priest was a sign of chastisement but it is wise to remember God's judgments are always tempered by mercy.

> And it came to pass, that as soon as the days of his ministration were accomplished, he departed to his own house. And after those days, his wife Elizabeth conceived; and hid herself five months, saying, Thus hath the Lord dealt with me in the days wherein he looked on me, to take away my reproach among men (vv. 23-25).

It is not difficult to imagine the amazement of Elizabeth when her husband arrived home dumb. When he wrote all the details of his strange but thrilling experience, his wife's incredulity gave place to increasing joy. It would appear from verse 36 that this devout lady had often heard the taunts of her neighbours. ". . . her *WHO WAS CALLED BARREN*" seems to be indicative of what had transpired. As though it was not enough to carry her secret disappointment, the people of the district taunted her.

Throughout the ages much speculation has been made as to the reason for Elizabeth's five months of seclusion. Origen and Ambrose thought she was dominated by a false modesty. De Wette said she went in order to safeguard her health during the early months of pregnancy. Paulus affirmed she had but little faith, and went away in order to await the assurance of pregnancy ere she announced the matter to her friends. Bleek and Oosterzee thought she was so filled with gratitude that she retired into seclusion to worship and return thanks without the fuss and ostentation which would have been unavoidable at home. Godet and others see in the text even deeper meanings. She who had suffered so long the insults of men, now had no need to suffer their taunts. She had been delivered; why then stay amidst people whose perverted minds might spoil the sanctity of the most blessed moments of her life? After five months, the condition of a pregnant woman becomes apparent, and therefore it was at this time, she decided to return to her home. Men could hardly sneer now for what had taken place could only be the result of a miracle. Probably, prior to this time had she confessed to being pregnant they would have laughed her to scorn; now her very appearance would indicate the favour of God. He alone could have done this for her. *He had taken away her reproach among men.*


HOMILIES

Study No. 2

### DELAYED ANSWERS TO PRAYER

We know that God answers prayer but it is always well to remember that He does so in His own way and in His own time. Faith and impatience are never good partners. "Now faith is the substance of things hoped for, the evidence of things not seen" (Hebrews 11 : 1). Impatience is the hand that would turn the key even before God has completed the building. The saint whose prayers are terminated by an increasing dissatisfaction with God's methods does not exhibit the characteristics of a true believer. Real faith looks at the Lord and not primarily at that which He might do. True faith presents a petition before the throne of Grace, and rejoices if God sees fit to answer. The same faith also rejoices when He declines to grant the request knowing that the Lord's ways are higher—and better—than our ways. The Bible presents many facts in support of this claim.

*Hannah . . . who prayed for a son* (I Samuel 1: 10–11)

"And Hannah was in bitterness of soul, and prayed unto the Lord, and wept sore." Language is inadequate to describe the torture of this woman's mind. Frustration, tauntings from the other wife, and the incessant yearning for a son played havoc with her peace of mind. She had prayed for many years; was it any use waiting upon God again? Alas, this noble woman was waiting for God but all the while He was waiting for her. She was looking for a son; He was looking for a Saviour. If she wanted a boy, the Lord wanted and needed the lad even more. God was waiting for Hannah to become willing to surrender her dearest treasure and when ". . . she vowed a vow and said, O Lord of Hosts, if thou wilt indeed look on the affliction of thine handmaid, and remember me, and not forget thine handmaid, but wilt give unto thine handmaid a man child, then I will give him unto the Lord all the days of his life . . ." then surely the Lord smiled. It was no longer necessary to delay the answer to her prayer.

*Daniel . . . who prayed for three weeks* (Daniel 10: 2, 12)

The Book of Daniel makes exciting reading, for this man of God had spent most of his time in an alien land. Great matters of state were brought to him and much was expected of this Hebrew. That Daniel was a man of prayer we all know for it was in answer to his supplication God revealed the king's dream and thereby prevented wholesale slaughter of innocent men. It was never difficult for this man to pray for he was in the habit of *opening his windows toward Jerusalem.* Yet there came a time when unusual difficulties interfered with the freedom of Daniel's expressions. This prayer warrior continued for three weeks, and had it been necessary he would have prayed for three months! Suddenly the explanation came that there had been opposition from the realms of evil. It had been easier for Daniel's prayer to reach heaven than for the answer to reach earth. *Persistent* prayer reminded God that something had to be done in the matter, and finally the situation was resolved. This emphasizes the Saviour's statement that *men ought ALWAYS TO PRAY AND NOT TO FAINT.*

*Elizabeth and Zacharias . . . who prayed for years* (Luke 1: 6–13)

The preceding expository notes explained much about this poignant story. That the apparent refusal of God to answer prayer had been taken calmly is obvious, for it is written of these wonderful people

"they were both righteous before God, walking in all the commandments and ordinances of the Lord blameless." God's refusal was
dictated by wisdom. He had planned for this aged couple more happiness than they thought possible. They were not only to enjoy the thrill
of parenthood; their child would be owned and blessed by God from
the moment of conception. God always gives the best to those who
leave the choice with Him.

*The Lord Jesus Christ. . . . Who prayed for help* (Hebrews 5: 7)

Here are unfathomable depths of mystery, and it might be well first
to consider the language used in Hebrews 5: 7. "Who in the days of
his flesh, when he had offered up prayers and supplications with *strong
crying and tears* unto him that was able to save him from death, and
was heard in that he feared." This was no ordinary prayer. Knowing
that the Cross would bring disaster to the kingdom of evil, Satan was
trying hard to kill Christ in the garden. The cup from which the Lord
sought release was not the Death of the Cross. He came to die and
never for a moment lost His desire to give His life a ransom for many.
Yet, if the Saviour died prematurely, His purpose in coming to earth
would have been thwarted. This was Satan's greatest attack, for in the
garden of Gethsemane, the Lord's life was threatened. Fearing momentarily, as the text indicates, that death might come too soon, the Lord
prayed for help. Luke 22: 43 reveals that this help came to Him, but
Mark adds the significant detail that it did not arrive until the Lord
had agonized in prayer at least in two sessions (Mark 14: 33–40). There
is reason to believe we are impoverished because we do not know how
to pray. Sometimes answers to prayer are delayed—not because God
has to be persuaded to heed our requests, but because terrible forces
of evil need to be overcome ere our prayers can be answered.

*The Disciples . . . who prayed for ten days* (Acts 1: 14; 2: 1)

Luke in the first chapter of the Acts of the Apostles tells how the
disciples returned to the city of Jerusalem to await the coming of the
Holy Spirit. "These all continued with one accord in prayer and supplication, with the women, and Mary the mother of Jesus, and with
his brethren" (Acts 1: 14). The Feast of Pentecost was set in the Jewish
Calendar and the great day could not be advanced to shorten the
waiting period of that band of believers. Probably they did not even
wish it could; they had so much to tell their Lord; they had so many
petitions to place before God's throne that the time went all too
quickly. However the point at issue here is that they *continued* praying
until God rent the heavens and poured His strength into their impotence. Only simple locks open with one turn of a key! The safety
doors guarding the bank's treasure have more complicated mechanism.

Sometimes the man responsible for the opening and closing of these huge steel barriers has to turn wheels and keys in various directions, but when he knows what he is doing, the end is never in doubt.

"Lord, teach us how to pray."

SECTION THREE

*A Necessary Introduction to the Study of the Virgin Birth of Jesus*

Throughout the centuries, and at frequent intervals, the authenticity of the Incarnation has been challenged by men of every type. Infidels ridiculed the story and attempted to turn the Bethlehem story into an account of ill repute. On the other hand, many scholars professing themselves to be Christians sought to explain the event in ways more compatible with science. There was a period when the sharp line of demarcation dividing Christianity and Infidelity was clearly drawn, but alas, today that is not the case. The rejection of the miraculous element in the birth of Christ slowly penetrated into Christian thought and at the present time many commentaries and colleges consider the story to be false.

It has been said repeatedly that the virgin birth of Jesus was not essential to the Gospel; redemption of mankind was based upon the death and resurrection of the Lord and not upon His incarnation. Furthermore extensive articles were written to prove that Paul, the great missionary-author of the first century, seldom, if ever mentioned the matter; that none of the other Gospels afford to the story the same space and importance. The early church never taught the doctrine, and consequently it can be of very little importance. Against this rather dubious background, the assertion was made that the entire account was fictitious, the vapouring of some energetic imagination. It was only beautiful poetry which appealed to the ascetic mind of the physician.

Not so very long ago this interpretation would have been rejected by all Christians, who would have considered it to be blasphemous. Under the guise of higher education, the doctrine steadily advanced until today many preachers have serious doubts as to whether the ancient account may be accepted as authentic. Other writers explained that birth without sexual intercourse was not impossible, and cases were cited to prove the assertion. At other times, conception was made possible by artificial insemination, and thus, in one way or another, theologians endeavoured to explain why they challenged the biblical account. Against this background we must discuss the veracity of Luke's Gospel. Some leaders deny the miraculous in the Book of books, but never explain the impotence of their own ministry. It is not possible to reduce God to decimal points and equations of doubtful value. It is never the ultimate in wisdom to declare that two and two make four; sometimes those numbers make twenty-two. The whole of the Christian Faith rests upon the supernatural. Conversion itself is a miracle for what else could change a man's nature; remove the burning desire for certain evils, and change a renegade into a child of the Highest?

Nevertheless for those who earnestly seek a solution to this thorny problem the following facts are cited. Luke was the travelling companion of Paul; the beloved physician remained with the apostle to the end. It is accepted that Luke gleaned some of his material, and much of his evangelistic zeal from the untiring preacher; that Paul knew of, and was acquainted with Luke's literary endeavour. That he would read the message and discuss it with his friend there can be no doubt. Had Luke been expressing something untrue, the very nature of Paul's ministry would have produced a scathing denial of the falsehood.

Matthew, Mark and John had no need to dwell upon the intimate details of Christ's birth, for even if they knew all the facts concerning the pregnancy of the two famous women, the details were not necessary for the story each had to tell. Matthew wrote of the Messiah, and only mentioned the birth of Jesus in so much as it referred to his theme. Matthew, for example, told of the arrival of the Magi and of their question which caused excitement in Jerusalem. Mark explained how Christ made Himself of no reputation and stooped to become a servant. The birth of a slave was unimportant; John was hardly interested for he saw the beginning of Christ's story in the eternal ages and not in the village of Bethlehem.

It is true that little mention was made of the birth of Christ throughout the early decades of the Christian era, but it should be remembered that Mary was still alive. Perhaps the apostles should be commended for the wisdom which made them by-pass a most important theme. They exalted Christ, and endeavoured constantly to give to Him the pre-eminence in all things. When the Roman Catholic church came into existence, its leaders sought to correct what they thought was a fault, and the entire world knows how Mary is now covered with a Glory she would have shunned. Mary's spirituality would have demanded that her son should have the pre-eminence in all things; that as with John the Baptist, she should decrease that the Lord might increase.

Nevertheless, to bring this debatable issue to a very decisive head, the question must be asked, What is the alternative to this old story? If Christ were not born as Luke described, then *how was He born?* Mary was engaged to Joseph, and in Jewish law an engagement was as binding as a wedding ceremony. Either party guilty of breaking that contract was liable to severe punishment. The New English Bible translates Matthew 1 : 18–21 as follows : "This is the story of the birth of the Messiah. Mary his mother was betrothed to Joseph; before the marriage she found that she was with child by the Holy Spirit. Being a man of principle, and at the same time wanting to save her from exposure, Joseph desired to have the marriage contract set aside quietly. He had resolved on this when an angel appeared to him in a dream. 'Joseph, son of David' said the angel, 'do not be afraid to take Mary home with you as your wife. It is by the Holy Spirit that she has conceived this child. She will bear a son, and you shall give him the name Jesus (Saviour) for he will save his people from their sins'." It is very evident that Joseph was not the father of this child. If the miraculous element be denied, then who was the father? These are not pleasant thoughts but the time has come when students must decide what they intend to believe and preach. There are no illegitimate children on earth; there are only illegitimate parents, and if modern interpretations are to be accepted then we must go the whole way and admit once for all that Mary was an unfortunate young woman whose moral lapse initiated her into the ranks of unmarried mothers. Some-where along the line, unknown to her sweetheart, she had associations with another man, but her unwanted child ultimately overcame this social handicap to become the most famous figure in Jewish history. Maybe some of the critics who reject the story of the virgin birth would like to spend time explaining to a waiting world how the second miracle was even greater than the one they rejected as impossible.

There is another angle of importance in regard to the Incarnation. The statement has been made that the Virgin Birth was of secondary importance for it was not essential to the Gospel. This is not true. Without the beginning there would have been no end. All readers of this message are urged to give serious consideration to the following fact. Within the Bible *sin is revealed as a nature and not merely as an act*. A man commits evil because his nature is evil. This was not always the case.

When God created Adam, man was without blemish. God never produced anything less than the best, and therefore man was created perfect. It was not possible for any suggestion of evil to arise from his soul or to emanate from his mind. Purity in its scintillating loveliness resided within Adam's being and it was necessary for the temptation to come from without. Thus we read how Satan came to tempt him. This however was not the case with Adam's children. Their parent transmitted to them a life that was already tainted. Had Adam after his failure observed faithfully every law of God, the end would never have been in doubt for the damage had already been done. The first spot of moral poison had tainted his soul. The sinless one became a sinner. When Adam begat children, he begat sinful children. Years

later Cain murdered his brother but it is not said Satan came to tempt
him. The idea originated within his own mind; he himself was responsible for his treacherous action. It is not fantastic to add that even
before a child knows the difference between good and evil, it is sometimes possible to see a manifestation of evil in the tiny body. Even
very young children have minds of their own, and frequently when a
parent tries to make the infant do something against its will, a domestic
storm breaks within the home. David apparently knew this for he said,
"Behold, I was shapen in iniquity; and in sin did my mother conceive
me" (Psalm 51: 5). Sin therefore is a nature transmitted from one
generation to another, and that is precisely the reason why salvation
has to be a miracle. The purpose of God in Christ is not the improvement of the old nature. Salvation means the transmission of a new life
—the very life of God. Thus the Saviour said to Nicodemus, "That
which is born of the flesh is flesh; and that which is born of the Spirit
is spirit. Marvel not that I said unto thee, Ye must be born again." An
earthly father can only transmit the life he possesses. Even so, the
Heavenly Father transmits His life. To receive that gift is to be born;
to be born is to commence living the spiritual life. Now since sin is a
nature continuing through successive generations, it follows that if
Christ had been born as we were born, He would have been born a
sinner. Had He received from His parents their tainted nature, He
would have received something upon which the sentence of death had
already been passed. If this had been the case, He would have needed
someone to redeem Him.

Readers must not be too surprised to read that Jesus was NOT a Jew;
neither was He a Gentile. The Lord Jesus Christ was the God-Man,
the Last Adam for Whom, as it has been said, "A body hast thou prepared for me." Therefore to make salvation possible for men and
women, God of necessity had to perform a miracle, and this He did,
when within the womb of Mary, the great Creator did what had to be
done. Thus, and only thus was the will of God fulfilled, and to say that
the virgin birth was in no way necessary to the Gospel story is to reveal
superficial thinking unworthy of the Christian ministry.

### Expository Notes on the Angel's Appearance to Mary

**And in the sixth month the angel Gabriel was sent from God unto a
city of Galilee, named Nazareth, To a virgin espoused to a man whose
name was Joseph, of the house of David: and the virgin's name was
Mary. And the angel came in unto her, and said, "Greetings, most
favoured one: The Lord is with you" (vv. 26–28. New English Bible).**

The term *the sixth month* relates to the pregnancy of Elizabeth, or
more precisely to the period which immediately followed the end of

her seclusion. Her secret was now revealed, and the scene was set for
God to proceed with His plans. See earlier notes for the function and
purpose of Gabriel's calling. Nazareth, a small but important village of
Galilee, was situated between sixty and seventy miles to the North-
East of Jerusalem, and was reached from the valley of Jezreel by a
mountain gorge running from South to North. Ultimately the traveller
arrived in a most beautiful plain which measured, in time of transit,
some twenty minutes by ten minutes. The village was situated on the
hills which sheltered the valley on its northern side. Not so very long
ago the total population only numbered about three thousand, but in
later years this number has increased to ten thousand. It is possible
to obtain excellent views from the surrounding hills, and of this panor-
amic view, Caiger has written, "Winding in and out among the hills,
the great highways from Egypt to Damascus; from Jerusalem to the
north, could clearly be seen in the New Testament times, white ribbons
of road, now floating in the dust of merchant caravans, now glittering
with the diamond-headed spears of soldiery. Towering skyward in the
distance were three of the most noted mountains in Scripture—the
rounded dome of Tabor, Hermon's snow-clad peak, and the historic
heights of Carmel" (S. L. Caiger, *In His Steps*, p. 639).

It was to this entrancing place the Angel was sent to announce glad
tidings to a betrothed couple. From every point of view the position
into which the message placed Mary was fraught with great peril. The
law of Moses was most explicit in its commands concerning an engaged
young woman found to be with child by any other than her husband
to be. "If any man take a wife, and go in unto her, and hate her, and
give occasion of speech against her . . . and say . . . when I came to
her, I found her not a maid: Then shall the father of the damsel, and
her mother, take and bring forth the evidence of the damsel's virginity
unto the elders of the city in the gate . . . But if this thing be true,
and the evidence of virginity be not found for the damsel, Then they
shall bring out the damsel to the door of her father's house, and the
men of her city shall stone her with stones that she die; because
she hath wrought folly in Israel, to play the whore in her father's
house; so shalt thou put evil away from among you" (Deuteronomy
22 : 13–22).

The final sentence of the message "blessed art thou among women"
appears to be an additional; it is not found in the early manuscripts.
It belongs to verse 42, and in that setting appears authentic. Here too
we have a throw-back to arguments expressed in the introduction to
this study. If the Virgin Birth were the figment of an imagination; if
Mary had consorted with an unknown man, the Lord could hardly
have greeted her as He did, when, according to His own law, she was
guilty of an unpardonable sin.

And when she saw him, she was troubled at his saying, and wondered what manner of salutation this should be. And the angel said unto her, Fear not, Mary: for thou hast found favour with God. And, behold, thou shalt conceive in thy womb, and bring forth a son, and shalt call his name Jesus. He shall be great, and shall be called the Son of the Highest: and the Lord God shall give unto him the throne of his father David: And he shall reign over the house of Jacob for ever, and of his kingdom there shall be no end (vv. 29–33).

It is perfectly understandable why this young woman was worried by the appearance and announcement of the angel. Godet thinks she might have been engaged in the act of prayer; that her home had become a sanctuary, and that suddenly her prayer was answered in a way completely unexpected. The reassurance of peace and the amazing prediction that she should bring forth the Messiah filled her with holy wonder. There were many women in Israel at that time but for some singularly great reason, God chose Mary. Why? We might also ask why such appearances are not made today? Are we so earth-bound, so materialistically minded that our attitude creates barriers through which it is difficult for spiritual manifestations to penetrate?

The promise of the angel might well be divided into three sections: (a) *The Greatness of Christ's Mission.* "Thou shalt call his name, Jesus" (Saviour). Matthew adds, ". . . for he shall save his people from their sins" (Matthew 1: 21). (b) *The Greatness of His Majesty.* "He shall be called the Son of the Highest: and the Lord God shall give unto him the throne of his father David." The fact that these two statements are linked together provides food for thought. God is careful to indicate the unique qualities of the coming Messiah. He is not only the Man of God's choice, for indeed that would have been acceptable to the majority of the people; the Messiah was to be infinitely MORE than the man of God's choice, He was to be "Son of the Highest." It should also be remembered that the throne of David was something tangible and real. This promise still awaits fulfilment and that is the reason why the Saviour must return to earth. Let it also be remembered that the Old Testament predictions concerning the Messianic reign also await fulfilment. (c) *The Greatness of His Might.* "And he shall reign over the house of Jacob forever, and of his kingdom there shall be no end." History has much to say of great kingdoms which ultimately crumbled and fell. Christ's kingdom will last for ever. No enemy will be able to overthrow it; no internal weakness will undermine its strength. It has been said that for a while at least He will rule with a rod of iron, but the hand that holds the rod will be motivated by compassion.

Then said Mary unto the angel, How shall this be, seeing I know not a man? (when I have no husband. N.E.B.) And the angel answered and said unto her, The Holy Spirit shall come upon thee, and the power of the Highest shall overshadow thee: therefore also that holy thing (Child) which shall be born of thee shall be called the Son of God (vv. 34-35).

Mary did not challenge the veracity of the announcement; she merely enquired as to the method by which the impossible would become real. Without physical association with a man, birth was not possible. How then could these things come to pass? Were there things she should know? Had the angel any instructions to give to her? The word translated overshadow is *episkiasei* which means to overshadow as with a cloud. The same word is used in Matthew 17: 5 where it reads, ". . . behold, a bright cloud overshadowed them." The Holy Spirit would hover above; would stay as did the cloud above the ancient Tabernacle in the Wilderness. God was never visibly perceived for His personality was veiled in the awe-inspiring cloud; nevertheless the very thing that hid Him from the eyes of His people assured them that He was there. Thus in the incarnation, there was no visible manifestation of the creative power of the Almighty, nevertheless, the hovering Spirit was unmistakably there, and in the fullness of time, the evidence needed to substantiate His creative power was forthcoming in the Person of the infant Christ.

Godet has expressed this in a most beautiful manner. "The Holy Spirit denotes here the divine power, the life-giving breath which calls into developed existence the germ of human personality slumbering in Mary's womb. This germ is the link which unites Jesus to human nature, and makes Him a member of the race He came to save. Thus in His birth the miracle of the first creation is repeated on a scale of greater power. Two elements concurred in the formation of man; a body taken from the ground, and the divine breath. With these two elements correspond here the germ derived from the womb of Mary, and the Holy Spirit who fertilizes it. The absolute purity of this birth results, on the one hand, from the perfect holiness of the divine principle which is its infinite cause; on the other, from the absence of every impure motion in her who becomes a mother under such a principle." (F. L. Godet, *Commentary on the Gospel of Luke*, p. 93.)

And behold, thy cousin Elizabeth, she hath also conceived a son in her old age: and this is the sixth month with her, who was called barren. For with God nothing shall be impossible. And Mary said, Behold, the handmaid of the Lord; be it unto me according to thy word. And the angel departed from her (vv. 36-38).

To the everlasting credit of Mary it must be said that she required no sign. Her mind was pure; her heart clean; her faith so strong that she co-operated in all God's wishes and fully yielded to His control. The Greek word *idou* (behold) does not express amazement, surprise or doubt, rather it indicates the complete surrender of her body to the Almighty. She was His handmaid; He could do with her as He chose. Her sublime faith probably recognised that He alone had created the cradle within her being; He could, if He so desired, place a baby in that cradle. With God nothing was impossible. A little reflection on the testimony of this young lady enables us to decide why God did not have difficulty in deciding which woman in Israel should have the honour of bearing His Son. It is not without interest that God did not intrude upon the privacy of Elizabeth. We have been told (verse 24) that the aged cousin hid herself, or withdrew herself to a realm of seclusion. Did she do this according to the guidance of God, or did she go away for reasons expressed in the earlier expository notes? It matters not, whatever her reason, God co-operated with her as she did with Him. Happy indeed is the offspring of such union. When God and His people are in perfect harmony, anything can happen. *And the angel departed from her.* As far as we know, that angel never returned. He came to introduce the Christ, and having completed his mission, retired. In any case, when the Son of God is near, who wants to see an angel? How very different are the appearances of God's messengers from those illuminating spirits said to frequent the sittings of the spiritist mediums. It is never said that an angel came to thump on a table; to carry a chair across a room, or to produce signs of one kind or another destined to make headlines in the newspapers. There is a satisfying, reassuring sanity about all God's dealings with men, and it is this characteristic which lends credence to the account written by Luke. There has always been something challenging and gloriously different between authentic writings and the efforts of other authors. Church history cites many examples and even the New Testament Apocalypse provides notable instances of the spurious art of the forger. Dating from the first century comes the account of one named Jesus. He wrote in his *evangelium*, "Fear not, said the angel to Mary; for thou hast found grace before the Master of all things, and thou shalt conceive by His word. Having heard that, she doubted and said within herself: Shall I conceive of the Lord, of the living God, and shall I give birth as every woman gives birth? And the angel of the Lord said to her, No, not thus, Mary, for the power of God shall . . ." Somehow, this message does not ring true. Somewhere along the line of descent, the original message had been changed; what was being written then was a very poor second best, a lamentable imitation of that which was without question the best in purity, poetry, and spiritual experience.

HOMILIES

Study No. 3

### THE WOMEN WHO LAUGHED

The Lord said unto Abraham, "Where is Sarah thy wife? And he said, Behold, in the tent. And the Lord said, I will certainly return unto thee according to the time of life; and, lo, Sarah thy wife shall have a son. And Sarah heard it in the tent door, which was behind him . . . Therefore Sarah laughed within herself, saying, After I am waxed old shall I have pleasure, my lord being old also? And the Lord said unto Abraham, Wherefore did Sarah laugh, saying, Shall I of a surety bear a child, which am old? Is anything too hard for the Lord?"

*Thou shalt have a son, and shalt call his name Isaac* (Genesis 18 : 9–15)
Poor Sarah! She could hardly believe her ears as she stood in the doorway of her tent. She was preparing her meal, but the apparent stupidity of the visitor had momentarily halted her activities. The words were still ringing in her ears—Sarah thy wife shall have a son! Amazed, she turned to look toward the strangers; and then her old shoulders silently shook. It was funny! The old lady tried hard to suppress her mirth but the task was almost beyond her capabilities. She remembered the long years when the joys of motherhood had been denied, and the thought of nursing a baby now seemed ridiculous. Quietly she stole away, lest her silent laughter should become more boisterous; but even as her hands prepared the meal, her wrinkled face betrayed the humour of her soul. "Sarah thy wife shall have a son." What nonsense! The stranger had taken leave of his senses. Then suddenly she was afraid, for beyond the door a voice was asking, "Wherefore did Sarah laugh?" Abraham's eyes were wrathful as they silently searched for his wife. The Stranger was also displeased; and instantly embarrassed and guilty, Sarah said, "I laughed not." The Lord quietly replied, "Nay, but thou didst laugh," and Sarah was glad to escape from the tent. She realised that God had spoken: but it was impossible—or was it?

*Thou shalt have a son, and shalt call his name John* (Luke 1)
Poor Elizabeth! She was old and very disappointed. Her greatest longings had never been realised, for a baby's smiles had never thrilled her soul. The home had remained silent and empty. Her husband was a priest, and together they walked uprightly before the Lord. They had persistently presented their requests for a child, but alas, their

prayers had not been answered. "They had no child, because that Elizabeth was barren, and they both were now well stricken in years" (Luke 1: 7). And while she sat at home patiently trusting in God, Zacharias went to follow his high and holy calling in the sanctuary. "And there appeared unto him an angel of the Lord standing on the right side of the altar of incense . . . and said, Fear not, Zacharias: for thy prayer is heard; and thy wife Elizabeth shall bear thee a son." He was astonished as he muttered to himself, "Impossible! I am an old man and my wife is well stricken in years. A son! I'm dreaming." And if old Sarah could have been present, she would have laughed again: but this time her mirth would have been unrestrained. And when she recovered she would probably have looked at the priest and asked, "Didn't you hear about me? Priest, you have lots to learn." "And the angel answering said unto Zacharias . . . Behold thou shalt be dumb and not able to speak . . . because thou believest not my words . . ."

*Thou shalt have a son, and shalt call his name Jesus* (Luke 1: 30–33)

Poor Mary! She was greatly stirred, for the angel had said unto her, "Fear not, Mary: for thou hast found favour with God. And, behold, thou shalt conceive in thy womb, and bring forth a son, and shalt call his name Jesus . . . Then said Mary unto the angel, How shall this be, seeing I know not a man? And the angel answered and said unto her, The Holy Spirit shall come upon thee, and the power of the Highest shall overshadow thee: therefore also that holy thing which shall be born of thee shall be called the Son of God." It was fantastic; it was impossible—or was it? Then Mary laughed, but hers was the laugh of faith. She said, "Behold the handmaid of the Lord; be it unto me according to thy word." Her heart was filled with joy as she sang, "My soul doth magnify the Lord, and my spirit hath rejoiced in God my Saviour."

Sarah, Elizabeth and Zacharias, and Mary—they all laughed; but she "who laughed last, laughed best." (Reprinted from *Bible Pinnacles*, p. 7.)

SECTION FOUR

*Expository Notes on Mary's Visit to Elizabeth*

And Mary arose in those days, and went into the hill country with haste into a city of Judah; and entered into the house of Zacharias and saluted Elizabeth.

The term "in those days" probably infers it took Mary a little time to prepare for this vacation but as soon as possible she went quickly to join her kinswoman. She was not commanded to go, but the angel's message surely gave a hint that it might be good to make the journey. Either woman would be able to contribute something to the faith of the other. It is extremely problematical whether any person would have believed Mary's amazing story. Even Joseph, at this early stage, might have had doubts regarding the truthfulness of Mary's testimony. Matthew 1: 19–20 reveals it was necessary for the angel to intercede on Mary's behalf; to explain to this upright man his sweetheart had not been unfaithful. Had Mary paused to explain what had taken place she might have encountered all kinds of problems. This virtuous woman believed God was more competent at explaining difficult problems than she could ever be, so with perfect confidence, she allowed the Lord to deal with her man. The only person completely able to understand Mary's experience was the kinswoman in the hills, and to her the young lady went as quickly as possible. The journey probably took about three days.

> And it came to pass, that, when Elizabeth heard the salutation of Mary, the baby leaped in her womb; and Elizabeth was filled with the Holy Spirit; And she spake out with a loud voice, and said, Blessed art thou among women, and blessed is the fruit of thy womb. And whence is this to me, that the mother of my Lord should come to me? For, lo, as soon as the voice of thy salutation sounded in my ears, the baby leaped in my womb for joy. And blessed is she that believed: for there shall be a performance of those things which were told her from the Lord (vv. 41–45).

It is not too difficult to imagine the scene as the two women met. Perhaps Mary was just a little nervous, maybe shy, but the overwhelming welcome and the glad cry of joy coming from the kinswoman not only filled her with wonder; it removed any reserve which might have been within her soul. It is not unusual for an unborn child to make movements during this time of pregnancy but this occurrence was somewhat out of the ordinary. Elizabeth was in a state of extreme exultation and in ways undefined and inexplicable, her ecstasy was imparted to the form cradled within her womb. These are great mysteries but we are surrounded by mysteries; life itself is a mystery. The expression, "blessed is the fruit of thy womb" seems to imply The Incarnation was already an established fact; that conception had already taken place. Later, Mary testified, "For he that is mighty *hath done to me* great things." Probably this memorable transmission was made as soon as Mary's triumphant faith exclaimed "Be it unto me according to thy word," and as the miracle took place within her being, this delightful woman knew the deed had been accomplished. Verse 43 is noteworthy in that it reveals two outstanding things. (*a*) *The deep humility* of Elizabeth was manifest when she voluntarily placed herself beneath the younger woman. From every natural viewpoint, her age, her prestige as a senior kinswoman would have compelled the utmost respect from any young woman, yet this wife of the priest confessed she was not worthy of a visit from her Lord's mother. (*b*) *The keen perception* of the old lady was apparent when she looked beyond Mary to see in the unborn child, the Lord of Glory. Surely the key to the full understanding of all this is found in the one potent statement ". . . and Elizabeth was filled with the Holy Spirit." It has been well said that the greatest proof of the authenticity of this account is its wonderful simplicity. No forger would have had sufficient wisdom to create a story filled with these delicate touches of grace. Oftentimes truth is stranger than fiction. For other notes on "Blessed is she that believed" see the homily at the end of section three of this chapter.

And Mary said, My soul doth magnify the Lord, And my spirit hath rejoiced in God my Saviour, For he hath regarded the low estate of his handmaiden. . . . He hath holpen his servant Israel, in remembrance of his mercy. As he spake to our fathers, to Abraham, and to his seed for ever (vv. 46–55).

This poem or song of Mary has been used by the church throughout the ages. It has inspired thought and thrilled souls in every century, and will forever remain one of the choicest portions of New Testament literature. The New English Bible translates the song as follows:

> Tell out my soul, the greatness of the Lord,
>     Rejoice, rejoice, my spirit, in God my saviour;
> So tenderly has he looked upon his servant,
>     Humble as she is.
> For from this day forth,
>     All generations will count me blessed,
> So wonderfully has he dealt with me,
>     The Lord, the Mighty One.
>
> His name is Holy;
>     His mercy sure from generation to generation
> Toward those who fear him;
>     The deeds his own right hand hath done
> Disclose his might:
>     The arrogant of heart and mind he hath put to rout,
> He has torn imperial powers from their thrones,
>     But the humble have been lifted high.
> The hungry he has satisfied with good things,
>     The rich sent empty away.

He has ranged himself at the side of Israel his servant;
Firm in his promise to our forefathers,
He has not forgotten to show mercy to Abraham
And his children's children for ever.

In common with everything else of exquisite beauty within the Bible, this song of Mary has been attacked from many angles. Critics noticed it was almost entirely made up of quotations from the Old Testament, and sarcastically asked if Mary's scriptures were before her as she sang. Probably the critics did not consider that even from infancy, Hebrew children were taught to memorize scripture; that thereafter they heard the same scriptures being sung over and over again in the synagogues. Certainly Mary had her scriptures before her as she sang, but she had no need of a printed page; the words were engraved upon her heart. It is interesting to observe that Zacharias and Elizabeth were filled with the Spirit at specific times for special tasks. This is not said of Mary. When the Cloud was seen hovering above the Tabernacle, Israel knew God was in residence. It is not said that Mary was filled with the spirit. There was no need of special anointings for He came to hover above her—that is, to be the constant symbol of the Lord's abiding presence. Her body had become a tabernacle; her womb the sacred mercy seat in the Holiest of All. She was permanently filled with the Spirit of God. As the manna from heaven had been placed within the sanctuary, so Mary had hidden the written word in her heart. When the Holy Spirit needed words for her song, He had only to take what she had provided, and the immortal message was soon flowing from her lips.

The Tabernacle in the Wilderness was divided into three sections and these represent the divisions in the human temple. The outer court into which all could come signified the body of the believer; that part of the Christian to which all have access. The Holy Place where only priests entered represented that spiritual part of a man, his soul where only fellow believers enjoy the fellowship. The Holiest of All would be that inner sanctum, the spirit, where God dwells. The opening stanzas of Mary's hymn of praise refers to this fine distinction of soul and spirit. *"My soul doth magnify the Lord* refers to the personal emotions of Mary, to her feelings as a woman and a mother; . . . *My spirit hath rejoiced* indicates the moment when in the profoundest depths of her being, by the touch of the Divine Spirit, the promise of the angel was accomplished in her" (Godet). Thus the final statement might be paraphrased: "My spirit hath rejoiced in the presence of God my Saviour"—He was already there, enthroned in embryonic form within her most intimate consciousness. Students might wish to analyse this passage under four headings: (a) *Her Sanctity.* God surely had a special reason for choosing this woman before all the others in Israel. (*b*) *Her Submission*. She had no objections; she did not argue. Her soul responded in the admirable words: "Be it unto me according to thy word." (*c*) *Her Serenity*. Such intimate fellowship with the Lord promotes joy of the deepest kind. It was naturally that she should sing to His praise, "My soul doth magnify the Lord, and my spirit hath rejoiced in God my Saviour." (*d*) *Her Song*. This was an outpouring of her knowledge of the holy scriptures, and as verse succeeded verse, she provided word pictures of her own faith. *God was observant* to see the low estate of His handmaiden. *God was gracious* to reward her for it. *God was powerful* for He had done to her great things. *God was pure;* holy was His name. *God was kind* for His mercy was upon His people from one generation to another. *God was just* for He deposed the mighty, and exalted them of low degree. *God was faithful* in that He filled the hungry with good things, but sent the rich empty away. Throughout the ages, He had remembered His covenant, and this He would do for ever.

**And Mary abode with her about three months, and returned to her own house.**

Some discussion has taken place over the time of Mary's departure. Some writers believe she did not depart until after the birth of Elizabeth's child. Godet, for example, thinks it would have been unnatural for Mary to leave on the eve of the most important event in Elizabeth's life. She did not arrive until the sixth month of the old lady's pregnancy; she stayed another three months, so obviously the birth of John was to be expected at any time. Great anticipation would be filling the priest's home; how then could Mary leave prematurely? Other writers say the birth of John Baptist would be publicized in all parts of the hilly regions and many people would flock to the city. Therefore Mary probably departed early in order to escape the attention of inquisitive people.

HOMILIES

Study No. 4

## THE SONGS OF THE BLESSED

It is as natural for a happy soul to sing as for a bird to fly. The birds greet the dawn with a paean of praise, and in like manner those who love the Lord announce their triumphs. The Bible cites many instances in support of this truth.

### Moses and his original choir

"Then sang Moses and the children of Israel this song unto the Lord, and spake, saying, I will sing unto the Lord, for he hath triumphed gloriously: the horse and his rider hath he thrown into the sea" (Exodus 15: 1). This was a command performance for the Lord was sitting in the seat of honour! Deep baritones and thrilling tenors; sweet sopranos and rich contraltos harmonized as they sang their song of praise: "The Lord is my strength and song, and he is become my salvation. He is my God and *I will prepare him an habitation* . . ." Even the choirs in heaven were hushed as this original anthem re-echoed from the earth. Surely something had happened. Whence this sweet music? God had redeemed His people with the blood of the lamb; with His strong stretched-out arm He had delivered a nation. If Israel had not sung, the stones would have registered a protest.

### Deborah who sang a duet with Barak

"Then sang Deborah and Barak the son of Ahinoam on that day, saying, Praise ye the Lord . . ." (Judges 5: 1–31). As far as we are able to judge this was the first duet, unrehearsed, unannounced, but thrilling and wonderful to hear. This was an operatic effort of the highest order, where the lead was sung by a prophetess, and the supporting role taken by a rugged captain. Behind them the land was ravaged by heathens, but Jehovah had rescued His people. Who else could have made this possible? The Lord had been gracious and as the singers' souls filled with ecstasy, they sang their thrilling message, "Praise ye the Lord." Had they remained silent, the angels would have veiled their faces.

### Hannah who sang a solo to the Lord

"And Hannah prayed and said . . . I rejoice in thy salvation . . . The Lord maketh poor, and maketh rich; he bringeth low, and lifteth up. He raiseth up the poor out of the dust, and lifteth up the beggar from the dunghill, to set them among princes, and to make them inherit the throne of glory; for the pillars of the earth are the Lord's, and he hath set the world upon them. He will keep the feet of his saints . . ." (I Samuel 2: 1–9). The woman of a bygone age had known a marvellous experience. The bitter anguish of years had almost been forgotten in the gift of the boy Samuel. A decadent nation was about to be rescued for God had sent a saviour. As this woman considered the wonderful works of the Lord, her soul filled with rapture and her prayer became a song. She could not have remained silent even had she tried.

*Solomon who had a professional choir*

"It came even to pass, as the trumpeters and singers were as one, to make one sound to be heard in praising and thanking the Lord; when they lifted up their voice with the trumpets and cymbals and instruments of music, and praised the Lord saying, For he is good; for his mercy endureth for ever; that then the house was filled with a cloud, even the house of the Lord; So that the priests could not stand to minister by reason of the cloud; for the glory of the Lord had filled the house of God" (II Chronicles 5: 13–14). This was surely a great day in Israel. The House of the Lord had been erected and consecrated, but the crowning point in the celebrations came when in response to the prayer and praise of the people, the Lord, the Redeemer came down to live among them. The quality of the anthems suited the occasion. If Solomon had not provided the choir, the angels would have filled the breach.

*Elizabeth and Mary sang separate songs of praise*

See the expositional notes. These two women were privileged indeed in that the Lord had permitted them to have a special part in His programme for a needy world. The elderly lady in the hills had seen the impossible coming to pass when the Creator allowed her to become the mother of the Lord's forerunner. Mary, also, had been touched by the Hand of God. These two saints were filled with thanksgiving and had they been unable to sing, their souls might have burst.

*The Angelic Choir which performed for the shepherds*

"And suddenly there was with the angel a multitude of the heavenly host praising God and saying, Glory to God in the highest, and on earth, peace, goodwill toward men" (Luke 2: 13–14). The shepherds were astounded for amidst the beauty of that eastern night, the sweetest harmony came down from the stars. Their astonishment gave place to peace; their bewilderment to ecstasy. God had sent angels to announce the birth of the Saviour. How marvellous! The Redeemer had come to Israel; the world had not been abandoned in spite of its sin. This was glorious; this was unspeakably marvellous. These men were so entranced they probably forgot to sing, so the angels did it for them.

*Paul and Silas who sang a duet at midnight*

"And at midnight Paul and Silas prayed, and sang praises unto God: and the prisoners heard them" (Acts 16: 25). To sing in the morning is to provide a good start for the work of the day. To sing in the afternoon is a pleasant pastime if elderly people are not resting. To sing at night can be entertaining if the audience is appreciative, but to sing at midnight is an abomination especially when the concert is in a prison where disgruntled prisoners are trying to sleep! Yet circumstances alter cases. Here were two men whose backs were bleeding, whose wounds were painful, yet they possessed joy which pain could not destroy. Their Saviour had not only come to earth, He now resided within their hearts. They were in excellent company. It was better to sing the praise of God than to listen to moans. Even God was thrilled, but He detected the need for a little base harmony, and to provide what was lacking, sent an earthquake.

### The Eternal Choir from every nation

"And they sang a new song, saying . . . thou hast redeemed us to God by thy blood out of every kindred, and tongue, and people, and nation: And hast made us unto our God kings and priests: and we shall reign on the earth . . . and the number of them was ten thousand times ten thousand and thousands of thousands" (Revelation 5: 9-11). This choir will break all records. Never before, and never again will there be an assembly of singers as large, as diverse in nationality, as exuberant in thrilling praise. Probably Heaven will have its song writers; its musicians; its superlative artists, but if sometimes they remember earth and desire to sing one of the old songs, someone might suggest and even begin the melody:

> Redeemed, how I love to proclaim it!
> Redeemed by the blood of the Lamb;
> Redeemed through His infinite mercy,
> His child and forever I am.

> Redeemed and so happy in Jesus,
> No language my rapture can tell;
> I know that the light of His presence
> With me doth continually dwell.

> I think of my blessed Redeemer;
> I think of Him all the day long:
> I sing, for I cannot be silent;
> His love is the theme of my song.

> And now I can see in His beauty
> The King in whose law I delight:
> Who lovingly guarded my footsteps,
> And gave to me songs in the night.

> Redeemed, redeemed,
> Redeemed by the blood of the Lamb;
> Redeemed, redeemed,
> His child, now, forever I am.

SECTION FIVE

*Expository Notes on the Birth and Circumcision of John the Baptist*

**Now Elizabeth's full time came that she should be delivered; and she brought forth a son. And her neighbours and her cousin heard how the Lord had shewed great mercy upon her; and they rejoiced with her (vv. 57–58).**

This provides a simple but charming picture of life in a Jewish home. The news of the imminent birth of a child to Elizabeth had reached the neighbourhood, and everyone waited expectantly for the great event. When the announcement was made that she had given birth to a boy, it was all the evidence needed to prove the Lord had been exceedingly gracious. Both Elizabeth and her husband had known all the time that the child would be a boy for the name had been chosen in heaven. The neighbours, however, even if they had heard this fact, would have no irrefutable proof until a boy was actually born. This was the last detail needed to endorse the testimony of the aged priest. This was truly God's work and the event was marvellous in the eyes of the people.

**And it came to pass, that on the eighth day they came to circumcise the child; and they called him Zacharias, after the name of his father. And his mother answered and said, Not so; but he shall be called John. And they said unto her, There is none of thy kindred that is called by this name. And they made signs to his father how he would have him called. And he asked for a writing table, and wrote, saying, His name is John. And they marvelled all. And his mouth was opened immediately, and his tongue loosed, and he spake and praised God (vv. 59–64).**

The circumcision of a child always took place on the eighth day, and it was customary within Jewish circles for this to be a joyous event when the child was officially named. To such gatherings friends and relatives came, for this was considered a most important occasion. Following the custom which is still prevalent today, the relatives proceeded to name the baby after his father, but this was opposed by Elizabeth. During the time when Mary visited the home, the events of the previous months were constantly under discussion and there can be no doubt through the medium of writing Zacharias had mentioned the naming of the baby. It is worthy of consideration that after Elizabeth had voiced an objection to the naming of her child Zacharias, the old priest quickly put an end to the argument by writing, HIS NAME IS JOHN. He did not express an opinion; neither did he ask that they should call him by that name. If they had only gathered for the naming ceremony they had wasted their time for the job had already been done. Thus did the old man exhibit an affinity with the purposes of God. It was customary in those days to write upon pieces of waxed wood; the pen was of the stilleto type, and the words were traced or scratched in the wax. When the priest proceeded to make known his decision, the people marvelled, but their wonderment increased when suddenly his power of speech returned. Thus did God endorse what had been written.

It has been suggested that since the people made signs to the father, Zacharias must have been deaf as well as dumb. This was by no means conclusive as most writers indicate. A dumb man, for the most part in those days, could only communicate thought by writing or by making signs with the hands. It would not always be convenient to write messages and on the spur of the moment, a man would use his hands by pointing, or beckoning, or making signs suitable for the occasion. It would be natural for others to emulate his example. There was nothing startling about the fact that the people used sign language even as did the priest. It was truly interesting that the returning speech was first used to thank God. Happy indeed was the man whose first expression was gratitude; whose first word was praise.

**And fear came on all who dwelt round about them. . . . The New English Bible translates this and the following verses thus: All the neighbours were struck with awe, and everywhere in the uplands of Judea the whole story became common talk. All who heard it were deeply impressed and said, What will this child become? For indeed the hand of the Lord was (or is) upon him (vv. 65–66).**

This was the natural outcome of the amazing events taking place in their midst. Long before John reached the age of maturity many of those hillside people would be dead, but it should be remembered that children would have listened to the excited talk of their parents; that these boys and girls grew up with the child of Zacharias and Elizabeth. When the time arrived for the public ministry of the Baptist, these folk would remember the events of his childhood and their testimony would increase the receptivity of many people. When God does something, He does it well! He who sees the end from the beginning knows how to plan for the future of His children.

**And his father Zacharias was filled with the Holy Spirit, and prophesied saying, Blessed be the Lord God of Israel; for he hath visited and redeemed his people, And hath raised up an horn of salvation for us in the house of his servant David . . . And thou child shall be called the prophet of the Highest; for thou shalt go before the face of the Lord to**

prepare his ways; to give knowledge of salvation unto his people by
the remission of their sins . . . the dayspring from on high hath visited
us, To give light to them that sit in darkness and in the shadow of
death, to guide our feet into the way of peace (vv. 67-79).

Luke has been careful to indicate this song was only made possible
through the infilling of the Holy Spirit. Probably the words were sung
over and over again and finally written upon a piece of wood. When
Luke needed the song for his Gospel, he was able to copy the script
from the original. The reference to the Saviour in verse 68 implies
that Zacharias was fully aware of Mary's pregnancy and saw in her
conception the intervention of God on behalf of the human race. For
additional notes on *"the horn of salvation"* see the homily at the end
of this section.

The student should carefully notice the key words of this poem.
*Redemption. Salvation. The Word of God. Mercy. Deliverance. Service. Holiness. Righteousness* leading to *Faithfulness.*

The reference to his own child as translated in the New English
Bible is:

"And you, my child, you shall be called the Prophet of the Highest,
for you will be the Lord's forerunner, to prepare his way and lead
his people to salvation through knowledge of him, by the forgiveness
of their sins."

Probably this is the most concise definition of the Christian ministry
ever given to man; it provides an example for all ministers and should
be written upon the ordination certificates of all churches.

F. L. Godet on page 116 of his commentary on Luke's Gospel suggests that the statements "To give light to them that sit in darkness
and in the shadow of death, to guide our feet into the way of peace"
provides a word-picture of extreme beauty. He says, "All the images
in the picture portrayed in verses 78-79 appear to be borrowed from
the following comparison. A caravan misses its way and is lost in the
desert; the unfortunate pilgrims, overtaken by night, are sitting down
in the midst of this fearful darkness, expecting death. All at once a
bright star rises in the horizon and lights up the plain; the travellers,
taking courage at this sight, arise, and by the light of this star find
the road which leads them to the end of their journey."

And the child grew, and waxed strong in spirit, and was in the deserts
till the day of his shewing unto Israel (v. 80).

This one verse covers a gap of almost thirty years in the life of John
Baptist. Luke, the descriptive physician, probably meant to suggest

the infant developed not only a muscular frame but also a deepening consciousness of God's presence. He became one in whom resided resolute convictions; he was a man of destiny. At this particular period, ascetic people known as the Essenes lived in their monasteries throughout the desert area of Judea. Actually, this was not a desert, in the sense that we understand deserts; the countryside abounded in deep crevices which are common today in some parts of southern Africa. There were many creviced valleys and numerous caves, and at intervals across the terrain were the monasteries in which the Essenes lived. Some writers think John became a recluse and lived with these people. This, however, is hardly possible for when John began to preach, he enunciated doctrines the very reverse of those taught by the hermits. The text "he . . . was in the deserts" is best interpreted by the idea that he spent his time in solitary places. It is unthinkable that he forsook his parents and spent thirty years apart from all other human beings. Probably the whole of his early life was spent under the watchful eyes of his devoted parents, and that as he grew older, he developed a love for the solitudes and sought every opportunity to walk and talk with God far from the listening ears of inquisitive people. Thus did the Lord train His servant and when the day of his initial appearance arrived, John was ready to become the greatest evangelist the world ever knew.

## HOMILIES

Study No. 5

### The Horn of Salvation

The image of a horn was often used by ancient writers to describe certain facets of truth. The figure was also used in a Messianic sense to indicate that one possessed of superlative strength would one day descend from the house of David. Psalm 132: 17 reads: "There will I make the horn of David to bud: I have ordained a lamp for mine anointed. His enemies will I clothe with shame: but upon himself shall his crown flourish." The scriptures reveal that under the title of "the horn" great truth is taught, and this, in the light of the utterance of Zacharias assumes great importance.

### The Horns of Salvation

"And Adonijah feared because of Solomon, and arose, and went, and caught hold on the horns of the altar" (I Kings 1: 50). The blood of sacrifice was always sprinkled or smeared upon the horns of the altar,

(Leviticus 8: 15) and it was to this refuge the guilty prince fled for safety. He recognized that if there could be one place of mercy in the kingdom, the horns of the altar would provide it. He was correct for when Solomon heard of his action, he announced forgiveness for the desperate insurrectionist. Thus Zacharias announced for all to hear that God had raised up one to whom sinful men could fly for refuge.

*The Horn of Sovereignty*

Throughout the prophetic era, the term, *horn* was used to indicate royalty; a king was described as a horn: the seat of strength. "Then lifted I up mine eyes, and saw, and behold four horns. And I said unto the angel that talked with me. What are these? And he answered me, These are the horns which have scattered Judah, Israel, and Jerusalem" (Zechariah 1: 18–19). The same imagery may be found throughout the book of Daniel. Thus when the husband of Elizabeth announced the Lord had raised up a horn of salvation, he indicated the coming Redeemer would be a Royal Redeemer, the King of Glory. Men could come to Him for pardon and thereafter remain to worship. Sinners by faith could seek entrance into His kingdom and afterward enjoy the privilege of service within the kingdom.

*The Horn of Special Anointing*

During the Old Testament ages the symbol of a man's being set apart for special service was anointing with holy oil. "And the Lord said unto Samuel, How long wilt thou mourn for Saul, seeing I have rejected him from reigning over Israel? fill thine horn with oil, and go, I will send thee to Jesse the Bethlehemite: for I have provided me a king among his sons . . . Then Samuel took the horn of oil, and anointed David in the midst of his brethren: and the Spirit of the Lord came upon David from that day forward . . ." (I Samuel 16: 1 and 13). Thus was David approved by God and set aside for a very special task. He was destined to become the leader of God's people. The same order of ordination was repeated with the appointment of Solomon (See I Kings 1: 39). Thus in the song of Zacharias, the Spirit of the Lord revealed that Jesus was the Man of God's choice; from His lips would pour words of wisdom to surpass even the utterances of Solomon.

*The Horns of Sublime Praise*

"And seven priests shall bear before the ark seven trumpets of rams' horns . . . and the priests shall blow with the trumpets. And it shall come to pass, that when they make a long blast with the rams' horn, and when ye hear the sound of the trumpet, all the people shall shout with a great shout; and the wall of the city shall fall down flat . . ." (Joshua 6: 4–5). Ahead of the advancing Israelites was an apparently impregnable fortress, but the people of God treated it with disdain. The Ark, the symbol of the presence of God went before them, and before that went the trumpeters. The rams' horns had been obtained through sacrifice. The blood had been shed and from the offering, now arose praise. The same ram whose blood had made forgiveness possible, now provided the means whereby faith could challenge the walls of Jericho. "Blow with the trumpets" commanded Moses, and the barriers were removed. Thus would God have His people realize that when they follow in the footsteps of the Lord, nothing can be impossible.

# The Second Chapter of Luke

THEME: *Early Events in the Life of Jesus*

OUTLINE:

      I. A Baby is Born. Verses 1–20
     II. A Child is Consecrated. Verses 21–40
    III. A Lad is Lost. Verses 41–52

SECTION ONE

*Expository Notes on the Birth of Jesus*

**And it came to pass in those days, that there went out a decree from Caesar Augustus, that all the world should be taxed. And this taxing was first made when Cyrenius was governor of Syria. And all went to be taxed everyone to his own city (vv. 1–3).**

The term "in those days" refers to the period already covered by the events recorded in the first chapter. God was at work in the hill country of Judea, and His Spirit was also moving in other parts of the world. During the ages, God had planned the coming of His Son to earth, and now that the time was approaching for the event to take place, the pieces of the master plan were falling into position as if they belonged to a jigsaw puzzle. Centuries earlier, Micah had prophesied saying, "But thou, Beth-lehem Ephratah, though thou be little among the thousands of Judah, yet out of thee shall he come forth unto me that is to be ruler in Israel; whose goings forth have been from of old, from everlasting" (Micah 5: 2). As the prophet indicated there were very many villages in Israel but Bethlehem Ephratah had been chosen as the birthplace of the Messiah. This necessitated something resembling a miracle, for Joseph and Mary had no intention of leaving their home in Nazareth. Therefore it became necessary for the Spirit of God to operate in the mind of the Emperor in Rome. There were no accidental occurrences in the realm of the Spirit for He who saw the end from the beginning was able to plan according to His foreknowledge. Had the Emperor Augustus made his decision three months earlier, or indeed three months later, the unfolding of the plans of God would have been thrown into confusion. God knew how long it would take to set the registration machinery of the Empire into action; He knew precisely how long it would take for officials to reach their place of duty, and when every detail had been finalized, things began to move, not primarily as the Emperor decreed, but according to the will of the Almighty. The term *Apographe* translated *taxed* would be better expressed *registered*. Among the Romans this indicated a general registration of citizens, when the heads of the various households were required to reveal their name, age, occupation, and the size of their family. These details were required as an aid to the assessment of taxes. It would appear that the Emperor ordered this registration with a view to the raising of money necessary for the extension and maintenance of the Empire. That all this came to pass in time to bring Joseph and Mary to the appointed place, Bethlehem, for the birth of Jesus provides food for thought. As God planned in bygone ages, so He plans now. Happy indeed is the man whose future rests in the hand of the Lord.

Within scholastic circles much criticism has been aimed at the historical details recorded in this text. Entire chapters could be written about the various statements made both for and against the historicity of Luke's narrative. Probably Godet best condenses the facts for he states: "From the commencement of his reign, Augustus always aimed at a stronger centralization of the empire. Already under Julius Caesar, there had been undertaken, with a view to a more exact assessment of taxation, a great statistical work, a complete survey of the empire. This work, which occupied thirty-two years, was only finished under Augustus. This prince never ceased to labour in the same direction. After his death, Tiberias caused to be read in the Senate, in accordance with instructions contained in the will of Augustus, a statistical document, which applied not only to the empire so called, but also the allied kingdoms—a category to which the states of Herod belonged. This document, called *Breviarium totius imperii*, was written entirely by Augustus' own hand. It gave the number of citizens and of allies under arms, of the fleets, of the kingdoms, of the provinces, *of the tributes or taxes*. The compilation of such a document as this, necessarily supposes a previous statistical labour, comprehending not only the empire proper, but also the allied states. And if Augustus had ordered this work, Herod, whose kingdom belonged to the number of *regna reddita,* could not have refused to take part in it . . ." Later, Suidas the famous writer said, "Caesar Augustus, having chosen twenty men of the greatest ability, sent them into all the countries of the subject nations, and caused them to make a registration of men and property" (*Commentary on John's Gospel,*

F. L. Godet, pages 120–121). Very much more could be added but this will enable students to know Luke was not writing fiction. There *was* a registration of the subject nations and men were required to visit the appointed places in order to comply with the demands of the law.

> And Joseph also went up from Galilee, out of the city of Nazareth, into Judea, unto the city of David, which is called Bethlehem; (because he was of the house and lineage of David) . . . and with him went Mary who was betrothed to him. She was pregnant, and while they were there, the time came for her child to be born, and she gave birth to a son, her first-born. She wrapped him round, and laid him in a manger, because there was no room for them to lodge in the house (vv. 4–7. New English Bible).

All Jews were very exacting in regard to their ancestry and it was not surprising that Joseph could trace his lineage to David. Even in Babylon the records were faithfully preserved. See Ezra Chapter two, and note particularly verse 62 where the omission of certain names from the authorized register had serious repercussions. Bethlehem was the birthplace of David (I Samuel 16: 1–13). Luke continues to refer to Mary as one who was engaged to be married and this appears to conflict with the account supplied by Matthew. After the angel's appearance to Joseph, the reassured man took Mary as his wife but the Gospel indicates "he knew her not till she had brought forth her first-born son . . ." (Matthew 1: 25). Probably Luke continued to speak of Mary as an engaged girl because thereby he emphasized that although she was the legal wife of her husband, they continued to live as betrothed people because the child she carried was not the fruit of their own intercourse. They lived together as man and wife only in the sense that Joseph had taken her into his home to shelter her from the evil insinuations of those who otherwise would have accused her of sinful conduct. It was not required that a woman should be present at the registration of a family, and some critics have challenged this detail in Luke's narrative. Mary was no stranger to the Scriptures; her song had already proved the sacred words were written upon her heart. She would therefore know that God had predicted the Messiah would be born in Bethlehem. Realizing her child would fulfil this prediction, she saw in the command of the Emperor the unfolding of the divine plan. Her time was at hand; it was necessary to accompany her husband for how else would the promises of the Lord be fulfilled? Students should remember this story describes an intelligent young woman completely controlled by the Spirit of God. She was not an unfortunate maiden adrift on the seas of circumstance. It is also necessary to remember that had she stayed at home, her child would have been born during the absence of her husband. They had been married for considerably less than nine months, and the arrival of a baby at such an early date in their marital relations would occasion gossip. The spiritual vision of this noble young woman was equalled only by the watchful care of her husband.

Since the decree of the Emperor required all men to register at specified places throughout the country, the number of travellers would be considerable. Every inn or hostelry within miles of Bethlehem would have been crowded. The inn-keeper must have been a very worried man, but alas, all his rooms were occupied; what could he do? Some writers think he might have surrendered his own apartment, but there exists the possibility that this had already been occupied, for the command of the Emperor had created a glorious opportunity for inn-keepers to make money! It could be argued that some of the travellers might have vacated their rooms to help a lady in distress, but we have no way of knowing if they were ever aware of the need. If the inn-keeper told them of the young woman probably already in labour, and if they refused to help her, then they missed for all eternity the chance to become famous.

The birthplace of Jesus was probably a stable, a cave in the nearby hill where animals found shelter. Justin Martyr, one of the leaders of the church in the second century, stated that this was so, and toward the middle of the fourth century, the Emperor Constantine caused a church to be built over a Bethlehem cave. Perhaps this was indeed the original place in which Christ was born, but unfortunately so many claims have been made about ancient sites and buildings that it is understandable why some statements issued by the church have been held in contempt. At a later date, Constantine's church was remodelled and rebuilt as a most beautiful edifice, and this, more or less, is the same place visited annually by thousands of pilgrims.

Unexpected visitors to a stable are apt to find anything but cleanliness. The fantasy of the modern Christmas card has destroyed the true meaning of the event in Bethlehem. It is well that we remember there were no fairy lights; no brilliantly decorated trees. That stable was dirty—probably very dirty, and whilst Mary anxiously stood waiting, Joseph went to work. Animal excretions were removed; cobwebs were probably pulled from the walls, and somewhere in a corner, this marvellous man made a bed of hay. There was no doctor in attendance; there was no nurse standing by; there was no anaesthetic, and unless some unknown woman came from the nearby inn, there was no other to assist at the birth. Together, Joseph and Mary waited. He probably held her hand and smoothed her brow, and during the silent hours of that night, the sudden cry of a new-born babe announced the King of Glory had arrived. Probably the angelic hosts had also waited for the announcement and when they knew the King was born, they sang for joy.

And there were in the same country shepherds abiding in the field, keeping watch over their flocks by night. And, lo, the angel of the Lord came upon them, and the glory of the Lord shone round about them: and they were sore afraid. And the angel said unto them, Fear not: for, behold, I bring you good tidings of great joy, which shall be to all people. For unto you is born this day in the city of David a Saviour which is Christ the Lord (vv. 8–11).

The Jews for some strange reason despised shepherds. Whether or not they were ashamed of their insignificant beginnings, or whether the people who tended the flocks were considered ignorant men unfit for more demanding occupations, we do not know. It has been affirmed that the testimony of the shepherds was never permitted in a court of law, and in some circles at least, succour was never granted to shepherds and heathen. Oftentimes when there were no wild beasts in an area; when thieves were not prevalent, the shepherding of sheep was entrusted to children. The talents and strength of men were required for more important tasks. It would seem then that the people who cared for the sheep were considered unfit for greater tasks. These men did the work of children! This is all the more strange to understand since their revered ancestors had been obliged to confess to Pharaoh, "Thy servants are shepherds, both we, and also our fathers" (Genesis 47 : 3).

To such men, came the announcement of the birth of Christ: probably in those early hours of that never to be forgotten morning, no other men were awake. The city would be silent, and very few, if any, travellers would be on the roads at such an hour. Out in the fields, sitting together near their flocks, these men sat and talked. It is not the wish of this author to read into the story things which are not there, but the fact remains that some of those sheep might eventually have become offerings in the temple. The shepherds were guarding animals which temporarily, at least, would make possible communion between God and man. Whilst other more important people made money, these simple folk remained in the solitudes guarding the sheep and lambs for which guilty people would soon be seeking. It was appropriate that the announcement of the Saviour's birth should be first made to them. Perhaps God was trying to teach everybody that sometimes there is more wealth in the fields of Bethlehem than in the courts of Caesar.

It was natural for the men to be afraid when the shining one

stood in their midst. Probably a translucent glow emanated from
his person, and "the glory of the Lord shone round about them."
The advice "Fear not" was given to Zacharias, 1: 13! to Mary,
1: 30; to the shepherds 2: 10. There is never need to be afraid of
the Lord when one's heart is clean. The good news of the Christ
demanded that it should be told to the waiting world. The angels
became preachers in their own right, and soon the shepherds followed
their example. To know the Saviour is to desire to tell others about
Him.

> And this shall be a sign unto you; ye shall find the babe wrapped in
> swaddling clothes, lying in a manger. And suddenly there was with the
> angel a multitude of the heavenly host praising God and saying, Glory
> to God in the highest, and on earth, peace, goodwill toward men (vv.
> 12–14). Some translations have: "Peace to men of good will" or "Peace
> to men on whom His favour rests" or "Peace to the men who are the
> objects of God's good pleasure."

It was possible that other babies might have been born in Bethlehem
that night, but it was nevertheless most unlikely that any other child
would be cradled in a manger. If any doubt of identification existed,
this simple sign was sufficient to identify the Christ-child. The message
of the angels was expressed in three phases. (i) *A Great Praise.* "Glory
to God in the Highest Places." The events taking place that night in
Bethlehem were conducive to the highest praise. There had been
many occasions when God displayed His graciousness; when undeserved favour was extended to guilty men, yet nothing had ever
equalled in mercy the gift of God's dear Son. Heaven and earth
should sing the praise of the Infinite. (ii) *A Great Peace.* ". . . on earth
peace." The coming of Christ to earth would result in perfect peace.
A measure of national peace was already known for the strength of
the Caesars had temporarily outlawed war, yet as Epictetus, the
philosopher of the first century wrote: "while the emperor may give
peace from war on land or sea, he is unable to give peace from
passion, grief and envy. He cannot give peace of heart, for which
man yearns more than for outward peace." Peace for a tortured
conscience; rest for a troubled soul: these are the treasures
obtained only through the coming of Christ. (iii) *A Great Purpose.*
This peace would become the possession of a select company of
people—the objects of God's good pleasure. God in Christ was
about to make salvation possible. The coming of the Christ removed
barriers of sin and opened a way by which the benediction of the
Highest could come to men. Some people would neither participate
nor co-operate; these men would therefore not know the peace of

God. Others by their choice of righteousness were recipients of God's favour, and enjoyed the peace of God which passeth understanding.

**And it came to pass, as the angels were gone away from them into heaven, the shepherds said one to another, Let us now go even unto Bethlehem, and see this thing which is come to pass, which the Lord hath made known unto us. And they came with haste, and found Mary and Joseph, and the babe lying in a manger, and when they had seen it, they made known the saying which was told them concerning this child. And all they that heard it wondered at those things which were told them by the shepherds (vv. 16–18).**

The shepherds were not expressly commanded to go in search of the child; they acted on their own initiative as all sensible men would have done. We are not told if they drove their sheep to the outskirts of the city, or whether they left their charges in the care of others. Neither are we told if they had any difficulty in locating the birthplace, nor how long it took to find the stable. Perhaps the wisdom of God veiled these things in order to stress the fact that whatever difficulties stood in the way, these men permitted nothing to terminate their search for Jesus. Mountains are made to be climbed; obstacles are challenges to the resourcefulness of individuals. The man who truly wants to find Christ will never rest until he has done so. And when this has been accomplished, the same man tells to others the news which thrilled his own soul. Every sincere Christian possesses a missionary heart.

**But Mary kept all these things, and pondered them in her heart. And the shepherds returned, glorifying and praising God for all the things that they had heard and seen. "It had all happened as they had been told" (vv. 19–20. New English Bible).**

Mary's mind was quickly becoming a treasure-house where jewels were being stored. Perhaps for other people these events were a "nine days' wonder," something to cause excitement and then to be forgotten. Mary was quite different from the people by whom she was surrounded. Every detail was stored within her memory; every exciting detail of the unfolding of the Divine Plan continued to stir her soul. These marvellous events could never be forgotten and that explained the ease with which, after many years, she was able to reiterate the story to the doctor who was planning to write a Gospel. The shepherds probably talked of these events for a considerable time, and their praises to God were not soon hushed. Yet with Mary, things were different. She did no talking; she was too busy remembering the things which had happened to her. Her radiant life was a thank offering, a sweet savour of praise continually ascending from the altar of her sanctified soul.


HOMILIES

Study No. 6

### Spotlight on Bethlehem

The story of Bethlehem is the most amazing story ever told, but its wonder can never be fully comprehended until all the facts relating to it are brought into bold relief. To appreciate the miracle of Bethlehem it is necessary to project our thoughts back into the eternal ages where the Divine Family met in conference. If it be permissible and wise for mere mortals to imagine what took place, we must see the Triune God calmly anticipating what would happen in the ages to come. Critics questioned the wisdom of God in creating man when at the same time, He was aware of the tragedy to follow. There are always two sides to a picture. Would God have been justified in NOT creating man when by so doing, eternal happiness would ultimately be known by countless millions? Should God refuse to do good because some of His creatures prefer evil?

### How Exacting His Plans

The New Testament speaks of the Lamb slain before the foundation of the world; it therefore follows that the Incarnation and subsequent events were in the mind of God before the beginning of time. Within the eternal conference chambers the Participants decided the thrilling entry should be accomplished by the co-operation of a virgin. "Therefore the Lord himself shall give you a sign; behold a virgin shall conceive, and bear a son, and shall call his name Immanuel" (Isaiah 7 : 14). It was also decided that the birth should take place at a small village called Bethlehem, and this was all the more remarkable for at the time of the decision even the planet on which the village would stand had not yet been called into being. "But thou, Bethlehem Ephratah, though thou be little among the thousands of Judah, yet out of thee shall he come forth unto me that is to be ruler in Israel; whose goings forth have been from of old, from everlasting" (Micah 5 : 2). Finally the time of His coming was also considered. This is evident from the fact that Daniel was able to predict the time of Messiah's death. Obviously then, since His decease was to be accomplished at a precise time, the birth of the Messiah would also be planned to co-ordinate with that event. "Know therefore and understand, that from the going forth of the commandment to restore and to build Jerusalem unto the Messiah the Prince shall be seven weeks, and three score and two weeks; the street shall be built again, and the wall even in troublous time. And after three score and two weeks SHALL MESSIAH BE CUT OFF . . ." (Daniel 9: 26). The same minds which designed the universe planned the details of the coming of Christ.

## How Extreme His Power

It is one thing to make plans; it is quite another to guarantee those plans be fulfilled. The Creation of the world was but an introductory measure making subsequent events possible. Bethlehem would need solid foundations, therefore God made the earth. The place would need a name, therefore God decided what it should be and in due course suggested this to the mind of an unknown official. Bethlehem for many reasons had to be a royal city, therefore God arranged that David should be born there (I Samuel 16: 1). At first there appeared no likelihood that Jesus would be born in this historic place for Mary and Joseph resided elsewhere. The only thing to make them go there at that inconvenient time would be something truly unavoidable. This was occasioned when the Emperor in far away Rome decided to take a census of his people. Joseph was left with no alternative; he was obliged to make the journey to Bethlehem. The events of those days fitted as sections of a jigsaw puzzle into a master pattern; the hand that moved the pieces, the hand of God.

## How Exciting His Promise

"For unto you is born this day in the city of David a Saviour, which is Christ the Lord." The presence of Christ in Bethlehem would have been completely futile if God had preserved this as His own secret. Unless the news be told near and far how could the divine purpose be fulfilled? What God has done, He must reveal. The shepherds of New Testament days were despised; their occupation merely demanded rugged courage; brains were not necessary! It is not without interest that the tidings of salvation were first announced to men of this type. Why did God choose the shepherds to be the first evangelists? There were other people in Bethlehem who lived closer to the stable. There were more prominent people whose testimony would have carried more weight with the citizens. There were men whose wealth might have greatly assisted the new parents. Why then did God choose unlearned, uninteresting men of the field? The announcement was indeed exciting; it might be even more thrilling if we discover the answer to the aforegoing question.

*How Expansive His Provision*

"And the angel said unto them, Fear not: for, behold, I bring you good tidings of great joy, *WHICH SHALL BE TO ALL PEOPLE.*" God always planned that His children should be united and for this great achievement the Saviour prayed (John 17: 11). Already, even in those early days, men's bitterness had segregated certain sections of the community. Jews had no dealings with Samaritans. Unfortunately in the following centuries, this evil practice was to grow into an international menace. There was, not so long ago, a denominational meeting in South Africa when black representatives of the native churches sat on one side of the centre aisle, and white representatives of the European churches sat on the other. The dividing line was only about three feet in width but it represented a gulf which few men were able to cross. One native speaker asked a startling question of the entire audience. "If the Lord Jesus entered this meeting, on which side of the aisle would He sit?" God recognizes no racial barriers for in Christ there is neither Jew nor Gentile; British nor German; American nor Russian; Black nor White; East nor West; IN CHRIST, all men are brothers, members of the true church which is His Body. It should be a cause of thanksgiving that this great message was announced by God in that first communication to the Shepherds.

*How Extraordinary His Peace*

"In the first, GLORY TO GOD IN THE HIGHEST PLACES, the angels demand that, from the lower regions to which they have just come down, from the bosom of humanity, praise shall arise . . . the second, PEACE ON EARTH, is the counterpart of the first" (Godet). The New English Translation interprets the passage: ". . . peace for men on whom his favour rests." It would seem that this peace is somewhat conditional. When men begin to praise God and thank Him for the gift of His Son, then in the greatest sense, the peace of God becomes their inward experience. Upon such, the true worshippers, the favour of the Lord rests. They recognize in the Babe the gift of the Highest and reverently adore the Lord. Thus the peace of God which passeth understanding settles upon their souls, and they cease to be troubled. Unless the intimate recognition of Christ be followed by praise in the Highest Places, peace is but a fantasy.

*How Exuberant His Praise*

"And the shepherds returned, glorifying and praising God for all the things which they had heard and seen, as it was told unto them." The story of the shepherds provides thrilling progression. (i) They heard. (ii) They came. (iii) They saw. (iv) They testified. (v) They rejoiced and glorified God. They did nothing to merit their salvation; they had no share in making it possible. Everything appertaining to the Incarnation began in Heaven. God was both the Author and the Finisher of those events. The shepherds recognised what God had done, and shared their good tidings with those with whom they came into contact.

## SECTION TWO

*Expository Notes on the Events at the Dedication of the Child Jesus*

And when eight days were accomplished for the circumcising of the child, his name was called Jesus, which was so named of the angel before he was conceived in the womb. And when the days of her purification according to the law of Moses were accomplished, they brought him to Jerusalem to present him to the Lord. As it is written in the law of the Lord, Every male that openeth the womb shall be called holy to the Lord. And to offer a sacrifice according to that which is said in the law of the Lord, A pair of turtledoves, or two young pigeons (vv. 21–24).

The naming ceremony of a child always took place eight days after birth; that was on the corresponding day of the following week. See also Luke 1: 59. The purification ceremonies mentioned here were in accordance with the commands set forth in the twelfth chapter of the book of Leviticus. "And the Lord spake unto Moses saying, Speak unto the children of Israel saying, If a woman have conceived seed, and born a man child: then she shall be unclean seven days; according to the days of the separation for her infirmity shall she be unclean. And in the eighth day the flesh of his foreskin shall be circumcised. And she shall then continue . . . her purifying three and thirty days; she shall touch no hallowed thing, nor come into the sanctuary, until the days of her purifying be fulfilled . . . and when the days of her purifying are fulfilled . . . she shall bring a lamb of the first year for a burnt offering, and a young pigeon or turtledove for a sin offering, unto the door of the tabernacle of the congregation, unto the priest: Who shall offer it before the Lord, and make an atonement for her . . . And if she be not able to bring a lamb, then she shall bring two turtles, or two young pigeons; the one for a burnt offering, and the other for a sin offering . . . and she shall be clean" (Leviticus 12: 1–8). It should be carefully noted how meticulously Mary and Joseph observed the letter of the law. That they were unable to bring a lamb reflects the poverty with which this betrothed couple began their married life. In a very realistic sense, "He who was rich, became poor, that we through His poverty, might become rich." That the thank offering and the sin offering were united in this one presentation seemed to suggest gratitude and penitence were blending when the suppliants came to the altar of God. All students should give careful consideration to the following passages: Exodus 12:2; Numbers 8:16; Numbers 18:15. The first-born of man and beast were considered to be the property of God, but in the case of a child, redemption was possible at the price of five shekels. How complete was the identification of Christ with sinful man even from the beginning of His earthly career. Far beyond the powers of mortal comprehension was the humiliation to which the King of Glory was subjected.

> And behold there was a man in Jerusalem, whose name was Simeon; and the same man was just and devout, waiting for the consolation of Israel: and the Holy Spirit was upon him. And it was revealed unto him by the Holy Spirit, that he should not see death before he had seen the Lord's Christ. And he came by the Spirit into the temple . . . (vv. 25-27).

God was never without a witness, and the apostasy of a religious movement was no guarantee that all God's people were bankrupt! Here and there amidst the shadows were Simeons and Annas whose eyes, ears, and hearts were open toward God. The religious life in the temple was not all that saints would have wished; yet they never made this an excuse to start a rival movement. Apparently Simeon was neither a great preacher nor an inspired singer. He was the type of man whose name would never be in the headlines of a national newspaper. Probably he never occupied a place on any select committee nor represented his organization at any important conference. He would never have been the President of a bank; nor mentioned in any vital dispatches, for apart from this brief mention on the pages of the New Testament, he was an unknown man who resided somewhere in the city of Jerusalem. The greatest things ever said about him was that he was an intimate friend of the Holy Spirit. Probably he had no time to visit conferences; he was too busy at home. Perhaps he did no public speaking; he had a full-time listening job. He was not a world conqueror for the cause of God; but he was a bondslave watching eagerly for the rising of the sun. (i) The Spirit was upon him. (ii) The Spirit talked with him. (iii) The Spirit led him. Simeon was in excellent company. Most people are not as wise in their choice of a companion! The word translated *consolation*—"waiting for the consolation of Israel" is paraklesin and it is noteworthy that this is the same word used by Christ of the coming of the Holy Spirit at Pentecost. Speaking of this Greek word, Dr. J. H. Thayer says it means: *"Summoned, called to one's side, especially to one's aid.* One *who pleads a cause before a judge, a pleader, a counsel for the defence; a legal assistant, an advocate."* Simeon recognised that his nation was in great danger. There was need that One should come alongside a guilty people, to understand their problems, to render assistance, to plead their cause before the bar of Divine Justice; to help, to advise, to save from death. Deep within his consciousness was the conviction that one day he would actually see this Comforter, the Lord's Christ. How he knew, we are not told, other than that the Holy Spirit begat the conviction. By what means he would recognise the Messiah when the moment arrived, we are not told. Probably he never worried about the matter. He never crossed his bridges before he reached them. We might be wise to follow his example.

... and when the parents brought in the child Jesus, to do for him after the custom of the law, Then took he him up in his arms, and blessed God, and said, "This day, Master, thou givest thy servant his discharge in peace; now thy promise is fulfilled. For I have seen with my own eyes the deliverance which thou hast made ready in full view of all the nations; A light which will be a revelation to the heathen, and glory to thy people Israel" (vv. 27–32. New English Bible).

It is surely amazing that every priest was by-passed in the revelation of God; that it was to an insignificant old man this great honour came. That particular morning an impelling urge carried him to the sanctuary. We are not told whether he had heard stories of the events in Bethlehem; we only know "he came by the Spirit into the temple." He was just in time to be in time! Probably he had seen very many mothers and their children but a thrilling elation warned him the day star was rising! The beauty of his song equalled anything found in Scripture. It was filled with eternal harmonies. This was to be expected from a man so intimately linked with the Author of all inspired music. The word translated *servant* in verse 20 is doulos which is very much stronger than that indicated by the English word. Actually it means *bondslave*. The entire setting provides a word picture of scintillating beauty. Simeon had been keeping vigil throughout the long dark hours. His Master had commanded him to watch, and whilst other things might have tempted him to leave his post, loving obedience sustained his faithfulness. After long hours of impenetrable darkness, the sky was beginning to brighten; the Sun of Righteousness was arising with healing in His wings. Now the bondslave could be relieved of his task; he was free to undertake other assignments; to go to live in the Palace of His eternal Friend.

Godet has an engaging paragraph concerning the terminology of Simeon's song. "The term soteerion which we can only translate by *salvation,* is equivalent neither to *soteer,* Saviour, nor to *soteeria,* *salvation.* This word, the neuter of the adjective *soterios,* saving, *denotes an apparatus fitted to save.* Simeon sees in this little child *the means of deliverance* which God is giving to the world." *Commentary on the Gospel of Luke,* p. 139. The worldwide mission of the Saviour; the far-reaching effects of His glorious message are clearly reflected in the closing statements of Simeon's thrilling utterance.

> And Joseph and his mother marvelled at those things which were spoken of him. And Simeon blessed them, and said unto Mary his mother, Behold, this child is set for the fall and rising again of many in Israel; and for a sign which shall be spoken against. Yea a sword shall pierce through thine own soul also, that the thoughts of many hearts may be revealed (vv. 34-35).

The parents of Jesus were probably surprised that a stranger should be so acquainted with facts relating to their son. It was true that the shepherds had been aware of His presence but the appearance of the angels accounted for their enlightenment. Whence came the knowledge of this man? It was not new teaching that the Messiah, whom they believed to be their son, should bring blessing to the Jews, but this strange man in the temple spoke of "A light to lighten the Gentiles." This was new, and therefore both Joseph and Mary marvelled at the stranger's message. Possibly Simeon was well aware of Isaiah 8: 14. "And he shall be for a sanctuary; but for a stone of stumbling, and for a rock of offence to both the houses of Israel, for a gin and for a snare to the inhabitants of Jerusalem." To be able to fall over the rock presupposes that one is standing; to be able to rise from the dust suggests that some souls in their humility resemble the publican who cried, "God be merciful to me a sinner." Simeon's song suddenly becomes prophetic announcing the effect of the future ministry of the Messiah. The New English Bible translates as follows: "Many in Israel will stand or fall because of him, and thus the secret thoughts of many will be laid bare." Some theologians, especially those belonging to the Roman Catholic church reject this rendering for it contradicts the cherished teachings of their church. They assert that the Cross of Christ brought such suffering to the Lord's mother, that now she has become the confidante of all saints. The thoughts of millions of hearts may be revealed as suppliants pour their requests into her ever-open ears. This is not good exegesis; this is not supported by the text. The only logical interpretation of the narrative is that through the death of Christ, which in itself would be a supreme sorrow to the mother, the evil hearts of the enemies would be made bare. Sin, which for long had been hidden beneath a thin veneer of religious respectability, would be hidden no more. This new manifestation of evil would only deepen the wounds already in the heart of Mary.

**And there was one Anna, a prophetess, the daughter of Phanuel, of the tribe of Aser: she was of a great age, and had lived with an husband seven years from her virginity; and she was a widow of about fourscore and four years, which departed not from the temple, but served God with fastings and prayers night and day (vv. 36–37).**

This elderly lady was undoubtedly one of the most virtuous women in Israel. There is some doubt as to her exact age for the narrative admits of two interpretations. Was she a widow eighty-four years old, or had she been without her husband for that length of time? Luke maintains that she had been married seven years when her husband died; that thereafter she lived in the temple, possibly in some room set apart for her use. It has been conjectured that if she married at the age of fifteen, which was not unusual, and if after seven years of married life, she commenced eighty-four years of widowhood, her age at the time of Christ's coming to the temple would have been one hundred and six. Probably this is more compatible with the statement, "she was of a great age." Other young widows had sought family life in another marriage, but this lonely woman had instinctively drawn nearer to God. When her own home appeared to be in jeopardy, she went to live in God's house, and perhaps even worked there, helping to keep the place clean. When age interfered with her service, she retired to her room and interceded for the cause of God in such a way that even the Lord decided she was worthy of mention in the immortal story of His Son. The clearest revelations of God were always given to those in whose experience fasting and prayers were not unknown.

**And she coming in at that instant gave thanks likewise unto the Lord, and spake of him to all them that looked for redemption in Jerusalem. And when they had performed all things according to the law of the Lord, they returned into Galilee, to their own city Nazareth (vv. 38–39).**

Thus at the very first coming of the child Jesus to the temple, God used a man and a woman to announce the greatness of the event. This should surely teach us that the job of proclaiming Christ is for every Christian. Even in those days the testimony of a woman was not held in very great esteem; her place was at home where she was expected to learn in silence. There are those who still claim this was to be the eternal example for all true believers. This procedure is neither sane nor scriptural. If it were followed strictly, all foreign missions could close immediately, and most Sunday School classes would be without teachers.

Their mission accomplished, Mary and Joseph returned home. There are obvious gaps in the story. Luke does not profess to supply ALL the details of the life of his Lord; he wrote the things which in his estimation were necessary for an ordered authentic record of the life and ministry of Jesus. There are details in Matthew's Gospel which are not found here. Probably the chronological order of the various events would be as follows.

1. Christ was born in the stable (Luke 2 : 7).
2. The shepherds arrived to tell their story (Luke 2 : 15–17).
3. The child was circumcised after eight days (Luke 2 : 21).
4. Joseph, Mary, and the Child visited the temple (Luke 2 : 22).
5. The family returned to live in a house at Bethlehem (Matthew 2 : 11).
6. The wise men arrived to pay homage (Matthew 2 : 11).
7. Joseph is warned to flee to Egypt (Matthew 2 : 13).
8. The family returned to live in Nazareth (Matthew 2 : 23).


HOMILIES

Study No. 7

### PRESENTING CHRIST

What a beginning! Within a hillside cave in which animals were probably still tethered; where cobwebs and spiders filled the corners; where draughts, dust, and smells were in permanent residence, there, this young woman gave birth to her baby. Unless a woman came from the inn to render assistance in the time of need, only Joseph was in attendance. Hurriedly he made a rough bed of hay; carefully he placed a lantern so that its light would render some help, and when the moment came, he was ready to do his best. When the tiny sacred body lay in his hands, he gently slapped its back until a baby's cry thrilled his soul, and then with loving care he poured water into a bowl and washed the little child. Probably he showed the child to the waiting mother and then with adoring wonder wrapped the prepared garments around the boy and gently placed him in a bed of hay. That wonderful man then went to work to clean up the place and when he had finished, he mopped his brow and sat beside his wife. And far above in the vaults of heaven the stars twinkled, and the angels sang, whilst the gentle winds of an eastern night provided the lullaby to send the Christ child to sleep. And so it all commenced. Seldom could any child have had such a humble beginning. Had it happened to us we might be ashamed to speak of the event.

## The Redeemer Redeemed

She was a delightful young mother, very poor; very pious; very proud. She had no expensive garments in which to wrap her child; she had no ornate carriage in which to ride to the temple. Maybe she sat on the back of a slow-moving donkey, but within her arms she held treasure. Her baby had arrived; He was marvellous! But certain things had to be done; the law of Moses had given explicit commandments concerning the first-born. Jesus was not entirely her's yet—the first-born belonged to God. She had saved her money and we may never know how great was the sacrifice behind her action. To provide a lamb for an offering was quite out of the question; she and her husband could only manage two turtle doves. Their savings, such as they were, had been kept for a very special reason: her son had to be redeemed! The law said, "Every thing that openeth the matrix in all flesh, which they bring unto the Lord, whether it be of men or beasts, shall be thine: nevertheless the first-born of man shalt thou surely redeem . . . And those that are to be redeemed from a month old, shalt thou redeem according to thine estimation, for the money of five shekels, after the shekel of the sanctuary, which is twenty gerahs" (Numbers 18: 15–16).

Thus those devout parents made their way to the sanctuary, to place the redemption money before the official appointed to receive it. Then they offered their sacrifices and knowing now He was truly their own, they took Him home. Then, as always, He was identified with sinners. Thirty years later when John the Baptist expressed reluctance to baptize the Lord, saying, "I have need to be baptized of thee, and comest thou to me?" the Saviour replied, "Suffer it to be so now for thus it becometh us to fulfil all righteousness" (Matthew 3: 14–15). Later still He instructed Simon Peter to pay the taxes "for me and for thee," and this was done in spite of the fact He had explained He was exempt from such taxing. He had chosen to become one with the people, and this He did to the end. He who lived with us, died for us.

## The Redeemer Recognized

This is the evidence of all true goodness. Sensible people need no coercion to promote faith in Christ. They who revel in beauty find no difficulty in admiring the Rose of Sharon. They who reside in the shadow of the Almighty have no difficulty in recognizing their Neighbour. When Christ was brought into the temple, the stranger from the city lifted the child from the arms of the young mother, and said,

"Lord, I'm ready to come home. At last, I have seen Him." Later, in her own inimitable way, Anna, the prophetess exultantly spoke of Him to all the people. There appears to be a strange difference between these two people. We are not told how old Simeon was; he might have been much younger than Anna for she definitely was very old. Yet suddenly the younger person spoke of dying whilst she recaptured youthful vitality. Simeon testified that having met the Saviour, the way was now open for him to proceed into the presence of God—he had the strength to die. Anna in contrast testified to the people and indicated that because He had come, it was now possible to live. Redemption had come to Israel.

## The Redeemer Redeeming

The expository notes explained that Simeon cried, "For mine eyes have seen the means of—the instrument whereby thy salvation has come." Later he indicated that opposition would be encountered, through "*a sign*" which would be rejected, criticized, and hated. This would mean pain even to His mother; a sword would pierce her heart. Thus did the shadow of the cross fall upon Him even from the beginning. He who had been barred from Bethlehem's inn would be excluded from Israel's heart; He who had found refuge in a stable would seek a home in the despised realms of the Gentiles. The angels had rejoiced at His birth; His enemies would gloat at His death. The wise men had given Him gold; the soldiers would give Him iron in the form of spikes. Saints had placed treasures at His feet; sinners would place thorns on His head. At His coming, His mother lay calm, serene, happy; at His death, the same woman would be pensive, heart-broken and lonely. The path to the sunrise first made its way through the darkest night, yet although many embittered people fell beside the way, millions of others would see in Christ the Light of the world. Simeon must have been very thrilled when he exclaimed, "Behold this child is set for the . . . rising again of many in Israel." Thus did a layman from the city of Jerusalem present Christ, and if every layman in the church today did as remarkable a job as he, the world would be turned upside down!

## SECTION THREE

*Expository Notes about the Losing of the Child Jesus*

And the child grew, and waxed strong in spirit, filled with wisdom; and the grace of God was upon him. The New English Bible renders the passage: "The child grew big, and strong, and full of wisdom; and God's favour was upon him" (v. 40).

Here we appear to have a literary window through which we not only see the growing child but also the author who wrote about Him. The doctor was describing a growing boy, and the very way in which he did so, helps us appreciate the physical, intellectual, and spiritual progress being made. The child was healthy, but within the growing body was a keen sense of perception; He was mentally alert; He gave promise of becoming exceedingly wise. Yet there was more—much more. His eyes reflected the blue of the heavens; He was good, wholesome, and attractive. The hand of God was upon Him; the boy Jesus was destined to reach high places. Students should compare and contrast the accounts of the boyhood development of both Samuel and Jesus. At what age did Jesus become absolutely and completely aware of His identity and mission? In some strange indefinable, inexplicable way, did He, even as a small infant comprehend the magnitude of what was taking place? Were His humanity and Deity things apart so that whilst He was truly human, yet in that other realm He knew exactly what was taking place? Were divinity and humanity welded together, wedded, merged, joined, so that with the physical and mental development of the child, understanding came gradually as rays of light at the dawn of a new day? We do not know, and rather than debate the issue, we prefer to worship.

Now his parents went to Jerusalem every year at the feast of the passover. And when he was twelve years old, they went up to Jerusalem, as was their custom (vv. 41–42).

It was required by law that all Jews present themselves annually before the Lord in Jerusalem. There were certain feasts at which attendance was obligatory, and the feast of the passover was one of these. It is not said that Joseph and Mary took their baby each time they visited the city, but there exists the possibility that they did so. Mary would feel He would be safer in her care than in that of any other.

And when they had fulfilled the days, as they returned, the child Jesus tarried behind in Jerusalem; and Joseph and his mother knew not of it. But they supposing him to have been in the company, went a day's journey; and they sought him among their kinsfolk and acquaintance. And when they found him not they turned back again to Jerusalem, seeking him (vv. 43–45).

Major, Godet, and others state that it was at the age of twelve a Jewish boy became "a son of the law," and therefore the child Jesus had come to Jerusalem for that specific purpose. However, there are other writers who disagree with the point of view stating this particular ordinance took place when a lad reached the age of thirteen. If this were the case, then Jesus was brought to the city at this time that he might be prepared for what would take place twelve months later. The duration of the feast was seven days (Exodus 13: 6) and we can only imagine how the Saviour spent His time during that period. With increasing awareness of His identity and Mission, He walked all around the city knowing He was upon Holy Ground. Nevertheless the events which occurred at the end of the week almost defy explanation. It is inconceivable that parents could start the journey home; continue on the highway for a whole day SUPPOSING their child was somewhere among the company. Geldenhuys in *The New International Commentary on Luke's Gospel* at page 126 suggests: "It is possible that it was the custom in those days that when a company of festival pilgrims went on their return journey, the women went on ahead with the younger children and the men followed them. The bigger boys then travelled either along with the fathers or with the mothers. Joseph therefore may have thought, when he did not notice Jesus, that He was with Mary, and Mary probably thought He was with Joseph. In addition it was a definite custom that in the evening, after the day's journey, the whole of the travelling company came together for the night at a place previously arranged. At the end of the day's journey Joseph and Mary then noticed to their consternation that Jesus was not with the company and must have remained behind in Jerusalem." To be fair to this gifted author, we must observe that he admits this is but a possibility, but in any case the explanation does not absolve these parents from the guilt of negligence. It is by no means certain that the women folk were allowed to travel unescorted. Robber bands and some philanderers frequented certain localities and there were occasions when unattended women might be confronted with danger. In any case that either parent could SUPPOSE their child was with the other seems to suggest they were supposing far too much. Their action was contrary to human nature, and was a violation of parental responsibility.

In view of the dangers of travelling unescorted it seems more probable that pilgrims journeyed together. We do not know whether they travelled by ox wagons or whether they rode on asses or even walked. It would be possible that a long line of travellers reached out along the highway and at lunchtime it would be necessary to halt in order to feed and rest the animals. Joseph and Mary ate their midday meal SUPPOSING their boy was eating with other children somewhere along the line of pilgrims. It does not particularly matter how far they travelled—the main point is that they travelled ALL DAY without their Boy. After lunch the journey was continued, but the stars were beginning to shine in the heavens ere they discovered Jesus was missing. Then a frantic search among the travellers revealed their loss, and desperately they returned to Jerusalem seeking Him.

**And it came to pass, that after three days they found him in the temple, sitting in the midst of the doctors, both hearing them, and asking them questions. And all that heard him were astonished at his understanding and answers (vv. 46–47).**

The three days probably refer to the first day used to travel away from the city; the second day used in returning, and the third day at the end of which they found the Lord in the temple. Lightfoot speaks of three synagogues within the temple precincts. One was at the gate of the Court of the Gentiles; another was situated at the entrance of the Court of the Israelites; the third was in the south eastern part of the Inner Court. Within the third, the Rabbis or Teachers explained the law. For the most part students were required to sit around listening to the discussions, asking questions when such were essential, and "to glean crumbs as they fell from the masters' table." It was not unknown for boys to sit in the seats of the mighty. Josephus told of an occurrence when the eminent men of the nation came to ask him questions relating to certain legal matters. At that time, Josephus was fourteen years of age. Surprise was occasioned therefore not by the presence of one so young among the learned professors, but by the quality of the Boy's statements.

**And when they saw him they were amazed; and his mother said unto him, Son why hast thou thus dealt with us? Behold, thy father and I have sought thee sorrowing. And he said unto them, How is it ye sought me? Wist ye not that I must be about my Father's business? (vv. 48–49).**

There is something disappointing about Mary's testimony. How hard it is for humans to confess their own fault. Mary might have expressed regret that she had allowed other things to crowd Him out of her consciousness (see the homily at the end of this section), instead she vaguely charged her Son for acting unreasonably. His calm dignified answer revealed an awareness of His purpose in life. He referred to God as His Father, and these words surely made Joseph consider the implications of the statement. The Boy had grown up already! What manner of man was He likely to become?

**And they understood not the saying which he spake unto them. And he went down with them, and came to Nazareth, and was subject unto them: but his mother kept all these sayings in her heart. And Jesus increased in wisdom and stature, and in favour with God and man (vv. 50–52).**

That they failed to understand and appreciate the full significance of His statements was no cause for amazement, yet Mary was closer to truth than Joseph. He probably frowned, shook his head and finally went about his business. His wife looked hard at the child, and then sat down to think about what she had heard. The accumulative effect of all her stored memories was destined to beget faith. Compare this with John 2: 5. "Then Jesus went back with them to Nazareth, and continued to be under their authority" (New English Bible). This should be the shining example for all teen-age Christians. We assume there must have been moments of tension within that ancient home; probably there were occasions when the growing Jesus knew He could have done better than His parents. Nevertheless, He was under their authority, and we may be sure there was never any domestic strife because the Child was impertinent, rude, aggressive, or self-centred. How wonderful it would be if all young Christians gave adequate consideration to this important scripture. "Jesus INCREASED in wisdom and stature." Here was a perfectly healthy boy growing into mature manhood. He was no fake; no sensational pocket-edition of some phoney genius. He was an intelligent, lovely, lovable boy. It was easy therefore to understand why He increased in favour both with God and man.

HOMILIES

Study No. 8

## LOSING CHRIST

There are many problems in the Scriptures, but most of them can be solved by serious thought. The intricacies of theology are apt to simplify when concentrated study can be brought to bear upon the text. Here, however, is a problem beyond explanation. It baffles me because it is contrary to humanity. It is the account of two parents who lost their little boy. I do not understand it.

*DISCOVERY 1. They had lost Jesus.*

The feast had just ended, and every road leading from the holy city was thronged with travellers. Friends laughed and chatted, business men seized the opportunity for selling goods; and while jocularly they jostled and pushed each other, here and there, a smiling man endeavoured to make his way through the milling throng. They had all had a grand time, and hoped it would not be too long before they returned once again. Mary and Joseph belonged to the party from

Nazareth, and as the sun climbed the sky, they went under the old archway, through the gate, and the journey had begun. "And the child Jesus tarried behind in Jerusalem; and Joseph and his mother knew not of it. But they, *supposing him to have been in the company,* went a day's journey; and they sought him among their kinsfolk and acquaintance." Somehow I have never been able to visualize my mother returning from a holiday, and going a day's journey without seeing me. It matters not *how far* that journey had taken these parents from the city, the fact remains they had breakfast, lunch, and possibly a late afternoon meal, and never once had they seen His face. They had not lost their *love* for Him; they had not lost their *faith;* THEY HAD LOST HIM. The greatest help in trying to understand the story comes in remembering that often we also lose Him as we journey along the road of life. We have boundless faith, but we go long distances without seeing His face. It is always a silly thing to do.

*DISCOVERY 2. It was their own fault.*

This was very difficult to admit; and even when He had been restored to them, His mother asked, "Son, why hast THOU thus dealt with us?" It would have been more appropriate had she confessed, "Son, we were wrong to forget you." They had allowed Him to be crowded from their thoughts; they had been so interested in the material things of life. The feast; the services; the temple; the crowds; and the fellowship had banished all other thoughts from their minds. There was no sin in thinking of those soul-thrilling experiences, but first things in life should always occupy first place. When something comes between the Saviour and the soul, that something immediately becomes a sin. We dare not go one step without Christ's aid. Many things manage to steal our thoughts for lengthy periods in this modern restless age. We make time for the bowling alleys; the television programmes; many avenues of sporting life, politics, clubs, lodges, and many functions, and the Lord is very fortunate indeed if we have a few words to say to Him just before we get into bed.

*DISCOVERY 3. They found Him where they least expected Him to be.*

"And it came to pass that after three days they found him in the temple, sitting in the midst of the doctors, both hearing them, and asking them questions." *AFTER THREE DAYS.* Even if two of these three days were spent in travelling, the third was spent in desperate searches along the many streets. This is a vital item of information for it appears they only sought Him in the temple when there was no other place in which to look. Finally, as a last resort, they came into the temple, and behold, He was there speaking with the leaders of the nation. Had they gone first to the House of God they would have saved themselves a great amount of time and heartache. We should remember that Christ can always be found close to the altar of God. If we find Him there, He will be ready to accompany us as we start the homeward journey.

(Taken from *Bible Cameos*, p. 105)

# The Third Chapter of Luke

THEME: *Stirring Events in the Jordan Valley*

OUTLINE:
      I. The Announcements of John. Verses 1–20
     II. The Anointing and Ancestry of Jesus. Verses 21–38

SECTION ONE

*Expository Notes on the Appearance of John the Baptist*

Now in the fifteenth year of the reign of Tiberias Caesar, Pontius Pilate being governor of Judea, and Herod being tetrarch of Galilee, and his brother Philip being tetrarch of Iturea and of the region of Trachonitis, and Lysanias the tetrarch of Abilene, Annas and Caiaphas being the high priests, the word of God came unto John the son of Zacharias in the wilderness (vv. 1–2).

It is clear from this passage that among the writers of the Gospels, Luke alone was the true historian. What others considered to be unessential to the completeness of their narratives, Luke decided was indispensable. To him it was not enough to say the Saviour had come; Luke was fascinated by the fact that Jesus arrived when He was most needed. The holy land and its people had become subject to a foreign and heathen power. Within the country itself, a people meant to be one, had been divided and placed under separate rulers. A nation over which God alone should have reigned, now had no king; no unity; and not much hope.

Herod the Great decreed in his will that after his death, the kingdom should be divided into four sections. The first share was given to Archelaus with the title *ethnarch*. This did not equal Herod's own title of *king*, but it was nevertheless greater than the title *tetrarch* which was bestowed upon the other beneficiaries. This first part of the kingdom included Judea which without doubt represented the most important part of the nation. During the sixth year of our era, Archelaus was deprived of his inheritance, and his domain was confiscated by the Romans who installed their own governor. None of these early governors lasted very long and it was about the middle of the third decade of our era, that Pilate, the fifth governor arrived on the scene. The second part of Herod's bequest went to his son Herod Antipas. This comprised Galilee and Peraea, and with it went the title *tetrarch* which meant "*sovereign of a fourth.*" This prince reigned for forty-two years and the entire ministry of our Lord was accomplished during this time. The third share was given to Philip, another of Herod's sons. He also was given the title *tetrarch* but he reigned over territory much farther to the north. A. R. Fausset states: "It stretched from Mount Hermon toward the northeast, i.e. toward Hauran, and from Damascus to northern Bashan." The fourth section was governed by a certain Lysanius and this fact is as intriguing as it is difficult. For many years, the secular historians charged Luke with having made a great error, for the only Lysanius known to history, reigned many years before the time allocated to him by the Gospel. Now, however, the archaeologists have unearthed tablets upon which the ancient inscriptions indicate there was indeed another Lysanius, probably the descendent of the earlier one, and that he reigned at the time of John's appearing. F. L. Godet reminds us on page 169 of his commentary on Luke's Gospel, that Augustus Caesar delighted in restoring to the children of deposed sovereigns, that which his predecessors took away. Probably, since the first Lysanius might have been deprived of his kingdom, in later years, one of his descendants accepted the gift of the Emperor, and took back what should have been his from the beginning. If this interpretation be correct, then the possibility exists that the decisions of Herod were, in part, dictated by the wish of the Emperor.

When Augustus died, Tiberias became the new Emperor, and Luke declares it was in the fifteenth year of his reign that John the Baptist appeared in the Jordan valley. It will be noticed therefore that the people of God were in bondage; they who were meant to be free were the slaves of a foreign potentate. It might well be that the reason for this was expressed in Luke's next statement: Annas and Caiaphas being *the high priest.* It is not without significance that Luke uses the singular—Two men occupied one office, and this had been strictly forbidden in the law. During the year 14, Valerius Gratus, the predecessor of Pontius Pilate deposed the high priest Annas. Within a few years, four other men were appointed and finally deposed until Caiaphas was appointed about the year 17. Probably since the law made a man high priest for the entire period of his life, the nation continued to regard Annas as their rightful leader; Caiaphas was only tolerated as a nominee of the Romans. It was against this rather saddening, sordid background, Luke displayed God's imperishable truth. When aliens occupied the throne and hypocrisy reigned in the sanctuary, God brought a man from the wilderness. Luke had already indicated that "John was in the deserts till the day of his shewing unto Israel" (Luke 1: 80). It was there at the proper time God found and ordained him to begin his ministry.

And he came into all the country about Jordan, preaching the baptism of repentance for the remission of sins: As it is written in the book of the words of Esaias the prophet, saying, The voice of one crying in the wilderness, Prepare ye the way of the Lord, make his paths straight. Every valley shall be filled, and every mountain and hill shall be brought low; and the crooked shall be made straight, and the rough ways shall be made smooth; And all flesh shall see the salvation of God (vv. 3-6).

The appearance of John was both startling and thrilling. The voice of a prophet in Israel had been unheard for four centuries and the cause of righteousness was at an exceedingly low ebb. The statement *"the word of God came unto John"* should read: "the word of God came upon John" and since this indicates the experience known by Old Testament prophets, it signifies John had a vision; or at least some soul stirring experience when the realization of a new commission terminated his seclusion. Centuries earlier the same conviction brought Elijah from the hill country of Gilead; now his counterpart of a later age was told to leave the desert country of Judea. The fact that it is said *"he came into all the country about Jordan"* suggests he became an itinerant evangelist. Probably at first he preached to travellers who had paused to partake of a meal; later as crowds came from near and far to hear his message, he was able to choose his own preaching places, and since he practised the ordinance of baptism, necessity demanded his services be held near the river. *"The country about Jordan"* probably indicates the rather bleak and desolate plains which existed near the mouth of the Jordan. Godet thinks that since Matthew and Mark wrote of "the wilderness of Judea" reference was being made to the mountainous country which formed the western boundary of the plain of the Jordan. Such obscure beginnings appear to be incompatible with the greatness of the occasion. When the Son of God came to earth, His appearance was made—not in a royal palace, but in a stable. His tiny form was placed—not in linens, lace, and luxury, but on a bed of hay. When, after many years, his forerunner appeared, the first sermon was not preached to a great audience of notabilities but to a few weary travellers who probably looked with amazement at the strange evangelist. Such are the ways and wonders of God; sometimes, they are past finding out!

A great amount of discussion has centred around the fact that John preached *baptism unto repentance*. A very important part of Jewish ritual included the washing of the body with water, but such ablutions seem to be taken a little further in the rite practised by John. Godet and many others admit the baptism practised by John "consisted in the plunging of the body, more or less completely into water." He goes on to say: "this was not at this period in use among the Jews, neither for the Jews themselves, for whom the law only prescribed lustrations, nor for proselytes from paganism, to whom, according to the testimony of history, baptism was not applied until after the fall of Jerusalem" (Godet's *Commentary on Luke*, p. 172).

Other writers take issue with the famous Swiss theologian on this matter affirming that baptism was indeed practised by Jews each time a Gentile renounced his former faith and applied for admission into the ranks of the chosen people of God. John 1: 24–25 indicates that whilst the emissaries sent by the Pharisees questioned the authority of John to practise the rite of baptism, they never challenged the rite itself. If this were a new ordinance, it would follow that all people seeking an excuse to criticize the preacher would challenge this new custom. Moses had never commanded this; then why should John or any other man introduce that of which the lawgiver had said nothing? Yet, in the final analysis, whether this act of baptism was in common use among the Jews, or whether John himself initiated the rite, the fact remains *he did baptize*. Furthermore according to the preacher's own testimony, *God sent him to baptize* (John 1: 33). If baptism were known as the confession of a pagan that he had renounced his former faith in order to embrace the new; if the act of being immersed signified death and resurrection, then John's baptism furnished the testimony that all recipients similarly were abandoning their former habits in order to embrace a life of true godliness. If John indeed initiated the rite, his insistence on an unashamed confession of faith in the water of baptism signified he was not content to hear words of acceptance spoken in secret. Faith must not be shackled by shame. Thayer expresses this "*a hearty* amending of their ways with abhorence for past wrongdoing." Such faith leading to open confession of guilt, was, according to John's message, the guarantee that pardon would be granted to the sinner. His was indeed a Baptism *unto* repentance. Three vital features are expressed in this text. A living faith; a determination to amend one's conduct; an unashamed confession. Any one without the others, falls short of God's requirements. Faith alone suggests a disobedient child of God. Baptism alone suggests an empty ordinance. The secret desire to live a life, *alone*, reveals a man trying to accomplish the impossible.

Luke saw in the appearance of John the fulfilment of that which had been uttered seven centuries earlier. John himself claimed that this was the case (see Isaiah 40: 3–5). Probably we have here one of the most charming word pictures of the Bible. Isaiah spoke of making a highway for God, and the thought suggests preparation for a king's journey. John was the herald announcing the imminency of the King's approach. Ravines had to be filled, hindering hills levelled, rough, stony places made smooth, and every awkward and dangerous bend replaced by a long straight road. The preaching of John the Baptist charged the hearers with the responsibility of getting on with this task of road building. There were chasms of evil within their own hearts which needed attention. Crooked actions; mountainous hindrances and unpleasant paths of life would displease and hinder the coming King. Thus John stood and cried, "Repent." The urgency of his ministry proclaimed no time should be lost; the King was at hand! The coming One would bring God's salvation and all flesh would see Him.

**Then said he to the multitude that came forth to be baptized of him, O generation of vipers, who hath warned you to flee from the wrath to come? Bring forth therefore fruits worthy of repentance, and begin not to say within yourselves, We have Abraham to our father: for I say unto you, That God is able of these stones to raise up children unto Abraham. And now also the axe is laid unto the root of the trees: every tree therefore which bringeth not forth good fruit is hewn down, and cast into the fire (vv. 7-9).**

There was something completely fascinating about the preaching of this anointed man. One cannot help but wonder what reactions would follow if a modern preacher similarly addressed his congregation. It should be noticed carefully that this multitude did not come to *hear* John; they came *to be baptized*. Yet, John who might have been overwhelmed with delight, looked at the people and called them vipers. Observance of any ordinance, if not accompanied by true repentance is only a sham. The word picture suggests snakes hurrying from a prairie fire. They were actuated only by terror which threatened their existence. Extinguish the flames and they would return whence they came. The evangelist was quick to detect this, and his scathing words of condemnation made bare their souls. When compared with other scriptures the statement "offspring or generation of vipers" becomes pregnant with meaning. The evil one, Satan, is called *the serpent*. "And the great dragon was cast out, that old serpent, called the Devil and Satan, which deceiveth the whole world, he was cast out into the earth, and his angels were cast out with him" (Revelation 12: 9). With this we must consider another verse: "Ye are of your father the devil, and the lusts of your father ye will do . . ." (John 8: 44). John the Baptist was saying in actual fact that the people who had come to his baptism were in reality the children of Satan; that before he could baptize them they would need to show evidence of true repentance. Thus he went on to say ". . . begin not to say within yourselves. We have Abraham to our father, for I say unto you, That God is able of these stones to raise up children unto Abraham." Many years later Paul developed this theme in his fourth chapter of the epistle to the Romans. The true children of Abraham were not those who had by heredity received a Jewish nature. Abraham became a child of God by faith—he was justified by faith, and thereafter all who truly believed were his spiritual children. The crowds assembling in the Jordan valley were actuated by fear and not faith, and therefore in the deepest sense, they were not the children of Abraham. The surrounding stones of the wilderness were dead things, things often trodden under foot. In some senses they resembled the Gentiles who were considered to be far from God, and dead in sins. Yet even from among the despised and unwanted, God could raise up children to Abraham for even those who were afar off were to be made nigh by the blood of Christ. This was a startling message accentuated by the challenge which followed immediately. The axe laid unto the root of the trees suggests an exacting cleansing of an orchard. A barren tree occupied a position which might be used to better advantage by another tree yielding fruit. The husbandman would take the axe and cut it down *to the very roots.* The fact that it had descended from a long line of famous trees meant nothing. The owner judged it—not by its pedigree, but by its present condition. John knew there had been saints among the ancestors of his audience, yet ancient virtue could not atone for present hypocrisy. The axe of God was about to be laid to the root of the trees; the only hope for the people was repentance.

And the people asked him saying, What shall we do then? He answereth and saith unto them, He that hath two coats, let him impart to him that hath none; and he that hath meat, let him do likewise. Then came also the publicans to be baptized, and said unto him, Master, what shall we do? And he said unto them, Exact no more than that which is appointed you. And the soldiers likewise demanded of him, saying, And what shall we do? And he said unto them, Do violence to no man, neither accuse any falsely; and be content with your wages (vv. 10-14).

John the Baptist and James would have appreciated each other's ministry. James affirmed that faith without works was dead. John insisted that the faith requisite for baptism could only be recognized by positive action in the reformation of their lives. It must not be forgotten that underlying all this preaching was the basic thought of preparing a highway for the King. Hills had to be removed; ravines filled, and every hindrance removed by the road builders. John brings into bold relief more of the details of the work expected from the road builders. Long afterward, another John wrote: "But whoso hath this world's good, and seeth his brother have need, and shutteth up his bowels of compassion from him, how dwelleth the love of God in him?" (I John 3: 17). The words *accuse falsely* are the translation of *sukophantesete* from *sukophanteo*. Dr. Thayer points out that at Athens "those were called sukophantai whose business it was to inform against any one whom they might detect exporting figs out of Attica; and as sometimes they seem to have extorted money from those loath to be exposed, the name sukophantes, from Aristophenes down, was a general term to designate *a malignant informer . . . a base accuser for love of gain.*" The word *violence* is the translation of the Greek word *diaseio,* which again, according to Thayer means *to shake thoroughly, to make to tremble, to terrify.* Godet also thinks this word has connections with the Latin word *concutere* from which we get the term concussion. It will be seen therefore that underlying this statement of John is the naked fact that these men went to any length in order to gain their desired end. The New English Bible has translated this part of John's message as follows: ". . . no bullying, no blackmail." The term *be content with your wages* should not be interpreted that to desire additional wages is wrong. The idea expressed is that the soldiers supplemented their wages by extortion.

And as the people were in suspense, and waited expectantly (The Amplified New Testament) The people were on the tip-toe of expectation (New English Bible) And all men mused in their hearts of John, whether he were the Christ, or not; John answered, saying unto them all, I indeed baptize you with water; but one mightier than I cometh, the latchet of whose shoes I am not worthy to unloose: he shall baptize you with the Holy Spirit and with fire. Whose fan is in his hand, and he will throughly purge his floor, and will gather the wheat into his garner; but the chaff he will burn with fire unquenchable (vv. 15–17).

At this time the district in which John was ministering was filled with excitement. Rumours were being circulated and many people considered the preacher to be the Messiah. Others doubted this possibility, and whilst the entire audience speculated in regard to this and other issues, John resolutely supplied the information they sought. He was not the Christ, and even his baptism was only the introduction to a baptism of greater importance. As he, the forerunner, would be followed by the King, so his ordinance would be superseded by another. The baptism of water signified a true repentance on the part of the sinner; the baptism and filling with the Holy Spirit would supply the power whereby the sinner could overcome sin and become a saint. Happy is the man who has seen the need to confess guilt, but privileged beyond word is he whose heart has become a

temple of God. The terms: ". . . he shall baptize you with the Holy
Spirit *and with* fire" are thought-provoking. See the homily at the
end of this section.

The final word picture in these verses depicts the threshing floor
where the workman, winnowing-fan in hand, patiently separates grain
from the chaff. The wheat is placed in the garner; the chaff is destroyed immediately. John's message appeared to be the harbinger
of doom; it reminded them of the necessity of giving urgent attention
to the salvation of their souls. They were in danger of being lost.

**And many other things in his exhortation preached he unto the people,
But Herod the tetrarch, being reproved by him for Herodias his brother
Philip's wife, and for all the evils which Herod had done, added yet
this above all, that he shut up John in prison (vv. 18–20).**

It would appear as if Luke suddenly developed a desire to terminate his account of the activities of John. The text vaguely suggests Luke became increasingly aware he was writing of the Christ;
that it was desirable to proceed with his task. Therefore, almost
without warning, he sums up the rest of John's ministry and with a
parenthesis, included the story of the imprisonment of the great
preacher. Matthew in the fourteenth chapter of his Gospel tells the
story of that sad event, but the most striking confirmation of the
historicity of both Matthew and Luke's writings comes from the works
of Flavius Josephus. The historian described the defeat inflicted upon
Herod's armies by the forces of Aretas, the father of his first wife,
and then went on to say: "This disaster was attributed by many of
the Jews to the displeasure of God, who smote Herod for the murder
of John, surnamed the Baptist; for Herod had put to death this good
man, who exhorted the Jews to the practice of virtue, inviting them
to come to his baptism . . . And when a great multitude of people
came to him, and were deeply moved by his discourses, Herod, fearing lest he might use his influence to urge them to revolt,—for he
well knew that they would do whatever he advised them,—thought
that the best course for him to take was to put him to death before
he attempted anything of the kind. So he put him in chains, and
sent him to the castle of Machaerus, and there put him to death. The
Jews therefore were convinced that his army was destroyed as a
punishment for this murder, God being incensed against Herod."
(*Antiquities of Josephus,* Book 18, chapter 5, 1–2.)

HOMILIES

Study No. 9

### YE SHALL BE BAPTIZED . . . WITH FIRE

Throughout the Scriptures the work of the Holy Spirit is revealed in various word pictures. For example, each time God appointed someone to special service, the man was anointed with oil. This was the symbol of the Divine Spirit soon to come upon the recipient to enable him to perform that which God desired. Yet of all the synonyms used, none is so expressive as that of fire. John the Baptist promised that Christ would baptize people with the Holy Spirit *and with fire*. Rich spiritual truth was enshrined in the statement and this becomes apparent when we consider the bi-products of this element.

*Fire Destroys*

A forest fire is an unforgettable sight; a furnace is a place of absolute destruction. Perhaps it is fitting that we begin with this simile for it is only as the power of the Holy Spirit fills a man's being that the evil within his soul can be conquered. The force of evil diminishes as God controls His children.

*Fire Softens*

The hardest and most stubborn piece of wax begins to yield as the heat of a fire reaches its surface. Then the craftsman goes to work and the wax is moulded to the desired design. Unfortunately we must admit there is much about the human heart which is stubborn and unyielding. It is the plan of God that all Christians be conformed to the image of His Dear Son; yet this is impossible until the Holy Spirit makes us responsive to the Divine Will.

*Fire Purifies*

Malachi asked, "But who may abide the day of his coming? and who shall stand when he appeareth? for he is like a refiner's fire . . ." (Malachi 3 : 2). The best known way of removing dross from gold is to make it white hot. When the dross rises to the surface, the refiner removes it. The Spirit of God is the Spirit of Holiness; His task is to make us like Christ. His fires may be hot and disconcerting, but the end is never in doubt, He plans to make us like the Lord.

*Fire Cheers*

After a journey through a stormy night, when gales made the countryside a cheerless, desolate wilderness, a cosy hearth, an attractive fire, and pleasant company are things of superlative worth. They offer the chilled traveller comfort and joy. Probably this explains why the early church was so happy. They performed miracles and saw the unmistakable triumphs of Christ, but deep within their hearts was a strange and almost mystical warmth. They were in the divine will; they were home; they were at the Father's fireside.

*Fire Heals*

We live in days when television and radio programmes constantly advertise the benefits derived from deep heat treatment. What ordinary medicine cannot do, the new methods are said to accomplish. The deep heat reaches the affected parts and begins its ministry of healing. There is no balm like the balm of Gilead. Wounded spirits, crushed souls, despondent hearts, are all cheered when the gentle soothing touch of the indwelling Spirit reaches the place of pain. He is the great Healer and there is reason to believe that if He had full control of our bodies, doctors would have more time for their vacations.

*Fire Defends*

One of the safest and most effective ways of killing a forest fire is to send another fire against it. Thus well-trained men are often dropped by parachute into the path of an advancing inferno. Feverishly they fell trees in order to fight fire with fire, and in this way vast timberlands have been saved from destruction. When the fire of the Holy Spirit fills and thrills a man, it becomes increasingly difficult for evil to rage unrestrained within his soul. When I fight alone, I fail, when God takes control, the fires of holiness extinguish the fires of evil.

*Fire Illumines*

Only light can dispel darkness. The Lord Jesus predicted the Holy Spirit would lead the disciples into deeper understanding of truth. Even the lessons which He taught were not clearly understood until Pentecost. Unfortunately many Christians consider the Bible hard to understand. They read it, and failing to grasp its message, hope the Pastor's sermons will supply what is lacking. This should never be the case. To be filled with the Holy Spirit is to possess a key to unlock the treasures of God's word.

*Fire Supplies Power*

Long ago a man saw steam lifting the lid of a tea kettle and stumbled upon one of the greatest discoveries of all time. Experimentation gave birth to the first railway engine and a world was enthralled by the first train. Today in innumerable places throughout the earth, machinery draws its power from fire, and whilst electricity now appears to be more desirable, the fact remains fire produces power. One has only to watch the launching of a rocket to understand that someday, fire will take men to the moon. "Ye shall receive power after that the Holy Spirit is come upon you." That a small band of unlearned and illiterate men could challenge pagan citadels and register triumphs hitherto thought to be impossible was incomprehensible. How did they do it—they did not; God did. Long ago He declared: ". . . Not by might, nor by power, but by my spirit, saith the Lord of Hosts" (Zechariah 4: 6).

A high-powered automobile without fuel; a becalmed yacht without a breeze; a high-flying plane without engines suggest a marvellously organized church without the power of the Holy Spirit!

SECTION TWO

*Expository Notes about the Baptism and Ancestry of Jesus*

Now when all the people were baptized, it came to pass that Jesus also being baptized, and praying, the heaven was opened, And the Holy Spirit descended in a bodily shape like a dove upon him, and a voice came from heaven, which said, Thou art my beloved son; in thee I am well pleased (vv. 21–22).

The statement "all the people" must be interpreted as "all the candidates" who had gone forward to be baptized. There were Pharisees and others who did not avail themselves of John's baptism and therefore this statement must be limited to those who were present for that particular purpose. Both Matthew and Mark wrote of the baptism of Christ, but Luke adds an important detail. He affirmed that Christ was praying. Indisputably this was the major door by which Christ entered into His ministry. This Gospel sets forth the Lord Jesus as the Absolute in perfect humanity, yet even in that exalted role, He depended upon God. Thus throughout the entire Gospel, prayer occupies a place of importance. The Lord had chosen to identify Himself with the sons of men, and the whole of this narrative must be considered in the light of that fact. Matthew's Gospel reveals John's reluctance to baptize Jesus. This baptism was one of repentance

unto the forgiveness of sin. Some writers express the belief that Christ
was confessing his own sin in the hope of obtaining the Father's
forgiveness, but this is totally unacceptable, and completely contradictory to the Scriptures. If confession of sin were being made, He was
confessing the sin of the people whom He had come to help. His
identification with sinners was just another piece of evidence suggesting He had come to supply the forgiveness they needed.

Much discussion has centred around the fact that the Holy Spirit
descended in a bodily shape. Some affirm that it was at this precise
moment Jesus became aware of the magnitude of His mission; that
He was truly the Son of God. Yet this could hardly have been the
case for even at twelve years of age, Jesus was aware of His true
identity. The Lord had been filled with the Holy Spirit from the
beginning, and therefore we are obliged to consider the possibility
that this manifestation was more for the sake of John and the people
gathered around, than for Jesus Himself. They needed to see and
hear; He already knew what was taking place. John had been warned:
". . . Upon whom thou shalt see the Spirit of God descending, and
remaining on him, the same is he which baptizeth with the Holy
Spirit." This event then was necessary for the purposes of identification. The attestation from Heaven was necessary also for the law
required that testimony was only acceptable when it came from two
witnesses. Thus God the Father, and God the Spirit witnessed to
the Oneness of God the Son; no other was able to give such testimony.
At page 187 of his commentary on Luke's Gospel, Godet writes:
"While Jesus is praying, with his eyes fixed on high, the vault of
heaven is rent before His gaze, and His glance penetrates the abode
of eternal light. The spiritual fact contained under this sensible
phenomenon is the perfect understanding accorded to Jesus of God's
plan in the work of salvation . . . the fertilizing and persevering incu-
bation of the dove is an admirable type of the life-giving energy
whereby the Spirit develops in the human soul the germs of the new
life. It is in this way that the new creation, deposited in all its powers
in the soul of Jesus is to extend itself around Him, under the influence
of this creative principle . . . At Pentecost the Holy Spirit appears
under the form of a *divided* (diamerizomenai) tongues of fire, emblems
of special gifts, of particular *charismata* shared among the disciples.
But in the baptism of Jesus it is not a portion only, it is the fulness
of the Spirit which is given . . . John the Baptist understood this
emblem: 'For God giveth not,' he says, 'the Spirit *by measure* unto
Him'" (John 3: 34).

The term "Son" is one of affinity. It does not always follow that a
son is inferior to his father. A son may be greater, wiser, more
influential in every way than the one who begat him. The term *son*

is used to express affinity of nature. The son is of the same essence as the father, and this, of course, is the underlying truth behind the attestation which came from heaven. God was bearing witness to the character and purity of that member of the Divine Family who had made Himself of no reputation in order to become identified with those He wished to redeem.

**And Jesus himself began to be about thirty years of age, being (as was supposed) the son of Joseph, which was the son of Eli . . . which was the son of Adam, which was the son of God (vv. 23-38).**

It was at the age of thirty years that the priests were commissioned to begin their public ministry, and it may not therefore be without significance that this was the time of the commencement of Christ's official ministry to a sinful world. Both Matthew and Luke supply the long lists of names essential to the tracing of the ancestry of the Saviour. Luke produced the genealogical list as it extended back through the generations of Mary. Matthew, who wrote of the King of Israel, traced the succession through the lineage of Joseph. This is no reason for surprise, for among the Jewish people the ability to trace one's lineage was a thing of supreme importance. Luke probably obtained from Mary the facts which he included in his Gospel. The importance of such records are also revealed in Ezra 2: 62. "These sought their register among those that were reckoned by genealogy, but they were not found: therefore were they, as polluted, put from the priesthood." Each claim in these matters had to be verified and supported by authentic records, and there can be no doubt whatsoever that if the genealogical tables relating to the descent of Jesus from David had not been available, the priests would have challenged any claim to Messianic authority made on His behalf. That these denials were never forthcoming bares adequate testimony to the value of the documents here reproduced.

Preachers have produced the most fascinating sermons relating to the meanings of the names in these extended lists. However, there have been occasions when thoughtful listeners wondered if the preachers were guilty of too much spiritualizing; of trying to find in the text something not supposed to be there. It is with deliberation therefore that this commentary avoids the danger of making the same error.

## HOMILIES

For the special homily "*The Witness of God Concerning His Son*" see "Sermons from the Sky" in the companion volume, *John's Wonderful Gospel*, page 271.

# The Fourth Chapter of Luke

THEME: *Christ begins His Public Ministry*

OUTLINE:

    I. Christ and His Temptation. Verses 1–13
    II. Christ and His Testimony. Verses 14–30
    III. Christ and His Triumphs. Verses 31–44

SECTION ONE

*Expository Notes on the Temptation of Jesus*

**And Jesus being full of the Holy Spirit returned from Jordan, and was led by the Spirit into the wilderness, Being forty days tempted of the devil. And in those days he did eat nothing: and when they were ended, he afterward hungered (vv. 1–2).**

The word translated *full* is pleerees, which according to Dr. Thayer means *"to be thoroughly permeated with."* Luke 5:12 describes a man who was *"thoroughly permeated"* with *leprosy*; that is, he was sick as it was possible to be; the disease had reached every part of his body. The Father's testimony at the Baptism of Jesus revealed the absolute perfection of the Son, and therefore it was to be expected that Jesus would be saturated by the power of the Holy Spirit. Yet the degree of power can never be known until it is tested. Virtue tested and proved is tangible, attractive, inspiring. There was all the difference in the world between the law which told men how to live, and Christ who *showed* them how to do it. It should be noticed that the blessing at the Jordan was the prelude of a vicious attack of evil. Triumph is often followed by continuous temptation and the only safe way to meet the onslaught is to be filled with the Holy Spirit.

Luke mentions the three major temptations which followed the forty days in the wilderness. Prior to the attacks here mentioned, Satan tried to break the Saviour's resistance over a period of nearly six weeks. A mantle of silence has been permitted to fall over this time, but there are one or two details which shed light on the otherwise obscure picture. So great had been the Lord's concentration; so continuous the strain of resisting evil, that throughout the temptations, He had eaten

98

no food. A prolonged fast had been maintained, and since *"Jesus was led of the Spirit into the wilderness"* we are safe in the assumption that the fasting was suggested by the Holy Spirit Himself. The ancients believed fastings to be a means of grace; that he who deprived himself of food for a season, generally gleaned spiritual strength forever. During the forty days the Lord concentrated all His powers on the conquest of evil, but since He also was a man, virtue went out of Him, and increasing weakness gave warning of a premature death. This happened on another occasion. See the expository notes on Chapter 22 : 43. It is not without significance that both at the beginning and end of the Lord's ministry, it was necessary for angels to minister strength to the Saviour. Throughout the entire period that Jesus was upon the earth, Satan tried to kill him. When Herod's edict threatened the infant Christ with destruction, an angel suggested to His parents that they take the young child to a place of safety. Here is evidence to support the assertion that Angels are ministering spirits sent forth to minister to the elect of God. The wilderness here mentioned was probably the wild and uninhabited region adjacent to the Jerusalem to Jericho road. Within a short distance from Jericho was a mountainous peak which bore the name *Quarantania*; the entire area abounded with caves and ravines. This district was a continuation of the desert of Judea, and was probably the place in which the Lord was tempted.

**And the devil said unto him, If thou be the Son of God, command this stone that it be made bread. And Jesus answered him, saying, It is written, That man shall not live by bread alone, but by every word of God (vv. 3–4).**

Much thought has been given to two major issues. (i) The individuality of Satan; (ii) The ability of Christ to commit sin. Throughout the earliest periods of church history arguments were fierce and long, and so embittered became the debates, the unity of the church was completely destroyed. This evil legacy was bequeathed to us and echoes of the ancient controversies can still be heard. Some internationally known scientists who freely admit the possibility of life on remote planets, reject the idea of Satan's existence. They admit the reality of evil but assert that its personification in one identity is the vapouring of an overwrought imagination. Other teachers believe he exists and even blame him for their own folly.

The Bible teaches that Satan was created by God and given a place of importance in the control of the universe. When his pride led to insurrection the devil was expelled from his place of honour. Every student should give careful consideration to the following verses. "How art thou fallen from heaven, O Lucifer, son of the morning! how art thou cut down to the ground, which did weaken the nations? For thou hast said in thine heart, I will ascend into heaven, I will exalt my throne above the stars of God; I will sit also upon the mount of the congregation, in the sides of the north; I will ascend above the heights of the clouds; I will be like the Most High" (Isaiah 14 : 12–14). Probably the next quotation is even more informative. "Thou hast been in Eden the garden of God ... Thou art the anointed cherub that covereth: and I have set thee so: thou wast upon the holy mountain of God; thou hast walked up and down in the midst of the stones of fire. Thou wast perfect in thy ways from the day that thou wast created, till iniquity was found in thee" (Ezekiel 28 : 13–15). The picture became complete when John wrote: "And there was war in heaven; Michael and his angels fought against the dragon; and the dragon fought and his angels, and prevailed not; neither was there place found any more in heaven. And the great dragon was cast out, that old serpent called the Devil, and Satan, which deceiveth the whole world; he was cast out into the earth, and his angels were cast out with him" (Revelation 12: 7–9).

Adam was created to be the head of a new earthly race, and had he maintained his purity he would not have died. Unfortunately he sold out to Satan, and that probably accounts for the fact that instead of Adam, the son of God by creation appearing with other *sons of God* at the holy conclave described in Job 1: 6, Satan took his place for through submission the rulership of this planet had passed from Adam to Satan. Thus a planet suddenly became at war with God, and unless the Lord were willing to admit failure in His Universal Empire, it was necessary for a way to be found by which the damage could be repaired. A lost world had to be won back from Satan's clutches. Therefore we accept what Luke wrote. Satan was a living personality at war with the Son of God. This account of the temptation in the wilderness merely describes one phase of an age-long conflict.

It has been affirmed that God cannot be tempted; that if Jesus were really God, then the temptations were superficial. Other teachers err in another direction. They assert that since Christ was truly tempted, He could not have been God. He was a created being who stepped into the breach when Lucifer, Son of the Morning, fell. Therefore to demonstrate fitness for high office, Jesus had to be subjected to the most severe testing; in other words, He had to be worthy to occupy the position vacated by Satan.

Christians find no insurmountable barriers in these statements. He who WAS GOD, also became human; He combined in one body the two natures. Had He remained exclusively *divine,* He could never have been tempted. Had He been merely human, His power would have been limited. That He was tempted in all points as we are, guaranteed He was able to succour all those who were tempted. "For in that He Himself hath suffered being tempted, he is able to succour them that are tempted" (Hebrews 2: 18). That He was also God suggests the strength with which He holds us, and supplies the assurance that some day He will present His church faultless before the throne of His Father with exceeding joy.

Luke and Matthew agree that this was the first temptation. This was to be expected for if through sheer fatigue the Lord was in danger of death; if progressive starvation had undermined His strength, his greatest physical desire at that time would have been for food. Yet after prolonged fasting, the intake of solid food can be extremely hazardous, and must be made according to medical direction. This suggestion contained another veiled threat on the Lord's life. It would not have been wrong to turn stones into bread unless there was an underlying motive of selfishness. See the homily at the end of this section. The Lord never argued with His enemy; He never compromised. His actions were always decisive; knowing the commands of God He obeyed them fully. This alone was the path of victory.

> And he brought him to Jerusalem, and set him on a pinnacle of the temple, and said unto him, If thou be the Son of God, cast thyself down from hence: for it is written, He shall give his angels charge over thee, to keep thee. And in their hands they shall bear thee up, lest at any time thou dash thy foot against a stone. And Jesus answering said unto him, It is said, Thou shalt not tempt the Lord thy God (vv. 9-12).

Godet thinks that *the place of temptation* was ". . . either *Solomon's Porch*, which was situated on the eastern side of the temple platform, and commanded the gorge of the Kedron, or the *Royal Porch* built on the south side of this platform, and from which, as Josephus says, the eye looked down into an abyss" (*Godet on Luke*, p. 218). When the first attacks were defeated by reference to the word of God, Satan changed his tactics when he also referred to the Scripture. Nevertheless, he omitted the most essential part of the quotation from Psalm 91: 11. "For he shall give his angels charge over thee, to keep thee IN ALL THY WAYS." The fact that divine help was keeping Christ *in all His ways* was the reason why Jesus could never compromise with His enemy. It is a strange but solemn fact that practically every movement under the sun will from time to time utter quotations from the Bible. Yet when these quotations are examined, they are either mis-quotations or removed from the settings to which they belong. The fact that men quote the Scripture is no guarantee they are sent by God. Even Satan had the word of God in his mind, but unfortunately it never reached his heart. When the Lord said, ". . . Thou shalt not tempt the Lord thy God," He claimed to be divine. The careful student will know that NEVER on any occasion did an evil spirit deny the deity of Christ—only men did that.

What might have happened to Christ had He indeed cast Himself down from the pinnacle of the temple? Faith in God is no licenee for irresponsibility. If without reason I place an arm into a fire, not even the omnipotence of God will prevent a burn. There is calm prevailing sanity about all the working of the Lord, and this must ever be the standard by which Christians live. Christ came to earth to become the Son of man—as the last Adam He demonstrated to humans how they could live triumphantly. The body of Jesus would have been destroyed by a senseless leap from the pinnacle of the temple. God would hardly be justified in breaking the laws of gravity because fanatical faith dared any man to take a death plunge. Behind all the evil suggestions was the cunning mind of the tempter whose one desire was to prevent Christ reaching His cross. The marvellous way in which the Lord Jesus overcame every attempt to undermine His sinlessness suggests strength of character hard indeed even to describe.

**And when the devil had ended all the temptation, he departed from him for a season (v. 13).**

The battle was over; the campaign would continue. Satan never yields an inch of battle-ground until he must. When utterly defeated, the Christian should pray; when oppressed on all sides, he should pray even more, but when conscious of glorious triumph, the saint should pray most of all—for then his danger is greatest. It is well to remember that Satan's vacations are always short!

HOMILIES

Study No. 10

### REFUSING TO TAKE A SHORT CUT

The Lord Jesus Christ came into this world with a passion to win the lost. He had no illusions as to what this might mean, and even from the beginning contemplated His crucifixion. Yet in one sinister moment, Satan revealed a plan to solve all the problems of evangelism. "Again, the devil . . . sheweth him all the kingdoms of the world, and the glory of them; and saith unto him, All these will I give thee, if thou wilt fall down and worship me" (Matthew 4: 8–10; Luke 4: 5–8). In those vital moments the world seemed to be spread as a map at the feet of the Saviour. He saw India, China, and Japan. He saw the jungle villages of Central Africa; He saw the crowded cities of western civilization; He saw the lonely islands of the sea, and realized that in all these places Satan would resist the eternal purposes of God. Bitter would be the conflict, long would be the campaign ere the world could be won; and even then the victory would hardly be complete, for many souls would have passed into eternity. Against this background Satan made his insidious offer.

*PURITY ... the foundation of all true usefulness*

We do well to consider that Christ never challenged Satan's ability to do as was suggested. Luke's record is even more pointed than Matthew's: "And the devil said unto him, All this power will I give thee, and the glory of them, for that is delivered unto me; and to whomsoever I will give it. If thou therefore wilt worship me, all shall be thine" (Luke 4: 6-7). The temptation suggests that Satan offered to withdraw all opposition. There would be no more surging passions; no more vice, wickedness, godlessness. The heart of Africa would be open and free from superstition; the underworld of the great cities would become clean overnight; and the entire world would be released from the thraldom of sin and brought back to God. "All this will I give thee, if——" From every human angle, the offer was most attractive; but the Lord Jesus refused. It therefore became clear that He considered the integrity of His own soul to be of more importance than the winning of the world. The end never justifies the means if the means destroy the sanctity of the soul. The evil one offers many attractive rewards, but his conditional *if* is always the prelude to disaster. In this connection it might be well to remember Esau who in a moment of temptation sold his birthright, and afterward, although he sought to regain it with many tears, discovered his mistake had ruined him.

*PREACHING ... the forerunner of all true blessedness*

After His triumph, "Jesus returned in the power of the Spirit into Galilee" (Luke 4: 14). "And from that time began to preach and to say, Repent . . ." (Matthew 4: 17). There can never be any substitute for preaching delivered in the power of the Holy Spirit. When the church loses this dynamic; when the services become glorified entertainments; when the message is subservient to all the other details introduced to captivate the superficial section of the congregation, the Church is on the road to suicide. "And Jesus walking by the sea of Galilee . . . called Peter and Andrew . . . and he saith unto them, Follow me and I will make you fishers of men." These men were only converts themselves, and yet before them was the prospect of catching men as they had always caught fish. The Lord meant to train these converts as quickly as possible, so that they also could go in search of kindred souls. Evangelism has always been the greatest weapon in the hands of the church. A church without a pulpit becomes a hall!

*POWER . . . the feature of all true godliness*

"And Jesus went about all Galilee, teaching in their synagogues, and preaching the gospel of the kingdom, and healing all manner of sickness, and all manner of disease among the people. And his fame went throughout all Syria: and they brought unto him all sick people that were taken with diverse diseases and torments, and those which were possessed with devils, and those which were lunatic, and those that had the palsy; and he healed them." And against all these remarkable statements, we must consider another promise. "And greater things than these shall ye do, because I go unto my Father" (John 14: 12). It would seem that something has gone wrong with the church. We may speak of opening the blind eyes of unbelief; of cleansing the moral leprosy from the great cities; but are these the final words in the fulfilment of Christ's promise? The power of the church could be increased immeasurably if we resisted every attempt of Satan to impair the sanctity of our souls. Preaching is a great weapon; holiness is also a great weapon, but when these two are combined and used in the power of the Holy Spirit, even the gates of hell cannot resist the advance of God's people.

(Taken from *Bible Highways*, p. 89.)

## SECTION TWO

*Expository Notes on Christ's Visit to the Synagogue at Nazareth*

**And Jesus returned in the power of the Spirit into Galilee: and there went out a fame of him through all the region round about. And he taught in their synagogues, being glorified of all (vv. 14–15).**

The Lord Jesus was (i) baptized with the Spirit; (ii) filled with the Spirit; (iii) led by the Spirit; (iv) energized by the Spirit. It is written, "And Jesus returned in the power of the Spirit into Galilee." This appears to be the royal highway to a successful ministry. A well-stocked mind can never be a worthy substitute for a flaming soul. There is a great difference between wood, dead and cold in the wood-shed and fiercely burning logs on the hearth. The appearance of the new preacher caused great excitement, and large audiences thronged the meetings. Jesus was not deceived. The brilliance of His sunrise was soon to be obliterated by storms of criticism and spite.

And he came to Nazareth, where he had been brought up, and as his custom was, he went into the synagogue on the sabbath day, and stood up for to read (v. 16).

Nazareth is ". . . in a basin among hills descending into Esdraelon from Lebanon, and forming a valley which runs in a wavy line East and West. On the northern side of the valley the rounded limestone hills rise from 400 to 500 feet. The valley and hillsides abound in gay flowers as the hollyhock growing wild, fig trees, olives, and oranges, gardens with cactus hedges, and cornfields. Now *en Nazirah* on a hill of Galilee (Mark 1: 9), with a precipice nigh (Luke 4: 29); near Cana (John 2: 1-11). Its population of 4,000 is partly Mahomedan, but mainly of Latin and Greek Christians. It has a mosque, a Maronite, a Greek, and a Protestant church, and a large Franciscan convent. The rain pouring down the hills would sweep away a house founded on the surface, and often leaves the streets impassable with mud. So the houses generally are of stone, founded, after digging deep, upon the rock (Luke 6: 47). On a hill behind is the tomb of *neby Ismail,* commanding one of the most lovely prospects in the world, Lebanon and Snowy Hermon on the North, Carmel and the Mediterranean and Acca on the West, Gilead and Tabor on the South-East, the Esdraelon plain and the Samaria mountains on the South, and villages on every side; Cana, Nain, Endor, Jezreel, and (Zerin), etc. Doubtless in early life Jesus often stood on this spot and held communion with His Father who, by His Son had created this glorious scene" (*The Bible Encyclopedia and Dictionary,* A. R. Fauset, p. 496).

Whilst John the Baptist was growing up in the obscurity of the deserts, Jesus was maturing in this quiet town of Nazareth. He had become well known to the citizens for His parents owned a carpenter's shop. Regularly He had attended the synagogue services, and in His quiet moments He explored every path in the surrounding hills. When the exciting news of the fame of one of their citizens reached this picturesque city, the population discussed the facts and were ready to give him a rousing welcome. Most congregations are charmed by a great preacher, but any message which leaves an audience unmoved remains suspect. It is better to see an audience incensed than indifferent.

It was customary for any visiting rabbi to be afforded the chance to speak or read within the synagogue precincts. Generally, on such occasions, the visitor rose to his feet to indicate he had something to say, and it is against this setting that we must consider the present text. Already Jesus was becoming known as a teacher or young rabbi; He was known by all the people present, and with strange rumours concerning His ability circulating through the city, it was to be expected

that the audience would welcome an opportunity to hear what He had
to say. When the Lord rose to His feet, interest increased, and this was
accentuated when the presiding rabbi handed the scroll to Jesus.

> And there was delivered unto him the book of the prophet Esaias. And
> when he had opened the book, he found the place where it was written,
> The Spirit of the Lord is upon me, because he hath anointed me to
> preach the gospel to the poor; he hath sent me to heal the broken-
> hearted, to preach deliverance to the captives, and recovering of sight
> to the blind, to set at liberty them that are bruised, to preach the
> acceptable year of the Lord. And he closed the book, and he gave it
> again to the minister, and sat down. And the eyes of all them that were
> in the synagague were fastened on him (vv. 17-20).

There exists the possibility that this portion of the Scripture might
have been the lesson to be read on that particular day; however some
commentators believe the Lord deliberately chose this reading. The
text came from Isaiah 61: 1-2. The Lord also included a statement
from Isaiah 58: 6 for this also was applicable to His message. There
is nothing contradictory about the statement which indicates his
address was given from a sitting position. The written word of God
was held in such high esteem that all who read its message in any
public service stood as a sign of deep respect. After the reading was
completed, the minister sat down either to deliver his oration or to
answer questions forthcoming from the audience. There is hardly need
to dwell on the varying aspects of the ministry of Christ for it is not
difficult to find illustrations in support of every part of the scripture
read. Probably it is more important to consider *what He did not say*
than to dwell at length upon His utterances. Had the Lord continued
for one more sentence, He would have read: ". . . *and the day of
vengeance of our God* . . ." (Isaiah 61: 2). Had He read this statement
it would have been impossible to add: "This day is this scripture
fulfilled in your ears." The wrath of God was not about to be poured
upon sinners; Christ had come to save men, not to slay them. For the
special notes on "The acceptable year of the Lord" see the homily at
the end of this section.

> And he began to say unto them, This day is this scripture fulfilled in
> your ears. And all bare him witness, and wondered at the gracious
> words which proceeded out of His mouth. And they said, Is not this
> Joseph's son? (vv. 21-22).

The word *ethaumazon* signifies the people were utterly astonished;
it should not be assumed that they were swept off their feet with
enthusiasm. They had heard rumours of this Carpenter and had greatly

desired to hear Him for themselves, but when that opportunity came they were astounded by the resolute purpose and conviction with which He made His announcements. Godet thinks *the gracious words* would be better understood as *the words of grace* or *the works result-ing from the grace of God.* If enthusiasm, of any sort, did exist, it was quickly chilled by the doubt which began to fill their souls. After all this speaker was only the son of one of their working citizens. It was this increasing scepticism which produced the. Lord's sermon. He recognized the unbelief spreading across their faces, and realised the evil one was about to renew his attack. Yet He who dwelt in the secret place of the Most High, remained beneath the shadow of the Almighty. Trees that stand on the edge of a cliff need to send their roots deep; Jesus who stood in constant danger knew how to send His roots deep into the will of God.

> And he said unto them, Ye will surely say unto me this proverb, Physician, heal thyself; whatsoever we have heard done in Capernaum, do also here in thy country. And he said, Verily I say unto you, No prophet is accepted in his own country. But I tell you of a truth, many widows were in Israel in the days of Elias, when the heaven was shut up three years and six months, when great famine was throughout all the land; But unto none of them was Elias sent, save unto Sarepta, a city of Sidon, unto a woman that was a widow. And many lepers were in Israel in the time of Eliseus the prophet; and none of them was cleansed, saving Naaman the Syrian (vv. 23–27).

Luke does not include any of the miracles reputed to have been per-formed already in Capernaum and for that reason some critics declare his chronological order to be faulty. This is by no means certain for John who makes no reference to the temptation and events at Nazareth does however point out that miracles were performed in the initial part of Christ's ministry. Furthermore, John also indicates that Christ had resided for a short time in the city of Capernaum. John concluded his gospel with the statement: "And there are also many other things which Jesus did . . ." Possibly in the crowded days at the commence-ment of the Lord's work, many things were apt to become overlooked and forgotten, and probably we are indebted to Luke for rescuing something which might otherwise have been lost forever. If this con-jecture be correct, the events in Cana and Capernaum would have taken place in the interim between verses 15 and 16. The quotation of the proverb *Physician, heal thyself* refers back to the reading which the Lord had just given. Jesus had affirmed *"Today, in your very hearing, this text has come true"* (New English Bible). He had come to help those who needed help; therefore since His own history had probably revealed a struggle against poverty, He would continue His meritorious work by helping those who were nearest to Him. Furthermore since His miracles had brought fame to a rival city, it was His duty to honour the place of His upbringing as He had just honoured Capernaum. All this signified selfishness; and a yielding to personal ambition. They desired a miracle of ostentation but this was only an old temptation in a new form. Jesus did not come to please Himself; He desired to do the will of God, and any temptation suggesting an alternative was resolutely resisted. He recognized the evil symptoms in their hearts, and His reference to the sacred writings revealed the Scripture had an abiding place in His affections. He referred to His Bible and even a brief study of His citations produces food for thought. Elisha the great prophet had been easily accessible to the many lepers in Israel, yet none ever came to him. Unbelief hastened their death. Yet a Gentile came from Syria to find and accept that which Israel despised. God was also aware of this fact for when relief was urgently needed by multitudes of His own people, He by-passed them and sent a prophet to meet a woman in a city of Sidon. Unrecognized by their own people, the ministry of the men of God had been extended to the Gentiles. None of God's prophets had been popular at home. Within the synagogue at Nazareth unbelief had already appeared; the people had said, "Is not this Joseph's son?" Their statement was the prelude to murder.

**And all they in the synagogue, when they heard these things, were filled with wrath, And rose up, and thrust him out of the city, and led him unto the brow of the hill whereon their city was built, that they might cast him down headlong. But he passing through the midst of them went his way (vv. 28–30).**

The Greek word *ekballein* was generally used to describe the act of determined sailors who in the midst of storm threw their cargo overboard. In its present setting therefore it signifies they violently laid hands upon the Lord in a determined effort to get rid of Him. With a dignity and majesty which rendered them incapable of aggression, Jesus calmly walked through their midst to safety. Nazareth is built on the spreading surface of the hillsides, and not very far from the city is a perpendicular face of rock rising to a height of between forty and fifty feet. This is probably the authentic site of the murderous attack on the Saviour. His hour had not yet come, and therefore it was quite impossible either for demons or men to terminate His ministry.

HOMILIES

Study No. 11

### IN THE DAY OF ATONEMENT MAKE THE TRUMPET SOUND

There were many great days in Israel but none equalled the day of liberation, which came in the year of Jubilee, once in every fifty years. During twelve months all kinds of amazing things took place, and joy thrilled the nation. No crops were sown and none harvested, and in preparation for this, God always granted a triple harvest in the forty-ninth year. Slaves were liberated, and land returned to former owners. The year of Jubilee was without question the greatest event in the life-time of a Hebrew. This was the acceptable year of the Lord, and only against this truth is it possible to appreciate the forcefulness of Christ's utterance in the synagague at Nazareth.

*Shiloh*

As far as the eye could see in every direction vast crowds were looking toward the Tabernacle. Trumpeters stood on distant mountains waiting for the moment when their announcements would sound over the valleys; when other men still farther away would relay their messages throughout the nation. This was the great day when after the offering had been made, the High Priest commanded that the trumpets be blown. First, however, the priest had to place his hands upon the head of the goat to be offered for the sins of the people. Then its blood would be carried within the Holy of Holies, and a second goat would carry the sins of the people into the wilderness. When atonement had been made; when forgiveness was an accomplished fact, then and not before the priest would nod approval, and men would lift their trumpets to their lips to announce glad tidings of liberation for all slaves. Certain things stand out in bold relief.

(1) *True joy began with redemption* . . . The trumpets did not sound until the offerings had been completed. (2) *Grace superseded law.* During the forty-nine years which preceded the year of liberation, law demanded that slaves remain in bondage; debts had to be paid, agreements honoured. Then suddenly these laws were abrogated, and undeserving men were freed. (3) *Self effort died.* During this particular year no crops were planted; no work was done. Happiness was entirely dependent upon the provision of God. In every way people were not saved by their works but by the free grace of God. (4) *This was a time of opportunity,* for men who were previously slaves had the chance to lay a new foundation upon which to build a brighter

future. The liberation experienced on the day of atonement could be consolidated and expanded until the life of freedom would last forever. (5) *This could be a year of tragedy* for if men wasted their opportunities, within twelve months the blessings would cease and their latter end might be worse than the beginning.

## Nazareth

It was the Sabbath day; the synagogue was filled with people. Every eye was focussed upon the presiding rabbi, when suddenly, another young man rose to His feet to read the Scripture. His rich and beautiful voice reached every part of the sanctuary, and soon people were enthralled. They heard Him say, "The Spirit of the Lord is upon me because he hath anointed me to preach . . . THE ACCEPTABLE YEAR OF THE LORD . . ." Then He sat down, calmly looked at the people around Him and in measured tones added, "Today, in your very hearing, this text has come true." After nearly two thousand years of Christian preaching, the modern church can look back with a greater degree of appreciation than could have been expected from the ancient congregation in Nazareth. The Lord had come to fulfil that of which the year of jubilee was a foreshadowing. He had come to release captives from the bondage of sin; to give hope to the hopeless; that spiritual debts might be cancelled forever; that on the basis of the redemption which He would accomplish at the Cross, men and women everywhere could begin a new and glorious life of freedom. He, through the Grace of God would provide an opportunity for men to begin a new life. Nevertheless, He warned the people that opportunities lost might never return. Most Hebrews only lived to see one year of Jubilee.

## Heaven

Redemption is more than the forgiveness of a man's sin. Reconciliation was obtained at the altar, but its liberating influence was felt in every part of the land. Similarly redemption was obtained by the precious blood of Christ at the Cross, but its saving power must reach every part of a man's life. Even our bodies must be cleansed from every taint of evil ere He can "present us faultless before the throne of His Father with exceeding joy." Paul wrote: "In whom ye also trusted, after that ye heard the word of truth, the gospel of your salvation: in whom also after that ye believed, ye were sealed with that Holy Spirit of promise, which is the earnest of our inheritance *UNTIL THE REDEMPTION OF THE PURCHASED POS-SESSION*, unto the praise of his glory" (Ephesians 1: 13–14). There is a sense in which, in spite of our redemption we remain in bondage. There are saints who suffer; there are bodies not free from the limitations of the flesh. It is part of the eternal purposes of God that complete and liberating redemption shall reach every portion of the purchased possession. Redemption obtained and proclaimed at Shiloh was destined to reach the very frontiers of the nation. The healing of a man's soul is a most wonderful thing, but his body must also know the transforming touch of divine power if he is to be fully conformed to the image of God's dear Son. This must be accomplished or the entire work of redemption will have been thwarted. There is to be a day when the glad and glorious call of the archangel's trumpet will sound throughout the universe. It will announce the greatest year of jubilee ever known in the history of mankind. "For the Lord himself shall descend from heaven with a shout, with the voice of the archangel, AND WITH THE TRUMP OF GOD: and the dead in Christ shall rise first: Then we which are alive and remain shall be caught up together with them in the clouds, to meet the Lord in the air: and so shall we ever be with the Lord" (I Thessalonians 4: 16–17). This will consummate the redemption of the purchased possession. Christ purchased us at the Cross, but His redemptive work will reach its glorious climax when He makes us like Himself. "Beloved," said John, "now are we the sons of God, and it doth not yet appear what we shall be: but we know that, when he shall appear, WE SHALL BE LIKE HIM; for we shall see him as he is" (I John 3: 2).

This is marvellous news; let every Christian reach for his trumpet.

## SECTION THREE

### Expository Notes on Christ's Miracles in Capernaum

And came down to Capernaum, a city of Galilee, and taught them on the sabbath days. And they were astonished at his doctrine: for his word was with power. And in the synagogue there was a man which had a spirit of an unclean devil, and cried out with a loud voice, Saying, Let us alone; what have we to do with thee, Jesus of Nazareth? art thou come to destroy us? I know thee who thou art; the Holy One of God (vv. 31–34).

The city of Capernaum stood on the banks of the lake, and since Nazareth was situated on the side of the hill, it was necessary for Jesus to go down to the city. It was a place of considerable importance for it was the Jewish capital of Galilee. Agriculture, fishing and various other interests were helped greatly by the road which ran from Damascus to Ptolemais. This was easily accessible from Capernaum and was one of the chief outlets for the city's industry. We are not told what the Lord did during the week days, probably He engaged in the work of private counselling or spent the time communing with His Father. The sabbath day brought special and unique opportunities to preach His message. His utterances were easily understood; His delivery so bold and uncompromising, that from the beginning of His ministry the people were astonished. Surely a prophet had arisen in Israel! This conviction deepened and intensified when the Lord was confronted by a man possessed of demons.

Many scholars dismiss this as an ancient way of describing epilepsy. The existence of demons, spirits, and even of Satan himself has been denied. It is therefore not without interest that Doctor Luke referred to demons. Throughout his writings, he makes copious use of medical terms, and frequently stresses the nature of the ailment of certain sufferers who came to Jesus. Yet this same physician is careful to emphasize that certain people were not only sick in body; they were possessed with evil spirits. The suggestion will doubtless be made that even ancient doctors could have been mistaken, but such an objection does not answer the questions arising from this and other texts. Never did demons deny the deity of Christ; indeed whenever they came face to face with Him, they cried out in terror acknowledging His ability to expel them. Must we be expected to believe that it took attacks of epilepsy to make men wise? Why did not the lame, the blind, and the withered confess the same thing?

The Bible teaches that when God originally created the universe, He created angels, and possibly very much more of which we have but limited, if any, knowledge. Lucifer, known as "The Son of the Morning" apparently was an angel of great importance. "How art thou fallen from heaven, O Lucifer, son of the morning? How art thou cut down to the ground which didst weaken the nations. For thou hast said in thine heart, I will ascend into heaven, I will exalt my throne above the stars of God . . . I will be like the most High" (Isaiah 14: 12–14). Probably Satan was given control of the original earth, but when judgment fell upon him and his followers, the earth became a waste and void, and it was necessary for God to restore it. This work of creative restoration is described in the first chapter of the book of Genesis. Yet a measure of freedom was still granted to the evil hosts, and apart from certain angels who kept not their first estate, (Jude 6) these evil agencies were still free when Jesus came to earth. They lived within humans, and even preferred to live within animals rather than be expelled to realms of permanent impotence. Many writers affirm this New Testament eruption of evil was Satan's challenge to the supremacy of Christ; that such manifestations are not known today because Christ no longer walks the earth. It might be better to say these beings were exposed by the majestic utterances of Christ; *they appear to be absent today*, because the impotence of the church never threatens their domain. Every evangelical missionary

THE FOURTH CHAPTER OF LUKE

tells stories of demon possession as he has seen it in heathen strongholds. Probably, if Jesus walked in some of our churches, we might be shocked that some of the members might not appear as good as we considered them to be. Sometimes Satan prefers to reside in homes that are *empty, swept and garnished* (Matthew 12: 43–45).

Within the synagogue at Nazareth was an unfortunate man whose being had been invaded by a demon. How, or when this took place we do not know. The outburst which came from his mouth would hardly be the expression of someone suffering from a commonplace malady. Here there was recognition; here there was abject fear. The term *"what have we to do with thee"* might be best rendered, "What have we to fight about: We never did thee any harm." The *we* of the text included all who belong to this realm of evil. There could not have been open defiance for even demons were afraid of Christ's power. See notes on Luke 8: 31. *Anekrazen* from *krazo* has the primary meaning of *to croak* (as with the cry of a raven). The encounter with the Saviour temporarily robbed this demon of clear articulation. Dread seized him, but as he recovered, his cry was loud and desperate. His earthly domain was in jeopardy; One had arrived whose word could destroy him.

And Jesus rebuked him, saying, Hold thy peace, and come out of him. And when the devil had thrown him in the midst, he came out of him, and hurt him not. And they were all amazed, and spake among themselves, saying, What a word is this! for with authority and power he commandeth the unclean spirits, and they come out. And the fame of him went out into every place of the country round about (vv. 35–37).

Thus did the Saviour commence His public ministry in the synagogues of Galilee. The completeness of His mastery over evil was manifest not only in His ability to expel the enemy but also in the fact that the expulsion revealed the powerlessness of the outgoing demon. We live in an age when retreating enemies become infamous for the scorched earth policies which devastate the territory they abandon. These demons were unable to hurt the afflicted man for Jesus completed that which He had gloriously commenced. The population had never seen a preacher to be compared with Him, and it was to be expected therefore that His fame would spread throughout the region.

And he arose out of the synagogue, and entered into Simon's house. And Simon's wife's mother was taken with a great fever; and they besought him for her. And he stood over her and rebuked the fever; and it left her: and immediately she arose and ministered unto them (vv. 38–39).

Matthew and Mark also refer to the events recorded in this final part of the fourth chapter of Luke's Gospel, but their accounts appear to differ in regard to certain details. There is no serious difference of opinion here. For example, Jesus could have stood over, stooped down, and also taken the hand of the woman in order to lift her from her bed of sickness. It would appear from John 1: 44 that Simon had lived at Bethsaida, but since Capernaum was not very far away, he might have moved to a new abode. Some writers think the two places might have had a common synagogue and thus Simon in some senses belonged to both places. The reference to the greatness of the fever suggests the writer's acquaintance with medical terms. This was not a slight cold but a harassing fever, and the fact that Jesus *rebuked* it suggests He considered it to be an enemy which had no right to occupy a saint's body. That the relatives told Jesus about her and even *besought Him for her* indicates real faith was already beginning to fill their souls. Instantly His power restored the woman to health, and she immediately expressed her gratitude in faithful service. The term *them* would mean Jesus and His followers and all present in the house at that time. Christians should see in this miracle an example by which to live. Converts who forget to pay their debt of gratitude are in need of further healing!

Now when the sun was setting, all they that had any sick with diverse diseases brought them unto him; and he laid his hands on every one of them, and healed them. And devils came out of many, crying out, and saying, Thou art Christ the Son of God. And he rebuking them, suffered them not to speak: for they knew that he was the Christ (vv. 40–41).

Jewish days began and ended with sunset, and since the carrying of any body was considered to be unnecessary work on the sabbath (John 5: 10) the population therefore waited until the sabbath ended. Then they came in crowds hoping to "glean crumbs which fell from the Master's table." Once again the difference is seen between the sick in body, and those possessed with demons. Yet Jesus was equal to every demand made upon Him for He healed them all. Sickness was removed, and demons were expelled when the benediction of God came from heaven. For reasons best known to Himself, the Lord commanded the demons to refrain from public acknowledgement of His greatness. Soon the leaders of the nation would say He was in league with Beelzebub, and perhaps had demons been permitted to acclaim His greatness, their testimony would have been used by the priests as evidence in support of their charge.

And when it was day, he departed and went into a desert place: and the people sought him and came unto him, and stayed him, that he should not depart from them. And he said unto them, I must preach the kingdom of God to other cities also: for therefore am I sent. And he preached in the synagogue of Galilee (vv. 42–44).

It was not possible for Jesus to maintain the high quality of His daily ministry without communion with His Father. Therefore because each and every day was filled with important acts of ministry, the Lord deliberately rose early to pray. Thus He found the strength with which to offset Satan's attacks, and to heal the needy who came seeking help. Praying is far more important than preaching; without intercession, healing is impossible. No man can heal bodies when his own soul is sick. Jesus never sought opportunities to preach; they came naturally; however it was necessary to make time to pray. We do well to consider this fact. Some ministers have so many irons in the fire they seldom see the fire! Some counsellors are so busy telling people what ought to be done that they themselves have no time to listen to any but their own voices. If Jesus needed spiritual refreshment in the quiet place, so do we. These people had seen only the miracles wrought by their illustrious Visitor; He had not yet preached to them. They had no objection to the healing of their bodies as long as He did not interfere with their consciences. If Jesus would mind His own business, He could stay forever! How fickle is unregenerate man! Healing meetings have always been more popular than penitent forms! The Lord looked at the people and recognized the full extent of His ministry. News repeatedly told to the same people ceased to be news. Many and varied have been the explanations of the *kingdom of God,* but for the present purpose it is sufficient to believe Jesus envisaged the entire plans of the Father; that within man, and within Palestine too, the sovereignty of God should be acknowledged. His message related to these very essentials, and since it was imperative that all men should hear the message it would have been wrong to linger in one place.

## HOMILIES

Study No. 12

### A DELIGHTFUL MOTHER-IN-LAW

Years ago I was thrilled when an old lady called me into her living room to announce the marvellous news she had just made a new will in which I was her only beneficiary. She had been in my services, had been charmed by the youthful preacher, and now planned to leave her considerable fortune to the young evangelist. That night I lay awake planning what I would do with the money. Alas, she did not die in time, for I discovered afterward she made a new will every month. Each time she took a liking to a preacher, she permitted him to depose his predecessor. No will can become effective until the testator dies. "For where a testament is, there must also of necessity be the death of the testator. *For a testament is of force after men are dead; otherwise it is of no strength at all while the testator liveth*" (Hebrews 9: 16–17).

Paul, in the first chapter of his epistle to the Ephesians wrote of a two-fold inheritance: (1) Our inheritance in Christ; (2) Christ's inheritance in us (Ephesians 1: 11 and 18). Through the death of the Saviour we inherit eternal life and many other things which accompany it. It was in the divine mind that we should know these blessings but the Testator had to die ere His will became effective. Similarly there is an inheritance which He can receive from us, but this is impossible until we die—we must be crucified together with Christ. These truths are clearly revealed in the story of Peter's mother-in-law.

## Our Inheritance in Christ

The house was very silent; the people were sad; Peter's mother-in-law was gravely ill. Her fever had become progressively worse and there were fears she might die. Already Simon had become acquainted with Jesus and the news that the travellers were approaching the house increased the hope that the Healer might help the stricken woman. Three things demand attention: (1) *A Serious Position.* The woman was very sick; she had *a great fever.* Her condition was extremely grave. (2) *A Sincere Prayer.* "And they besought Him for her." He had hardly entered the homestead when someone told Him their friend was very ill. Could He render assistance? Happy indeed is the person who has interceding friends. (3) *A Sublime Power.* The Lord Jesus went to the side of the sick woman, and within seconds His mighty power banished the fever. This was an example of other desires existing deep within His heart. He believed the whole world was sick of a great fever; and had come to earth to minister healing to the needy. He loved to be asked to do this. Need should beget faith, and faith should promote prayer. When these prerequisites are forthcoming anything is possible. *His touch has still its ancient power; no word from Him can fruitless fall.*

## Christ's Inheritance in Us

The people who were near the bedside were surely astonished for within moments the fever was obviously dying. When signs of health returned to the face of the sick woman, an intense gratitude thrilled

her heart. ". . . *and immediately she arose and ministered unto them.*"
Once again there are three things which invite our attention: (1) *Her
Demanding Devotion.* As she looked into the face of Jesus, her heart
throbbed with wonderful exhilaration. She was now in His debt; He
had done for her what no other could have done. She would always
be grateful, but that was not enough. Whereas others might have
said, "Lord, I hope that someday I shall have the chance to do something for you," she recognized something could be done immediately.
(2) *Her Dedicated Deeds.* "She arose and ministered unto them." We
are not told precisely what other people might have been included
in the "them," but we may be assured that in serving others she also
served Him. Probably she prepared a meal, and the possibility exists
that there were other tasks also which she performed on His behalf.
Mothers-in-law can be an awful burden, but when these ladies dedicate their talents to Christ, they are angels in disguise. (3) *Her Deepening Delight.* When she saw smiles upon His face, and noticed how
He appreciated the meal, her heart filled with joy. She had been able
to do something for her Lord, and this was all the compensation
needed for a task well done. Nevertheless, in a deeper sense, she
had died to self. Some people arising from a sick bed would have
found all manner of excuses to avoid going into the kitchen. They
would need time to recuperate! They would need to rest lest the
symptoms of sickness return. Some people expect a lot of attention
even after they get well! This delightful woman gently pushed the
people out of her path. Her Lord was hungry; something had to be
done about it! Thus any idea of self gratification was forgotten. Her
self-life—if such it may be called, had been absorbed in her increasing
love for Jesus. She was dead, and yet she was alive; in another sense
she was not living: His life was filling her. It would be very difficult
to say who was the happier that day, Peter's wife's mother, or the Lord
Jesus. Both received an inheritance, perhaps of equal worth.

# The Fifth Chapter of Luke

THEME: *The Call of the First Disciples*

OUTLINE:

    I.   Jesus Calls Simon, James and John. Verses 1–11
    II.  Jesus Cleanses a Leper. Verses 12–16
    III. Jesus and a Jewish Convention! Verses 17–26
    IV. Jesus Attends Levi's Feast. Verses 27–39

SECTION ONE

*Expository Notes on the Events in Simon Peter's Fishing-boat*

And it came to pass, that, as the people pressed upon him to hear the word of God, he stood by the lake of Gennesaret, and saw two ships standing by the lake: but the fishermen were gone out of them and were washing their nets. And he entered into one of the ships, which was Simon's, and prayed him that he would thrust out a little from the land, And he sat down, and taught the people out of the ship (vv. 1–3).

The sea of Galilee was also called the *lake of Gennesaret* because the fertile plain of Gennesaret stood at its north-west angle. Faussett gives its measurements as three and a half miles long by two and a half miles broad. The *Sea of Tiberias* was another name given to the same body of water; these names were drawn from the places which lined the shore. The presence of a large number of listeners created problems for the Lord for their proximity made preaching difficult. They were crowding Him, and therefore to gain more room, Jesus asked for the use of a fishing-boat. Some discrepancies have been imagined in the first three Gospels. The differences are negligible and are easily explained. Possibly the boat had been pulled from the water, but one of the men could still have been sitting in it mending his net. Simon was probably standing alongside, and as he examined his net, he threw it over the water. There are no contradictions here. These men were faithfully recording what had been orally handed down, and the details expressed a particular viewpoint.

118

Simon, although acquainted with Jesus, and indebted to Him for the healing of his mother-in-law, had not yet become a permanent disciple. It was to be expected that he would co-operate with the Lord for in this way he could express gratitude to the Healer. Peter therefore pushed his boat into the water, and whilst he skilfully used his oars to keep the ship at a convenient distance from the beach, the Lord sat in the stern and preached to the congregation.

Now when he had finished speaking, he said unto Simon, Launch out into the deep, and let down your nets for a draught. And Simon answering said unto him, We have toiled all the night, and have taken nothing: nevertheless at thy word, I will let down the net. And when they had this done, they inclosed a great multitude of fishes: and their nets were beginning to break (vv. 4-6).

The Greek word *dierreegnuto* has been rendered in the Englishman's Greek Testament: *was breaking*. The Amplified New Testament renders the text: *was at the point of breaking*. The New English Bible translates as follows, "their net began to split." So great was the catch of fish, the net was strained to its limit, and signs of damage began to appear. This was to be expected for Simon's faith had not been equal to the occasion. He had been told to let down the NETS, but unfortunately, he considered this to be a waste of time. Since the regular fishing during the night hours had been fruitless, it was fantastic to expect to catch fish in the morning hours when fish were not known to bite or be taken in the nets. He did not wish to be discourteous and therefore expressed willingness to put down ONE net. The fish which might have been caught in several nets were crowded into one, and the strain was too great.

Certain cynics have written words rejecting the miraculous element in this story, but once again there is no difficulty here. It is not even certain that this was a miracle. "The thickness of the shoals of fish in the lake of Gennesaret is almost incredible to anyone who has not witnessed them. They often cover an area of more than an acre; and when the fish move slowly forward in a mass, and are rising out of the water, they are packed so close together, that it appears as if a heavy rain was beating down on the surface of the water" (Tristram in *The Natural History of the Bible*, p. 285).

And they beckoned unto their partners, which were in the other ship, that they should come and help them. And they came, and filled both the ships, so that they began to sink. When Simon Peter saw it, he fell down at Jesus' knees, saying, Depart from me; for I am a sinful man, O Lord. For he was astonished, and all that were with him, at the draught of the fishes which they had taken (vv. 7-9).

The emotional disturbance within Simon's soul was instantaneous and overwhelming. His sudden outburst indicated he had been greatly affected by what he had just witnessed. Nevertheless we must ask the question, What had he seen? If, as Tristram states, it was no uncommon sight to see immense shoals of fish in the lake of Gennesaret, then Simon must have seen this often during his years as a fisherman. Furthermore it could hardly be accepted that the sight of two over-laden boats could have produced such a testimony. Some teachers believe the Lord specially commanded these fish to arrive at the proper time, but it is doubtful whether Peter would have believed this. It must surely be that having seen all these details fitting into the perfect picture, Simon looked at the Lord to see again the calm serenity of a Teacher in perfect union with God. Christ realized the fish were often seen in vast numbers, but He also knew *they would be seen THAT DAY*. He had known of their coming whilst He was still at the water's edge, and this was something not explicable by natural causes. Matthew Henry says, *"Jesus commanded both the waves and the wealth of the sea."* Confronted by the overwhelming magnificence of Christ, Simon felt extremely sinful and believing his unworthiness rendered him incapable and unworthy of being a friend of Jesus, he said, "Depart from me, O Lord." Simon had still to learn that a man is never as pleasing to God as when a sense of shame makes him hide his face. Wise indeed is the man who has no good to say of himself; happy is the man who has no ill to say of others.

**And so were also James and John, the sons of Zebedee, which were partners with Simon. And Jesus said unto Simon, Fear not, from hence-forth thou shalt catch men. And when they had brought their ships to land, they forsook all, and followed him (vv. 10-11).**

Matthew and Mark state the call was addressed to four disciples present at the time; Luke says the call was given to Simon Peter. However, the fact that the entire party forsook all and followed Jesus, indicates they all understood that what had been spoken to Peter was meant for each of the party. At this time Jesus reached a crucial point in His association with men. He realized the time was swiftly approaching when disciples would need special training to attempt impossible things for God. Henceforth He would be their Teacher and so prepare them for the days when the affairs of the kingdom of God would rest entirely in their hands. We have not been told what happened to the fish but there are one or two possibilities which deserve consideration. The great congregation, or at least part of it, would still be on the beach awaiting the return of the ship. Maybe the fish was used to supply a meal for hungry people. In view of the fact that Simon and his colleagues had families to support, the fish might have been sold to the people on the beach so that the dependant families would be reimbursed for the loss of their supporting sons. If the Lord were now to take away the bread winners from the homes some compensation would be given to the families concerned. The enormous catch taken that morning probably met the financial needs of those people for many days. Within that time, other arrangements could have been made for the continuation of the fishing. The boats and the nets were still there; it only remained for the other members of the family to hire fishermen and their problems would be solved.

## HOMILIES

### Study No. 13

#### EVALUATING AN EVANGELIST

The man who handles the tools should always be greater than the tools—for without him they would be impotent. Had fishing universities been in existence long ago, Simon Peter would have been an honoured graduate. His hands were probably hardened and calloused by the constant pulling of the nets. His keen eyes were capable of reading the weather directions in the sky, and his knowledge of the movement of fish shoals possibly surpassed that of many of his colleagues. Among the fishermen along the shores of Galilee, Simon was probably one of the most efficient workmen, and it was not surprising when the Lord Jesus found and commissioned him. Yet for the new task Simon needed special training. Sometimes an ounce of experience was worth more than a ton of knowledge; sometimes the most brilliant student failed because of his inability to work harmoniously with other people. Unfortunately some fishermen returned with empty baskets because they endeavoured to attract fish with bricks, not worms!

#### CONFIDENT . . . Christ can supply one's needs

The stillness of the morning air was probably unbroken except for the sweet tones of the Master's voice, and the breaking of the waves on the beach. Along the water's edge an enthralled crowd listened to the great Teacher, and even Peter, who skilfully handled the floating pulpit, sat as a man in a trance. Jesus was an astonishing preacher for He knew the short cut to the consciences of His hearers. Then suddenly the sermon ended, and before Simon knew what was happening, the Speaker was ordering him to take the boat on a fishing expedition.

Obviously the Lord desired to pay for the services rendered, and since no collection had been taken at the beach service, the Saviour had other methods of paying a debt. Simon was about to get his first lesson in the ways of God; he was about to discover that no man ever works for God for nothing.

*CONFIDENT . . . Christ's word cannot return void*

Poor Simon was frowning; the entire project seemed to be a little stupid . He had been at the fishing grounds all night and had caught nothing—the fish were on vacation! Yet the Speaker had asked him to let down the nets; Simon could hardly be rude. "Master, we have toiled all the night and have taken nothing : nevertheless, at thy word, I will let down the net." And probably beneath his breath, he told himself, "But we'll never get a fish." Poor Peter, his lack of faith was about to hurt his pocket! When the Lord commanded to let down the nets for a draught, He obviously meant to catch fish, and not merely to wash the nets! All the fish in the oceans were there by His command, and the same authority could bring them to any net—if such were the Lord's desire. God's fishermen should have better ears than eyes. Fishing conditions may be unfavourable, but when God says "Fish" we should let down the nets.

*CONFIDENT . . . that unity with the brethren is beneficial*

The man who tries to do everything himself deserves to fall overboard! God gave Eve to Adam; Aaron to Moses; disciples to Jesus; Silas to Paul; John Mark to Simon Peter; Charles Wesley to John Wesley, Sankey to Moody. Fellowship is one of the grandest things in the world and the man who prefers to live alone is generally left alone. "Where the brethren dwell together in unity, there the Lord commandeth the blessing." The overwhelming tragedy of modern Christendom is that many people use more time criticizing their brethren than in exalting the Lord. When Christ goes fishing, no one man can safely handle the catch. Happy is the fisherman who can ask other partners to help haul the nets. Christ was able to fill both boats but unfortunately today some misguided men prefer to have one boat filled rather than to permit some of the fish to land in another convention!

*CONFIDENT . . . that a sense of unworthiness is no insurmountable barrier*

There must always be hope for the fisherman who considers himself useless. A man is seldom as tall as when he kneels before his Maker. A self-asserting ego can be a great nuisance when the Master Potter tries to mould unyielding clay! When Peter said, "Depart from me, for I am a sinful man, O Lord," he revealed he had reached the place where Christ could do something with Him. Happy indeed is the man who knows nothing; it is not difficult to fill an empty vessel. The man who has everything can hardly increase his possessions. "If we confess our sins, He is faithful and just to forgive us our sins, and to cleanse us from all unrighteousness" (I John 1: 9).

*CONFIDENT . . . that absolute surrender is the gateway to successful service*

The two boats had been brought safely to land, and the disposal of the catch probably turned the beach into an open-air market. A strange light was already shining in the eyes of the fishermen; their hearts were singing. Yet their strange exhilaration did not deprive them of sanity for it has always been the will of God that things should be done decently and in order. The imminent call to full-time service for Christ would deprive families of their means of livelihood. Some urgent adjustments would have to be made, and this would take time. If the boats were to be taken to the fishing grounds again, hired help would be necessary. Money would be needed to help the family make the necessary adjustments, and the great haul of fish seemed providential. The job was done; the farewells had been said; "Master, we are ready," and "they forsook all and followed Jesus." That day initiated a new era; they saw an open door, and walking through it, made history.

SECTION TWO

*Expository Notes on the Cleansing of the Leper*

**And it came to pass, when he was in a certain city, behold a man full of leprosy: who seeing Jesus fell on his face, and besought him saying, Lord, if thou wilt, thou canst make me clean. And he put forth his hand, saying, I will: be thou clean. And immediately the leprosy departed from him (vv. 12–13).**

Both Matthew (Matthew 8: 1–4) and Mark (Mark 1: 40–45) described this event, but their accounts differed slightly from Luke's record. The term "full of leprosy" was used to translate the Greek word *pleerees*. This was the word used to express that Jesus was *filled* with the Holy Spirit. It signifies therefore that the man was full of disease; that the leprosy had reached a very advanced stage; in fact the man was probably a hopeless case, nearing death. Many and varied have been the descriptions of lepers, but probably Godet's is among the best. He says: "Leprosy was in every point of view, a most frightful malady. (i) In its physical aspects it was a whitish pustule, eating away the flesh, attacking member after member, and at last eating away the very bones; it was attended with burning fever, sleeplessness, and night-mare, without scarcely the slightest hope of cure. (ii) In the social point of view, in consequence of the excessively contagious nature of his malady, the leper was separated from his family, and from inter-course with men, and had no other company than that of others as un-happy as himself. Lepers ordinarily lived in bands, at a certain distance from human habitations (II Kings 7 : 3; Luke 17 : 12). Their food was deposited for them in convenient places. They went with their head uncovered, and their chin wrapped up; and on the approach of any persons whom they met, they had to announce themselves as lepers. (iii) In the religious point of view, the leper was Levitically unclean, and consequently excommunicate. His malady was considered a direct chastisement from God . . ." Trench says: "Leprosy was nothing short of a living death, a corruption of all the humors, a poisoning of the very springs of life; a dissolution, little by little of the whole body, so that one limb after another actually decayed and fell away." The Levitical law envisaged the possibility of cleansing even in the worst stages of the disease; even when sickness had made a leper "as white as snow." Probably this was God's way of stimulating the faith of all. Such extreme cases of cleansing were practically unknown, and it should be remembered that this was the first known case of a Hebrew being cleansed since the law was given centuries earlier. The Greek text is almost startling: *kai idou aneer*—and behold a man! Lepers were warned never to endanger the lives of others by getting too close to them. And leper seen approaching citizens would have been punished by law. The text suggests that although desperation had made the man bold; wisdom made him careful. Probably he secreted himself in some hiding place until Jesus was passing by, and then with an abruptness truly astonishing, made his appearance. One moment he was not there; the next he was. *And behold a man!* The leper knew that if his venture did not succeed he would be stoned to death, but in any case he was destined to die of his malady, and death by stoning was preferable to lingering relentless agony. His beseeching cry brought an instant response from the Lord, for with great compassion, Jesus even touched the suppliant. To touch a leper was not only to become defiled; it was to invite disaster; the disease was most con-tageous. Dr. Herbert Lockyer in his great book *All the Miracles of the Bible* on page 267, has a telling statement. "The sun shines on earth's pollution, but remains unscathed in its own purity and splendour." So it was with Christ. He was the sun of righteousness; healing was in His wings. Instead of disease finding its way through a touch into the

Lord's body; the strength of divine omnipotence through His touch found its way into the germ-filled leper. If we may be permitted to paraphrase a test: *Where disease abounded, the healing power of Christ much more abounded.*

**And he charged him to tell no man: but go, and shew thyself to the priest, and offer for thy cleansing, according as Moses commanded, for a testimony unto them. But so much the more went there a fame abroad of him: and great multitudes came together to hear, and to be healed by him of their infirmities. And he withdrew himself into the wilderness and prayed (vv. 14-16).**

To this account we must add the details as supplied by Mark. "*And having strictly charged him, Jesus sent him away, saying, See thou say nothing to any man . . .*" "*But he having gone out, began to proclaim much and to spread abroad the matter . . .*"
Unfortunately the man's enthusiasm overshadowed his memory; intense excitement gave birth to indiscretion. This passage may best be understood under four headings. (i) *A Solemn Duty.* The fourteenth chapter of the book of Leviticus gave stringent instructions regarding the procedure to be adopted when a leper became clean. Realizing that many enemies would try to undermine the value of this miracle and fully conscious of the fact that some people would even harm the convert to destroy his testimony, the Lord gave strict instructions that the command of Moses be fulfilled as soon as possible. At a later date, those same enemies would desire the death of Lazarus to defeat the influence of the Saviour. See John 12: 10–11. This man would have been wise to follow the instructions of Christ for in so doing he would have safeguarded his own life. (ii) *A Stimulating Declaration.* Somewhere within or near the city was the abode of the priests, and since it was the will of God that all men should hear the truth, this testimony might have done much to bring these men into the kingdom of God. See the homily at the end of this section. (iii) *A Serious Danger.* The man's exuberance of enthusiasm not only endangered his own life, it hindered the purposes of Him by whose power he had been cleansed. Converts should help not hinder their Saviour. This startling story of healing could summon immense crowds and stir a false enthusiasm. A crowd out of hand could easily become a mob. Rumours spreading through the nation could bring persecution from the authorities and the time was not yet ripe for such things to happen. If the Romans heard of noisy demonstrations in support of a would-be king, their armies might bring death to some of the people whom Christ wished to reach with His message. He desired to do His own work in His own way; He was more anxious to win the love of the people than to rouse their

enthusiasm. (iv) A Sublime Discernment. The people were coming from all directions; sensational rumours were spreading through the countryside, and all the while Satan was watching for one false move on the part of Jesus. Real danger existed, and therefore the Lord quietly withdrew into the places of solitude. Once before He had shown His enemy that He would accept no easy road to world dominion; He would show him the truth again. Somewhere away from the prying eyes of men, Jesus knelt to pray, and as He communed with His Father, the danger diminished.

## HOMILIES

Study No. 14

### THE PRIESTS ... who became converts (Acts 6: 7)

"And the work of God increased; and the number of the disciples multiplied in Jerusalem greatly; *and a great company of the priests were obedient to the faith.*" It is not unlikely that the final statement in this verse represents a triumph of patient perseverance in the art of soul-winning.

*Testimony Number One* (Matthew 8: 4)

Perhaps some of the priests were sitting around their table when the ominous knock sounded at the door. Someone was in a hurry! When one of the number opened the door, he saw a rather dilapidated beggar —or so he thought. Here was another fellow who thought the priests were millionaires! "Yes, and what do you want?" "I want to give you something, Sir. Moses said that if a leper were cleansed, he should offer certain things according to the law, and I want to do that." The words tumbled from the man's lips, and he seemed possessed by a strange excitement. The priest looked at him. A leper—cleansed. What nonsense! "Yes, priest, I was a leper without hope when Jesus found me. Perhaps I should say that I found Him, for I ran and fell at His feet and said, 'Lord, if thou wilt, thou canst make me clean,' and He touched me, and I was cleansed immediately. Then He reminded me of my duty to go to the priests; and here I am." When the priest had attended to the requirements of the stranger he returned to his colleagues; and that evening they surely had great discussions. Then, as always it was one thing to dismiss Jesus of Nazareth as a fanatical impostor, but quite another to account for the wonder of His miracles.

*Testimony Number Two* (Luke 17 : 14)

The priest could hardly believe his ears. Nine men standing around the doorway maintained they had all been lepers. They were very poor; their garments were tattered, and everything about their appearance suggested hardship—but lepers, No! "Yes, sir, we were all lepers; and we stood and cried, 'Jesus, Master, have mercy on us.' He heard us, and told us to come and see you." "And were you cleansed then?" "No, sir, we heard His voice but we were still lepers. Yet, He commanded us to come. We obeyed, and as we walked along the street, power came into our bodies and we were made clean." Some time later, the priest was recalled to the door to find another man who claimed he was the tenth of the original party. He had returned to Christ to give thanks, and was a little late in presenting himself before the priest. He reiterated all that had already been told to the leader, and once again the great men of the temple faced the challenge of the Nazarene. We shall never know how near they came to believing in Christ at that time; but when Jesus died it seemed the new movement would die with Him.

*Testimony Number Three* (Acts 3 : 1–8)

It was the hour of prayer, and some of the priests would be officiating within the sacred house. Outside, the city was agog with excitement. People were saying that Jesus of Nazareth had risen from the dead, and great public meetings had brought the enthusiasm of the crowds to fever pitch. Everywhere men and women talked of the great occurrence and it was being rumoured that thousands of converts had been won for the new movement. The priests waited expectantly, for some of the strange preachers would be coming to pray. Suddenly there was a great commotion outside the building, and as the door opened, the waiting men saw a great crowd being led by an apparently hysterical man who jumped, and danced, and shouted. "And they knew that it was he which sat for alms at the Beautiful gate of the temple : and they were filled with wonder and amazement at that which had happened to him." When Peter explained how the lame man had been made whole, the priests realized that once again the power of Jesus had been made manifest. And this time the great leaders refused to postpone their decision. They could not remain secret followers of Christ when their hearts thrilled at the mention of His Name. That day they left all, and followed the Saviour. And the moral of the story for all soul winners is, "If at first you don't succeed, try, try again." (Taken from *Bible Pinnacles*, p. 141.)

Section Three

*Expository Notes on the Healing of the Man sick with a Palsy*

**And it came to pass on a certain day, as he was teaching, that there were Pharisees and doctors of the law sitting by; which were come out of every town of Galilee, and Judea, and Jerusalem; and the power of the Lord was present to heal them (v. 17).**

This is an interesting verse which calls for some explanation. Luke was careful to indicate when certain things happened on a Sabbath day (6:1). Here, this event occurred on a weekday. It would appear that Jesus was doing the work of an itinerant evangelist and using every opportunity to proclaim His message. The meeting was being held in a private building, and this pre-supposes the co-operation of an unknown friend. The presence of such a large number of religious leaders added importance to the occasion. If these men had come from one or two cities, or even from Jerusalem itself, the natural explanation would be that they had come to spy upon the Lord; to seek evidence in support of any charge which might be brought against Him. That they had been drawn from *every* place in the country indicates another drawing power. Let it be emphasized instantly that no man can be sure of the precise reason for their presence in this service, but the idea cannot be ignored that perhaps some special convention was being held at that time in that place. If this were the case, then representatives and delegates would naturally come from EVERY place in the land. Recognizing that such a gathering would present an opportunity to reach many people at one time, the Lord may have planned deliberately to be in the vicinity during the convention days. This is but an idea, but to this author it appears to be the most reasonable explanation for a very challenging text. Furthermore the verse says: ". . . and the power of the Lord was present to heal *them*." Throughout the centuries various renderings have been made of this text, and even now the correct interpretation or translation remains vague. The Englishman's Greek New Testament renders it *"Kai dunamis kuriou een eis to iasthai autous." "And the power of the Lord was there to heal them."* A footnote to this text reminds the reader that some manuscripts carry the singular *auton*—and the power of the Lord was present to heal him—the paralytic. However, this hardly makes sense, for this man had not yet been introduced to the story. Other translations suggest that the power of the Lord was present so that Christ would be able to heal anybody. This offers difficulty also for this fact hardly needed a special announcement. Being permanently filled with the Holy Spirit, the Lord was capable of healing anybody anywhere. The possibility exists that Luke meant precisely what he wrote, that delegates from every part of the land were present and God's power was sufficient to meet their needs. Unfortunately they missed their blessing, and finally the paralytic went away with something originally designed for others. See the homily at the end of this section.

**And, behold, men brought in a bed a man which was taken with a palsy; and they sought means to bring him in, and to lay him before Jesus. And when they could not find by what way they might bring him in because of the multitude, they went upon the housetop, and let him down through the tiling with his couch into the midst before Jesus (vv. 18–19).**

Once again the chronological order is not identical with those of Matthew and Mark (Matthew 9: 1–8; Mark 2: 3–12) but this is not of importance. This is an account of the ministry of Jesus written that Theophilus might *"know the certainty of those things wherein he had been instructed."* See Luke 1: 1–4. Nevertheless it is important that we have an understanding of the dwelling in which this event took place. Strauss and certain other writers have objected to this narrative asserting that it would have endangered the people sitting beneath the roof. Other critics suggest the historicity of this story is doubtful. Yet again it may be affirmed there is little if any difficulty in the text. Today in the uncovered remains of the ancient city of Pompeii, it is possible to see many houses which were actually standing during the life and ministry of Christ. The city was buried by an eruption of Mount Vesuvius in the year 79, but the untiring work of the archaeologist has provided us with remains of an ancient civilization. The Roman houses were often built around an open cistern; that is, their rooms opened on to an enclosed square, large enough to accommodate many people. Above the square was an opening through the roof. When sunlight was necessary, the aperture was allowed to remain uncovered; when fresh air was necessary, the same opening in the roof provided the ventilation. Yet on the other hand, in winter time the vent was closed. Sometimes the covering was of a temporary nature consisting of a piece of canvas; at other times, the roof was of a more permanent design. Probably this varied according to the weather likely to be experienced. Whenever the house was sheltered, there would be no need for a strong covering. If, on the other hand, strong winds endangered the roofs of the homes, it would be necessary to have a roof capable of resisting the onslaught of the weather. This was the kind of building in which the Romans lived, and whilst the Jews had their own kind of architecture, it must be remembered that Palestine in the time of Christ had many Roman dwelling places.

We are unaware of the kind of building in which Christ was teaching at this time. It might have been a public hall built by and for the Romans; in fact it could have been any type of structure, but Luke's account suggests it conformed to the pattern known throughout the Roman empire. Let us then visualize a large building with the customary opening in the roof. Beneath was a large hall, built as it were around the open cistern—the equivalent of an ornate fish-pond so decorative in large buildings today. Often an outside stairway led to the flat roof or terrace where people sat in the sunshine. The opening had been covered either to keep the bad weather out or to prevent people falling through. This would account for the statements of the Gospels. Luke says the paralytic was let down through the tiling; Mark adds it was necessary to break up the roof. Delitszch says in *Ein Tag in Capernaum*, pages 40–46, "Two bearers ascend the roof by a ladder and, by means of cords, draw up the sick man after them, assisted by the other two bearers. In the middle of the house was a square place open in summer to give light and air to the house, but closed with tiles during the rainy season. Having opened this passage, the bearers let down the sick man into the large inner court immediately below, where Jesus was teaching near the cistern fixed as usual in the court. The trap-stairs which lead down from the terrace into the house would have been too narrow for their use, and would not have taken them into the court, but into the apartments which overlooked it from all sides" (Quoted from Godet's *Commentary on Luke*, page 266). This detailed and descriptive paragraph might well describe what happened; however, since styles in architecture were never completely identical, an outside stairway might easily have facilitated the bringing of the sick man to the roof of the building. A. R. Fausset describes the palsy thus: "Paralysis affecting part of the body. The *grievously tormented*, Matthew 8:6, refers to the convulsions, foaming, and heavy breathing of the sufferer, giving the appearance of torment, whether himself conscious of pain or not."

And when he saw their faith, he said unto him, Man, thy sins are forgiven thee. And the scribes and Pharisees began to reason, saying, Who is this which speaketh blasphemies? Who can forgive sins but God alone. But when Jesus perceived their thoughts, he answering said unto them, What reason ye in your hearts? Whether it is easier, to say, Thy sins be forgiven thee; or to say, Rise up and walk? But that ye may know that the Son of Man hath power upon earth to forgive sins, (he said unto the sick of the palsy) I say unto thee, Arise, and take up thy couch, and go into thine house. And immediately he rose up before them, and took up that whereon he lay, and departed to his own house, glorifying God (vv. 20-25).

The Amplified New Testament renders the text: "And when He saw their confidence in Him, the confidence which sprang from their faith . . ." Faith has always been the key to unlock the treasure house of heaven. "Without faith it is impossible to please God." Yet there is order in the dealings of God with men. Some teachers assert every malady is the direct outcome of personal sin. This we reject. Job, for example, endured one of the most terrible physical experiences ever known by man, but this did not take place because he himself had violated the laws of God. He became sick—not because he was a sinner, but because he was a saint whom God could trust under any circumstances. *See the first chapter in the Book of Job.* Here, however, the man's sin had impaired his health. First, Christ would deal with the *cause* of the trouble, and then with its *effects*.

The scribes were the lawyers; the Pharisees were the leaders of one of the two religious parties within the nation. Although the Prince of Glory was within sight of their needy souls, they preferred to open their minds to evil. They began to question the validity of His utterances. Since God alone could grant pardon, his statements were blasphemous! The Lord was aware of their criticism, and proceeded to challenge their assertions. In regard to His forgiving the sins of the paralytic, it was His word against their word. He had nothing to lose. If He failed to heal the man after having encouraged the sufferer to believe He could do so, He would be revealed as a charlatan, an impostor. The evidence of His spiritual authority lay in His ability to do the impossible. To substantiate this claim He proceeded to heal the sufferer. This is the first time Luke uses the title "Son of man" but we must remember that he had this idea in mind from the beginning. Luke saw in Christ the fulness of sanctified manhood; He who had been with God, had voluntarily come to earth to be a Man and live among men. In heaven, He belonged to the divine Family; on earth, He was the official representative of the Godhead. He had always been the Son of God, but He became the Son of man through the miracle of the incarnation. Nevertheless, His eternal abilities, His divine attributes were unchanging. He who had been able to place the stars in the firmament was also capable of placing forgiveness in a man's soul. Then, as now, the greatest evidence in support of His teaching was the dynamic by which He transformed lives.

**And they were all amazed, and they glorified God, and were filled with fear, saying, We have seen strange things today (v. 26).**

The New English Bible renders this text as follows: "They were all lost in amazement and praised God; filled with awe, they said, 'You would never believe the things we have seen today'." The Greek word translated *fear* is a very strong word meaning *to terrify*—they were terrified. God was being magnified by the things which had taken place; yet they were astounded; bewildered; frightened. His teaching was diametrically opposed to anything they had ever heard; His acts were beyond anything they imagined; what would happen next? There is reason to believe that in spite of all the marvellous things they had witnessed, the strangest phenomenon had passed unnoticed. A paralytic had gone home with somebody else's blessing!

HOMILIES

Study No. 15

### THE RABBIS' CONVENTION!

"And it came to pass on a certain day, as He was teaching, that there were Pharisees and doctors of the Law sitting by, which were come out of every town of Galilee, and Judea, and Jerusalem: and the power of the Lord was present to heal them." This verse suggests certain questions. (1) What attraction brought together this select company of religious dignitaries from every town in the country? Why did these celebrated people converge on one central spot? I have often thought of our denominational assemblies, to which all the churches send their representatives. I have wondered if something of the sort were being held in this town, and if these ministers far from their congregations seized the opportunity of hearing the new Teacher—a privilege they would have shunned nearer home? (2) Why did God specially prepare for the coming of these men—the power of the Lord was present to heal *them*? (3) What hindrances prevented the receiving of the blessing?

*A Personal Need*

Somewhere in the district, the Lord Jesus addressed His audience; and it must have been a wonderful meeting. The building was packed to its utmost capacity, and it is not too much to suggest that the special visitors arrived early. A late-comer found it necessary to enter through the ceiling! They claimed their seats and waited for the sermon. It would be most interesting to know their reactions to His message. Ignorant of the fact that God had planned to draw near to them, they listened critically and went away unblessed. (1) Were they too blind to recognize their own need? Were they watching others, and not considering they might have been His first converts? (2) Even if they knew their need, were they too proud to admit it? Did the dignity of the synagogue forbid bowing before a Carpenter? (3) Did the fear of men hold them back? Were they conscious of the presence of colleagues and were they mindful of the repercussions which would follow any rash action? These questions are interesting because all these types still exist.

## A Personal Appeal

The story provides a glorious contrast. Elsewhere in the district, a man lay at home sick of the palsy. He was desperately anxious to meet Jesus of Nazareth, but had no means of transport until four friends volunteered to carry him to the meeting. (1) Unlike the priests, he already knew his need of Christ. His case had baffled other healers. (2) He was not too proud for his fellow men to know his desire, for he chose to enter the service in such a novel fashion that the world has never ceased talking about him. (3) He also knew his action would lead to expensive repercussions. He was damaging the property of some other man—a man who in all probability would have much to say concerning it. In blissful abandon the sufferer urged his friends to lift the tiles. Perhaps even God smiled as He watched from Heaven.

## A Personal Saviour

This man had obviously determined to meet Christ. He intended to present his own petition, whatever the cost. The Lord Jesus ceased preaching as dirt commenced to fall. It would have been futile to speak whilst the audience stared upward at an ever increasing hole in the ceiling. "And when he saw their faith, He said unto the sick of the palsy, Man, thy sins are forgiven thee. And the scribes and Pharisees began to reason, saying, Who is this that speaketh blasphemies? Who can forgive sins but God alone?" Thus their Bethel became a debating chamber. The power of God was present to heal *them*—and not one was healed. I do not know if the convert were ever required to pay damages; nor do I know what hard words might have been spoken to him. Yet, however great his account, it never equalled the other account settled when Christ said, "Thy sins are forgiven thee." How sad is the thought—a man may only be a step from the Kingdom, and yet miss it by a mile! *Taken from Bible Cameos*, page 107. See also homily at the end of Section One, Chapter Six.

Section Four

*Expository Notes on the Call of Levi*

**And after these things he went forth, and saw a publican, named Levi, sitting at the receipt of custom: and he said unto him, Follow me. And he left all, rose up, and followed him (v. 28).**

There has been much discussion and some controversy regarding the identity of Levi. Matthew 9: 9 tells the story of the call of Matthew, and the two stories are practically identical. Possibly the Lord gave to Levi another name—Matthew. This is quite feasible for to Simon the Lord gave the surname Peter. A very important highway ran through or near Matthew's city, and much toll had to be collected from the business caravans which used it. Both Herod, and the foreign powers to whom he was subject, were despised by the Jews, and any man employed by the hated regime was considered excommunicate, a publican, a sinner. Matthew was a toll collector, and was probably seated outside his office when Jesus was passing by. The Greek word translated *saw* is very suggestive. *Ethiasato* means *to gaze intently upon; to stare; to fix one's eyes constantly upon an object.* Godet thinks it was at this moment a directive came from heaven, instructing Christ to call Levi, but one wonders if this were necessary. He who lived in constant communion with the Father would hardly need to be surprised into calling anybody. It might be better to assume that this was no casual glance, but a deep searching look of appraisal and approval giving birth to a definite call to service. This call was expressed through the eyes of the Lord as much as by His voice, and deeply stirred by what he felt and heard, the publican rose to accept the challenge.

**And Levi made him a great feast in his own house: and there was a great company of publicans and of others that sat down with them. But their scribes and Pharisees murmured against his disciples, saying, Why do ye eat and drink with publicans and sinners? And Jesus answering said unto them, They that are whole need not a physician; but they that are sick. I came not to call the righteous, but sinners to repentance (vv. 29-32).**

Levi was indisputably a man of rare discernment. His feast suggests three vital things. He desired more of *the presence of Christ;* therefore he took the Lord to his own home. He desired to increase *the pleasure of Christ,* and therefore he planned the greatest feast possible. He gave the best he had: It was "a *great* feast." (3) He desired to assist *the purposes of Christ* and therefore provided a congregation to hear the Great Teacher. This was a great occasion and it is not difficult to imagine the excitement which prevailed during the time of preparation. This was Levi's first missionary effort; it would have been a marvellous beginning had he been able at one service to bring all his friends to Christ. He had no idea what their reactions would be; he had no way of knowing what would happen at the feast, but at least he was determined that his friends should meet the Master. This set the pattern for modern disciples. When missions are held in these days, unfortunately most disciples treat the occasion as a time for personal feasting rather than an occasion when the lost may be brought to Christ.

When the scribes and Pharisees raised objections regarding the virtue of the guests, the Lord countered their veiled accusations with an illustration. All were sick, for all had sinned. Unfortunately the Pharisees remained unaware of their need. They began to criticise; it would have been better had they knelt to pray! It is not sufficient *to call* sinners to repentance for alas, some sinners are deaf! As a shepherd goes in search of lost sheep; so Christ must search for lost souls. When a patient cannot be brought to the physician, the doctor must go to the patient. This was precisely what the Lord was doing.

> And they said unto him, Why do the disciples of John fast often, and make prayers, and likewise the disciples of the Pharisees; but thine eat and drink? And he said unto them, Can ye make the children of the bride-chamber fast, while the bridegroom is with them? But the days will come when the bridegroom shall be taken away from them, and then shall they fast in those days (vv. 33–35).

The synoptic writers appear to be at variance in regard to the details of this event. Mark says, *"the disciples of John and the Pharisees were fasting."* This might mean they were in the habit of fasting, or that they were actually fasting at that time. There were occasions when the relationship between John's disciples and the followers of Jesus appeared to be strained; it is therefore easy to believe that these men would question procedure not aligned to their own. Matthew makes no mention of the Pharisees and states the disciples of John came to ask their question. It is possible that all three writers were expressing various phases of the same event. Maybe the disciples of John suddenly appeared to ask their pertinent question. Hearing them, other people might have added: "Yes, that is a good question. Why do they do these things?"

The Lord's answer was most illuminating. On another occasion John the Baptist said, "He that hath the bride is the bridegroom: but

the friend of the bridegroom, which standeth and heareth him, re-
joiceth greatly because of the bridegroom's voice: this my joy therefore is fulfilled" (John 3: 29). We have not been told whether this
statement had already been made, nor indeed if John had often
uttered the same words. However it is against this setting the Lord's
answer must be considered. Christ was the Bridegroom; His purpose
in coming into the world was that of wooing and winning His bride,
the church. Much would happen ere His joys would be consum-
mated, but even then he had the marriage in view. He also had
friends who were willing to assist Him; they belonged to the marriage
party. How could they be expected to weep when happiness should
be filling their hearts? Through the sovereign mercy of God, those
rejoicing friends were destined to become part of the Bride. To make
this possible, the Bridegroom would be taken away, and that would
be the time to fast.

And he spake also a parable unto them; No man putteth a piece of a
new garment upon an old; if otherwise! then both the new maketh a
rent, and the piece that was taken out of the new agreeth not with
the old. And no man putteth new wine into old bottles; else the new
wine will burst the old bottles, and be spilled, and the bottles shall
perish. But new wine must be put into new bottles; and both are preserved. No man also having drunk old wine straightway desireth new;
for he saith, The old is better (vv. 36–39).

These verses are a goldmine, which, alas, is seldom discovered by
those seeking spiritual treasure. Obviously, these parables of the
Lord referred to that which He had already uttered. The question
had been raised about the necessity and advisability of fasting, but
the questioners had apparently lost sight of the fact that fasting,
according to the law, was only commanded for the day of atonement.
The dictates of the fathers, and the traditions increasing through the
centuries had obscured the true meaning of the act. Originally fasting
was a sign of deep penitence; unfortunately it had become a meritorious deed of which men could boast (Luke 18: 11–12). Jesus had
come to institute a new form of worship, completely opposed to the
old ways practised by the fathers. To try and patch up the old and
disappointing garments of Jewish practice by adding to them pieces
of the new faith would only spoil the both. Jesus had not come to
repair an old system; He had come to give the world something
entirely new. If decaying portions of a worn-out system were grafted
or sown on the fabric of the new life, neither the faded design nor
the age-old texture would be in harmony with that which had come
fresh from the looms of Heaven. Therefore why should the followers
of the new order emulate the slaves of the old? Fastings there would

undoubtedly be, but they would be voluntary; self-imposed; begotten not by the commands of the law but by an inherent desire to emulate Christ's example.

Within the framework of these two parables, the one garment seems to be opposed to the many bottles! This calls for investigation. The people of the East have long preserved their liquids in leather bottles made generally from the skin of a goat. These have the rare quality of preserving the water untainted. Yet, to place unfermented wine in old bottles would be stupid for the increasing pressure within the leather containers would burst the goatskins. New wine must therefore be placed within a new goatskin. The spotlight of emphasis is now upon the container—not upon the wine. Godet correctly says, "The new wine represents that living and healthy spirituality which flows so abundantly through the teaching of Jesus; and the bottles, the men who are to become depositories of this principle, and to preserve it for mankind." Jesus knew that He would need new men for the new message. Had he chosen Pharisees, the danger would ever have been present that their preconceived notions might have ruined the entire project. Their warped minds would not have been able to preserve the sweetness of the new wine; it would have become sour; tainted; unpalatable. It was therefore necessary to store the new wine in new men, and to do this Jesus by-passed the officials in the temple and went forth to the seashore to find fishermen. The final portion of this great utterance of Christ suggests that one of the chief virtues of His followers must be patience. Men who have drunk old and mature wine may not take kindly to a new vintage. Many of the Pharisees would soon be comparing the old and new systems and at first would reject the new message. Some men are converted in a moment of time; others are the product of long and patient labour. If the new vessels preserved the new wine, the entire world would one day be able to substantiate the testimony of Christ and rejoice in that which God had sent to his people. The text therefore contains a warning to His followers. The word *eutheos*—translated, *straightway* suggests the reluctance of men who had long drunk of the old wine even to try the new wine—*they will say "The old is better."* Therefore it was to be expected that the protagonists of the law would refuse to yield to the claims of the new message. The disciples needed to consider this, for to be forewarned was to be forearmed.

HOMILIES

Study No. 16

## MATTHEW . . . THE MASTER'S MAN

He was always the master's man—even before he met the Saviour. Matthew the toll collector was probably known to all the travellers who journeyed through the great city alongside the lake. They knew him by name; they probably spat in the dust when he was mentioned. He had sold out to the rulers; he squeezed taxes out of his brethren; they suspected that some of their money went into his pockets! He was a sinner but they seldom expressed their feelings; he was in a position to increase their tolls. Bah, all such men should die!

*Matthew . . . the man with a pen. A Great Day*

Business was possibly a little slack; the toll collector was sitting outside his office. Not far away the shops in the city were open for business; within sight, the waters of the lake stretched to distant horizons. One caravan had just gone; another would soon be coming. Matthew put the finishing touches to that particular account. Probably he had no idea why he had become a toll-collector for a man with his talents could have found a job with any responsible firm. He had a brain, and a pen, and a knowledge of book keeping. He handled money with care, and his accounts were reliable. He knew the people hated him, but it took all men to make a world. If his task were distasteful, at least, he would try to be honest and do his duty. Few men are as good as they think, and none so bad as others declare. Matthew was due for a shock. God had found a new job for the tax collector, but as yet He had been unable to tell him.

*Matthew . . . the man with a problem. A Great Decision*

People were coming down the road; but they were walking. Where were their wagons? What were they carrying? How much would they have to pay? Matthew watched as the strangers drew nearer. One Man was a little ahead of the others—He was different, dignified, commanding in appearance, His face was kindly, but his eyes were alive with the joy of living. What did He desire? He had neither bags nor laden donkeys. Matthew waited expectantly. The Stranger approached and for awhile stood gazing intently at the man seated beside the office. His eyes were speculative as if they were appraising the man before them. The toll collector shifted uneasily; something was happening to him. A strange warmth was permeating his being, fear—of a kind, the premonition of something tremendous made his nerves tingle. This was Jesus the Carpenter; the others were His disciples. Most men frowned when they came to the tax station; Jesus was radiant, and His smile was lovelier than a sunrise over the lake. Then the Master said, "Follow me," and suddenly Matthew's heart was on fire! His job; his accounts; his money; his reputation; the upkeep of his home failed to quieten the commotion in his soul. Could he, should he obey the call? He was on his feet. What fool could play with pennies when a treasure house was being opened?

*Matthew . . . the man with a plan. A Great Devotion*

As yet he had received nothing from the Stranger but a command to follow. He had heard no sermon; had witnessed no healings. He had received no promises of life everlasting, nor of amenities soon to be forthcoming. He had seen the Master's face, heard His marvellous invitation, and that was enough. Excitement which raged as a fire out of control, surged through his being. Who wanted to get when it was possible to give? *"And Matthew made him a great feast in his own house."* It would have been less work had the party gone to an inn, or some eating place, but Matthew had a home where the Lord could both eat and rest. Beside, what place offered the kind of feast Matthew wanted. This had to be a GREAT feast befitting a great occasion. He would give to the Lord the best that money could buy for only thus could he express the gratitude filling his soul. "Servants, prepare the greatest meal you ever prepared. Spare no cost, and place the best pottery on the table. This shall be a royal occasion, the King is coming to dinner!"

*Matthew . . . the man with a passion. A Great Desire*

Matthew had suddenly become silent. Obviously something had occurred to him. Formerly he had taken so much from men; it was now possible to give something back to them. It was said that Jesus was the friend of sinners; that He loved to speak to people. This banquet could become an evangelistic meeting if only a congregation could be provided. "What about it, Matthew?" His eyes were shining; this was the best idea he had ever had. "Servants, send for the scribes, and be ready to take out invitations." And when the feast was about to begin, *"there was a great company of publicans and of others that sat down with them"* (Luke 5: 29). Matthew proved himself to be a capable organizer even before he tried to preach. And when he saw the crowd listening to the Lord, something stirred within his soul. This was his first attempt to bring souls within the sound of the Gospel; it should not be his last. During the Lord's sojourn on earth, Matthew did what he could to preach the Gospel of the Kingdom; later, when the Holy Spirit prompted him, he wrote a Gospel so that other evangelists would have something to preach. When this task was successfully concluded, he went forth into the highways and byways of a big world urging people to worship the King of kings. According to the testimony of ancient authors, Matthew spent the closing part of his life preaching the Gospel in Ethiopia. When he vacated his seat outside the tax office, he began to travel a highway to a place of honour within the kingdom of God. It was a long road, with many twists and turns; with dangers and difficulties abounding; but the toll collector was true to the end. He who had written so many names in his own book was sure his name had been written in the Lamb's Book of Life.

# The Sixth Chapter of Luke

THEME: *The Lordship of Christ*

OUTLINE:

      I. The Controversies on the Sabbaths. Verses 1–11
     II. The Choice of His Servants. Verses 12–19
   III. The Challenge of His Sermon. Verses 20–49

*Expository Notes on the Supposed Violations of the Sabbath Laws*

**And it came to pass on the second sabbath after the first, that he went through the corn fields; and his disciples plucked the ears of corn, and did eat, rubbing them in their hands (v. 1).**

It is of interest that Luke identifies these events with a specific date. The term *deuteroproto* (the second first) is a rare word and is not found elsewhere in the Testament. Many interpretations have been given concerning it but none are absolutely authentic. Quoting Strack-Billerbeck, Norval Geldenhuys in his *Commentary on the Gospel of Luke*, at page 201, says, "It is presumably a technical expression of the Jewish calendar. We cannot be sure what it meant, though Strack-Billerbeck are probably right in taking the term to indicate, 'A Sabbath which comes second in a series of Sabbaths, the numbering of which begins with the first Sabbath—The situation of Luke 6: 1, the time when the corn was ripe, requires us to think of a series of Sabbaths which lay in the neighbourhood of the Passover. At this time, the days and the weeks were in fact numbered, according to Leviticus 23: 15, and so were the Sabbaths between Easter and Whitsuntide. So the *second-first* Sabbath would mean the second Sabbath after the fifteenth of Nisan, the first Sabbath being that which fell in Passover week itself. The numbering of the days between Easter and Whitsuntide began on the evening of the fifteenth of Nisan with the commencement on the sixteenth of Nisan."

The objection raised by the Pharisees was shallow and trivial; their murmurings were based not on the laws of God but upon the traditions of the fathers. Deuteronomy 23: 25 says, "*When thou comest into the standing corn of thy neighbour, then thou mayest pluck the ears with thine hand; but thou shalt not move a sickle unto thy neighbour's standing corn.*" It was not illegal to pluck the corn when this was needed for food; it would have been stealing and unjustifiable interference to begin cutting the corn of another farmer. However, during the passing of the centuries, the Pharisees had obscured the true meaning of the law stating that the act of rubbing out corn in one's hand constituted work, and since the law commanded that no work should be done on the Sabbath, this was prohibited. By the same standards, the breaking of a piece of bread would have been illegal; the ˙carrying of food to animals, or the milking of cows would have been violations of the divine code. The objection of these men indicated they were more concerned with accusing Christ than obeying God.

> And certain of the Pharisees said unto them, Why do ye that which is not lawful to do on the sabbath days? And Jesus answering them said, Have ye not read so much as this, what David did, when himself was an hungered, and they which were with him; How he went into the house of God, and did take and eat the shewbread, and gave also to them that were with him; which it is not lawful to eat but for the priests alone? And he said unto them, That the Son of man is Lord also of the sabbath (vv. 2-5).

The original version *Oude touto anegnote* has been rendered in the Englishman's Greek New Testament, *"Not even this did ye read . . . ?"* The Lord might have argued with them concerning the accuracy of their statements, but instead, in one devastating question He revealed their ignorance, not only of the letter of the word, but also of its meaning. The Author of the Word was greater than His works. The scriptures were second only in importance to Him Who breathed life into the written characters. It was possible to become a slave to commandments; to strain at a gnat and swallow a camel, and yet at the same time to be out of harmony with the Spirit of Him who taught that God is love. Christ quoted from I Samuel 21: 1-6, and as Godet suggests, revealed "the conduct of David rested upon this principle, that in exceptional cases, when a moral obligation clashes with a ceremonial law, *the latter ought to yield.*" God gave the law that it should be a guide and not a slave master; a light shining in the darkness and not a chain binding one to a prison wall. Thus did Christ indicate He was above the ceremonial dictates of the hierarchy. He was Lord of the universe; Lord of the sabbath, and the final authority in matters pertaining to the kingdom of God.

> And it came to pass also on another sabbath, that he entered into the synagogue and taught: and there was a man whose right hand was withered. And the scribes and Pharisees watched him, whether he

would heal on the sabbath day; that they might find an accusation against him (vv. 6-7).

Once again the Saviour made His way to the synagogue for He attended regularly the sabbath services; ". . . and as his custom was, he went into the synagogue on the sabbath day . . ." (Luke 4: 16). If He were present to do this in our generation He would probably be shunned by people who profess to be His friends. It is strange to relate that some Christians who send the Gospel to unevangelized heathen, ignore the heathen nearer home. If, as some would have us believe, the church is apostate and without the true Gospel, there is all the. more reason for the message to be carried within the sanctuary. Christ went wherever He could find an audience, and some of His followers might be of greater use in the kingdom of God if they followed His example. And to those who criticize the church members, it only remains to say, "If ever you find a perfect church, don't join it—you would ruin it!" Luke states the man's *right* hand was withered. See the homily at the end of this section.

But he knew their thoughts and said to the man which had the withered hand, Rise up, and stand forth in the midst. And he arose and stood forth. Then said Jesus unto them, I will ask you one thing, Is it lawful on the sabbath days to do good, or to do evil? to save life or to destroy it? And looking round about upon them all, he said unto the man, Stretch forth thine hand. And he did so: and his hand was restored whole as the other. And they were filled with madness; and communed one with another what they might do to Jesus (vv. 8-11).

The Greek word translated *watched* in verse 7 is pareteeroun; it is derived from pareteereo; and is made from two words: *para,* a preposition denoting nearness or close proximity, and *teereo* which means *to guard; to watch carefully.* Dr. Thayer suggests a word picture: *to watch and to guard carefully in order to preserve the state in which one is already.* For example, the assiduous attention of a father in order to preserve the virginity of a well-beloved daughter; to safeguard the child from rape. This was far more than a casual observance of what Christ was doing at the time. They were spying on Him with an attentiveness which suggested their lives depended upon their findings. Christ knew their thoughts and calmly ordered the sufferer to stand forth in front of the congregation. The unassailable logic of His question negatived their criticisms, and when He healed the man their anger was unrestrained. *Anoias* translated *"with madness"* is also an interesting word with a dual meaning: (1) *to be devoid of understanding;* (2) *to be mad.* The bitterness of the Pharisees revealed the bankruptcy of their thinking.

HOMILIES

Study No. 17

## PARALYSIS IN THE PEW!

"And it came to pass also on another sabbath, that he entered into the synagogue and taught: and there was a man whose right hand was withered." This is a typical Dr. Luke text, and the beloved physician carefully pointed out it was the man's right hand and not his left which was useless. The fellow was very much alive; and as far as we can judge from the Scriptures, his eyesight was not impaired! All his trouble centred in that right hand, which would not respond to his will. The right hand is the hand of service, and for most people the loss of this valuable member would be inestimable. A man might endeavour to work with his left hand, but he would never accomplish all he wished to do unless he could also use the other member which dangled helplessly at his side. He reminds us of Christians whose service is not up to standard. They have received eternal life and are no longer dead in sin; they see clearly and discern between true and false teaching; yet in actual service, spiritual paralysis has withered the right hand. The Bible has several illustrations of this type; and from the sacred record we may now learn the causes of this infirmity.

*Sinfulness . . .* (Luke 5: 18–20)

"And, behold, men brought in a bed a man which was taken with a palsy . . . and when Jesus saw their faith, he said unto him, Man, thy sins are forgiven thee." This statement seemed out of place, for the unfortunate sufferer was not seeking the forgiveness of his sins. Paralysis had deprived him of the joy of living. His problem was not spiritual, but something practical and physical. The Lord Jesus realized the cause of the man's helplessness was secret sin. It would appear that somewhere in his former experiences, the fellow had permitted evil to predominate, and physical infirmity resulted. The Great Physician dealt with the secret sins before He finally removed the irksome malady. Here was a man who could neither walk, nor work, because sin had paralysed him. We are reminded of the outstanding facts of Christian experience. "If I regard iniquity in my heart the Lord will not hear me" (Psalm 66: 18).

*Prayerlessness . . .* (Matthew 17: 19–21)

"Then came the disciples to Jesus apart, and said, Why could we not cast him out? And Jesus said unto them, Because of your unbelief;

for verily I say unto you . . . this kind goeth not out but by prayer and fasting." The Lord Jesus revealed eternal truth in that one great statement. While His disciples slept, He had prayed. Their impotence and failure to cast out the demon provided a strange contrast to the amazing power of their Lord. Omnipotence and impotence were never so near as on that day. Prayer is a great mystery, and we shall never understand all its secrets until life's journey has been completed. Yet the facts of history and the teachings of the Bible agree that prayer—real believing prayer—is the greatest weapon given by God to man. *Prayer changes the man who prays.* It makes him more usable for the purposes of God. Eloquence may be the machinery, but prayer is the power which drives it. A church without a prayer meeting—is not a church!

*Nervousness* . . . (John 9: 20–22)

"The parents of the blind man answered them and said, We know that this is our son, and that he was born blind: But by what means he now seeth, we know not; or who hath opened his eyes, we know not: he is of age; ask him: he shall speak for himself. These words spake his parents, because they feared the Jews: for the Jews had agreed already that if any man did confess that he was Christ, he should be put out of the synagogue." Thus two cowardly people failed their boy and dishonoured their Lord. We shall never know what great things might have been accomplished that day if those parents had courageously given their testimony. Supposing they had said, "Gentlemen, our hearts have been aching for years. Our boy was blind, and we brought him regularly to the synagogue. Yet you could do nothing for us. Then, Jesus came!" Such a testimony, given in the power of the Holy Spirit, might have performed an even greater miracle than the one already accomplished. Alas, they were too nervous to do their duty. Their right hands were useless and thus they lost their greatest opportunity. (Taken from *Bible Treasures,* p. 95.)

SECTION TWO

*Expository Notes on the Call of the Twelve Apostles*

**And it came to pass in those days, that he went out into a mountain to pray, and continued all night in prayer to God. And when it was day, he called his disciples: and of them he chose twelve, whom also he named apostles (vv. 12–13).**

Godet is at his scintillating best when he says, "Luke has already brought before us more than once the need of prayer, which so often drew Jesus away into the solitude (4: 42 and 5: 16). But the expressions he makes use of here are intended to carry weight. *Dianuktereuein, to pass the night in watching,* is a word rarely used in Greek, and which in all the New Testament is only found here. The choice of this unusual term, as well as the analytical form (the imperfect with the participle) express the persevering energy of this vigil. The term *proseuchee tou Theou,* literally, *prayer of God,* is also a unique expression in the New Testament. It does not denote any special request, but a state of wrapt contemplation of God's presence, a prayer arising out of the most profound communion with Him. The development of the work of Jesus having now reached a critical point, during this night He laid it before God, and took counsel with Him. The choosing of the twelve apostles was the fruit of this lengthened season of prayer; in that higher light in which Jesus stood, it appeared the only measure answering to the exigencies of the present situation." (Godet's *Commentary on the Gospel of Luke,* p. 299.)

This scripture may best be understood under five headings. (1) *The Passion for Prayer:* ". . . in those days." What days? The days when special dangers awaited the Saviour; when unique opportunities needed to be grasped; when vital decisions had to be made. Prayer was not a passing thought in the mind of Jesus; it was a consuming fire keeping Him aware of the need for the closest fellowship with God. He prayed, not merely because He needed to pray, but because He could not exist without it. It was as indispensable to His soul as fresh air was for His lungs! (2) *The Place of Prayer:* ". . . he went out into a mountain."* Prayer meetings within the church are excellent; prayer meetings within the family circle are even better, but the greatest times of communion can only be known when the soul is alone with God. Within the sanctuary one is privileged to listen to many voices; on the hilltop, one hears only the voice of the Father. The valleys of our continuous toil are apt to be filled with smog; happy indeed is the Christian who knows how to climb God's mountains. (3) *The Persistence of Prayer:* ". . . and continued all night in prayer to God." Great battles are never won in a single moment of time; high mountains cannot be crossed by taking one step! The divine art of perseverance was never seen to better advantage than in this text. The Lord was confronted by many problems; the future of the world would be settled by what would take place the following morning. There was so much at stake that He could not afford to make a mistake! That He could have chosen His own disciples, we have no doubt, but let us remember Luke was presenting the thrilling portrait of a fully consecrated Man, and as a MAN Jesus was utterly dependent upon God. Therefore He carried His problems to the throne of grace, and wise indeed is the man who emulates His example. (4) *The Purpose of Prayer:* "And when it was day . . ." How significant these words appear to become in the light of what has just been expressed. When the Lord ascended the mountain, the valleys were enshrouded in gloom; when He had prayed, the sun was shining. The same valleys were bathed in radiance; the roads were clearly visible; the way was open; He knew what He had to do. The best way to solve problems is to pray about them—to pray until they disappear before the rising sun! (5) *The Power of Prayer:* "... he called his disciples: and of them he chose twelve." His action on that beautiful morning brought a measure of organization to His followers; suddenly the embryonic church began to make its appearance. The enemies were organizing for their evil attacks; He would safeguard His followers so that in the moment of danger, they would have leaders whose counsel would be of inestimable worth. The fact that after such prolonged communion He chose Judas demands special attention. See the notes on verse 16.

**Simon (whom he also named Peter) and Andrew his brother, James and John, Philip and Bartholomew, Matthew and Thomas, James the son of Alpheus, and Simon called Zelotes, and Judas the brother of James, and Judas Iscariot, which also was the traitor (vv. 13–16).**

Matthew 10: 2–4; Mark 3: 16–19; Luke 6: 13–16; and Acts 1: 13 all list the names of the Apostles and each time Simon Peter is named first, presumably because he was the recognized earthly leader of the group. Bartholomew was not a real name but rather a patronymic term relating to the descent of the person mentioned; thus Bartholomew was the son of Tholomai. The true name of this apostle was Nathaniel. Levi's other name was Matthew. Thus the Lord chose twelve disciples and the inference was obvious. He was beginning a new society and not improving the old! Formerly, the people of God had been marshalled under twelve earthly heads, the tribes of Israel. Now the new people of God would also have twelve leaders. The ancient leaders had been responsible under God to interpret the law and lead the nation in its attacks upon sinful enemies. Within the framework of the church, the twelve apostles would be responsible, under the guidance of the Holy Spirit, to interpret the mind of Christ and lead the saints to the conquest of a sinful world. The Lord Jesus thus announced the fact that He was initiating a new era destined to be completely divorced from its predecessor. *Its laws would be greater and holier.* The commandments of the new life would make demands upon a man's thoughts and not merely his actions. *Its citizens would be more representative* for they would include people from every nation. *Even its day of rest would be different.* The New Testament Church would observe the resurrection day as their Holy Day, and thus the break with the old regime would be complete. There are people who claim that the Church was wrong to do this; that they went out of the Will of God, but alas, those same critics do not explain how the Lord used these Christians to turn the world upside down!

Why did the Lord appoint Judas Iscariot to be an apostle, when He knew the man would eventually become the traitor? Was it fair and just of Christ to expose a man to temptation, when He knew beforehand Judas would lose his soul in the battles to come? These pertinent questions have been debated at length, and many strange ideas have been advanced by theological writers. This author is of the opinion that if Christ could have avoided the call of Judas, He would have done so. Judas, was called *the son of perdition,* and there are many responsible teachers who say he was the child of Satan. That he was the devil's challenge to Christ, none can deny. It might be better to consider Judas to have been the choice of Satan, rather than the choice of Christ. The Lord was instructing His followers how to behave under every circumstance, but it was one thing to teach them these things, and another to show them! Could He, the Son of God, remain calm, serene, and holy, when a traitor lived in His presence? It is easier to deal with enemies without the camp than to tolerate hypocrisy within the heart of a professed friend. Perhaps Jesus *had* to accept Judas for otherwise He would have been avoiding a direct challenge from Satan.

And he came down with them, and stood in the plain, and the company of his disciples, and a great multitude of people out of all Judea, and Jerusalem, and from the sea coast of Tyre and Sidon, which came to hear him, and to be healed of their diseases; And they that were vexed with unclean spirits; and they were healed. And the whole multitude sought to touch him; for there went virtue out of him, and healed all (vv. 17–19).

Surrounded by His disciples, the Lord came down to a level place among the lower slopes of the hill, and seeing His opportunity, began preaching His immortal message—The Sermon on the Mount. Certain writers have stressed the differing features in the Gospels of Matthew and Luke but there is no real problem in these accounts. It is worthy of mention that some of the people present that day had come from the twin towns Tyre and Sidon and their presence indicated the influence of the Saviour was spreading out in ever widening circles. The future was bright with prospect and hope but the increasing size of the kingdom would necessitate officials responsible for the carrying out of the King's wishes. The Lord was content; His appointed officers were around Him; they would be trained and ready when the responsibility of managing His affairs fell upon their shoulders.

HOMILIES

Study No. 18

## THE ALL-SUFFICIENT CHRIST

Luke provides one of the most comprehensive pictures of Christ ever given to man. Very many people throughout the Christian era have wistfully longed that some ancient artist had persuaded Jesus of Nazareth to sit for a painting. If indeed there could be an authentic picture of the Master its sales would supersede anything ever known. God evidently desired the image of His Son to be engraved on our hearts, and not painted on canvas! Luke in his admirable manner endeavoured to meet this need when he described for us the ministry of Him whom the ancients described as *the altogether lovely One; the chiefest among ten thousand.*

*The Great Preacher:* "... and a great multitude of people ... came to hear him."

It is significant in the text that the quality of His preaching had a greater effect upon His hearers than did His miracles. These people had sick relatives and friends whom they greatly desired to be restored to health, yet they came primarily to hear Christ preach. This is truly astonishing, especially in the light of present day events. When a modern preacher advertises his ability to heal the sick, and promises beforehand that this will be done in the regular meetings, crowds attend in the hope of seeing something sensational. Without the so-called "drawing card" even the greatest orator might preach to empty seats! Modern evangelists must have a programme, and gimmicks with which to attract outsiders. How very far the modern church seems to have wandered; how poverty stricken are some of her instruments. Jesus of Nazareth was just a preacher of the Word of God, and to hear His amazing message, men and women came from all parts of the nation.

*The Great Healer:* "... and to be healed of their diseases."

The Bible has promised that if we seek first the kingdom of God and His righteousness, all other things shall be added unto us. This was singularly illustrated when having preached to the listening audience, the Lord commenced to heal their sick friends. There appears to be a quiet dignity, a commendable charm about Luke's narrative. This Man from Nazareth was no showman; no charlatan; He did not grab people and shake them until they were dizzy. He had no need to impress onlookers with His antics; He spoke, and the disease died. Why does not this happen today? Has God changed His methods? Has disease become invincible? No! God is the same; His power has not diminished. We remain impotent because innumerable committee meetings; the ceaseless endeavour to make a dollar; the attraction of the ball games, and other things take our time and we seldom climb God's mountain. We believe in God but we never meet Him.

*The Great Deliverer:* ". . . they that were vexed with unclean spirits . . . were healed."

The disease of the soul must always be worse than the ills of the body. Sometimes it is easier to paint a house than to expel its tenant! Often the spiritual physicians prescribe a box of pills when they should be supplying a key to unlock prison doors. The power of the evil one is a reality, and this fact should ever be in the view of those who seek to be the Lord's disciples. If our preaching does not challenge as well as encourage; if our ministry does not rout as well as dismay the enemy, then something must be wrong. We are engaged in holy warfare, and unless we are the channels through which the mighty power of God flows, those with whom we come into contact will remain in bondage.

*The Great Saviour:* ". . . for there went virtue out of him and healed all."

Luke does not mention any specific ailment; he saw and described a crowd with innumerable needs. There were adults and children; freemen and slaves; possibly Jews and Gentiles; wealthy and poor; educated and illiterate; religious and indifferent, but in one never-to-be-forgotten moment, barriers disappeared, and that cosmopolitan crowd became a family before God. Arguments were unheard, criticisms were forgotten, for men ceased looking at men—they saw only Christ. And as faith silently prayed, healing influences emanated from His overflowing soul, and God's benediction turned the hillside into an open-air cathedral. Need knows no racial barriers; men can hardly be segregated in death! Christ takes all people and unites them within the fellowship of His everlasting purposes. It is tragic that we apply to the marriage service alone the potent words: "Whom the Lord hath joined together, let no man put asunder." He who breaks up a marriage is an enemy of the church; he who divides the church cannot be the friend of Christ.

## SECTION THREE

### A Necessary Introduction to the Study of Christ's Sermon on the Mount

Throughout the centuries much argument has revolved around the two versions of Christ's sermon on the mount. Matthew devotes three complete chapters to the message whereas Luke needs only thirty verses to describe the entire oration. Matthew 5: 1 says Jesus went up into the mountain before He began to preach; Luke 6: 17 says He descended from the mountain to a level place ere He began to preach. Obviously at first there appears to be a clash of opinions and some writers have stated that either Luke or Matthew was in error. Other theologians have tried to harmonize these versions by suggesting Jesus made two speeches; one on the mountain, and another in the valley. The similarity of certain parts of the two accounts makes this improbable. Reference has already been made to the fact that Jesus probably descended to a level place somewhere in the hill—that is, to a plain which was higher than the valley itself. Matthew may have ascended with another section of the crowd, and thus from his viewpoint, Jesus had *gone up* into the mountain to preach. Luke, who in after days, probably went across to see the place about which he was to write, saw the location and truthfully wrote that Jesus came down from the mountain to the level place and there delivered His speech. There is no great difficulty in bringing together these two apparently conflicting versions. Matthew was certainly an eyewitness of the entire proceedings; Luke either copied from an earlier manuscript or gleaned his information from oral sources. No one can be sure. If Luke had Matthew's manuscript before him, he would probably consider there was hardly need to repeat what his fellow Christian had already written; he would choose salient points necessary to his subject, and omit the rest. On the other hand, someone might have described from memory those parts of Christ's sermon which appeared to be unforgettable, and hearing these, Luke faithfully wrote them in his Gospel. There can be no doubt that Matthew's account is the greater of the two, but since Luke never professed to write everything that Jesus ever uttered, there is no serious omission in his description. It is necessary for the purpose of understanding this part of the chapter to see clearly that the Lord's audience was divided into three sections. (1) the disciples whom He had just chosen to be apostles; (2) the larger number of professed disciples who were not apostles; (3) the vast number of spectators whom Luke describes as "the *whole multitude*." Let us then visualize the Lord descending from the higher parts of the

mountain. He is accompanied by the chosen leaders of the new movement. Many other disciples, either with Him or waiting for Him, join
the party, and the entire procession proceeds to the level place among
the hills. Hearing that Jesus has come to the lower parts of the
mountains, many interested people, and possibly Matthew with them,
climb from the valley to join the large crowd already assembled. As
the people increase in number, and as expectation mounts higher,
Jesus looks around for a natural pulpit—on a similar occasion, He had
asked for the use of Simon Peter's boat (see Luke 5: 1–3)—and climbing a little higher so that the audience could see and hear, He proceeded to preach his sermon.

## SUB-SECTION ONE

### *Expository Notes on Christ's Message to the New Apostles* (vv. 20–23)

**And he lifted up his eyes on his disciples, and said, Blessed be ye poor;
for yours is the kingdom of God. Blessed are ye that hunger now: for
ye shall be filled. Blessed are ye that weep now: for ye shall laugh.
Blessed are ye when men shall hate you, and when they shall separate
you and reproach you, and cast out your name as evil, for the Son of
man's sake. Rejoice ye in that day, and leap for joy: for, behold, your
reward is great in heaven: for in like manner did their fathers unto the
prophets (vv. 20–23).**

The *ye* in this part of the sermon indicates this message was
addressed to a particular group of people. There is no mention of sin,
and no condemnation can be found in the utterance. The recipients
of this message were acceptable to Jesus and this supports the assertion
that these words were spoken to the apostles There are four *blesseds*
in the section, and these appear to be filled with deep meaning.
*Blessed are ye poor* . . . the word translating *poor* is *ptochoi*. It comes
from *ptosso* and means more than being without money. Dr. J. H.
Thayer mentions four of these words and they are all closely related:
*ptosis; ptocheia; ptocheuo; ptosso*. There is certainly the idea of
poverty, but the word also means *to be frightened, cowed,* and in a
broader sense, *to be destitute of influence, position, honours.* The
picture suggested by the text therefore is of a man, who in the estimation of the world, is *nothing!* He has forsaken all to follow Christ; and
is now despised by his former friends. Deprived of the customary
means of livelihood, the man resembles an itinerant beggar asking alms
and obtaining food wherever he can. Acceptance of the invitation of
Jesus had already brought the apostles into this unenviable position,
but the benediction of Christ was meant to compensate them for their

losses. Poverty in itself is no guarantee of entry into the Kingdom of
God. Care must be taken to understand that the *cause* of this particular poverty—that is, *their allegiance to Christ*—this and this alone
led to the promise, *"yours is the kingdom of God."* Matthew simplifies
the meaning of this text: "Blessed are the poor in *spirit.*" Similarly
he increases the scope of the second *blessed*: "Blessed are they which
do hunger and thirst *after righteousness*: for they shall be filled."
The text reveals that the disciples had become aware of an intense
desire to partake of the bread of life; they were conscious of deep
yearnings for spiritual food, and this in itself would be a blessed and
hallowed experience. Such hunger could never be ignored; it would
be incumbent on God to satisfy it. Matthew reports the third *blessed*
thus: "Blessed are they that mourn; for they shall be comforted."
Luke interprets the passage: "Blessed are ye that weep now for ye
shall laugh." Obviously the underlying idea is that of suffering for the
kingdom's sake. It was upon such texts that Pauline doctrine rested.
"For I reckon that the suffering of this present time are not worthy to
be compared with the glory which shall be revealed in us" (Romans
8: 18). The idea of separation from fellow men refers to excommunica-
tion from the synagogue. Their names would be erased from the rolls
of membership; they would become outcasts. (See John 9: 34.) When
this happened, the disciples should jump for joy for the treatment
being endured indicated they were in excellent company. The prophets
similarly had suffered. In this manner Christ instructed and warned
His friends; it was His charge to those whom He had just ordained
to the ministry.

### SUB-SECTION TWO

*Expository Notes on Christ's Message to the Larger Company*
*of Disciples* (vv. 24–38)

**But woe unto you that are rich! for ye have received your consolation.
Woe unto you that are full! for ye shall hunger. Woe unto you that
laugh now! for ye shall mourn and weep. Woe unto you when all men
shall speak well of you! for so did their fathers unto the false prophets
(vv. 24-26).**

It should not be assumed from the text that Christ was speaking
against all people who possessed wealth. It was not a crime to be
wealthy—unless the wealth were gained by illegitimate means. It
should be remembered the Lord was now addressing a greater number
of disciples, some of whom would desert Him as soon as the opposition
to His teaching increased. Many of these people professed to be close
followers of the Lord, but they still belonged to the multitude. For the

most part wealth in those days belonged to the rulers and unfortunately many of these were already criticizing the Lord. It was to them primarily that these words were being directed. The wealthy who had striven to become wealthy had already received their reward. Every prediction of Christ was literally fulfilled when Jerusalem fell.

> But I say unto you which hear, Love your enemies, do good to them which hate you. Bless them that curse you, and pray for them which despitefully use you. And unto him that smiteth thee on the one cheek offer also the other; and him that taketh away thy cloak forbid not to take thy coat also. Give to every man that asketh of thee; and of him that taketh away thy goods ask not again. And as ye would that men should do to you, do ye also to them likewise (vv. 27-31).

The Lord Jesus was now enunciating the laws of His kingdom, and at once it became obvious that His commandments were vastly different from and infinitely superior to, anything expressed in the laws of Moses. Under Mosaic law, men could apply to the judges and be sure their grievances would be heard. Debts had to be paid, and thieves were punished. Christ issued new commandments, and the startling difference between the two systems is even more noticeable when one considers the word translated cheek really means *the jaw*. It is *siagon*; *the jaw or jawbone*. Christ is referring to a heavy punch to the jaw, and urges that even in this extreme case of violence, retaliatory passion should be subservient to love. When people continue to say that Christians must never forsake the ancient standards set by Moses; when they affirm that these are still the alpha and the omega of the Christian faith, they exhibit ignorance of the greater message proclaimed by Christ. If man did all that Moses commanded, inevitably he would need to do things expressly forbidden by Jesus. An understanding of these features enables us to appreciate the reason for the growing opposition of the leaders who actually heard the enunciation of these new principles. Were these laws ever meant for an unregenerate world; would they work in a modern society? We return to the assumption with which we began this study. Christ was now speaking to professed disciples; some of whom were destined to forsake His cause. Active allegiance to Christ meant conformity to His will. No man should seek citizenship in the Kingdom of God unless he be willing to live as a true citizen. There are responsibilities as well as privileges in being a Christian.

> For if ye love them which love you, what credit is that to you? for sinners also love those that love them. And if ye do good to them which do good to you, what credit have ye? for sinners also lend to sinners, to receive as much again. But love ye your enemies and do good, and

lend, hoping for nothing again; and your reward shall be great, and ye shall be the children of the Highest: for he is kind unto the unthankful and the evil (vv. 32–35).

Verse 34 is rendered in the Amplified New Testament as follows: "And if you lend money at interest to those from whom ye hope to receive, what quality of credit and thanks is that to you? Even notorious sinners lend money at interest to sinners, so as to recover as much again." The striking difference between a kindly benefactor and a shrewd money lender is brought into bold relief: compassion and not cleverness is the hallmark of a true child of God. The passage may best be understood under three headings: (1) *God's Commandments:* ". . . love your enemies, and do good . . ." (2) *God's Compensations:* ". . . and your reward shall be great, and ye shall be the children of the Highest." One point here needs clarification. A man does not become a child of God simply because his actions conform to the teachings of the sermon on the mount. He might easily do these things and NOT be a child of the Highest. If the man does these things— because he loves the Lord and desires to obey Him—then, he becomes a child of God. It is not the action that leads to acceptance with God but rather the motive behind the deed. A man might do good because he desires to have his name in the newspapers or because he needs support at a forthcoming election! The will of Christ may never even be considered in his doing unto others as he himself would have them do to him. This is a salient point demanding consideration. (3) *God's Conformity*—to His own laws. Matthew 5: 44–45 extends the scope of this text: "Love your enemies . . . That ye may be the children of your Father which is in heaven: for he maketh his sun to rise on the evil, and on the good, and sendeth rain on the just and on the unjust." Man is so prone to assess the greatness of his conduct by a comparison with the less virtuous deeds of his fellow men. This is a great mistake. Our example must be God Himself. As He is kind to all, so must we be.

Be ye therefore merciful, as your Father also is merciful. Judge not, and ye shall not be judged: condemn not, and ye shall not be condemned: forgive, and ye shall be forgiven: Give, and it shall be given unto you; good measure, pressed down, and shaken together, and running over, shall men give into your bosom. For with the same measure that ye mete withal it shall be measured to you again (vv. 36–38).

The Lord was aware of the critical attitude of many of the Scribes and Pharisees who were standing near; they had already judged, and their preconceived opinions had produced an unfair decision. They had condemned without a cause, Him from whom someday they would need forgiveness. Against this forbidding background, Christ advocated a better way of living. The measure to which He referred was that used for measuring solids, and the idea of running over does not contradict this fact. I often saw the natives in Africa coming to the trading store to buy meal. They watched carefully as the container was filled; then they expected the trader to shake the receptacle so that the meal could settle into greater compactness. Finally the container had to be filled to the brim. Christ indicated an even greater reward. The meal would be pressed down, and shaken together, and finally the super-abundance of the supply would be too much for the container; some would fall over the sides. Thus would God give to those who gave to Him. This was, and still is a basic law of the Kingdom. No man can outgive the Lord. I once heard the late Dr. Frank Boreham say, "If you possess something indispensable, *give it* away." It was good advice. The best way to increase one's possessions is to share what we have.

## SUB-SECTION THREE

*Expository Notes on Christ's Message to the Multitude* (vv. 39–49)

And he spake a parable unto them, Can the blind lead the blind? shall they not both fall into the ditch? The disciple is not above his master: but every one that is perfect shall be as his master. And why beholdest thou the mote that is in thy brother's eye, but perceivest not the beam that is in thine own eye? Either, how canst thou say to thy brother, Brother, let me pull out the mote that is in thine eye, when thou thyself beholdest not the beam that is in thine own eye? Thou hypocrite, cast out first the beam out of thine own eye, and then shalt thou see clearly to pull out the mote that is in thy brother's eye (vv. 39–42).

The Lord was now looking beyond the inner circle of disciples. Many of the Pharisees were blind leaders; how could they lead other people who were similarly in the darkness of sin? No man should ever try to lead perishing souls into the kingdom of God until he himself has passed from darkness into the marvellous light of the Gospel. The original meaning of the word *disciple* was *pupil or scholar*. The master to whom reference was made in verse 40 was the Pharisee— the disciples or pupils of the Pharisees were not above, nor greater in importance than their teachers, yet every student who desired to be perfect set his eyes on his master and hoped some day to be like him. Thus in one devastating statement the Lord revealed the utter uselessness of a system which at best could only produce graduates as blind as its own professors. Those teachers were employed to instruct students and correct errors by imparting knowledge. They were aware of the mote (a small piece of hay) which had somehow blurred the vision of their hearers, and yet at the same time they remained ignorant of the beam (a false image; a mirage!) which ruined their own sight. Christ taught the wisdom of self-examination and the necessity of being ruthless with self. The man who erected homes whilst his own fell into a state of disrepair was surely stupid!

For a good tree bringeth not forth corrupt fruit; neither doth a corrupt tree bring forth good fruit. For every tree is known by his own fruit. For of thorns men do not gather figs, nor of a bramble bush gather they grapes. A good man out of the good treasure of his heart bringeth forth that which is good; and an evil man out of the evil treasure of his heart bringeth forth that which is evil: for of the abundance of the heart his mouth speaketh (vv. 43–45).

This simple illustration about trees, bushes, and fruit, sheds light on a central theme. Let us remember again that this part of the discourse was being preached to unregenerate people. Many of them had a form of godliness but their hearts remained critical, envious, evil. A corrupt tree is one infected with disease; a tree incapable of producing luscious fruit. Sometimes, even today, it is possible to see a fig tree almost completely covered with the climbing tendrils of vine branches. A tree may be poisoned from within, or strangled from without, but the results are identical. A healthy tree must be free from all encumbrances. Christ used this parable to emphasize the important parts of His message. When He spoke of the evil heart, He meant precisely what He said. Man had sinned; man needed a new heart, and it was to make this possible the Lord came to earth. All this, and possibly much more, was expressed in Ezekiel 36: 25–27. "Then I will sprinkle clean water upon you, and ye shall be clean: from all your filthiness, and from all your idols, will I cleanse you. A new heart also will I give you, and a new spirit will I put within you: and I will take away the stony heart out of your flesh, and I will give you a heart of flesh. And I will put my Spirit within you, and cause you to walk in my statutes, and ye shall keep my judgments, and do them."

And why call ye me, Lord, Lord, and do not the things which I say? Whosoever cometh to me, and heareth my sayings, and doeth them, I will shew you to whom he is like: He is like a man which built an house, and digged deep, and laid the foundation on a rock: and when the flood arose, the stream beat vehemently upon that house, and could not shake it: for it was founded upon a rock. But he that heareth, and doeth not, is like a man that without a foundation built an house upon the earth; against which the stream did beat vehemently, and immediately it fell; and the ruin of that house was great (vv. 46-49).

This passage must be considered in the light of the geographical features of the district in which Christ was preaching. There were hills around the Sea of Galilee in which the layers of shelf-like rocks came to within a few feet of the surface. The wise builder removed the surface soil in order to place the foundations of his home upon the solid rock. Less prudent men erected their buildings in shallow trenches. There were times when severe storms broke in the tops of the mountains, when raging torrents of water rushed down the ravines to cover the plains. These surging floods undermined and weakened flimsy foundations, and when the hurricane increased, the house toppled over and the ruin was complete. Homes erected on the rock were able to withstand the onslaught of Nature.

The people who heard these things were able at the same moment to look beyond the Lord to see evidence in support of His statements. Let us remember the meeting was being held on a level piece of land somewhere in the lower area of the hills. The congregation would therefore be able to look up the natural ravines down which the torrent would flow; they would be able to see places where homes had been destroyed. The good foundation about which Jesus spoke was likened unto His own teaching. *"Whosoever cometh to me, and heareth my sayings, and doeth them"*—He is the man who built on the rock. The solid foundation then is the Word of Christ, and not the commandments of Moses. Christ was indeed initiating a new era, and unless He was what He claimed to be—THE SON OF GOD, He was guilty of violating everything considered sacred in Israel. See the following homily.

HOMILIES

Study No. 19

### WITHOUT A FOUNDATION

I once met a person who appeared to have everything this world offers—money, position, friends. She was a very charming woman who delighted in helping other people, but she seldom went to any church. Apparently the lady was doing so well without God, it would have been difficult to persuade her she needed Him. Then one day she became conscious that something was wrong, and her visit to the doctor confirmed her worst suspicions. I heard her thought-provoking testimony—"I nearly went mad!" How does a person pray to an unknown God? How does a woman find strength in a non-existent faith? Her beautiful house of satisfaction suddenly crumbled and fell because it had no foundation.

## Foundations of Sand

This parable was used as a conclusion to the Lord's sermon on the mount. He had spoken to people who knew the will of God but seldom did it. It was difficult to teach them because they knew everything! It was impossible to lead them; they would not follow. It was hard to convince them; they only argued. They were like the man who built his house upon sand; he was very satisfied, very sincere, very stupid. (1) *This is an age of broken homes.* We may well ask the reason for continuing domestic unhappiness. Every bride hopes her marriage will succeed but many forget that the strength of matrimony is the foundation upon which it rests. The novelty of marital union has a short life. Nerves become strained, and the glamour of a honeymoon quickly disappears. Then either sex may be attracted by illegitimate associations, and inherent desires are expressed along unethical channels. It is only the strength of a continuing Christian faith that offsets the challenge to this type of temptation. (2) *This is an age of broken thrones.* A nation built upon corruption is doomed. Even the empire of the Caesars fell because its foundations were undermined by evil. Greed begets enemies; persecution begets bitterness. History provides many examples of this fact, but it is good to remember the kingdom of Christ continually extends its borders. Love begets brethren; kindness conquers enemies. "Happy is that nation whose God is the Lord." (2) *This is an age of broken lives.* Any evangelistic mission in the Skid Row of a large city supplies evidence in support of this conclusion. Men who once enjoyed the comfort of a beautiful home now exist in the squalor of a slum. People who knew the benefits of a first-class education are now enslaved to the power of sin. Life abounds with illustrations of men and women whose lives were unable to withstand the onslaught of evil. Alas, the structure of their good intentions disintegrated and fell before their eyes.

## Foundations of Salt

Years ago during a visit to Northwich, a small town outside of Manchester in England, I was astounded to find huge buildings in the main street leaning at a most fantastic angle. Local friends explained this was the result of subsidence throughout the district. Every building in the place was sinking. I was told that Northwich had vast salt deposits through the area, but no man ever went down the mine, for there was no salt-mine! At one end of the town, water was pumped at high pressure into the salt deposits. At the other end— after the water had become brine, it was brought back to the surface. Then the water was evaporated and the salt obtained for commercial purposes. The discovery of the salt deposits brought great prosperity to Northwich; business houses flourished, the population increased, and every one was happy until the homes began to sink! There was never an earthquake, nor an explosion. Everything was dignified, peaceful, and quiet, but as the water dissolved the salty foundations, the town began to push its way into the earth. Then the local council had to decide whether to abandon their new-found wealth, or devise ways and means to restore the place to an even keel. To give up the salt-mines was unthinkable; the officials therefore employed engineers who were experts in the art of lifting sinking buildings! I have known this to happen to humans, but the system is deadly! Instead of erecting barriers along the tops of the dangerous cliffs, we build hospitals at the bottom so that our doctors will not be unemployed! Instead of abolishing drink traffic, we open homes for alcoholics. Instead of banishing smoking, we appeal for funds to find a cure for cancer of the lungs!

### Foundations of Stone

Wise men build upon the precepts of Christ, for "other foundation can no man lay, than that is laid, Jesus Christ." One of the greatest dangers confronting the free world is the steady infiltration of evil; against this there is no bulwark except the principles taught by Jesus. His word is from everlasting to everlasting; it has been tested on innumerable occasions and has never been found wanting. Italy is a strange but delightful land of contrasts. The Tower of Pisa, for example, has to be lifted every two years and to accomplish this tremendous undertaking the greatest engineers in the nation are employed. Apparently this great tower was erected over a fault in the earth's strata and although fabulous amounts of cement have been poured into the foundations, the tower continues to sink. Yet the Italians love it; the Tower of Pisa is a magnificent dollar earner! On the other hand, the entire city of Venice, which the Venicians proudly call *The Pearl*, rests exclusively upon hundreds of thousands of pylons driven thirty-eight feet through mud, water, and slime to the underlying beds of solid rock. The streets of Venice are canals; the means of transport barges, boats and gondolas. The sidewalks, the shops, the bazaars, the marvellous St. Mark's Cathedral, everything rests on pylons. Formerly these were made of wood—huge tree trunks driven into the water, but these are now being replaced by cement pylons.

Nevertheless, in spite of the colossal weight of the entire city, it never sinks—it rests upon the rock. Safe indeed are those people who build upon the Rock of Ages.

> My hope is built on nothing less
> Than Jesus' blood and righteousness:
> I dare not trust the sweetest frame,
> But wholly lean on Jesus' Name.

> On Christ the solid rock I stand,
> All other ground is sinking sand.

# The Seventh Chapter of Luke

THEME: *Christ continues His Ministry in Galilee*

OUTLINE:

    I. Christ strengthens a Faith. Verses 1–10
    II. Christ stops a Funeral. Verses 11–17
    III. Christ supports a Friend. Verses 18–35
    IV. Christ stays for a Feast. Verses 36–50

## SECTION ONE

*Expository Notes on the Healing of the Centurion's Servant*

Now when he had ended all his sayings in the audience of the people, he entered into Capernaum. And a certain centurion's servant, who was dear unto him, was sick, and ready to die. And when he heard of Jesus, he sent unto him the elders of the Jews, beseeching him that he would come and heal his servant. And when they came to Jesus, they besought him instantly, saying, That he was worthy for whom he should do this: For he loveth our nation, and he hath built us a synagogue (vv. 1–5).

The two versions of this event, Matthew 8: 5–13, and Luke 7: 1–10, should be read and studied together for either account has something to contribute to the other. When Christ had finished preaching to the multitude, He proceeded to Capernaum and soon a deputation of Jewish elders arrived to present a very special request. The fact that the elders (*presbuterous*) were willing to swallow their pride and ask a favour of One whom they were already criticising, indicates the greatness of their esteem for this unknown Gentile. A slave boy was critically ill in the centurion's home, and there were fears that unless the Healer could do something quickly, the lad's life might be lost. Luke uses the Greek word *doulos* which means *a slave*; Matthew uses another word *pais* which means *a child; a boy or girl;* and in a secondary sense, *a servant or slave*. There must have been special reasons why this slave boy had captured the affections of the Roman captain. The word *entimos* translated "was *dear* unto him" offers a different shade of meaning. Dr. Thayer says it means: *held in honour; prized; precious.* The Amplified New Testament renders the passage: *"Now a centurion had a bond servant."* The lad who might have been liberated had chosen to remain with his master; either one was intensely precious to the other. This youth therefore was sick, and the anxious centurion hearing of the approach of Jesus sent the elders of the Jews to ask Him to heal the servant. It is possible that this man heard of the healing of the nobleman's son (John 4: 46–54), for this miracle had also taken place within the city of Capernaum. Some writers suggest these two events were actually the same, but a comparison of the accounts makes it clear this would have been impossible. Encouraged by what he had heard, but conscious of the fact that he was a Gentile, this centurion sought the help of the elders of the synagogue —the synagogue for which he had been responsible. The use of the definite article—"for he loved our nation, and *the* synagogue he built . . ." suggests that at that time there was only one synagogue in Capernaum and this had been made possible by the Centurion's generosity.

**Then Jesus went with them. And when he was now not far from the house, the centurion sent friends to him, saying unto him, Lord, trouble not thyself: for I am not worthy that thou shouldest enter under my roof: Wherefore neither thought I myself worthy to come unto thee: but say in a word, and my servant shall be healed. For I also am a man set under authority, having under me soldiers, and I say unto one, Go, and he goeth; and to another, Come, and he cometh; and to my servant, Do this, and he doeth it (vv. 6–8).**

It would seem from the comparative readings that the man first sent the Jewish elders; then when Christ could be seen approaching the home, the humble centurion asked his friends to intercept and stop the Visitor. Then, overwhelmed by his sense of unworthiness, and fearing that his friends might not convey the right idea, the anxious man hurried down the street to do himself what he had asked others to do. His conception of Christ's authority within the Kingdom of God, and the word-picture by which he illustrated his faith, are indeed worthy of their place within the canon of Holy Scripture. As he represented Caesar, and as the power of the empire was vested in him to the extent that men hastened to do his bidding, so Christ represented an eternal empire; the authority and power of God were vested in Him. It was therefore only necessary for Jesus to utter a command and an unseen angel would hasten to fulfil His desire. It was indeed problematical whether any of Christ's disciples at that time had faith and vision equal to this.

**When Jesus heard these things, he marvelled at him, and turned him about, and said unto the people that followed him, I say unto you, I**

have not found so great faith, no, not in Israel. And they that were sent, returning to the house, found the servant whole that had been sick (vv. 9–10).

Godet thinks the sickness to which reference is made in Matthew 8 : 6 was chronic rheumatism affecting the heart. Others may disagree with this diagnosis, but whatever might have been the trouble, the power of Christ was able to heal the sufferer. Matthew supplies additional details of Christ's message, but since Luke was not particularly interested in the verbatim reports of sermons, it is not difficult to understand why he omitted certain incidentals in order to emphasize the thrilling qualities of the Master. If Luke had been a painter, this would have been his finest work. The scintillating faith of the centurion was second only in importance to the matchless power of Christ. All other details, however beautiful or important in themselves were but minor parts of a great masterpiece. Luke therefore made no attempt to supply every word that Jesus uttered; he was content to portray as much as possible of his thrilling Christ. The word translated *marvelled* is *othaumasen* and this would be better translated *admired,* "And having heard these things, Jesus admired him . . ." The Lord who had so often seen displeasing things in the minds and hearts of people, suddenly saw shining faith, and responded to the sight. The elders of the synagogue had probably been filled with their own importance when they came on the man's behalf—the Teacher should feel honoured that they had come to His meeting, and furthermore, even if He would not do this thing for other reasons, He would surely do it for them. Against this dark background the centurion's humility shines as a brilliant star in the night sky. The Lord saw it and was thrilled, and moved with compassion did as the centurion desired.

## HOMILIES

Study No. 20

### THE CENTURION WHO WON BATTLES PEACEFULLY

This Gentile soldier of a bygone age has won the admiration of the world. His restraint in face of provocation; his dignity in spite of insult and enmity; his forbearance and tolerance when open aggression might have been excusable, gained for him the respect of those whose land he had come to dominate. He was a man of outstanding quality.

*Kindness Overcoming Hatred*

Racial pride was a supreme characteristic in Israel, and patriotic Jews found it extremely difficult to beg from the Carpenter of Nazareth. The elders of the synagogue constantly urged their followers to boycott the meetings of Christ, and it was a startling sight when these same elders came to seek the Master's help. "And a certain centurion's servant, who was dear unto him, was sick and ready to die. And when he heard of Jesus, *he sent unto him the elders of the Jews,* beseeching him that he would come and heal his servant. And when they came to Jesus, they besought him instantly, saying, that he was worthy for whom he should do this thing: for he loveth our nation, and he hath built us a synagogue." Their testimony gave eloquent evidence of the power of human kindness. All their bitter resentment and passionate opposition had been challenged and overcome by the kindliness of this Roman. The sunlight of his gracious personality had opened the flowers of appreciation which had been fast closed in their night of bitterness. They put aside their prejudice; swallowed their pride, and on behalf of their Gentile friend sought the help of the Saviour.

*Humility Overcoming Pride*

The man for whom they sought assistance was a centurion—a captain in Caesar's army of occupation. He was no ordinary man, and his qualities had been recognized by his superiors. His promotion to higher rank had not spoiled him, and when necessity arose, he was not above seeking the help of a humble Carpenter whose exploits had aroused the enmity of many of his friends. Finally, he openly confessed his unworthiness of the approach of Christ, and said his home was no fit place for the Son of God. Humility is a flower which blooms in the garden of graciousness. In some climates it is a very rare orchid.

*Faith Overcoming Doubt*

"Then Jesus went with them. And when he was now not far from the house, the centurion sent friends to him, saying unto him, Lord, trouble not thyself: for I am not worthy that thou shouldest enter under my roof . . . say in a word, and my servant shall be healed. For I also am a man set under authority, having under me soldiers, and I say unto one, Go, and he goeth; and to another, Come, and he cometh; and to my servant, Do this, and he doeth it." The officer saw Caesar's kingdom and recognized that the weight of his own commands was only explained by the authority he represented. He saw also a greater empire in which Jesus of Nazareth held high office. The Teacher represented eternal powers, and unseen angelic servants were waiting to fulfil His desires. "Speak the word only, and my servant shall be healed." Real faith sees the invisible; laughs at the impossible and cries aloud in thanksgiving even before the deed is accomplished.

## Grace Overcoming Need

"And they that were sent, returning to the house found the servant whole that had been sick." It would appear from Matthew's account of the incident that as a last desperate measure, the captain himself went to the roadway to voice his humble protest against the unworthiness of his own abode. Thus the Lord was able to say to him, "Go thy way; and as thou hast believed, so be it done unto thee. And his servant was healed in the selfsame hour" (Matthew 8: 13). This ancient story is rich in truth. (1) The centurion was one of the best people of his day, yet he still had need of Christ. (2) The grace of God as manifest in Christ was both able and willing to respond to the appeal for help. (3) The Lord Jesus is "the same yesterday, and today, and forever." Therefore I can follow the example of the centurion, remembering that what might be lacking in faith, will be more than supplied by the kindness of God.

(Taken from *Bible Pinnacles,* page 101)

SECTION TWO

*Expository Notes on the Raising of the Widow's Son at Nain*

And it came to pass the day after, that he went into a city called Nain; and many of his disciples went with him, and much people. Now when he came nigh to the gate of the city, behold, there was a dead man carried out, the only son of his mother, and she was a widow: and much people of the city was with her (vv. 11–12).

Nain "now called Nein on the north-west verge of *Jebel ed Duhy* (Little Hermon) where it slopes down to the Esdraelon plain. The rock west of the village abounds in cave tombs. . . . Eighteen miles from Capernaum. . . . Josephus (*Antiquities of Josephus,* Chapter 5, paragraph 1) mentions Nain as on the way from Galilee to Jerusalem." *Fausset's Bible Encyclopaedia,* page 494. These details corroborate the account supplied by Luke. It is obvious that after the healing of the centurion's servant, the Lord began His journey to Nain and arrived in time to meet a funeral. Much criticism has been directed toward this miracle because none of the other Gospels makes any reference to this event. This is the only time that Christ is said to have entered the city, and whilst there may have been other occasions, it is nevertheless noteworthy that no reference has been made to any other visit. If this were indeed the one and only visit made to Nain, it is of great significance that He arrived at the right moment. All places of habitation in Palestine were surrounded by walls. Entry and exit were made through gates placed at convenient places. Luke says the funeral procession was actually going through the gateway when Jesus arrived. Had the Lord arrived two minutes earlier, He would have passed through the narrow opening and proceeded into the streets. Had He arrived two minutes later, the funeral would have been through the gate and on its way to the burial ground. Godet speaks of the Prince of Life meeting the victim of death, but the intriguing question arises: was this meeting accidental or was it planned by Christ? Did He know of this woman's need even before He came within sight of the procession? Did He hasten to be there in time to solve her problems? This was the second time she had been bereaved; now, she was alone in an empty world! That she was accompanied by much people, suggests she was either a very well-known citizen, or news of her loss had awakened a great sense of sympathy throughout the city.

**And when the Lord saw her, he had compassion on her, and said unto her, Weep not. And he came and touched the bier: and they that carried, stood still. And he said, Young man, I say unto thee, Arise. And he that was dead sat up and began to speak. And he delivered him to his mother (vv. 13-15).**

The Jews did not enclose a corpse in a casket or coffin; they placed the forms of their loved ones on a plank that had raised edges to prevent the body rolling off. Thus in this funeral at Nain, the young man's body was clearly visible. Seeing the sorrow of the mother, the Lord stepped across to the men who were carrying the corpse to the burial grounds, and commanded them to stand still. His mighty power challenged death, and emerged from the contest victoriously. The young man sat up on the plank whilst the people stared in amazement. Then slowly, as understanding came to the fellow, he commenced to speak and any doubt which might have lingered in the minds of the bystanders quickly disappeared. Man's body is but a house, and at death, the tenant moves from his home to other spheres. Certain critics have expressed the opinion that this was not a miracle; but rather a case of a man who was in a very deep sleep or coma. But, as Godet so aptly says, "*If this were so, the miracle of power would only disappear to be replaced by a miracle of knowledge quite as incomprehensible.*" Quoting Zeller (*Apostelgesch*, page 177) Godet proceeds to negative the ancient rationalistic explanation by saying, "In order to admit it, it must be thought credible, that, within the short period embraced by the evangelical and apostolic history, there took place five times over, thrice in the Gospels, and twice in the Acts, this same circumstance, this same remarkable chance of a lethargy, which, though unperceived by those who were engaged about the dead, yields to the first word of the divine messenger, and gives rise to a belief in a real resurrection." As a voice of command is often sufficient to arouse men from a deep sleep, so the authoritive command of Christ was sufficient to recall the man's spirit, to reunite the man with his body, and as full consciousness returned, he sat up and began to speak. It would be a most interesting thing if we could know what he said, but perhaps the Lord has hidden this from us in order to teach a greater truth—that all people who have been raised from the deadness of sins should begin to testify. If the young man had remained dumb for the rest of his life, his miraculous resurrection would have begotten scorn and not praise for Christ. Possibly the Lord remembered that someday His own mother would be bereaved and there would be no one to heal her broken heart. Thus, moved with compassion He hastened to help the forlorn widow.

**And there came a fear on all: and they glorified God, saying, That a great prophet is risen up among us; and, That God hath visited his people. And this rumour of him went forth throughout all Judea, and throughout all the region round about (vv. 16-17).**

No mention has been made of any call to discipleship issued to this young man, That Christ's raising him from the dead placed the man under a moral and spiritual obligation to the Saviour, no one could ever doubt. Nevertheless there was need for him to remain at home with his mother; she was a widow, and the possibility exists that her only son was her sole means of livelihood. There is prevailing sanity about all Christ's works and wishes. It is true that elsewhere in the Testament, the Lord spoke of leaving father and mother in order to become a permanent member of the disciple band, but there is also reason to believe that no dependent relative or, for that matter, anyone else, was ever made to suffer because of the acceptance of Christ's call by any member of the family. God has never been any man's debtor; He pays in full anything ever borrowed from those who work in His kingdom (See the notes on chapter 5, verse 11). The raising of this young man increased the enthusiasm of the crowds and soon news of the event spread throughout the nation.

HOMILIES

Study No. 21

### SPOILING A FUNERAL!

Few men ever dared to interrupt a funeral, for when people mourn, onlookers silently remove their hats and stand motionless until the cortege has passed. Yet Jesus did what others never thought of doing, and, furthermore, Luke has described the occurrence. Doctors are' only concerned with the living; the dead are left to the undertakers! The author of the third Gospel was different from other physicians; periodically he was more concerned with the dead—especially when Jesus was near. There were many other miracles, but always the mighty demonstrations of God's power were the outcome of faith which refused to yield. Here, however, there was no believing person; here apparently there was no plea for help. What He did, He did because of something happening within His own soul.

### A Dead Man

The pitiful wails of the mourners were already sounding within the house; the breadwinner had just died. We have not been told the cause of death, nor how long the victim had been sick. A widowed mother had passed this way before, but when her husband died, she became increasingly devoted to her only son. Now the outlook was bleak indeed; God apparently had forsaken her for the young man was soon to be buried. Somehow it did not seem right that one so young should die. Life had just begun, why should it end prematurely? And Christ agreed with the sentiment. When the widow was probably thinking God had left her, the Son of God was already on His way to the funeral!

### A Distracted Mourner

The procession was slowly making its way toward the city gate. The hired musicians and the women went first, for Jewish traditions declared that since women brought men into the world, women should also lead them out of it! Just ahead of the plank upon which the boy's body rested, walked the woman whose heart was breaking. Tears blinded her eyes and sorrow devastated her soul. She had no faith; she had no knowledge of what was soon to take place. Her son was dead. The outlook was completely bleak, but Christ was coming toward the gateway. Sometimes in our ignorance we think an out-pouring of His power depends exclusively upon the strength of man's faith. God has not to be coerced into doing things, and the story of the raising of this boy provides a glowing example of the truth.

### A Discerning Master

There is evidence to support the assertion that Christ came specially to meet that funeral. Climatic conditions in Palestine made it imperative that bodies be interred soon after death took place. Therefore there would not have been time for any message to summon Christ from Capernaum, eighteen miles away. Jesus had commenced the journey to Nain even before the boy died. Had He commenced His journey a little later, the burial service would have been finished. Was it by accident that He arrived when He did? Did not God who planned the constellations, plan also that another star should shine amidst the darkness of this woman's sorrow? And if Christ could see her, even when she was out of sight—cannot He see us?

### A Delightful Meeting

It was all over, and everybody was gasping. Jesus had ruined a funeral; the hired musicians might never be paid for a job fully completed! People were beginning to run toward the gate for already even from yards away they could see the corpse sitting upon the bier. The funeral bandages must be removed; Jesus probably superintended the task; then gracefully He extended a hand to lift the youth to his feet. When all had been accomplished, the Lord turned toward the mother and with indescribable charm, gave the son back into her arms. What a reunion! Even the angels in heaven must have been filled with ecstacy. Without even the key of faith, Christ had unlocked eternal treasure chests. Perhaps He did this deliberately to teach us that someday even though we are not present on earth to exercise faith, He will make the grave yield its victims; our bodies will be raised again, and claimed as we return from the skies in company with our wonderful Lord. "For the Lord Himself shall descend from heaven with a shout, with the voice of the archangel, and with the trump of God: and the dead in Christ shall rise first. Then we which are alive and remain shall be caught up together with them in the clouds, to meet the Lord in the air: and so shall we ever be with the Lord. WHEREFORE COMFORT ONE ANOTHER WITH THESE WORDS (I Thessalonians 4: 16–18). What a meeting! He will give our loved ones back to us and us to them, and forever we shall live together in His presence. It is well to remember that as was the case in Nain, He will do this, not because *our mighty faith makes him do so*—He will do it because this was decided in the eternal council meetings of the Godhead. This will be the normal unfolding of the divine purposes and happy indeed are those people who will be present to witness this gathering in the sky.

## SECTION THREE

*Expository Notes on the Question asked by John the Baptist*

**And the disciples of John shewed him of all these things. And John calling two of his disciples sent to Jesus saying, Art thou he that should come? or look we for another? When the men were come unto him, they said, John Baptist hath sent us unto thee, saying, Art thou he that should come? or look we for another? (vv. 18-20).**

Matthew 11: 2 supplies an additional detail: "Now when John had heard in prison the works of Christ, he sent two of his disciples. . . ." This is a thought-provoking passage and some of the best minds in the church express conflicting interpretations of John's question. John had come in the spirit and power of Elijah, but even Elijah after moments of thrilling triumph had plunged into depths of despair. It is well to remember that a period of eighteen months might have elapsed since the glorious days when John first preached in the Jordan Valley; things had certainly changed. Instead of preaching beneath the blue of God's far-flung heavens, John sat beneath a dirty prison ceiling. The soul-stirring experiences of the revival meetings had been superceded by the lonely hours in a disgusting dungeon. Formerly with holy eloquence John had announced the arrival of the Messiah, and a wave of intense expectation had swept through the nation. Now, after many months of continuing silence; the frustrated hopes; the absence of any manifestation of Messianic power might have been undermining the confidence so characteristic of John in his earlier and possibly happier days. Separated from the outside world, and permitted only to see some of his closest friends, John gleaned information from the reports these disciples brought into the dungeon. He was told that Jesus was eating and drinking with publicans and sinners; he was informed that the call to repentance was not as pronounced as it had been during his own meetings. Things were not running according to plan! Could this be the Messiah? Was it possible that John had been mistaken in establishing the identity of the Coming One? Geldenhuys says: "John had expected that Christ would speedily destroy the powers of darkness, and judge the unrighteous. But instead of doing this, Jesus leaves him, His forerunner, helpless in prison; and it is clear to John that even the Jewish people did not follow Him on a great scale and did not believe in Him.

All these things made John impatient and dissatisfied, and even cast shadows of doubt over his mind."

*(The New International Commentary on the New Testament,*
Luke, page 226)

Nevertheless whilst Geldenhuys expresses the thoughts of many writers, his utterance is certainly not the final word on the subject. Chrysostom, Calvin, Brotius and in more recent times, Dr. Campbell Morgan, categorically rejected this interpretation. They maintain that John sent His disciples to Jesus realizing that Christ was far more competent at solving their problems than he could ever hope to be.

When the men were come unto him, they said, John Baptist hath sent us unto thee, saying, Art thou he that should come? or look we for another? And in that same hour he cured many of their infirmities and plagues, and of evil spirits; and unto many that were blind he gave sight. Then Jesus answering said unto them, Go your way, and tell John what things ye have seen and heard; how that the blind see, the lame walk, the lepers are cleansed, the deaf hear, the dead are raised, to the poor the gospel is preached. And blessed is he whosoever shall not be offended in me (vv. 20–23).

John might have wasted a great amount of time and effort trying to persuade disgruntled men that they were wrong in criticizing Jesus. It is always better to take complaints to the one most intimately concerned, than to jump to hasty conclusions. There is reason to believe John still had the utmost confidence in the Lord and that he sent the questioners to the Saviour firmly believing Christ could do in five minutes what he could not do in hours. It is noteworthy that Jesus continued His works of healing, and finally cited these as evidence of His identity. There are times when one miracle is worth a thousand sermons; when a man's deeds far outweigh the value of his utterances. The greatest evidence for Christ must always be His power to save. Souter translates the final part of the Lord's answer as follows: "... *to be envied is he who takes no offense in Me, and who is not hurt, nor resentful nor annoyed, nor repelled, nor made to stumble, whatever may occur"* (*The Amplified New Testament*).

And when the messengers of John were departed, he began to speak unto the people concerning John, What went ye out into the wilderness for to see? A reed shaken by the wind? But what went ye out for to see? A man clothed in soft raiment? Behold, they which are gorgeously apparelled, and live delicately, are in king's courts. But what went ye out for to see? A prophet? Yea, I say unto you, and much more than a prophet (vv. 24–26).

The term *a reed shaken by the wind* is most suggestive. John was not a man whose instability was displayed each time the wind changed. His constancy was not undermined each time his circumstances altered. It was this very characteristic which attracted people from their homes and made them hurry into the wilderness to hear the remarkable preacher. To say the least, unless the Lord was being exceedingly gracious in covering John's lapse of faith, it is very difficult to make this word picture fit the man of whom Christ speaks. If John Baptist had been sure of his predictions and announcements in the Jordan valley, and if that same preacher had now lost his assurance because his own circumstances had changed for the worst, then surely, he must have appeared to be a reed shaken by the wind. By the same standards we might be allowed to infer that had John been suddenly released from his cell, his faith might have returned only to disappear again had he been arrested again the following week. John was not a man of this calibre, and the verses now being considered endorse that opinion.

This is he, of whom it is written, Behold I send my messenger before thy face, which shall prepare thy way before thee. For I say unto you, Among those that are born of women there is not a greater prophet than John the Baptist; but he that is least in the kingdom of God is greater than he (vv. 27-28).

The appearance of John was the fulfilment of the predictions made by Malachi centuries earlier. It was in this sense that John was greater than all his predecessors. It must not be understood that John surpassed in holiness and spiritual understanding Moses, Elijah, Elisha and many others. He was greater *in privilege,* for to him, and to him alone was given the honour of being the Lord's forerunner. We are able to see in John the fulfilment of thousands of years of prophecy; whereas others had merely spoken of the coming One; John actually saw Him. The wilderness preacher had not seen him with the eye of faith from afar off: John had touched the Blessed One; had listened to Him; learned of Him; and immersed Him in the waters of the Jordan. No other prophet could claim these inestimable privileges. John was therefore the Prince among the Prophets, yet, strange to relate, the forerunner did not equal the least in the kingdom of God! This cannot mean that the poorest, the most disappointing Christian surpasses the great Forerunner of the Lord, for the fact is indisputable that John the Baptist was a far greater man than some of us are ever likely to become. John foreran the Lord; the Lord came to establish a kingdom, and in the fulness of time, through faith in His name, sinners were able to enter into that realm of blessedness. Even John, in due course, was able to enter into the kingdom of God. When Jesus declared John to be the greatest of all the prophets, he measured his stature according to Old Testament standards when the kingdom was something promised; something still in the future. John the Baptist belonged, so to speak, to two ages; the old and the new. John at his best *in the old age* never equalled the youngest or most immature Christian who knew the privilege of being within the fellowship of the kingdom of God. The new order began where the old terminated; therefore even a child who had taken one step into the kingdom was indeed that one step further on, than John had been, even at the peak of Old Testament prophetic perfection. Nevertheless, *and this is very important,* when by the mercy of God, and by faith in the Lord, John entered into the kingdom, he also became a far more wonderful person than he ever had been previously. John *WITHIN* the kingdom was a better man than he could ever have been *OUTSIDE* the kingdom. This expresses one of the greatest truths in the Gospel. *If being within the kingdom of God means so much to humans,* then no effort should be spared in the supreme endeavour to reach that hallowed place.

**And all the people that heard, and the publicans, justified God, being baptized with the baptism of John. But the Pharisees and lawyers rejected the counsel of God against themselves, being not baptized of him (vv. 29–30).**

This passage has been rendered in the *Amplified New Testament:* "And all the people who heard him, even the tax collectors, acknowledged the justice of God (in calling them to repentance, and in pronouncing future wrath on the impenitent) being baptized with the baptism of John. But the Pharisees and the lawyers (of the Mosaic Law) annulled, and rejected, and brought to nothing, God's purpose concerning themselves, by refusing and not being baptized (by John)." Godet says, "*To justify God* is to recognize and to proclaim by word and deed the excellence of His ways for the salvation of men. The expression: *they have annulled for themselves the divine degree,* signifies that, although man cannot foil God's plan for the world, he might render it vain for himself." The symbol of the acceptance of John's preaching was conformity to the requirements of his ordinance. Those who believed and accepted his message obeyed his commands; they were baptized. This became the pattern for all who followed, and it is an irrefutable fact that the New Testament church knew nothing of unbaptized believers. When the proud Pharisees refused to be baptized they revealed the sad fact that their hearts were not in harmony with the purposes of the preacher.

And the Lord said, Whereunto then shall I liken the men of this generation? and to what are they like? They are like unto children sitting in
the market place, and calling one to another, and saying, We have piped
unto you, and ye have not danced; we have mourned to you, and ye
have not wept. For John the Baptist came neither eating and drinking
wine; and ye say, He hath a devil. The Son of man is come eating and
drinking; and ye say, Behold, a gluttonous man, and a winebibber, a
friend of publicans and sinners! But wisdom is justified of her children
(vv. 31-35).

This was a reference to the game played by the children of that time;
perhaps even the Lord Himself had joined in the game during His
childhood in Nazareth. The youthful players divided into two teams
to play-act certain scenes which the opposing team had to complete.
When one team began to depict a wedding; they piped or pretended
to play the instruments expecting the others quickly to recognize the
signs and to continue the acting or representation of the marriage
procession. In like manner, when their turn came, the other children
began to play a funeral game, expecting their friends to recognize
what was taking place and to complete the representation of the
solemn event. However, for reasons of their own, the watching young-
sters refused to co-operate. Thus the cries went back and forth "calling one to another"—"We played weddings to you, and you did not
dance"; "We sang dirges and wailed, playing funeral, and you did not
weep." The whole point in the illustration was that whatever happened, there were people who had already made up their minds not
to co-operate. Whether the preacher laughed or cried; preached long
or short sermons; spoke of the happiness of the blessed or the sorrow
of the damned—he would never be able to please his listeners. Their
prejudice and preconceived ideas had already closed the door of their
hearts. Unfortunately their descendants appear to have lived a very
long time! True wisdom is always justified by her children; the attitude of the listeners obviously revealed they were not the children
of wisdom—they were foolish, arrogant and evil.


HOMILIES

Study No. 22

JOHN THE BAPTIST . . . AND A STUDY IN SHAKING REEDS!

There are two interpretations of John the Baptist's question, "Art
thou he that should come, or look we for another?" Some declare that
after eighteen months' imprisonment, his faith was beginning to waver;

that his doubts found expression in this question. He had become a
reed shaken by the wind. The Bible has much to say of the winds
that shake souls.

### The Wind of Adversity

If this interpretation be correct, John's faith and courage had been
undermined by the things he endured. Amid the soul-thrilling excitement of the Jordan meetings, he had cried, "Behold the Lamb of God
which taketh away the sins of the world." During those memorable
meetings he had been a light to a darkened nation; but now, so it is
suggested, he had slipped into the shadows. Adversity is a cold, wintry
blast, and only men with a super-abundance of backbone can resist
the temptation to lean away from it. Then blue skies of vision are
apt to become overcast; inspiring songs of victorious faith are apt to
be hushed, and amid the perplexities of current events, the soul pauses
to ask, "Why has God permitted this to happen? Did I make a mistake
in trusting Christ? Art thou he that should come, or look we for
another?"

### The Wind of Hypocrisy

Our example comes from Old Testament literature. We are told in
I Samuel 2 : 12–17 that the sins of Eli's sons had become very great
before the Lord and before Israel. Their disgusting behaviour had
made the people "abhor the offering of God." It is surely not difficult
to understand the repercussions of such dislike. Recognizing the
hypocrisy of the priests, men turned from the house of God, and
abstained from fulfilling His laws. Much might be said on their behalf,
but the fact remains that they had looked too long at hypocrites and
had lost their vision of God. The strong wind of hypocrisy proved
them to be reeds. They permitted poor, disappointing priests to spoil
the service of the sanctuary. And are not their type still with us? Are
there not multitudes of people who complain about the presence of
hypocrites within the churches, and do they not offer this as an excuse
for their own non-attendance at the sanctuary? Alas, they are reeds
shaken by the wind.

### The Wind of Worldliness

There is something supremely pathetic about Paul's last message to
Timothy : "Do thy diligence to come shortly unto me : for Demas hath
forsaken me, having loved this present world, and is departed unto
Thessalonica." How sad it is to relate that he who had been Paul's
companion in the work of evangelism failed to stay at his post. He had
weathered many storms, but suddenly, permitting his eyes to remain
on the enjoyments of sin, he went away in search of carnal pleasures.

"He loved this present world." Let us feel profoundly sorry for Demas. The Cross would have ruined his taste for worldly pleasure, and worldliness would have come between him and the Cross. He would be in no-man's-land, friendless and alone. Poor Demas! He had proved to be a reed shaken by the wind. He lacked the stiffening effect of a good backbone, and bowed at the wrong altar.

Was John the Baptist a man of this type? Surely not. Did not Christ look at the crowd and say, "What went ye out into the wilderness for to see? A reed shaken with the wind? But what went ye out for to see? A man clothed in soft raiment? What went ye out for to see? A prophet? Yea, and much more than a prophet. . . . Among those that are born of women there is not a greater prophet than John the Baptist. John was not a shaking reed. He had listened to the complaints of the disciples, and realizing that Christ alone could solve their problems, he was too wise to argue with them. He probably smiled and said, "Go and ask the Master, and tell Him that I sent you." Well done, John! You came to point men to Christ, and you did it to the end. (Taken from *Bible Cameos,* p. 113.)

SECTION FOUR

*Expository Notes about the Woman who came Uninvited to Simon's Banquet*

**And one of the Pharisees desired him that he would eat with him. And he went into the Pharisee's house, and sat down to meat (v. 36).**

There is no way by which we can be completely sure why this invitation was given. Godet thinks the man was appreciative of the Lord's ministry; that the invitation to supper was given by one who was beginning to love the Saviour. However, if this were the case, it is hard to explain why the Pharisee omitted the customary signs of welcome offered to any guest. ". . . Thou gavest me no water for my feet. . . . Thou gavest me no kiss. . . . My head with oil thou didst not anoint . . ." Other commentators think the man was curious to know more of Him whom the Pharisees were beginning to hate. He was not hostile himself, and this might have accounted for the fact that an unmistakable tenderness seemed to be reflected in certain parts of the parable which the Lord used during the supper. There are still other writers who believe the man issued the invitation in order to spy upon Christ, and that by so doing he would be able to win favour with the leaders of his party. It was customary for all guests at such feasts to sit in a recumbent position with their feet stretched out backward. First the sandals were removed; then the guest sat on the floor with his legs passing close to the body away from the table. It was therefore an easy matter for the woman to approach from behind the Lord and to express her act of contrition in the way Luke described.

> And behold, a woman in the city, which was a sinner (an especially wicked sinner—The Amplified New Testament), when she knew that Jesus sat at meat in the Pharisee's house, brought an alabaster box of ointment, and stood at his feet behind him weeping, and began to wash his feet with tears, and did wipe them with the hairs of her head, and kissed his feet, and anointed them with the ointment (vv. 37-38).

The Greek word used to describe this woman is used to describe all who have come short of the glory of God, but the sense of the parable seems to suggest that she was a notorious sinner. The Alexandrian reading is somewhat startling: "A woman who was a sinner in that city" or "A woman who practised in that very city her shameful profession." By modern interpretation she was probably a woman of the streets; a prostitute. Her precious ointment of perfume would have been the symbol of her profession. Its rich and fragrant odour would have been used to entice fools. We are not told how she became attracted and then indebted to Jesus. The very nature of her work would necessitate her being in the streets, and possibly seeing a crowd, she approached to discover a Stranger addressing an open-air audience. Let it be admitted that this is only conjecture, but somewhere, this sinful woman was stirred by the message of the Saviour. See the homily at the end of this section. Verse 45 indicates she entered the house almost, if not as soon as the Lord—". . . since the time I came in, she hath not ceased to kiss my feet." We must therefore consider the possibility that the woman's contact with Christ might have taken place hours earlier. Sufficient time had elapsed for her to see the folly of her ways, and to feel within her soul the desire to live a new life. Stealing up behind the recumbent Christ, she looked down at him, but remembering her shameful past, suddenly commenced to weep. Her tears fell upon the feet of the Master, and as He turned to look into her tear-filled eyes, she became aware of what had happened. She knelt, untied her hair, and used her tresses as a towel. But it was too late to hide her feelings. A victim of her own emotions, her tears were falling faster than she could wipe them away, and finally she placed her lips against the Saviour's feet and covered them with kisses. It is well to remember that no Hebrew woman was ever seen in public with her hair down. This was an act of abasement, of deep humiliation. Any vestige of pride or self respect which she might have desired was completely destroyed by her action.

Now when the Pharisee which had bidden him saw it, he spake within himself saying, This man, if he were a prophet, would have known, who and what manner of woman this is that toucheth him: for she is a sinner (v. 39).

The word translated ointment is *muron*. Dr. Thayer says this has been derived from *muro*—to flow; a trickling juice or sap. There is also a connection with the oriental word *murra* which means *to smear*, hence the translation *ointment*. With cold calculating eyes the Pharisee had watched the unexpected demonstration of the woman's gratitude to Christ, but his secret thoughts indicated criticism and not admiration. Obviously he had not as yet been convinced that he had invited a true prophet to supper.

And Jesus answering said unto him, Simon, I have somewhat to say unto thee. And he saith, Master, say on. There was a certain creditor which had two debtors: the one owed five hundred pence, and the other fifty. And when they had nothing to pay, he frankly forgave them both. Tell me therefore, which of them will love him more (vv. 40-42).

The money or coinage mentioned here is the denarius, a silver coin. To appreciate its worth one should consider Matthew 20: 10 for there we are told it represented a day's wages. Since no man worked on the sabbath, the five hundred pence would therefore represent wages for twenty months of toil. The question placed before Simon presented a word picture of considerable challenge. Let us say that one man owed twenty months of service in the vineyards; the other man owed seven or eight weeks. To default in such matters could only lead to punishment and lengthy imprisonment. It would be inconceivable that any master would be willing to overlook such grave charges. "Simon" said Jesus, "if the man forgave his debtors, which man would love him the more?"

Simon answered and said, I suppose that he, to whom he forgave more. And Jesus said unto him, Thou hast rightly judged. And he turned to the woman, and saith unto Simon, Seest thou this woman? I entered into thine house, thou gavest me no water for my feet: but she hath washed my feet with tears, and wiped them with the hairs of her head. Thou gavest me no kiss: but this woman since the time I came in hath not ceased to kiss my feet. My head with oil thou didst not anoint: but this woman hath anointed my feet with ointment. Wherefore I say unto thee, Her sins which are many, are forgiven; for she loved much: but to whom little is forgiven, the same loveth little (vv. 43-47).

This is probably one of the most charming passages to be found in Luke's gospel for here the Master places two sinners side by side in

order to reveal to a waiting world some of the greatest principles of
the kingdom He had come to establish. The cold, calculating demeanour of the critical host is contrasted with the spontaneous outburst
of the woman's contrition. Nevertheless the passage demands serious
thought for it is possible even amidst the wonder of the woman's forgiveness to misinterpret certain things which Jesus said. It is true that
she washed, wiped, and kissed His feet, but in order to discover the
means whereby forgiveness reaches a guilty soul we are forced to seek
the reasons for her actions. Is forgiveness the reward of sincere service?
Was the Pharisee partially forgiven because he only partially loved?
The parable was spoken, and the resultant question asked, in order to
reveal the state of the debtors' minds. Forgiveness is indisputably
the gift of God, but is this dispensed wholesale as is the rain from
heaven? Does it fall upon the just and upon the unjust? It would
appear that the Lord was endeavouring to bring into bold relief the
fact that whereas this woman was overwhelmed with a dual sense of
shame and gratitude, the critical Pharisee had little if any sense of
guilt, and probably no real affection for Christ. If he had received
anything from Jesus, he considered it to be insignificant compared with
the honour he himself had bestowed upon the Carpenter. Jesus should
feel greatly honoured in that he had been permitted to attend a feast
in the house of such a great man! If indeed God had granted forgiveness to the Pharisee, it had certainly not strained the riches of divine
mercy—the Pharisee's debt was only trivial. Opposed to all this was
the overwhelming contrition of this repentant woman. She recognized
that her debt was enormous; that nothing short of the boundless mercy
of God could ever meet her need. When relief came through Christ,
her soul began to overflow with gratitude, and in the final analysis this
was the true ointment which gladdened the heart of God.

And he said unto her, Thy sins are forgiven. And they that sat at meat
with him began to say within themselves, Who is this that forgiveth
sins also? And he said to the woman, Thy faith hath saved thee; go
in peace (vv. 48–50).

As far as we know she made no request; she uttered no audible
confession of her sins. She did not comply with the requirements of
the Mosaic law for she never took any offering to the temple, nor expressed regret to any priest. Yet the peace of God flooded her soul,
and forgiveness of her sins resulted from her faith in Christ. The
crushing of her box of ointment was evidence that she would never
need its attracting values again. She had decided once and for all to
abandon her previous ways. If her tears reflected the sincerity of her
faith, her kisses expressed the strength of her love. This surely was

a new woman. Nevertheless in the eyes of the onlookers she was still a sinful woman, and it was to meet this need that Jesus publicly announced her forgiveness. It is one thing to kneel in the privacy of our own apartment to ask for pardon, it is altogether another to come out into the open to make a public confession of faith in Christ. The Lord Jesus appreciates both. Actually the Saviour did not say He personally forgave her; He merely announced that she had been forgiven. He claimed to be so close to God that He was fully aware of God's attitude toward a penitent soul. By the same token He demonstrated a new truth, real faith in the Son of God was infinitely more than observance of Mosaic law. He did not command her to hurry to the temple to offer a lamb as a sacrifice—the true sacrifice was that of a contrite heart; this she had already offered. At other times He commanded the lepers to go and offer those things which were required. This, however, He did to stifle opposition for any breach of the ceremonial and civil laws would have brought unpleasant repercussions upon the heads of the offenders. This woman's sin concerned only God, and since He was capable of handling the matter, it only remained to pronounce her clean, and to urge her to go in peace. The Lord spoke of her faith. This surely was a white lily appearing from what had once been a very slimy pond. Simon's critical attitude spread to his guests for they began to say, "Who is this that forgiveth sins also?" Whilst they talked of a treasure, the woman walked away with it.

## HOMILIES

Study No. 23

### A BROKEN HEART IN A BROKEN BOX

How can a man obtain the forgiveness of his sin? There have been numerous answers to this important question. It has been suggested that man must endeavour by his own merit to increase his credit account in the bank of heaven. It has also been taught that the granting of forgiveness is the prerogative of certain ecclesiastical leaders; that one must conform to particular church laws in order to obtain the coveted treasure. Other people prefer to seek their answer within the message of Holy Scriptures.

### A Woman's Contrition

Somewhere within the shadowy hovels of an eastern city, a poor woman prepared for her nightly escapade. She was a great sinner and regularly went out to break the heart of God. We do not know what ugly combination of circumstances brought her to such a low level of morality; nor do we know whether or not she cared. She took from its resting place her box of perfume, and appreciating its powers of attraction, used it to adorn her person. Then, extinguishing the lamp, she stepped into the street, and her night had begun. Somewhere she probably saw a crowd, and hearing the voice of a Stranger, drew near and came face to face with Jesus. We can only guess as to the nature of His message, but we are sure His words reached her soul. Soon she forgot the purpose of her coming into the city, and retraced her steps homeward. She had met Jesus and His words could never be forgotten. . . . She felt unclean; and hardly knew what to do; she loathed herself. This was her first step along the pathway to pardon.

*A Woman's Contrition*

Mechanically she lifted her precious box of ointment, and as her fingers closed around her treasure, she made her greatest decision. If she accepted and followed the Teacher's way of life, she would never again need this questionable adornment. The purpose for which it was meant would be non-existent in her life. If she took it to Him how would she earn her living? It was sufficient to know her need for cleansing. She made enquiries at the meeting place, and ascertaining that Jesus had gone to dine with Simon the Pharisee, followed to the well known house. "And behold, a woman in the city, which was a sinner, when she knew that Jesus sat at meat in the Pharisee's house, brought an alabaster box of ointment, and stood at his feet behind him weeping, and began to wash his feet with tears, and did wipe them with the hairs of her head. Her conviction had deepened to contrition. We must not confuse these two steps. Conviction revealed sinfulness; contrition revealed sorrow. Many people know conviction of soul, yet persistently follow the path of evil. Contrition is much closer to God's heart than conviction.

*A Woman's Confession*

"She anointed his feet with the ointment." Bowing before the mounting storm of criticism, she listened to the words of the Lord, and found peace. He alone read aright the confession behind the broken box. The other guests looked into it and saw fragrant perfume; Christ looked and saw a broken heart and a contrite spirit. He knew that she was trying to say, "Lord, I shall never need this again, for the old life is now dead," "And he said unto her, Thy sins are forgiven . . . Thy faith hath saved thee; go in peace." He saw her broken heart and tenderly healed it. The perfume of that box of ointment slowly filled the room, and then escaped to fill the world: it is still with us. We imagine the woman's homegoing; and if sleep seemed elusive that night, maybe, she continued to remember His words: "Thy sins are forgiven . . . go in peace." She was not commanded to reach new heights of morality in order to atone for former failures; nor was she instructed to bow before the priest in the synagogue. The only confessional box she ever knew was the small one broken in His presence. How can a man obtain the forgiveness of sins? He must realize his need; be ashamed of his guilt; and in sincerity of soul seek the Saviour.

"None who to Jesus came were ever turned away."

# The Eighth Chapter of Luke

THEME: *The Mighty Power of Jesus*

SECTION ONE

*Expository Notes on the Parable of the Sower*

And it came to pass afterward, that he went throughout every city and village, preaching and shewing the glad tidings of the kingdom of God: and the twelve were with him. And certain women which had been healed of evil spirits and infirmities, Mary, called Magdalene, out of whom went seven devils, and Joanna, the wife of Chuza Herod's steward, and Susanna, and many others, which ministered unto him of their substance (vv. 1–3).

We have now reached a most important part in the unfolding of Luke's story. Hitherto, the Lord had exercised most of His ministry in the environs of the city of Capernaum; now the time had arrived to move onward. The time would come when the world-wide commission for evangelism must be given to the disciples; meanwhile, the Lord sets the example for their life work. It might have been advantageous to remain within the well known city, but the Lord had become increasingly aware of the need of distant villages. Therefore, gathering His disciples around Him, He commenced His first missionary journey. This was something new in the affairs of evangelism. In after days, the disciples, and especially Paul, were to emulate this shining example, until the whole of the known world heard the glad tidings of the kingdom of God. Nevertheless, even for the Lord Himself, this undertaking presented problems. As the little band moved from place to place, preaching, visiting, healing, they needed food and finance. There is no mention that the Lord ever appealed for money; there is no evidence to support the idea that He took collections at the meetings. How then could the disciples live? By what means could they pay their bills? There was an occasion when Peter was instructed to go to the lake to catch a fish, for in its mouth would be sufficient money to pay the taxes for both Peter and the Lord. Nevertheless, Peter could hardly be expected to spend most of his time fishing for coins: the fish were not always as co-operative! This passage is most illuminating for it reveals the disciples' source of income. Attached to the band of itinerant preachers were a few wealthy women *who ministered unto Him of their substance.* The word translated *ministered* is *dieekonoun* which is derived from *diakonos.* Primarily it means to serve, as for example, a deacon, who by reason of his office attends to the needs of the poor. From this old word we derive our modern word *deacon.* Paul uses the same word in Romans 15: 25-26: "But now I go unto Jerusalem *to minister* (diakonoon) unto the saints. For it hath pleased them of Macedonia and Achaia to make a certain contribution for the poor saints which are at Jerusalem." The presence of these generous women in the disciple band is a most interesting detail. Most men would be far too independent to accept monetary gifts from women; their pride would forbid the act. That Christ permitted them to aid in this manner reveals he was not above accepting the love gifts of His followers; neither did He wish to deprive them of their greatest joy—that of giving to God. But there is also another detail which deserves to be mentioned. Within a few days of the departure of this small band of preachers, their enemies were searching for anything which could be used against the Preacher. They said abominable things about Him, and even suggested He was in league with the Prince of Demons; yet never on any occasion was there any suggestion of scandal; no critic ever cited the fact that women lived, moved, and had their being among a band of men who were not their husbands. How careful the Lord must have been, and how wonderful in all His ways.

It would be interesting if we could know how Mary of Magdala first made contact with the Lord. We know she was possessed of demons, but in the first instance, was she driven into His meeting to upset the proceedings? We cannot tell. When the power of Christ freed her from the thraldom of evil, a convert was gained who was destined to remain for ever. Joanna was the wife of Herod's steward. This man probably held high office in the administration of the kingdom, and some suggest he might have been the nobleman whose son was healed in Capernaum. As the steward of the king, Chuza was probably a man of means, and this accounts for the fact that his wife, who obviously became a dedicated follower of Jesus, was able to help finance the party of preachers. Acts 13: 1 reveals that there was also another man of high estate who became a Christian. Manaen, who had been adopted by Herod, and had grown up with Herod's son, would have the most intimate knowledge of affairs within the palace. Perhaps some of the details written in this Gospel were obtained by Luke when he conversed with the converted Prince. If I were a woman I would be very proud of these sisters of a bygone age; I would be very thrilled to remember that nowhere in the New Testament is mentioned any woman who opposed the Saviour. Susanna of whom nothing more has been said, represents that vast army of consecrated women whose dedication made the evangelization of the world a glorious accomplishment.

And when much people were gathered together, and were come to him out of every city, he spake by a parable: A sower went out to sow his seed: and as he sowed, some fell by the way side; and it was trodden down, and the fowls of the air devoured it. And some fell upon a rock; and as soon as it was sprung up, it withered away, because it lacked moisture. And some fell among thorns; and the thorns sprang up with it, and choked it. And other fell on good ground, and sprang up, and bare fruit an hundred-fold. And when he had said these things, he cried, He that hath ears to hear, let him hear (vv. 4–8).

As the itinerant band went from village to village, the excitement grew; the crowds increased. People came out of the cities, towns and villages in ever increasing numbers, and this presented another problem. What was to be done with them? The future of the kingdom would depend not upon numbers but on quality; not upon superficial enthusiasm but upon constant dedication. As a gardener weeds his garden in order to promote the growth of his valuable plants, so Christ recognized the need of weeding His audience. Since a stitch in time is said to save nine, the Lord probably recognized the need to get rid of certain undesirable elements before they could cause trouble. His first parable and the explanation He offered certainly did this. Both Matthew (13: 1–23) and Mark (4: 1–10) also recorded this parable, and whilst from this time on the Lord made frequent use of preaching through parables, it would seem this was the best loved; the most easily remembered of them all. Matthew and Mark agree that this message was given at the seaside; that because of the proximity of a great audience, the Lord entered into a boat and preached from a floating pulpit. The Lord sat facing the beach and the hills beyond, and thus the scene at which He gazed supplied the illustration used in His sermon. The lowlands running up from the sea would be suitable for cultivation; further up where farming would be somewhat difficult, weeds and thistles abounded. Further up still where the rocky slopes were very prominent and where the depth of soil was negligible, the production of crops would be impossible. At the very top of the cliff where in all probability a path would be found, the ground would be hard and uncultivated. Any seeds which fell there would be food for the birds. Beyond that high path would be other fields where crops were sown and harvested. Any farmer sowing seeds on such terrain would be aware that some of the seeds would be swept by the wind over the cliff and would fall on all kinds of ground. When Jesus uttered His parable and probably indicated the illustration before His eyes, the audience easily understood His sermon. See the homily at the end of this section. Matthew cites the fruitful increase as "A hundred fold; sixty fold; thirty fold." Mark cites the same differences but reverses the order. Luke is content to mention the fact that some seeds produced a hundred fold. There are no contradictions here. These varying viewpoints indicate that God was using *men* to tell the Good News and not *robots*. The Lord was speaking through the intellects of humans and not tapping out messages on the keys of typewriters!

**And his disciples asked him saying, What might this parable be? And he said, Unto you it is given to know the mysteries of the kingdom of God: but to others in parables; that seeing they might not see, and hearing they might not understand (vv. 9-10).**

At first this appears to be a very difficult passage, for what would be the use of preaching anything if the people were not to understand? The reader should consider the following passages from the Old Testamen: Isaiah 6: 9-10; Jeremiah 5: 21; Ezekiel 12: 2. The Saviour was merely quoting scriptures with which most of His hearers would be conversant. If they knew the texts to which He referred, they would also know why the words were first spoken by God and the prophets. The basic cause of their unenlightened minds and deaf ears was rebellious hearts. They were stiff-necked, and ultimately they stoned the messengers whom God sent. To waste time trying to teach them would be tantamount to casting pearls before swine; they listened because they wished to argue; they watched in order to criticize. Such people would be a menace to any cause. Further back still in ancient history, Pharaoh the ruler of Egypt had similarly acted in his relationship to Israel, and finally recognizing the folly of trying to persuade a man who did not wish to be persuaded, the Lord hardened the ruler in order to hasten the deliverance of those receptive to the message. It is against this background that we must consider the Saviour's statement. He had just enunciated certain principles of the kingdom. Those whose hearts were receptive to the message would be able to understand; the Lord would illumine their understanding. Others who were enemies of the faith; who waited to destroy what they did not desire, would hear in parables, and failing to be attracted by His sermons would eventually go away and leave the disciples in peace.

> Now the parable is this: The seed is the word of God. Those by the wayside are they that hear; then cometh the devil, and taketh away the word out of their hearts, lest they should believe and be saved. They on the rock are they, which, when they hear, receive the word with joy; and these have no root, which for a while believe, and in time of temptation fall away. And that which fell among thorns are they, which, when they have heard, go forth, and are choked with cares and riches and pleasures of this life, and bring no fruit to perfection. But that on the good ground are they, which in an honest and good heart, having heard the word, keep it, and bring forth fruit with patience (vv. 11-15).

Throughout the ages of christendom evangelists have been criticized because some of their converts failed to continue in the service of the church. It would be well for critics to study this parable. The Saviour was the greatest preacher the world ever knew, yet even from Him, so it is written, the people turned back and followed Him no more. He was fully aware of this possibility and admitted that most of the seed sown failed to produce the desired results. Yet should He have ceased sowing the Word of Life because 75 per cent of His effort was destined to be wasted? God's mathematics are exceedingly thrilling. If four bushels of wheat are sown, and if three bushels are lost, this would seem to be a colossal waste, but that is only part of the story. If the other bushel produces a hundredfold, the farmer is left with a hundred bushels, and in spite of his loss, finished with twenty-five times more than that with which he started. History is filled with shining examples of this fact. There was a minister who preached on a very wintry night in England, and probably believed most of his sermon had fallen upon deaf ears. Yet one small boy, Charles Haddon Spurgeon, had listened. His heart was very fertile soil from which one seed produced ten-thousandfold, and even more. There was a missionary who felt that his service for Christ had not been what it should have been, but again and again he told his story to listening people. He said he had seen the smoke of a thousand villages in Africa where the Gospel had never been preached. One young fellow heard that missionary and decided something should be done to meet Africa's need. The boy was David Livingstone who afterward wrote the name of Christ across a continent. Spiritual comptometers would be needed to calculate the size of the increase from the seed planted in his heart by Robert Morrison. If one soul is of more value than the whole world, critics would be better employed seeking such souls than in finding fault with God's workmen, who following their Lord's footsteps have to admit the possibility of losing 75 per cent of the seed sown. See the homily at the end of this section.

No man, when he hath lighted a candle, covereth it with a vessel, or putteth it under a bed; but setteth it on a candlestick, that they which enter in may see the light. For nothing is secret, that shall not be made manifest; neither anything hid, that shall not be known and come abroad. Take heed therefore how ye hear: for whosoever hath, to him shall be given; and whosoever hath not, from him shall be taken away even that which he seemeth to have (vv. 16–18).

The word *lucknon* translated *candle* really means lamp, and this referred to the shallow saucer-like piece of pottery in common use throughout Palestine at that time. A wick lay in the oil, and this when lighted gave off a small light. Thus it could have safely been left lighted beneath any vessel. Beds for the most part were actually down on the floor where most of the poor people slept. There were however small beds or frames upon which beds were placed which stood on legs some four or five inches high. A divan was often used. This was made of wood and covered with oriental cushions among which people reclined during the day. So small a flame would not have been any cause of danger had it been placed beneath the divan. The illustration was perfectly understandable to Christ's listeners. The Lord had just lit the light of truth; it was not for His disciples to hide this, but rather to use it, guard it, and by all means possible, to walk in its radiance. Thus He urged them to listen carefully, for otherwise, His message would have been spoken in vain; their carelessness would be tantamount to placing the lamp under a vessel. Plummer interprets the passage by saying: "Whoever gives a welcome to the word and appropriates it becomes worthy and capable of receiving more. But by not appropriating truth when we recognize it, we lose hold of it, and have less power of recognizing it in the future."

Then cometh to him his mother and his brethren, and could not, because of the crowd. And it was told him by certain which said, Thy mother and thy brethren stand without, desiring to see thee. And he answered and said unto them, My mother and my brethren are these which hear the word of God and do it (vv. 19–21).

Matthew (12: 46-50) and Mark (3: 31-35) also record this visit of the relatives of the Lord. Mark supplies additional details which enable us to understand the reasons for this visit. The Greek text "Hoi par' autou ezeethon krateesai auton" those belonging to him went out to lay hold on him has been rendered in the Amplified New Testament: "And when those who belonged to him, that is, His kinsmen, heard it, they went out to take him by force, for they kept saying, He is out of His mind—beside Himself; deranged." This really is the force of the word krateesai—"to seize in order to bring into one's power." It is clear that reports had reached the family of Jesus which to some extent undermined what little faith they might have possessed. Fearing that Jesus was becoming overwrought; that His constant work might lead to a breakdown in health, they went out determined to bring Him home even if force were necessary to accomplish that purpose. Much has been spoken and written about the brethren of the Lord, but an honest interpretation of the New Testament admits that Mary had other children. See Matthew 13: 55-56. Norval Geldenhuys correctly points out: ". . . there can be no doubt that the Lord really had blood brothers and sisters. The Roman Catholic opinion that 'the brethren and sisters' were step-brothers and step-sisters (children of Joseph by a former wife), or 'His cousins' is unfounded, and would never have existed had it not been for Epiphanius, Jerome and later Roman leaders who embraced a false asceticism and regarded Mary as a woman who had remained a virgin all her life. Even Tertullian insisted on taking 'the brethren and sisters' of Jesus as real children of Mary." (De Carne Christi. vii) The New International Commentary on The New Testament, page 250.

When the Lord heard of the mission and request of His family, He emphasized that spiritual ties are even more binding than those of the flesh. The family of God is a more closely-knit fellowship, and in the final analysis a brother in Christ should mean more to a Christian than those who are his natural kinsmen.


HOMILIES

Study No. 24

### CHRIST . . . AND HIS COMMENTARY ON PREACHING

The parable of the sower was perhaps the best known of the Saviour's sermons. The Lord explained how the sowing of the seed represented the preaching of the Gospel, and His remarks were both stimulating and challenging.

*The Stolen Seed*

"A sower went out to sow his seed . . . and it was trodden down, and the fowls of the air devoured it." It was good seed, which was never allowed to germinate and take root. When Christ interpreted this section of the parable, He indicated that in like manner, Satan takes the word of Truth from the hearts of people lest they should believe and be saved. And in that one great statement the Lord revealed the setting of Biblical doctrines. Man is at the heart of all spiritual struggle, and the Lord would hardly have mentioned Satan if He had not believed in his existence. The object of divine love, and the desire of the great Sower, humanity needs the word of God; yet every attempt to sow the good seed in human hearts is challenged by evil. The Pharisees present in every evangelistic service supply evidence in support of Christ's statement.

*The Starved Seed*

"And some fell upon a rock; and as soon as it was sprung up, it withered away, because it lacked moisture." The profession of abundant life was not equalled by its depth of root. The results were superficial; they were on the surface, and consequently the plant was unable to survive. "These," said the Master, "have no root, which for a while believe, and in time of temptation fall away." Even the Lord had such people among His many followers. At a certain point in His ministry, "they turned back and followed him no more." Real evangelism is recognized by the depth of the work done, and not by its seeming popularity. Judas illustrates this type of follower. He received the word with joy and appeared to be a most sincere disciple; yet in the hour of testing he revealed that his profession of faith did not rest upon spiritual reality.

*The Strangled Seed*

"And some fell among thorns; and the thorns sprung up with it, and choked it." Jesus continued, "These are they which, when they have heard, go forth and are choked with cares and riches and pleasures of this life, and bring no fruit to perfection." It is not said that the seed failed to germinate; neither is it suggested that a harvest was non-existent. The growth of the plant was seriously hindered, because parasites drained the earth of energy. Every church has its quota of people who belong to this disappointing category. The rich young ruler never brought fruit to spiritual perfection, because love of riches ruined his spiritual perception. Demas, one of the most promising of Paul's associates ultimately left the apostle, because the pleasures of the world attracted his soul. This young man might have become eternally famous; but alas, he disappeared in a wilderness of over-growing worldliness.

## The Successful Seed

"And other fell on good ground, and sprang up, and bare fruit an hundredfold." The disciples easily understood this kind of seed represented "they, which in an honest and good heart, having heard the word, keep it, and bring forth fruit with patience." And in this way Christ summed up the results of preaching the Gospel. Perhaps every minister should be reluctant to count heads! It would be safer to count hearts. Spontaneous responses can be most thrilling but sometimes the better converts are they who at first are slow to respond. An up-lifted hand is insufficient unless it be propelled by a broken heart. In like manner, every minister should be hesitant before he becomes disheartened. No one sees seed taking root; one must have patience, and learn to believe that the unseen is really taking place. A faithful sower is always of more value than a successful reaper. Without the former, the latter might be unemployed. And if Demas provided the example of disappointing seed, Timothy may provide another illustration of seed well sown in a boy's heart. He had "known the holy scriptures from his youth up" and because divine truth had taken root in his soul, the boy grew to be a man of God, whose consecrated service influenced the world. The realization that some seed might be lost did not prevent the farmer from getting on with his task. He probably made allowances for possible loss by sowing extra seed. We must emulate his example. Let us sow to our maximum capacity; then we shall not enter God's presence empty-handed. The fields are very large; the seed is very plentiful; unfortunately, there is a shortage of sowers! I wonder why?

## SECTION TWO

### Expository Notes on the Stilling of the Storm

**Now it came to pass on a certain day, that he went into a ship with his disciples: and he said unto them, Let us go over unto the other side of the lake. And they launched forth. But as they sailed he fell asleep; and there came down a storm of wind on the lake; and they were filled with water, and were in jeopardy (vv. 22–23).**

*The Amplified New Testament* supplies a remarkable word picture of this event: "And a whirlwind revolving from below upwards swept down on the lake, and the boat was filling with water, and they were in great danger." Matthew, Mark and Luke all record this important occurrence, but in some details appear to be at variance. It is well to remember that each writer tried to present the story as he knew it. His ambition was not that of an author who wished to be microscopically correct, and in harmony with contemporary writers—each author to the best of his ability, tried to direct attention to the astounding fact that Christ was able to do the impossible. Strauss and other critics treated this narrative with disdain, affirming the stilling of the storm was a falsehood. For a while, it was considered evidence of higher education when preachers dismissed the story as a fantasy, but in recent years a remarkable change has come to the realm of scholarship. The ancient story has been endorsed by modern circumstances for what happened in the days of the Christ still happens on that same lake. Thompson says: "Storms of wind rush wildly through the deep mountain gorges which descend from the north and northeast, and are not only violent, but sudden; they often take place when the weather is clear" (*The Land and the Book*, page 375). Geldenhuys quoting Plummer says of the hills around the lake: "These are furrowed with ravines like funnels, down which the winds rush with great velocity" (*The New International Commentary on the New Testament*, Luke, page 243).

It is not without significance that the Creator of Heaven and earth could be utterly exhausted. A comparison of the three Gospels leaves no doubt that this happened at the end of an exacting time of preaching. Various sermons in parables had been delivered and virtue had gone from the Master. When He sat in the boat to be taken to the other side of the lake, the gentle movements of the craft rocked Him to sleep. It is truly thoughtful that whereas the accumulated noises of the storm; the fearsome slapping of the waves against the sides of the boat; the howling and shrieking of the tempest; the frantic movements of the crew; failed to disturb Jesus, He awakened instantly when one of his followers appealed for help.

**And they came to him, and awoke him, saying, Master, master, we perish. Then he arose, and rebuked the wind and the raging of the water: and they ceased, and there was a calm. And he said unto them, Where is your faith. And they being afraid wondered, saying one to another, What manner of man is this! for he commandeth even the winds and water, and they obey him (vv. 24–25).**

The word translated rebuked is *epetimeesen* and this is both strong and suggestive. *The Amplified New Testament* renders the passage: "And He, being thoroughly awakened, *censured*, and *blamed*, and *rebuked* the wind and the raging waves . . ." It is impossible to censure an insensible thing; to scold, as it were, an inanimate object. To blame the wind for blowing would be ludicrous and therefore we are obliged to give added consideration to this text. Could it have been that the Lord recognized in the unfriendly elements the handiwork of His greatest enemy, Satan? Was this another attempt to kill him, this time by drowning? Throughout the itineraries of the Lord, the devil constantly tried to end Christ's life prematurely. This text suggests the Lord rebuked not the storm itself, but the hand which controlled the elements. Maybe it is not without reason that Satan is called, "The Prince of the Power of the air." Matthew quotes the Lord as saying, "Why are ye fearful, O ye of little faith?" Ministers may find interest in the homily at the end of this section. Here we have A Great Storm; A Great Saviour; A Great Stillness. How nice it is to know that He remains the same yesterday, and today, and forever.

## HOMILIES

Study No. 25

### Faith . . . the Eternal Bulldozer

Faith is heaven's bulldozer which removes every obstacle and makes a highway to the throne of God. Yet faith is far more than an intellectual assent. It is a vital apprehension of things unseen; it laughs at impossibilities.

### No Faith

The ship was sinking, and even the experienced fishermen were scared. Their skilled seamanship was unequal to the task of keeping the vessel on an even keel, and at any moment the frail craft might capsize in the turbulent waters. The winds shrieked through the rigging; the mast threatened to break. Frantic bailing made little impression on the swirling waters in the bottom of the boat; the position was untenable. The fishermen disciples were beginning to despair, when they remembered their Master. They could hardly believe their eyes when they saw Him peacefully sleeping at the back of their boat. "And they awake him, and say unto him, Master, carest thou not that we perish? And he arose, and rebuked the wind, and said unto the sea, Peace, be still. And the wind ceased, and there was a great calm. And he said unto them, Why are ye so fearful? How is it that ye have *no faith*? (Mark 4: 37–40).

### Little Faith

A remarkable stillness rested upon the holy hill; the crowd was enthralled. This was the greatest sermon they had ever heard. Slowly, but with rare power, the Preacher from Nazareth spoke about faith. "Therefore I say unto you, Take no thought for your life, what ye shall eat, or what ye shall drink; nor yet for your body, what ye shall put on. Is not the life more than meat, and the body than raiment?" He paused, and the ensuing stillness was as eloquent as His speech. No one moved; no one desired to move. This was wonderful preaching. He was so sure; He really believed what He was saying; and what was much more to the point, He had the ability to make them believe. Their emotions were strangely stirred. He continued, "And why take ye thought for raiment? Consider the lilies of the field, how they grow; they toil not, neither do they spin: And yet I say unto you, That even Solomon in all his glory was not arrayed like one of these. Wherefore, if God so clothe the grass of the field, which today is, and tomorrow is cast into the oven, shall he not much more clothe you, O ye of *little faith*?" (Matthew 6: 25-30). It is very foolish to worry when the promises of God are reliable.

### Great Faith

The Lord Jesus was very interested: something unique had taken place. The elders of the synagogue had swallowed their pride in seeking a favour, but all their plans had been ruined by the very man on whose behalf they had acted. They had persuaded Christ to visit the home of the Gentile officer; but now, he had said, "Lord, trouble not thyself; for I am not worthy that thou shouldest enter under my roof . . . say in a word, and my servant shall be healed." "Master, because I represent Caesar's empire, I command men to do certain things and they obey. You represent God's empire, and if you issue a command, that will be sufficient. Some angel will hasten to do your bidding, and my servant shall be healed." "When Jesus heard these things, he marvelled . . . and said . . . I have not found so *great faith*, no, not in Israel" (Luke 7: 1-10). Within the spiritual realm, the Capernaum centurion had a twin sister—she was the woman of Canaan who tried to deceive the Lord. See Matthew 15: 22-28. She clung to the belief that Christ would help her, even though her appeals for help met with no immediate response. "But he answered and said, I am not sent but unto the lost sheep of the house of Israel. Then came she and worshipped him saying, Lord, help me. But he answered and said, It is not meet to take the children's bread and cast it to dogs. And she said, truth, Lord, but even the dogs eat of the crumbs which fall from their master's table. Then Jesus answered and said unto her, O woman, GREAT IS THY FAITH: be it unto thee even as thou wilt. And her daughter was made whole from that very hour." Faith is a great bulldozer—it can remove mountains. But what is faith? Someone has supplied a most illuminating acrostic: F A I T H—

*F*orsaking *All I* Take *Him.* These texts placed together represent the
royal highway. No automobiles travel there. Travellers must walk—by
faith; and those who walk by faith, walk with God.

(Taken from *Bible Treasures,* page 81)

SECTION THREE

*Expository Notes on the Deliverance of the Maniac of Gadara*

**And they arrived at the country of the Gadarenes, which is over against
Galilee (v. 26).**

Matthew calls this place ". . . the country of the Gergesenes" and
the varying names have produced confusion. Godet goes into much
detail outlining the arguments directed against this narrative. However a brief extract from his notes should be sufficient for the student.
". . . the recent discovery of ruins bearing the name of Gersa of Khersa,
towards the embouchure of the Wady Semakh. The course of the
walls is still visible, according to Thompson (*The Land and the Book,*
page 375). This traveller also says, that 'the sea is so near the foot
of the mountain at this spot, that animals having once got fairly on
to the incline, could not help rolling down into the water.' . . . The
true reading therefore would be *Gergeseenon* or *Gergesaion.* This
name, so little known, must have been altered first into *Geraseenon,*
which has some semblance to it, and then into *Gadareenon*" (*Godet on
John,* page 383).

**And when he went forth to land, there met him out of the city a cer-
tain man, which had devils long time, and ware no clothes, neither
abode in any house, but in the tombs. When he saw Jesus, he cried
out, and fell down before him, and with a loud voice said, What have
I to do with thee, Jesus, Son of God most high? I beseech thee, torment me not. (For he had commanded the unclean spirit to come out
of the man. For oftentimes it had caught him: and he was kept bound
with chains and in fetters; and he brake the bands, and was driven of
the devil into the wilderness) (vv. 27–29).**

Matthew insists that there were two demoniacs (Matthew 8: 28) and
there is no reason to doubt his statement. Although two men were
delivered, for reasons unknown, one disappeared from the scene; probably he had gone to rejoin his family and in the highly-exciting reunion
forgot to return to give thanks. These men, or as Luke describes, this
man was completely subjected to evil. A strange restlessness had
driven him from society, and without clothing he made his home
among the tombs. There had been an occasion when the citizens,

resenting the presence of a naked man in their district went out in force to clothe him; they also sought to restrain him with fetters, but the demoniac's superhuman strength destroyed the chains, and all efforts to bind the man were then abandoned. His long, untidy hair, his uncouth appearance; his wild eyes, and noisy outbursts were sufficient to arouse pity in the heart of anyone. He was among the tombs when the Lord and His small band of disciples arrived on the beach. As the party slowly ascended the hill, the surging emotions of the demoniac overwhelmed him, and suddenly his piercing cry echoed across the hillside. *The Amplified New Testament* renders the passage: "And when he saw Jesus, he raised a deep, terrible cry from the depths of his throat, and fell down before him in terror. . . ." We do not know when this tragedy had occurred but to say the least, it was a shame that a man whom God meant to be a temple should become the abode of demons. It is an even greater tragedy that unlike the Lord who was able to deliver the afflicted sufferer, the modern church is impotent in the face of similar situations. This was not a case of mental illness; according to the teaching and actions of Christ, this man was indwelt by demons. The Lord did not send him to an institution specially devoted to the care of such unfortunates: Jesus delivered him instantly. One cannot help but wonder what repercussions would follow if Christ could truly live with us for a few weeks. Jesus was already commanding the evil tenant to vacate the premises when the demoniac fell at His feet. The Great Physician was quick to diagnose the cause of the man's sickness, and quicker still to begin His work of deliverance.

And Jesus asked him saying, What is thy name? And he said, Legion: because many devils were entered into him, And they besought him that he would not command them to go out into the deep (the bottomless pit—the abyss). And there was there an herd of many swine feeding on the mountain: and they besought him that he would suffer them to enter into them. And he suffered them. Then went the devils out of the man, and entered into the swine: and the herd ran violently down a steep place into the lake, and were choked (vv. 30-33).

It is thought-provoking that the Saviour asked for a name which was not supplied. What is THY name? The poor fellow was unable to reply accurately for even his tongue was controlled by the evil within him. Yet we must enquire why the Lord asked this question; surely He knew already. Probably the Master was trying to focus attention on the fact that the man, although subjugated by demons, was nevertheless still a man. He did have a name; he did possess an individuality. A soul may be submerged by evil but no man can sink out of

God's sight. Obviously these demons were terrified that they might be consigned to the abyss—the bottomless pit. The Greek word is *abusson* and this is the ·same word used in Revelation 20: 1. We can only infer then that these demons were afraid they were to be banished to a realm where they would be helpless and imprisoned. It is a startling thought that such beings should exist for the sole purpose off deluding and estranging men from God. It is a dangerous practice indeed for Christians to leave their minds unguarded. Convinced that this is the only way to obtain the fulness of the Holy Spirit some sincere but deluded men have urged their fellows to "let themselves go" to "become blank in the mind." Then, so it has been taught, the Holy Spirit can enter to claim and occupy the unresisting mind. This is both wrong and unscriptural. If we may judge from some of the very sad events which followed the cases mentioned, other spirits occupied the empty mind of the misguided seeker. God gave man a mind to use, and not to abandon. The way to the fulness of blessing is not to abandon all intellectual sanity, but rather to place intelligently one's all upon the altar of sacrifice. "I beseech you therefore, brethren, by the mercies of God, that ye present your bodies a living sacrifice, holy, acceptable unto God, which is your reasonable service" (Romans 12: 1). There is no need to appeal constantly to God that we might be filled with the Holy Spirit. The long continuous prayers of certain Christians suggest that God is reluctant to grant the request. God is more anxious to fill His people than they are to be filled—BUT—He refuses to fill hearts that are already filled with cobwebs! If Christians were as keen to springclean their temples as they are for God to come in to occupy the premises, God would have answered their prayers long ago.

Men have asked if it were fair for Jesus to deprive citizens of their swine in order to deliver this demoniac. *Readers are urged to study the homily at the end of this section.* We do not know what physical impact might have been made upon these animals as the evil spirits made contact with them. That they were suddenly frightened seems obvious for the peaceful herd suddenly became restless, and losing their balance on the steep slopes, rolled into the waters in which they were drowned. What happened to the demons? Probably they were banished to the realms they feared, for Christ would never have permitted their entering into any other human being.

When they that fed them saw what was done, they fled, and went and told it in the city and in the country. Then they went out to see what was done; and came to Jesus, and found the man, out of whom the devils were departed, sitting at the feet of Jesus, clothed, and in his right mind: and they were afraid (vv. 34–35).

The story of the herdsmen aroused great alarm throughout the city; the citizens rushed to the hillside overlooking the sea. The empty hills were most eloquent, and the delivered man at the feet of Jesus more than endorsed the news that had been given. Consider three things: (1) A *New Relationship.* He who had been afar off, had been brought nigh. (2) A *New Raiment.* Within a matter of moments, he who had resisted clothing, accepted a garment: he was no longer naked. (3) A *New Realization.* He was in his right mind; a new and wonderful Master had suddenly come into his life. He was at the feet of Jesus. This is one of the most entrancing Gospel pictures. Adam and Eve made flimsy garments with which to clothe themselves but remained unaware of their true nakedness until God came to walk in the garden. Then they ran to hide among the trees. Yet, when God made for them garments of skins, Adam and his wife were glad to accept God's offered gift. This demoniac did not realize his nakedness until Christ came, but when that alarming realization dawned upon his mind, he was glad to accept the garment Jesus offered. An overwhelming sense of need is always a prerequisite to the acceptance of God's gift of salvation. We can never see God's outstretched hand until our eyes are opened. Where did Christ obtain the garments with which to clothe this man? We can only assume that since He came to this place specially to deliver the unfortunate victim, the same love, foreseeing the need would have made provision. Christ would never deliver the fellow only to leave him confused and embarrassed before the citizens.

**They also which saw it told them by what means he that was possessed of the devils was healed. Then the whole multitude of the country of the Gadarenes round about besought him to depart from them; for they were taken with great fear: and he went up into the ship and returned back again (vv. 36-37).**

The excited comments as the herdsmen retold their story ultimately died away and in its place a deadly fear took possession of the people. Possibly they were very superstitious and wondered what new misfortunes might occur if they allowed this Stranger to tarry in their country. It was a gratifying sight to see the demoniac turned into a fine citizen, but the miracle had cost two thousand swine. This probably represented a lifetime of work. A farmer who had been rich in the morning was now bankrupt. Everybody agreed it was a shame, but each man silently considered the sober possibility that if Jesus continued this work, other swine might be drowned in the lake. There would be no objection to Christ's staying among them, if He would use different methods of producing miracles! This He might not be willing to do, so they asked Him to depart.

Now the man out of whom the devils were departed besought him
that he might be with him: but Jesus sent him away, saying, Return
to thine own house, and shew how great things God hath done unto
thee. And he went his way and published throughout the whole city
how great things Jesus had done unto him (vv. 38–39).

The term "the man *besought* him" is weak. The Greek Testament
renders the passage: *edeeto de autou "and was begging him."* This
man probably could not understand why his Benefactor was making
such a hurried departure, but when the full import of the events taking
place dawned upon his mind, the convert made his decision. To be
able to rejoin his loved ones, and associate with former friends, must
have seemed singularly attractive, yet nothing could compensate for
the loss of his Saviour. He earnestly continued to beg for permission
to accompany the Lord. Probably this would have given Christ very
much pleasure, but all things must be subservient to the ultimate responsibility of doing the will of God. This was and still is, that all men
should hear the Gospel, and when one door closes, God seeks to open
another. An initial setback must never mean the abandonment of a
project. The simple ordination service there on the beach turned a
new convert into a first-class missionary, and since there is no record
of Christ ever having made a second visit to this locality, the mission
of this former demoniac assumed even greater proportions. The man
was told to proclaim all that *God* had done for him; he went his way
and told what *Jesus* had done. Although he had not studied theology
in a seminary, obviously, he had an aptitude for learning.

## HOMILIES

Study No. 26

### WHICH SHALL I CHOOSE—THE SWINE OR THE SAVIOUR?

He was mad and completely terrifying, and no one ever approached
his home among the tombs. His long, untidy hair reached to his massive shoulders; his eyes, furtive and restless, were alternately light
with excitement, and dark with depression; and his only pleasure—
if pleasure we may call it—came when he was near the dead. The
desolation of his surroundings matched that of his heart. He was a
haunted, hunted man, the mention of whose name made the citizens
tremble. They said he was possessed of devils. And then the Lord
Jesus came. . . .

## The Peace

When the Master appeared over the brow of the hill, the demented captive stared; something snapped in his brain, and with a wild, vehement cry he rushed toward the invader. Unperturbed, the Lord awaited the onrushing maniac, and suddenly a surprising thing took place. The watching disciples hardly knew how it happened, for in some mysterious fashion the running man hesitated, and fell at the feet of their Master. When the prostrate fellow lifted his head, the dawn of a new day was shining in his eyes. Christ had challenged and expelled the indwelling demons; the power of sin had been broken, and into the liberated soul poured the boundless peace of God. How wonderful it is to remember that this Christ is unchanging. The greatest evidence for Christ and the Gospel is not in the multiplicity of churches, but in His word that breaks the power of sin.

## The Price

In a little while the people came out to see what had been done, and there at the feet of his Deliverer, they found the demoniac, "clothed, and in his right mind; *and they were afraid.*" One might ask of what were they afraid? Surely this wonderful day should have been recognized as the greatest in the history of their seaside homes. They looked at the gently moving waters of the lake, and shuddered as they recalled how two thousand swine had disappeared beneath the waves. This much-to-be-desired miracle had been expensive! One of their comrades had suffered irretrievable loss, and if Jesus of Nazareth continued His mission of healing, other farmers would soon be bankrupt. They looked at Jesus "and besought him to depart." Probably they did not realize this was one of the Lord's most powerful sermons. This was a notable illustration of the old saying "Actions speak louder than words." The entire district, so history affirms, was thickly populated by Gentiles, and such people would have no scruples about eating swineflesh. Yet all Jews believed this meat to be unclean. If these farmers were Jews, and there is no evidence to the contrary, they probably stifled their consciences by the excuse that there was no harm in supplying others as long as they did not eat the swine. The whole point of the incident appears to be that Christ was trying to teach that before the Benediction of Heaven can rest upon a community, evil things must be driven out. According to their own teaching, God and swine could not live together in the same house. It would appear that the people of our modern age need to learn the same lesson.

## The Poverty

That day, as far as we are able to tell from the record, they lost a priceless opportunity. When the tiny craft sailed out over the lake, it carried far more than men. No one can be certain, but this at least can be said: there is no reference to any later visit made by Christ. Possibly He never returned, and we shall never know how many miracles might have been performed among those people if they had not preferred swine.

> Rabbi, begone. Thy powers
> Bring loss to us and ours.
> Our ways are not thine:
> Thou lovest men; we—swine.
>
> Oh, get thee hence, Omnipotence,
> And take this fool of thine;
> His soul, what care we for his soul?
> What good to us that thou hast made him whole,
> Since we have lost our swine?
>
> And Christ went sadly.
> He had wrought for them a sign
> Of love, and hope, and tenderness divine:
> They wanted swine.
>
> Christ stands without your door
>    and gently knocks;
> But if your gold or swine
>    the entrance blocks,
> He forces no man's hold; He will depart
> And leave you to the pleasures of your heart.
>                    "Author Unknown."

And so this Stranger comes to us. Sometimes in the most unexpected of ways, and often unannounced, He draws near. Let us be sure that He never comes empty-handed. Should His coming mean sacrifice, we shall do well to remember that ultimately "no good thing will He withhold from them who walk uprightly."

### SECTION FOUR

### *Expository Notes on the Woman who Touched the Hem of His Garment*

**And a woman having an issue of blood twelve years, which had spent all her living upon physicians, neither could be healed of any, came**

behind him and touched the border of his garment: and immediately
her issue of blood staunched (vv. 43-44).

F. L. Godet quotes Eusebius as saying this woman was a heathen
and dwelt at Paneas, near the source of the Jordan, and that in his
time her house was still shown, having at its entrance two brass statues
on a stone pedestal. One represented a woman on her knees, with her
hands held out before her, in the attitude of a suppliant; the other,
a man standing with his cloak thrown over his shoulder, and his hand
extended toward the woman. Eusebius had been into the house himself, and had seen this statue, which represented, it was said, the
features of Jesus (*Godet on John*, page 393). It is difficult to estimate
how much reliability may be placed on this statement handed down
from a bygone age. One thing remains indisputable; this woman
was in an unenviable position. Over a period of twelve years she
had suffered from recurring haemorrhages, and her continuing visits
to the physicians had impoverished her beyond measure. The fifteenth
chapter of the book of Leviticus has much to say of a woman in this
condition. She was not only considered to be unclean herself; she
also defiled anyone or anything she touched. If she were a Jewess,
she would be an unfortunate woman with whom no one would wish
to associate. The fact that her condition had continued over a period
of twelve years would suggest this was a judgment from God. If she
were a Gentile, a heathen, as Eusebius suggests, then she would be
even more unclean in the estimation of her Jewish neighbours. Thus,
viewed from any angle, this woman was an object of pity, a desolate,
dejected case for whom the physicians could do nothing. The fees
which she had been obliged to pay her doctors had left her impoverished and helpless. Some theologians suggest her faith was more
in keeping with a heathen superstition; that she sought to touch him
by stealth believing some magical process would cure her ills. There
is nothing to support the theory that superstition made her touch the
Lord's garment for even the Lord commended her faith. The Greek
word translated *the border* of his garment is *kraspedou*, and this according to Dr. J. H. Thayer means "a little appendage, hanging down from
the edge of the mantle or cloak, made of twisted wool; a tassel or
tuft." The Jews wore these in accordance with the commands of God.
"Speak unto the children of Israel, and bid them that they make them
fringes in the border of their garment. . . . And it shall be unto you
for a fringe, that ye may look upon it, and remember all the commandments of the Lord, and do them" (Numbers 15: 38–39). The robe
customarily worn by the Jews resembled in some ways a woman's
shawl. Two corners hung down at the back and to these would be
attached the tassels. When the woman heard of the approach of

Jesus, and knowing that He was her last hope of healing, she waited anxiously for Him, and as He proceeded on His way, stole up behind him, and reaching forth her hand touched one of the tassels.

**And Jesus said, Who touched me? When all denied, Peter and they that were with him, said, Master, the multitude throng thee and press thee, and sayest thou, Who touched me? And Jesus said, Somebody hath touched me: for I perceive that virtue is gone out of me (vv. 45–46).**

Momentarily the scene almost beggared description for the crowds were so large that it was hard to make progress. *The Amplified Testament* renders the foregoing passage : "As Jesus went, the people pressed around him—*almost suffocating Him.*" Therefore it follows that within the space of a few yards many people had touched Him. He was in the position of having to force a way through the crowds. It was for this very reason that the disciples were probably dumbfounded when the Lord asked, Who touched Me? Her touch might have been unnoticed; but her faith gripped His heart. It was the magnetic quality of her sincere desire which drew from His boundless resources the healing she desperately needed. He felt virtue going out of Him; someone's need was being met; His life was being drained to help another; He was giving a spiritual blood transfusion in a very real way, and since this could not happen by chance, there had to be a cause. Could He who knew so much, be ignorant of the woman's identity? Did He ask His question because He did not know who touched Him? Did He ask in order to help this woman come out into the open to make her first unashamed confession of faith? There would be people in that crowd who knew her condition. She was unclean, but even of more consequence was the fact that she was contaminating other people. The scripture to which reference has already been made forbade what she was now doing. Unless this woman's case be publicised, there could be serious repercussions. It would not be safe to let her go away unnoticed, for someone might have seen her, and that someone might inform the authorities. The Lord's action was kindness in disguise.

**And when the woman saw that she was not hid, she came trembling, and falling down before him, she declared unto him before all the people for what cause she had touched him, and how she was healed immediately. And he said unto her, Daughter, be of good comfort: thy faith hath made thee whole; go in peace (vv. 47–48).**

There was now no escape; the woman realized He was aware of her action; she felt guilty. The Lord's smiles must have been very attractive as He looked at the kneeling woman; she was making her first confession and the people were listening. At that moment blessing came to her in triplicate. (1) Faith in her soul. (2) Health in her body. (3) Peace in her mind. Thus would He teach all His followers that they who are healed by His grace should tell their story to a waiting world.

HOMILIES

Study No. 27

### THE WOMAN WHO PAID DOCTOR'S BILLS

"And a woman having an issue of blood twelve years, which had spent all her living upon physicians, neither could be healed of any, came behind him, and touched the border of his garment: and immediately, her issue of blood staunched." And in these few simple sentences, Luke recorded one of the most suggestive of all Christ's miracles. "*A woman who had spent all her living upon physicians.*" Day after day, and week after week, this worried soul had visited surgeries; time after time, she had waited her turn, and had gone away with new hopes rising in her heart. But all her efforts had been in vain. She paid her doctor bills, and then started saving money to be ready to pay the next doctor. Her temperature probably went up as fast as her bank balance went down. This is the type of story in which John Bunyan would have revelled. He would have visited that woman in her home; and accompanied her on every trip to the doctor. He would have written down the names of all the physicians, and found them to be most illuminating. To him, quite obviously this woman would have represented the sinner: someone needing relief from inbred sin; the doctors would have been the physicians of a pagan world; the grand climax would have been the moment of supreme relief when the impoverished one knelt at the feet of the Lord. This story has been used again and again by the ministers of all churches; this commentary and others of its type will be filled with the orthodox presentation of pulpit homiletics. Let that be the justification—if justification be necessary for a startling application of a very old account.

### THE PSYCHIATRIST—Dr. Don't Worry

This doctor is always very gracious; very wise; very methodical, and sometimes very cunning. He explores the unknown and comes up with tremendous discoveries. He remembers what most men forget; he passes his hands over a molehill, and behold a mountain! He's a genius, but he knows his business. Sometimes his home is palatial;

sometimes it is not. Yet always the shining plate at the door announces the presence of a man who is keen, clean, and very popular. The Gospel of Christ always begets a sense of need, and in the desperate struggle which follows, the sinner has either to yield to the insistent pleadings of the Saviour or seek relief elsewhere. Sometimes the home of the spiritual psychiatrist is a haven of refuge for the modern Jonahs who try to run away from God. A change of environment, a visit to fresh surroundings, a complete relaxation from the cares and strain of life may work wonders in any patient—providing the cause of the malady is not too deep-seated. Many people therefore stay away from religious meetings, deciding that conviction is a disease of the mind; an unnecessary stirring of one's emotions. They endeavour to cure this by excessive worldliness. The treatment is most expensive, especially since it provides no cure.

### THE DIETICIAN—Dr. Diet

This physician is very famous. His treatment promises permanent cure through elimination. His is the method of giving up things! The patient is urged to adhere strictly to diet, for through complete denial of certain commodities, both body and soul may be purified. In the spiritual realm, these doctors thrive—they are always wealthy! The sinner is urged to forsake every appearance of evil; to avoid anything even remotely detrimental to spiritual health. He must shun the world and all its allurements; he is urged to live the life of a recluse, for by the continuance of religious exercises, admittance may be gained to the realms of the blessed. These doctors have their busiest season just before Easter when thousands of their patients are in the most co-operative mood of the entire year. Yet immediate joy is quite unobtainable under this treatment, and every doctor is careful to explain that only those who endure to the end can be saved.

### THE SPECIALIST—Dr. Know-all

This is the wisest of all earth's physicians. With particular care he examines his patients, and outlines methods by which health may become a reality. Sometimes his countenance can be frightening as he speaks of a scalpel; at other times he is most endearing as he dispenses the balm of Gilead! A little of this, and for a change, a little of that. Sufficient religion to satisfy the qualms of conscience; sufficient worldliness to appease the demands of the flesh. The mountain top for fresh air and an occasional glimpse of the eternal; a vacation in Egypt where the entertainment is exciting, the food is ravishing, and the people strangers! Everything is all right in moderation—be sure to give a tenth of your income to the church, and then go out and have a ball with the other nine-tenths. The Lord will not mind, He has already had His share! Oh yes, Dr. Know-all is a great doctor; the woman with the issue of blood helped to buy his second Cadillac. Yes, John Bunyan with his love for allegories would have visualized all these men. But since Bunyan was also a preacher, he might have indicated that the ancient story divided into three sections. (1) *The Trial of her Faith*—she had an issue of blood twelve years. (2) *The Touch of her Faith*. She came *behind* Him; she could not see His face to know if He were smiling. A man's back is never very attractive, and God's back can be frightening, but she believed and touched His garment. (3) *The Triumph of her Faith*. She was healed immediately. It is a great thing to know a doctor whose reputation is matched by his ability. Even the people of Palestine recognized this when they called Jesus "The Great Physician."

> Oh, touch the hem of His garment!
> And thou too shalt be free;
> His saving power, this very hour,
> Shall give new life to thee.

## SECTION FIVE

*Expository Notes on the Raising of the Daughter of Jairus*

And it came to pass when Jesus was returned, the people gladly received him; for they were all waiting for him. And, behold, there came a man named Jairus, and he was a ruler of the synagogue: and he fell down at Jesus' feet, and besought him that he would come into his house: For he had one only daughter, about twelve years of age, and she lay dying. But as he went, the people thronged him. And a woman . . . (vv. 40–43).

The case of the woman who touched the hem has already been considered for this took place as Christ was accompanying the ruler of the synagogue. The woman's healing came as an interruption in the journey, and the ensuing delay only emphasized the greatness of the man's faith. It was for this cause, the study of the woman's healing was considered first.

The immense crowd had waited for the return of the Lord and the moment he stepped ashore, the excitement began to increase, for the ruler of the synagogue was seen making his way to Jesus. This in itself was truly startling for it would have been this man's duty to warn the synagogue congregations against any one considered a menace to the cause of Israel. We do not know whether or not this man had been among the enemies of the Saviour; if he had, then his daughter's sickness helped to destroy his prejudice. There is a thought-provoking

contrast here. The woman who had touched his garment had been
dying for twelve years; this maiden had lived twelve years. Christ was
equal to the needs of both.

> While he yet spake (that is to the woman who touched His garment)
> there cometh one from the ruler of the synagogue's house, saying to
> him, Thy daughter is dead; trouble not the Master. But when Jesus
> heard it, he answered him, saying, Fear not: believe only, and she
> shall be made whole. And when he came into the house, he suffered
> no man to go in, save Peter, and James, and John, and the father and
> the mother of the maiden (vv. 49–51).

The delay occasioned when the woman touched the tassel on Christ's
garment must have been heart rending to the anxious parent, but
there was nothing he could do to hasten proceedings. The Teacher
would not be hurried, and beside, the woman also had great need.
He could only stand and wait, and perhaps pray. When the message
arrived announcing the death of his only daughter, his faith received
its greatest test. We may never know what he felt for Christ immediately reassured him that all was well. *The Amplified New Testament*
renders the passage beautifully, "Do not be seized with alarm—
simply believe in Me." The next moment the party continued the
journey toward the stricken home. The professional musicians had
gathered, but the superficiality of their mournful songs was seen in
bold relief when they forgot the agony of the parents and laughed
aloud at the apparent stupidity of the Carpenter they already hated.
Faith and unbelief cannot live together. The Lord therefore refused
to admit these people to the sick room. The disciples were admitted
for through their lips the story would ultimately be told to the world.
The tenderness and thoughtfulness of the Lord were seen to great
advantage when He allowed the parents to witness what was about
to take place. A little girl awaking from the sleep of death might be
startled to see strange men around her bed; the presence of her parents
would calm and comfort her. The Lord knew exactly what He was
doing.

> And all wept and bewailed her: but he said, Weep not; she is not
> dead, but sleepeth. And they laughed him to scorn, knowing that she
> was dead. And he put them all out, and took her by the hand, and
> called saying, Maid, arise. And her spirit came again, and she arose
> straightway: and he commanded to give her meat. And her parents
> were astonished: but he charged them that they should tell no man
> what was done (vv. 52–56).

Ever mindful of the need of His people, the Lord was careful to
command that this girl be fed. God may give life, but man must sustain

it. Probably He commanded that the parents refrain from broadcasting the news of the miracle because He knew His enemies would only endeavour to make this event another cause for sarcastic comment. If they were capable of laughing when the parents were breaking their hearts, they would also be capable of saying the girl was never dead. The entire episode might have become an object of ridicule as embittered men accused the parents of being sensationalists, fools, people who hastily jumped to conclusions. There are times when silence can be golden.

## HOMILIES

### Study No. 28

#### JAIRUS . . . WHO PROBABLY BROKE ALL HIS VOWS

One of the strangest things in life is the way in which man is often made to do things he had no intention of doing. Centuries ago Naaman in great rage vowed he would never wash in Jordan—but he did. Probably the Christian Church often prayed for Saul of Tarsus, and if the mad zealot heard of their intercessions, he too would have vowed never to bow before the Nazarene—but he did. And so it proved to be with Jairus. As the ruler of the synagogue, his entire attitude would be antagonistic toward the new Teacher, and he would warn his people against attending the Lord's meetings. He himself was determined never to appeal to this enemy of Israel—but he did.

### The Father's Desperation bringing him to Christ

Jairus was a ruler of the synagogue, and all matters of social and religious importance rested in his hands. Proud of his ancestry, loving his faith, serving his God, and hating all heresy, he was a Hebrew of the Hebrews. He lived in the nearby home, where for twelve wonderful years, his charming little daughter had brightened his life. Dignity and love walked hand in hand through the life of this favoured man; but when his daughter became critically ill, the matter of her preservation swept all else aside. When Jairus heard of Jesus, his heart became a battle ground where love and pride fought to the death. Love suggested an appeal to the Great Physician; pride reminded of the warnings which in all probability had been given continually to the congregation. "And behold, there cometh one of the rulers of the synagogue, Jairus by name; and when he saw Jesus, he fell at his feet." How helpless—how humble—how hopeful; these were the three stages through which this man fought his way to victory.

### The Friend's Doubt blinding him to Christ

"And Jesus went with him; and much people followed him, and thronged him. And a certain woman, which had an issue of blood twelve years . . . came in the press behind, and touched his garment." The healing of the woman occasioned a little delay, and to the anxious father this was tragic. "Then came there from the ruler of the synagogue's house, certain which said, Thy daughter is dead: why troublest thou the Master any further?" These words were possibly spoken in sincerity, but they might have been injurious to the faith of the desperate father. The people said, "The case is now hopeless. If only Jesus had come earlier something might have been done. Come home, therefore, and arrange for the funeral." There are still many people who seem strangely related to these people of a bygone age. They limit the power of God, and believe that beyond certain limits, every case becomes hopeless. Their unbelief says, "Trouble not the Master any further."

### The Fool's Disdain banishing him from Christ

"As soon as Jesus heard the word that was spoken, he saith unto the ruler of the synagogue, Be not afraid, only believe . . . and when he was come in, he saith unto them, Why make ye this ado, and weep? the damsel is not dead but sleepeth. And they laughed him to scorn." And never was laughter so ill-timed as in that stricken home. Possibly, the people were angry because their leader had apparently betrayed the cause of Israel—he had gone to solicit help from the accursed Carpenter. They looked at the grieving ruler, and scornfully chuckled at the stupidity of Christ's statement. Their foolishness robbed them of an inestimable privilege. Christ put them all out and closed the door. Such sin could never be permitted to linger in His presence, either there or in eternity. Should He ever deem it necessary to close an eternal door, the consequences would be most grave for those left on the outside, "He taketh the father and mother of the damsel, and them that were with him, and entereth in where the damsel was lying. And he took the damsel by the hand." His whispered words were as the balm of Heaven to wounded souls. Slowly the colour came back into the ashen cheeks of the little girl; slowly two sleepy eyes opened, and in the following moments, peace returned to the sorrowful parents. Yes, Jairus probably broke all of his earlier vows when he came to Christ; but it was better to do that then than to break his heart for ever. (Taken from *Bible Cameos*, p. 99.)

Study No. 28

## THE CHARACTERISTICS OF THE NEW LIFE IN CHRIST

*Confession.* Taken from the story of the raising of the widow's son at Nain. "He that was dead sat up and *began to speak*" (Luke 7: 15).

*Communion.* Taken from the story of the raising of the daughter of Jairus. "And her spirit came again, and she arose straightway: and *he commanded to give her meat*" (Luke 8: 55). Converts need food.

*Consecration.* Taken from the story of the raising of Lazarus. "And he that was dead came forth *bound hand and foot with graveclothes: and his face was bound about with a napkin*; Jesus saith unto them, LOOSE HIM AND LET HIM GO" (John 11: 44).

The new life should never be hindered by graveclothes brought from the old life.

For details of this study see my commentary on *John's Wonderful Gospel*, pp. 246–248.

# The Ninth Chapter of Luke

*Expository Notes on the Commissioning of the Twelve Apostles*

SECTION ONE

*Expository Notes on the Commissioning of the Twelve Apostles*

**Then he called his twelve disciples together, and gave them power and authority over all devils, and to cure diseases. And he sent them to preach the kingdom of God, and to heal the sick (vv. 1–2).**

The Lord had now reached a crucial place in His ministry. He and His followers had stayed in Galilee for a considerable period of time; but before the small band of preachers moved to another area, it was the Master's desire to address one final appeal to the people among whom He had laboured so long. Furthermore, the Saviour was aware that the work of evangelism would soon be the task of these men whom He had called to be His disciples. They had, so to speak, been receiving His tuition in a special classroom. The time had now come when they should go on a field trip! It would be an invaluable lesson for them to go forth without His immediate presence; to meet and solve their problems alone; then, when the time came for the Lord to leave them, they would not be completely devoid of the experience of depending upon an absent Christ.

Godet says: "There is something greater than preaching—this is to make preachers; there is something greater than performing miracles; this is to impart the power to perform them." Christ's earlier ministry revealed the possibility of such events; His special gifts to them at this time imparted the power which they had considered to be His alone. Foolish indeed would be the man who tried to accomplish the impossible, but even more foolish would be the employer who sent his workmen to do what he alone could do. Therefore the Saviour called the disciples; commissioned, empowered, instructed, and finally blessed them. Yet in spite of the power with which they had been invested, they were to remain humble servants of the Christ. Even their power would diminish if they failed in this important phase of daily living. See verse 40 and Matthew 17: 19–21.

And he said unto them, Take nothing for your journey, neither stave nor scrip, neither bread, neither money; neither have two coats apiece, And whatsoever house ye enter into, there abide, and thence depart. And whosoever will not receive you, when ye go out of that city, shake off the very dust from your feet for a testimony against them. And they departed and went through the towns, preaching the gospel, and healing everywhere (vv. 3–6).

At first glance Luke appears to be at variance with Mark. Mark 6: 8 represents Christ as saying: ". . . they should take nothing for their journey *save a staff only.* . . ." Luke indicates that no staff was to be taken. Quoting Ebrard, Godet says, "Ebrard makes the acute observation that in Aramaean Jesus probably used an elliptical form also much used in Hebrew, and which may be filled up in two ways: 'For if you take a staff, this of itself is quite sufficient' (Mark); or, 'this of itself is too much' (Matthew and Luke). This saying of Jesus might therefore be reproduced in Greek either in one way or the other (*Godet on John,* p. 399). Thus the import of the command would be that the men thus sent forth to preach should trust more on the promises of God than upon their own resources. A staff could and would be a most helpful instrument if the owner's eyes were focused upon God. Yet if the disciple, even for one moment, considered his safety exclusively dependent upon the staff, then the staff itself would be dangerous. The Greek word translated *staff* is somewhat interesting in that it is used in various ways throughout the Scriptures. Hebrews 9: 4 uses the word to indicate Aaron's rod that budded. There the idea is of a staff usually held in the hand of a traveller—the equivalent of a walking stick. Revelation 2: 27 using the same word *rhabdos* indicates the sceptre of a king.

Quesnel wrote an illuminating paragraph concerning this verse. His words deserve consideration. "Men will never be able to establish the kingdom of God in the hearts of people, so long as they do not appear fully persuaded themselves of those truths which they preach. And how can they appear so, if they plainly contradict them in their practice and behaviour? In order to persuade others to be unconcerned for superfluities, a man must not himself appear too much concerned, even about necessaries." The commission of the disciples should be considered in this way. This obvious poverty provided an opportunity to exercise faith. Their power to perform miracles would attract many people, and offers of hospitality would be forthcoming. It would thus became possible to take the message into the homes of the very people they wished to reach. Other people, in supplying the needs of the disciples, would share the joys of the crusade and in ever-widening circles, the power of the Saviour's words would reach increasing audiences. Yet it must be remembered that these words were spoken to men who went forth into a quiet, agricultural countryside nearly two thousand years ago. It is extremely problematical whether the Lord would issue today's commission in identical terms. God always honours true faith, but true faith is not stupidity in action. God also honours preparation. The disciple who rode a donkey on the freeways of California would soon be preaching to angels or talking to a high court judge! The evangelist who did nothing to prepare for his modern crusade would have the dubious honour of addressing non-existent congregations in a spacious, but empty, auditorium. The original commission must be considered in the light of its true setting. Nevertheless, even today's evangelists should remember that the Lord is "the same yesterday, and today, and forever." The original disciples were told not to take scrip, that is, they were not to take the little wallet usually carried by beggars. They were not to make appeals for money, nor take collections. The continuous appeals for financial assistance coming from modern preachers leaves the impression that God is somewhat hard of hearing! It is easier, quicker, and safer to beg for money, than to hope God might remember His children can get hungry! The shaking of the dust from one's feet was a well known custom by which irate visitors displayed displeasure against a community. When the Saviour commanded His followers to be content with the hospitality of one homestead, He probably considered this would be the best way to avoid rivalry and gossip. It was better to establish a church in one home than to put on weight in twenty.

Now Herod the tetrarch heard of all that was done by him: and he was perplexed, because that it was said of some, that John was risen from the dead; And of some, that Elias had appeared; and of others, that one of the old prophets was risen again. And Herod said, John have I beheaded: but who is this, of whom I hear such things? And he desired to see him (vv. 7–9).

Herod ruled over that part of the country now traversed by the itinerant band of preachers, and the fact that interest was aroused even within the palace indicates the overwhelming success of the missionary venture. Hitherto, only certain privileged places had known the manifestation of Christ's power to heal, and to those centres huge crowds had journeyed to witness the spectacle. Now things had changed. The disciples had systematically journeyed from village to village until the entire region heard the good news. Those who had been unable to go to Christ, were left without excuse, for the Gospel had been preached in their own streets; miracles had been performed almost on their doorstep. Throughout Galilee there was only one topic of conversation; all men spoke of Christ. All true preaching does this. When the population became excited by what was taking place, it was to be expected that someone would tell Herod. Here we have the only indication within Luke's Gospel that John the Baptist had been murdered. Herod had succeeded in stilling the voice of the wilderness preacher, but he had not been as successful in quietening the clamour of his conscience. The testimony and speculation of the crowds increased his agitation, and finally the uneasy ruler decided it was necessary to see this Jesus.

**And the apostles, when they were returned, told him all that they had done. And he took them, and went aside privately into a desert place belonging to the city called Bethsaida (v. 10).**

Defeat is often dangerous, but success can be deadly. Defeat sometimes overwhelms the heart; success often inflates the head! The preacher who prefers the pulpit to the desert has very much to learn. Bishop J. C. Ryle wrote: "Occasional retirement, self-enquiry, meditation, and secret communion with God, are absolutely essential to spiritual health. The man who neglects them is in great danger of a fall. To be always preaching, teaching, speaking, writing, and working public works, is, unquestionably, a sign of zeal. But it is not always a sign of zeal according to knowledge. It often leads to untoward consequences. We *must* make time occasionally for sitting down and calmly looking within, and examining how matters stand between our own selves and Christ. The omission of the practice is the true account of many a backsliding which shocks the church, and gives occasion to the world to blaspheme." (*Ryle's Expository Thoughts on the Gospels.* Luke, p. 297.)

HOMILIES

Study No. 29

## THE NEED FOR THE SECRET PLACE

It is one of the anomalies of life that men who are faithful in some things are faithless in others. The carpenter who is anxious to complete a job in a distant house is often slow at finishing a task at home. The builder whose workmanship merits the highest honours, will often have broken-down walls in his own garden. Perhaps these men could appreciate the words of the unknown husbandman who said, ". . . they made me the keeper of the vineyards; but mine own vineyard have I not kept" (Song of Solomon 1: 6). This is something that every Christian worker needs to consider. It is a great privilege to help our friends keep their vineyards clean and attractive, but unless our own vines are healthy and productive, our service must be suspect. My ministry can never be greater than the sanctity of my soul. My vineyard is the place of testing, experimentation, triumph; my neighbour's vineyard is the place to extend that which has been brought to perfection at home.

*ABRAHAM . . . the man of faith who lost his faith*

"By faith Abraham, when he was called to go out into a place which he should afterward receive for an inheritance, obeyed; and he went out, not knowing whither he went. By faith he sojourned in the land of promise . . ." (Hebrews 11: 8–9). Yes, FAITH brought him to the land of promise and enabled him to pitch his tent close to the altar at Bethel, but stupidity ruined his tranquillity. When he went down into Egypt, he urged Sarai to lie on his behalf. His success in coming to the land of promise would have been seen to better advantage had he gone into the desert to commune with his God. The lights of Egypt can be clearly seen even from the altar—if our backs are toward the hills of God. See Genesis 12: 13–20.

*MOSES . . . the meekest man on earth who lost his meekness* (Numbers 12: 3)

A man's strength is often in his weakness; but sometimes his weakness is in his strength. It has been said that a chain is no stronger than its weakest link. This is true, but in the greatest experiences of life, our chief weaknesses are sometimes hidden within what appears to be the strongest link. Trees that grow on the highest mountains need to send their roots deep; men who live in exalted positions are often the targets of hell's hurricanes. There was a time when God placed Moses in a lofty crevice in the rocks, and from that place of sanctified seclusion the great leader saw the Lord. The glow on the cheeks of Moses reflected the glow within his heart, and at such times he was safe. This was triumph, but unfortunately, even the best of men cannot be hermits all their lives. Moses came down the mountain to become contaminated by the people who watched his every movement. The great saint momentarily forgot the exaltation in the mountain and passionately struck the rock destined to become a fountain. The sparkling fountain of water slaked his thirst but could not remove the stain from his soul. Blessed is the man who brings the mountain crevice into the smoky valley! (Numbers 20: 7–12).

### ELIJAH ... the man of prayer who forgot to pray

"Elias was a man subject to like passions as we are, and he prayed earnestly that it might not rain, and it rained not on the earth by the space of three years and six months. And he prayed again, and the heaven gave rain, and the earth brought forth her fruit" (James 5: 17–18). Prayer is spiritual electricity. It gives light, power, and warmth to the soul of the believer. Elijah knew all this, but one day he forgot to press the switch! When Jezebel threatened his life, the strong man of God became unutterably weak, and ". . . arose and went for his life" (I Kings 19: 3). Earlier he had resided in a place of divine choosing; a small canyon had been his cathedral, and the babbling brook provided his music. There he had known serenity of soul; there, his spirit remained calm for he was with God. Unfortunately he only charged his batteries when he might have linked himself eternally with the unfailing resources of God. He who had so often tended the vineyards of others, neglected his own, and consequently his nationwide ministry had a premature ending. With great grace God took Elijah, but the need at that moment was on earth and not in heaven.

### JONAH ... the preacher who refused to preach

"Now the word of the Lord came unto Jonah the son of Amittai saying, Arise, go to Nineveh, that great city, and cry against it; for their wickedness is come up before me. But Jonah rose up to flee . . ." (Jonah 1: 1–3). It is not the purpose of this commentary to explain the reasons for this flight; it is sufficient to remember that whatever his reason, Jonah was disobeying God. Unquestionably he was a man of great courage, great oratorical ability, great zeal, but his rash action not only threatened the entire population of Nineveh; it endangered his own soul. The law made it clear that if a watchman knew of the approach of an enemy and omitted to warn the city, the blood of its citizens would be required of the watchman. Jonah ran the risk of losing his precious soul. It would have been wiser to walk to the quiet place in the hills, rather than to visit the booking office of the ships sailing to Tarshish. Sometimes a holiday in the hills is better than a sea voyage.

## PETER THE GREAT . . . who became Peter the less

It is almost inconceivable that the same man who exultantly cried, "Thou art the Christ" should ultimately deny his Lord. It seems a long, long way between these extremes, but actually, the one is only just around the corner from the other. It is with this in mind that we should remember the warning, "Let him that thinketh he standeth take heed lest he fall." Simon Peter was indisputably a preacher, and all preachers of note stand in the limelight. This is dangerous, and often disastrous. A man is only tall when he kneels before his Maker. Sometimes, boys grow too fast, and die too quickly! The most eloquent speaker is not always the most Christ-like saint. It is easier to get one's name in the newspapers than to engrave it on the hearts of grateful listeners. It must remain a cause for great grief that some who once influenced great congregations now serve behind counters! Some husbandmen who could see the smallest pest in the neighbour's vineyard failed to detect the presence of kangaroos in their own backyard! Unfortunately, some of the fiercest denunciators of secret sin succumbed to the charms of a temptress. No man should stand before a congregation until he has knelt before his Lord.

## DEMAS . . . who stayed long enough to run away

"Luke the beloved physician, and Demas, greet you" (Colossians 4 : 14). "For Demas hath forsaken me, having loved this present world, and is departed unto Thessalonica" (II Timothy 4 : 10). Poor Demas he was a promising athlete, but he strayed from the course and became stuck in the mud! Day after day he ministered to Paul in the Roman prison, but when Paul bowed his head to thank God for his food, Demas looked through the window toward the beckoning lights of worldliness. Possibly, if he were a gifted musician, he would have been thrilled to conduct Heaven's greatest orchestra. Had he been a prince of preachers, he would have preached day and night without a complaint. Had he been a mighty warrior, he would have led spiritual armies into the fiercest battles and would have waged holy war until the devil was dead—but who wants to wash dishes, cook meals, and be faithful, rusting out in the room next door to a prisoner's cell? Poor Demas! Paul's cell could have been a pinnacle from which to view the heights of Canaan; unfortunately the young man saw only the pleasures of Thessalonica. He stayed long enough to run away, but however far he ran, it is doubtful if he ever ran beyond the reach of his conscience. Probably the Lord was well aware of the dangers besetting the returning band of victorious disciples, and this accounted for His thought-provoking action when, ". . . he took them, and went aside privately into a desert place belonging to a city called Bethsaida" (Luke 9: 10).

SECTION TWO

*Expository Notes on the Feeding of the Multitude*

**And the people, when they knew it, followed him: and he received them, and spake unto them of the kingdom of God, and healed them that had need of healing (v. 11).**

It might be that this was one of the less publicised testings of the Saviour. With great care and deliberation He planned this retreat so that His followers could be refreshed and made ready for future service. Probably He too anticipated a quiet time away from the demands of the great congregations, but suddenly the crowd invaded the resting place; seclusion became impossible, and the peacefulness was shattered by the appeals of the needy. How easy it would have been for a man of smaller stature to become irritable, critical, and frustrated. With characteristic charm and grace, the Lord received the people and ministered to their physical needs. He was careful to meet first the need of their souls; afterward, and not before, He healed their sick. Thus would He teach men that spiritual health is more important than physical strength.

**And when the day began to wear away, then came the twelve, and said unto him, Send the multitude away, that they may go into the towns and country round about, and lodge, and get victuals: for we are here in a desert place. But he said unto them, Give ye them to eat. And they said, We have no more but five loaves and two fishes; except we should go and buy meat for all this people. For they were about five thousand men (vv. 12–14).**

The Jewish day begins to "wear away" immediately after midday. The disciples were probably concerned by the fact that many in this great audience would be aged, tired and weary. If they had already been standing in the sun for some hours, the continuance of this procedure might be disastrous for some of the company. Furthermore it was obvious that to find accommodation for such a crowd would be impossible at short notice. Some preparation would need to be made, and therefore the request to the Lord was perfectly legitimate. The importance of this miracle is emphasized by the fact that all the evangelists record the event. The four records vary a little but this only endorses the individuality of each author. Each reported the event as he was able to understand its implications. Probably this has been the hardest of all the miracles to refute; there were so many reliable witnesses of the mighty event. Following the oriental custom by which women and children were apart, only the men were counted. However, the presence of a great number of women and children was indicated by Matthew (Matthew 14: 21).

**And he said to his disciples, Make them sit down by fifties in a company. And they did so, and made them all sit down. Then he took the five loaves and two fishes, and looking up to heaven, he blessed them, and brake, and gave to the disciples to set before the multitude. And they did eat, and were all filled: and there was taken up of the fragments that remained to them twelve baskets (vv. 14–17).**

Christ was careful to have the audience seated before He performed His miracle. Had He neglected to do this, the scene might have beggared description. Had they been standing in a closely packed throng all around him, the startling news of what He was doing might have turned that crowd into a rushing multitude of fanatics. The people would have pressed from all sides to see what was taking place; children might have been injured in the crush, and the whole scene would have become the object of criticism. Therefore with the aid of his disciples the Lord arranged that the people be seated in groups of fifty (Matthew) or by double rows of fifty—hundreds (Mark). This exhibited orderliness in the Master's methods; it provided an easy way by which the people could be counted, and each individual was able to see clearly what Christ intended to do. Thus a catastrophe was averted and a benediction rested upon the scene. John supplies the information that the food was provided by a lad. The basket was probably the small receptacle carried by strict Jews. Unwilling to purchase provisions from pagans, orthodox Jews took bread on every journey. This suggested to certain critics that the miracle was fraudulent; each traveller surrendered his small store of provisions and the people had a "basket lunch." This absurd suggestion is unworthy of comment, except perhaps for one detail. The critics might have told us if any of the donors ever claimed their portions from the abundance left over in the twelve baskets! The surplus was probably used to help people who had special needs. The account provides a picture of a greater faith. Christ the Bread of Life sees the multitude before Him, and dispensing the good news to His disciples, commands that they go forth to supply that which is needed. The disciples, the Church, can only give what they first receive from Him. Their own resources are too small and inadequate. Unless the preacher obtains the food from the hand of Christ, congregations go home hungry. Furthermore, the provision of Christ and the co-operation of His followers cannot avail unless hungry people accept what is offered. Christ supplies the banquet but He never FORCES His guests to eat.

## HOMILIES

Study No. 30

### PAUL . . . AND HIS SPECIAL KIND OF BREAD

This is a homily of a different kind. One of the greatest sermons I ever heard preached came from the lips of an African leper. The following is an extract taken from my book *Silent Challenge*, pages 89–101. "When my friend, Dr. C. M. Doke, Professor of Bantu languages in the Witwatersrand University, Johannesburg, paused before the door of a mud hut and said, "This is it," I knew that my great moment had come; my long journey to the border of the Belgian Congo had terminated. Inside that hut, a hut so strangely like a sanctuary— was Paul Kaputula, the disfigured African leper who for so long had been an Apostle to the Lamba people. Two thousand miles to the south I had received the disturbing news that the life of the revered leader was in danger, and I had fervently hoped that God would spare him. My prayer had been answered. My journey along the apparently endless roads had been worthwhile. The famous leper was in that hut. Stepping across the threshold, Dr. Doke said, "Twaisa"—We have come. A resonant voice replied, "Injileni"—Come ye in. And then a strange thing happened. I who had waited so long and travelled so far for the supreme purpose of entering that hut, was reluctant to cross the doorstep. . . . Beyond the door I saw a small room about six feet square, and completely devoid of furniture. The walls were made of mud bricks, and the floor was earth trampled hard . . . Dr. Doke stood in an inner doorway, and as I turned toward him, I discovered another room—a bedroom leading off from the apartment I had just entered. "This is Paul." As his pitiable stump of an arm touched his chest in the customary greeting of Lambaland, the leper said, "Mutende, Mutende." Accepting the chair which had been brought for me, I sat in the second doorway and listened as my friend conversed with his old mission boy. It was easy to recognize the affection shining in the eyes of the leper. Dr. Doke had been one of the pioneer missionaries who first took the Gospel to the people of Lambaland, and through his untiring efforts, the Word of God had been given to the people in their own language. . . . Here there was no Apartheid—no man-made barriers; here was real affection, for the eminent University Professor and the African leper were strangely and completely united in the love of Christ. My emotions were beginning to run riot, so I bit my lip—hard.

Paul sat on a low deck chair just inside the second door, and perhaps the darkness of the hut accounted for the fact that I first saw the white of his eyes. Then I saw the long narrow face and detected the evidence of the dread disease. The high cheek bones were rather too prominent; the eyes were kindly but piercing; but his huge leprous lips were out of all proportion to the rest of his face. His white shirt was torn at the collar, and his long khaki trousers effectively hid his toeless feet. I shuddered when I saw what once had been hands. They were just two horrifying stumps—black stumps with white marks where once fingers and thumbs had been. They were like two misshapen potatoes fastened to the end of long bony forearms. Paul was just a poor African leper, and yet nowhere in Lambaland did any man, black or white, command more respect. His hut was like a sanctuary . . . Dr. Doke ceased his conversation and indicated that I could ask my questions. . . . "Ask him which is his favourite Bible story?" I wondered what the answer would be, and half expected Paul to reply, "The story of the Cross." To my surprise he looked up, and without a smile, gravely said, "I like the story of the feeding of the five thousand." I was so completely surprised that I wanted to discuss the relative value of Bible stories. I was so certain that this eminent leader of the African church would have chosen the story of the death of the Saviour. How could he choose this in preference to the greatest of all stories? "Doctor," I whispered, "please ask him why he likes that one." Paul's swollen lips pouted for a brief moment; his poor arm rubbed his cheek-bone, and then he said : "I like that story because it's a parable of how God breaks up his mercy. There is some for every man who will take it." His answer was so deliberate; so dignified, so inspiring. . . .

Just over Paul's bed a small text hung on the wall. Every morning he looked at it, and constantly it supplied new courage. On it were the immortal words, "He is able to keep." I shall always remember how Paul looked at me and said, "When I think of Christ, and what He did, it helps me—it helps me—when, when I'm like this." And he lifted his two fingerless hands. . . .

## SECTION THREE

### *Expository Notes on Christ's Prediction of His Death*

**And it came to pass, as he was alone praying, his disciples were with him: and he asked them saying, Whom say the people that I am? They**

answering said, John the Baptist; but some say, Elias; and others say, that one of the old prophets is risen again. He said unto them, But whom say ye that I am? Peter answering said, The Christ of God. And he straightly charged them, and commanded them to tell no man that thing; Saying, The Son of man must suffer many things, and be rejected of the elders and chief priests and scribes, and be slain, and be raised the third day (vv. 18–22).

Verse ten of this chapter explains that Christ had taken His friends into a place of seclusion in the hope that they might rest and be refreshed. That purpose had been defeated when the crowd arrived to ask for healing. Nevertheless, and it is important that this should be remembered, although the project had temporarily been abandoned, the idea had not been forgotten. At the earliest possible moment, the Lord carried through to completion the plans made earlier. When unexpected demands upon our time take us from the place of prayer, we should return as quickly as possible to commune with the Father. Satan is far more anxious to keep us off our knees than he is to keep us off our feet! Let us remember that Luke set out to reveal Christ as the expression of perfect manhood. It was incumbent upon the author to explain how this high standard of moral excellence was maintained. Luke therefore was careful to emphasize that Jesus was a Man of prayer. When the constant demands of needy people drained His resources, Christ recharged His spiritual batteries by direct contact with Heaven's power house.

A careful examination of the synoptics reveals the fact that all three Evangelists recorded their versions of this conversation with Simon Peter, but the accounts vary. Matthew indisputably gives the most comprehensive version of the utterances of the Lord. Mark, and let it be remembered that he was the emanuensis of Simon Peter, gives some of the facts, but omits the more personal details connected with his great friend. Luke only mentions the mere framework of the conversation, and this has begotten much speculation and some criticism. Why did Luke omit so much from the conversation of Jesus and Simon Peter? To repeat what has just been said, Luke had a specific theme for his Gospel; he set out to portray Christ as the perfect Man, and it was to be expected that the material chosen for the manuscript would have some bearing upon the subject. There were many things which might have been written, but no man could write them all. The comments of Norval Geldenhuys are worthy of consideration; his explanation is among the best. "Out of many items of information, Luke produces only those which, under the guidance of the Spirit of God, he regards as the most important in composing his Gospel. We should remember that Luke could not make his writing unlimited in length—among other things he had to consider the question of not exceeding the limits of a normal papyrus roll. As it is, his Gospel is the longest book in the New Testament. So he used his space economically and recorded only the parts which were most necessary for his purpose" (*The New International Commentary on the New Testament. Luke*, p. 273).

Why did the Lord seek information from His followers? It could hardly have been that He was unaware of the opinions of the multitudes. The intimate contacts of the previous days afforded ample opportunities to gather the facts He required. Could it have been that this was a veiled way of helping the disciples to grow in grace; to express the faith which had been slowly developing. Simon, the accepted leader of the band at that time, impulsively expressed what they were all beginning to feel. Their Master was the Christ of God. It should never be forgotten that Simon Peter was a great man. The Protestant Church has made a great mistake in that it has allowed the teaching of the Roman Catholics to overshadow its thinking. It is true that Peter has been exalted to occupy realms that he himself would have rejected, for he who refused to have his feet washed by Jesus, would object more vehemently to having his big toe kissed by innumerable pilgrims to Rome. Nevertheless, we must remember that. *Peter was a great man*, and his confession to the Lord Jesus Christ clearly reveals that at that particular time, he was ahead of all others in his conception of the true identity of his Master.

John 6: 15 sheds light on the reason for the Saviour's prohibition. There existed real grounds for believing the crowds would insist on the Lord's coronation, and any premature move in that direction would have set the Roman legions against a defenceless population. In addition to this, the Lord's own ministry was by no means complete; much remained to be done. It was necessary to exercise care that impetuosity should not hinder the unfolding of God's plans. The Greek word *apodokimastheenai* is rather strong. It is used in verse 22 and is translated *to be rejected*. This word means *to test; to examine; to scrutinize; to recognize as genuine or fradulent after careful examination*. The ultimate rejection of Jesus would not be any hurried decision of misled men; it would be the cold calculated decision of those who considered carefully what they wanted to do. For such men in the day of judgment there will be no excuse. It is thrilling to note that even at this early part of the Lord's ministry, the end was never for a moment in doubt. He saw the Cross, and beyond it, the glory of the sunrise.

And he said to them all, If any man will come after me, let him deny himself, and take up his cross daily, and follow me. For whosoever will save his life shall lose it; but whosoever will lose his life for my

sake, the same shall save it. For what is a man advantaged, if he gain
the whole world, and lose himself, or be cast away? For whosoever
shall be ashamed of me and of my words, of him shall the Son of man
be ashamed, when he shall come in his own glory, and in his Father's,
and of the holy angels (vv. 23-26).

Crucifixion was the type of execution used by the Romans, and
whenever a man was condemned to this kind of death, he was compelled by law to carry his own cross to the place of execution. The
word translated *let him deny* is *aparneesastho* and this is a very strong
expression. Used with the *heauton* it means *to deny oneself; to forget
or lose sight of one's self; to forget that one exists.* If this is the standard
of discipleship, we need to learn the principles of our faith anew.
There are three things a man may do with the Cross. First, if his vision
be sufficiently keen, *he may believe on it.* Secondly, if his heart be
stout enough, *he may carry it.* Finally, if his soul be truly dedicated,
*he may die on it.* The original cross was not a sombre ornament to
sanctify a building; it was something to be stained by blood. Unfortunately, many believers endeavour to see its beauty but shrink from
its cutting edge. The cross challenges our self life and destroys that
which is carnal. The cross is the avowed enemy of selfishness and
pride; it is God's weapon of destruction. *Believing on the Cross* leads
to salvation. *Carrying the Cross* brings shame. *Dying upon the Cross*
produces sanctification, for then we are like Christ. Stage one secures
entrance into God's school; stage two indicates we are proceeding with
our lessons; stage three is graduation. Unless, with Paul, we can say,
"I die daily," we are still in the kindergarten.

There are those who prefer to save their lives in the sense that they
desire to retain their time, their talents, their possessions. To do this
is to lose them, for only what is truly given to Christ endures. What
we give to Him we keep forever. That which we refuse to give, we
eventually lose forever. The fact that Christ spoke of the grim possibility of losing one's soul proves this is possible. If all men are to be
saved, why speak about the possibility of the eternal tragedy? Verse
twenty-six reveals three kinds of glory. The glory of the Father; the
Glory of the Son; the Glory of the holy angels. The simple Greek word
translated *glory* is in itself most colourful. It is a diamond with many
facets. Its shades of meaning are expressed by such words as: praise;
honour; glory; magnificence; pre-eminence; dignity, grace. It is one
of the windows through which the revelation of God shines upon us.
(1) The Glory of the Father is something which in all probability we
cannot fully comprehend. Paul said, "I give thee charge in the sight
of God . . . Who only hath immortality, dwelling in the light which no
man can approach unto; whom no man hath seen, nor can see, to whom

be honour and power everlasting" (I Timothy 1 : 16). Even the most elementary study of the firmament with its billions of fiery planets makes one gasp with awe and wonder; yet all this, and much more, was made by God, for "In the beginning God created the heaven and the earth." The Glory of God is surpassing excellence in the absolute, and yet it belongs to Christ. When He returns to this earth, the praise, the excellence, the pre-eminence of the Godhead will be shining from His resplendent face. (2) The Glory of the Son possibly refers to another phase of His excellence—a glory acquired, for when He had finished the work which God gave Him to do, when He ascended again to the place from which He had come, "God crowned Him with glory and honour." Then, the excellence of creation was wedded to the glory of redemption, and the offspring of this was translucent radiance which thrilled the eternal world. Although Christ was the Lamb slain from before the foundation of the world, He was not always the Man of Calvary—except in the mind of God. When the purposes of God were fulfilled upon the green hill, that which had been a hope, a yearning, was now an actual reality. (3) The Glory of the Angels might well express the unanimous approbation of the angelic hosts. They who had been witnesses of His glory from the first; they who had watched every phase of the unfolding drama both in heaven and on earth, could and would testify to the eternal majesty of Him whom they delighted to own as King. When Christ returns, all men will honour His Name; sing His praise, and do His will.

**But I tell you of a truth, there be some standing here, which shall not taste of death, till they see the kingdom of God (v. 27).**

This verse has caused a great deal of discussion, and many have been the interpretations offered to the church. Bishop Ryle says: "These words are interpreted two ways. Some think that they mean 'They shall not die until they see the Church of Christ established and settled on earth'. This is a very unsatisfactory explanation. The right view appears to be that which connects the verse with the transfiguration, and regards the glorious vision of the kingdom, which the transfiguration supplied, as the fulfilment of the promise of this verse. This is the view of Jerome, Hilary, Chrysostom, Theophylact, and many more." Bishop Ryle was an eminent scholar and a great theologian, but one wonders if his view is truly compatible with Scripture. The term *geusontai thanatou—taste of death* is a most interesting expression and it is used at least three times in the New Testament (Luke 9: 27; Hebrews 2: 9; John 8: 52). It refers to that experience when the soul is separated from God. It also expresses what Christ endured to bring men to God, and finally announces the glad relief known by all Christians when through faith in Christ they are saved for ever. For further details of this great truth see the homily "The Nastiest Taste in the World." This is found in my commentary, *John's Wonderful Gospel*, page 194.

## SECTION FOUR

### *Expository Notes on the Transfiguration of the Lord*

And it came to pass about eight days after these sayings, he took Peter and John and James, and went up into a mountain to pray. And as he prayed, the fashion of his countenance was altered, and his raiment was white and glistening. And behold there talked with him two men, which were Moses and Elias: Who appeared in glory, and spake of his decease which he should accomplish at Jerusalem (vv. 28-31).

Matthew and Mark (17: 1 and 9: 2) are more precise in regard to the time lapse between the Lord's earlier statements and this great event. They state that the transfiguration took place six days after the Lord's predictions; Luke is content to be approximate in his estimate of the days which had intervened. Possibly he counted the day when Christ delivered His message, and also the first day in the mountain. Many theologians endeavour to identify the mountain upon which this event took place but there is no authoritative information on the subject. Certain commentators cite Mount Tabor but this has been refuted by Godet who says: "The summit of Mount Tabor was at that time, as Robinson has proved, occupied by a fortified town, which would scarcely agree with the tranquillity which Jesus sought." Others think the event took place on Mount Hermon, but the distance between this mountain and the place from which Jesus commenced His journey seems to offer certain problems. The point is not important.

This was one of the occasions where for reasons best known to Himself the Lord chose to take only three disciples into the hill. The same men accompanied Him on two other missions (Luke 8: 51; Matthew 26: 37). Did the Lord actually choose these men to become His most intimate associates, or did they exhibit an interest in advance of their colleagues? Was this an endeavour to provide special training for men who were destined to become leaders in the field of evangelism, or was it the spontaneous expression of a love which yearned to be as near as possible to the Master at all times? Here is food for thought, for whatever the reason, the fact remains that many modern disciples appear to miss the greatest experiences of the Christian life.

As the Lord continued in prayer, His appearance was changed and even His garments shone with unearthly splendour. The force of the Greek word suggests the flashing brilliance of lightning, and for awhile it must have appeared as if His body had put on the scintillating garments of immortality. When Moses and Elias came to converse with Him, the disciples thought the kingdom was at hand. This was the greatest moment they had ever known, and in the absorbing wonder which filled and thrilled their hearts, anything might have been possible. Momentarily Heaven ceased to be far away; it had come to earth. This was the reason why Peter would have gladly stayed on the mountain forever. Throughout the Lord's sojourn upon earth, the glory of divine kingship had remained hidden beneath human tissue. A body had been prepared for the Eternal Son, and this frail barrier of flesh had hidden the effulgence of His other nature. Yet, when the penetrating light of the eternal shone down upon Him, the hidden suddenly became visible, and the disciples saw the clear shining glory of the matchless Son of God.

In view of the fact that soon after the episode had ended, the journey back into the valley commenced, it would appear that the disciples had slept for most of the night. They had been *"oppressed; bowed down with sleep; overcome by fatigue;"* they had struggled to keep their eyes open, but had succumbed to weakness. We may never know therefore all that happened on that occasion. Yet it is a cause for praise, that they awakened in time to see what was afterward recorded. It is necessary to consider this scripture under four heads. (1) *There is life beyond the grave.* Critics have said the transfiguration was a dream or a nightmare which troubled the sleep of the weary men; but the independence of the various narratives outlaws the suggestion. Moses represented the *Law,* Elias represented the *Prophets,* and both these agencies had witnessed to the coming of the Messiah. Those who had spoken of Him in bygone ages were now speaking face to face; if the disciples needed confirmation that their Master was the fulfilment of the prophetic promise, the appearance of these men provided what was necessary. He who had died, and he who had been caught up into the clouds, were present with the Lord in Glory. This surely was a type of that other great event described by Paul in I Thessalonians 4:16-17: "For the Lord himself shall descend from heaven with a shout, with the voice of the archangel, and with the trump of God; and *the dead in Christ* shall rise first: Then *we which are alive* and remain *shall be caught up together with them in the clouds,* to meet the Lord in the air: and so shall we ever be with the Lord."

(2) *There is intelligent life beyond the grave.* These visitors from the other world were able to speak, to move, to converse with Christ concerning the future. We are not given precise details as to the nature of their remarks; we know only that they discussed "the Lord's exodus which He should accomplish at Jerusalem." The word trans-

lated *accomplished* reveals that the death to take place in Jerusalem would not be a succumbing to natural weakness; the result of any accident or unexpected catastrophe. This was a part of the plans of God; *this was something to be done.* It could not be accomplished without purpose and effort. The representatives of the earlier ages were aware of the nature of Christ's mission to earth. The doctrine of *soul sleep* as taught by certain movements cannot be supported from Scripture.

(3) *There is glorious life beyond the grave.* It is true that Moses had died and had been buried by God (Deuteronomy 34: 6), but on the Mount of Transfiguration this man appeared in glory; that is, his mortal had put on the garments of immortality. Elijah had been carried to Heaven in a chariot of splendour. Probably he had been changed in a moment, in the twinkling of an eye, but he too was living in the power of an endless life. We have not been told how the disciples recognized the Patriarchs. Perhaps the identity of Moses and Elias was revealed to the watchers by revelation, or maybe something was said by Christ which enabled the listening disciples to identify the Lord's companions. Charles Haddon Spurgeon was once asked if Christians would be able to recognize each other in heaven. His answer was somewhat startling, "Madam, do you think we shall be bigger fools up there than we are down here?"

(4) *There is useful life beyond the grave.* We cannot be expected to know all that was said during the conversation in the mountain. Were Moses and Elias learning of Christ, encouraging Christ; or even carrying some message to Him? One thing is beyond doubt. Their coming to earth was essential or they would not have been sent. They were speaking with Christ concerning His exodus—this might have been exclusively confined to His death or it might have embraced His resurrection and ascension from the Mount of Olives. The "going out of" this world might be either one of these. In any case, the ancients were probably ministering to the Lord in some way or another. The old idea of saints playing harps throughout eternity has long since been discarded. The eternal world will be a place of progress, and whilst at present our finite minds may be unable to conceive of what might transpire in the Hereafter, we may be assured our interests will revolve around the person of the Christ, without whom we would never be there.

**But Peter and they that were with him were heavy with sleep; and when they were awake, they saw his glory, and the two men that stood with him. And it came to pass that as they departed from him, Peter said unto Jesus, Master, it is good for us to be here: and let us make three tabernacles; one for thee, and one for Moses . . . and one for**

**Elias: not knowing what he said. While he thus spake, there came a cloud, and overshadowed them: and they feared as they entered into the cloud (vv. 32–34).**

See the special homily at the end of this section. It must be remembered that the transfiguration of the Lord took place after the Saviour's remarks concerning the crucifixion. If the watching disciples were able to follow the conversation regarding the exodus to be accomplished in Jerusalem, they would have been reminded of the Lord's earlier message. Moses and Elias were beginning to withdraw when Peter's sincere but irresponsible outburst revealed he preferred the glory of the mountain to the blood of the cross. "Lord, let us stay here, all three of us, and we can be your servants forever." In saner moments, even Peter would have deplored the sentiments. Momentarily the need of the people in the valley had been forgotten. Peter thought only of self. It was then that the cloud cast a shadow over the disciples' face. Momentarily the radiance had subsided as though God had ceased to smile.

**And there came a voice out of the cloud saying, This is my beloved Son: hear him. And when the voice was past, Jesus was found alone. And they kept it close, and told no man in those days any of those things which they had seen (vv. 35–36).**

This was the second time God witnessed from heaven concerning His Son. After the baptism in the Jordan, God witnessed to the purity of His Son by saying, "This is my beloved Son, in whom I am well pleased" (Matthew 3: 17). At that point in the ministry of Jesus, this was all that was necessary. The preaching of Jesus had never been challenged, for the Lord's experiences had more or less been limited to Nazareth. At this later date much had happened. The Saviour had announced His doctrines in many places and the antagonism of the hierarchy had been aroused. There were those who vehemently denied His teachings; there were some who accused Him of being in league with the prince of demons. The time had therefore come for God to endorse the utterances of His Son, and this He did when He spoke at the transfiguration. Jesus was THE WORD—that is, the *vehicle of expression* used by God, for "God, who at sundry times and in divers manners spake in time past unto the fathers by the prophets, Hath in these last days spoken unto us by his Son . . ." (Hebrews 1: 1). Bishop Ryle thinks this refers to the prophecy of Moses, *"Unto him shall ye hearken"* (Deuteronomy 18: 15). Calvin says, "We are placed under His tuition alone, and commanded from Him alone to seek the doctrine of salvation, to depend upon, and to listen to One—to adhere to One—in a word, as the terms import, to hearken to ONE only."

It is worthy of note that the word of Christ now superseded the commandments of Moses. The disciples were commanded to listen to Christ and not primarily to deepen their studies of the written law. However, let us be careful to remember that this was not meant to infer that the laws of Moses were wrong, or that God had changed His mind and altered His opinions from those of former ages. The law was good; the word of Christ was better. The law brought students to God's school, but within that school, Jesus was head teacher! Moses through the medium of his doctrines was able to initiate believers into the realms of God's will. Where the law fell short, the teaching of Christ was available to help students graduate. God said, HEAR YE HIM, and by this one tremendous utterance, He forever endorsed what His Son was about to say to a needy world. Mark 9: 9 explains why the disciples did not immediately broadcast the news of the event in the mountain. The Lord indisputably had His reasons for commanding the disciples to remain silent about the transfiguration. Unbelievers would have ridiculed the whole affair.

## HOMILIES

Study No. 31

### SLEEPING SICKNESS

"But Peter and they that were with him were heavy with sleep: and when they were awake, they saw his glory . . ." (Luke 9: 32). There are three instances of sleeping disciples mentioned in the New Testament, and in each case the time spent in slumber proved to be exceeding costly. When the Lord Jesus led His faithful followers into the Mount of Transfiguration they did not realize what amazing events were about to take place. Determined to remain with Him during the night watches, they sat upon the ground and were soon asleep. That they awakened just in time to see a transfigured Lord, and then to accompany Him into the valley seems to suggest they had slept for most of the night. We shall never know how much they missed.

*They slept and missed His Glory*

"*When they were awake, they saw his glory*, and the two men that stood with him." Their brief vision left such an indelible impression upon their memories that even after thirty years the apostle Peter wrote, "We were with Him in the Holy Mount" (II Peter 1: 18). The disciples never forgot the soul-stirring vision of the face that shone as the sun, and the garments which were white and glistening. They

remembered how God said, "This is my beloved Son: hear him."
With awe and amazement they recalled how "Moses and Elias spake
of the decease which he should accomplish at Jerusalem," and probably speculated as to the reason why both the Law and the Prophets
were so informed of the Messiah's death. The glory of that resplendent
scene was indescribable. Radiance emanated from their beloved
Master, and He seemed more like the King of Angels than the hero
of poor fishermen. All this happened just prior to the dawn, and we
are obliged to ask what untold revelations might have been theirs
had they remained awake and watchful. Perhaps their slumbers
accounted for their subsequent defeat in the valley.

*They slept and missed His Passion*

There was a strange and eerie silence in the garden of Gethsemane
on the night when Jesus was betrayed. The stillness preceding the
breaking of the storm only accentuated the heartbreaks of the Lord
Jesus. Fully conscious of His great need, He temporarily withdrew
from the crowds and, accompanied by three disciples, "went, as he
was wont, up to the mount of Olives . . . and being in an agony he
prayed more earnestly: and his sweat was as it were great drops of
blood falling down to the ground. And when he rose up from prayer,
and was come to his disciples, he found them sleeping from sorrow"
(Luke 22: 39–45). If these men were sleeping, who witnessed the
sufferings of Christ? Possibly one of the men who had been left outside the garden became a little impatient and came in search of his
friends. If this happened, then he arrived in time to witness the
indescribable. The love of God's heart was overflowing, and the
streams of compassion were reaching out to earth's remotest end. Yet
if the disciples had remained awake during those moments of agonizing conflict, their appreciation of the price paid for our redemption
might have increased immeasurably. Their sleep in the garden preceded the fear that made them forsake their Lord.

*They slept and missed Eternal Joys*

When the disciples asked for signs of the Lord's return, He described
ten virgins going forth in anticipation of a wedding (Matthew 25:
1–13). While the bridegroom tarried they all slumbered and slept, but
when the cry went forth, "Behold, the bridegroom cometh," they arose
immediately and went forth to meet him. Thereafter five foolish virgins
became aware of their great need, and while they vainly endeavoured
to prepare for the future, their moment of opportunity passed by. The
five wise virgins entered into the marriage, and had great joy in the
presence of the bridegroom. Yet each one of the five should have been
accompanied by a convert! The Lord Jesus cited this as an indica-

tion of conditions to exist in the world prior to His return. Souls would be perishing while Christendom remained inactive and sleepy. His word has been fulfilled. "Watch therefore, for in such an hour . . . the Son of man cometh."

SECTION FIVE

*Expository Notes about the Events in the Valley*

**And it came to pass, that on the next day, when they were come down from the hill, much people met him. And, behold a man of the company cried out saying, Master, I beseech thee, look upon my son: for he is mine only child. And, lo, a spirit taketh him, and he suddenly crieth out; and it teareth him that he foameth again, and bruising him hardly departeth from him. And I besought thy disciples to cast him out; and they could not (vv. 37-40).**

The word used by Matthew to describe the state of the unfortunate son is *seleeniazetai* which means to be *moonstruck; to be lunatic;* to be *epileptic.* It would appear as if this malady afflicted the lad each time the moon approached its fulness. The ever-recurring tragedy had driven the father to the point of despair and his deepening distress brought him as a suppliant to the men whose healing of the sick was now being discussed throughout the land. It was a well-known fact that on a recent missionary journey they had healed the sick; this begat hope within the man's breast that what they had done for others, they might do for him. Alas, their impotence became apparent when their prayers failed to deliver the youthful sufferer. The sudden appearance of the Saviour came at a most opportune moment, for the man instead of villifying the helpless disciples brought a new request to Christ. It has always been better to look hopefully to Jesus than to gaze critically at His followers.

**And Jesus answering said, O faithless and perverse generation, how long shall I be with you, and suffer you? Bring thy son hither. And as he was yet a coming, the devil threw him down, and tare him. And Jesus rebuked the unclean spirit, and healed the child, and delivered him again to his father. And they were all amazed at the mighty power of God (vv. 41-43).**

Godet reminds us that "The severe exclamation of Jesus: *faithless and perverse generation,* etc., has been applied to the disciples (Meyer); to the scribes (Calvin); to the father, (Chrysostom, Grotius, Neander, De Wette); to the people, (Olshausen)." Some of these suggestions are not in harmony with the text. There is a sense in which we are all lacking in faith, but the most likely interpretation of this utterance is that Jesus confronted with this great need sighed, looked sadly at the religious world represented by the people standing around, and then said: "Oh faithless—O people without faith—if only your power from God could equal your knowledge about God, no father would ever need to bring such a boy to my feet." It is not without interest that Luke, the doctor, the man who would have been quite conversant with epilepsy and similar maladies insisted in describing this case as one of demon possession. At least in this instance, Luke was convinced that behind the infirmity lay the crippling power of evil. Yet Christ was equal to the sinister challenge, for having dismissed the evil occupant of the youthful body, He healed the boy and delivered the lad to a grateful parent. Luke seemed to find interest in the fact that the widow at Nain had *one only* son (Luke 7: 12); Jairus had *one only* daughter (Luke 8: 42); this man had *one only* child (Luke 9: 38). He who was the only Son of God knew what an only child meant to a father. It is thought-provoking to remember that although He hastened to help the suffering parents, when His own time came, there was none to help. God the sorrowing Father in Heaven, and Christ, the only Son, bore the burden alone, and yet they were not alone, for "God was in Christ reconciling the world unto himself." *They were all amazed at the mighty power of God.* How near can a man get to the kingdom of God and yet be lost? These people saw, heard, and marvelled, and yet some of them ultimately rejected the Saviour. When the day of judgment dawns they will be without excuse.

> But while they wondered every one at all things which Jesus did, he said unto his disciples, Let these sayings sink down into your ears: for the Son of man shall be delivered into the hands of men. But they understood not this saying, and it was hid from them, that they perceived it not; and they feared to ask him of that saying (vv. 43–45).

Some of the greatest lessons in God's school are learned slowly! Each new demonstration of the power of Christ increased the fervent expectation that the establishing of the kingdom was imminent. Neither the oft-repeated instruction of Christ, nor the sombre lessons from the mount succeeded in making an impact on the preconceived ideas of the disciples. They looked for the coming of the kingdom and anything opposed to that idea was unwelcome. There are none so blind as the people who have no wish to see, and none so limited in vision as those whose eyes are focused on one spot. Their reluctance to discuss the subject might be explained by their fear that He might rebuke them for being poor listeners, or by the horror of having to listen to something they thought better left unsaid.

> Then there arose a reasoning among them, which of them should be greatest. And Jesus, perceiving the thought of their heart, took a child,

and set him by him. And said unto them, whosoever receiveth this child in my name, receiveth me, and whosoever receiveth me, receiveth him that sent me: for he that is least among you all, the same shall be great (vv. 46-48).

The complete story of the events leading to this episode can only be obtained when the three Gospels are considered together. During the journey to Capernaum, the disciples had argued as to who should be the greatest in the coming kingdom. The argument had been somewhat heated, and finally on reaching their destination the disciples brought their question to Jesus. They did not confess that they had been quarrelling; they merely asked their question, "Who is the greatest in the kingdom of heaven?" Then, or at least soon afterward, Jesus replied with a question of His own, "What was it that ye disputed among yourselves by the way?" When guilt filled their souls, they failed to supply an answer. Then the Lord set a small child in their midst and proceeded to give His object lesson (Compare Matthew 18: 1-6; Mark 9: 33-37; Luke 9: 46-48). It is necessary to recognize and admit the folly of the disciples, and yet when viewed from another angle there is something wonderfully comforting about this scripture. These men were truly human and were "subject to like passions as we are." How stimulating to remember the Lord did not choose angels, nor even men with a flawless record, to carry out His purposes on earth; He chose ordinary men who made the same mistakes that we make; they could be jealous; argumentative; self-seeking; ambitious; proud; but the Lord was patient with them. He rebuked and chastened them, but never abandoned them. To Him they were as little children, and with great affection He watched their development. "He knoweth our frame and remembereth that we are dust." "His mercy is from everlasting to everlasting upon them that fear Him." The Lord set a small child in the midst of these big men and proceeded to explain that greatness is dependent upon humility. He who learns how to be nothing will surely be something! He who would rule others must first rule himself. When men become angry about anything, they prove they are smaller than the thing which upset them. Dependability is more to be desired than talent; the grace of humility is infinitely above boastful self-confidence.

> Oh to be nothing, nothing!
>     Simply to lie at His feet:
> An emptied and broken vessel
>     For the Master's use made meet.
> Emptied that He might fill me
>     As forth to His service I go;
> Broken that so unhindered
>     His life through me might flow.

And John answered and said, Master, we saw one casting out devils in thy name; and we forbad him, because he followeth not with us. And Jesus said unto him, Forbid him not: for he that is not against us is for us (vv. 49–50).

There is some doubt as to the proper reading of this text, and it is extremely difficult to be dogmatic in regard to interpretation. Mark and Luke use the aorist tense of the verb, that is *ekolusamen,* denoting something completed in the past. This would mean that when the disciples found this man casting out demons in the name of their Master, they rebuked him, and told him to cease. He had no right to work in the name of One whom he did not follow. However, some manuscripts have the imperfect tense of the verb *ekoluomen,* "We were forbidding him, and thought we were doing right; were we wrong?" If this version be correct, then the passage would indeed follow on the episode of the child. John having heard the discourse about humility suddenly remembered the arrogance with which the stranger had been denounced. Meyer says, "Outside the circle of the permanent disciples of Jesus were men in whom His words and works had called forth a higher and miraculous power; these sparks, which fell beyond the circle of His disciples, had made flames burst forth here and there away from the central fire." At first the disciples had challenged the right of any man to use power which had been usurped. Why should men attract to themselves praise which belonged to Christ? If this unknown exorcist wished to serve the Christ in this fashion he should align himself with the orthodox band of disciples, and shoulder some of the responsibilities of the disciple family. This freelance evangelism had not been sanctioned, therefore he should cease his endeavours until he had obtained an official permit from the right office! There exists the possibility that afterwards, John wondered if indeed the disciples themselves had been in greater error than the stranger.

The kingdom of God is always bigger than the men who represent it. God's family is as broad as His heart, but in that family are strange children. Alas, the family of God is divided into well-defined camps and between them are barbed-wire fences of separation. Both colour and creed have become insuperable barriers. We proclaim that all men in Christ are our brethren but we treat them as strangers; we love the glorious Gospel but doubt whether any other church can really do justice to its message. There are meetings where strangers are unwelcome unless they carry a letter of introduction. There are places where it is far harder to reach the communion table than it is to reach the heart of God. There are men who should be skilled in bringing others to Christ, but they spend all their time decapitating their brethren. This is wrong; this is not Christlike; this is a sad throwback to the text under consideration. It should be constantly remembered that it is far easier to preach the Cross than to die on it!

## HOMILIES

Study No. 32

### LITTLE GIANTS

God is the God of little things! Nevertheless it is almost incomprehensible that He who is so great can become attached to small things. Man makes huge sugar mills, but God made bees! Man with his ever-increasing desire for fragrance makes ornate perfume factories, but God planted flowers! Communities organize and finance operatic and philharmonic societies, God created birds. Little things can be tremendous. Man has rare vision and through the aid offered by high-powered telescopes now studies the planets, yet one speck of dust in his eye, and the planets become invisible. Man is a genius. His creative skill brings into being immense structures and the most unbelievable creations, yet one germ fells the giant, and he who might have conquered the world suddenly leaves it. Humans make bulldozers to demolish and destroy; God made ants—particularly white ants, and left alone, these tiny things destroy palaces. Yes, God is the God of little things. It is true that He made the universe, the far-flung heavens, the innumerable planets, the countless stars, but He made them out of atoms! In some senses the acorn is greater than the mighty oak, for without it, the oak would never exist. Similarly, the greatest preachers grew from childhood, and all this might be reflected in the ancient utterance. "Bring up a child in the way he should go, and when he is old, he will not depart from thee."

*Be like this child—trusting*

Perhaps the most satisfying thing in a normal, healthy child is the trusting devotion he exhibits for his father. Dad is the greatest; dad can do anything. He is so big that he reaches to the sky; he is so small, he can kneel on the rug to play with his child. He can tell stories, play cowboys and Indians; shoot, hunt, fish, and play ball better than anyone else. No journey is too dangerous as long as Dad is there; no task too great as long as he offers help. Impossibilities do not exist when he is about, and if somebody contradicts these things, the little child argues to the end that they are so. This childlike veneration is born of simple faith; it promotes a trust that endures to the end. If only our Heavenly Father could occupy such a place in the centre of our affection.

*Be like this child—innocent*

Unfortunately this characteristic has a short life, for a child is quicker at acquiring evil than learning his lessons. Firmly implanted within the fertile soil of his young heart are seeds which are destined to germinate in record time. His selflessness will soon become tainted; his pure, lovely guilelessness will soon be marred; he will become selfish, peeved; prone to tantrums. Yet in the early days he knows nothing of the moral smogs destined to invade his soul. He is unaware of the unpleasantness of the world into which he has come. His little soul is clean, sweet, and wholesome. He has no desire to abuse that which is good; he has not become a slave to money, for give it to him, and he will probably chuckle with glee as he throws it away. Alas, all this is to change, and sometimes the most adorable child becomes the most disagreeable man. If only adults could preserve the innocence of youth, and be "perfect even as their father in heaven is perfect."

*Be like this child—anxious to learn*

No child knows everything! The child goes to school to learn, but even before that auspicious day arrives, the baby, one syllable at a time, learns from its mother how to say small words and understand those words when they are spoken. To the ever-opening mind of a boy or a girl the whole world is waiting to be discovered; and each day reveals a path into the unknown. He may never climb the highest mountains, but meanwhile he is climbing the mountainous obstacles confronting him within his lessons. To grown people these are insignificant things but men and women would do well to carry these characteristics into the world they occupy. Even a home can become a class-room, and every day can be a journey with God into a new world. "Learn of me," was one of the most important things ever uttered by the Saviour, but unfortunately, and so unlike the child, we often think we know everything. Some are even reluctant to learn anything from Christ lest their knowledge lead to further employment!

*Be like this child—respond when I call you*

When the Lord took the child and placed him in the midst of the disciples, the lad did not complain, stating he wished to play with other children. Many modern children would not even have been there to hear the Master's call! Life, even for children is so regimented, from the kindergarten to the grave, time is at a premium. This child responded, and remained at the Saviour's side as long as Christ desired that he should be there. Jesus made the youngster the subject of a sermon which became immortal. Unfortunately, the Lord was never able to take a man or a woman, and then to say to others, "Be like this one." It might help preachers to remember that God used the testimony of a sweet maid from Israel to bring cleansing to one of the greatest men in Syria (II Kings 5: 2–3). God made an unwanted boy the saviour of the world (Genesis 37: 23–28). When the prophet Samuel went to Bethlehem to find a king for Israel, he never succeeded until an almost forgotten lad was brought from the fields. The child was David (I Samuel 16: 4–12). And what more needs to be said? The Lord used the willingness of a lad to feed thousands of people; the Lord used a boy's testimony to save the life of his uncle, Paul, and all through the ages, God has demonstrated again and again that He is the God of little things. Someone has said that a Cross is nothing but an "I" crossed out! A man is never quite as secure as in the moments when desperation makes him cling to the outstretched hand of God; a Christian is never as effective as in the moments when his sense of inadequacy makes him depend completely upon the sufficiency of His Lord.

## SECTION SIX

### Expository Notes about the Journey to Jerusalem

And it came to pass, when the time was come that he should be received up, he steadfastly set his face to go to Jerusalem, And sent messengers before his face: and they went and entered into a village of the Samaritans to make ready for him. And they did not receive him, because his face was as though he would go to Jerusalem (vv. 51–53).

The feud between the Samaritans and the Jews dated back many centuries. Any student wishing to know more of this bitterness should read II Kings 17 and Ezra 4. The conflict had reached serious proportions during our Lord's life and this is indicated by the text. Jesus was no stranger to the Samaritans (see John 4: 39–41), but He was only popular to the Samaritan masses as long as He appeared to be their prophet. The itinerary to Jerusalem necessitated special preparations. Accommodation had to be sought, and provisions provided, and it was for this purpose the Lord sent disciples ahead with the instructions to what was required. Goodness was sacrificed upon the altar of prejudice; sick people remained sick, and dying people died because of the short-sighted stupidity of folk who only thought of self. And yet it is extremely difficult to think of these people without seeing the same situation as it is today. It must be a real grief to the Saviour that there exists churches professedly evangelical and sound in doctrine who reject any child of God from a convention other than their own. If the entire church of Christ had been united in the bonds of love, hell would have been subdued long ago; alas, quarrelsome Christians provide entertainment for the devil. The Lord had steadfastly set His face toward Jerusalem; that is, He had firmly made up His mind that nothing should prevent His going to the Cross. The time was coming when He would be received up; that is, when through the Cross and the resurrection He would triumphantly enter into the presence of His Father. On many occasions, He had recognized that "his hour had not yet come." Now the hour was at hand, and the Saviour would permit nothing to turn Him from the appointed journey.

And when his disciples James and John saw this, they said, Lord, wilt thou that we command fire to come down from heaven, and consume them, even as Elias did? But he turned and rebuked them, and said, Ye know not what manner of spirit ye are of. For the Son of man is not come to destroy men's lives, but to save them. And they went to another village (vv. 54–56).

It must be inferred from the test that these two disciples were not among the men who had received the chilling reception in the village of the Samaritans. As ever, they had stayed near the Master, and only heard the news when the Lord and the rest of the band overtook the others who had tried in vain to secure accommodation. The fiery outburst of James and John revealed they were indeed "sons of thunder." This zeal for Christ was out of all proportion to the demands of the occasion; they were exceedingly good Bible students but disappointing saints. They remembered the exploits of the prophet Elijah but remained partially ignorant of the love of their Lord. How marvellous it is to be able to relate that this man whose wrath could have destroyed the people of Samaria, later returned to their towns to preach the glorious Gospel of God's grace (Acts 8: 14). It is wise to remember that in the event of one place refusing to accept the message, there is always "another village." Nothing can ever excuse the unemployment of God's chosen vessels.

And it came to pass that as they went in the way, a certain man said unto him, Lord, I will follow thee whithersoever thou goest. And Jesus said unto him, Foxes have holes, and the birds of the air have nests; but the Son of man hath not where to lay his head. And he said unto another, Follow me. But he said, Lord, suffer me first to go and bury my father. Jesus said unto him, Let the dead bury their dead: but go thou and preach the kingdom of God. And another also said, Lord I will follow thee, but let me first go bid them farewell, which are at home at my house. And Jesus said unto him, No man, having put his hand to the plough, and looking back, is fit for the kingdom of God (vv. 57–62).

There has been much discussion about the time of these events for Matthew also cites two of these interviews. The first Gospel places these at a different time in the Lord's ministry (Matthew 8: 19–22). It should be remembered that Luke is portraying a theme, and deliberately groups certain incidents. Here, for example, he places incidents together which relate to discipleship; in chapter fifteen, as we shall see eventually, he groups parables because they all have something to contribute to the theme under discussion. The beginning of Luke's ninth chapter cites the sending out of the twelve disciples to preach; the beginning of the tenth chapter cites the sending out of the seventy on a similar mission. This group of incidents is sandwiched between the two, probably to indicate the kind of men that made true disciples. Matthew reveals that the first man was a scribe. Probably he listened to the Lord's messages and had witnessed certain miracles. Finally overwhelmed with enthusiasm he approached the Master to make a spontaneous declaration of faith. Such a convert would make the modern preachers delirious with joy, but Jesus with sombre reflection gazed at the man and realized his faith was shallow. True conversion is not merely an oral confession of Christ, nor the coming forward to avow allegiance at some special moment of soul elation. True conversion is the embracing of a new way of life; it signifies not the acceptance of a glittering uniform, but a readiness to go forth to battle. The great tragedy of modern missions is that under the sway of eloquent speakers crowds of people surge forward to confess publicly their willingness to become soldiers of Christ, yet within a few days, those same people disappear. They welcome the publicity; they even rejoice in the evangel, but ultimately shirk the true responsibilities of discipleship. When they discover that following Christ means participation in His work; identification with His task; growing in grace through the ordinances of the church; the financial support of similar missions to reach other souls; the joys of tithing income; the glorious privilege of sharing fellowship at a prayer meeting; they hesitate, make excuses, and finally disappear. These people attend all the crusade meetings, but it is doubtful if they ever carry the cross. The scribe mentioned was of this type. His confession indicated he was ready to go anywhere, but when the Preacher explained the meaning of discipleship, a disappointing silence fell on the scene. It is not said that he refused to co-operate; neither is it said that he followed to become one of the seventy. We may be sure the words of the Lord revealed to the man that discipleship was infinitely more than a picnic on the way to heaven. Jesus said, "Foxes have holes, and the birds of the air have nests; but the Son of man hath not where to lay his head." The Greek word translated *nests* is *kataskeenoseis*; it is an interesting expression meaning to pitch one's tent; to encamp; to tarry; to dwell; the haunt of birds, etc., etc. The other word *kataskizo* means *to overshadow; to cover with shade.* This accounts for the fact that F. L. Godet declares this utterance of Jesus *"denotes shelter under foliage as opposed to holes in the earth."* Even the foxes and the birds had places which they could recognize as home; that is they had a permanent place of rest to which they could retire; it was indeed their own habitation, but in this respect, Jesus had none. The Bedouins had tents which could be moved from one place to another; He had nothing. Discipleship meant loneliness, frustration, poverty, pain, and any man desirous of becoming a follower of Christ needed to count the cost ere he embarked on the venture.

There appears to be a great difference between the first two men. The former was exuberant; nothing would hold him back; he would follow Christ anywhere! The second man was sombre, unemotional, rigid. He needed that someone should help him, talk to him, encourage him. Therefore Jesus took the initiative and called him. It should be remembered that the Lord had no set way of dealing with people; He took a man as He found him, and assessing the individual's temperament, dealt with him accordingly. The reply, "Lord suffer me first to go and bury my father" has begotten much comment. Throughout the East it was the recognized duty of the first-born to be responsible for the burial of the father. Probably the old man was not even sick, but the age-old custom provided the ready excuse whereby the son could avoid a direct refusal of Christ's invitation. He was playing for time, feeling that when the old man had succumbed to the ravages of age, Jesus would be far away. Had the parent been dead, the son would hardly have been spending time listening to an itinerant Preacher; he would have been home attending to the funeral arrangements. Climatic conditions of Eastern countries demand that funerals take place as quickly as possible after death. Bishop Ryle quoting the Fathers says: "Theophylact and Pellican think that it means: 'To take care of a father until he is dead' and that it implies a wish to attend upon an aged father during all the infirmities of his latter days, until he was released by death. Heinsius thinks there is a reference to the many tedious and superstitious practices of the Jews in connection with deaths and funerals, such as a seven days' lamentation before interment and a year's special mourning after his funeral'" (*Ryle's Expository Thoughts on the Gospels.* John, page 343). These suppositions might carry an element of truth for whilst it was customary to bury a body as quickly as possible after death, there were special occasions when even though the body had been embalmed or enclosed within a coffin, the ultimate funeral was not completed for a considerable length of time. It will be remembered that the body of Joseph was carried by the Israelites for many years until it could be buried in the land of promise. However, the main point about this incident was the man's unwillingness to respond immediately to the call and claims of Christ. His excuse brought from Jesus the words, "Let the dead bury their dead: but go thou and preach the kingdom of God." Those who were dead in trespasses and sins could undertake such work without difficulty; meanwhile there were more important tasks to be undertaken. A good soldier accepts orders; the man's answer revealed he was unfit for service.

We cannot be sure that the third man was present at the time the second man made his lamentable excuse; indeed the incident might have happened in some other place, but Luke undoubtedly includes it here because it related to discipleship. If he were present, then partially disgusted with what had just taken place, the man said, "Lord, I will follow thee; but . . ." Exuberance produced a spontaneous confessing of allegiance, but this proved to be disappointing for it was limited by restrictions of the man's own making. Let it be remembered that Matthew the publican also desired to follow Christ, and that ere he did so he actually arranged a feast in his home. It was a farewell feast given in honour of the Lord. The Saviour did not forbid this; he graced that feast by His own presence. Probably in this instance the Lord recognized it would be fatal if the would-be disciple returned to his home; the family would talk him out of the project! No man is able to plough a straight furrow when he spends half his time looking back. See the following homily.

## HOMILIES

Study No. 33

### THE PLOUGHMAN . . . WHO HAD EYES IN THE BACK OF HIS HEAD

"And Jesus said . . . No man having put his hand to the plough, and looking back, is fit for the kingdom of God." It is not without significance that this statement was made at the end of three interviews with the Saviour. Young men had been confronted by the challenge of discipleship, and apparently all three had missed the opportunity of following the Lord Jesus. This suggested to the Lord the picture of the half-hearted ploughman.

*Discipleship Demands Resolution*

"And it came to pass, that, as they went in the way, a certain man said unto him, Lord, I will follow thee whithersoever thou goest. And

Jesus said unto him, "Foxes have holes, and the birds of the air have nests, but the Son of man hath not where to lay his head." The silence that followed the announcement seemed ominous. Amid the prevailing excitement of a revival service, an impressionable soul spontaneously responded to the call of Christ. It should be noted that he came on his own initiative. Stirred to the depths of his heart, he hastened to pledge allegiance to the cause of the new Teacher. Christ's sombre warning was as the chilly blast of a midwinter's wind. The fervour of the meetings had thrilled the young man, and he could not understand how the future could be any different from the present. The Lord Jesus knew that such a disciple would be useless unless he was prepared to endure hardness. The ploughman who sets out to plough a field must be prepared for difficult places. Stones, roots, and rough ground may soon be encountered, and any half-hearted attempt at such an enterprise would only damage the plough and spoil the job.

*Discipleship Demands Readiness*

"And Jesus said unto another, Follow me. But he said, Lord, suffer me first to go and bury my father." Not all men are alike. Some impulsively rush to offer service; others retire into seclusion, fearing their talents are unequal to the demands of the new life. The former needs to be retarded; the latter must always be encouraged. This man's excuse only revealed his unfitness of soul. Had his father been dead, he himself would have been attending to the funeral arrangements. It was considered the duty of the firstborn to lay the father's body to rest. The call to follow Christ was secondary to that of waiting to bury his—perhaps—still healthy father. Thus, in one request, he demonstrated that as a ploughman or as a disciple, he would be useless. A farmer cannot plough a field at any time. The state of the soil, and the weather dictate the time for ploughing, and the wise farmer hurries to the task when the time is opportune. These things are also true in regard to discipleship. There are occasions when the cares of this world hinder the Spirit; there are days when our hearts are hard. God is best able to decide when His Spirit can work successfully, and every wise man will be ready to answer His call immediately. In farming or discipleship it is never safe to put off until tomorrow what should be done today.

*Discipleship Demands Resignation*

Probably greatly stirred, the third man hastened to say, "Lord, I will follow thee; but let me first go bid them farewell, which are at home at my house." And Jesus, realizing the dangers of such a procedure, replied, "No man, having put his hand to the plough and looking back, is fit for the kingdom of God." And if any casual reader should consider this attitude to be severe, let ft be remembered that Jesus Himself loved to visit the homes of His followers. Such an answer is a sure guarantee that, had the man returned home, his family would have argued him out of his proposal. How can any man take up his cross to follow Christ, if all the while, the eyes in the back of his head are hungrily searching for the alluring pleasures left behind in a home, a business, or in some other place? Following Christ demands resignation—deliberate, sacrificial resignation. The successful disciple is the one who says, "I must be a Christian or die." Every ploughman worthy of the name will recognize conditions suited to his enterprise, and stay at his plough until the task is completed. When a man is moved to exclaim, "Lord, I will follow thee whithersoever thou goest," nothing should be permitted to prevent the fulfilment of his vow.

(Taken from *Bible Pinnacles*, page 109)

# The Tenth Chapter Of Luke

THEME: *The Intensification of Christ's Ministry*

OUTLINE:

      I. Christ Addresses the Seventy. Verses 1–24
     II. Christ Answers the Lawyer. Verses 25–37
    III. Christ Accepts an Invitation. Verses 38–42

## SECTION ONE

*Expository Notes on the Commissioning of the Seventy Disciples*

> After these things the Lord appointed other seventy also, and sent them
> two and two before his face into every city and place, whither he himself
> would come (v. 1).

There is some uncertainty about the number of the new missionaries
commissioned at this time. Some manuscripts state seventy, but others
quote the number as seventy-two. This has caused argument and
speculation. Probably Godet's explanation is among the best. "The
oscillation which prevails in the MSS. between the numbers seventy
and seventy-two, and which is reproduced in verse 17, exists equally
in several other cases where this number appears, e.g. the seventy or
seventy-two Alexandrine translations of the Old Testament. This is
due to the fact that the numbers 70 and 72 are both multiples of
numbers very frequently used in sacred symbolism—7 times 10 and 6
times 12. The authorities are in favour of seventy, the reading in
particular of the *Sinaiticus*. Does this number contain an allusion to
that of the Sanhedrin (71, including the President), a number which
appears in its turn to correspond with that of the seventy elders chosen
by Moses? (Numbers 11: 16–25.) In this case, it would be, so to speak,
an anti-Sanhedrin which Jesus constituted, as in the naming of the
Twelve, He had set over against the twelve sons of Jacob, twelve new
spiritual patriarchs. . . ." No commentator can be dogmatic in his
interpretation of this vague passage, but some things appear to be
obvious. One dispensation was ending and another beginning. As God
had appointed the twelve patriarchs to be the leaders of His earthly
people, so now the Son of God was instituting a new era: He was
replacing the old leaders with His own appointed men. To these the

246

church of the future would look for guidance. As the patriarchs were commissioned to interpret the law: the apostles would similarly be authorized to interpret the word of Christ. Similarly, as the affairs of the earthly kingdom had more or less been managed by the council of seventy, so the spread of the Gospel and the establishing of the new kingdom would begin to take shape as the new council of seventy began its mission. From all this we deduce but one thing—"For the law was given by Moses, but grace and truth came by Jesus Christ" (John 1: 17).

This then was the burden of the commission: these men were to go forth with a message demanding new responsibilities of the people to whom they were to preach. It would no longer be sufficient for men to affirm they kept the law: much more was now being demanded by Christ. Nothing has been said about the identity of the new band of workers except that they were "other" than the original twelve. There were men who, having responded to the claims of Christ, had lost their employment: there were some who had been excommunicated by the Jews. See John 9: 34. What would have happened to these men? As in the case of the blind beggar, to return to his home was out of the question for his parents had already made their unfortunate decision not to confess allegiance to Jesus. The convert could not beg for he was no longer blind. No Jewish employer would offer work for this would have invited the attention of the Jewish leaders who had denounced the man. What then could the beggar do? How would he earn his living? There exists the possibility that with others of his type, he became one of the seventy. This is mere speculation, but it would be very difficult to believe that Christ would be unconcerned about the man's economic problems. That the seventy were sent forth in couples exhibits true wisdom. The road ahead would be rough; sometimes the reception would be chilling. Ecclesiastes 4: 9 states, "Two are better than one," and obviously the Lord believed the statement.

It should be remembered the countryside of Galilee had been well traversed by the disciple band; the people had received every chance to hear the Gospel and see the Saviour. Now, the Lord planned to proceed to Jerusalem, and the time for the additional training of His servants was limited. Between His present location and Jerusalem were many villages. The area of the Trans-Jordan included many small places where the Good News had not been announced, and knowing this, the Lord intensified His efforts to reach the unreached. He intended to visit these places, and knowing the value of adequate preparation, commissioned the new preachers to go ahead in His name. This has always supplied inspiration for the missionary societies. Where the preacher goes, Christ follows; where Christ goes, the Kingdom is established.

Therefore said he unto them, The harvest truly is great, but the labourers are few: pray ye therefore the Lord of the harvest, that he would send forth labourers into his harvest. Go your ways: behold I send you forth as lambs among wolves. Carry neither purse nor scrip, nor shoes: and salute no man by the way. And into whatsoever house ye enter, first say, Peace be to this house. And if the son of peace be there, your peace shall rest upon it: if not, it shall turn to you again. And in the same house remain, eating and drinking such things as they give: for the labourer is worthy of his hire. Go not from house to house. And into whatsoever city ye enter, and they receive you, eat such things as are set before you; And heal the sick that are therein, and say unto them, The kingdom of God is come nigh unto you. But into whatsoever city ye enter, and they receive you not, go your ways out into the streets of the same, and say, Even the very dust of your city, which cleaveth on us, we do wipe off against you: notwithstanding be ye sure of this, that the kingdom of God is come nigh unto you (vv. 2-11).

The most important word in verse two is *pray*. The tasks ahead would be difficult whatever happened, but if the disciples forgot to pray, the work would be impossible. It should be noticed that the details of the commission, to some extent at least, followed the same order as set forth in the charge to the Twelve. Poverty would be their best advertisement; it advertised their complete and constant dependence upon God; and attracted people who desired to participate in the work of the kingdom. Some of the commands of the two commissions seem to be in opposition. "But be shod with sandals" (Mark 6: 9) seems to be at variance with "Carry . . . no shoes" (Luke 10: 4). The sandal was the simple protection for the sole of the foot, the flat piece of leather attached by thongs to the toes of the wearer. The shoe was a most expensive and elegant thing which covered the entire foot. The one indicated the owner to be a simple itinerant peasant; the other generally belonged to a man of means. The term "son of peace" was often expressed in Israel. A man who loved to go forth to battle was called "a son of war." A man tired of life would be known as "a son of death" (II Samuel 12: 5). Wicked men were sometimes called "the children of wrath" (Ephesians 2: 3). Therefore *the son of peace* would be a peace lover, a peace maker. He was kindly disposed; not argumentative, quarrelsome, embittered, evil. Such men were to be blessed with the benediction of peace. Christ had given peace to His followers; they in turn were authorized to pass this on to others. Within these homes the disciples were commanded to stay. It would be better to light one great fire, than to strike matches in twenty different homes! Quality was to be the key word in their ministry—not quantity. Some people are great statisticians; they make thousands of calls, but seldom reach anybody. Others whose figures are not as astronomical, establish churches. It must be remembered too that under law, certain foods were prohibited. The command "eat such things as are set before you" was surely the forerunner of that other statement, "What God hath cleansed, that call not thou common" (Acts 10: 15). Under law this would have been inadmissable; now, a whole new world was opening before the eyes of the disciples. The statement, "for the labourer is worthy of his hire" is interesting in that it is the only part of the Gospels quoted in the epistles. This suggests the Gospel of Luke had been finished prior to the time of Paul's writing to Timothy. See I Timothy 5: 18. The fact that of this, and the earlier statement, Paul says: "For the scripture saith," suggests that Luke's Gospel had already been recognized as an integral part of God's revelation. Special attention should be afforded to the statement: "The Kingdom of God is come nigh you." That this was to be said both to the favourably inclined and to the antagonists of the message indicates the Kingdom is intimately linked with the coming of Christ. There were people who welcomed the visitors; opened their homes to the preachers, fed them, listened to them, and even saw the sick being healed; yet even to them, the kingdom only came near. Entrance into the kingdom was secured by real faith in the Son of God and not by the friendliness exhibited toward those who preached the Gospel. It was planned that the kingdom should come nigh unto all men; all would have the chance to enter; but what they did with their opportunities was their responsibility.

But I say unto you, that it shall be more tolerable in that day for Sodom, than for that city. Woe unto thee Chorazin! Woe unto thee Bethsaida! for if the mighty works had been done in Tyre and Sidon, which have been done in you, they had a great while ago repented, sitting in sackcloth and ashes. But it shall be more tolerable for Tyre and Sidon at the judgment, than for you. And thou, Capernaum, which art exalted to heaven, shalt be thrust down to hell (vv. 12–15).

This is a sombre scripture. Chorazin is not mentioned anywhere else in the Bible, but according to Eusebius the city was situated about twelve miles from Capernaum. This corresponds with the remains of Bir-Kirazeh. It was therefore in the centre of the district where the power of God had been manifested. Nothing more has been said of the miracles performed there. The blind man had been given sight in Bethsaida, but at Capernaum many miracles had been performed. Scholars have debated the interpretation given of the exaltation of Capernaum. Matthew 9: 1 reveals this to have been the city in which Jesus had made his temporary headquarters; from this centre, in ever-expanding circles, the power of God had radiated into the countryside. Therefore its citizens had been in the most privileged part of the

country. "They had been exalted unto heaven." Alas, they were soon
to descend to abasement and shame. See the homily at the end of this
section.

He that heareth you heareth me; and he that despiseth you despiseth me;
and he that despiseth me despiseth him that sent me. And the seventy
returned again with joy, saying, Lord even the devils are subject to us
through thy name. And he said unto them, I beheld Satan as lightning
fall from heaven. Behold, I give unto you power to tread on serpents
and scorpions; and over all the power of the enemy: and nothing shall
by any means hurt you. Notwithstanding in this rejoice not, that the
spirits are subject unto you; but rather rejoice, because your names are
written in heaven (vv. 16-20).

The authority of these disciples was beyond question for, identified
with their Master, they were also one with God. As God was to be in
Christ reconciling the world unto Himself, so also Christ was to be
with, and in them, reaching out to save the lost. Unseen, He would
be with them; unheard, His voice would re-echo in their tones. Such
an enterprise could not fail. The Lord probably arranged a rendezvous
where they could meet after the journey. Let it be remembered that
the disciples were sent to preach whither He Himself desired to go.
We are not told what He did during their absence; either He went on
a short journey of His own, or He sought seclusion in order to prepare
for the days ahead.

The statement, "I beheld Satan as lightning fall from heaven," invites
attention. The Lord had listened to the thrilling report of His returning
messengers, and when they announced their wonderful triumphs, He
said, "I beheld Satan as lightning fall from heaven." The theological
outlook of the church has been divided into three sections—the past,
the present, the future. Some teachers state the Lord, stimulated by
the success of His servants, was anticipating that great day when Satan
would be utterly overcome; when eternal deliverance would be brought
to the world. However the tense of the Greek verb hardly supports
this viewpoint. Godet more or less believed the second interpretation
for he wrote, "The word *etheoroun—I was contemplating,* denotes an
intuition, not a vision, 'While you were expelling the subordinates, I
was seeing the Master fall' . . . The fall of Satan, which He con-
templates, symbolizes the complete destruction of his kingdom. . . ."
All this might well have been included in the text, but I cannot believe
this to be the final answer. As Greydanus points out, the aorist tense of
the Greek verb denotes something completed in the past, and this is
the tense used. *Etheoroun ton satanan . . . pesonta.* The New English
Bible translates this: "I watched how Satan *fell,* like lightning, out of
the sky." Greydanus goes on to say: "The point at issue here is the

concept of having fallen, not the act of falling while it is taking place, nor its result, namely, lying down. Satan had been cast out, thrown down from his exalted position of power." Bishop Ryle's comments are even more illuminating. "Some think that our Lord is speaking of the effect produced on Satan's kingdom by the preaching of the seventy disciples: 'I saw in spirit, or with my mind's eye, Satan's power declining, and himself rapidly losing his dominion over men in consequence of your ministry.' This is the view held by many modern commentators, but it does not seem satisfactory. The strong language used by our Lord can hardly be explained . . . by such an interpretation. Others think our Lord was speaking of what He had witnessed when Satan and his angels fell from heaven. . . . 'There was a time, when I saw Satan, great and mighty as he was, fall suddenly from his high position, and become a lost spirit.' This latter interpretation appears to me far the more satisfactory of the two, and is that which is held by Cyprian, Ambrose, Chrysostom, Jerome, Gregory, Bede, Theophylact, Bernard, Erasmus, Pellican, Doddridge, Gill, and Alford." (*Bishop J. C. Ryle on Luke*, p. 362.)

I am of the opinion that this is the only feasible interpretation. Away in eternal ages, Satan rebelled against the Most High, and was expelled from his place of power. As a blinding flash of brilliance disappearing into the darkness of the sky, Satan had fallen. The Son of God had witnessed the catastrophy. It was not surprising that these disciples had triumphed. God was still supreme; when confronted by divine authority demons were helpless. Satan had fallen because of his pride (I Timothy 3: 6). The Lord probably reminded the disciples that unless they remained humble, even their astonishing powers might become a snare. Some of the church fathers interpreted the text as follows: "Be not puffed up because the devils are subject to you. Remember that Satan fell through pride as I myself saw. Rejoice then, not merely because you have been able to accomplish such mighty deeds; rejoice humbly because the Grace of God saved you; your names are written in heaven." It should be remembered that the Jews carefully preserved their written records. The names of all who belonged to Israel were carefully inscribed in the rolls. See Ezra 2: 62. They believed God also did this, and the thought is expressed throughout the New Testament. See Revelation 20: 11–15.

> In that hour Jesus rejoiced in spirit, and said, I thank thee, O Father, Lord of heaven and earth, that thou hast hid these things from the wise and prudent, and hast revealed them unto babes: even so, Father; for so it seemed good in thy sight. All things are delivered to me of my Father; and no man knoweth who the Son is, but the Father: and who the Father is, but the Son, and he to whom the Son will reveal him (vv. 21–22).

This verse is remarkable for it mentions the only occasion when Jesus is said to have rejoiced. The evangelists were careful to tell us that He wept—at Nain, over Jerusalem, and in the garden of Gethsemane. Yet in no other place do we read of the Lord rejoicing. The New English Bible translates: "At that moment Jesus *exulted* in the Holy Spirit . . ." The Lord was thrilled; His great heart was overwhelmed with happiness; His face radiated joy; His soul was exultant:—and why? He had just heard of the deliverance of precious souls. Nothing ever brought joy to Christ as did the redemption of the lost. The wise and the prudent were the bigoted religious leaders. They knew everything, and consequently learned nothing! Yet in His great wisdom, God had found the little people of the earth, and to these had revealed the riches of the eternal world. Within the eternal family, was an intimacy shared by none outside. From everlasting to everlasting, God is indivisible. The Father and the Son were one; Either knew the Other in the fullest possible way. As the Father and the Son were one; so the Son could and would reveal the Father. Such was the miracle of Grace; men who were afar off would be brought nigh; strangers would be able to say, "Abba Father."

And he turned unto his disciples, and said privately, Blessed are the eyes which see the things that ye see: for I tell you, that many prophets and kings have desired to see those things which ye see, and have not seen them; and to hear those things which ye hear, and have not heard them (vv. 23–24).

The privileges enjoyed by the disciples were inestimable. The prophets and kings were obviously the saints of former ages. They had seen through a glass darkly; the disciples had seen face to face the matchless Son of God. Nothing could be more eloquent in expressing the greatness of Christ. He had always been one with the Father; He had shared in the eternal counsels of the Godhead; He had been the object of veneration for the saints of all ages. Kings had been His subjects; prophets had been His messengers. Yet, to poor undeserving sinners had come the privilege of being the friends of the Highest. They were *blessed* indeed.

HOMILIES

Study No. 34

### A TALE OF TWO CITIES (Mark 6: 7–12)

The synagogue was in an uproar; the citizens of Nazareth were angry. It was disgraceful that their one-time carpenter should have defiled the holy place with his abominable utterances. He had a swollen head—he was an arrogant young fool—he was a disgrace to his parents and the community in general. He should have been thrown over the precipice, but perhaps it was providential that he had escaped. The good name of Israel might have been stained with murder. Good riddance to him! And outside the city of sin, the Lord Jesus sorrowfully looked back at His old home, and sighed. "And he called unto him the twelve, and began to send them forth by two and two. . . . They were ready to depart when He reminded them of two cities.

### The City of Disgusting Passion

Lot sat in the gateway of the ancient city, and watched the approach of two strangers. Where would they spend the night? They were in danger but were unaware of the perils of entering Sodom. He would offer them shelter. "Gentlemen, follow me quickly, or else—Ah, we are too late. That hateful mob saw us. Excuse me, I'll be back in a moment." And he closed the door behind him. Poor man, he had gone to turn wolves from their victims. The angels opened the door to pull him to safety. He was rather startled, but outside the lewd cries of filthy men echoed through the night. Hell was abroad! Those beastly men were a blot on God's fair world. "Then the Lord rained upon Sodom and Gomorrah brimstone and fire from the Lord out of heaven." When the disciples shuddered, the Saviour reminded them of the other place.

### The City of Dignified Pride

"Can you see it, children? It has elaborate, ornate synagogues, and the elders are men of standing. They fast twice in the week, and give tithes of all they possess. They are dignified and true to the traditions of the fathers. Yet, watch them now, as two preachers begin to speak in the market place. They frown. 'What is this? Are those itinerant evangelists telling us to repent? Disgraceful! We are children of Abraham. Hidden sin in our hearts! Such unwarranted interference! Preacher, mind your own business, and repent of your own wickedness. And leave our city; we don't want your noise nor your religion!'" Jesus paused to ask, "Can you see those two cities? Now listen again, And whosoever shall not receive you, nor hear you, when ye depart thence, shake off the dust under your feet for a testimony against them. Verily I say unto you, *It shall be more tolerable for Sodom and Gomorrah in the day of judgment, than for that city.*"

### (1) The Day of Judgment—how sure

Unless there is to be a day of final reckoning, this statement of Christ is utterly misleading. This part of His teaching coincides with other messages. He believed that ultimately all men will stand before God to account for the things done in this world. He believed too, that men could be lost; and it was to save such people He came.

### (2) The Decision of the Judge—how surprising

Why should Sodom have a better chance than the city of a later date? Sodom had no Gospel, no preachers to warn of the consequences of sin, no church in which services were held. Sodom never heard of the Lord Jesus, and had never witnessed His amazing miracles. The other city had heard of Christ and had met His ambassadors. They had seen the miracles of redeeming grace, and had no excuse for their ignorance. God can only judge a man according to the light which the man possesses. When the books are opened the relative advantages and opportunities of men must be taken into consideration. The Bible teaches that there are degrees of rewards for the faithful. See I Corinthians 3: 12-15. The Bible also teaches that there will be degrees of punishment.

### (3) The Desires of Jesus—how sincere

"And they went out, and preached that men should repent. And they cast out many devils, and anointed with oil many that were sick, and healed them." The Lord Jesus desired to save men. He wanted them to hear the way of truth, and be unashamed before the throne of God. Have I heard the Gospel? Have I been reared in a godly home and a Christian church? Could it be possible that in the day of judgment it will be more tolerable for untutored, black heathen, than it will be for me?

> When I soar to worlds unknown
> See Thee on Thy judgment throne;
> Rock of Ages, cleft for me,
> Let me hide myself in Thee.

### SECTION TWO

### Expository Notes on the Parable of the Good Samaritan

And, behold, a certain lawyer stood up, and tempted him, saying, Master, what shall I do to inherit eternal life. He said unto him, What is written in the law? how readest thou? And he answering said, Thou shalt love the Lord thy God with all thy heart, and with all thy soul, and with all thy strength, and with all thy mind; and thy neighbour as thyself. And he said unto him, Thou hast answered right: this do, and thou shalt live (vv. 25-28).

A lawyer in New Testament days was a man who devoted all his time to the study of the ancient manuscripts; he was considered to be an expert in the legal affairs of the nation. We do not know if he had been hired for the purpose of disputing with Jesus, or whether his own self-confidence encouraged him to try and defeat Christ in an argument. That his question was tantamount to a tempting or testing reveals his motives were impure. The Lord was wise—He turned the question back on the questioner. There was another occasion when a wealthy young ruler asked a similar question, but as we shall see shortly, the Lord's reactions were totally different on that occasion. It was to be expected that the lawyer would reply as he did, for Jews were required to recite, morning and evening, the scripture which he quoted. The Saviour's methods momentarily caught the questioner off balance, and realizing the purpose of his attack had been thwarted, the lawyer quickly thought of another way to pursue his aims. That he was told to keep the commandments suggests he was not living up to the high standards set forth in his own textbook. He who told others what to do failed to practise what he preached. The chief thing about the law was that it proved man's guilt. Had the lawyer conscientiously tried to fulfil the multitudinous commandments set forth in the writings of the fathers, he would have discovered the task was beyond his capabilities. When the rich young ruler asked a similar question, he did so with a very different thought in mind. He had already become aware that keeping the law did not provide life eternal (Matthew 19: 20). Therefore the Lord told him to forsake all and become a disciple. This final part of the message was never given to the lawyer, for he would have scoffed at the idea. Men are more likely to obey the commands of a doctor when they know they are dying! The lawyer considered himself to be in the best of spiritual health; the young ruler knew he was sick in his soul.

But he willing to justify himself, said unto Jesus, And who is my neighbour? And Jesus answering said, A certain man went down from Jerusalem to Jericho, and fell among thieves, who stripped him of his raiment, and wounded him, and departed, leaving him half dead. And by chance there came down a certain priest that way: and when he saw him, he passed by on the other side. And likewise, a Levite, when he was at the place, came and looked on him, and passed by on the other side. But a certain Samaritan, as he journeyed, came where he was: and when he saw him, he had compassion. And went to him, and bound up his wounds, pouring in oil and wine, and set him on his own beast, and brought him to an inn, and took care of him. And on the morrow when he departed, he took out two pence, and gave them to the host, and said unto him, Take care of him: and whatsoever thou spendest more, when I come again, I will repay thee (vv. 29–35).

The word *willing* would be better expressed *desiring*—"but he desiring to justify himself . . ." "*determined to acquit himself of re-*

*proach"* (*The Amplified New Testament*). *"Wanting to vindicate him-self"* (The New English Bible). Jews considered their neighbours to be only those of their own race. The Gentiles and particularly the half-Gentiles (the Samaritans), were unclean—dogs. If they were citizens—they were second or even third-class citizens and it was not to be expected that any Jew would defile himself by associating with them. It would be easy for us to condemn their attitude, but before we do so let us remember that the same situation exists today. Alas, the colour of a man's skin; his social upbringing; the western equivalent of the Indian caste system have done more to hinder the cause of Christ than any-thing else on earth. We proclaim that all men in Christ are our brethren, but we are so thankful they live the other side of the city. As the lawyer of old we are experts at formulating arguments where-by we may vindicate our actions—justify ourselves—for passing by on the other side.

There were other legal men who asked Jesus similar questions. See Matthew 22: 35–40; and Mark 12: 28–32. The road from Jerusalem to Jericho was exceedingly notorious in that it ran through wild and desolate country, the habitual haunt of bandits. Jerome called it "The bloody way." The lawyer understood the implications of the Lord's illustration for at that time Jericho was a city of priests. It was neces-sary for them to travel this road frequently, for in turn they all went to Jerusalem to perform their monthly courses. Lightfoot states that no fewer than twelve thousand priests resided in the city. The Lord cited three men who had dealings with the unfortunate victim. The priest possibly thinking the man was dead, and having no wish to be defiled by contact with a corpse, "passed by on the other side." The Levite actually approached the body, but finally decided that he too might be in jeopardy if he lingered too long in a vicinity where bandits were active. The Good Samaritan threw caution to the winds and did what his conscience commanded. Against this colourful background the Lord was able to propound a question of His own. Some critics question the fact that the Samaritan was able at short notice to supply oil and wine, but there is no difficulty here. Believing that oil and wine were a means of healing for the body, most travellers carried supplies. Obviously this practice had been known from antiquity for even Jacob was able to pour oil upon the pillar which he set up in the wilderness. The two pence, today, suggests the Good Samaritan was not too generous! It should be remembered that in those days, one penny was consider fair wages for a whole day's work (Matthew 20: 2). This message of the Saviour is recognized as being one of the most sug-gestive, most thrilling illustrations ever given. We cannot authentically state it was a parable; it could have been an actual occurrence which took place on the dangerous road to Jericho.

Which now of these three, thinkest thou, was neighbour unto him that fell among the thieves. And he said, He that shewed mercy on him. Then said Jesus unto him, Go, and do thou likewise (vv. 36–37).

The Lord was adept at answering awkward questions; His replies made questioners consider facts which they wished to avoid. Legal men often thrive on telling others what needs to be done; it was certainly a change for the lawyer to be told that he needed to do something. The story of the events on the Jericho road has been used extensively throughout the ages, and all kinds of sermons have been preached around its details. Unfortunately some of the preachers went to extremes, and brought the noble art of homiletics into disrepute. Whatever the opinions of my readers might be, the following homilies are supplied as a stimulant to productive thought.

## HOMILIES

Study No. 35

### Travellers who Fell Among Thieves

"A certain man went down from Jerusalem to Jericho, and fell among thieves, which stripped him of his raiment, and wounded him, and departed, leaving him half dead." And, as Dr. Parker once said, "He asked for it!" It is not possible to walk from Jerusalem to Jericho without *first turning one's back upon the sanctuary.* Jericho was "the city of the curse"—it had been so from the days of Joshua, and any man walking in that direction could expect to fall among thieves. The Bible has several examples of such foolish travellers.

### The Ephesian Elder who Lost his First Love

There are travellers who set out with the fixed purpose of reaching a desired destination; there are others who stroll along aimlessly. Probably the man from Ephesus belonged to the latter class. Perfectly satisfied with the abundance of church services, and a little conceited over the obvious superiority of his church connections, the revered saint sauntered along without a care; and while he walked in his sleep, the evil thieves stole his greatest jewel. The Lord Jesus said of the man and the church he represented, "I know thy works, and thy labour, and thy patience, and how thou canst not bear them that are evil . . . Nevertheless, I have somewhat against thee, because thou hast left thy first love" (Revelation 2: 2–4). If love warms the heart and cheers the assembly, then the church at Ephesus had no heating apparatus.

### The Psalmist who lost the joy of his Salvation

King David was one of those unfortunate men whose eyes were permitted to rest too long upon prohibited pleasures. His vision kindled an unholy fire upon the altar of his heart, and in those fires he sacrificed his peace of mind. The sordid story of murder reveals David walking away from his sanctuary. He had forgotten his former vows, and sought attractions along the road to Jericho. And then came the thugs! When the soul of David struggled back to consciousness, he discovered that serious harm had befallen his spiritual raiment. He had been stripped and left naked in his guilt before God. The accusing eyes of the prophet were focused upon him, and the unwavering finger pointing at his heart added emphasis to the accusation, "Thou art the man." Broken-hearted, David bowed in despair, and discovered that the Jericho thieves had taken his fairest treasure. Psalm 51 tells how he prayed, "Restore unto me the joy of thy salvation." Poor David, he should have known better.

### The Prodigal who lost his Father's Fellowship

As he whistled his way along the road that led to the far country, the prodigal smiled. Bah! His father was old-fashioned and stodgy. The home was too circumscribed. He had left it forever. Ahead, lay another country and a great time. Instinctively he lengthened his stride. The road was hazy. Visibility was never very good in the Jericho area, and some of the smog entered the mind of the boy. He was unable to recognize his own stupidity; he could not see what awaited him in the glamorous city, and he was too short-sighted to discern the base hypocrisy of the thieves who posed as his friends. He fell among thieves who left him bewildered and penniless in a pig-sty. When the disillusioned fellow began taking stock of his position, he discovered he had lost many treasures, including the fellowship of his father. In comparison with that tragedy, the loss of his money seemed insignificant.

### The Crown of Life—the Greatest Jewel of All

"And to the angel of the church in Philadelphia write . . . Because thou hast kept the word of my patience, I also will keep thee from the hour of temptation . . . Behold I come quickly: hold that fast which thou hast, that no man take thy crown" (Revelation 3: 7–11). This constitutes the greatest warning given to the church. No man can afford to lose his eternal crown of life, and the undivided attention of every individual should be devoted to the guarding of this great treasure. Jericho has never been a health resort, and the man of old should be a warning to all travellers.

Study No. 36

## THE GREAT EVANGELIST . . . AND THE CHURCH HE COULD TRUST
### (Luke 10: 34)

The stories or parables of the Saviour were always filled with abounding interest, but few can be more intimately related to the problems of modern evangelism than the account of the Good Samaritan. How he went forth on the Jericho road, and there found an unfortunate traveller, is known to all Bible students; but strange to relate, many readers have missed a vital part of the account. When the Samaritan saw his potential convert ". . . he had compassion on him, and went to him, and bound up his wounds, pouring in oil and wine, and set him on his own beast"—and then probably asked himself a most important question. "What shall I do with him now?" *"And he brought him to an inn."*

### The Church of the Open Road

What would the Good Samaritan have done with his convert if the inn had not existed? The traveller's life was in danger; his physical condition forbade removal either to distant Jerusalem or to Jericho. He needed urgent attention. Here was a problem of the first magnitude. "What can be done with my convert? Have I rescued him only to see him die in my arms?" "And he brought him to an inn . . . and said unto the host, Take care of him . . ." And there we have the crux of the problems of modern evangelism. The church has been built alongside the road of life to be a haven for travellers who need succour. Gifted evangelists may go forth seeking the lost, but without the church, much of their best effort will be fruitless. To build an inn in such an isolated and dangerous place surely seemed a ludicrous venture. That he was a man of rare vision, none will deny. Possibly he had travelled that way and had first-hand information of the need for such accommodation. This account teaches that the ministry of the church is of equal importance with that of the man who brings the lost from the highways of life.

### The Church of the Open Door

It would appear that the Good Samaritan knew the type of reception he would receive at the innkeeper's door. Here was a man whose hospitality was known far and wide. None who came were ever turned away. The innkeeper could not afford to turn people away. This was not a thriving seaside resort, nor a place of majestic scenic beauty. Wealthy citizens did not come here to retire. The inn was on the Jericho road where robber bands terrorized travellers. If people were refused admission there would be the possibility that the innkeeper would go out of business. And in like manner the same truth applies to the church. Without the fruits of successful evangelism, the modern church may become an eventide home for the aged. The function of the church is to keep open doors for all people—segregation is a word not found in God's dictionary. The clarion call of the church must always be: "Whosoever will may come, and him that cometh, I will in no wise cast out." Where the church has departed from this ancient standard, she has ceased to be of spiritual value. The text, "Take care of him," should be mentioned in the assembly each time a new member is received into fellowship.

### The Church of The Open Heart

The dawn was breaking; the Good Samaritan was about to leave. The innkeeper was smiling. "Friend, why not stay longer?" "Mr. Innkeeper, I cannot. Other travellers may be needing help. Yet soon I shall return. Take care of my convert, 'And whatsoever thou spendest . . . when I come again, I will repay thee.'" Thus was a man commissioned to continue the work which the Saviour had commenced. The best possible attention was given to the sufferer; nothing was too much trouble, and at any time of the day or night, the kind host was ready to respond to a call for assistance. The care of the convert is the duty and privilege of the church; and thus we arrive back where we started. Evangelism without the church is a flop; the church without evangelism is a social club with a religious flavour. To bring souls into the fellowship of the Assembly is the prerogative of evangelism; to prepare wholesome meals enabling souls to grow into a measure of spiritual health, is the task of the church itself. The Lord gave to the church, apostles, prophets, evangelists, pastors, and teachers—"for the perfecting of the saints, for the work of the ministry, for the edifying of the body of Christ" (Ephesians 4: 11–12). When the evangelist and the church begin to quarrel, both commit suicide. (Taken from *Bible Highways*, p. 105.)

SECTION THREE

### *Expository Notes on the Acceptance of Martha's Invitation*

**Now it came to pass as they went, that he entered into a certain village: and a certain woman named Martha received him into her house. And she had a sister called Mary, which also sat at Jesus' feet, and heard his word (vv. 38–39).**

Luke alone of the Gospel writers mentions this absorbing account. At first it seems a little difficult to place the story into the general pattern of the itineraries of the Lord, for we know that Martha lived with her sister and brother in Bethany. The possibility exists that whilst the seventy went forth on their preaching mission, the Lord used the time for a quick visit to Jerusalem, and that this event took place either going to, or returning from the city. It should not be forgotten that Martha received Jesus into her house. Martha means *mistress*; some have conjectured that she was the wife of Simon the leper, but of this there is no proof. The text infers that she was mistress of the home, and that it was at her invitation the Lord, for the first time, met the family destined to become famous. Martha was industrious, Mary was contemplative.

**But Martha was cumbered about much serving, and came to him, and said, Lord, dost thou not care that my sister hath left me to serve alone? bid her therefore that she help me. And Jesus answered and said unto her, Martha, Martha, thou art careful and troubled about many things: But one thing is needful: and Mary hath chosen that good part, which shall not be taken away from her (vv. 40-42).**

Two words provide a clear picture of what transpired. Martha said, ". . . my sister hath LEFT me to serve ALONE . . ." The scripture says that Mary ALSO sat at the Lord's feet to hear His word." At the beginning of the meal, both sisters were busy attending to the requirements of the guests. At some point during the meal, Mary probably thought that everyone was well supplied and grasped the opportunity to sit near the Lord to listen to His conversation. The Master would have been reclining, with His feet doubled beneath His body, and extending behind Him. There Mary sat; from her position she was close enough to hear His word, and near enough to respond to any need for service. For this great act, she was to be commended, and when the time came, the Lord was not slow in speaking on her behalf. The word translated *"thou art careful"* is *merimnas*. This is a colourful term which means *"to be drawn in different directions."* "Martha, your mind is in a turmoil for your thoughts are being pulled two ways at once. You try to listen to me; you continue to think about the tasks in the kitchen. You are agitated beyond measure. Martha, Martha!" Two things are obvious: Christ would never have condoned the laziness of Mary; neither could He excuse the needless exertions of her sister. Perhaps the best way to understand this ancient story is to interpret it in the light of modern customs. The Lord has been invited to dinner; the wonderful meal has almost ended. The need for further service has disappeared, and Mary, deeply interested in the Lord's remarks, sits down to listen. Poor Martha is thinking of the accumulation of dirty dishes in the kitchen. The fact that the Lord will soon continue His journey; that there will be all the time in the world to wash the dishes, apparently does not occur to her. How can she sit down doing nothing when the sink is full of dirty utensils? This plays upon her mind until she becomes unforgivably agitated. She is unwilling to stay with Jesus; she is equally unwilling to let her sister stay. Hence, her outburst. Momentarily she forgets even to be courteous for she reminds the Lord that He should rebuke her sister. Indeed, there is a vague apportionment of blame, for she says: "Lord, *is it no concern to thee,* that my sister hath left me?" Poor Martha, she is truly a wonderful soul, but her symptoms, if left unchecked, might lead to a nervous breakdown!

There has been a very great amount of discussion concerning the Lord's statement, "One thing is needful," but even such able commentators as Ryle and Godet are at variance with their interpretations. Godet thinks the Lord was saying that one course already served was sufficient for the needs of the body. Ryle flatly rejects this idea, and states the thing needful was the seeking of food for the soul. In fairness to Godet it should be mentioned that he also mentions this point, and thinks that Christ contrasted the two. As one course would be enough to meet the needs of the body, so the one desire for close communion with Christ, would be sufficient to meet spiritual needs. Readers will doubtless have their own ideas on this thorny problem. Possibly Christ was trying to teach Martha, and the others present, that whilst many things were desirable and legitimate, there were others of far more importance. It was not wrong to supply a wonderful meal; it was not wrong to admire a clean kitchen; it was splendid to see an industrious woman desirous of getting the dishes washed, but first things should come first. To say the least, it seemed stupid to play with pennies when gold nuggets were all over the place! All need to learn this lesson, for some are so busy working for Christ, they have no time to sit at His feet.

## HOMILIES

See *The Need for the Secret Place,* Chapter 9, Section 1.

Study No. 37

### FIVE HEADS WITH A SINGLE THOUGHT

It is far better to have one aim in life, and to achieve an ambition, than to attempt innumerable things and miss them all. Centrality of purpose is always a commendable feature, and it is truly significant that five of the leading Bible characters excelled in this respect. When these are grouped together, we are provided with a sequence of thought which embraces the entire range of Christian experience.

## *"One thing thou lackest"* (Mark 10: 21)

When the Lord Jesus told the rich young ruler to keep the Commandments, the earnest seeker replied, "Master, all these have I observed from my youth. Then Jesus beholding him loved him, and said unto him, *One thing thou lackest:* go thy way, sell whatsoever thou hast, and give to the poor, and thou shalt have treasure in heaven: and come, take up the cross, and follow me. And he was sad at that saying, and went away grieved; for he had great possessions." This illustrious young man possessed everything except that which mattered most. His home was filled with valuables, while his soul remained poor. Life begins when man responds to the call of discipleship. No amount of money, no degree of popularity, no worldly honours can ever compensate for the loss of eternal treasure.

## *"One thing I know"* (John 9: 25)

The street was filled with people; the religious leaders were protesting against the enthusiasm aroused by the latest miracle of Jesus. The people were fools swayed by every wind of doctrine! This was a storm in a teacup! "Then again called they the man that was blind, and said unto him, Give God the praise: we know that this man is a sinner. He answered and said, Whether he be a sinner or not, I know not: *one thing I know,* that, whereas I was blind, now I see." In contrast to the rich young ruler, this man was willing to sacrifice anything in order to follow Christ; and his unashamed testimony surely brought joy to the Saviour's heart. Military leaders say that attack is often the best defence. This is true of spiritual warfare.

## *"One thing is needful"* (Luke 10: 42)

The charming home in Bethany had suddenly become a place of strain. The atmosphere was tense, and there seemed every likelihood of a first-class quarrel. When twenty people were waiting for their meal, and many tasks demanded attention in the kitchen, "Mary sat at Jesus' feet, and heard his word." Martha's patience suddenly failed, and looking into the Lord's face, she said, "Dost thou not care that my sister hath left me to serve alone? bid her therefore that she help me. And Jesus answered. . . . Thou art careful and troubled about many things: but *one thing is needful:* and Mary hath chosen that good part, which shall not be taken away from her." Spiritual appetite is always an indication of a healthy soul. In any case, Mary would have been useless in the kitchen, when her heart was in the parlour.

*"One thing have I desired"* (Psalm 27 : 4)

David's soul was a ship adrift on turbulent waters. Surging emotions played havoc with his peace of mind, and memories of spiritual lapses haunted him. He had reason to know that "in his body dwelt no good thing"; he had been born in sin and shapen in iniquity; evil was ever present with him. "His heart and his flesh cried out for the living God." Where could he find eternal security? Where could the yearnings of his soul be fully satisfied? When his eyes instinctively turned toward the sanctuary, he cried, *"One thing have I desired* of the Lord, that will I seek after; that I may dwell in the house of the Lord all the days of my life, to behold the beauty of the Lord and to enquire in his temple." David might have been the elder brother of Mary of Bethany. They attended the same school—only he was in a higher standard. Of course, after all, he was a bit older!

*"One thing I do"* (Philippians 3 : 13)

It is fitting that Paul, the indomitable missionary should provide the final link in this chain of spiritual desire. He had graduated in God's school, and was determined to translate his lessons into ceaseless endeavour. He said, "Brethren . . . *this one thing I do,* forgetting those things which are behind, and reaching forth unto those things which are before, I press toward the mark for the prize of the high calling of God in Christ Jesus." Paul never permitted interference with the realization of his greatest ambitions, and ultimately he was able to say, "I have finished my course . . . henceforth there is laid up for me a crown." To a traveller, one guiding star is better than a million comets which have no meaning.

# The Eleventh Chapter of Luke

THEME: *Jesus continues His Teaching*

OUTLINE:

      I. Jesus speaks about prayer. Verses 1–13
     II. Jesus refutes an allegation. Verses 14–28
    III. Jesus warns of coming judgment. Verses 29–36
    IV. Jesus denounces hypocrisy. Verses 37–54

SECTION ONE

*Expository Notes on the Disciples' request concerning Prayer*

**And it came to pass, that, as he was praying in a certain place, when he ceased, one of his disciples said unto him, Lord, teach us to pray, as John also taught his disciples (v. 1).**

It must have been a constant source of wonder to the watching disciples how the Lord, in spite of His busy schedule, made time to pray. They could not have remained unaware that often whilst they slept, He arose early and went into the hillside to commune with His Father. Probably they had also detected the strange thrilling power which always emanated from His Person when He returned to meet the demands made upon His time and energy. Prayer was not a new exercise, but the way Jesus prayed surely challenged their thinking. Rabbis often taught their followers a prayer which could be said on special occasions, and the scriptures suggest John the Baptist had emulated this example. We have not been told of the type of prayer used by the wilderness preacher; neither can we be sure of the motives which prompted this request of the disciples. They wanted to master the art of prayer, and their request to the Lord elicited an instant response.

**And he said unto them, When ye pray, say, Our Father which art in heaven, Hallowed be thy name. Thy kingdom come. Thy will be done, as in heaven, so in earth. Give us day by day our daily bread. And forgive us our sins; for we also forgive every one that is indebted to us. And lead us not into temptation; but deliver us from evil (vv. 2–4).**

This is the prayer known throughout the church as "The Lord's Prayer," but actually it would be wiser to call this *the disciples' prayer*. This was the standard by which the followers of the Lord were to model their petitions; for the Lord's prayer we should examine the seventeenth chapter of John's Gospel. It has been well said that familiarity breeds contempt, and probably that is the reason why so many Christians fail to see spiritual beauty in this utterance. Oftentimes our prayers are selfish; we come to God because we desperately need something, and therefore, most of what we express to God is an appeal for something we very much desire. Students must notice that in this prayer, nothing is requested for self until certain important details have been handled. First, the disciples are reminded of *the Majesty of God. HALLOWED BE THY NAME.* The Almighty is to be addressed as a Father, and to say the least, this was the introduction of a new relationship. The God whose power had shaken Mount Sinai; whose laws made the people tremble, could hardly have been addressed in this manner. The coming of the Lord Jesus had unveiled new characteristics in the Godhead. It was still true that God was holy, but the approach to His throne should be that of love for a parent and not fear for a Creator. It was the constant consideration of this important fact that produced within the suppliant the right frame of mind in which true prayer could be offered. Secondly, the prayer suggests *the Purposes of God.* It was true that the suppliant earnestly desired certain things, but the will of God always has priority in the hearts of true believers. Shortly, the praying soul will ask for certain commodities, but the fact that this request had precedence was a confession that if God desired something else, even the prayers to follow could be forgotten. This was another instance of the Lord teaching His followers to say, "Not my will but Thine be done." Nevertheless, if the purposes of the Almighty could be fulfilled, and at the same time, these other requests could find favour with the Father, then it was the desire of the believer to ask for certain things. These requests were divided into three categories. (1) Food for the body; (2) Forgiveness for the soul; (3) Fortitude for the spirit. If the believer has to help in establishing the kingdom of God, he will need sustenance for his body, it would not be possible to work without strength. Food was an essential and not a luxury; therefore this request comes first. The appeal for forgiveness reveals two things. (1) Living men are prone to sin, and work in establishing the kingdom would never attain to the standards desired unless the workmen be pleasing to the Father. (2) But the forgiveness sought is the forgiveness shared —*forgive us—as we forgive every one indebted to us.* The man who expects forgiveness from God and who at the same time remains embittered toward his brother is a hypocrite. Finally, because in himself man is unable to withstand the onslaughts of the evil one, he should seek strength; strength to be able to stand in the day of testing. ". . . deliver us from evil." The believer could not be expected to be above his Lord. As the Master had been tempted, so would the followers. To survive the testings and attacks of hell would be of supreme importance; therefore the disciples of Jesus were urged to pray for God's help.

And he said unto them, Which of you shall have a friend, and shall go unto him at midnight, and say unto him, Friend, lend me three loaves; For a friend of mine in his journey is come to me, and I have nothing to set before him? And he from within shall answer and say, Trouble me not: the door is now shut, and my children are with me in bed; I cannot rise and give thee. I say unto you, Though he will not rise and give him, because he is his friend, yet because of his importunity he will rise and give him as many as he needeth. And I say unto you, Ask, and it shall be given you; seek, and ye shall find; knock and it shall be opened unto you. For every one that asketh receiveth; and he that seeketh findeth; and to him that knocketh, it shall be opened (vv. 5-10).

The homes of the peasants were very simple indeed, consisting of a two-level apartment. The one section was raised somewhat above the other, and there was very little privacy. Often—as is still the case in certain parts of the middle-east, even the domestic animals were brought into the house during the night. This was the safest way of preventing their being stolen. The upper or raised platform was the bedroom, where the family lay upon the floor. The animals occupied the lower deck of the apartment, and when the entire household had retired, it would indeed be a nuisance to respond to the requests of any man who decided to come calling at midnight. If the family were large, it would be necessary to step over or between the sleeping people; the animals would be disturbed, and by the time the operation had been completed, everybody would be disturbed and probably grumbling. The Lord Jesus was an expert in finding illustrations, and each of the listening disciples would fully appreciate the problem being set forth in the Saviour's message. The man at the door was a nuisance, but his continued knocking proclaimed the fact that he was determined to remain a nuisance unless somebody in that house opened the door. He needed something; he needed it urgently. His friend in bed was able to supply what was necessary, so he had better get up first as last! If he did not the whole village would wonder if he were dead. Thus did the Lord describe the art of prayer. He did not mean to infer that God had to be coaxed into responding to the cry of His children. Jesus was teaching by contrasts. If ordinary men would do this thing, *how much more could God be expected to do it?* However, the three stages of prayer as outlined in the text suggest we miss many answers to prayers because we are not in earnest about the thing we desire done. *Asking* is but a petition; *Seeking* implies persistent petitioning; *Knocking* indicates force—persevering force. Either the man will get out of bed, or the door will come off its hinges! "This," said Jesus, "is the prayer that brings results."

> If a son shall ask bread of any of you that is a father, will he give him a stone? or if he ask a fish, will he for a fish, give him a serpent? Or if he ask an egg, will he offer him a scorpion. If ye then being evil, know how to give good gifts unto your children: how much more shall your heavenly Father give the Holy Spirit to them that ask him? (vv. 11-13).

It is not without significance that in contrast to the staple items of diet mentioned by the Lord in this paragraph, He cites as the provision made by His Father—THE HOLY SPIRIT. In the final analysis, is not this the complete answer to the petitions already expressed in the prayer given to the disciples? If the Holy Spirit truly resides within us, His presence is indicative of the fact that we have found favour with God. If He goes with us each day to battle for Christ, could we be in better company? What the Captain of the Lord's host was to Joshua throughout the crusade to conquer Canaan, so the Holy Spirit will be to us. This, and only this is the sure way to be "delivered from the evil one." To repeat the earlier statement, the Lord was at this time teaching superlative truth by means of contrasts.


HOMILIES

Study No. 38

### DR. FRANK BOREHAM'S SERMON

During my wanderings around the world I met very many choice Christians; their presence was a delight; their advice invaluable. Yet, as in retrospect I review my host of friends, I see the late Dr. Boreham standing head and shoulders above them all. He was a great man; a marvellous preacher; a very gifted author, but above all a Christlike believer. I treasure above all other memories those of the time I spent in his presence. His words were always a benediction; his sermons immortal. He loved the story of the man who came knocking at his friend's door at midnight. Dr. Boreham had his own inimitable way of handling texts, and the following provides a shining example of that fact. He cited the three main characters in the story and gave them special names.

*Mr. Gold*

This was the householder; the man who had the bread; the man who had retired for the night. Yes, he knew the man who was knocking at the door; his name was Mr. Silver: he lived up the street. Mr. Gold did not know the other friend who had suddenly arrived at Mr. Silver's house, but it was obvious that the stranger's name was Mr. Copper. Probably this third man knew nothing whatsoever about Mr. Gold; they had never met, but at least, he did know Mr. Silver, who proved to be the go-between the first and the third man. Mr. Gold, represented God. He had plenty of bread, and was in the marvellous place where He could meet the need of all the hungry. Nevertheless abundant supplies in Heaven's storehouse were quite useless unless some of the provision could be brought to earth to meet the need of Mr. Copper.

*Mr. Silver*

He has nothing. Alas, whether it be his fault or not, he has nothing to offer Mr. Copper. The situation has become desperate, but suddenly Mr. Silver remembers that his friend Gold has bread enough and to spare. Could he possibly obtain a few loaves to meet this urgent need. He would try. The hour was late; the night was dark. Gold's door was shut, but his neighbour had excellent hearing and he had sound knuckles to knock on the closed door. Soon the bangs in the night told everybody that somebody was in trouble. Mr. Silver represents the church. We have nothing to set before our hungry neighbours unless we obtain supplies from God. We may offer a bed, but alas blankets are not food; one cannot fill an empty stomach with pillow cases! We may offer entertainment, but when the caller is starving, a solo on a flute will never satisfy his appetite. Mr. Copper needs food, not entertainment, and since Mr. Silver is bankrupt in this department, it becomes very necessary to get Mr. Gold out of bed. No church can dispense the bread of life to the hungry unless that same church knows how to obtain supplies from God. Without His aid, the traveller in the night might starve.

*Mr. Copper*

This is the world. This man cannot be expected to call upon Mr. Gold, for after all, he hardly knows of his existence. "Is there a Mr. Gold? Sure, I have heard something about him, but I never met him. But I do know my friend Silver, and feel sure he will not fail me in this hour of need." Thus did Dr. Frank Boreham weave his web and cast his marvellous spell around these three characters from the story of Jesus. He spoke about the sufficiency of God; the responsibility of the church, and the desperate plight of the traveller in the dark. Mr. Copper had no other to whom he could go for assistance; if Mr. Silver failed, he would remain hungry and perhaps even die. Against this background we should study the claims of evangelism and the mission of the church. Unless we know how to obtain supplies from heaven, our ministry on earth will be vain. The church stands between God and a perishing world; if we fail in our mission, the results will be tragic.

## SECTION TWO

### Expository Notes on the Accusations of the Lord's Enemies

**And he was casting out a devil, and it was dumb. And it came to pass, when the devil was gone out, the dumb spake; and the people wondered. But some of them said, He casteth out devils through Beelzebub the chief of the devils. And others tempting him, sought of him a sign from heaven (vv. 14–16).**

Each miracle performed by the Saviour increased the problems of the Pharisees. It was one thing to refute His teachings but quite another to deny the miracles which thrilled people every day. They could argue against His teachings, but it was impossible to ignore the miracles about which the entire population had become enthusiastic. What then could they do to prevent the spread of something they considered to be heresy? When someone suggested this power came from an allegiance with Satan, it seemed they had found what they sought. The name Beelzebub means *The God of Flies* and reference to this heathen god is made in II Kings 1: 3. Just how this title should be given to Satan by the people of New Testament days remains a mystery. All travellers are aware of the annoying flies which plague the middle-east, and it might well be that the people who suffered daily from these pests blamed their misfortune upon *the god of flies.* Perhaps on that never-to-be-forgotten day when Jesus expelled the demon, the flies were more noticeable than ever, and someone said this particular god was the chief of all their enemies. This is mere conjecture but the fact remains that for some reason or other they identified Satan with this infuriating deity whose winged subjects continually annoyed them. When men cannot hurt their rivals in any other way, they resort to slander.

The Lord was very careful and very clever in the moments which followed their charge. Josephus speaks of certain Jews who had been able to expel demons, and Acts 19: 13 proves there were Jews who still practised the art. When Christ asked the source of power known by the Jews of His day, His antagonists were left without an answer.

If they continued to charge that he was in league with the Prince of Demons, they were admitting the possibility that some of their own family were guilty of the same crime.

But he knowing their thoughts, said unto them, Every kingdom divided against itself is brought to desolation; and a house divided against itsself falleth. If Satan also be divided against himself, how shall his kingdom stand? Because ye say that I cast out devils through Beelzebub. And if I by Beelzebub cast out devils, by whom do your sons cast them out? therefore shall they be your judges. But if I with the finger of God cast out devils, no doubt, the kingdom of God is come upon you. When a strong man armed keepeth his palace, his goods are in peace: But when a stronger than he shall come upon him, and overcome him, he taketh from him all his armour wherein he trusted, and divideth his spoils. He that is not with me is against me: and he that gathereth not with me scattereth (vv. 17-23).

It was impossible to defeat or offset the arguments of the Lord. Each statement He ever made was a thrust into the conscience of His listeners. Everybody knew that civil war impoverished a kingdom; every listener knew that when a family began to kill each other, long life became an impossibility. These were simple truths with a tremendous application. If Satan had decided to help Jesus expel demons, then he was committing suicide. If the Pharisees desired an explanation for the power by which Jesus expelled demons they would have to look elsewhere. Yet to save their time, Christ supplied the answer immediately. Until that moment, Satan had kept his palace and kingdom intact; there had been none sufficiently strong to challenge him. Now things had changed. One stronger than he had come forth from the presence of God, and before the conflict was over, the powers of darkness would be put to flight. Here again is the veiled reference to the glorious fact that Jesus was God's man; indeed He was manhood at its thrilling best. All true men would recognise this and follow him; others with less vision would refuse to do so. Nevertheless everybody would do something for the word *neutrality* could not be found in heaven's vocabulary.

When the unclean spirit is gone out of a man, he walketh through dry places, seeking rest; and finding none, he saith, I will return unto my house whence I came out. And when he cometh, he findeth it swept and garnished. Then goeth he, and taketh to him seven other spirits more wicked than himself; and they enter in and dwell there; and the last state of that man is worse than the first (vv. 24-26).

Matthew (12: 43-45) adds one important detail. He says that when the unclean spirit came back to his old home, the house was empty.

This then is the story of an empty house, and in its true setting, it
supplies food for thought. See the homily at the end of this section.

> And it came to pass, as he spake these things, a certain woman of the
> company lifted up her voice, and said unto him, Blessed is the womb
> that bare thee, and the paps which thou hast sucked. But he said, Yea
> rather, blessed are they that hear the word of God, and keep it (vv.
> 27–28).

The identiy of this woman was never revealed; probably she was
an impressionable Jewess who had watched with increasing interest.
When her admiration had been greatly aroused, she made her statement. The Lord did not scold her neither did He deny the truth of
her remarks. Appreciating the sincerity of her soul He directed her
thoughts to higher and greater goals. There was nothing wrong in
her confession, but had she followed through to the end along the
pathway outlined by the Master her admiration might have become
adoration.


## HOMILIES FOR PREACHERS AND TEACHERS

Study No. 39

### THE PROBLEM OF AN EMPTY HOUSE

This Scripture belongs to one of the most fascinating of the Lord's
sermons. Christ was a great student of human nature, and it is said of
Him that He did not commit himself unto the people because He
knew all men. Constantly He came face to face with all types, and
here in this challenging message, He centres attention on one class—
the man who says, he could never live the Christian life even though
he tried.

### The Parable

The house was a study in contrasts. It seemed impossible that this
could be one home, for its two ends were two extremes. One was as
beautiful as the other was ugly. Seen through modern eyes, one end
was charmingly decorated, beautifully curtained, and a sight to gladden the heart. The other was bleak and barren and exceedingly dirty.
*But it was one house.* The good householder occupied one portion,
and a devil occupied the other. The good man desired to throw out
his evil neighbour, but felt unequal to the task. They continued to
live side by side. We are reminded of a human heart where so often

the good and bad impulses live together. Paul said, "When I would do good, evil is present with me"; and Studdart Kennedy once wrote:

> There's summat that pulls us up,
> And summat that pulls us down;
> And the consequence is that we wobble
> 'Twixt muck and a golden crown.

If we could only be rid of the evil within us, our entire house could be beautified according to our noblest desires.

## The Problem

A great inspiration energised the householder, and in one supreme moment of triumph he ejected the unwanted devil. Probably he was more surprised than the evil one, but after a little while the devil said, "I will return into my house from whence I came out." Then he discovered it to be empty, swept, and garnished; and realizing that the householder might expel him once again, he took with him seven other spirits more wicked than himself. Thus, said Christ, "the last state of that man was worse than the first." There is something peculiarly suggestive about this scene. It is obvious that Christ appreciated the difficulties of sincere souls. It seemed so futile to make any decision which in after days might return as a boomerang to create dismay. It is easy at times to cry, "Lord, I will follow thee whithersoever thou goest," and yet to fail when subsequently the road is long and steep. In the glorious ecstasy of His presence we can brave unlimited perils; but, alas, we are mindful that the expelled demon might someday return with reinforcements. Our philosophy says, "Better be content with the presence of one devil than run the risk of his bringing seven others."

## The Preaching

The weakness of the story seems to be in that, having expelled the demon, *the householder was content to live alone.* If he could have found a companion whose power exceeded that of many devils, he would have had a chance of maintaining the freedom of his home. And however imaginative this may seem, it is nevertheless the real fact behind this message. Matthew 12: 22–24 tells of the deliverance of a demoniac, and no one could deny the actuality of the miracle. Even the Lord's enemies admitted He had performed the impossible, but they cunningly suggested He was in league with Beelzebub, the prince of the devils. But let us remember that He had established beyond all doubt His superiority over demons. He thereupon proceeded to describe the harassed householder, and to this there can only be one feasible explanation. If such a man could invite Christ to live in his heart, he would find security in the new fellowship. And that is the crux of the Gospel message. If the Lord tarries with me, His strength will be made perfect in my weakness. How silly it is to live in the shadow of nameless fears. I must seek the companionship of the new Guest.

SECTION THREE

*Expository Notes on the Witnesses at the Judgment Day*

> And when the people were gathered thick together, he began to say, This is an evil generation: they seek a sign; and there shall no sign be given it, but the sign of Jonas the prophet. For as Jonas was a sign unto the Ninevites, so shall also the Son of man be to this generation. The queen of the south shall rise up in the judgment with the men of this generation, and condemn them: for she came from the uttermost parts of the earth to hear the wisdom of Solomon: and, behold a greater than Solomon is here. The men of Nineve shall rise up in the judgment with this generation and shall condemn it: for they repented at the preaching of Jonas; and, behold, a greater than Jonas is here (vv. 29-32).

We must remember that verse 16 informed us that certain people were asking from Jesus a sign. They ignored His miracles; they forgot all that had gone before; for the want of something else to say, they asked for a sign as an aid to faith. Yet there is reason to think that even had He given them many additional signs they would have only examined them to find ways and means of bringing accusations against Him. The Lord was not unmindful of their presence in the audience, and suddenly turning toward the questioners He began to speak of the day of judgment. At first He did not speak of *the testimony* of Jonah, but rather of *his appearance.* As a matter of fact it is extremely problematical whether any preaching could have turned that great city to God in such a short time. The Ninevites worshipped the fish god and when Jonah suddenly appeared on the seashore bearing upon his person the marks of the ordeal through which he had passed, they recognised he was a man who had returned from the dead. Their sea-god probably lay dead in the shallow water, and yet this resurrected man was there to speak to them. They were willing to listen even before he uttered a word. The queen of Sheba came from her distant home to hear the wisdom of Solomon because tidings of the great king had stirred her soul. Having heard about the great king, she could not rest until she came to see if the reports were accurate. Obviously the Lord Jesus believed His Bible. These stories from a bygone age were not legends; stories; the product of the overwrought imaginations of ancient authors. They were true; they were factual. (See the homily at the end of this section.)

**No man when he hath lighted a candle, putteth it in a secret place, neither under a bushel, but on a candlestick, that they which come in may see the light. The light of the body is the eye: therefore when thine eye is single, thy whole body also is full of light; but when thine eye is evil, thy body also is full of darkness. If thy whole body therefore be full of light, having no part dark, the whole shall be full of light, as when the bright shining of a candle doth give thee light (vv. 33-36).**

If these words represent the conclusion of the Lord's message then they appear very appropriate. There are none so blind as the people who have no wish to see. Quoting various writers, J. C. Ryle says: "Parkhurst says that the Greek word rendered *single,* when applied to the eye, means clear. Doddridge says, 'It is opposed to an eye overgrown with film.' Campbell says: 'it means sound and healthy,' and that both Chrysostom and Theophylact interpret it in that sense." Sin places cataracts on the eyes of the soul, and the Lord appeared to teach that if this had happened, it would not matter how many signs were given, the end would never be in doubt—the critics would never recognize what was being done. On the other hand, if their eyes were single; if their bodies were indeed radiant temples, there was no need to ask for signs, already evidences of God's power were all over the place.

## HOMILIES

Study No. 40

### THE WITNESSES FOR THE PROSECUTION

In the year A.D. 79 Vesuvius erupted, to bury the city of Pompeii beneath a sea of lava and ashes. Slaves chained to their posts perished; the people who fled into their homes were suffocated; in a few hours, a city disappeared. For some inscrutable reason Pompeii was forgotten, until centuries later certain monuments attracted the archaeologists, and the uncovering of the ruins commenced. In June 1957, I walked through this scene of devastation asking why God permitted the catastrophe. Then the guide, accompanied only by men, went into the ancient house of Vetii, and my question was answered. The eruption of Vesuvius destroyed a city of lust. The Bible declared that God will judge the world in righteousness; and when we consider the various statements of the Lord Jesus, it is possible to trace the trend of events as they are to be revealed at the final great assize.

## Call the Men of Nineveh (Matthew 12: 41)

Let us consider that judgment day; let us see the opening of the books, and watch as the accused are brought to trial. Then, "The men of Nineveh shall rise in the judgment with this generation, and shall condemn it: because they repented at the preaching of Jonas; and behold, a greater than Jonas is here." Perhaps on God's eternal television screen will be flashed the ancient scene. We may see Jonah standing close to the sea; we may see the great mammal gently rolling in the shallow waters, while nearby the onlookers marvel at the phenomenon which brought Jonah from his watery grave. The fish-god was dead; the preacher had returned from another world; his message was a supernatural warning. "And they repented at the preaching of Jonas." The ministry of the Lord Jesus Christ, His resurrection from the dead, the reiteration of His warning through the ages, will all unite in the condemnation of this unrepentant generation. And when the accused ask "But how were we to know whether the message was authentic?" the recording angel will summon the next witness.

## Call the Queen of Sheba (Matthew 12: 42)

If the ancient scene is recaptured in all its scintillating brilliance, we shall see a sight probably unsurpassed in ancient history. We shall consider again how the news of Solomon's magnificence was carried by merchants to distant lands, and how the queen of Sheba heard the story, and smiled. Such fantasy was surely the product of over-wrought minds; the effervescence of vivid imagination. Yet the reports continued to be given, and unable to silence her doubts, "she came from the uttermost parts of the earth to hear the wisdom of Solomon." "Queen of Sheba! Was it not beneath your dignity to travel so far on such an errand?" and the regal lady of a bygone age gracefully bows and replies, "I had nothing to lose; I had much to gain. I discovered that the half had never been told." Continues the prosecuting counsel: "Let me ask another question: What would you think of people who heard a similar message thousands of times, of people who only had a short distance to travel, and yet they lived and died debating whether the message were true or false?" The Lord Jesus said, "The queen of Sheba shall rise up in the judgment with this generation, and shall condemn it . . ."

## Call the People of Sodom (Mark 6: 11)

Sodom was the most indecent of all the ancient cities, and its evil practices led to disaster. Yet the Saviour stated that in the day of judgment Sodom would be more acceptable than some of the modern respectable cities with which our present world abounds. "Men of Sodom, why did you not heed the warning of Holy Scripture?" "We had no Scripture." "Did you not attend the evangelistic meetings?" "We never had any meetings." "Did you not go to church—to Sunday-school; did you not hear a preacher?" "We never knew any of these blessings. We never saw a Bible, we never heard a hymn, we had no Gospel, no preacher. Perhaps if we had known these wonderful things, Sodom might have been a holy city." "Men of Sodom, what would you say of people who had all these advantages—a church in every street, a Bible in every home, a preacher in every pulpit? Men of Sodom, what would you say of modern folk who only had to turn a knob on a radio panel to hear as many preachers as they desired, and yet, who remain indifferent to every warning?" "Surely, such people would be fools." And before this array of witnesses sinful man must inevitably be condemned. "It is appointed unto man once to die, and after death the judgment." To be forewarned is to be forearmed. If I must appear before God's throne, I shall need the services of a competent lawyer; and it is worthy of note that the Lord Jesus offers His services without money and without price. I should consult Him before it is too late.

## SECTION FOUR

*Expository Notes on the Lord's Sermon at the Pharisee's Dinner Table*

And as he spake, a certain Pharisee besought him to dine with him: and he went in, and sat down to meat. And when the Pharisee saw it, he marvelled that he had not first washed before dinner. And the Lord said unto him, Now do ye Pharisees make clean the outside of the cup and the platter, but your inward part is full of ravening and wickedness. Ye fools, did not he that made that which is without make that which is within also? But rather give alms of such things as ye have; and, behold, all things are clean unto you (vv. 37-41).

It is not possible to understand the criticism of the Pharisee nor appreciate the scathing denunciation of Jesus until one has become acquainted with the ridiculous requirements of the man-made laws of the Jews. This was not a casual washing of the hands in normal preparation for a meal. If that had been the point in question the Lord would not have reprimanded His host in such a way. Many writers have tried to express the details of the ceremonial law but probably Barclay's account is among the most informative. This author in his delightful *Daily Study Bible*, at page 158, says, "The law laid it down that before a man ate, he must wash his hands in a certain way, and that he must also wash them between courses. As usual every littlest detail was worked out. Large stone vessels were specially kept for the purpose because ordinary water might be unclean. The amount of water used must be at least a quarter of a log, that is enough to fill one and a half eggshells. First the water must be poured over the hands, beginning at the tips of the fingers and continuing right up to the wrists. Then the palm of each hand must be cleansed by rubbing the fist of the other into it. Finally, water must again be poured over the hand, this time beginning at the wrist and running right down to the finger tips. To the Pharisee to omit the slightest detail of this was to commit sin." Thus the beauty of the Mosaic law had been spoiled by man-made additions, and when the Lord failed to comply with the requirements of these ceremonial laws, the watching host began to criticize. It was this unfortunate state of affairs which occasioned the scathing denunciation of Jesus. He reminded His hearers that God is more concerned with the state of a man's heart than with the appearance of his hands. Holiness is a quality within the soul; sin is greater than a speck of dust on the hand. One kind act is of more value in the sight of God than all the ceremonial washing preceding any feast.

> But woe unto you Pharisees! for ye tithe mint and rue, and all manner of herbs, and pass over judgment and the love of God: these ought ye to have done, and not to leave the other undone. Woe unto you, Pharisees! for ye love the uppermost seats in the synagogues, and greetings in the markets. Woe unto you, scribes and Pharisees, hypocrites! for ye are as graves which appear not, and the men that walk over them are not aware of them (vv. 42–44).

It should be remembered that Jesus came to earth when the religious life of the nation was at its lowest ebb. Spirituality had been buried beneath the dictates of legalism. James 1: 27, says "Pure religion and undefiled before God and the Father is this, To visit the fatherless and the widows in their affliction, and to keep himself unspotted from the world." Love is the hallmark of true godliness, but unfortunately this was missing from the exercises of the Pharisees. They were critical, spiteful, legalistic, and often their attitude toward fellow men was exactly the opposite of what might have been expected from men so anxious to observe the traditions of the fathers. Ostentatiously they tithed even the herbs from their gardens, but they forgot or ignored the weightier matters of virtue, kindness, and true humility. They would argue about seats of importance at any function; they expected people to recognize them as they walked in the market places; they desired and demanded public acclamation, and yet they were obnoxious in the sight of God. Even though a traveller innocently contacted an ancient tomb, he was still defiled and as such was deprived of certain privileges. These men not only contaminated the people with whom they came into contact; they themselves were vaults of decay and putrefaction. Their hearts were filthy.

Then answered one of the lawyers and said unto him, Master, thus saying thou reproachest us also. And he said, Woe unto you also, ye lawyers! for ye lade men with burdens too grievous to be borne, and ye yourselves touch not the burdens with one of your fingers. Woe unto you! for ye build the sepulchres of the prophets, and your fathers killed them. Truly ye bare witness that ye allow the deeds of your fathers: for they indeed killed them, and ye build their sepulchres. Therefore also said the wisdom of God, I will send them prophets and apostles, and some of them they shall slay and persecute; That the blood of all the prophets, which was shed from the foundation of the world, may be required of this generation; From the blood of Abel unto the blood of Zacharias which perished between the altar and the temple: verily I say unto you, It shall be required of this generation (vv. 45-51).

The paragraph more or less is self-explanatory. The lawyers were experts in finding fault with other people; it was a startling change when they discovered they themselves were being criticized. One cannot read these utterances of the Lord without admiring the continuing courage with which He faced His task. Men of smaller stature would have modified the denunciation feeling the influential people in the audience might thereby be won. Jesus never played to the gallery; when He saw sin in arrogant hearts, He denounced it. The death of Zechariah is described in II Chronicles 24. This was the closing book in the Jewish canon of Holy Writings, and therefore we are safe in assuming that Jesus was speaking of the first and last murders to be mentioned in their own records. His terrifying statement inferred they would be held responsible for all that had happened because their sin was identical with that of the ancient murderers. They were as bad as the worst. This was indeed a terrible indictment; if they had possessed any wisdom they would have asked God for pardon. The statement THE WISDOM OF GOD is certainly interesting and during the centuries it has occasioned much speculation. The parallel passage is in Matthew 23: 34 where Christ says, "Behold, I SEND unto you prophets . . ." Christ claimed to be the embodiment of the wisdom of God. He Who had been in the counsels of the Godhead; He who expressed the mind of the Father was able to speak authoritatively. This was just another of those thrilling scriptures in which the Saviour identified Himself with the Almighty and claimed equality with the One by Whom He had been sent.

Woe unto you, lawyers! for ye have taken away the key of knowledge: ye entered not in yourselves, and them that were entering in ye hindered. And as he said these things unto them, the scribes and the Pharisees began to urge him vehemently, and to provoke him to speak of many things; Laying wait for him, and seeking to catch something out of his mouth, that they might accuse him (vv. 51-54).

The lawyers were the men responsible for the study of the law, and the enunciation of any new details connected therewith. They constantly reminded other people what ought to be done, but they seldom did much themselves. They knew all the loopholes and were experts at evasion. Here are some of their evasions. The limit of a sabbath day's journey was two thousand cubits (1,000 yards) from a man's residence. But if a rope were tied across the end of the street, the end of the street became his residence and he could go 1,000 yards beyond that. If on the Friday evening he left at any given point enough food for two meals, that point technically became his residence and he could go 1,000 yards beyond that. One of the forbidden works on the sabbath was the tying of knots, sailors' or camel drivers' knots, and knots in ropes. But a woman might tie the knot in her girdle. Therefore, if a bucket of water had to be raised from a well, a rope could not be knotted to it, but a woman's girdle could. . . . To carry a burden was forbidden, but the codified law lays it down, "he who carried anything, whether it be in his right hand, or in his left hand, or in his bosom, or on his shoulder is guilty; but he who carried anything on the back of his hand, with his foot or with his mouth, or with his elbow, or with his ear, or with his hair, or with his money-bag turned upside down, or between his money-bag and his shirt, or in the fold of his shirt, or in his shoe, or in his sandal is guiltless" (William Barclay, *Daily Study Bible.* Luke, pages 161-162). The lawyers to whom Christ addressed His remarks were the men responsible for many of these stupid ideas; they placed intolerable burdens upon suffering people whilst they themselves cited reasons to explain their non-observance of their own laws. The Master's denunciation aroused their bitter opposition, and the words used to describe their reactions were exceedingly strong. The shadow of the Cross was beginning to fall across the soul of the Saviour.

# The Twelfth Chapter of Luke

THEME: *Christ's Interrupted Sermon*

OUTLINE:

    I. Be careful . . . lest Satan hinder you. Verses 1–12
    II. Be confident . . . God will not fail you. Verses 13–34
    III. Be consistent . . . in preparing for Christ's return.

                              Verses 35–39

## SECTION ONE

*Expository Notes on Christ's Warnings to His Friends*

In the meantime, when there were gathered together an innumerable multitude of people, insomuch that they trod one upon another, he began to say unto his disciples first of all, Beware ye of the leaven of the Pharisees, which is hypocrisy. For there is nothing covered that shall not be revealed; neither hid, that shall not be known. Therefore whatsoever ye have spoken in darkness shall be heard in the light: and that which ye have spoken in the ear in closets shall be proclaimed upon the housetops (vv. 1–3).

Barclay reminds us that the Jews had a special term by which they described preaching. It was *Charaz* which meant *stringing pearls*. The implication of this term was obvious. Unlike modern homiletics in which the speaker is expected to develop a theme, the ancients gathered their wisdom from many sources, and whether or not the jewels of thought were connected, they were "strung together" in an extended oration. This chapter provided an outstanding example of this kind of preaching, and if we may assume from Luke that the discourse was delivered at one time, then the utterance was interrupted at least twice. At verse thirteen, we read, "And one of the company said unto him, Master speak to my brother . . ." Then at verse forty-one, Peter said unto Him, "Lord, speakest thou this parable unto us, or even to all." However, we should not lose sight of the fact that as Burgen said, "Of the fifty-nine verses which compose the present chapter, no less than thirty-five prove to have been delivered on quite distinct occasions; not in single verses only, but by seven, eight, or even ten verses at a time." Perhaps the Lord repeated some of these sayings many times in many places, and the possibility exists that he might on some special occasion have uttered them all together. The point is not really important. The phrase, *an innumerable number of people* is somewhat strong and must be regarded as a hyperbolical expression. Literally it means myriads of people—a crowd so vast that the people were trampling upon each other. The Lord began to speak about the danger of hypocrisy, and indicated it was never safe to be two-faced! The Pharisees often professed one thing and practised another! The homes of that day had flat rooftops, and it was easy for the listeners to visualise the horror of a householder if some of the secrets of the home were suddenly shouted from the roof. The implications were that what men did secretly in hypocrisy, God would proclaim publicly.

> And I say unto you my friends, be not afraid of them that kill the body, and after that have no more that they can do. But I will forewarn you whom ye shall fear: Fear him, which after he has killed hath power to cast into hell; yea, I say unto you, Fear him. Are not five sparrows sold for two farthings, and not one of them is forgotten before God. But even the very hairs of your head are all numbered. Fear not therefore: ye are of more value than many sparrows (vv. 4-7).

This passage is as remarkable for its beauty as for its teaching. The introductory note "My friends" suggests that tenderness had been expressed in the Saviour's voice. He could not promise immunity from suffering for He knew some of His followers would die for their faith. Nevertheless they were not to fear their enemies. Death was not final, but a channel through which they would enter a larger world. Viewed from the highest pinnacle of faith, martyrdom would be the means by which the enemies would promote saints to glory. The disciples were not to be afraid of such men. God alone commanded fear—reverential fear, for His power extended not only to the physical frames of humans but to their immortal souls. The body and the soul; time and infinity are closely related in this scripture. The fear of God is immediately offset by the superb reference to the sparrows. These birds were common pests. Matthew says that two were sold for one farthing. Luke adds the suggestive detail that if a man bought double that number, the seller gave one extra sparrow for nothing. Although the bird was insignificant and worthless, God cared for it. The Creator loved the sparrows, therefore it was inconceivable that He could ever forget or forsake man. Fear, when tempered by love, becomes adoration. Someone made a study of hairs and claimed that a blond person has about 145,000 hairs; a brunette 120,000, and a red-head 90,000. This is another hyperbolical expression. Jesus was emphasizing that God was mindful of insignificant things; individuals were never lost in the crowd. If He were interested in one hair, obviously that interest increaséd enormously when He considered the whole man. If He loved the tiny sparrow, then He loved man very much more. Fear disappears when love looks into the face of a Heavenly Father.

> God feedeth the sparrows that fly in the air.
> They are never in trouble but what He is there.
> If God with these creatures His blessings doth share
> Then I surely can trust such infinite care.

The term *Gehenna* translated *hell* or *hades* originally referred to *the Valley of Hinnom.* This in ancient times had been a fair and beautiful valley to the south of the hill of Zion. The king's gardens were there, and for a while this was the most attractive place in the kingdom. However, the idolatrous kings worshipped Molock in that area, and afterwards, as a mark of the divine displeasure, Josiah made it the city dump where fires smouldered and burned day and night. Jesus used this as an illustration in many of His sermons.

> Also I say unto you, Whosoever shall confess me before men, him shall the Son of man also confess before the angels of God: But he that denieth me before men, shall be denied before the angels of God. And whosoever shall speak a word against the Son of man, it shall be forgiven him: but unto him that blasphemeth against the Holy Spirit, it shall not be forgiven (vv. 8–10).

Throughout the Christian era this passage has often been taken from its context, and misused to destroy the confidence of earnest people. It is true that Christ encouraged His followers to witness unashamedly, and that He also warned against the folly of denial, but He did not state that some of His followers in error might be eternally damned. The chief work of the Holy Spirit is the presentation of Christ. ". . . he shall not speak of himself . . . he shall glorify me" (John 16: 13–14). Throughout the ministry of the Lord, the Holy Spirit presented Christ through the medium of the body which had been prepared for the eternal Son; thereafter, the Holy Spirit continued the work by presenting Christ through the preaching of the apostles. The alpha and the omega of this ministry was the exaltation of Jesus. It should be remembered that Matthew (12: 31–32) and Mark (3: 28) place this utterance after the Jews had ascribed the works of the Lord to Beelzebub, the prince of devils. The Holy Spirit had manifested the power of God in the works of Jesus, but in spite of the fact the Holy Trinity had combined to produce a miracle, the Jews insisted this was the work of Satan. The Greek word used is *blaspheemeesanti*; this is the aorist participle denoting finality. These people had reached a verdict—and the decision appears to be irrevocable. That is the sense of the aorist tense of a Greek verb—something completed in the past. Jesus indicated this kind of sin was beyond forgiveness. This was not through any deficiency in the Grace of God, but because sinners had reached the point of no return! It would be impossible for them to repent for they were dead toward God. The Holy Spirit no longer strove with them. The man who worries lest he has committed the unpardonable sin, *is the one man who has not*. When there is any sign of repentance within the soul, this in itself is evidence that the Holy Spirit is still working there. God has too much wisdom to try to bring souls to repentance when repentance is impossible.

And when they bring you unto the synagogues, and unto magistrates and powers, take ye no thought how or what thing ye shall answer, or what ye shall say. For the Holy Spirit shall teach you in that same hour what ye ought to say (vv. 11-12).

These words were never meant to be an indulgence against laziness. The preacher who affirms he has no need to study has either too small a brain or too large a mouth. This message was meant to be a stimulant against the dangers of excessive care and worry. The prisoners would be unaware of the nature of all the charges which would be brought against them. Therefore if they spent days trying to form some kind of defence, they might be wasting time considering things never to be mentioned. Yet even if they did not know the charges to be brought against them by the rulers, God did. It was essential therefore that the disciples keep open the channels by which God communicated thought. A clean heart; a listening spirit; a readiness to obey the Lord, would in the final analysis, be better than a lengthy document drawn up through the long exacting hours of anxious preparation. The Holy Spirit would be the Paraclete, the Counsellor called alongside to help. When the prisoner stood in the courtroom, he would have a skilled Attorney at his side. With this assurance the disciples were encouraged to march into the future.

## HOMILIES

Study No. 41

### THE UNPARDONABLE SIN

The Lord Jesus said, "Wherefore I say unto you, All manner of sin and blasphemy shall be forgiven unto men : but the blasphemy against the Holy Spirit shall not be forgiven unto men. And whosoever speaketh a word against the Son of man, it shall be forgiven him, but whosoever speaketh against the Holy Spirit, it shall not be forgiven him, neither in this world, nor in the world to come (Matthew 12: 31–32). This great utterance often leads to error and fear. In various parts of the world, despairing people confess their terror because they believe they have committed the unpardonable sin. The judgment of God appears to be a guillotine. The eternal death sentence has already been passed, and life is but the interim before the execution takes place. These poor people are utterly miserable, very foolish, and do not understand the Scriptures.

### An Unaccepted Testimony

All who believe they belong to this category should consider the circumstances in which Christ uttered the words. He had just delivered a man possessed of a devil, and excitement prevailed among the onlookers. "But when the Pharisees heard it, they said, This fellow doth not cast out devils, but by Beelzebub the prince of the devils" (Matthew 12 : 24). They recognized Christ was the medium through whom power was manifested, but they failed to recognize whence that power came. In actual fact the last Adam had come to show the fallen first Adam what might be accomplished when man fully surrenders to the Holy Spirit. Thus it is written that Christ was born of the Spirit—led of the Spirit—returned in the power of the Spirit—spake of the Spirit— and ultimately offered Himself to God through the Spirit. When man ascribed to Satan the deeds of the Holy Spirit, they endangered their souls. The Lord knew that soon a major change would take place in the workings of God. He Himself would return to heaven in order that the Comforter might come to earth as the representative of the Godhead. He would have a unique commission, and would constantly witness of Christ. ". . . He shall not speak of himself . . . he shall glorify me . . ." Christ knew that many people would continue to reject this testimony.

### An Unending Tragedy

If the Holy Spirit constantly affirms the truth of redemption as found in Christ; if as Christ taught, "He shall receive of mine and shall show it unto you"—if this ministry came forth from God the Father, and men rejected it, what more could be done for them? Christ was God's answer to human need. The Holy Spirit was God's method of bringing Christ to human need. To reject His message and to spurn Christ would mean immeasurable guilt. Since Jesus alone can deal with human sin, a man without Him must remain unpardoned. Thus the statement was made: "It shall not be forgiven him, neither in this world, neither in the world to come." The unpardonable sin is the rejection of the Lord Jesus Christ. Language is inadequate to express the disaster of a lost soul.

### An Unnecessary Terror

When God finally abandons man, all spiritual promptings will cease. The soul will be dead; the opportunities gone forever. When a man is worried about this matter, it is evident that some power is at work in his consciousness. A whisper says, "You need Christ," and fear responds, "It's too late now; you have committed the unpardonable sin." Whence came the first whisper? If God has departed, would He return to torment the guilty soul? If the prompting be heard, there is reason to believe the Lord is still seeking the man's soul. The objection represents Satan's greatest effort to thwart the purposes of God in man's salvation. It may be safely assumed that *all who have committed the unpardonable sin are not the least worried about it.* The souls who are tormented by such thoughts have the least reason to fear. If God has come near enough to whisper "Jesus," He cannot be far away. Let us kneel to pray, and the sun will shine through the clouds. God is a Father, a wonderful Father—not a tyrant!

### SECTION TWO

*Expository Notes on Christ's Attitude toward Wealth*

And one of the company said unto him, Master, speak to my brother, that he divide the inheritance with me. And he said unto him, Man, who made me a judge or a divider over you? And he said unto them, Take heed, and beware of covetousness; for a man's life consisteth not in the abundance of things which he possesseth (vv. 13-15).

Possibly the best way to understand the underlying motives of this request is to consider the story of the Prodigal Son. Under Jewish law, the first-born received as his birthright twice the inheritance received by any other member of the family. The eldest brother was responsible for the support of his mother and the unmarried sisters in the family. Usually the division of the inheritance took place at the father's death, but there were occasions when the younger brother or brothers desired to be *bought out*—that is, they desired to receive their share of the inheritance before they were legally entitled to claim it. The Prodigal Son asked for his share and then departed to squander his possessions in a far country. It would appear from the test that this man had similar ideas. He was obviously covetous for the Lord used the occasion to warn the listeners against this sin. The Lord's refusal to help the fellow made it more difficult for him to embark upon what might have been a life of sin. Life in all its fulness means more than material prosperity. Some people are so poor they only have money. Sometimes a man's overcrowded barns are indicative of an impoverished soul.

And he spake a parable unto them, saying, The ground of a certain rich man brought forth plentifully: And he thought within himself saying, What shall I do, because I have no room where to bestow my fruits. And he said, This will I do: I will pull down my barns, and build greater; and there will I bestow all my fruits and my goods. And I will say to my soul, Soul, thou hast much goods laid up for many years; take thine ease, eat, drink, and be merry. But God said unto him, Thou fool, this night thy soul shall be required of thee: then whose shall those things be, which thou hast provided. So is he that layeth up treasure for himself, and is not rich toward God (vv. 16-21).

Someone said of this stupid man, "There was too much ego in his cosmos." His world was bounded on all sides by himself. He made three statements but in so doing, used the personal pronoun *I* six times and the possessive pronoun *my* five times. He was self-made deity who worshipped at his own shrine. Nevertheless this story was told by the Saviour that a contrast might be drawn between the man who possessing everything, enjoyed nothing, and the man who having nothing, could lay claim to unlimited wealth. Of all his assets, only one had any continuing value. His great crops would be gathered by others; his new granaries he would never see; the many years of which he so fondly dreamed would never arrive. His soul, alone, was destined to live on. Yet in the final analysis, he was not even master of his own house, for the messengers of God—the angels of death, were to visit his homestead that night. It was easy to appreciate the forcefulness of the Saviour's message for He had just been asked to assist such a man in obtaining a premature share of an inheritance. Sometimes, it is very dangerous to become wealthy!

And he said unto his disciples, Therefore, I say unto you, Take no thought for your life, what ye shall eat; neither for the body, what ye shall put on. The life is more than meat, and the body is more than raiment. Consider the ravens: for they neither sow nor reap; which neither have storehouse nor barn: and God feedeth them; how much more are ye better than the fowls? And which of you with taking thought can add to his stature one cubit? If ye then be not able to do that thing which is least, why take ye thought for the rest? (vv. 22-26).

These words of Jesus should never be taken from their context. They were meant to teach the folly of excessive worry. God's children should never be over-anxious about daily subsistence. At all times to grasp firmly the hand of God is better than to be building larger barns. Nevertheless, this is not a licence for negligence. There are people who take this text literally and never plant anything. They live from day to day honestly believing that God will provide all their needs; they only have to wait for the modern ravens to bring the daily meals. This is wrong. Farmers must plough their fields or see them become a wilderness. Fishermen must use their nets or starve; men must do their daily work. Let it be repeated and emphasized that this is a warning against harassing anxieties and not a permit for indolence. Yet, on the other hand, there was a literal fulfilment of these promises in the experiences of the disciples. They were commissioned by their Master to go into the highways and byways of a lost world to proclaim the Gospel. They could not plough nor fish, and thus as necessity arose, God supplied their needs. Nevertheless, let us remember that even though God similarly met the needs of the apostle Paul, when the great preacher stayed for a while in a city, he did not ask the Lord to perform miracles in sending bread; he probably asked for a different miracle —customers to buy the tents he was making—for Paul was a tent maker by trade. Faith without works is dead. The trusting soul is the man who does his best at all times. He looks for the movement of the divine hands only when the task is too complicated for his own.

The idea of being able or unable to add to one's stature one cubit is strange, and the consensus of opinion is this might be an unfortunate translation. The Greek word is *heelikian* and there can be little doubt that the primary meaning of this word refers not to height but to *length of life*. Thus stature ought not to have been translated *life* or *age*. It is so translated in John 9: 21 and 23, and in Hebrews 11: 11. The idea of a person being anxious to increase his stature is undoubtedly somewhat strange, and the addition of a cubit to it would hardly be called in the following verse "that which is least." Anxiety about a longer term of life is much more common and intelligible. The application of the word *cubit* to an increase of life is quite justified by the expression in the Psalms, "Thou hast made my days as an handbreadth" (Psalm 39: 5, *Ryle's Expository Thoughts on Luke*, p. 82). However as a contrast to this, Godet thinks the term applies to the growth of plants; that within a short space of time, a small plant can greatly increase its height. This to the plant is very easy, and yet to man it remains an impossibility, if man cannot do—what to the plant is easy—why should he grow weary trying to do the hard things?

Consider the lilies how they grow: they toil not, they spin not; and yet I say unto you, that Solomon in all his glory was not arrayed like one of these. If then God so clothe the grass, which is today in the field, and tomorrow is cast into the oven; how much more will he clothe you, O ye of little faith. And seek not ye what ye shall eat, or what ye drink, neither be ye of doubtful mind. For all these things do the nations of the world seek after: and your Father knoweth that ye have need of these things. But rather seek ye the kingdom of God; and all these things shall be added unto you (vv. 27–31).

It has become extremely difficult to identify the lily to which Christ referred. It might have been the *Amaryllis Lutea* or Autumnal Narcissus for this flower grows all over the country and fills the fields with golden glory during the months of Autumn. Yet the works of M. F. Bovet seem to suggest that the lily was the *Anemone Coronaria*, the magnificent red anemone with which on occasion the fields of Palestine were carpeted. Then there were the *Lilum Candidum* the beautiful white lily, and also the *Lilium Rebrum* an elegant red lily. These were not quite so common, but they were indescribably lovely. Any or all of these lilies might have been mentioned by the Saviour, for "Solomon in all his glory was never arrayed like one of these."

Wood was always hard to obtain in Palestine and therefore dry grass was used as a substitute to feed the fires. It will be remembered that the Hebrew word for preaching suggested stringing pearls together. The idea is evident in this sermon. God clothed the lilies; God made the grass, and these things were very trivial compared with man. If God could exhibit such watchful care over the insignificant things of nature, He could hardly forsake the crown of all His creation. The nations of the world might be subject to overwhelming stress and strain for they were strangers to the covenant promises of the Almighty. God's children should be wiser; happier, and safer. Their constant seeking the mind of God would in itself be the guarantee they would want for nothing. Their faith was the key to the granaries of God's never-diminishing supplies.

**Fear not, little flock; for it is your Father's good pleasure to give you the kingdom. Sell that ye have, and give alms; provide yourselves bags which wax not old, a treasure in the heavens that faileth not, where no thief approacheth, neither moth corrupteth. For where your treasure is, there will your heart be also (vv. 32–34).**

This added note of tenderness—*little flock*—was obvious. Each flock had a shepherd, therefore, though small in number, the disciples could be assured of the presence of their Lord. They were not to be afraid. The continuing interest displayed in them by the Father was the guarantee that He intended to complete that which He had commenced. He who had brought them to the kingdom planned to promote them within it. Obviously the following statements were not to be taken literally for how could any believer provide himself with an eternal bag. This is indeed *a string of pearls*. Assured of the support which the Kingdom of God could offer, the disciple, as he was led of God's Spirit, could afford to sell some of his unnecessary possessions in order to give alms, and by so doing he would be laying up treasure in heaven. Earthly treasure in those days was often indicated by the rich clothes and sparkling jewels of the owner. Clothes could become moth-eaten; jewels might be stolen; treasure could easily disappear. Spiritual treasure laid up in the bank of Heaven never deteriorated; thieves never gained admittance to eternal vaults. Jesus brought this part of His sermon to a great conclusion when He said, "Place your treasure in Heaven, and your heart will be there also." By the same token, if a disciple be fascinated by the stock markets of Sodom, he will probably spend more time studying the market reports than in reading the Word of God. It is exceedingly difficult to separate the heart from its treasure, and therefore we must be very careful where we deposit our valuables!

See "A Dream in Three Acts" the special homily at the end of section two, chapter sixteen, p. 357.

## SECTION THREE

*Expository Notes on the Essential Readiness for the Lord's Return*

Let your loins be girded about and your lights burning. And ye yourselves like unto men who wait for their lord, when he will return from the wedding; that when he cometh and knocketh, they may open unto him immediately. Blessed are those servants, whom the lord when he cometh shall find watching; verily I say unto you, that he shall gird himself, and make them to sit down to meat, and will come forth and serve them (vv. 35–37).

The customary garments of the men of the east were long flowing robes, and these often became a nuisance when certain tasks had to be done. Therefore it was necessary to have a girdle around the waist, and into this when occasion demanded, the lower parts of the robe were tucked. The lamp was a small piece of pottery sometimes resembling a sauce-boat and often as small as the palm of the hand. The wick floated on the top of the oil. The parable of the ten virgins in Matthew 25 supplies the background information necessary for the correct understanding of this text. Believers had to be unhindered; their feet had to be free from encumbrances and their lights shining in a dark world, for only thus could they be as men expecting the return of their Master. Quoting Pearce, Bishop Ryle said, ". . . it was the custom in those days for the bridegroom . . . to wait upon the guests as a servant." The returning master, delighted at the faithfulness of his watchful servants, honoured them by an invitation to his table when he personally attended to all their needs. The inference of these sayings of Christ was that similarly He intends to reward all who faithfully await His return.

And if he shall come in the second watch, or come in the third watch, and find them so, blessed are those servants. And this know, that if the goodman of the house had known in what hour the thief would come, he would have watched, and not have suffered his house to be broken through. Be ye therefore ready also: for the Son of man cometh at an hour when ye think not (vv. 38-40).

The Jewish night was divided into four watches. The first was from sunset or dark until nine o'clock; the second from nine until midnight; the third from midnight until three in the morning, and the fourth from three until dawn. No man can continue to watch the clock around, but even though some slept, the watching servant would have time to awaken the others so that all would be ready to meet the Master. When the Lord changed the simile to that of a thief coming in the night, He introduced a note of danger. Again the suggestion is made that this scripture be linked with the parable of the virgins. Five virgins actually expected to rejoice with the bridegroom but alas, their joys were turned to sorrow. A thief stole their greatest jewels!

Then Peter said unto him, Lord, speakest thou this parable unto us, or even to all? And the Lord said, Who then is that faithful and wise steward, whom his lord shall make ruler over his household, to give them their portion of meat in due season? Blessed is that servant, whom his lord when he cometh shall find so doing. Of a truth I say unto you, that he shall make him ruler of all that he hath (vv. 41-44).

Peter's question was apparently never answered—at least not to him personally. The Lord knew that in days to come some teachers would state certain scriptures only applied to specific classes of men—this for the Jews—that for the Gentiles. In the greatest possible sense all scripture is for all people, and the manner in which the Lord handled Peter's question provides food for thought. Two great words stand out in bold relief. They are *watching* and *working*. If watching is the evidence of faith; working is the evidence of faith in action. *Watching* for the Lord's coming may prepare the soul for the great day; but *working* for the Lord's coming is the sure way of bringing additional guests to the wedding feast. It must ever be a cause for regret that so many brethren spend weeks searching for signs of the Lord's appearing, but never go forth into the highways and byways seeking the lost for Christ. They prefer to pay missionaries to seek the lost in

Africa rather than to go forth themselves seeking the lost in their own neighbourhood. Watching and Working are the twin sons of faith. Both must develop and become strong. Happy indeed is the believer in whose heart this is taking place; he is destined for promotion in the coming kingdom.

> But and if that servant say in his heart, My lord delayeth his coming; and shall begin to beat the men servants and maidens, and to eat and drink, and be drunken; The lord of that servant will come in a day when he looketh not for him, and at an hour when he is not aware, and will cut him in sunder, and will appoint him his portion with the unbeliever's. And that servant, which knew the lord's will, and prepared not, neither did according to his will, shall be beaten with many stripes. But he that knew not, and did commit things worthy of stripes, shall be beaten with few stripes. For unto whomsoever much is given, of him shall be much required: and to whom men have committed much, of him they will ask the more (vv. 45-48).

The Greek word translated "cut in sunder" is very strong and probably relates to the form of punishment practised among ancient peoples. It literally means *to cleave in two*. The meaning must be modified here for further mention is made of the offender. Possibly the idea which the Lord tried to convey to the listeners was that this sin merited the greatest punishment—the sinner would be beaten with many stripes. It is also worthy of note that Christ differentiated between those who knew the lord's will and those who did not. Knowledge of the revealed will of God is a standard by which men will be judged, but ignorance of that will is something which cannot always be condoned. When a man ignores the sources of knowledge; when he refrains from reaching for that which is near, he will be responsible for his indifference. When men such as the unevangelized heathen never have a chance to become acquainted with the Will of God, there must be other standards by which they will be judged. All men have a conscience, and it is not too much to state that in the absence of the written word of truth, the Spirit of God works through the consciences of those who walk in darkness. However, although these may still prefer their evil ways, their guilt cannot equal that of the men who saw the light and rejected it. This line of demarcation is clearly drawn in the text; the second class of offenders are beaten—but with few stripes. The Bible teaches there are degrees of punishment for the guilty as there are degrees of rewards for the saints.

> I am come to send fire on the earth; and what will I, if it be already kindled! But I have a baptism to be baptized with; and how am I straightened till it be accomplished! Suppose ye that I am come to give

peace on earth? I tell you, Nay; but rather division. For from henceforth, there shall be five in one house divided, three against two, and two against three. The father shall be divided against the son, and the son against the father; the mother against the daughter, and the daughter against the mother; the mother in law against her daughter in law, and the daughter in law against her mother in law (vv. 49–53).

The New English Bible renders the passage: "I have come to set fire to the earth, and how I wish it were already kindled! I have a baptism to undergo, and how hampered I am until the ordeal is over." Fire destroys and purifies and both these ideas may be expressed in the text. Christ came to destroy the works of darkness; He came also to purify the people who would be won through His death. The divisive qualities of His ministry were already being witnessed, but since the full effect of His power could not be known until He had been crucified, the Lord felt the restraint which hindered the fulfilment of His desires. The word translated *baptism* was the word commonly used for the ordinance of baptism by which believers were received into the fellowship of the church. That is, they were immersed—submerged—covered—overwhelmed. The experience confronting the Lord was complete. He would be submerged in sorrow. *"All thy waves and thy billows are gone over me"* (Psalm 42: 7). One of the main Roman objections to the Gospel was that it divided families. Acceptance of Christ demanded allegiance to Him and this always brought the convert to the place of decision. When other gods, movements, societies, people expected the allegiance formerly given, the convert had to choose between the new faith and the old customs. When relatives persisted in their efforts to dissuade him and he refused to compromise, the unity of the family was shattered. (See the homily at the end of this section.)

And he said also to the people, When ye see a cloud rise out of the west, straightway ye say, There cometh a shower; and so it is. And when ye see the south wind blow, ye say, There will be heat; and it cometh to pass. Ye hypocrites, ye can discern the face of the sky and of the earth; but how is it that ye do not discern the time? Yea, and why even of yourselves judge ye not what is right? (vv. 54–57).

To the west of Palestine lay the Mediterranean Sea; when the wind came from that direction, the weather prophets predicted showers. To the south of the country lay the desert, and the winds from that direction were the harbingers of heat. These things were well-known and were discussed freely by all the people. Unfortunately, as now, so then, there were none so blind as those who had no desire to see. The other signs were ignored even by the religious people who professed to be expecting the coming of God's kingdom.

When thou goest with thine adversary to the magistrate, as thou art in the way, give diligence that thou mayest be delivered from him; lest he hail thee to the judge, and the judge deliver thee to the officer, and the officer cast thee into prison. I tell thee, thou shalt not depart thence, till thou hast paid the very last mite (vv. 58-59).

Some commentators turn this story into a sermon. That there is material for thought here none can deny but there is also danger that we stretch the sayings of Christ to make them express our doctrines rather than His. Surely the main point here is that the Lord was urging upon His listeners the necessity of making wise judgments. He had just condemned them for their inability to read the signs of the times, and this utterance came out of what had already been said. The word picture described two people taking a case to law. There was never any doubt in the Lord's mind concerning the guilt of the person addressed. Because the man was unquestionably guilty, he would have been wise to prevent the case going to the magistrate, and thereafter to the judge. It would be in the man's best interest to settle the matter out-of-court, for if the case actually went to the judge, the end would never be in doubt. Jesus was therefore urging His listeners to study their own needs; they were guilty before God; they had need of repentance, and the matter should never be postponed until the last moment. When men stood before God, penitence would be useless. Through the Grace manifested in Christ there existed a way by which all matters could be settled out of court. Wise men gave heed to the message of Jesus. "They shall not come into condemnation" (see John 5: 24).

## HOMILIES

Study No. 42

### THE SAVIOUR'S STRANGEST UTTERANCE
(Matthew 10: 34-36; Luke 12: 51)

The coming of Christ stirred the hearts of Israel as they had never previously been stirred, and from all parts of the country, crowds rushed to hear the new Teacher. Every miracle gave promise of greater things to come, and the fact that He gave peace to innumerable sufferers seemed to guarantee that soon He would bring peace to the troubled nation. Then to the consternation of His followers, He said, "Think not that I am come to send peace on earth: I came not to send peace but a sword. For I am come to set a man at variance against his father, and the daughter against her mother . . . And a man's foes shall be they of his own household."

### The Sword that Wounds

The Bible has three things to say of the usefulness of a sword. In the first place it wounds. The Saviour came to act as a great surgeon, and knowing the need of His patients, He liberated a Gospel destined to become a two-edged scalpel. Recognizing the need of sinners, the Lord Jesus did not hesitate to hurt them, for only by so doing could He bring healing to their sick hearts. He also warned His disciples that the forceful presentation of the Gospel message would arouse resentment, for the sword of truth would penetrate into the secret places of the conscience to reveal those things which most people would prefer to remain hidden. He said, "Woe unto you, when all men shall speak well of you." Holy warfare must always precede the healing of souls, for until the hidden, secret cancer of the soul be exposed and overcome, healing will be an impossibility.

### The Sword Separates

"For I am come to set a man at variance against his father, and the daughter against her mother," and we might add "a friend against a friend." The incoming of the message of the Gospel leads to a complete transformation in the outlook of men. The convert's former associates will probably misunderstand his motives, and might even persecute him in the new faith. In order to follow the Lord Jesus, the Christian may find it necessary to renounce his old delights, and forsake many of his former friends. The business man may find it necessary to revise all his ideas of trading, and if this should lead to a serious reduction in the profits, his partners are very likely to become critical. A wife who has accepted Christ as her Saviour may find it impossible to accompany her husband in the ways of sin, and her refusal to co-operate may lead to domestic unpleasantness. The sword of the Gospel may sever ties that might have been in existence for years. The early history of the Church provided ample evidence of the truth of Christ's prediction.

### The Sword that Ministers

The inspired Old Testament prophet recognized another use for the sword, and embodied his vision in his thrilling utterance concerning the coming of the King. "And he shall judge among the nations, and shall rebuke many people: and they shall beat their swords into ploughshares, and their spears into pruning hooks: nation shall not lift up sword against nation, neither shall they learn war any more" (Isaiah 2: 4). The prophet saw that the coronation of the Messiah would change the steel weapons of war and make them to serve a new purpose in the production of food. People who had been hurt by the sword would suddenly be fed by the new instrument. And in like manner this is true concerning the Gospel of Christ. The message of redemption will hurt, and then separate the sinner from his evil ways. Yet when this operation has been completed, and Christ occupies the throne of the man's affection, the Bible suddenly becomes the greatest Book in the world, for within its pages the Christian discovers the Bread of Life. It will minister to his deepest needs, and satisfy his hungry soul. The universal coronation of the Lord Jesus will lead to a new world, and the greatest proof of this sublime fact is found when a similar transformation takes place within the kingdom of a human heart.

(Taken from the Author's Book, *Bible Pinnacles*, page 85.)

# The Thirteenth Chapter of Luke

THEME : *The Need for Repentance*

OUTLINE :

    I. Jesus tells a story . . . of a fig tree. Verses 1–9
    II. Jesus delivers a woman . . . in the synagogue.
                                          Verses 10–21
    III. Jesus answers a question . . . with a sermon.
                                          Verses 22–30
    IV. Jesus counters a threat . . . with a forecast.
                                          Verses 31–34

## SECTION ONE

*Expository Notes about the Report Concerning the Death of the Galileans*

**There were present at that season some that told him of the Galileans, whose blood Pilate had mingled with their sacrifices. And Jesus answering said unto them, Suppose ye that these Galileans were sinners above all the Galileans, because they suffered such things? I tell you, Nay: but, except ye repent, ye shall all likewise perish (vv. 1–3).**

There is not a great amount of information available concerning this incident. Josephus does not mention it, and no one speaks authoritatively about it. Obviously the people were referring to an act of Pilate which had infuriated the nation. The Samaritans were excitable and very prone to become entangled in any political upheaval; if a fight were in the offing, these inflammatory folk were sure to be present. It was about this time that Pilate became involved in serious trouble with the Jewish leaders. The shortage of water in Jerusalem had always been a problem, and the administration planned to build an aqueduct to meet the increasing needs of the population. It was further proposed to offset the cost of this improvement by using certain funds allocated to the temple. The Jews, however, desired both the penny and the bun; they cried insistently for more water, but they thought the over-lords of the country should pay for it with their own currency. Thus the situation quickly became dangerous. When the crowds gathered in the city, the Roman soldiers were instructed to move among the people and be prepared to take action against the trouble-makers. They wore cloaks over their battle dress so that they might pass unnoticed. Probably these men exceeded their rights and even abused their profession by being ruthless. Instead of controlling the crowds they became brutal and in the ensuing battles, certain Samaritans were slain even as they prepared to offer their sacrifices to God. Many writers think this was the cause of the dispute which existed between Herod and Pilate,—the dispute which continued until the trial of Jesus (Luke 23: 6–12). Undoubtedly there were those who asked if these men had been forsaken by God because of some personal sin. Had the Almighty refused to come to their assistance because they were Samaritans—or because they had been guilty of some misdemeanour? The Lord quickly seized the opportunity to remind His informants of their own need for repentance.

> Or those eighteen, upon whom the tower in Siloam fell, and slew them, think ye that they were sinners above all men that dwelt in Jerusalem? I tell you, Nay: but, except ye repent, ye shall all likewise perish (vv. 4–5).

The word translated *sinners* is different from the word used in the preceding scripture. Actually this verse should read: ". . . think ye that they were debtors above . . ." This is another historical event veiled in obscurity. Obviously there had been an accident when a tower—possibly a defence tower built into the walls of the city—had collapsed causing the death of eighteen people. T. W. Manson says: "The accident described in this verse is not mentioned elsewhere, which is not surprising, since *it was an accident and not an incident!*" There have always been those people who connect personal suffering with personal sin. Even in the days of Job, Eliphaz the Temanite said, "Remember, I pray thee, *whoever perished being innocent? or where were the righteous cut off?*" (Job 4: 7). God is seen as a vindictive taskmaster waiting to punish the guilty. The Lord Jesus denied this. Sometimes the greatest saints have been permitted to suffer whilst the wicked prospered. This, to some, has been a great problem, but all must remember that gold is purified by fire, and as David remarked, there are times when the wicked spread themselves as a green bay tree, but it is only a matter of time before "they are not." It is the end that counts. Once again the Lord used the illustration to reveal the need for true repentance.

> He spake also this parable; A certain man had a fig tree planted in his vineyard; and he came and sought fruit thereon, and found none. Then said he unto the dresser of his vineyard, Behold, these three years I come seeking fruit on this fig tree and find none: cut it down; why

cumbereth it the ground? And he answering said unto him, Lord, let it alone this year also, till I shall dig about it and manure it. And if it bear fruit, well: and if not, then after that, thou shalt cut it down (vv. 6–9).

Matthew 21: 18–20 forms a suitable setting against which this passage may be seen in its true perspective. It was not unusual for fig trees to be planted in vineyards. However, its presence amongst the vines indicated strong personal desires of the husbandman to have it there. The vineyards were an industry providing the finances necessary for the maintenance of the home; the solitary fig tree could hardly be placed in this category. It was probably there because the family liked figs. The surrounding vines were objects of the husbandman's care; the fig tree was the object of his affection. Upon it he lavished his attention; its fruit was not for the market but for his own delight. It is hard to ignore the implications of this strange situation for the Lord was speaking to people who firmly believed they were the apple of God's eye. Within the far-reaching international vineyards of the earth, God had planted a special race of people—His own chosen nation from which He would receive that which would gladden His heart. The outflow of their appreciation was expected to compensate for the inflow of the divine paternal care. Unfortunately God's desires were not being realized. The fig tree reached full productiveness after three years and therefore the Lord's indictment was fully justified. However, one wonders if the three years mentioned contained a veiled reference to the three years during which the Son of God ministered to this nation. Yet when the people exhibited nothing but hatred; when the fig tree might have been cut down, the mercy of God extended the time of grace into the fourth year. It was of no avail for the barrenness of the tree continued until Israel cried, "His blood be on us and on our children." It was only then that the nation was dispersed and scattered; it was then that the national fig tree was cut down. The mercy of God is as far-reaching as His patience, but the judgment of God is as certain as His predictions. The doctrine of *another chance* was never meant to blind men to the fact that someday will come the *last chance*.

(See the special homily at the end of the chapter.)

## SECTION TWO

*Expository Notes on the Woman Loosed from an Infirmity*

And he was teaching in one of the synagogues on the sabbath. And, behold, there was a woman which had a spirit of infirmity eighteen years, and was bowed together, and could in no wise lift up herself.

And when Jesus saw her, he called her to him, and said unto her, Woman, thou art loosed from thine infirmity. And he laid his hands on her: and immediately she was made straight, and glorified God (vv. 10-13).

The story of this suffering woman is as remarkable as its thoughts are challenging. The Lord later referred to her as "a daughter of Abraham" and this indicated more than her Jewish descendancy. Her presence in the synagogue surely denoted her nationality. As we shall see later, the Lord used this term in regard to Zaccheus, and this seems to indicate that those of whom it was said, were the offspring of Abraham in so much as they also exhibited the same kind of faith which characterised the patriarch. This woman was a believer. In spite of the fact that her crippled condition made movements extremely awkward; in spite of the fact that her appearance invited attention and made her the object of pity, she continued to attend the house of the Lord on the sabbath day. Others suffering from a mild headache might have taken—had they been available in those days—two aspirin tablets and gone to bed! Dr. A. Rendle Short in his book, *Modern Discovery and the Bible*, suggests her condition might be attributed to *spondylitis deformans*, that is, *"the bones of her spine were fused into a rigid mass."* Thus she was unable to straighten herself, and was obliged to shuffle around doubled up and helpless. The Lord saw her in the sanctuary and calling her to Him, proceeded to perform a most marvellous miracle. The scene which followed almost beggared description. The woman hearing her name called, shuffled from her seat, and trying to turn her head, looked up sideways at the Saviour. Then she struggled to obey His command. When the Lord's hand rested upon her bent body; when His wonderful voice whispered the benediction, the matchless grace of God flooded her soul and thrilled an audience. Suddenly she was straight. It should be noted she did not at first thank the Lord for His gracious act—she thanked God. Probably she learned much in after days, but at the moment of her deliverance she was as a babe beginning a new life. She would come to know that God had come down to earth in the Person of His Son, but during those initial moments of deliverance she remembered only that however she might be indebted to the instrument used in her healing, she was first indebted to God who had used this gracious Preacher— *"she glorified God."* She was indeed a daughter of Abraham.

And the ruler of the synagogue answered with indignation, because Jesus had healed on the sabbath day, and said unto the people, There are six days in which men ought to work: in them therefore come and be healed, and not on the sabbath day. The Lord then answered and said, Hypocrite, doth not each one of you on the sabbath loose his ox or his ass from the stall, and lead him away to watering? And ought not this woman being a daughter of Abraham, whom Satan hath bound, lo, these eighteen years, be loosed from this bond on the sabbath day? And when he had said these things, all his adversaries were ashamed: and all the people rejoiced for all the glorious things that were done by him (vv. 14-17).

The Jewish laws relating to work on the sabbath day were both confusing and ridiculous, but the statement made by the President of the Synagogue was even more stupid. Had the people taken his advice and returned to the synagogue the following day, they would have gone away again as impotent as when they arrived. Probably some of those people had been there on many occasions but the rulers of the synagogue had been unable to meet their need. This time, Christ was there and His presence was sufficient to make any day God's day. The Lord, strong and resolute, turned to face the man. Christ was no weakling; His face would be set in manly determination as He said, "Hypocrite." To address the synagogue dignitary in this manner required courage, but the Son of Man was never afraid to denounce evil. He never shirked responsibility nor turned aside from the path of duty. He believed in His mission; He believed in goodness. This was no time for a tactful approach to a difficult complaining man; this was not an occasion to exhibit care for one who was mentally ill; this was a time to denounce hypocrisy, and Jesus did that. The idea of keeping this poor woman in her pain for another twenty-four hours was obnoxious. Had she not suffered enough already—every day for eighteen years? There is every reason to believe that His eyes were hard, his finger was pointing straight at the heart of the hypocrite, when He faced the ruler of that synagogue. If it were right to help animals on the sabbath could it be wrong to assist one of God's children? Maybe the word "Hypocrite" was spoken in a whisper, but we may be sure it was heard in every part of the synagogue.

Here is a problem, for even Christ admitted that Satan had bound the woman for eighteen years. If she were a daughter of Abraham, why should Satan be allowed to spoil her life? Do we have here evidence of the permissive will of God? The problem of suffering has long disturbed the thoughts of the church, and sometimes it has been hard to harmonize the intense agony of a trusting soul with the delayed delivering powers of a loving Father. Millions of people have asked, Why? And the simple answer is that no one knows—if we knew everything, faith would be unnecessary. Had this woman committed some sin? Had Satan been able to take possession of her? Had her deep faith in God commenced at some later date; had her soul been healed whereas her body remained crippled? Had the woman known great remorse even when she worshipped because she remembered that her condition might have been avoided if she had *believed* earlier in life? We do not know. It is sufficient that she carried her burden with fortitude; whilst she could not repair the past; she determined to build the future, and with this thought in mind came to the sanctuary. Such faith and hope can never go unnoticed. Jesus called her to him, and the rest we know.


HOMILIES

Study No. 43

### A CHILD OF ABRAHAM

Degrees, however honorary, have to be earned. Some men attain to greatness after years of exacting research; others have degrees conferred upon them as an appreciation of superlative service in the cause of a country or convention. Nevertheless the fact remains that degrees of worth must always be earned. Throughout the New Testament story it becomes obvious that certain splendid people were honoured by God's University. Oftentimes the mark of greatness was unnoticed, but the keen reader easily observes that certain people might justifiably have written the letters C.A. after their names. They were in very deed and truth *Children of Abraham.* Paul wrote, "Cometh this blessedness then upon the circumcision only, or upon the uncircumcision also? for we say that faith was reckoned to Abraham for righteousness. . . . And he received the sign of circumcision, a seal of the righteousness of the faith which he had yet being uncircumcised : *that he might be the father of all them that believe,* though they be not circumcised; that righteousness might be imputed unto them also. And the father of circumcision to them who are not of the circumcision, but who also walk in the steps of that faith of our father Abraham, which he had being yet uncircumcised" (Romans 4 : 9–12).

*She suffered long when God only watched: but her faith continued.*

According to the testimony of the Saviour, this woman was a daughter of Abraham; that is, she believed, and righteousness was imputed unto her. Eighteen years are a very long time. We cannot ascertain her correct age at this time but the period through which she suffered surely represented a major portion of her lifetime. There is no record of her reactions to her sickness but the continued attendance at the sanctuary was not without meaning. It was hard to suffer year after year and not complain; it was harder still to maintain a buoyant faith when the waves of circumstance threatened to destroy her. It was surely stimulating to watch for the dawn, but when her night continued unbroken for eighteen years, surely doubt suggested the darkness would never end. Where was God? Why did He not do something? He had promised His kindness should never depart from those who trusted Him. Had He forgotten to be gracious? Probably she shook her head in perplexity, but her eyes shone through the tears. She could not understand the ways of God, but she believed He understood hers.

*She prayed often when God only heard: but her faith increased.*

A woman could attend a lot of services in eighteen years if she so desired, and obviously this one did. It will never be known how often she earnestly asked the Lord to help and heal her, but all the while the nagging pains in her back continued. She believed her soul stood upright in the sight of God; why should not her body be upright in the sight of men? To those with a heart she was an object of pity; to the heartless she was an object of ridicule, but she prayed, and for eighteen years, God seemed as helpless and indifferent as the idols of the heathen. Was it any use to pray? Was she wasting her time? If God ever answered prayer, He did so for those who were wealthy and able to do more for His cause! Surely God could not be bothered with a cripple, so why pester Him with prayers He never intended to answer? When she bowed her head in the sanctuary; when she tried to kneel at her bedside, the haunting thoughts returned. Why? Why? Why? Perhaps there were times when doubts produced tears, but always in the end she prayed. If she could not pray for healing she could at least pray for grace; and whether God answered or not she probably felt a lot happier when she had finished.

*She attended the sanctuary services even when God seemed to be absent, for her faith was in the Lord, not in the minister.*

The ruler of the synagogue was not exactly well known for his sympathetic understanding, and the orations which came regularly from the pulpit were not destined to make the blood run a little more freely in the veins of the listeners. Perhaps there were days when certain families were missing from the services. The exacting laws of sabbath-day travel forbad their going too far away on the sacred day, but a man can travel a long way without difficulty when he knows how to relax and dream in a comfortable armchair. Yet every sabbath day this lonely woman doubled over with infirmity shuffled up the street, and when the cantor began the service, she was in the usual seat. Probably she was unable to look into the preacher's face during the sermon, but she had long since learned to look into the face of God even when her eyes were closed. Other people on the slightest provocation would have found excuses for non-attendance, or reasons for going to another synagogue, but this woman had worshipped in that same pew for years; other places would now be unattractive. This was the place where she expected to meet God.

*She was miraculously delivered by a Visitor, but faith saw Him only as the instrument of her heavenly Father.*

It was a great day; rumour had it that a special preacher would be delivering the sermon. At least He would be a change from the weekly routine with which she and others were so accustomed. She found her place in the building and waited. Then suddenly she heard her name. Was she dreaming? Painfully she lifted her head until she saw the Stranger who was calling. That she responded to His invitation is obvious for within a matter of moments she was close enough for Christ to place His hands upon her body. Then suddenly something happened to her back; Prison bars were broken; the key of health opened a bright new future; it was unbelievable but true, God had healed her. Momentarily she forgot the Man who had done this marvellous thing. The nearest Person at that moment was God; she had seen Him regularly for eighteen years; she knew how to recognise His hand. Yes, God had done this thing and she instinctively praised Him. And then she remembered God's instrument: the Almighty had used the Visitor, and she looked again at the Preacher. His kindness was shining through His eyes; the power of God was flowing through His touch; the music of the eternal world was echoing in His tones. He was so wonderful, surely He was like God—and faith was indeed teaching the first lesson in the Christian experience. And Christ smiled. He had cared a great deal for Abraham; He cared no less for Abraham's daughter.

## SECTION THREE

### *Expository Notes on Christ's Answer to a Question*

**Then said he, Unto what is the kingdom of God like? and whereunto shall I resemble it? It is like a grain of mustard seed, which a man took, and cast into his garden; and it grew, and waxed a great tree; and the fowls of the air lodged in the branches of it. And again he said, Whereunto shall I liken the kingdom of God? It is like leaven, which a woman took and hid in three measures of meal, till the whole was leavened (vv. 18-21).**

Matthew and Mark place these parables in a different setting and this has led to controversy. There is no evidence to suggest that Christ only used the illustration once during His ministry. These were details vitally linked with the daily life of the people and probably Christ spoke of the mustard seed and the leaven on many occasions. Furthermore the lessons extracted from the illustrations were not identical. Matthew and Mark emphasized the smallness of the mustard seed and likened it to faith which can remove mountains. Luke had no such thought in mind. He emphasized the amazing growth of the kingdom of God which began with a small handful of unlearned men and ultimately encompassed the known world.

The mustard seed is indeed very small but in the Middle East where the climatic conditions favour the plant, the mustard tree has been known to reach a height of twelve feet. Its offshoots or branches are often so strong that the birds can indeed find shelter in the foliage. This then was commonplace and the listeners fully appreciated what Christ was saying. The fantastic growth of the tree has been likened to organised Christendom, and the birds to the various stages of apostasy which plague the work of God in the latter days. The exponents of this doctrine also point out that leaven, for the most part is spoken of as an evil influence; therefore in the parable of the measures of meal, it is made to represent the evil which works from within to contaminate the entire church. I do not think this is rightly dividing the Word of Truth. It must be remembered that Christ was endeavouring to indicate what the Kingdom would be like, and let it also be remembered that at that time, the kingdom had hardly begun. To a handful of unlearned men the gigantic task of evangelizing the world was being entrusted. There would be many setbacks and some of the disciples would give their lives for the cause of Christ. The Lord in this passage not only forecast the success of their mission; He spoke words which after sober reflection, could only be a source of encouragement and comfort. Their mission would succeed beyond their wildest dreams. Throughout the Old Testament, kingdoms are often likened to trees, and there are teachers who believe that the birds of the air were meant to indicate the Gentile nations who would find refuge within the shadow of God's church.

The parable of the leaven was something that every person in Palestine would have fully understood for each household made its own bread. Leaven was simply fermented dough—possibly retained from a prior baking. Jesus surely had seen Mary placing it into her dough and probably had watched the entire character of the bread changing because of the dynamic action of that small piece of leaven. Working quietly from within, the fermented dough worked to produce something wholesome, sweet, and desirable. Jesus saw in this an illustration of what would happen within the confines of the kingdom. His band of followers seemed so insignificant, and by many would even be denounced as unclean, but with the help of God they would challenge the citadels of Satan. The Holy Spirit would intensify and bless their efforts until growing from practically nothing, the kingdom would be established throughout the world.

> And he went through the cities and villages, teaching, and journeying toward Jerusalem. Then said one unto him, Lord, are there few that be saved? And he said unto them, Strive to enter in at the strait gate: for many, I say unto you, will seek to enter in, and shall not be able. When once the master of the house is risen up, and hath shut the door, and ye begin to stand without, and to knock at the door saying, Lord, Lord, open unto us; and he shall answer and say unto you, I know ye not whence ye are. Then shall ye begin to say, We have eaten and drunk in thy presence, and thou hast taught in our streets. But he shall say, I tell you, I know ye not whence ye are: depart from me, all ye workers of iniquity. There shall be weeping and gnashing of teeth, when ye shall see Abraham, and Isaac, and Jacob, and all the prophets, in the kingdom of God, and ye yourselves shut out. And they shall come from the east, and from the west, and from the north, and from the south, and shall sit down in the kingdom of God. And behold, there are last which shall be first, and there are first which shall be last (vv. 22-30).

The Lord had now returned to His itinerant evangelism. At verse 10 we read of His being in the synagogue; that was the last time Jesus entered the normal place of worship. The people had rejected Him; it would almost appear as if recognizing the uselessness of further effort, the Saviour turned away from them. From village to village the little band of preachers travelled, and everywhere people came to hear His message. Then suddenly from the ranks of the bystanders came someone to ask a question. His identity has not been revealed but it is almost certain that he shared the common belief that only Jews could be sure of admittance into the Kingdom of God. The Lord's reply surely startled the questioner. The task of getting into the kingdom of God was not only something of superlative importance; it was exceedingly difficult—so difficult that unless a man exerted all his strength, there was danger he would be excluded. The word translated *"strive"* is very strong. It is *agonizesthe*, which, according to Schlatter, means *the exerting of concentrated strength.* Jamieson, Fausset and Brown say: "The word is expressive of the difficulty of being saved— as if one *would have to force his way in."* Thayer says the word means: *to enter a contest; to contend in the olympic games; to contend with adversaries; to fight.* Liddle and Scott add another word picture; they suggest the word conveys the desperation of a lawyer *as he struggles to offset a capital charge.* Thus we arrive back where we started. To get into the kingdom of God is such a matter of importance that one should exert his concentrated strength to surmount any obstacle in the way.

This idea was diametrically opposed to the popular conception that Jews would inherit the kingdom by right of their birth into the Hebrew nation. Major suggests "In these verses allusion is made to nuptial feasts. These were celebrated by night. The house was filled with lights . . . the guests entered by a narrow wicket gate, at which the porter stood to prevent the unbidden from rushing in. When all that had been invited had arrived, the door was shut, and not opened to those who stood without, however much they knocked." There is also the possibility that the Lord had in mind the fact that city gates closed at sunset, and all cameliers desiring to enter, had need to arrive before closing time. Sometimes it was necessary to exert great effort to reach the gate, but unless the traveller succeeded, he was obliged to remain outside all night. Whichever is correct, the basic thought is identical. Nothing could be taken for granted. It was imperative that men should strive to enter God's kingdom whatever the cost. Even some participation in the work of God on earth is no guarantee that a man will enjoy the blessedness of the eternal kingdom. Unless men be born again, they will never see the kingdom (John 3 : 3).

The reference to Abraham, Isaac, and Jacob lends credence to the suggestion that this question had been asked by a Jew who believed all Jews would automatically be received into the kingdom. It was a startling thought that people who called themselves the descendants of Abraham, might in the last day be separated from their ancestor. It has also been taught that verses 29 and 30 were literally fulfilled for the spread of the Gospel and the establishment of the church proceeded first to the east, then to the west—along the Mediterranean coast; then to the north—to Europe; and finally to the South and the uttermost parts of the earth. It is also true that whereas the first churches in the East flourished greatly, today they appear to be the last, and in like manner the insignificant, and at that time, the unborn churches of the Western Nations—the last to come into being, are today the foremost in the work of evangelizing the world. This is an interesting idea, but probably there is greater depth of meaning in these words of the Saviour. Perhaps when the kingdom is eternally established, some of the great citizens of earth will find they are unimportant and obscure in the realms of the Lord, and by the same token, some insignificant Christians might thrill to hear the Lord saying, "Well done thou good and faithful servant . . . Come ye blessed of my Father . . . inherit the kingdom. . . ."

HOMILIES

Study No. 44

### STRIVING TO ENTER THE KINGDOM

There are two Bible words, which, pregnant with meaning, offer the most suggestive word pictures. Dr. Strong declares that the Hebrew word doon or dun, translated to *strive* really means to struggle, to resist *a charge of murder*. Liddle and Scott maintain that the Greek word agonizomai which is also translated *to strive*, means precisely the same thing. Therefore in order to appreciate the full significance of these Scriptures, one must endeavour to see a court of law where a desperate lawyer anxiously examines the records, sifts each piece of evidence, and does everything possible to gain a verdict on behalf of the accused.

### *The Case that was Lost*

The court-house was in the open air, and possibly near to the forests that lined the sides of a mountain. In the valley stood the skeleton of a huge ship; and not far away was the ancient saw-mill, alongside of which stood piles of sawdust. Nearby stood a strange old man, who always refused to work on the sabbath. His name was Noah. His ship was truly fantastic, but his preaching was even more so. All the people knew him, and probably thought he was mad. When he insisted that God would pour judgment upon the nation, they laughed him to scorn. What right had Noah, or even God to interfere in their pleasures? They loved to do that which Noah condemned; he should mind his own business! They failed to understand that they were figures in a court of law. The judge was God; the prosecuting counsel was Righteousness; the counsel for the defence was the Holy Spirit; the junior counsel was Noah; the accused was a guilty world. Possibly a rowdy meeting had just ended when God said, "My Spirit shall not always *strive* with man." The word used was *dun* and might be translated, "My Spirit shall not always struggle desperately to save the lives of sinful people." *How righteous are the laws of God.* The Holy Spirit acted as Counsel for the defence; yet when no righteous escape could be found, love yielded to law, and the sentence was passed. *How wonderful is the love of God.* That He should even try to save such people reveals a compassion beyond degree. *How persistent is the Spirit of God.* He continued year after year, and only gave up the struggle when to con-tinue was virtually impossible.

*The Case that was Won*

Once again the court-house was in the open air, where beneath the star-lit heavens, the Son of God lay prostrate. Describing the scene, Luke declared, "And being in an *agony* he prayed more earnestly: and his sweat was as it were great drops of blood falling down to the ground" (Luke 22:44). The word translated *agony* is the Greek equivalent to the Hebrew word already considered. It suggests the desperation of trying to offset a capital charge. Man was in danger; the forces of righteousness were about to pass sentence. The time was short, but Christ was making the supreme effort to discover a loophole whereby the guilty could be saved from death. This was the climax of the epic struggle which had continued throughout the Saviour's life. Continually the forces of evil had tried to defeat this great Lawyer, but when victory seemed within their grasp, He seized the sin of the accused, suffered in his stead, and satisfied every requirement of divine justice. The Saviour of men died in His own court-house and the prisoner went out free.

*The Case that is Still in Doubt*

There was a day when someone asked the Lord, "Are there few that be saved?" and His reply presented another word-picture. The disciples saw a city on a hill-top; the sun was setting, and the gates were about to be closed. Certain travellers who were late, were struggling desperately to reach the gate before it closed for the night, but some were finding difficulty climbing the hill. They were hurrying; they were breathless: but to enter in time was a matter of supreme importance. The disciples were still visualising the scene when the Saviour said, "Strive (agonize) to enter in at the strait gate: for many, I say unto you, will seek to enter in, and shall not be able." The same desperation exhibited in the efforts of the Holy Spirit in Noah's day, and in Christ's struggle in the garden of Gethsemane, should be found in our untiring desire to get into the Kingdom of God. There is so much at stake; there is no time to lose. This case may be either won or lost, and we shall be the deciding factors. What shall it profit a man if he gain the whole world and lose his soul? (Taken from the Author's book: *Bible Highways*, p. 9.)

## SECTION FOUR

*Expository Notes on Christ's Reactions to Herod's Threat*

**The same day there came certain of the Pharisees, saying unto him, Get thee out, and depart hence: for Herod will kill thee. And he said unto them, Go ye, and tell that fox, Behold, I cast out devils, and I do cures**

today and tomorrow, and the third day I shall be perfected Nevertheless
I must walk today, and tomorrow, and the day following: for it cannot
be that a prophet perish out of Jerusalem (vv. 31-33).

The motivating force of these Pharisees has long been the subject of
debate. It has been suggested that they were sincere men who
earnestly warned the Lord of impending disaster. Others think that
they were in league with the king, and this was an effort to drive the
Saviour into places where He would more easily be captured. Still
others think that this was an effort on the part of Herod to frighten the
Preacher and thereby to undermine the effectiveness of His ministry.
It is hardly possible to be dogmatic in interpreting this passage.
William Barclay has an illuminating passage in his *Daily Study Bible*.
"The Jews divided the Pharisees into seven different classes. (1) *The
Shoulder Pharisees*. These wore their good deeds on their shoulder,
and performed them to be seen of men. (2) *The Wait-a-Little Pharisees*.
They could always find a good excuse for putting off a good deed until
tomorrow. (3) *The Bruised or Bleeding Pharisee*. They would not even
look at a woman in the street. They even shut their eyes to avoid
seeing a woman. They therefore knocked into walls and houses and
bruised themselves, and then exhibited their bruises as special badges
of extraordinary piety. (4) *The Hump-backed Pharisees*. They walked
bent double in a false and cringing humility. (5) *The Ever-Reckoning
Pharisees*. They were ever reckoning up their good deeds and striking
a balance sheet of profit and loss with God. (6) *The Timid Pharisees*.
They went in fear of the wrath of God. (7) *The God-loving Pharisees*.
They were copies of Abraham, and lived in faith and charity. There
may have been six bad Pharisees to every good one: but this passage
shows that even among the Pharisees there were those who admired
and respected Jesus."

The Lord Jesus refused to be intimidated. Again various interpretations have been given concerning His answer, but it is wisest and best
to declare He had a definite path to follow, and nothing would be
permitted to drive Him from His course. It should not be inferred that
Jesus was stating the impossibility of a prophet being killed anywhere
but in Jerusalem. John the Baptist had already been killed away from
that city. The Lord was stating that because of the history and spiritual
decline of this city it was extremely unlikely that God's servants would
ever be permitted to die elsewhere. Having uttered these solemn
words the Saviour proceeded to speak again concerning Jerusalem.

O Jerusalem, Jerusalem, which killest the prophets, and stonest them
that are sent unto thee; how often would I have gathered thy children
together, as a hen doth gather her brood under her wings, and ye would

not! Behold, your house is left unto you desolate: and verily, I say unto you, Ye shall not see me, until the time come when ye shall say, Blessed is he that cometh in the name of the Lord (vv. 34-35).

This has been called "The Heart-Break Passage": its word picture is both pathetic and striking. Preachers may like to consider these verses under the three heads: *His Plan*—to gather and protect Israel. *His Plea*—He called the people but *they would not* respond. *His Prediction* —"your house is left desolate." The world is aware of the fulfilment of those sad words of Jesus. The city of glory became in A.D. 70 the place of unrelenting destruction; the place of abject desolation and sorrow. Those who refuse to welcome Christ must surely learn to live without Him—to exist without the Light of the World is to remain in the shadows for ever. There is every reason to believe that the final and complete fulfilment of the closing part of the verse can only come when at the end of the age, Israel will accept the Saviour as their Messiah. Then the earth shall be filled with the glory of God as the waters cover the sea. See Zechariah 12: 9–13: 1.

## HOMILIES

### Study No. 45

#### ONE THING LEADS TO ANOTHER

There is a strange sequence of thought in the thirteenth chapter of Luke's Gospel for here three pictures are brought together to form what might be called a composite picture of the evangelical message. That each one of the three is complete in itself, none would deny; but investigation reveals that each of the trio belongs to its companions. They are meant to contribute to each other, for united they present to mankind the most important message ever told.

*Opportunities will not last for ever* (vv. 6-9)
The fig tree seemed a little out of place; many people surely wondered why it was ever allowed to stay. A fig tree in the middle of a vineyard seemed as incongruous as an elephant in a greenhouse. Yet for some inscrutable reason, the owner of the vineyard permitted it to stay. Surely he loved figs! Yet his liking for this fruit gave place to disappointment, and ultimately he said, "Behold, these three years I come seeking fruit on this fig tree, and find none: cut it down; why cumbereth it the ground? Then the dresser of the vineyard replied, Lord, let it alone this year also, till I shall dig about it and manure it: and if

it bear fruit, well: and if not, then after that thou shalt cut it down."
The vineyard represented the world; the fig tree, the Jewish nation.
That God loved the whole world was perfectly understandable, but why
He should select the Jewish nation to be His chosen race presented
problems. A fig tree in the midst of a vineyard! During three years,
the Lord sought fruit from the people He loved most; but alas, His
expectations were not realised. When Christ said, "Let it alone *this
year*," He possibly referred to the fourth year of His ministry—the
year in which He was to die. He was determined to make a final
attempt to influence Jewry but their destiny would be settled by their
reactions to His ministry. The God-sent opportunity could not be
expected to last for ever.

### Opportunities can quickly pass by (vv. 24-30)

The golden sun was setting. Soon the gold would change to pink,
and then to scarlet, and finally the ball of glory would sink beyond
Western horizons. The Guardian of the Gate stood ready to close the
doors; people were hurrying; no camel driver wished to stay outside
until dawn. Beasts were urged to greater speed and the sun continued
to sink. A short distance down the road two cameliers greeted each
other. They were probably old friends; many months had passed since
their last meeting. They talked of many things and time slipped by.
Soon a bugle sounded from the gate, and the great doors slowly swung
into the closed position. Then the incoming traveller urged his camels
to a trot, and approaching the gates cried for admittance. The im-
perturbable gateman calmly listened to the requests of the visitor and
said, "I never knew you. Were you not standing along the road talking? You are well acquainted with the law. You had every opportunity
to enter while the gates were open. Instead you wasted your time
talking of things of little consequence. I never knew you." The city
could be the Kingdom of God, for as the Lord Jesus described the
scene, He said, "Strive to enter in at the strait gate: for many, I say
unto you, will seek to enter in and shall not be able."

### Opportunities lost, seldom return (vv. 34-35)

The city seemed to be spread out as a cloth at His feet. O place of
memories; the city of God; so honoured; so guilty; so loved. And the
Lord sighed and said, "O Jerusalem, Jerusalem, which killest the
prophets, and stonest them that are sent unto thee; how often would I
have gathered thy children together, as a hen doth gather her brood
under her wings, and ye would not! Behold your house is left unto
you desolate. . . ." We are told that when He saw the city He wept
over it, and described the horrors soon to turn it into a place of misery.
He spoke of the destruction of the temple, and of the inhuman savagery

which would destroy mothers, and annihilate a generation even before its birth. And when He saw these things looming in Israel's future, the vision broke His heart. His people had been so near to salvation, but now they had missed it for ever. Never again would that generation be visited by the Son of God; never again would these people hear, "Come unto me, all ye that labour and are heavy laden, and I will give you rest." Israel's opportunity had gone, and even the Lord Himself could not bring it back to them. "And Jesus wept!" Herein is wisdom. Here is a warning. Our proverb says, "A stitch in time saves nine." A decision in time saves eternity.

# The Fourteenth Chapter of Luke

THEME: *Jesus Visits the Home of one of the Chief Pharisees*

OUTLINE:

I. Jesus speaks to the Lawyers in the Pharisee's house.
Verses 1–6
II. Jesus speaks to all the Guests in the Pharisee's house.
Verses 7–14
III. Jesus speaks to an unknown man in the Pharisee's
house. Verses 15–24
IV. Jesus speaks to the crowd outside the Pharisee's house.
Verses 25–35

SECTION ONE

*Expository Notes concerning the Man with the Dropsy*

And it came to pass, as he went into the house of one of the chief
Pharisees to eat bread on the sabbath day, that they were watching
him. And behold, there was a certain man before him which had the
dropsy. And Jesus answering spake unto the lawyers and Pharisees
saying, Is it lawful to heal on the sabbath day? And they held their
peace. And he took him, and healed him, and let him go. And answered
them saying, Which of you shall have an ass or an ox fallen into a pit,
and will not straightway pull him out on the sabbath day? And they
could not answer him again to these things (vv. 1–6).

Altogether there are seven instances in the Gospels where Christ
healed on the sabbath day (Luke 4: 38; Luke 6: 6; Luke 13: 14; Luke
14: 1; Mark 1: 21; John 5: 9; and John 9: 14). It is thought-provoking
that whilst the Lord realized His enemies would be watching His every
movement, He did not hesitate to do good on the sabbath even though
He knew His actions would arouse violent opposition. The word
translated *watching* is parateeroumenoi, and it means *to watch assidu-
ously; to observe carefully.* (Thayer) This word has been used in the
sense of *watching in espionage.* Under the guise of friendship and
hospitality, they were endeavouring to lure their Guest into a position
of insecurity; they were intent on trapping Him. The observance of
the Jewish sabbath was hedged around by insufferable regulations. It

314

was not permissible to cook food on the sabbath, and therefore such food was prepared on the Friday. Even the matter of keeping this warm or of reheating it for the sabbath mealtime was something strictly controlled by legalism. The food could not be placed in "oil dregs, manure, salt, chalk or sand, whether moist or dry, nor into straw, grape-skins, flock or vegetables, if these are damp, though it may be if they are dry. It may be, however, put into clothes, amidst fruit, pigeons' feathers and flax tow" (*The Daily Study Bible. Barclay*, p. 193). The law forbad working on the sabbath, and healing was considered to be work; therefore if Christ healed on the sabbath, He was working and thereby breaking the law. It is saddening to reflect that the warped minds of man make virtue appear as evil. They who look through dark glasses can make the sun to become dim, and they who continue to do this, in the end go blind.

There has been conjecture about the sick man's presence in the house at this particular time. Some expositors blame the Pharisees for deliberately arranging the scene; the dropsical man was bait in their trap! Yet others are inclined to believe the man was responsible for his own actions. He placed himself in the path of the Lord hoping the Saviour would heal him. If this interpretation be true, the Pharisees surreptitiously pleased with the turn of events, seized the opportunity to accuse the Preacher. Suddenly the Lord became aware of the challenge confronting Him, and seeing also the watchfulness of the other guests, asked His devastating question. Open cisterns or wells abounded in Palestine, and it was a common occurrence for an animal to fall into the holes. No farmer would hesitate about rescuing the animal whether the day were the sabbath or not. If such care were justified for a beast, could it be right to ignore the claims of a suffering man. There is doubt about the word translated ass or donkey. Some of the early manuscripts contain the word usually translated *son*; the probable rendering would be "*Which of you having a son or a donkey or an ox fallen into a pit . . .*" The Lord's question left them speechless. It taught that he who lives close to God need never fear being close to men. Christ never refused an invitation to dine in the homes of His enemies. Probably to some of us, those visits might suggest casting pearls before swine; certainly there were many hosts who only took advantage of the presence of Christ to intensify their criticisms. It would seem that sometimes the Lord's acceptance of the invitation never did any real good for those who invited Him. That may well be true but Christ found it difficult to abandon even the greatest sinners. When they asked Him to enter their homes, He did so, and at least, those people will never be able to blame Jesus for refusing to talk with them in the privacy of their dwellings.

HOMILIES

Study No. 46

## CHRIST IN THE LIONS' DEN!

Dr. Campbell Morgan used a great illustration concerning Paul's injunction to the Ephesian Christians: "see then that ye walk circumspectly . . ." (Ephesians 5: 15). He described a beautiful flower garden surrounded by a high wall, and indicated that the gardener, to keep out intruders, placed hundreds of pieces of broken glass into the cement top of the wall. Then finally, he described an old cat carefully placing its feet between the broken glass, always advancing, but never cutting its paws. That, according to Dr. Morgan, was walking circumspectly. There was a time when Daniel went into the den of lions, but mercifully, the animals were harmless. Long afterwards, Christ similarly went into a den of lions, but the lions were dangerous; every moment was filled with peril, and it was necessary for the Lord to walk with extreme care.

### The Danger of a Sabbath Meal

Probably Jesus would have enjoyed a snack on a lonely hillside far more than a sumptuous meal in the Pharisee's home; that He would have preferred to sit quietly with a few of His trusted friends enjoying a sandwich rather than to sit with the chief Pharisees eating the choicest food their larders could supply. The invitation to share a sabbath meal seemed an innocent and gracious gesture on the part of the would-be host, but his smiles were deceptive. His food might indeed be extremely tasteful but it was bait in a trap. When the Lord looked toward the distant solitudes, His heart yearned to take the upward path, but the stern necessity of God-given duties pointed to the home of danger. If He refused to accept the invitation, His action could be interpreted as an insult; if He accepted it and went into the home, some of the poorer citizens might become envious and accuse Him of fraternizing with the wealthy—of eating and drinking in luxury whilst His forerunner had languished and died in a dungeon. What should He do; for as now, so then, it was impossible to please everybody.

### The Danger of a Suffering Man

Just inside the door was a man with the dropsy, and it is not without significance that the man made no appeal whatsoever. Had he cried out for mercy, the reactions of the Lord would have been understood.

But according to Luke, the fellow merely sat in silence. His legs were probably swollen; his appearance was unattractive and sickly. Suddenly all the guests were attentive. Christ was looking at the sufferer and the Pharisees were watching both. When the Lord's eyes scanned the guests, He discerned their evil intentions. If He calmly proceeded to His seat; if He ignored the suffering of the man with the dropsy, the Pharisees would smile and accuse Him either of helplessness or indifference. Yet if He delivered the sufferer, they would accuse Him of working on the sabbath; of breaking the law. Heaven, and earth, watched as He calmly assessed the situation. What should He do; for as now, so then, it was impossible to please everybody.

## The Danger of a Striking Message

Luke says that Jesus *"answering spake unto the lawyers and Pharisees."* That He first addressed the legal experts seems to indicate He was well aware of the trap which lay at His feet. They were acquainted with the restrictions governing conduct on the sabbath day; they themselves had helped to formulate some of the exacting laws which forbad many things and permitted others. They were watching as vultures waiting to pounce on a defenceless victim. They were hypocrites, but if He said so, He would lay Himself open for further attacks upon His person. If He spoke the truth, His words would infuriate them; as human lions they would desire to pull Him to pieces. Yet if He remained silent, they would interpret His silence as weakness. If He healed the sufferer, they would charge Him with being a law breaker. One false move would bring disaster. There was urgent need to walk circumspectly. Maybe He remembered that it was written : "And if thou draw out thy soul to the hungry, and satisfy the afflicted soul; then shall thy light rise in obscurity, and thy darkness be as the noon day; And the Lord shall guide thee continually . . . and thou shalt be like a watered garden, and like a spring of water, whose waters fail not" (Isaiah 58: 10–11). As the Lord Jesus calmly looked to God for guidance, He knew what He had to say and do. "Which of you shall have a son, or an ass or an ox fallen into a pit, and will not straightway pull him out on the sabbath day? And they could not answer him again to these things."

> Hold Thou my hand: so weak I am and helpless;
> I dare not go one step without Thy aid.
> Hold Thou my hand, for then O loving Saviour,
> No thought of ill shall make my soul afraid.

SECTION TWO

*Expository Notes on the Virtue of Humility*

**And he put forth a parable to those that were bidden, when he marked how they chose out the chief rooms; saying unto them, When thou art bidden of any man to a wedding, sit not down in the highest room; lest a more honourable man than thou be bidden of him; And he that bade thee and him come and say unto thee, Give this man place; and thou begin with shame to take the lowest room. But when thou art bidden, go and sit down in the lowest room; that when he that bade thee cometh, he may say unto thee, Friend go up higher: then shalt thou have worship in the presence of them that sit at meat with thee. For whosoever exalteth himself shall be abased; and he that humbleth himself shall be exalted (vv. 7–11).**

It is not too difficult to imagine the scene as Jesus saw it. The Pharisee had invited many guests to his home for the sabbath meal, and these were seated at various places around the table. We cannot be sure exactly which were the important places. Major quotes an ancient writer stating, "The most honourable station at an entertainment among the Romans, was the middle part of the middle couch, each couch holding three." The Pharisee may have had different ideas concerning the relative value of the seats at the table. However it seems obvious that the Lord recognized that certain guests coveted the seats of eminence, and used the fact to illustrate the need for true humility. It could be extremely embarrassing for any man if he were asked by a host to vacate a seat in order that some other person might take his place. On the other hand to be exalted before others was truly something to be desired. The value of the lessons thus taught became obvious. Verse 14, as we shall see, speaks of the rewards to be issued at the resurrection of the just, and it is difficult to forget the earthly picture when we consider the heavenly. Some people will probably expect the most wonderful rewards but their expectations will not be realized; there may be those, who expecting nothing, will hear the Lord say, "Well done thou good and faithful servant . . ." Humility is the soil in which the flowers of grace bloom freely; humility is the atmosphere breathed by all Christ-like people. No Saint ever boasts of his humility; for he honestly believes himself to be nothing. I once knew a man who was intensely proud of his humility. He advertised the fact that he lived by prayer, and lest any of his visitors should be unaware of his great characteristic, ostentatiously he wore two very large patches over the knees of his trousers!

Then said he also to him that bade him, When thou makest a dinner or a supper, call not thy friends, nor thy brethren, neither thy kinsmen, nor thy rich neighbours; lest they also bid thee again, and a recompense be made thee. But when thou makest a feast, call the poor, the maimed, the lame, the blind: And thou shalt be blessed; for they cannot recompense thee: for thou shalt be recompensed at the resurrection of the just (vv. 12-14).

This passage cannot be taken literally, for nowhere does Christ advocate that one should ignore the claims of true friendship. To give anything in the hope that the recipient would return more, was not really to give. There could be no harm in inviting one's neighbour to a feast; it could hardly be displeasing to God to have fellowship with one's family. The man who ministers to the poor cannot hope for a reward—unless—even this be a part of his advertising campaign! The Lord spoke of the future day when the saints would be brought to the Judgment seat of Christ. See I Corinthians 3: 11–15. Christian works are to be tried as in a fire; when a man has lived for self and for self interests, even though his actions appeared to be the most commendable, they will be revealed for their true worth; they will perish in the fires of God's examining scrutiny. When a man has conscientiously striven to do that which is right, irrespective of whether or not he is ever to be recompensed for his actions, his deeds remain to shine forth as gold, silver, precious stones. This passage, it must be remembered, was delivered to men who coveted the chief places; they gave feasts that all men might mention the fact to others. The Lord advocated the wisdom of letting the right hand be unaware of what the left was doing. The self-life is best seen to advantage when it is crucified!

HOMILIES

Study No. 47

## ABRAHAM . . . AND A BUNCH OF ROGUES!

Self-esteem is rarely found in the heart of a true man of God, for the more virtuous a saint becomes, the less satisfied he will be with himself. Increasing love for God means increasing hatred of the self-life. The Bible has many examples of this fact.

*ABRAHAM "I am but dust and ashes"* (Genesis 18: 27)
Abraham was the friend of God, and the greatest character in the ancient world. Divine secrets were shared with the illustrious patriarch,

and in a sense unknown by ordinary men, he walked with God. Yet Abraham despised himself, and became increasingly conscious of his shortcomings. He considered himself unworthy to commune with God, and said he was dust and ashes.

## JOB "Behold, I am vile" (Job 40: 4)

We are left in no doubt as to the true greatness of this man. It is recorded that the Lord said of him, ". . . there is none like him in the earth, a perfect and upright man, one that feareth God, and escheweth evil" (Job 1: 8). When Job's friends declared him to be a hypocrite; that secret sin had brought about his misfortunes, he maintained that his heart was clean before God. Yet when he came face to face with his Maker, he whispered, "I am vile."

## DAVID "Behold, I was shapen in iniquity" (Psalm 51: 5)

The sweet psalmist of Israel was a man after God's own heart, and although certain indiscretions marred his fine record of devotion, his integrity and true consecration were always beyond question. Yet this great man sadly shook his head and denied his own virtues. Psalm 51 is a heart-throb in which we hear tears of anguish, cries of disappointment, and the moan of a man who feels that he is a complete failure.

## EZRA "I blush to lift up my face" (Ezra 9: 6)

Ezra was one of the greatest men of his day. He held an honourable place among the spiritual aristocracy of the nation. His courageous example at a time when Israel needed spiritual leadership lifted the nation to new heights of achievement. He and Nehemiah were the greatest men of that generation; yet Ezra's confession claimed for him a place in Rogue's Gallery. He said, "O my God, I am ashamed and blush to lift up my face."

## ISAIAH "I am undone . . . I am a man of unclean lips" (Isaiah 6: 5)

Isaiah was one of the major prophets who gave counsel and guidance to a stumbling nation, and at the same time, provided unerring information concerning the coming of the Messiah. He was a friend of the king, a father to the nation, and a trusted servant of the Most High. Yet of himself he had nothing good to say.

## SIMON PETER "I am a sinful man" (Luke 5: 8)

There is something delightfully human about Simon Peter, for at all times, he was unquestionably honest. Sometimes strong emotions and fierce temptations upset his equilibrium; but within minutes, the real man appeared again. He was a great man, an excellent preacher, and a brother beloved. Yet all who read the New Testament realize how very much Peter abhorred himself.

## THE CENTURION "I am not worthy" (Luke 7: 6)

This Gentile soldier won a place among the great immortals, for his spiritual perception enabled Christ to say, "I have not found so great faith, no, not in Israel." Although he was an officer in Caesar's army, and occupied a position of importance, he confessed his home to be unworthy of a visit from the Carpenter of Nazareth.

## PAUL "I am the chief of sinners" (I Timothy 1: 15)

Paul was undoubtedly the greatest of all Christian missionaries. He was the first to look beyond the narrow bounds of Israel's horizons, and with determination of purpose to penetrate into the unknown. His indomitable spirit and untiring energy took the Gospel to millions of heathen and with God's help he established the Christian Church. Yet Paul claimed to be the greatest sinner in the world.

God has strange ways of estimating the greatness of men. Sometimes the first are last, and the last first. Those who are great in their own estimation are far from the will of God, while others who are overwhelmed by a sense of unworthiness are ready for the Master's use. A Bunch of Rogues? No: some of God's great gentlemen! (Taken from the Author's book, *Bible Treasures,* p. 7.)

### SECTION THREE

### Expository Notes about the Great Supper

**And when one of them that sat at meat with him heard these things, he said unto him, Blessed is he that shall eat bread in the kingdom of God. Then he said unto him, A certain man made a great supper, and bade many. And sent his servants at supper time to say to them that were bidden, Come; for all things are now ready (vv. 15-17).**

It was commonly believed among Jews that the establishment of the Messianic kingdom would be followed by a great feast at which all pious Jews would be guests. Leviathan, the great monster of the deep would be served as food thus indicating that the Messiah ruled heaven and earth and seas. It is probable that when Jesus spoke of the resurrection of the just, one of His hearers immediately thought of the golden age still to come, and exclaimed, "Blessed is he that shall eat bread in the kingdom of God." At that moment the sumptuous feast arranged by the Pharisees was only a faint foreshadowing of the matchless feast to be arranged by God, and the speaker was sure that he, as a Jew, would be among the guests on that notable occasion.

The Lord immediately told the story of the Great Supper and its implications became very obvious. Every important feast was announced long beforehand for the invitations were sent to the guests sometimes weeks in advance of the actual feast day. When the invitations were accepted, the host knew how many would be attending, and was able to make provision accordingly. When the day of the feast finally arrived, and when all things were in readiness, servants were sent hurrying to the various homes to announce the time had come; and the guests were desired as quickly as possible in the banqueting chamber. To refuse to attend at that late hour, when preparation had already been completed was a great insult, and among the Arabs was tantamount to a declaration of war. All these details were well understood by the people to whom Christ told the story.

**And they all with one consent began to make excuse. The first said unto him, I have bought a piece of ground, and I must needs go and see it: I pray thee have me excused (v. 18).**

This excuse was as shallow as it was stupid. The great supper could begin, continue, and end; one day could follow another, but the piece of ground would still be there. There was no possibility that it would develop legs during the night and run away. Beside, any businessman who would only wish to see his new land AFTER he had bought it could hardly justify his actions. This was indeed an excuse; he did not wish to attend the supper, but on the spur of the moment this was the best reason he could supply to explain his absence. A man's love for Real Estate is often an indication of his real state before God.

**And another said, I have bought five yoke of oxen, and I go to prove them: I pray have me excused (v. 19).**

This man apparently permitted a new novelty to crowd out the more important things of life. If he had already seen the animals, he would have some idea of what they could do, but at this particular moment he was possessed with a passion to try them out. Of course they could wait for another day, but a fire was now burning in his soul—he wanted to try them out, and what was much more to the point, he wished to try them out immediately. The fact that a friend would be inconvenienced meant nothing. This man thought only of himself; no other mattered. His mantle fell on many of his descendants. A man buys a new car; the week-end provides the opportunity to try it out on a run to the seaside. A man buys a new set of golf clubs; the communion service does not have the facilities for testing them, so the Sunday morning is spent on the golf course!

**And another said, I have married a wife, and therefore I cannot come (v. 20).**

Either his new wife had tied his legs, or his love had paralysed them. He *could not* come—poor fellow, he was a slave already! Better by far had he remained single! A man who begins married life like this is destined to remain in bondage for ever. And yet after some sober reflection, it must be admitted that this man had some justification for his conduct. The law made special provision for newly weds. "When a man hath taken a new wife, he shall not go out to war, neither shall he be charged with any business, but he shall be free at home one year, and shall cheer up his wife which he hath taken" (Deuteronomy 24: 5). Ostensibly then, this fellow was within his rights to refuse, but with a little ingenuity, he might have brought his bride to the supper. Alas, he had no desire to come, a new affection had broken the old ties of friendship. He was as a stupid child who threw away an old and dependable toy because a cheap gaudily painted thing had temporarily attracted attention.

**So that servant came, and shewed his lord these things, Then the master of the house being angry said to the servant, Go out quickly into the streets and lanes of the city, and bring in hither the poor, and the maimed, and the halt, and the blind. And the servant said, Lord, it is done as thou hast commanded, and yet there is room. And the Lord said unto the servant, Go out into the highways and hedges, and compel them to come in, that my house may be filled. For I say unto you, That none of those men which were bidden shall taste of my supper (vv. 21-24).**

The streets and lanes of the city were the places, where those without the comfort of a permanent home would likely congregate. Market places; parks; gardens or any other such place would come within this category. Care must be taken in interpreting the Greek word *anagkason* translated *compel*. It is only used nine times in the New Testament and in four of these it is translated *constrain* (Matthew 14: 22; Mark 6: 45; Acts 28: 19; Galatians 6: 12). Men are to be constrained by argument and reason rather than by brute force. Christians are never won for the Saviour at the point of a gun! The only compulsion known within God's kingdom is the compulsion of love—"the love of Christ constrains us."

Probably the entire story was meant to unfold the vicissitudes of dispensational teaching. Throughout the ages God had given warning of the great supper with which He would honour His Son. The time had come when the preparations had been completed, and the servants of God were urging men to respond. Yet the Jews who had fully expected the coming of the great moment were now working hard to avoid the responsibility of attending the feast. Whilst the leaders were making excuses, the common people were hearing Christ gladly, and therefore were represented by the poor, the maimed, the halt and the blind. When the invitation was extended to others who inhabited the highways and hedges, this illustrated the truth that beyond the boundaries of Judaism awaited the Gentile nations who through matchless Grace would come to sit down at the Marriage Supper of the Lamb.

## HOMILIES

Study No. 48

### THE MEN WHO SAID "No" TO GOD!

The kindly host was very excited; his moment was at hand! Months before the announcement of a forthcoming feast had been well received by the city fathers, and his invitations had been accepted. This gave promise of a great occasion and determined that his food and entertainment should be of the highest quality, the man spared no expense to make his dream come true. The tables were attractively decorated; the musicians had been well rehearsed; the cooks had worked overtime! All that remained according to the custom of the East was to send the servants with the last-minute announcement that all was in readiness; the feast would soon begin.

*A Finished Work!*
Probably, as the Lord told His story, He thought of another Host. From time immemorial God had made known to His people that ultimately, Messiah would visit them. Throughout the centuries the message had been repeated and God's invitation accepted. Everywhere, Jews enthused about the coming days of celebration, and rejoiced in anticipation of the blessedness of the coming kingdom. Yet even the most instructed Jew could hardly have realized to what lengths God would go to meet the spiritual need of His people. Ultimately, on a green hill outside the city wall, the triumphant words would be spoken, "IT IS FINISHED," and only then in all its matchless wonder would the final invitation go forth to the bidden guests. This was something to supersede anything ever known in history. Every valley would be exalted; every mountain and hill would be made low; the crooked would be made straight, and the rough places plain, and the glory of the Lord revealed so that all flesh would see it together.

Among the indescribable wonders to be supplied would be the forgiveness of sin; reconciliation to God; the glorious gift of life eternal,
and an inheritance incorruptible which would never fade away. These
were the ingredients in the Bread of Life, and to supply this spiritual
banquet, God would even go to the expense of yielding His own Son.
The entire cost of providing this eternal salvation would be offset by
the Grace of God. Man had only to accept the divine invitation.

## A Faithful Witness!

"Then said he unto him, A certain man made a great supper, and
bade many. And sent his servant at supper time to say to them that
were bidden, Come; for all things are now ready." It was incumbent
upon the host to inform the guests when they should arrive, and therefore the servant was sent into the streets to broadcast the good news.
This was free; without money and without price; they were bidden to
come immediately. Probably it was with this same thought in mind
that Christ chose His disciples. Throughout the known world the early
Christians carried their message, and from those early beginnings, the
streams of witness flowed to the ends of the earth. All men must hear
the Gospel and the commission to go into all the world is as potent
today as when Christ first uttered the message. It is still incumbent
on God to bring the tidings to needy and waiting people, and as His
servants, the church must be ready to hurry forth to do the Master's
bidding. This alone is consecrated service; this alone is yieldedness.
What men do with God's message is their own responsibility, but at
least, we must do our part and communicate to them what God has
already told us.

## A Foolish Whim!

"And they all with one consent began to make excuses." The one
man had property trouble; the second had animal trouble; the last had
wife trouble. Yet no man had any insoluble problem. Probably they
worked harder trying to find a suitable excuse than they would have
done if they had attended the supper. "Where your heart it, there is
your treasure also." To the New Testament excuses we may add many
others. "I do not wish to yield to Christ. I am young; let me enjoy
myself. When I am old, I will think about the matter, and probably
become a Christian." "I do not wish to make my stand for Christ
because I would have to give up too many of my pleasures." "I could
never live that kind of life anyway." "I do not wish to attend the
Church; there are too many hypocrites—Pharisees among the guests!"
"Why should I come? I am far better than anybody there." "Do not
bother me; I am not interested." The list could be lengthened tre-
mendously. Men and women who do not desire to yield to the claims

of God have no difficulty finding an excuse for their actions. God never *makes* anyone accept His invitation; unless men desire to attend, they have the power to stay away.

## A Final Word!

". . . none of those men that were bidden shall taste of my supper." The implications of this last announcement are terrifying for God speaks with finality of purpose—THEY SHALL NOT TASTE OF MY SUPPER. Let it be remembered that the entire story was suggested by the unknown man who had exclaimed, "Blessed is he that shall eat bread in THE KINGDOM of God." Whatever Jesus said afterward, obviously was linked to that initial utterance, and therefore the implications of this final word are unmistakable. People who had heard the invitation; who were desired by the host; ultimately were excluded for ever. Had the parable been limited to earthly issues, the loss would not have been so tragic; the men who refused to attend might have missed an excellent supper and lost a good friend. But when the teaching of this story is seen in its fullest setting, then a man's stupidity in refusing to accept God's invitation could eventually cost him his soul. To be banished from the Light of the World could mean to languish in the gloom for ever. One is justified in asking: of what use would an acre of virgin soil be—or a team of unsurpassed oxen, or even the amorous felicitations of a woman, in the day when God says, "I never knew you"?

## SECTION FOUR

### Expository Notes on the Cost of Discipleship

And there went great multitudes with him: and he turned, and said unto them, If any man come to me, and hate not his father, and mother, and wife, and children, and brethren, and sisters, yea, and his own life also, he cannot be my disciple. And whosoever doth not bear his cross, and come after me, cannot be my disciple (vv. 25–27).

The passage before us is one of the most dynamic in the Gospel but it should be remembered that these words were spoken to crowds who were already eagerly anticipating the early establishment of the kingdom. Excitement was beginning to run high for it was obvious to all that Jesus was marching toward Jerusalem. It is very possible that even as He walked, the Lord was able to hear the conversation of those who accompanied Him. They were convinced that the glory of the Messianic kingdom was about to break over Israel, and therefore the Master felt constrained to correct their mistaken beliefs. He knew that the cross was awaiting Him within the city, and unless these eager people were prepared for what was to come, their faith would disintegrate. The term *hate* must be interpreted in a relative sense for it was never the will of God that hate should fill the heart of any believer. The idea here is that Christ should occupy the first place in the affections of His followers; that however much one might be endeared to one's family, they at best, could only take second place to the Saviour. Particular attention should be given to the Lord's statement that unless His followers were willing to reach these standards of discipleship, then discipleship was impossible. This truth devastatingly cuts across much that is practised in modern churches. Unfortunately most churches that are young and weak are apt to welcome anybody with open arms. We have become slaves to statistics, and quantity has superseded quality. It would be well if all preachers proclaimed as it were from the housetops that church membership does not necessarily mean discipleship.

For which of you, intending to build a tower, sitteth not down first, and counteth the cost, whether he have sufficient to finish it? Lest haply, after he hath laid the foundation, and is not able to finish it, and all that behold it begin to mock him, Saying, This man began to build and was not able to finish. Or what king going to make war against another king, sitteth not down first, and consulteth whether he be able with ten thousand to meet him that cometh against him with twenty thousand? Or else, while the other is yet a great way off, he sendeth an ambassage, and desireth conditions of peace. So likewise, whosoever he be of you that forsaketh not all that he hath, he cannot be my disciple (vv. 28-33).

The theme of this passage is indisputably *the cost of discipleship*. Many writers have spiritualized the verses to make them mean many things, but the only thing obvious here is that Christ was warning people about making hasty decisions. Following Christ meant deliberation and very much determination. No one ever had a picnic on a Cross! Probably the tower to which Christ referred was the usual tall tower often found in vineyards. This was a look-out tower from which the watchman could see any pilferer of the harvest. The husbandman who laid the foundation only to find that he had insufficient funds to finish the project ran the danger of being an object of ridicule. It was wise therefore for the builder to make an estimate of the costs and to ascertain whether or not his finances would be equal to the demands to be made upon them. Similarly the king, unable to face the overwhelming odds of overpowering enemies, would be wise to seek settlement at the bargaining table rather than on the field of battle. These illustrations primarily teach the same truth. The life of discipleship would make exacting demands upon all who decided to follow Christ. Prospective disciples were urged to count the cost for ultimately the claims of the cross would divide families, and even the dearest of earthly friends would oppose the dedicated Christian. Unless the disciple were willing to leave father and mother and friends —unless he would be willing to go all the way with the Lord, it would be better not to start. In the truest and fullest sense of the term, half-hearted disciples were not disciples, for unless Christ possessed them completely, He did not possess them at all.

> **Salt is good; but if the salt have lost his savour, wherewith shall it be seasoned? It is neither fit for the land, nor yet for the dung hill; but men cast it out. He that hath ears to hear, let him hear (vv. 34-35).**

Salt was one of the most valued commodities in the agricultural life of Palestine. It was used to preserve things—in the case of fish, etc.; it was used to season things—in the case of food; it was used to fertilize things in the form of manure which was spread upon the land. Yet salt was only of real value when it retained its potency. Salt exposed continually to the weather became useless in all of the three usages just mentioned. Salt that had lost its savour was totally unfit to do that which it was primarily meant to do. Then it was only fit to be trodden under foot of men; that is, it was thrown over wet and slippery pavements in order to prevent accidents. Christ used this illustration on at least two other occasions: Matthew 5: 13 and Mark 9: 50. Mark reminds us that Christ urged His followers to *"have salt in themselves"*. Therefore it becomes obvious that the prevailing characteristics of salt were likened to the attributes of a healthy Christian life. When the disciple completely yielded to his Master, even to the extent of leaving his dearest earthly friends, that abandonment preserved him from the evil which is in the world; sweetened and made attractive his own life, and produced within his heart those principles of holiness without which no man can please God. Yet, if the salt has lost its savour; if through continuous exposure to the winds and weather of worldliness, the quality of the Christian's spirituality deteriorates, he will be unfit to do God's work. Then there is grave danger that he might become a castaway. These are important words. This cannot mean that God will completely abandon the man who once trusted Him. Rather it means that "his candlestick will be removed"; that instead of occupying an important part in the ministry of sending light to those who sit in darkness, he will be demoted to lesser tasks.

HOMILIES

Study No. 49

### THINNING-OUT AN ARMY!

Crowds are both attractive and dangerous to any preacher. Attractive in that they recommend his ministry; dangerous in that they inflate his ego. The law of Biblical history seems to assert that God prefers to work through the few rather than the many—". . . lest Israel vaunt themselves, saying, Mine own hand hath saved me" (Judges 7: 2). That the Bible is one book seems to be demonstrated by the fact that the Old Testament stories are windows through which may be viewed to better advantage the stories of the New Testament. The exacting tests of discipleship are clearly illustrated in the manner by which Gideon's army was reduced to three hundred men.

### The Men who were Fearful

The two scenes we are about to consider were separated by almost thirteen hundred years, and yet they appear to be so related that it would be easy to believe they were identical. Gideon was confronted by a great problem. His people were in bondage; the arrogant enemy was overpowering and ruthless; his task frightening. Somehow the opposition had to be vanquished and the nation liberated. Thirty-two thousand fighting men had rallied to the standard, but even so, the number was insignificant and puny in proportion to the innumerable hordes of the enemy. "And the Midianites, and the Amalekites and all the children of the east lay along in the valley like grasshoppers for multitude; and their camels were without number, as the sand by the sea-side for multitude" (Judges 7: 12). Gideon surely trembled when God said, "You have too many soldiers." "Proclaim in the ears of the people saying, Whosoever is fearful and afraid, let him return . . ." Long afterward another Preacher faced the same problem. "And there went great multitudes with him : and he turned, and said unto them, If any man come to me and hate not his father and mother . . . and his own life also, he cannot be my disciple. And whosoever doth not bear his cross, and come after me, cannot be my disciple" (Luke 14: 25–27). Discipleship is more than a joyous excursion on a sunny afternoon; it is far more than a mammoth barbecue at which the Master of Ceremonies supplies entertainment for guests. The heart of the Christian faith, and the symbol of the unceasing warfare it conducts, is a Cross. When disciples carry the cross day after day, it cuts deeply into the self-life; it might cause tears; it could shed blood. No man dare follow Christ until he has fully counted the cost. Gideon's men would have been easy victims if their thoughts of a comfortable home robbed them of the will to fight. The early Christians would never have taken the Gospel to a pagan world if they had spent their time running away from every threatening circumstance. It is becoming increasingly obvious that at this point the modern church has failed. We are so anxious to increase our church membership, and thereby increase our finances that the thoughts of quality of soul have been relegated to the background. The Church has been likened to a school in which each new member is enrolled. One leading churchman said recently—"Forget about conversion; get people into the fellowship of the church, and with the passing years will come the chance to educate them into our way of thinking." Perhaps this system explains why thousands of our members only attend church on Easter Sunday, and thousands more never attend at all.

*The Men who were Forgetful*

"And the Lord said unto Gideon, The people are yet too many; bring them down unto the water; and I will try them for thee there . . ." Gideon listened intently as God issued the instructions by which the army would be decreased in size. The men who knelt to push their parched lips into the water proved they were more eager to drink than to watch for potential dangers. The quenching of their thirst seemed to be a matter of greater import than the cause they represented. Yet others stooped, and scooping the water in the palm of their hand, remained ready to fight the moment the necessity arose. "And the Lord said unto Gideon, By the three hundred men that lapped will I save you . . ." We read in the scriptures that after the Lord had sifted His followers, "many of them went back and followed him no more." They were *salt without savour* (Luke 14: 34); *clouds without water* (Jude 12); *branches without fruit* (John 15: 4–6). By a small band of unlearned and ignorant men, Christ challenged a pagan world, but He was only able to do so, because those men were completely yielded to His will. Any thought of self was ruthlessly nailed to the cross; they learned to die daily, and it was this blessed abandon that carried them and their message to the ends of the known world.

*The Men who were Faithful*

"And he divided the three hundred men into three companies, and he put a trumpet in every man's hand, with empty pitchers, and lamps within the pitchers. . . . So Gideon and the three hundred men that were with him came unto the outside of the camp in the beginning of the middle watch . . . and they blew the trumpets, and brake the pitchers that were in their hands . . . and they cried, The sword of the Lord and of Gideon . . . and the Lord set every man's sword against his fellow . . ." (Judges 7: 16–22). This was one of the strangest victories on record. Compared with modern standards of military achievement, the entire episode appears to be ludicrous, for the battle was won without a blow being struck. The light shone through the smashed earthen vessels, the triumphant testimony of the bugle announced that faith was active and God did the rest. Thus did the foolishness of men overcome a wise and mighty enemy, and this was precisely the lesson Christ endeavoured to teach His disciples. When Gideon's men forsook everything to sponsor the cause of God, their dedication enabled the Lord to do the impossible. This was, and still is, *discipleship*. These were men who were as salt that had not lost its usefulness. With such men, God shook the pagan world; with similar men, He could do it again.

# The Fifteenth Chapter of Luke

THEME: *Christ Speaks of Lost Treasures*

OUTLINE:

I. The Lost Sheep. Verses 1–7
II. The Lost Coin. Verses 8–10
III. The Lost Son. Verses 11–32

SECTIONS ONE AND TWO

*Expository Notes on the Parables of the Lost Sheep and the Lost Coin*

**Then drew near all the publicans and the sinners for to hear him. And the Pharisees and scribes, murmured, saying, This man receiveth sinners, and eateth with them (vv. 1–2).**

The term, *Publicans and sinners* refers to people considered to be outlaws in Israel. The publicans or tax-gatherers accepted employment from the Romans, and used their acquired authority to force taxes from the brethren. Thus they brought upon their heads the disdain of the nation, and were condemned as the most despicable of sinners. That this class should be drawn into the meetings of the Carpenter signified that in their estimation this Preacher was totally different from the ordinary Jewish orators. They repelled sinners; Christ attracted them. The Greek word *prosdexetai* translated *receives* means a little more than our English word is able to convey. Christ gave them a sincere welcome—He received them gladly; with open arms, not because He condoned their sin, but because their coming provided the opportunity to reveal to them a better way of living. The Pharisees who were always seeking ways by which to criticise Jesus, misinterpreted the Lord's motives, and charged Him with complicity in their crimes.

**And he spake this parable unto them, saying, What man of you, having an hundred sheep, if he lose one of them, doth not leave his ninety and nine in the wilderness, and go after that which is lost, until he find it. And when he hath found it, he layeth it on his shoulders, rejoicing. And when he cometh home, he calleth together his friends and neighbours, saying unto them, Rejoice with me: for I have found my sheep which was lost. I say unto you that likewise, joy shall be in heaven over one**

sinner that repenteth, more than over ninety and nine just persons, which have no need of repentance (vv. 3-7).

To understand the true import of this parable it is necessary to begin at its end rather than at its beginning. That the ninety and nine sheep had no need of repentance does not mean that they were without sin. This parable was the direct answer to the charge that He was committing a misdemeanour by associating wth publicans and sinners who had sinned in becoming the servants of the hated Romans. To illustrate these people the Lord spoke of a lost sheep, and in contrast, the ninety-and-nine who had not similarly strayed from the fold were the people to whom the Lord addressed this parable. They had no need to repent —of this sin—*because they had not committed it.* Yet as Christ continued His parables, they were guilty of even greater sins in that they constantly murmured against the One whom God was using to rescue the lost. The *wilderness* to which reference is here made was not the sandy wastes, but rather land which is today called *common land.* It belonged to no one in particular, and therefore any man had the right to graze his flocks upon it. The illustration was drawn from the daily life of the people and could not be misunderstood. The entire inference of the story is that whilst the publicans and sinners had wandered, they were still precious in the sight of God. No sheep should ever be abandoned whilst there remained a chance to reclaim it. It was for this reason, the Great Shepherd welcomed publicans and sinners to His meetings.

Various, and sometimes startling interpretations of this parable have been suggested. The ninety and nine which have no need of repentance, have been said to be sinless beings of other worlds, and the explanation has been offered that in the estimation of God, one redeemed sinner from earth is more precious than any number of celestial beings who never sinned. Other commentators likened the lost sheep to the church. They have said that Christ turned His back upon the fold of Israel where the ninety-nine were safely grazing; that redemptive love sent Him into the wilderness to rescue and create the Church. To support their theories they emphasized that when the lost sheep was found in the waste lands, the Shepherd placed it on His shoulders and carried it to His home where a party was immediately organized. This was likened to the great Home in Heaven where there is joy in the presence of the angels when a sinner returns to God.

However, since Christ links together the home of the shepherd and His own home in Heaven, one thing becomes very obvious. As the earthly shepherd calls together his friends to rejoice together, so the news is broadcast throughout Heaven each time a sinner is reclaimed for God. The earthly joy in the shepherd's home is but a faint echo of the superlative happiness thrilling eternity. Therefore knowledge of earthly affairs is one of the attributes of the life hereafter. If the angels are aware of the miracles which take place on earth; indeed if they are ministering spirits sent forth to minister to the heirs of salvation (Hebrews 1 : 13–14) then there exists the possibility that the eternal world is not as far removed from us as would at first appear. Perhaps our comprehension of the magnitude of God's world is limited only by our short-sightedness!

From the homiletical point of view the parable is most interesting for here we have : *disaster* in that a sheep had become lost; *desire* in that the shepherd yearned to reclaim it; *decision* in that his desire was expressed in action, he went forth to seek it; *determination* in that he searched until he found it; *discernment* in that having found it, he placed it upon his shoulders to carry it home. Probably the sheep was unable to walk. Here too we have *delight* in that it is said the shepherd placed the sheep on his shoulders *rejoicing*. This great happiness was shared with others for as soon as it was possible the man gathered his friends that they might rejoice together. Nothing is so effective in thrilling a church as the sight of sinners being won for Christ. If our evangelistic programme were more effective, our joy would be immeasurably greater.

Commenting on this parable, William Barclay said, "The shepherd was personally responsible for the sheep. If a sheep were lost the shepherd must at least bring home the fleece to show how it had died. These shepherds were expert at tracking, and could follow a straying sheep's footprint for miles across the hills. There was not a shepherd for whom it was not all in a day's work to lay down his life for his sheep. Many of the flocks were communal flocks, belonging not to individuals, but to villages. There would be two or three shepherds in charge. Those whose flocks were safe would arrive home on time, and they would bring news that one shepherd was still out on the mountainside searching for a sheep which was lost. The whole village would be upon the watch, and then, when in the distance they saw the shepherd striding home wth the lost sheep across his shoulders, there would rise from the whole community a shout of joy and thanksgiving. That is the picture that Jesus drew of God; 'that,' said Jesus, 'is what God is like. God is as glad when a lost sinner is found as a shepherd is when a strayed sheep is brought home.'" (*The Gospel of Luke* by William Barclay, p. 207.)

**Either what woman having ten pieces of silver, if she lose one piece, doth not light a candle, and sweep the house, and seek diligently until she find it? And when she hath found it, she calleth her friends and her neighbours together, saying, Rejoice with me; for I have found the**

piece which I had lost. Likewise, I say unto you, there is joy in the
presence of the angels of God over one sinner that repenteth (vv. 8-10).

"The anxiety of the woman to find her lost piece of money certainly
does not proceed from a feeling of pity; it is *self-interest* which leads
her to act. She had painfully earned it, and had kept it in reserve for
some important purpose; it is a real loss to her. Here is divine love
portrayed from an entirely different side. The sinner is not only, in
the eyes of God, a suffering being, like the sheep on whom He takes
pity; he is a *precious* being, created in His image, to whom He has
assigned a part in the accomplishment of His plans. A lost man is a
blank in His treasury. Is not this side of divine love, rightly understood, still more striking than the preceding?" (Godet. *The Gospel of
Luke*, p. 148.) The coin, a drachma, represented a day's wages, and
was possibly part of the woman's savings. The intensity of the search
reveals how much she desired to find it. She sought diligently; that
is, she moved the articles of furniture, looked into all the corners, and
explored every possible place in the house until she discovered her
coin. Surely this reflects the intensity of the search with which God
looks for the sinner. He even stoops to the dusty and dirty places of
earth in order to lift His treasure from the grime into which it has
fallen. It will be seen therefore that these parables belong to each
other. The parable of the lost sheep reveals the intense pity of the
Shepherd's heart; the parable of the lost coin reveals the tremendous
worth of the soul being sought.

The archaeologists have uncovered some of the ancient houses of
Palestine and therefore we have an idea of the type of home in which
this woman lived. The structure was in all probability made of mud
bricks, dried hard in the sun; it had a small window possibly not much
more than eighteen inches across, and the interior was very dark. The
floor would be of beaten earth—earth trampled hard, and finally
covered with dried reeds or rushes. Any articles of furniture would
stand on this. Usually there were two levels, the one just a little higher
than the other, and upon this the entire family slept. Any coin lost
among the reeds would be the equivalent of a needle lost in a hay-
stack! If the woman energetically swept that kind of floor it would
probably be in the hope that the coin would be turned and made to
glint in the light coming through the window. If the woman were very
poor, the silver coin would be too valuable to lose.

Yet we must not lose sight of the fact that there might have been
another reason why she looked so diligently for her lost treasure. The
ancient sign of a married woman was a head-dress in which ten silver
coins were linked together on a silver chain. This was a great possession signifying the status of its owner. She had been chosen; she be-

longed to a husband, she was desirable! This was the ancient equivalent of the modern wedding ring, and was so completely her own that it could not be confiscated even to pay a debt. Although the coin was only worth in our currency a few pennies, to this woman of a bygone age it represented far more than a fortune. Therefore when she found it, her heart filled with ecstasy, and she cried aloud to her neighbours that they might share her happiness. The Lord chose the most excellent illustrations for His sermons, but this story of the woman and her coin must be numbered among the best.

## HOMILIES

See the homily at the end of the following section.

### SECTION THREE

*Expository Notes on the Parable of the Prodigal Son*

**And he said, A certain man had two sons; And the younger of them said to his father, Father, give me the portion of goods that falleth to me. And he divided unto them his living. And not many days after the younger son gathered all together, and took his journey into a far country, and there wasted his substance with riotous living. And when he had spent all, there arose a mighty famine in that land; and he began to be in want (vv. 11–14).**

The story of the prodigal son is certainly the most widely known, the best loved and the most used of all the Lord's parables. It is indeed a Gospel within the Gospel, and expresses so much truth that this very fact is apt to be exploited by preachers. Whatever might be deduced from this story; whatever allegorical meanings men might find in its details, it should never be forgotten that this parable, like the first two, was spoken to the Pharisees and scribes who constantly murmured that Christ received sinners and ate with them. Already the Lord has spoken of a sheep which wandered away from the rest of the flock; already mention had been made of a coin separated from other coins. Now the Lord continues to teach identical truth—a son deliberately left the fellowship of a home. The numbers used may be very thought-provoking. Throughout the first parable the Lord spoke of one sheep out of a hundred; the second parable spoke of one coin out of ten; this story speaks of one son out of two. These details are too important to miss for in correct and true exegesis it is necessary to remember that the background of all this is the legalistic realm of Judaism from which the publicans and sinners had wandered. Let it also be emphasized that at the end of each parable the centre of activity is transferred from earth to heaven; the joy in both the households of the shepherd and the woman is used to illustrate the supreme happiness in the heavenly Home. Nevertheless the first two parables could not express all that Jesus wished to say, and therefore their teachings were deepened immeasurably in the final parable of the three.

The original charge was that publicans and sinners by their action of going astray had more or less forfeited the right to any welcome in Israel, and therefore the Lord had no excuse to fraternize with them. Primarily then, the prodigal son represents this class of people. That the Father could love this erring child, and even watch for his return every day, provided evidence that the lad's disgrace had not obliterated his worth; his failure had not destroyed his parent's love. Since this father indisputably represented the Great Father—then Jesus was more than justified in going forth to encourage the return of the prodigals for whom God anxiously waited. This illustration was the Lord's answer to the charge made against Him. This alone is correct exegesis.

Deuteronomy 21: 15–17 explains that under no circumstance could the second-born usurp or inherit the special portion provided for the first-born. The birthright, or double portion belonged exclusively to the first-born son, even though that son was not the offspring of the father's favourite wife. It was customary for the inheritance to be divided after the death of the father, but in New Testament days it was not uncommon for the inheritance to be divided earlier. There were occasions when, to use modern terms, the younger son "was bought out" that is, he received his share in cash, and afterward the first-born received the complete inheritance when the father died. This of course only applied in the case of a family in which there were only two sons.

**And he went and joined himself to a citizen of that country; and he sent him into his fields to feed swine. And he would fain have filled his belly with the husks that the swine did eat: and no man gave unto him (vv. 15–16).**

The Saviour was certainly a Master-Preacher. Let it be remembered again that His enemies had charged the Lord with fraternizing with Publicans and sinners, who had indeed joined themselves to citizens from the far country. It was true that at the moment they seemed to be prospering, but the veiled forecast in the text was not hard to detect. Even these Romans had no love for their hirelings and if ever circumstances changed, they too would not hesitate to insult their servants. The task of feeding swine was all the more abhorrent because swine-flesh was considered to be unclean. The Greek word translated *joined* s rather startling in its first meaning. It is *ekolleethee,* which literally means *to glue*; *to cement* or *fasten together*. The inference is that the prodigal's need was such that in desperation he pestered the citizen for employment of any kind, and that, possibly in irritation, the employer chose the most odious task for his workman. Dr. Thayer says of *keration*—translated *husks*, ". . . the name of the fruit . . . the *Ceratonia siliqua* or carob tree, called also *St. John's Bread*, from the notion that its pods, which resemble the locusts, constituted the food of the Baptist. This fruit is shaped like a horn and has a sweet taste; it was, and is used, not only in fattening swine, but as an article of food by the lower classes."

And when he came to himself, he said, how many hired servants of my father's have bread enough and to spare, and I perish with hunger. I will arise and go to my father, and will say unto him, Father, I have sinned against heaven, and before thee. And am no more worthy to be called thy son: make me as one of thy hired servants (vv. 17–19).

There is something singularly beautiful about the phrase, "And when he came to himself." Most people would have criticized this young man, and cited continually the evil things which he did. Yet the Lord with characteristic kindness revealed that *the* real young man had not been responsible for these unfortunate acts; the true man had been overshadowed by a cruel understudy. See the homily at the end of this section.

And he arose and came to his father. But when he was yet a great way off, his father saw him, and had compassion, and ran, and fell on his neck, and kissed him. And the son said unto him, Father, I have sinned against heaven, and in thy sight, and am no more worthy to be called thy son (vv. 20–21).

Let it be noted that the returning son did not finish the prayer which in all probability had been repeated until the suppliant was word-perfect. The petition "Make me as one of thy hired servants" was never presented. Was the boy overcome by surging emotions, or did the overjoyed father interrupt before the lad could finish? This we may never know. However, we cannot fail to see that whereas the Lord in the earlier parables had spoken of the joy among the angels at the return of a sinner, now He presents that picture in all its thrilling wonder. Preachers should stress the fact that whilst the prodigal had resolved to return, he could have repeated his resolution daily and remained among the swine. Nothing really commenced to happen until his resolve was translated into action. HE AROSE AND CAME.

But the father said to his servants, Bring forth the best robe, and put it on him; and put a ring on his hand, and shoes on his feet: And bring

hither the fatted calf, and kill it; and let us eat and be merry: For this
my son was dead, and is alive again; he was lost, and is found. And
they began to be merry (vv. 22-24).

Probably the significance of the robe and the ring is best understood
when this scripture is compared with Genesis 41: 41-42. "And Pharaoh
said unto Joseph, See, I have set thee over all the land of Egypt. And
Pharaoh took off his ring from his hand, and put it upon Joseph's hand,
and arrayed him in vestures of fine linen, and put a gold chain about
his neck." The prodigal was probably dressed in the poorest of garments; perhaps he was even in rags. Cleansed and clothed in the
resplendent garments of true sonship, the ring of authority was placed
upon his hand, and since slaves went barefoot, the final marks of the
poverty which had enslaved him were removed. Delivered, accepted,
free, he stood resplendent alongside his father. There is reason to
believe that no other parable or word-picture given by the Lord so
fully represented the basic truths of the Gospel. Students may want
to consider *the following ideas*: (1) *LOVE ENDURING.* It should
not be difficult to imagine the scene in the ancient homestead immediately prior to the departure of the erring son. We have not been given
many details concerning the behaviour of the younger son, but the
subsequent facts revealed in the scriptures make it very clear that
the loss of the boy had grieved the father's heart. *"Love suffereth long
and is kind."* Throughout the long and lonely months or years that
the boy remained in the far country, the love of the parent continued,
and this is a splendid picture of the love of God which yearns over,
and waits for, the return of His prodigals. (2) *LOVE EXPECTING.*
". . . when he was yet a great way off, his father saw him . . ." The
parent had been watching for him. There might have been many
mornings when the older man looked in vain, but successive disap-
pointments did not kill the expectancy within his heart. He firmly
believed that some day his boy would come home. All the father's
desire seemed to be concentrated on that one matter. He waited
eagerly for the moment when the sinful one would arrive. Is not this
the passionate hope of God? Was it not for this purpose that He permitted Christ to die? (3) *LOVE EXCITING.* ". . . and had compassion,
and *RAN* . . ." Eagerness, compelling enthusiasm flooded the father's
heart; his son was within sight; the boy was coming home. Dignity;
calmness; meticulous deliberation were forgotten. As glorious abandon
thrilled the man's soul, he rushed to meet his boy. One wonders if
there can ever be anything as exciting as the sight of a man yielding
to God. No church can ever sleep when its members are praising God.
This father of a bygone generation had prayed, worked, and waited
for this great moment. It had now arrived, and he was thrilled beyond

words. (4) *LOVE EMBRACING*. "... and fell on his neck and kissed him." If ever the prodigal entertained doubt as to whether or not he would be welcomed home, those doubts were banished the moment his father's arms went around his neck. This was love outpoured. Abraham Lincoln was once asked how he intended to treat the rebellious Southerners when they had been defeated and returned to the Union of the United States. Lincoln with characteristic grace answered, "I will treat them as if they had never been away." This is forgiveness; this is love; this is the only way to reflect the kindness of God. (5) *LOVE ENRICHING*. "Bring forth the best robe and put it on him, and put a ring on his hand, and shoes on his feet." The robe stood for honour and acceptance; the ring for authority; the shoes for freedom. Slaves always went barefoot, and since this boy had sunk to pitiable levels, he returned utterly impoverished. This appalling picture was soon changed. The dirt and grime of past experiences were washed away; the robe revealed the boy was back in favour; he was an accepted member of the family. The ring revealed he was indeed a son—he was being treated as though he had never been away. Let it be noted again that the boy never had the opportunity to complete his request —make me as one of thy hired servants. Even the slaves to a very small degree were recognized as being part of the family. In contrast to this *the hired servants* were strangers who could be dismissed at a moment's notice. The prodigal had not expected even to be welcomed as a new slave. His weak faith could only believe that within the old homestead would be a chance to work as a stranger. (6) *LOVE ENTHUSING*. "And bring hither the fatted calf, and kill it; and let us eat, and be merry." The fatted calf could always be found on a farm; it was the animal specially fattened in preparation for a festive day. This father could not imagine any day superseding the present one. Days of happiness there might well be but nothing could surpass the wonder of the time when his boy came home. Soon the home of silence became the home of song; the house of sorrow became the house of gladness, and even the darkness of the surrounding night seemed to be challenged by the light shining from every window. This matchless picture supplied by the Lord made Heaven to be a most desirable place. (7) *LOVE EXPLAINING*. "For this my son was dead, and is alive again; he was lost, and is found." No guest was left in doubt as to the reason for the festivities. The Father had a story to tell and he told it. The Lord explained there was joy in the presence of the angels when sinners returned from the far country. Heaven and earth appear to be in close accord. *UP THERE* God tells out the glad story; *DOWN HERE* we should be doing it.

PART TWO . . . THE OTHER PRODIGAL

Now his elder son was in the field: and as he came and drew nigh to the house, he heard musick and dancing. And he called one of the servants, and asked what these things meant. And he said unto him, Thy brother is come; and thy father hath killed the fatted calf, because he hath received him safe and sound. And he was angry, and would not go in: therefore came his father out, and entreated him. And he answering, said to his father, Lo, these many years do I serve thee, neither transgressed I at any time thy commandment: and yet thou never gavest me a kid, that I might make merry with my friends: But as soon as this thy son was come, which hath devoured thy living with harlots, thou hast killed for him the fatted calf (vv. 25-30).

At first glance, it would appear the older brother had grounds for his behaviour. He had indeed toiled at home whilst his younger brother, having taken his share of the inheritance squandered his money in a far country. If his testimony were true, there had never been an occasion when he had been able to make merry with his friends. The father was giving something to which the younger son was not entitled. He had already received his inheritance, why then should more be given to him? There exists the possibility that the older brother imagined a part of his own possessions would in some clandestine way be transferred to the pockets of the undeserving prodigal. It could be a sobering thought that we might have reacted just as he did.

*He was angry*

When he came in from the fields to see the house illuminated and to hear the music echoing through the night, his reactions became very violent. When a man becomes angry he reveals he is smaller than the thing which upsets him. For all he knew the brother might have returned a millionaire; the lad's coming might have enriched the estate a thousand fold. The elder brother did not wait to make enquiries; he never even thought of seeking an explanation from his father. *He* had not been consulted, and therefore this thing should not have taken place. His passion erupted, and as he stood beneath the stars his soul was in rebellion.

*He was stubborn*

Most angry people are stubborn. They instinctively argue for otherwise there is no justification for their conduct. They have to persuade others that they are right, and in the final analysis they find it necessary to persuade themselves! When the father came out to entreat him, the elder boy commenced to utter his complaints. He was not prepared to listen to reason; he had made up his mind on certain matters and his findings were beyond question.

### He was rebellious

Actually he made no real complaint against his brother; the complaint was against his father. ". . . *thou* never gavest me a kid that I might make merry with my friends." There is no record that he ever asked for a kid, and for that matter there is no evidence that he had any friends. Anybody whose volcanic soul is likely to erupt in unrestrained passion finds it very difficult to make or keep friends. It is not too difficult to believe the son was now blaming his father for the lack of friends for which he himself was directly responsible.

### He had an evil mind

His statement, "thy son . . . which hath devoured thy living with harlots . . ." was unjustified. This was mere supposition, and it should be remembered that his was the first and only mention of this abhorrent sin. It was true that the boy had "wasted his substance with riotous living," but no mention had ever been made of sexual relations. This was the product of the man's filthy mind. He had often imagined that this was taking place, and suddenly his secret thoughts were expressed openly.

### He was jealous

"Thou never gavest me a calf" revealed the flaming anger and overpowering jealousy which coloured his thinking. He referred to the prodigal as "thy son" and not as *his brother*. He cited the great amount of work which he had done, and inferred there had been very little compensation. The fact that the WHOLE of the inheritance was to become his; that whatever he had done on the farm, he had done for his own benefit; that every cent earned was destined for his own pocket, were ignored. He demonstrated how easy it was to work hard in the father's establishment and yet at the same time to be completely out of touch with his heart.

### He was mean

"Son . . . all that I have is thine." This was the truth. The loss of one calf was so small that it would hardly be missed. However there remained the haunting fear that the returning boy might desire something in excess of that which he had already received as his inheritance. He who keeps his hands closed can never receive anything. It was said, "Give and it shall be given unto you, pressed down, and running over." Unfortunately this elder brother had never studied that kind of virtue. He lived for himself, and he lived in vain.

*He was ? ? ?*

Perhaps this alone demonstrates the marvellous finesse of Jesus the story-teller. The end of the account is not given for perhaps it had not come. Did the older brother yield to the pleadings of the father? Did he eventually consent to joining the party? Was there a glad reunion between the two boys? We are not told for this belonged to the future. This is all the more pointed when we remember the occasion for the giving of this parable. The key figures at the beginning of this chapter were (1) the Pharisees and the scribes; (2) the publicans and the sinners; (3) The Saviour. Let us remember that the story was given as an answer to the charge brought against the Lord Jesus. The complaining Pharisees were therefore likened to the elder brother; the publicans and the sinners were portrayed by the prodigal son; the outshining love of the father reflected the concern shown by the Saviour toward these outcasts of society. The ultimate attitude of the Pharisees had not yet been revealed, and lest Christ should be condemned for pre-judging a situation, He wisely left the end of the parable untold. Christ was truly a magnificent preacher.


HOMILIES

Study No. 50

### THE SCHOOL IN THE PIGSTY!

God always says the best possible about a man, and in that respect His account of the prodigal is somewhat different from the many sermons preached in the pulpit. The preacher invariably speaks about the sin of the selfish boy who revelled in the lustful enjoyments of the far country. This is considered to be a great message for tramps and drunkards. Yet in His approach to the theme, God says that the REAL man was not responsible for the sins of the prodigal. These were brought about through the cruel activities of a deplorable understudy.

*The Real Man Submerged*

Yes, it is a thrilling thought that God always seeks the best in a man. He knew the prodigal would soon come to himself. Surging passions and tumultuous emotions had temporarily swamped the real man. Studdart Kennedy often said:

> There's summat that pulls us up
> And summat that pulls us down;
> And the consequence is that we wobble
> 'Twixt muck and a golden crown.

Here is the story of moments when the downward pull seemed to be the greater of the two. Thus a man had been ruined. He appeared to be utterly vile; but let us be patient—the real man will yet lift up his head.

### The Real Man Surviving

When we consider the awful moral and spiritual depravity of the prodigal, it appears difficult to find virtue in his character. "He spent all his substance in riotous living," and sank to depths where no decent citizen would help him. His entire background seems sordid and immoral, yet underneath his recklessness lay the soul of a real man. Someone has said,

> There's so much bad in the best of us,
> And so much good in the worst of us,
> It ill behoves any one of us
> To find fault with the rest of us.

We therefore do well to consider three vital facts. (1) *God's Vision.* He saw that the real man still existed. (2) *God's Faith.* He believed *the real man* would ultimately triumph. (3) *God's Patience.* He was willing to wait until such a miracle became possible.

### The Real Man Suggesting

Sometimes pigs can be splendid schoolmasters. They are expert tutors of the fact that they who never look up generally live in squalor and end in tragedy. The prodigal listened to their grunts and learned to appreciate the music of his home. *"And when he came to himself."* An identical expression is used to describe the trance or sleep-walking of Peter when by divine intervention he was brought out of prison (Acts 12: 11). Outside the city, he came to himself and realized that he had been a man doing and saying things for which he was not quite intellectually responsible. That phase had passed, and the sleepiness had vanished from his eyes. Similarly the prodigal awakened and realized (1) *His need for penitence*—"Father, I have sinned before heaven." (2) *His need for prayer*—"Make me as one of thy hired servants." (3) *His need to proceed immediately,* or his finest resolutions would be useless.

*The Real Man Supreme*

Once again we may profitably consider three things. (1) *How great his sincerity.* "Father, I have sinned against heaven and in thy sight, and am no more worthy to be called thy son." He realized that his greater sin was against God; the sin against his father was secondary. (2) *How great his salvation.* "But the father said to his servants, Bring forth the best robe . . . For this my son was dead, and is alive again; he was lost and is found." *"How great his service."* This surely provides a strange contrast to the half-hearted service rendered before he left home. This time it would be born of gratitude. His heart would strengthen his hands. The Lord Jesus loved to tell this story for He believed the real man existed in every fallen soul. To seek such men, He left His throne in glory and came to die on a cross. He is supremely thrilled each time a prodigal turns his face homeward. (Taken from the Author's book *Bible Cameos,* p. 117.)

# The Sixteenth Chapter of Luke

THEME: *Jesus Speaks of Two Rich Men*

OUTLINE:

      I. The Rich Man and the Steward. Verses 1–18
     II. The Rich Man and the Beggar. Verses 19–31

SECTION ONE

*Expository Notes about the Embezzling Steward*

> And he said also unto his disciples, There was a certain rich man, which had a steward; and the same was accused unto him that he had wasted his goods. And he called him, and said unto him, How is it that I hear this of thee? give an account of thy stewardship; for thou mayest be no longer steward. Then the steward said within himself, What shall I do? for my lord taketh away from me the stewardship: I cannot dig, to beg, I am ashamed, I am resolved what to do, that, when I am put out of the stewardship, they may receive me into their houses (vv. 1–4).

It must be candidly admitted, we are here confronted by one of the most surprising utterances of the Lord. What He meant to teach, and why Luke should place the scripture in this part of his narrative are questions which have engaged the minds of the church for centuries. The interpretations of the parable have been almost legion, but in spite of the many opinions expressed, it remains impossible to state categorically that any one idea is correct. J. C. Ryle in his commentary on Luke mentions sixteen different writers most of whom offer varying interpretations of the parable. Trench, on *The Parables,* mentions others. Both the steward and the master have been likened to many people and subjects, but there seems to be an increasing danger of trying to make the parable mean something that was never in the Saviour's mind. It is wise to stay with the simple facts expressed in the lesson, and thereby to avoid errors.

This is a story about two swindlers whose infamy almost beggared description. The few details mentioned here are indicative of the greater things they might have done had opportunity presented itself. There were many land-owners in Palestine who, for the most part, were content to leave their affairs in the hands of stewards. These

346

stewards were not slaves, but free men employed to administer the estate of their employers. Oftentimes, they collected rents, either in cash or kind; they paid the expenses of running the business, and even paid themselves. The residue of the profit was finally given to the landowner. The story before us tells of a steward who had embezzled money; he had been unfaithful in the discharge of his duties, and someone conversant with the facts, had accused him. The master thereupon dismissed his employee and ordered him to present his accounts for examination. Realizing that he had lost his job and that the future would be bleak, the scheming scoundrel devised an ingenious plan by which he would be able to blackmail his associates.

So he called every one of his lord's debtors unto him, and said unto the first, How much owest thou unto my lord? And he said, An hundred measures of oil. And he said unto him, Take thy bill, and sit down quickly and write fifty. Then said he to another, And how much owest thou? And he said, An hundred measures of wheat. And he said unto him, Take thy bill and write forescore (vv. 5-7).

T. W. Manson estimates that the one hundred measures or *baths* of oil would probably be about 868 gallons, and the one hundred measures or *cors* of wheat would be approximately 1,083 bushels. The scheming steward probably was an excellent, psychologist for without hesitation he reduced the debt of the first man by fifty per cent. Yet, when he faced the second man, he only reduced the debt twenty per cent. He was shrewd and expert in entangling the debtors in his scheme. When with their consent he falsified the entries, he instantly made grounds upon which in after days he could exercise blackmail. As long as he did not exert too much pressure upon his victims, they would yield to his requests. Otherwise, if he informed the landlord about their part in the conspiracy, they might lose their lands.

And the lord commended the unjust steward, because he had done wisely: for children of this world are in their generation wiser than the children of light. And I say unto you, Make to yourselves friends of the mammon of unrighteousness; that, when ye fail, they may receive you into the everlasting habitations (vv. 8-9).

Actually the employer was as great a swindler as the servant, for when he heard of the deeds of his employee, he commended him—it was probably the kind of thing he would have done himself under identical circumstances. Obviously the paramount truth here is that a man foreseeing danger made precautions to offset his peril. The Lord Jesus cited this instance as an illustration of an even greater truth. If the children of evil are so wise—even in their deceit and sin, how much wiser should the children of light be as they face the demands of eternity! Candidly let it be admitted that verse 9 presents problems. The derivation of the Aramaic word *mammon* is uncertain but the inference is clear. Jesus was referring to wealth of any kind, and in its present setting was indicating it was better to make friends of money— that is, by using it properly— than to use it in such a way that it would act as a boomerang and return to injure the man who had become its slave. Godet thinks the terms *"that . . . they may receive you into everlasting habitations"*, is a poetic expression. This may well be, but here is evidence that this is a most difficult passage to interpret. The Scriptures make it clear that no man encouraging friendship with sin and sinners can thereby earn an abiding place in the presence of God. Whatever the text DOES mean, at least we know it DOES NOT mean that. Certain teachers throughout the ages quoted this statement in an endeavour to prove assertions that Christ was without principles; that He also was morally unsound when He faced the greatest temptations of life. This, of course, we cannot accept. The passage is indisputably difficult, but it would appear from the context that He was advising His followers it would be better to have friends than to be without them; that to be prudent in the use of money or anything else, in the end would return the best dividends. The following verses suggest the spotlight was upon character rather than destiny.

**He that is faithful in that which is least is faithful also in much: and he that is unjust in the least is unjust also in much. If therefore ye have not been faithful in the unrighteousness mammon, who will commit to your trust the true riches? And if ye have not been faithful in that which is another man's, who shall give you that which is your own? No servant can serve two masters; for either he will hate the one, and love the other, or else he will hold to the one, and despise the other. Ye cannot serve God and mammon (vv. 10-13).**

A confirmed thief would hardly be trusted with the wealth of a bank; a man prone to pick the pockets of his friends could hardly be expected to safeguard their jewels! A man's character will sooner or later be revealed in his actions. The man who carefully counts his pennies will seldom squander his gold. There are certain gifts which God would bestow upon the sons of men; there are gifts which He longs to give to His disciples; therefore, in a sense, these would be *their own*, yet, would God grant to anyone such gifts if already the person had demonstrated his complete irresponsibility in the use of such gifts? There is a sense in which "even that which he hath, is taken away." No slave could have two masters. When a man owned a slave, *he owned him completely*. Today, it is possible for a man to have two jobs—to be a watchman by day and a janitor by night. Yet this was never the case in older days. A slave belonged exclusively to his master—he had no time of his own. At any time of the day or night the master could command him to do anything and there was never any court of appeal. What the master said was law. If such principles existed in the earthly sphere, how much more were they to be desired in the spiritual realm! Unless God possesses men completely—HE DOES NOT POSSESS THEM AT ALL.

And the Pharisees also, who were covetous, heard all these things: and they derided him. And he said unto them, Ye are they which justify yourselves before men; but God knoweth your hearts: for that which is highly esteemed among men is abomination in the sight of God. The law and the prophets were until John: since that time the kingdom of God is preached, and every man presseth into it. And it is easier for heaven and earth to pass, than one tittle of the law to fail (vv. 14-17).

It is not too difficult to understand why such preaching should offend the Pharisees. They were constantly urging people to obey the dictates of the law, and yet at the same time they were ignoring the great details of mercy, kindness, and grace. They appeared to be straining at gnats and swallowing camels, and when Christ insisted on the fundamental characteristics of honesty before God, their consciences were troubled, and they sought solace in criticism. The Saviour's words laid bare their inmost souls, and revealed the things they most desired were hateful in the estimation of God. And in any case, a new era had been introduced. The exacting laws of Moses had reached a goal in the appearance of John the Baptist. The coming of Christ had brought a new message; a new opportunity, and whilst the hypocritical Pharisees were critical and antagonistic, other men were more sensible—they were pressing into the kingdom of God. Even the publicans with their penitence were more acceptable than the Pharisees with their pride. Yet even in this strange and sad contrast the law was being fulfilled, for just as the ancients had been stiff-necked and hardened in heart, so also were their descendants. What God had predicted was surely being fulfilled.

Whosoever putteth away his wife, and marrieth another, committeth adultery: and whosoever marrieth her that is put away from her husband committeth adultery (v. 18).

We are unable to decide whether or not this utterance is in its proper chronological setting. We cannot tell why Luke should decide to place the text at this precise place in his narrative—unless divorce with all its ramifications provided an example of the thing Christ had just denounced. He had said that certain things were an abomination to God—did He mean to infer that high on the list of such things was the Pharisaic attitude toward marriage? The Mosaic teaching concerning this vexing question was based upon Deuteronomy 24: 1–4. "When a man hath taken a wife, and married her, and it come to pass that she find no favour in his eyes, because he hath found some uncleanness in her: then let him write a bill of divorcement, and give it into her hand, and send her out of his house. And when she is departed out of his house, she may go and be another man's wife. And if the latter husband hate her, and write her a bill of divorcement, and giveth it in her hand, and sendeth her out of his house; or if the latter husband die, which took her to be his wife; Her former husband, which sent her away may not take her again to be his wife, after that she is defiled; for that is an abomination before the Lord . . ." It will be seen at a glance that the present situation is vastly removed from those outlined by Moses. The law came through the patriarch, but grace and truth came by Jesus Christ. The standards which satisfied the ancient are no longer satisfactory to the Christian. Grace demands much much more than did the law. It was by the ancient standards that Jewish conduct was judged, but let it be remembered a woman was unimportant in the eyes of Jewish men. She cooked meals, bore children, and worked in the fields. She was very necessary but most expendable.

According to Jewish interpretation of the law, everything depended upon the meaning of the words *"because he hath found some uncleanness in her."* There were two schools of thought in Jewry. The school of Shammai insisted that it meant only adultery, but the school of Hillel insisted it meant "if she spoiled a dish of food; if she spun in the streets; if she talked to a strange man; if she spoke disrespectfully of her husband's relations in his presence, or if she were a brawler." One famous Rabbi, Rabbi Akiba insisted that a man could divorce his wife as soon as he found a woman fairer than she. As a result of these strange ideas, married life was in jeopardy. A woman's marital status was in constant danger for at any moment, and for the most superficial of reasons, the man could write a bill of divorcement before witnesses, and expel her from the home. Because of the ever-recurring problems of womanhood, there were those who refused to marry, and the future of the nation was thereby threatened. Alas, a woman was only a necessary evil, and the continuing insecurity of womanhood throughout the Moslem world at the present time bears eloquent testimony to the conditions which have prevailed in the Middle East since the days of Jesus. Aware of the outlook of some of the rabbis, the Lord spoke of divorce and endorsed certain principles which they had ignored. "It hath been said, Whosoever putteth away his wife, let him give her a bill of divorcement: But I say unto you, That whosoever shall put away his wife, saving for the cause of fornication, causeth her to commit adultery: and whosoever shall marry her that is divorced committeth adultery" (Matthew 5: 31–32). The sanctity of home life is one of the basic principles of national strength, and when a nation sacrifices these virtues upon the altars of lust, it commits suicide.

## HOMILIES

Study No. 51

### THE MAN WHO BLACKMAILED HIS FRIENDS

During the days when slavery was legal, it was quite impossible for any slave to belong to two masters. When a man purchased a slave, he did so completely. He bought him outright! Every moment of the slave's day; every inch of the slave's body; every talent the slave possessed, belonged exclusively to his master. The slave existed to obey the owner's commands, and however much he might have resented the situation, unfortunately there was no court of appeal. Therefore, when the Lord stated it was an impossibility to serve God and Mammon; that no man could serve two masters, His hearers knew exactly what He meant for they viewed His utterance against the background of slavery. Yet to understand fully the lessons Jesus desired to teach, it is necessary to consider also the strange and colourful story which introduced the Saviour's statement.

### God and My Conscience

The man should have been sent to prison! "There was a certain rich man who had a steward" and that steward was as great a rogue as may be found anywhere in the Scriptures. He was probably the trusted agent of a very wealthy land-owner; the entire estate was left in his hands. He was responsible for the upkeep of the property; he sub-let to tenants; he collected rents; he paid bills and did a little unscrupulous book-keeping; he was an adept at maintaining his master's happiness for the figures on the annual balance sheet were always pleasing. Yet his chief asset was the skill with which he paid money into his own account. He never asked for a raise in his salary for he was very well satisfied. Somewhere along the line, he made one mistake; he allowed someone to suspect the falsification of the company's books. That someone had probably been squeezed a little too much for taxes, and in an increasing desire to get even with the unscrupulous agent, the offended one carried his accusation to the wealthy landowner. Then the fat was in the fire! Angry and very indignant, the master demanded a full enquiry and ordered the agent to prepare to quit his job. The outlook was very stormy for everyone. If the money-loving agent ever had a conscience, he had long since learned to stifle it. The Lord Jesus Christ was a master story-teller, but ere we proceed with this absorbing account, we must consider that the Lord used this as an illustration of the impossibility of serving both God and Mammon. The chief characteristic of *the children of light* is that they *walk* as children of light. Truly dedicated, and existing to do the will of God, they abandon all thought of self. At home; in the business; at work and at play, they live that their Master might be pleased. If they make money, they delight in giving as much as possible to their Lord; if they have any spare time, they hasten to use it to further the cause of their Master. Whereas the man in the story only lived for the advance of self; they live, move, and have their being in the centre of the will of God.

## God and My Character

The steward was in great trouble. What could he do? His lucrative source of income was gone; he had lost his job. Of course he might have asked pardon from his master, but penitence was unknown in his make-up. He had lived by his wits for most of his life and he saw no reason to leave the boat now that it was beginning to rock! "What shall I do? for my lord taketh away from me the stewardship: I cannot dig; to beg I am ashamed." "Yes, Sir, I know what I will do. Let me proceed carefully, and my future will be assured." Soon he was sitting with one of the farmers—"Friend, how much do you owe the master? I see—one hundred measures of oil—that is a lot. Never mind, we can help each other. Sit down quickly and write fifty. The master will never know the difference for I will alter the figures in the accounts. Now friend keep your mouth shut, and we shall be all right. Now let me go and see your neighbour" . . . "And how much do you owe? Yes, that is correct. You owe one hundred measures of wheat. Yes, indeed that is a lot. Friend, let us look after ourselves. Suppose I change the figures to read eighty measures. You like that? Good. Keep your lips sealed and he will never know. If the Almighty helps those who help themselves, let's give Him some extra work!" And the man smiled and walked away. And as the Saviour told the story, He indicated such men could never be the servants of God. What a man does is only the reflection of what he is. This man lived by his wits; he was exceedingly shrewd; it mattered not what happened to anyone as long as he himself was pleased. He was unscrupulously selfish. Sacrifice was unknown; penitence and remorse were words never found in his vocabulary. The New Testament is particularly strong at this point. Had strong arguments been put to the swindler, or had excessive fear played havoc with his peace of mind, a temporary change of action might have been forthcoming. Yet as night follows day, so the man would have eventually returned to his evil ways when a greater chance to make money had come his way. He needed to be born again for otherwise he would have remained untrustworthy. Such people have no place in the kingdom of God.

## God and My Conduct

His plans were well made. He knew what he intended to do. He smiled as he visualized the scene. "Mr. So and So, do you think you could let me have some cash for I am in urgent need of funds? You cannot—well, that is most unfortunate. I was very kind to you. I actually risked punishment just to ease your taxation problems. I think I might be suitably rewarded if I went and told my former master that you still owe him a great amount of money. Yes, indeed, perhaps he would even reinstate me, or at least, he would exhibit his gratitude for the information by allowing me to take over your farm. Yes, it is a great pity that you are unable to let me have that money. I should be so grateful to you, and naturally, I would not even think of telling the landlord about your falsified accounts. Ah, you might be able to manage it. You are a gracious tenant; it is a pleasure to do business with you. And your neighbour, let me see, he had a very good crop this year. Perhaps he could help me a little for I have been so kind to him. I actually only asked for a small portion of what I so urgently need at the present time. Good day to you, Friend. You are very co-operative."

And Jesus sighed as He said, "If therefore we have not been faithful in the unrighteous mammon, who will commit to your trust the true riches?" The conflicting ways of the two systems—the earthly and the heavenly—were brought into bold relief when the Lord said, "And the lord commended the unjust steward because he had done wisely." Such are the ways of the children of this world—oftentimes, they are a bunch of rogues! To be used of God, the children of light have to exhibit character of a different kind. Mercy, truth, reliability, goodness, gentleness, faith—against such, there is no law. The Great Lord of the vineyard will never promote to high office anyone who has not revealed trustworthiness even in the minor details of His kingdom. His favourite commendation appears to be "Well done, thou good and FAITHFUL servant." It would be interesting to know if we shall ever earn that award.

SECTION TWO

*Expository Notes on the Rich Man and Lazarus*

**There was a certain rich man, which was clothed in purple and fine linen, and fared sumptuously every day; And there was a certain beggar named Lazarus, which was laid at his gate, full of sores, And desiring to be fed with the crumbs which fell from the rich man's table: moreover the dogs came and licked his sores (vv. 19–21).**

Bishop Ryle says of this passage: "From the very earliest days it has been a matter of dispute whether it ought to be regarded as a parable or real history. The truth seems to me to lie between the two extremes. I see no reason why it should not be regarded as a real history. And yet it may be a history employed to point a lesson." There is evidence to suggest that Ryle is correct, for whenever the Lord used a parable, He invariably made that point clear. However, in this instance no such term is used. The teaching expressed in these verses harmonizes with the doctrines of the Bible, and there appears to be no valid reason why the account should be dismissed merely as an illustration or parable. This is the story of two men who lived at opposite extremes of the social order. The one owning everything, possessed nothing. The other owning nothing, inherited everything. Some people are so poor they only have money! Each and every detail of the description of the rich man endorses the fact that he was very wealthy. He was clothed in purple and fine linen—this was the type of clothing worn by the High Priest and it was most costly. He fared sumptuously; that is, he had banquets every day. He was exceptionally fond of calories but never worried about counting them. The word translated *fared sumptuously* basically means *to make merry,* but Thayer explains it is the word generally used for the type of merriment known at a feast. This man was a glutton. Lazarus was an abject contrast for he had as little as the other man had much. Weak and helpless he lay at the rich man's gate hoping he would be able to glean crumbs which came out with the garbage. It should be remembered that knives and forks were unknown in those early days; that men ate with their hands. Therefore it was to be expected that as they broke their bread, crumbs would indeed fall from the table. Furthermore as Barclay points out, the very wealthy people wiped their fingers on thick pieces—chunks of bread which were afterward thrown away. Lazarus the hungry and helpless beggar hoped to be able to secure some of these. The poor fellow was so helpless that even the dogs bothered him.

And it came to pass, that the beggar died, and was carried by the angels into Abraham's bosom: the rich man also died, and was buried; And in hell he lift up his eyes, being in torments, and seeth Abraham afar off, and Lazarus in his bosom. And he cried and said, Father Abraham, have mercy on me, and send Lazarus, that he may dip the tip of his finger in water, and cool my tongue; for I am tormented in this flame. But Abraham said, Son, remember that thou in thy lifetime receivedst thy good things, and likewise Lazarus evil things: but now he is comforted, and thou art tormented. And beside all this, between us and you there is a great gulf fixed: so that they which would pass from hence to you cannot; neither can they pass to us, that would come from thence (vv. 22–26).

It should be remembered that throughout the Old Testament, it was taught that the dead at the cessation of their stay on earth went to *Sheol*—the place of the departed. This term was translated *Hades* in the New Testament. The Septuagint translated the word sixty-one times, and in all these places the texts referred to *the place of the dead*. However, there is a great depth of doctrine in the usage of these terms and students are exhorted to give earnest heed to this important study. Because the blood of beasts and bulls only provided *a covering* for sin —a means whereby sin could be temporarily hidden, men who were not truly cleansed from their iniquity were unable to proceed directly into the presence of God. The common Jewish belief expressed in this illustration indicated that the place of the departed was divided into two sections. One for the unrighteous dead, and the other for the righteous. That there was no fraternizing between the two sections is indicated by the presence of *a great gulf* separating either section from the other. It is further believed that when Christ offered Himself for sin; when He dealt with this enemy once and for all, the barrier which had excluded saints from the presence of God was removed. Thereafter, Christ went and freed the captives, and *"When He ascended up on high, he led captivity captive"*—that is, they who had been as captives were now liberated only to become His captives—they followed Him to Glory (Ephesians 4: 8). It follows from this that the section previously occupied by the righteous dead in Sheol is now empty. When Christians now die, they are *"absent from the body, and home with the Lord."* The New Testament teaches clearly that the Lord is seated at the right hand of the Majesty on High, and therefore it follows that if the saints are with Him, they are in heaven. The unrighteous dead remain in Hades, awaiting the final day of Judgment when the books will be opened and sinners will answer for the deeds done in the flesh.

These utterances of the Saviour graphically describe the teachings of the Old Testament and provide a most colourful picture of the

things believed by the Jews. The fact that the rich man spoke of torment seems to indicate that suffering is a very real thing in the hereafter. Whether or not these sayings are proverbial or poetic we do
not know. It might be that the hottest flame in Hades is that of a
seared conscience. The impossibility of crossing from one side to
another suggests that one's eternal destiny is settled here and not in
some future world. Throughout the story, Lazarus is never made to
utter a word, and some commentators believe this was indicative of
the graciousness with which he accepted his unfortunate lot in life.
He did not complain; he did not blame God; he did not even envy
the rich man. On the other hand, it is not said that the wealthy man
was a blasphemer, an idolater, an immoral man nor even an infidel.
Perhaps on occasion he even attended the synagogue. Nevertheless,
he loved himself more than any other man on earth. He did not drive
the beggar away; he did not begrudge the poor fellow any of the crusts
that found their way into his waiting hands. As long as he himself
was completely satisfied, nothing else mattered. He was a self-made
deity who worshipped at his own shrine. Probably it was not what he
did—but rather what he did not—which ultimately took him to Hades.

> Then he said, I pray thee therefore, father, that thou wouldest send
> him to my father's house: For I have five brethren; that he may testify
> unto them, lest they also come into this place of torment. Abraham
> saith unto him, They have Moses and the prophets; let them hear them.
> And he said, Nay, father Abraham: but if one went unto them from the
> dead, they will repent. And he said unto him, If they hear not Moses
> and the prophets, neither will they be persuaded, though one rose from
> the dead (vv. 27–31).

It has been argued that this petition of the lost man revealed an
improvement in his guilty soul. There is no basic proof that this is
correct. Some think the presence of the brothers would have increased
the man's misery for his regrettable actions had helped to ruin them.
Their being with him might have deepened his own anguish. Whatever may be the true reason we are left in no doubt as to the answer
given by the patriarch. The witness of God on earth is confined to
the realm of the written word and the men whose messages are based
thereon. If sinners neglect the scriptures, there is no other authorized
source of inspiration. It is impossible to ignore the difference between
the motives of this would-be messenger and the fantastic claims of
the spiritists. This man wished to warn his brethren of impending
disaster; the modern counterparts generally send back greetings of
the most dubious kinds; they would have us believe they are enjoying a picnic in summerland! That Abraham spoke accurately was
soon proved, for the Lord Jesus actually came back from the dead

only to discover that the Jewish nation preferred to continue in their unbelief.

Finally it should be noted that this message was given to the Pharisees who according to verse 14 loved their money. The terminology used throughout the narrative—*father Abraham*—suggests the words were being spoken by a Jew—a formerly wealthy Jew. It was therefore possible even for religious Jews to be lost, and to say the least, this was a thought-provoking doctrine for the people who were then being addressed.

## HOMILIES

Study No. 52

### A DRAMA . . . IN THREE ACTS

*Act One*

He was a splendid young man, and the villagers loved him. He was a ruler, but he was also a brother beloved; he had kept the commandments from his childhood days. His happiness must have been complete until Jesus came preaching in the little village. The ruler had never heard a preacher like this Stranger, upon whose countenance shone the light of Heaven, whose words had the ring of authority, and whose charm none could deny. It was not a cause for amazement when later he came running to ask, "Good Master, what must I do to inherit eternal life?" Jesus answered, "If thou wilt enter into life, keep the commandments." "But Master, all these have I kept from my youth up. What lack I yet?" Gravely the Teacher listened. This was a nice young man; so honest and so sincere. Eagerly, the ruler awaited an answer, and had he been able to thought-read, he probably would have read, "Well done. You have indeed made a great discovery. Keeping the commandments will never bring eternal life. Others will talk of their deeds and will measure themselves by the standards of earthly virtue, not knowing that their best righteousness is to God as filthy rags." Then Jesus said, "If thou wilt be perfect, go and sell that thou hast, and give to the poor, and thou shalt have treasure in Heaven: *and come and follow me.*" But when the young man heard that saying, he went away sorrowful: for he had great possessions. Did he ever reappear in the Gospel story?

*Act Two*

The farmhouse stood silently in the countryside, and from its chimneys the thin wisps of smoke lazily climbed into transparency. A wealthy man leaned on his gate and intently gazed at his crops. They were wonderful this year. Indeed, he had seldom seen such a harvest; it was obvious that his barns would be unable to store his possessions. What could he do? To give to the poor would be bad business. Let them work for their food. He would build larger barns, and then take his ease. His problem was settled. He smiled. He went to bed thinking about the new project, and wakened up in eternity. A voice had whispered in the stillness of the night, saying, "Thou fool, this night thy soul shall be required of thee." "What shall I do?" asked the rich young ruler. "What shall I do?" asked the older man. They spoke the same language—*were they the same man?* Of course, no one can be dogmatic about this and it does not really matter. There is truth here if we seek it. The rich pauper was buried, but the question arises once again—Did he ever reappear on the Gospel page?

*Act Three*

Some time later the Lord said, "The rich man also died, and was buried; And in hell he lift up his eyes being in torments." When we read the account in Luke 16, it becomes increasingly clear that once again the question in eternity was, "What shall I do?" There seems to be a continuity of thought in these three stories. The characters may not have been identical, nevertheless here is experience indeed. It is an established fact that the overwhelmng majority of Christians are won before they reach the age of twenty. Once a young man has passed this age, the possibility is that soon he will be engrossed in business, and most of his interests will be earthly. Many a successful businessman, who has no time for God, remembers the youthful days when his interests were loftier and holier. Alas, at the end of such a life is eternal frustration and boundless sorrow. Perhaps it was this fact which inspired the wise man to say: "Remember now thy creator in the days of thy youth, while the evil days come not, nor the years draw nigh when thou shalt say, I have no pleasure in them." Yesterday has gone for ever. Tomorrow, I may be gone—but where? Here is food for thought.

(Taken from the Author's book, *Bible Cameos*, page 115.)

# The Seventeenth Chapter of Luke

THEME: *The Continuation of Christ's Ministry*

OUTLINE:

    I. Jesus instructs His Disciples. Verses 1–10
   II. Jesus cleanses the Lepers. Verses 11–19
  III. Jesus predicts His Return. Verses 20–37

SECTION ONE

*Expository Notes on the Message to the Disciples*

Then said he unto the disciples, It is impossible but that offences will come: but woe unto him, through whom they come! It were better for him that a millstone were hanged about his neck, and he cast into the sea, than that he should offend one of these little ones (vv. 1–2).

The Greek word translated *offences* is *skandala* from which we get scandal; to speak evil concerning another person. Formerly the word did not mean this. Dr. Thayer points out that the word originally meant: *"the movable stick or trigger of a trap."* Later it came to mean *"any impediment placed in the way and causing one to stumble or fall."* Therefore the idea expressed in this text is that the expected offences will be snares deliberately placed in the path of the disciples; snares designed to trap the believer. Christ was aware that as the enemies had tried to trap Him, so would their descendants treat the Christians. The Saviour never promised a life of ease to those who would follow Him. He spoke of the necessity of taking up the cross daily. Yet with His warning came the unfailing promise that God's grace would be sufficient in every time of need. Even the times of hardship would be turned into a blessing, for God could make all things work together for good to those who loved the Lord. It could also be said that whilst God's watchful care would protect the believer, He would observe those through whom the trials would come, and in due course they would reap their reward.

Take heed to yourselves: If thy brother trespass against thee, rebuke him; and if he repent, forgive him. And if he trespass against thee

359

seven times in a day, and seven times in a day turn again to thee,
saying, I repent; thou shalt forgive him (vv. 3-4).

The Lord here reminded His followers of some of the basic principles
of the kingdom, in the establishment of which they were destined to
play such an important part. Discipleship demanded stern resolution.
Weaklings would either have to change or feel sadly out of place. If
wrong had been committed, the disciple was not to condone the fact.
There would be times when the Christian would need to rebuke his
brother—for the sake of the integrity and reputation of the kingdom.
Yet each rebuke had to be uttered in the spirit of love. Forgiveness
was to be the continuing sign of a grace-filled soul. And since within
the scriptures, seven is the number of perfection or completion, the
forgiveness offered by the disciple had to be absolute; grudges which
remained to poison the mind, had to be banished. This, and only this
could be true forgiveness.

> And the apostles said unto the Lord, Increase our faith. And the Lord
> said, If ye have faith as a grain of mustard seed, ye might say unto this
> sycamine tree, Be thou plucked up by the root, and be thou planted in
> the sea; and it should obey you (vv. 5-6).

Whether or not this request was the direct outcome of the preceding
verses, it is somewhat difficult to decide. Having listened to the Lord's
words about the necessity of continuing forgiveness, did the listeners
feel unequal to the spiritual demands thus made upon them? Did
they then ask for greater faith which would enable them to maintain
this high standard of daily living? On the other hand, we must ask
if this was something entirely apart from the preceding statements.
These disciples had listened to a great amount of doctrine, and perhaps
were beginning to feel unequal to the claims of true discipleship. Perhaps it is not possible to answer the question to the satisfaction of
every reader, but at least we know these men did the only wise thing
possible. Conscious of their limitations they brought their problem
to Christ.

> Oh what peace we often forfeit;
> Oh what needless pain we bear:
> All because we do not carry
> Everything to God in prayer.

The sycamine tree, or as some commentators think, the mulberry
tree, was well known for its tenacious roots which were exceedingly
difficult to uproot. That the smallest segment of faith was able to do
this indicated that nothing would be impossible for the man who truly
believed in his Lord.

But which of you, having a servant ploughing or feeding cattle, will say unto him by and by, when he is come from the field, Go and sit down to meat? And will not rather say unto him, Make ready wherewith I may sup, and gird thyself and serve me, till I have eaten and drunken; and afterward thou shalt eat and drink? Doth he thank that servant because he did the things that were commanded him? I trow not. So likewise ye, when ye have done all those things which were commanded you, say, We are unprofitable servants: we have done that which was our duty to do (vv. 7-10).

The fact that these verses follow the request for increasing faith seems to be exceedingly suggestive. Even if the prayer of the disciples were answered to the extent that they became the greatest of all the servants of God, there were still vital things to remember. A slave— strictly speaking—had no will of his own; he existed to do the bidding of his master. Against the accepted standards of those days, we must consider this text. A man who had been purchased was completely possessed. He was expected to think only of his master, and whether or not these standards would be applicable today, is beside the point. Christ was using an ancient situation to remind His followers it would never be safe to have an inflated ego. Then and always, they could never give more than God deserved; even their best would be insufficient to pay what they owed. The constant consideration of this never-changing fact would encourage the growth of humility. At best, they were to consider themselves unprofitable servants.

# HOMILIES

Study No. 53

## THE QUALIFICATIONS OF A GOOD SERVANT

The apostle Paul used some choice words to describe the Christian. Each one supplied a word picture, and three of these provide excellent progression of thought. Paul spoke of *the Bond-Slave or Servant of Jesus Christ* (Philippians 1: 1). This undoubtedly was based on the ancient custom by which a liberated slave indicated he wished to continue in the service of his master. The man who did not desire to be set free permitted a small hole to be drilled in the lobe of his ear, and thus signified to all people that he loved his master too much to leave him. He became a bond-slave. Paul referred to the believers as *Soldiers of Jesus Christ*, and thus expressed the fact that each disciple had embarked upon a holy war (2 Timothy 2: 3). Indeed, the conflict would be so severe that each Christian would need to take unto him the whole armour of God that he might be able to stand against the wiles of the devil. Christianity did not offer a lengthy vacation from the struggles of life; discipleship promised greater trials and stern opposition. Weaklings and cowards would have a hard time. Finally Paul referred to himself as *An Ambassador of Jesus Christ*, and this was one of his most colourful word pictures (Ephesians 6: 20). He was the representative of the eternal country; he had been appointed to represent the Government of Heaven in this world. His word was the authoritative message sent from the King of Heaven; he was determined to convey to earthly courts that which his Master wished to say. Furthermore, as an Ambassador he was also commissioned to speak on behalf of earth; he could intercede for sinners and thereby carry their requests to his Lord. The fact that he referred to himself as an Ambassador *in bonds* revealed a state of war had broken out between earth and heaven. Even Ambassadors are given safe conduct guarantees back to their own spheres, but Paul was imprisoned; even the elementary principles of decency had been violated. The god of this world was at war with the Prince of Heaven, and Heaven's Ambassador had been imprisoned. It will be recognized at a glance that becoming a follower of the Saviour makes certain demands upon the disciples. To become a good servant of Christ one must exhibit certain qualities; these are set forth clearly in the seventeenth chapter of Luke's Gospel.

### Watchful but Unafraid

"*It is impossible but that offences will come . . .*" People who desire a life of continuing ease should never climb the hill of Calvary. Men who shrink from difficult tasks should never take up the cross. Those who love the shouts of the world find great difficulty recognizing God's still small voice. If the ambassadors of Christ are to be imprisoned, the ordinary follower will be treated with even less courtesy. There will be persecution, suffering, and martyrdom. Let the coward therefore look the other way. The true servant of Christ must live with his eyes open; his brain alert, and his lips ready to bear testimony to the saving grace of God. If the Captain of Salvation orders the soldier suddenly to advance against a dangerous enemy, the soldier will not pause to debate the wisdom of the order. A rigid discipline; and unfailing confidence in his Leader; and a deep-rooted desire to be faithful even in battle conditions make the Christian a good soldier of Jesus Christ.

### Firm but Gentle

"*If thy brother trespass against thee, rebuke him; and if he repent, forgive him.*" Peace at any price is not always a good maxim, for sometimes the price to be paid for an uneasy truce is too high. Domestic strife is always to be deplored, but when a malignant cancer threatens the health of the church, it is necessary to use the scalpel. Yet, the hand to use the knife must be kind, gentle, and very careful. If a man has committed evil, he must be censored regardless of wealth, importance or position. Yet when he truly repents, no grudge should be held against him; spite within the heart or the church should be rooted out. "If any man be overtaken in a fault, ye which are spiritual restore such an one in the spirit of meekness considering thyself lest thou also be tempted."

### Believing but Bold

"If ye had faith . . . say unto this sycamine tree . . ." So many ask for faith but never do anything! So many people believe mightily, but they would never uproot a dandelion! We live in strange days when theologians talk eloquently about history but never make any! A quiet faith within the heart may produce wonderful experiences of eternal tranquillity, but this is not enough. A soldier may sit confidently in his trench fully persuaded his country will win the war, but that quiet faith must be strenuously expressed in hard combat if its presence is to be justified. The man who believes, but never speaks to any sycamine tree will never see changes in his immediate surroundings.

### Ready and Willing

". . . when ye have done all those things which are commanded you, say, We are unprofitable servants; we have done that which was our duty to do." No servant is ever tired when his beloved master asks a favour! No man begrudges time given to his best friend when he already knows he owes everything to his friend. The true Christian stands ready—at any time of the day or night; in fair weather or foul; when it is convenient and when it is inconvenient; the true Christian yearns to do his Master's will, and as soon as the message of Christ is relayed to his soul, he hastens on his errand. It is practically impossible to read Luke's descriptions without wondering what has happened to the church. If this is the standard of Christian service, many church members must have been paralysed from birth! When a professed Christian complains and invents excuses why he cannot do this and that for Christ and the church, it is obvious he has never seen the Cross, or at least, he has forgotten what it looks like.

### SECTION TWO

#### Expository Notes on the Cleansing of the Ten Lepers

And it came to pass, as he went to Jerusalem, that he passed through the midst of Samaria and Galilee. And as he entered into a certain

**village, there met him ten men that were lepers, which stood afar off:
And they lifted up their voices, and said, Jesus, Master, have mercy on
us. And when he saw them, he said unto them, Go shew yourselves
unto the priests. And it came to pass, that, as they went, they were
cleansed (vv. 11–14).**

There has been much discussion concerning the meaning of *dia
mesou*, the Greek words translated *through the midst of*. There were
two main highways along which south-bound travellers made their
way, but it appears Jesus did not use either of them. Commentators
emphasize that such travellers would first pass through Galilee and
then enter into Samaria. The order of places visited should then be
reversed. The text seems to indicate that Jesus was passing through
*the middle of*—or, *along the border of these two countries*. Some
writers think that Jesus encountered opposition from the local inhabitants, and as a result, followed the border; made his way toward the
Jordan valley, and there turned south toward Jericho. This would explain why he met a band of lepers in which both Jews and a Samaritan
were found.

Lepers were obliged by law to keep at a safe distance from other
people; the risk of contagion was thought to be exceptionally great and
therefore as Leviticus 13: 46 commanded, the lepers were required to
dwell alone, somewhere outside the camp. A common need had
banished all thoughts of racial bitterness; men who in health would
have been enemies were now united by adversity. There exists the
possibility that Christ deliberately took this unexpected road in order
to meet these unfortunate sufferers. These men therefore placed themselves in a place where their cries would attract His attention. Their
shouts brought an instant response, but the text is worthy of careful
examination. It must be stressed that the Lord did not cleanse them
immediately. Faith without works is dead. We are not told these
men had any faith in the Lordship of Christ; they had merely heard
He was capable of healing the sick, and as drowning men clutching at
a straw, they cried for mercy. There can be no doubt that the Saviour
desired to help them, but always He had the amazing gift of bringing
the best out of men. His command "Go and shew yourselves unto the
priests" was perfectly in keeping with the commands outlined in the
law. However, under the Mosaic order it would have been quite stupid
for any leper to go to the priest—as long as he remained a leper. To
present himself as the continuing victim of the dread disease would
only have elicited fierce condemnation; even priests were capable of
becoming lepers. When a man had reason to believe his leprosy had
vanished, he had grounds upon which to ask for a ceremonial pronouncement that he was fit to rejoin his fellow-men, but until his

petition was substantiated by actual fact, his journey to the priest was only a waste of time. Let it be noted clearly that although Christ told these men to report to the priest, they remained lepers. Thus they were faced with a problem. Reason said, "It is useless to do as He suggested." Faith replied, "Since He commanded us to go, He surely had a reason for issuing the command. Therefore let us go in simple dependance upon His word." *"And it came to pass that as they went, they were cleansed."* It is well to remember that hearing the Gospel never saved anybody. Faith must be followed by commitment; because a man believes, he acts, and as faith is thereby translated into intelligent response, the healing power of God does what needs to be done in the leper's life. This is just another of the many details which help to make the third Gospel one of the most thrilling documents in biblical writings.

**And one of them, when he saw that he was healed, turned back, and with a loud voice glorified God, And fell down on his face at his feet, giving him thanks: and he was a Samaritan. And Jesus answering said, Were there not ten cleansed? but where are the nine? There are not found that returned to give glory to God, save this stranger. And he said unto him, Arise, go thy way: thy faith hath made thee whole (vv. 15-19).**

Writing of this passage of scripture, Geldenhuys says: "After the carrying off of the kingdom of the Ten Tribes, a large number of Israelites remained behind in Samaria . . . and became interbred with the pagan immigrants who had been sent to the country by the Assyrians; thus a new race, the Samaritans, gradually originated . . . Until recently there were about a hundred Samaritans at Nablus in Palestine (the ancient Shechem) remaining faithful to their views and customs. These have now crossed into the territory of the state of Israel, and settled there. In New Testament times there prevailed a violent enmity between Jews and Samaritans. In the hour of common affliction, such differences are often wiped out, as in the case of this group of Jewish lepers, amongst whom there was at least one Samaritan." (*The New International Commentary on Luke*, p. 437.)

The sentence *he pistis sou sesoken se* has attracted the attention of theologians in every phase of church history. Thayer says the word translated *has cured* conveys the idea of being made *safe and sound,* but it would appear to be almost impossible to exhaust the meaning of that aspect of this remarkable incident. It is obvious that the returning Samaritan received a greater blessing than his companions. But to what extent are we justified in proceeding to explain the magnitude of his new blessing? The ten were cleansed, but this man was made safe and sound—he was made whole. Does that mean the disease was not only banished from his body—does it also imply that any member of the body which had suffered damage was restored to normal appearance and health? If hands had become deformed; if fingers had disappeared, were they suddenly and miraculously restored? We cannot tell. Does the text imply that the gratitude which brought the Samaritan to the feet of Jesus bore its own fruit and received its own reward in that physical cleansing was followed by spiritual enlightenment? Was the man made whole both in body and soul? Godet and several other writers think this is the only logical interpretation of the text. It is however thought-provoking that whereas the nine longed to claim their place in society, this Samaritan returned to express his thanks. Alas, for so many moderns, gratitude has become a forgotten art. See the homily at the end of Section 2, Chapter 5.

SECTION THREE

### Expository Notes on Christ's Teaching Concerning His Return to Earth

**And when he was demanded of the Pharisees, when the kingdom of God should come, he answered them and said, The kingdom of God cometh not with observation: Neither shall they say, Lo here! or, lo there! for, behold, the kingdom of God is within you (vv. 20-21).**

All commentators are agreed that this is a most difficult passage to interpret. It is not quite clear what Christ meant to infer; and cognizance must be taken of the two possible renderings of the text. The Amplified New Testament renders the passage thus: ". . . the kingdom of God is within you, (in your hearts) and among you (surrounding you). Historical records attest the simple fact that no matter of importance equalled that pertaining to the coming of the Messiah, and the establishment of His kingdom. The Pharisees discussed these matters continuously and their question to the Saviour was therefore to be expected. The Lord's answer seemed to suggest the impossibility of detecting the coming and the presence of the kingdom by sitting still watching for external signs. The word suggests a doctor sitting beside a patient, and looking, waiting for some signs which would assist a diagnosis. Two ideas seem to be in conflict here—the Pharisees looking without, and Christ looking within. They were only concerned with an earthly kingdom; with headquarters at Jerusalem; Christ thought more of a spiritual kingdom centred in men's hearts. If the former of the suggested interpretations be correct then He was trying to teach this very truth. If the latter be more acceptable, then He was endeavouring to explain that the kingdom of which they spoke had already come, for He in very deed and truth was the King. His followers were already increasing in number, and in a spiritual sense at least the true kingdom of God was beginning to take shape all around them. It cannot be claimed from the text that the kingdom of God was within the hearts of the proud, and sometimes, antagonistic Pharisees.

And he said unto the disciples, The days will come, when ye shall desire to see one of the days of the Son of man, and ye shall not see it. And they shall say to you, See here; or, see there: go not after them, nor follow them. For as the lightning, that lighteneth out of the one part under heaven, shineth unto the other part under heaven; so shall also the Son of man be in his day. But first must he suffer many things, and be rejected of this generation (vv. 22–25).

These statements seem to fall under three simple headings. (1) *BE COURAGEOUS*. The future will be fraught with peril and difficulties and the burdens to be carried will sometimes be intolerably heavy. So great will be the suffering that disciples will yearn for the coming of the kingdom if only to obtain relief. Jesus said, "Be courageous—carry your burdens with fortitude." (2) *BE CALM*. When things are going from bad to worse, there will always be those whose doctrines persuade you to run here, there, and everywhere in search of new revelation of truth. New movements will spiral from nowhere, and many of the saints will be swept along by every wind of doctrine. Jesus said, "Be calm—go not after them." (3) *BE CONFIDENT*. The Saviour will come. You may not be able to tell the exact moment, for as suddenly as the lightning flashes in the night, so suddenly will the Lord return. Therefore, at any moment, your tribulation might end. Jesus said, "Be confident, the Lord knoweth the way that you take, and when He has tried you, you will come forth as gold."

And as it was in the days of Noe, so shall it also be in the days of the Son of man. They did eat, they drank, they married wives, they were given in marriage, until the day that Noe entered into the ark, and the flood came, and destroyed them all. Likewise also, as it was in the days of Lot; they did eat, they drank, they bought, they sold, they planted, they builded; But the same day that Lot went out of Sodom it rained fire and brimstone from heaven, and destroyed them all. Even thus shall it be in the day when the Son of man is revealed. In that day, he which shall be upon the housetop, and his stuff in the house, let him not come down to take it away: and he that is in the field, let him likewise not return back. Remember Lot's wife (vv. 26–32).

For a long time the critics of the Scriptures maintained that much of the Old Testament was merely a collection of legends; that no educated man could be expected to accept its accounts as historically accurate. The flood, the ark, the experiences of Lot and his wife; the destruction of Sodom and Gomorrah were high on the list of incidents viewed with suspicion. Now, however, things have changed. The findings of the archaeologists have proved the reliability of the sacred records, and it is with increasing interest we are now able to consider the statements of the Lord. Evidently He believed and fully endorsed the accounts supplied by the book of Genesis. If there were no flood; no ark, no destruction of the ancient cities, why mislead people by referring to them as if they had really existed? Formerly the Lord had mentioned the suddenness with which the coming of the kingdom could be expected; these verses endorse the same teachings. See the homily at the end of this section.

> Whosoever shall seek to save his life shall lose it; and whosoever shall lose his life shall preserve it. I tell you, in that night, there shall be two men in one bed; the one shall be taken, and the other shall be left. Two women shall be grinding together; the one shall be taken, and the other left. Two men shall be in the field; the one shall be taken, and the other left. And they answered and said unto him, Where, Lord? And he said unto them, Wheresoever the body is, thither will the eagles be gathered together (vv. 33-37).

Once again we are confronted by a passage of scripture, part of which presents problems. That the coming of the Saviour will separate the just from the unjust is made clear throughout the entire realm of Holy Writings. Constantly the contrast is drawn between the good and the bad fish (Matthew 13: 48-49); the wheat and the tares (Matthew 13: 36-43). Let us remember also that these utterances were made when it was commonly believed that the world was flat; the idea of a round world where all the seasons—at some part or another —could be experienced at one and the same moment, was for the most part unknown. Day and night; working hours and sleeping periods are all mentioned in one breath, and every honest reader is forced to the conclusion that the Speaker knew what he was talking about. There is widespread belief that these verses have already partially been fulfilled, and that may well be true, for when the city of Jerusalem was taken by the Romans, some things predicted by Jesus were certainly fulfilled. However, we must remember that Christ spoke of the coming of His kingdom and of His appearance in glory; this certainly did *not* take place in the year A.D. 70. These utterances will never be completely fulfilled until Christ returns to earth. See I Thessalonians 4: 16-18. The Bible teaches that when Christ appears, the dead will be raised, and "we which are alive and remain shall be caught up together with them to meet the Lord in the air." Then, two men might be working side by side; the one will be taken and the other left. Then, two people may be sleeping in a bed; the one will be taken and the other left. It is obvious that this teaching harmonizes with the earlier parts of this same chapter.

The final verse of the chapter is very difficult, and we must admit it is impossible to be dogmatic in interpreting its message. Bishop Ryle in *Expository Thoughts on the Gospels* mentions fifty-six writers who hold different views in regard to the interpretation of this mysterious verse. The questions asked have been legion, and among them have been the following: What did Christ mean by *the body*? Whom did the eagles represent? When the disciples asked, "Where, Lord?" were they asking where the "caught away ones" would be taken —or at what part of the world would these events happen? Any commentator trying to be dogmatic and conclusive about these age-old questions would only succeed in advertising his stupidity. For what they are worth, the following observations are made. If the disciples were thinking of specific sites where the occurrences would take place, the answer must be they would happen wherever there was need for them to happen—that is, everywhere. If they were thinking of the future home of the "caught away ones" then the answer is supplied by other parts of the New Testament. The saints would be absent from the body and at home with the Lord. Throughout the Bible, the eagles or vultures are often mentioned in regard to their gathering around a carcass—a dead body—the place of putrefaction. Maybe Christ was thinking of the people who would be left behind; the people who through their corruption and sin would be unacceptable to God. If this were the case, then the eagles might represent the angels of judgment whose task it will be to separate the wheat from the tares; the good fish from the bad, at the end of the age. Thus the scripture would then infer that where the deadness of sin might be found, there would the harbingers of doom be gathered. As we approach the end of this age, the days may come when God will shed additional light upon these obscure texts; when God will proclaim from the housetops that which is now veiled in secrecy.

## HOMILIES

Study No. 54

### REMEMBER LOT'S WIFE

When the Saviour urged His listeners to remember Lot's wife, He turned the spotlight upon one of the most divided families in history.

When the Lord compared that scene to the situation as it will exist prior to the setting up of His kingdom, He indicated the study of the ancient situation might help us to remedy our evils. The family of Lot divided clearly into three groups, and the purpose of this homily is to bring each one into bold relief.

## The Soul That Laughed

When Lot rushed into the presence of his sons-in-law, they probably wondered what had happened to their respected father-in-law. He was agitated and almost desperate. When he informed them he had been visited by two angels; that the immorality of the Sodomites had angered Jehovah; that the cities of the plain were about to be overwhelmed by unprecedented disaster; the eyes of the listening men shone with incredulity. Had their honoured relative taken leave of his senses; had he sat alone too long in the sun? Surely, he was sick and needed medical attention. Yet when Lot insisted that his message was authentic, and urged his relatives to abandon their possessions and flee to the mountains, they could restrain their mirth no longer. If their father were not sick, then he was unspeakably funny—and they probably put back their heads and laughed. "He seemed as one that mocked." The offended holiness of God; the necessity for stern self-control; the certainty of judgment; these and other truths were unknown to these sinful citizens. They had certainly married into a respectable family, and possibly within the family circle, from time to time, had heard the strange beliefs of the father-in-law, but any idea of changing their habits and renouncing their lustful pleasures was totally obnoxious. The strange words of the preachers were fantastic; the result of some brainstorm; and if they yielded to the demands of such stupidity, they too would be foolish. So they laughed at the message; they scorned its warnings, and lived long enough to realize they had been fools after all. It is not too much to believe that their kind still exist.

## The Soul That Looked

Lot's wife was puzzled; naturally she had been closer to her man than the husbands of her daughters. She lived with him every day; she heard his views, and possibly had more than ordinary acquaintance with old Uncle Abraham. The New Testament indicates that Lot vexed his righteous soul every day he remained in the city of sin (II Peter 2: 7-8). It was therefore to be expected that his wife had a clearer insight into the faith and practices of her husband than any other in that city. Probably she had seen the angelic visitors who suddenly entered their home. She was certainly present during the final moments for the Bible says, "And while Lot lingered, the men laid hold upon his hand, AND UPON THE HAND OF HIS WIFE, and upon the hand of his two daughters; the Lord being merciful unto him, and they brought him forth, and set him without the city . . . and said, Escape for thy life . . ." As sudden panic seized her soul, she began to run, faster and faster until the doubts crept into her mind. Her man was running for his life, but she thought of her home; her sons; her friends —could those preachers be wrong? Then quite suddenly, she was looking back, and the delay proved fatal. All around the ground was shaking as a terrible earthquake rocked the countryside. Then great cracks opened in the face of the earth, and oil from the underground oil-field gushed through the openings. The tremendous pressure of the cities as they slipped between the vertical faults in the earth caused the greatest upsurge of power ever known, and as the limitless supplies of oil were forced from the depths of the ground, enormous supplies of rock salt was carried into the air, where, disintegrating, it began to fall as a gigantic snowstorm. Suddenly aware of her danger, Lot's wife began to run again, but now her progress was seriously hindered by what appeared to be deep snow drifts. She floundered and failed, and suddenly overwhelmed, she became the inside of a pillar of salt and was suffocated. These graphic details have been supplied by the arch-aeologists, but as we reconstruct the scene in our minds we are forced to admit the possibility of being close to the kingdom without gaining an entrance. Her husband was taken, but she was left, and it is not too difficult to understand why so often after telling such stories, Jesus said, "He that hath ears, let him hear."

## The Soul That Lingered

Soon Lot reached the safety of the little city near to the mountains, but as he looked back, his spirit was chilled. His former home was burning; the city was being razed to the ground. By morning the scene would be indescribably awesome; instead of proud cities would be black charred devastation. And Lot trembled, for he had been so near to destruction. Why had he been so stupid? Why had he been so slow to believe? Why had the Lord been so merciful to one totally undeserving? Month after month he had been unhappy as he listened to the filthy conversation of his neighbours. Constantly he had been miserable, for the increasing prosperity offered by the plains of Sodom had been unable to compensate for the loss of the fellowship with God which had been his normal daily experience when he resided in the hill country with Abraham. It almost seemed as if he had gained the world but lost his soul. Why then had God been so merciful? Maybe in after days he graduated in God's school and realized that ". . . when God destroyed the cities of the plain . . . God remembered Abraham, and sent Lot out of the midst of the overthrow, when he overthrew the cities in which Lot dwelt" (Genesis 19: 29). Unfortunately there are still many saints who vex their righteous souls as they sit in the gateways of the modern Sodoms. The love of money; the increasing thirst for prosperity; the splendid opportunities of promoting new business, etc., etc., etc., are often the only encouragement they need to turn their backs on the ancient hills of God. Stock markets are generally found in the thriving cities but so also is the smog; the dirt; the poison gases that ruin the health of the believer. Yet happy is the poor stupid Lot who has someone to pray for him! It is extremely doubtful if any believer can perish in the conflagration of judgment when that same believer has a loved one interceding before the throne of God. Nevertheless we must remember that Jesus said, "Remember Lot's wife." If she could perish within sight of the place of safety, so might we if we pay too much attention to the things from which we are supposed to be running.

# The Eighteenth Chapter of Luke

THEME: *Jesus Continues His Ministry*

OUTLINE:

    I. The Judge and the Widow. Verses 1–8
    II. The Pharisee and the Publican. Verses 9–14
    III. The Lord and the Children. Verses 15–17
    IV. The Ruler and his riches. Verses 18–30
    V. The Saviour and His Cross. Verses 31–34
    VI. The Beggar and his opportunity. Verses 35–43

## SECTION ONE

*Expository Notes on the Parable of the Unjust Judge*

And he spake a parable unto them that men ought always to pray, and not to faint; Saying, There was in a city a judge, which feared not God, neither regarded man: and there was a widow in that city; and she came unto him, saying, Avenge me of mine adversary. And he would not for a while; but afterward he said within himself, Though I fear not God, nor regard man; Yet because this widow troubleth me, I will avenge her, lest by her continual coming she weary me (vv. 1–5).

We cannot be sure that this parable was the continuation of the preceding discourse. There appears to be continuity of thought, but the possibility exists that Luke placed the story here because he considered its truth relevant to the other things the Lord had uttered. If, as chapter 17, verse 1 suggests, offences must come, and if the appearance of the Lord could take place at any moment, then of necessity, *men ought always to pray.* This cannot mean that they should spend every moment of the day and night pouring out petitions before the Lord. Orthodox Jews prayed publicly three times each day, and most people throughout the Arab world still follow this procedure. Probably the Lord was urging His disciples to develop an attitude of prayer; that is, to remain in the spirit of prayer; to maintain a conscious dependence upon the goodness of God rather than lapse into a feeling of self-sufficiency. To emphasize the importance of prayer He used the parable of the unjust judge.

373

There were two kinds of judges in Palestine. The first was the orthodox judge who upheld the principles of the Mosaic law; the man in whom most of the people trusted. The second was the one appointed either by the Romans or King Herod. These for the most part were scoundrels. Writing of them, Barclay says, "Such judges were notorious. Unless a plaintiff had influence and money to bribe his way to a verdict, he had no hope of ever getting his case settled. They were said to pervert justice for a dish of meat. People even punned on their title. Officially they were called *Dayyaneh Gezeroth*, which means, *judges of prohibitions or punishments*. Popularly they were called *Dayyaneh Gezeloth*, which means, *robber judges*." The judge in the text belonged to this category for of him it was said, "he feared not God, nor regarded man." This could not have been said of any man whose life was dedicated to the enactment of laws given by Jehovah. The unjust judge was one of the paid magistrates appointed by the local rulers.

The widow belonged to the poorer classes; she had no means to further her cause except by direct petition to the judge. We are not told the nature of her complaint, nor the identity of the accused. These details were unnecessary, for the theme here is prayer and not primarily injustice. She brought her request to the magistrate only to discover he intended to do nothing to help her. She had neither money nor influence, but as a persistent woman, she possessed a tongue and knew how to use it! Her persistence troubled the judge and forced him to take action. However, the Greek word used in this instance is very suggestive. The word is *hupopiazee* and it denotes (a) *that part of the face which is under the eyes;* (b) *a blow in that part of the face; a black and blue spot, a bruise; to beat black and blue; to smite so as to cause bruises and livid spots.* Thayer goes on to indicate that from this comes the idea of giving *intolerable annoyance—to beat one out; to wear one out by entreaties. The Amplified New Testament* expresses all this in the rendering, "Yet because this widow continues to bother me, I will defend, and protect, and avenge her; *lest she give me intolerable annoyance, and wear me out by her continual coming, or at last, she come and rail on me, or assault me, or strangle me.*"

The word picture of this woman is somewhat frightening. She was not a pathetic, insignificant, helpless widow. She not only had a tongue; she had muscles! She had a just cause, and did not intend to lose any battle without first giving a good account of herself. In short, *she meant business!* This surely must be one of the most marvellous pictures of prayer to be found anywhere in the Gospels.

**And the Lord said, Hear what the unjust judge saith. And shall not God avenge his own elect, which cry day and night unto him, though he bear long with them? I tell you that he will avenge them speedily.**

Nevertheless when the Son of man cometh, shall he find faith on the earth? (vv. 6-8).

Certain writers have objected to this parable. They do not like comparing this disgraceful judge with the Judge of all the earth. Their objections are superficial for the Lord Jesus did not liken this man to God. Christ was teaching by contrasts, and saying that if a man of this unreliable kind could be persuaded by the persistence of a suppliant woman—HOW MUCH MORE COULD SAINTS BE SURE GOD WOULD ANSWER PRAYER. God does not need to be persuaded; the Almighty has not to be coaxed! Saints are not strangers nor unknown widow women. Believers are the sons and daughters of God. Therefore, there is no need of "black eyes, and strangulation" to obtain results—we ask in faith, and God according to His wisdom answers.

The final statement concerning the lack of true faith on the earth prior to the appearance of the Son of man has attracted much attention. The consensus of opinion suggests that apostasy will precede the coming of the Saviour; that whilst there will be a form of Godliness in every place, true faith will be rare.


HOMILIES

Study No. 55

### THE PRAYER THAT PREVAILS

If believing prayer is the instrument to remove mountains and the key to unlock heaven's treasure house; if prayer can still the tempests of life; unlock prison doors; challenge pagan empires; and deliver innumerable souls from bondage, then surely the church has forgotten how to pray. One has only to turn the dial on a radio set, or switch on the television set any Sunday, and instantly the most beautifully phrased prayers pour forth from the loud speakers. Many clergymen have graduated in the noble art of using flowery speech, of expressing in the most artistic fashion the ever spreading needs of a dying world, but somehow, the needs continue to spread. Every denomination declares God can and does answer prayer, but whilst the church reiterates her doctrines, her pews are emptying fast. If the age-old teachings of the Bible are true, probably we should be asking: "Lord, teach us how to pray." And there is every reason to believe that in answering our prayer the Saviour would tell us to consider again the parable of the unjust judge who yielded to the demands of a very insistent woman.

## Her Conscientious Desire

She was a widow, but she was never a fool. Her man had been taken from her but she was not helpless. She was very annoyed; her seething indignation made rest impossible. The adversary had been ruthless, and this knowledge was a festering sore in her soul. The judge who fraternised with scoundrels had listened to her complaint, but his smiles eloquently proclaimed he intended to work hard doing nothing. She was furious! She desired no favours; she merely asked for justice, but unless she had the means with which to bribe the magistrate, her cause had died before it was born. Her neighbours probably asked, "What is the use of wasting time and money on him? Forget your grievance and be more careful next time." But she shook her head and asked, "Why should that man disgrace his office? My cause is just; I will not give up." Maybe this is the true basis of all effective prayer. James said, "Ye ask and receive not, *because ye ask amiss.*" It would be well if all prayers were prefaced by the questions: Is the petition justified? Am I asking for something in alignment with the will of God? If I am sure the prayer is justified, I should pray until the petition is answered.

## Her Continuing Determination

She was pounding on the door, and the noise of her insistent hammering echoed through the house. The servants had tried to dismiss her, but she was becoming more and more furious. Everybody was becoming a little apprehensive for this was no weakling. Her waving arms and loud voice suggested she was quite capable of punching them in the eye; furthermore, they suspected she would enjoy the exercise! Probably the old judge eavesdropped and what he heard startled him; the woman was a nuisance, but there was every possibility that she would soon be a menace. If she could not gain access to the house, she would stay on the sidewalk until the judge appeared. Yes, she would await His Honour, and provide a most boisterous welcome when he decided to leave the premises. His lordship would hear her complaint, or he might never have the chance to hear any others. Was she afraid? Certainly not. By the time she had finished, she would probably be in the prison, but at least it would afford some satisfaction to know the magistrate would be in the morgue! The eavesdropping judge heard all this, scratched his head, and murmured, "Maybe, I had better do something. It is the quickest and easiest way to get rid of her." And thus did the Lord Jesus teach that when we need something urgently, we should never give up. Mountains are made to be climbed; doors are made to open, and the suppliant who ceases to pray because his answer does not arrive immediately, proves his desires are shallow.

*Her Complete Deliverance*

She was returning to her home; her eyes were shining, but her experience still showed on her face. She had truly meant business, for if that old swindler had ignored her complaint, she would have made his life a misery. Yes, the deed was done; now she could resume her normal life. And Jesus said, "And shall not God avenge his own elect, which cry day and night unto him, though he bear long with them. I tell you that he will avenge them speedily." There is a most suggestive text in the prophecy of Isaiah and one cannot help but believe it is a companion text to the one now under consideration. ". . . ye that make mention of the Lord, keep not silence, AND GIVE HIM NO REST, till he establish, and till he make Jerusalem a praise in the earth" (Isaiah 62 : 6–7). Surely this is the companion picture to that presented in the Lord's parable. The emphasis is on persistent, prevailing prayer. We are enjoined to worry God—to remind Him continually, that His covenant promises have not been fulfilled. There are great mysteries about prayer, but rather than wait until all these have been explained, we should pray until miracles are being performed. It does not really matter how the Lord opens eyes, as long as blind men are made to see. It is a matter of minor importance how the Lord cleanses lepers, as long as He does. Luke's thrilling picture of the insistent woman suggests we should hammer at the gates of the celestial city until every angel asks, "When, O God, will thou answer that Christian?" Then the attention of Heaven will be focused on our problem; then and not before will it be proved that we mean business.

SECTION TWO

*Expository Notes on the Pharisee and the Publican*

And he spake this parable unto certain which trusted in themselves that they were righteous, and despised others: Two men went up into the temple to pray; the one a Pharisee, and the other a publican. The Pharisee stood and prayed thus with himself, God, I thank thee, that I am not as other men, extortioners, unjust, adulterous, or even as this publican. I fast twice in the week, I give tithes of all that I possess. And the publican, standing afar off, would not lift up so much as his eyes unto heaven, but smote upon his breast, saying, God be merciful to me a sinner. I tell you, this man went down to his house justified rather than the other, for every one that exalteth himself shall be abased; and he that humbleth himself shall be exalted (vv. 9–14).

This is one of the great parables peculiar to Luke's manuscript; it deserves special consideration. There is no conclusive proof by which

we may identify those to whom this parable was addressed, but we
may be fairly sure that among those who were following Jesus were
people whose hearts were filled with a false sense of their own importance. They might have been the Pharisees, but on the other hand
they might have been others who preferred to remain aloof from the
sinners who were finding acceptance in the disciple band. The Lord
mentions two men who occupied extremes in social importance. The
Pharisee stood alone; that is, in a place where he could be seen, and
prayed ostentatiously, so that his prayer could be heard. Nevertheless
we must be careful in our criticism of this man's conduct for he was
not a criminal. He might have been among the best of the citizens.
There was no law which commanded a man to fast twice a week. It
was obligatory that all should fast on the day of atonement, but those
wishing to gain special merit fasted on Mondays and Thursdays. When
they did, they sometimes whitened their faces to advertise their special
piety.

There was no law which commanded a man to tithe *ALL* his possessions. It was customary for a man to tithe his crops, but this
Pharisee did much more. According to the accepted standards of those
days, the man was a very fine fellow, and it ill behoves any modern to
criticize him, if that same critic refrains from making any effort to be
well pleasing in the sight of God. There are people who criticize this
Pharisee, and yet at the same time they would not even think of going
without anything in order to pray. There are those who find fault with
him, and yet at the same time, they conveniently forget to give anything approaching a tithe to help the work of God progress. It is
very easy to criticize a man who has only climbed half-way up a ladder,
but if we have not even left the ground, our mouths should remain
closed! The point at issue in this parable was not that this man was
bad, but that good as he was, he was not good enough. And by the
same token, the publican, bad as he undoubtedly was, had not fallen
too low to be lifted again by the mercy of God. This man was so
conscious of his guilt that he refrained from entering into the sacred
precincts of the sanctuary. He stood afar off, his eyes were downcast
with shame, and so great was his remorse that he continually beat
upon his chest, saying, "God be merciful to me, *the sinner.*"

It is significant that the definite article is used in the original script.
This man might have argued with Paul for the doubtful distinction of
being the chief among all sinners. He believed he was the greatest
sinner in the world, but there is much more depth in the text than
would at first appear. The Greek text: *Ho Theos hilastheeti moi to
hamatolo* is thought-provoking. The man prayed: "O God, be pro-
pitious to me the sinner." Hebrews 9:5 uses this same word to
describe the mercy seat where the blood of the offering was sprinkled.

This man was not without knowledge; there is evidence that he was an instructed Jew. As a tax gatherer he was obviously in the employment of the Romans, and the disdain of his fellow Jews had probably driven him from bad to worse. Yet even as he strayed from the accepted standards of Jewish piety, his conscience haunted him. He forsook the truth, but could not forget it. When remorse overwhelmed him, his earlier training found expression in this enlightened prayer. "O God, be toward me, as thou wouldest be at the mercy-seat." He was asking for forgiveness even though he had not presented a lamb as an offering; he was seeking forgiveness even although he had no priest to intercede for him. He was as one born out of due time! He saw his own unspeakable guilt; the magnificent mercy of God; and the simple faith that could bring both together.

When the Lord spoke of these two men, He provided one of the most potent sermons ever preached. The notorious sinner went away justified rather than the other—there are no degrees in justification; either a man is justified or he is not. "Therefore being justified by faith, we have peace with God through our Lord Jesus Christ" (Romans 5: 1). The Pharisee provided a news bulletin for God; the publican supplied a broken heart, and in that strange contrast is the secret of true happiness. "Every one that exalteth himself shall be abased, and he that humbleth himself shall be exalted." Actually little David with his superlative faith was a much taller man than Goliath, and the girl who went to work in Naaman's household exercised a far more effective ministry than that of her warrior master. See the special homily at the end of Section 5, Chapter 9.

## SECTION THREE

### Expository Notes on Jesus Blessing the Children

And they brought unto him also infants, that he would touch them: but when his disciples saw it, they rebuked them. But Jesus called them unto him, and said, Suffer little children to come unto me, and forbid them not: for of such is the kingdom of God. Verily I say unto you, Whosoever shall not receive the kingdom of God as a little child shall in no wise enter therein (vv. 15-17).

To obtain the complete account of what happened at this time it is necessary to read the descriptions supplied by all the synoptic records. Luke is content to say that Jesus called the little children to Him; Matthew adds that the Lord placed His hands on them (Matthew 19: 13-16); Mark states that Jesus took them into His arms and blessed them (Mark 10: 13-16). The Greek text suggests these children were babies, possibly approaching the age of twelve months. It was custom-

ary for Hebrew mothers to bring their children at this age to be blessed
by a rabbi. It was also customary for any head of a family or tribe,
to take the children and bless them. See Genesis 27 : 38. Bengel says:
*"Christ had no children that He might adopt all children."*

Let us not be critical of the disciples' action. Although Mark affirms
the Lord was moved with indignation because the children had been
dismissed, both Matthew and Luke omit this detail. Mark obtained
his information from Simon Peter who noticed the Lord was disappointed with the behaviour of His followers. Nevertheless even though
these men made a mistake, their motives might have been meritorious.
The Lord was on His way to the Cross; the journey had been long and
exacting; the Master was tired. Perhaps the disciples were trying to
protect their leader, to save Him from unnecessary exertion. Probably
had we been there we would have acted similarly, by saying, "The
Lord is very tired; please do not bother Him now. Some other time,
maybe!"

The Lord did not agree. Certainly He was tired, but He was never
too tired to welcome those who came to Him. Major in *The Mission
and Message of Jesus*, at page 128, says, "To judge by certain precepts
in the Wisdom literature, the attitude of the Jews to children was
disciplinary and severe. That of Jesus was tender and sympathetic.
He was undoubtedly interested in children and fond of them. His
reference to their playing at weddings and funerals in the market-
place; His refusal to order them to be silent when they sang Hosanna
in His honour in the temple; His citation of the words of the Psalmist:
'Out of the mouths of babes and sucklings hast thou perfected praise';
His citation of a little child as an example to His apostles; and also
the incident related here supports the view that Jesus may be justly
acclaimed as the lover of little children." His statement ". . . for of such
is the kingdom of God . . ." demands and deserves special attention.
See the following homily.


HOMILIES

Study No. 56

### THE LITTLE-BIG CITIZENS OF THE KINGDOM

When Jesus spoke about little children and indicated they represented the citizens of the kingdom of heaven, He did not mean to infer
that the hereafter will be filled with adolescents. Age will be unknown
in eternity, for those redeemed by the blood of the Lamb will know
the blessedness of perennial youth. The Lord was drawing attention

to the *characteristics* of the child rather than to its age. "Of such—of such qualities; with such attributes—is the kingdom of God made."

## The Child Who Responded

"And they brought young children to him . . . and he took them up in his arms . . . and blessed them" (Mark 10: 13–16). This simple and apparently unimportant act was among the most remarkable of all the deeds of that particular day. There can be no doubt that these children were strangers to the Lord Jesus; they had never been in His arms before. In similar circumstances children have been known to scream, fight, and turn away from the unknown man. It is hard to believe this could ever have happened in the case of Jesus. Perhaps the babies were too young to comprehend what was taking place; but on the other hand, they might have been old enough to know a Stranger was stretching out His hands. The fact remains that there was no protest. The Lord lifted the child and poured benedictions upon the tiny form. The baby did not object with innumerable questions; neither did the child make certain conditions the basis of its response. The beckoning arms of the Lord; the encouraging smile on His face were sufficient to dispel any fears. If only adults could master the art of being childlike!

## The Child Who Stood In The Midst

"And Jesus called a little child unto him, and set him in the midst of them, and said, Verily I say unto you, Except ye be converted, and become as little children, ye shall not enter into the kingdom of heaven" (Matthew 18: 2–3). Here the lessons suggested in section one are amplified, for this child was certainly old enough to understand what he was doing. Thus did Jesus set before His argumentative disciples one of the greatest object lessons they ever received. The suspicion, malice, and bitterness known in later years can seldom be seen in a baby. Daddy is the most wonderful man in the world, and whatever any other might suggest, he must always be the final court of appeal. What father says must be correct. The fantasy and charm of a little boy's world is something beyond description: when a story is told, horizons are meaningless; the youthful listener sees the invisible, and enters realms from which materialistic adults are excluded. Ambition has not had the chance to make the child ruthless; jealousy has not had the chance to make the child spiteful; love of money has had no opportunity to make the youngster mean. Sometimes it seems a shame when a charming child grows up!

### The Child Who Testified

"And the Syrians . . . brought away captive out of the land of Israel a little maid . . . And she said unto her mistress, Would God my Lord were with the prophet that is in Samaria! for he would recover him of his leprosy" (II Kings 5: 2–3). Certainly this child was no baby, but she could still be described as "little." We do not know how she fell into the hands of the invader. Perhaps her parents had been killed in the battle; maybe she had been kidnapped. We are not given the details of those unfortunate days for the ancient record merely says she was carried away captive. That she returned good for evil; that she desired the healing of her enemy rather than his death is worthy of consideration. An older person might not have shared her graciousness. She was sure of the prophet's ability to cleanse lepers; she was filled with pity for the man who had separated her from her homeland; she had marvellous news to tell, and found it impossible to remain silent. Her testimony led to the greatest day in the life of her master, and saved him from a premature death. I would like to meet that small girl for of such is the kingdom of heaven made.

### The Child Who Helped

"There is a little boy here which hath five barley loaves, and two small fishes; but what are they among so many?" (John 6: 9.) So spake Andrew, Simon Peter's brother to the Lord. The Authorized Version of the Bible renders the passage: "There is a lad here . . . " but the Greek word is *paidarion* which is better translated *a little boy*. He was probably having a day out with his friends. His mother had packed a small lunch, and sent him off for the morning. Seeing the crowds, the little fellow, drew near to become famous. Probably he overheard the disciples talking about the need for food and with an innocence which could not have belonged to an older child, offered to surrender his loaves and fishes. The stupidity of thinking his lunch could meet that particular need was something that never occurred to him; indeed if he were very small he would have been unable to comprehend the apparent futility of his action. He only knew that the great Man was asking about food, and he was willing to help. It was the best investment he was ever likely to make for it returned eternal dividends. Many others followed his example for in later years, boys and girls placed their meagre talents into the hands of Jesus, and then went forth to minister the bread of life to millions of starving heathens. I wonder what the boy said when he saw his lunch getting bigger and bigger until it was sufficient to feed thousands of people? His eyes surely became stars! Yes, I should like to speak with that lad for he possessed qualities essential for first-rate citizens in the kingdom of God.

*The Child Who Listened*

"And it came to pass . . . That the Lord called Samuel: and he answered, Here am I" (Samuel 3: 1–4). The story of the boy Samuel is well known. He belonged to God from the moment of his conception; his appearance within the sacred house was the fulfilment of a mother's vow. A nation was perishing and God urgently needed an instrument to arrest the downward tendencies of these sinful people. Then God found Hannah—and when at a later date, Hannah found God, the battle was won. Samuel was only a little boy but the quietness of the sanctuary helped to develop his excellent hearing. His limited company encouraged the desire for a new companion, and when God called the little fellow, Samuel knew he would never be lonely again. Each time he retired to bed, he wondered if the Lord would speak again that night, and life became a joyous new adventure. He grew up in the expectancy that his great Friend might appear at any moment, and when the will of God was revealed to him, nothing on earth could have prevented his co-operating with the Most High. Samuel saved a nation.

"And Jesus called a little child unto him, and set him in the midst of them, and said, . . . *except ye become as a little child, ye shall not enter . . .*"

## SECTION FOUR

### *Expository Notes on the Rich Young Ruler*

**And a certain ruler asked him, saying, Good Master, what shall I do to inherit eternal life? And Jesus said unto him, Why callest thou me good? none is good, save one, that is, God (vv. 18–19).**

Mark 10: 17 suggests the children were brought to Jesus when the Master was resting within some home; the rich young ruler therefore must have asked his question as the Lord was leaving that house to resume His journey toward Jerusalem. Mark also says that the young man was eager; he came running and kneeling down, asked the question, "Good Master, what shall I do that I may inherit eternal life?" It is interesting to remember that ordinary Rabbis were never addressed in this way for the Jews considered only God and the law to represent absolute goodness. Obviously, somewhere this young man, possibly a ruler of the synagogue, had heard the message of Jesus, and his desire to obtain eternal life brought him to the Teacher. The Lord's reply deserves much consideration. Jesus did not deny His own goodness; He merely stated that only God was good. It was as though He said, "Young man why do you call me Good?—only God is good. No, I am not saying you are mistaken, I merely ask if you suspect I might be more than a famous Rabbi?" This is the explanation suggested by Whitby for in his paraphrase, he writes, "Why givest thou me a title not ascribed to your reverend rabbis, nor due to any mere man? Thinkest thou there is anything in me more than human, or that the Father dwelleth in me? This thou oughtest to believe if thou conceivest the title 'Good' doth truly belong to me, seeing there is none good but one, that is God."

**Thou knowest the commandments. Do not commit adultery, Do not steal, Do not bear false witness, Honour thy father and thy mother. And he said, All these have I kept from my youth up (vv. 20-21).**

Mark 10: 21 adds the significant detail that when these words had been spoken, the Lord loved him. Obviously the warmth of appreciation and admiration shone from the Master's face. This young man was speaking the truth. To the best of his ability he had kept the commandments, and possibly could have said with Paul, "As touching the righteousness which is in the law, I was blameless." See Philippians 3: 6. Nevertheless although he was indisputably good according to the standards of men, he was far beneath the standards required by God. He was good, but not good enough. This realization was always a pre-requisite in the search for eternal salvation.

**Now when Jesus heard these things, he said unto him, Yet lackest thou one thing: sell all that thou hast, and distribute unto the poor, and thou shalt have treasure in heaven: and come, follow me (v. 22).**

This scripture is one of the most important in the Gospel for there have been men who affirmed Christians could never be wealthy. They taught that Christianity brought to men the obligation to share wealth among the poor and needy, and therefore any man who refused to obey, could not be a follower of Jesus. This is false. There was only one condition revealed by God to men for knowing the joys of life everlasting. Christ had to be first in every matter related to the life of the convert. Unless men crowned Him Lord of all, they did not crown Him Lord at all. It is obvious from the scriptures that this wealthy young ruler, in spite of the almsgiving for which he was probably well known, still attached more importance to his possessions than He did to the need of his soul. Jesus realized this was true and decided it was necessary to challenge him on this vital issue. The suppliant was asked to dethrone his wealth and enthrone the Saviour. The resultant refusal is known to all. The man was willing for Christ to occupy the second place, but if his possessions had to be renounced, then he preferred to lose his soul.

The Old Testament provides an interesting setting against which the decision of this young man can be seen to better advantage. Abraham's wealth, *his true wealth* was represented by his son, Isaac; and yet ere the patriarch could enter into the riches of friendship with God, he too had to be tested on this issue. He was commanded to offer his son as a sacrifice upon Mount Moriah. Perhaps we shall never be able to appreciate what this meant to the old man, but he came through triumphantly. He proved that the favour of God was more desirable than the presence of his own son. When this happened, God gave Isaac back to his delighted father. It was as though the Lord said, "Isaac will be far more useful to me alive than he ever could be dead —take him home, FRIEND OF GOD, I merely wanted to see who came first in your affection, and because thou hast done this thing, in blessing I will bless thee, and make thy seed as the sand upon the sea-shore." Probably if the rich young ruler had similarly reacted to the challenge of the Saviour—had he said, "Lord, should I die tonight, I would have to leave my wealth in any case, so just give me a few hours to settle my estate and I will be ready to follow you anywhere," then Jesus might have said, "Well done. Go thy way and remember to be a good steward of the things which God has entrusted to your care." The ruler would have retained the money he needed; he would have been the dispenser of great happiness to the needy; he would have had the commendation of Jesus, and best of all, he would have known the joy of possessing life everlasting. He might have found even greater joy in becoming a follower, for Jesus did leave that possibility open, when He said, "Come, and follow me."

**And when he heard this he was very sorrowful: for he was very rich. And when Jesus saw that he was very sorrowful, he said, How hardly shall they that have riches enter into the kingdom of God! For it is easier for a camel to go through a needle's eye, than for a rich man to enter into the kingdom of God. And they that heard it said, Who then can be saved? And he said, The things which are impossible with men are possible with God (vv. 23-27).**

Dr. Frank Boreham once said, "If you have anything which is indispensable, give it away." The rich young ruler held on to his riches but remained poor for ever. The reference to the camel passing through the needle's eye was well known in those days. Alongside the main entrance gates to a city, was a smaller gate used only by pedestrians. This served a two-fold purpose. When at sunset or on the sabbath the large gates were closed to keep out the cameliers with their animals, ordinary people could still either enter or leave by the smaller door. This entrance was said to be only about three or four feet high, and was called the needle's eye. There were occasions when an angry

camelier literally tried to get his camel through the eye of a needle—
that is, the small gate. This was not impossible, but nevertheless it was
exceedingly difficult. There were three pre-requisites. The animal had
to be small; the load had to be taken from its back, and the camel
somehow, had to go forward on its knees. It could be done, but it was
difficult. It was also possible for wealthy men to get into the kingdom
of God but the same three conditions applied. Those who desired
admittance had to be small in their own estimation; they had to offload
anything that would hinder progress; they had to kneel, and thus seek
entrance into the kingdom of God. The second interpretation comes
from the fact that two Greek words are very similar. *Kameelos* means
camel, but *Kamilos*, an unusual word, meant a ship's cable; that is a
rope. It will be readily understood that one word could easily be
mistaken for the other; that the tone of a man's voice; his accent; his
emphasis on either word might make it sound as though he had uttered
the other. Therefore some teachers think the Lord was referring to
the impossible task of threading a needle with a piece of rope.
This, I believe, is not the correct interpretation. To do this would
be *impossible* whereas it was possible to get a wealthy man into the
kingdom of God. From every angle the former interpretation seems
the more reasonable. The question asked by the disciples indicated
the strange wonder filling their souls, but the answer forthcoming
from their Leader was destined to give courage to saints in every
age.

> Then Peter said, Lo, we have left all, and followed thee. And he said
> unto them, Verily, I say unto you, There is no man that hath left house,
> or parents, or brethren, or wife, or children, for the kingdom of God's
> sake, Who shall not receive manifold more in this present time, and in
> the world to come life everlasting (vv. 28–30).

Simon Peter had watched the rich ruler departing, and had been
aware of the keen disappointment filling the Master's soul. Then suddenly he knew a sense of pride filling his own heart. He had not been
as stupid as the young ruler. His statement led the Saviour to utter
great truth. No man ever works for God without payment. Our
heavenly Father is no man's debtor, for if a cup of cold water given
to the Lord does not pass unnoticed, it is certain the greater sacrifices
outlined in Peter's statement will bring their own rewards. The inference here seems to suggest the ruler had lost tremendous blessings
in this life—and in the world to come, he would lose his soul.

HOMILIES

Study No. 57

### TWO MEN WHO ASKED THE SAME QUESTION
#### (Luke 10: 25; Luke 18: 18)

"What must I do to inherit eternal life?" It is not possible to understand the implications of this text until we appreciate the effect of the preaching of Jesus. Against the uncertainty of the theological thought of His day, Christ's utterances were as stars in a dark sky. The Sadducees and the Pharisees were opposed on the question of survival. The former said that death terminated existence; the latter declared death was an introduction to another world. And while these leaders argued, the ordinary wayfarer hardly knew what to believe. He saw loved ones taken from his side, but when he considered the possibility of reunion in another world, he could only hope for the best. Then Jesus came to preach in the villages of Galilee, and immediately His bold declarations stirred the hearts of Israel. The Sadducees detested the new doctrines, but the Pharisees were delighted; and it would appear that from these religious camps, two representatives came to ask an identical question. The fact that they received different answers provides food for thought.

### The Wise Lawyer

The Sadducees were annoyed. Their doctrines were being discounted; their enemies were jubilant. Something had to be done. A clever speaker must challenge the new Teacher. "And behold, a certain lawyer stood up, and tempted him, saying, Master, what shall I do to inherit eternal life? Jesus said unto him. What is written in the law? How readest thou? And he answering said, Thou shalt love the Lord thy God with all thy heart . . . and thy neighbour as thyself. And Jesus said unto him, Thou hast answered right: this do, and thou shalt live. But he, willing to justify himself, said unto Jesus, And who is my neighbour?" (Luke 10: 25-29). Then the Lord Jesus told the story of the Good Samaritan, and finally reminded the man of his duty to go and do likewise. At first, many evangelical teachers would denounce this teaching. Does a man obtain eternal life by fulfilling the requirements of the law? Does a man attain to the highest pinnacle of spiritual possession through self-achievement, when his best righteousness is said to be filthy rags?

## The Wealthy Leader

"And a certain ruler asked him saying, Good Master, what shall I do to inherit eternal life? And Jesus said . . . Thou knowest the commandments . . . And the ruler said, All these have I kept from my youth up" (Luke 18: 18–21). It is at this point that the one man differs from the other. How easy it would be to imagine the Lord Jesus saying, "Well done, young man; you have excelled at your learning. Many people really believe that human merit will gain the highest awards in heaven. They say their virtue equals and even excels that of many other people. They keep the law, and challenge any teaching which denies their right to eternal security. Yet you realise this is not true. You are good, but not good enough. You are conscious of spiritual need." And as Christ looked at the departing lawyer, He could have said, "Now that man asked the same question, but his motives were different. If one suggested that he had personal need, he would treat the statement as an insult. He's a lawyer, an expert at discovering flaws in other people. He has yet to discover his own need. You, rich young ruler, know your need. Well done."

## The Wonderful Lord

The Saviour continued, "Yet lackest thou one thing: sell all that thou hast, and distribute unto the poor, and thou shalt have treasure in heaven: and come, follow me" (verse 22). Why did not Christ repeat the story of the Good Samaritan to this ruler? And why did He not ask the lawyer to forsake all and follow Him? A little investigation reveals the fact that the answers to these questions supply a comprehensive view of the doctrines of God. The lawyer was told to keep the law, for if he conscientiously did this, his very nearness to God would beget a sense of personal need. The ruler had already discovered his need, and it only remained to find a remedy. He was given a new challenge, "Sell all that thou hast, and come, follow me." This was a test to ascertain whether or not he would permit the Lord to occupy the throne of his affections. Probably had he expressed willingness to obey the Master's command, he would have been sent home with a benediction. What must I do to inherit eternal life? I must recognize my need as a sinner, and then crown Christ Lord of my life.

Taken from the Author's book, *Bible Treasures*, page 101.

(See also the homily at Chapter 16, Section 2.)

## SECTION FIVE

*Expository Notes on Christ's prediction of His Death and Resurrection*

Then he took unto him the twelve, and said unto them, Behold we go up to Jerusalem, and all things that are written by the prophets concerning the Son of man shall be accomplished. For he shall be delivered unto the Gentiles, and shall be mocked, and spitefully entreated, and spitted on: And they shall scourge him, and put him to death: and the third day he shall rise again. And they understood none of these things: and this saying was hid from them, neither knew they the things which were spoken (vv. 31-34).

Mark 10 : 32 adds the significant detail that the disciples were afraid. The shadow of the cross was already beginning to fall across the little band of followers and certain premonitions warned them that things were not going according to their plans. A nameless dread was beginning to capture their hearts; the future was dark with foreboding and threats; it might be better to turn back. And it was at this moment their Leader, Who was walking ahead, paused, turned around, and addressed to them these remarks. (1) *How Calm.* He knew the dangers of His mission; there could be no turning back, for the moment was at hand when that planned in the eternal councils of the Godhead was to be fulfilled. The hope of all the ages was centred in Jerusalem at this time. He saw not the anguish but the glorious fulfilment of the desires of His Father. (2) *How Confident.* ". . . all things that are written by the prophets concerning the Son of man shall be accomplished." It is difficult to understand in the light of this claim how any man can refuse to believe in the deity of Christ. He claimed to be the One of whom the prophets spake; He claimed the law and the prophets witnessed of Him; that without Him their message would have been futile. (3) *How Contented.* He never spoke of His cross without mentioning the resurrection. He saw not merely the tragedy; He rejoiced in the certain triumph of that Easter day. His was courage personified for seeing clearly the menace of the future, He walked steadily toward His cross; nothing could turn Him from the path of duty. ". . . let us lay aside every weight, and the sin which doth so easily beset us, and let us run with patience the race that is set before us, Looking unto Jesus the author and finisher of our faith; who for the joy that was set before him, endured the cross, despising the shame, and is set down at the right hand of the throne of God" (Hebrews 12 : 1-2).

*Expository Notes on the Giving of Sight to the Beggar*

**And it came to pass, that as he was come nigh unto Jericho, a certain blind man sat by the wayside begging: And hearing the multitude pass by, he asked what it meant. And they told him that Jesus of Nazareth passeth by. And he cried, saying, Jesus thou Son of David, have mercy on me (vv. 35–38).**

A great amount of attention has been focussed upon this miracle for although Matthew, Mark, and Luke record the incident, their accounts differ. Matthew 20: 29–34 says that two men were given sight as the Lord departed from Jericho. Mark 10: 46–52 says that one man, Bartimaeus, the son of Timaeus, was given sight as the Lord was leaving the city. Luke 18: 35–43 says one beggar was given sight as the Lord was entering, or had come nigh to Jericho. Various explanations have been offered to solve these problems. The difference in numbers resembles the accounts of the deliverance of the demon-possessed men at Gadara; Matthew says that two demoniacs were delivered; Luke only mentions one. This is not a great problem. Probably the one was better known than the other; possibly the one went on to demonstrate greatness of soul, whilst the other ran off to join his family, and momentarily at least, forgot even to be grateful. However, the conflicting accounts of the place of the miracle provide a little more difficulty. Very many explanations have been suggested but of them all, only two deserve consideration. Josephus speaks of two Jerichos. He mentions the old Jericho, which perhaps was the site of the old Canaanitish city; he also speaks of the new Jericho, the Herodian city. It is possible that Jesus had just passed through the one Jericho, and was leaving in order to enter into the new adjoining Jericho. Thus, according to Matthew and Mark, the Lord was leaving the city when the blind man asked for mercy; yet according to Luke, the Lord was approaching Jericho when the incident took place. The other explanation offered by various writers suggests the blind man cried for help as the Lord was approaching the city, but his cries were drowned by the noise of the multitude. Therefore in desperation the blind beggar followed the disciple band, lingered outside the home of the tax-gatherer Zaccheus, and later, when the Lord was departing from the city, made a new appeal—a very desperate appeal for assistance. The fact that Luke used two different words to describe the shouts of the blind man lends credence to this interpretation.

The beggar hearing the approach of a great crowd asked what it meant, and when he was told the great Healer was in the vicinity, he cried with a loud voice; that is, he shouted, "Jesus, thou Son of David, have mercy on me." This indicated faith, for it was commonly believed Messiah would be the Son of David.

**And they which went before rebuked him, that he should hold his peace: but he cried so much the more, Son of David, have mercy on me (v. 39).**

*The Amplified New Testament* renders the passage: "They told him, Jesus of Nazareth is passing by. And he shouted saying, Jesus, Son of David, take pity and have mercy on me. But those that were in front, reproved him, telling him to keep quiet; *yet he screamed and shrieked* so much the more, Son of David, take pity and have mercy on me." This translation rests upon the fact that Luke uses two different words. *Eboeesen* translated *shout* or "he cried" means: *to lift up one's voice and cry aloud. Ekrazen,* the word used in verse 39, and translated, *he cried so much the more,* is a much stronger word. Thayer says it means *to cry out; to cry aloud; to vociferate particularly of inarticulate cries.* It is also used to express *a croak,* hence *a scream* or *desperate screech.* The first cry of the blind beggar was born of intense desire; the second by deepening despair. The first was produced by a longing for help; the second by the fear he might not get what he wanted. And when we recall that in the earlier chapters Luke emphasized the value of prayer, this incident adds to the quality of the manuscript. Luke spoke of the widow woman who threatened to give the unjust judge a black eye; she meant business and would not abandon her project until her request was granted. Now the same author speaks of a man who prayed until desperation echoed in every word he uttered. This is real prayer.

**And Jesus stood, and commanded him to be brought unto him: and when he was come near, he asked him, Saying, What wilt thou that I shall do unto thee? And he said, Lord, that I may receive my sight. And Jesus said unto him, Receive thy sight: thy faith hath saved thee. And immediately he received his sight, and followed him, glorifying God: and all the people, when they saw it, gave praise unto God (vv. 40–43).**

Throughout the storm on the Sea of Galilee the Master slept. The wind shrieked in the rigging, the waves slapped ceaselessly against the sides of the small boat, the men frantically tried to bail water out of the sinking craft, and yet all the while Jesus continued to sleep. Then one of the disciples said, "Master, we perish," and instantly Christ was ready to save them. The cry of a worried disciple did more than the entire storm—it awakened him out of sleep. The same truth appears in this account. The cheers of the crowd; the jostling and pushing of would-be sightseers; all this could have been somewhat distracting, but when the blind asked for help, the Saviour heard him. How wonderful it is to remember Jesus is never too pre-occupied to listen to our requests. He is never too busy to pause along the highway of life.

## HOMILIES

Study No. 58

### THE MAN WHO COULD SEE WITHOUT EYES

Through the Bible, and indeed in every-day experience, there appears to be a difference between sight and vision. Many people have excellent eyesight, but a little disappointment is sufficient to blot out the sun—something goes wrong, and instantly the sufferer jumps to the conclusion that God is unkind. There are other people who are quite unable to see, but they possess sufficient vision to look into another world. This is the story of a man who could see without eyes.

*He saw that his greatest need was to meet Jesus*

The ninth chapter of John describes another blind man, and emphasizes he had been born blind. That is not said of this beggar, so the possibility remains that he had once been able to see. Then disease struck, and from that first day, the unfortunate man was destined to go blind. The necessities of life required that he earn a living somehow, and therefore as the weeks passed by, he became known as the beggar who sat at the gate of the city. When people thronged the streets on market days, he sought alms; when the streets were quiet and empty, the beggar leaned against the wall to consider all he had heard from passers-by. It was said that a Carpenter possessed uncanny powers of healing; that He could cleanse lepers and even give sight to the blind! It is not possible to decide how much time elapsed ere the beggar saw clearly the first thing. We only know that ultimately he realized that above all else, he needed to meet that Carpenter. Some people undoubtedly would have argued saying, "He needs most to meet a wealthy patron whose generosity will make begging unnecessary." Others would have said, "Let him beg as long as he is able. His greatest need is to find someone who, in the eventide of life, or in times of sickness, will provide a home." The beggar would have answered, "No, I need to meet Jesus, for He alone can solve my problems." Have we ever seen this fact?

*He saw that his greatest opportunity had come*

Suddenly one day he heard the noise of approaching people and when he asked what all this meant, he was told Jesus of Nazareth was passing by. Probably he had often wondered how best he could reach the Healer, but it was extremely difficult to find any man who would volunteer to escort him on such a journey. There was no easy means of transport, and therefore the blind man was left alone with his frustration. Then quite suddenly, what he had never expected, came to pass—Jesus was in his street; Jesus was near; the opportunity to seek assistance had come. The unfortunate man could not see the people by whom he was surrounded; neither could he see the sky above, but he did see this moment presented the most wonderful opportunity of a lifetime. His cry for help announced the thrilling fact, that he intended to take advantage of this priceless chance to see. We must remember that ere the Lord Jesus returned to Heaven, he commissioned His disciples to go into all the world to preach, and with that same commission went a promise, "Lo, I am with you always." If that promise be true, then the Lord cannot be far from any who meet in His Name. It means He is present NOW. And if this be the case, then *our* greatest opportunity is near. Are we too blind to see it?

*He saw that if this opportunity were lost, he might not get another*

When the crowd appeared to be annoyed by his desperate shrieks; when they told him to be quiet, their attitude was almost frightening, but the beggar persisted for he was desperate. The people had said, "Jesus of Nazareth is PASSING by"; that meant He was on the move. Within two minutes, the Lord would be out of range. If the beggar intended to attract the Lord's attention it had to be NOW for if he missed this opportunity, the Saviour might never return. He was correct. The Lord Jesus was on His way to Jerusalem for the last time. The Cross was already waiting in some lumber yard; the spikes destined to nail Him to the tree had already been forged in the fires of some unknown blacksmith. Never again would the Carpenter pass through Jericho. It was all very well for the crowds to tell the suppliant to remain quiet, but the beggar could not afford to obey them. It was now or never, and raising his voice, again he begged for mercy. Someday we shall be presented with our final opportunity to seek from the Son of God that which we so urgently need. Have we ever thought of the sombre fact that sometime—perhaps today, He will pass our way for the final time? To miss that golden opportunity, is to remain in the dark for ever.

*He saw that following in Christ's way was better than going his own way*

When the Lord granted his request; when the darkness had been banished, the man was told to go his way. Possibly the Lord remembered that somewhere in that city would be relatives who would thrill to the news of this glorious miracle, and wishing to spread happiness, He told the man to go home. Yet Mark in giving his description of the event said, "And immediately he received his sight, and *followed Jesus* in the way." Possibly he countered the words of Jesus by saying, "Lord, my people will not be expecting me home for quite a time; they are probably in the streets somewhere trying to see you, so please, Lord, do not send me home. Wherever you are going, that is where I want to be. Are you going to preach? Then let me listen. Are you going to stay awhile; then perhaps I might be able to find some other blind man and bring him to you. Lord, I want to follow you." The man saw that continuing happiness was only possible in the presence and service of Jesus. It would have been exceedingly thrilling to run home with the good news, and thereby to have become the centre of attraction for hundreds of people. However, the beggar had no desire to become popular or important; he only desired to be with Jesus. He was to be commended for his intelligence. Some moderns do not appear to have graduated in that noble college of wisdom.

# The Nineteenth Chapter of Luke

THEME: *The Closing Stages of the Journey to Jerusalem*

OUTLINE:

SECTION ONE

*Expository Notes on the Conversion of Zacchaeus*

And Jesus entered and passed through Jericho. And, behold, there was a man named Zacchaeus, which was the chief among the publicans, and he was rich. And he sought to see Jesus who he was; and could not for the press, because he was little of stature. And he ran before, and climbed up into a sycamore tree to see him: for he was to pass that way (vv. 1–4).

This is an intriguing account presenting certain problems. Jericho was one of the most important cities of the ancient world for it was situated in one of the best agricultural districts of Palestine, and stood at one of the busiest crossings of the Jordan. Godet says, "There must have been at Jericho one of the busiest custom-houses, both on account of the export of the balm which grew at the oasis, and which was sold in all the countries of the world, and on account of the considerable traffic which took place on this road, by which lay the route from Peraea to Judea and Egypt." Barclay says, "Jericho had a great palm forest and world famous balsam groves which perfumed the air for miles around. Her gardens of roses were known far and wide." Josephus called the city: "A divine region." These details enable us to understand the great importance of Jericho as a taxation centre. There must have been several very important customs offices. The Bible infers there were numerous agents, but the chief tax gatherer was Zacchaeus. He held one of the major positions in that branch of the government. In spite of the adverse comments of some writers there is evidence to suggest this man was an honest official. The majority of the people despised him because he had become a servant of the hated Romans; because he enforced the payments of dues;

something which was bitterly resented by every household in Israel. His name means *the righteous one*; he was undoubtedly a Jew, and Clement of Alexandria stated he afterward became the Bishop of Caesarea.

Zacchaeus was very wealthy, but we must resist the temptation to assume this money represented illicit gains. Many preachers suggest this publican had been unscrupulous in his dealings with travellers; that he had become wealthy at the expense of those whom he swindled. There are doubts as to the validity of these assertions. Zacchaeus might have been wealthy in his own right; he could have inherited money, or since his position was extremely important, he might have received special wages, which, by careful management and wise investments had grown into a private fortune. A detailed examination of the story provides evidence to suggest this conclusion might be justified. When Zacchaeus heard of the approach of Jesus, his interest was aroused. When the people were in the street waiting to see the Visitor, business within the office was probably at a standstill, and thus the tax gatherer was able to join the crowds. Unfortunately, he was not very tall, and was unable to see over the broad shoulders which hemmed him in on all sides. Not to be outdone, this little man found a sycamore tree; climbed into the branches, and waited to see the Carpenter who was already coming down the street.

And when Jesus came to the place, he looked up, and saw him, and said unto him, Zacchaeus, make haste, and come down; for today I must abide at thy house. And he made haste, and came down, and received him joyfully. And when they saw it, they all murmured, saying, That he was gone to be guest with a man that is a sinner. And Zacchaeus stood, and said unto the Lord; Behold, Lord, the half of my goods I give to the poor; and if I have taken any thing from any man by false accusation, I restore him fourfold (vv. 5-8).

It is possible that the Lord heard the name of Zacchaeus from the people in the street; it is also possible that His attention was directed to the tree by the crowds who had watched the tax gatherer's climb into the foliage. The sycamore tree is known for its branches which spread out horizontally starting close to the base of the trunk. It was not a difficult tree for any man to climb, but the fact that the hated tax official had done so surely attracted attention. The Lord possibly saw this as He walked down the street, and overhearing the conversation of the bystanders, ascertained that the man in the branches was Zacchaeus. Moving across until He was standing beneath the tree, Jesus addressed the tax gatherer and announced His intention of dining with him. Whereupon Zacchaeus quickly descended to give his guest a royal welcome. His spontaneous confession startled the listeners, and divided the theological world! As we consider his statement we must not be influenced by the attitude of the crowd. Whether Zacchaeus was a man of integrity or a notorious swindler could not be ascertained from the attitude of the Jews. Any man, wealthy or poor; trustworthy or otherwise, would be considered an outcast from society if he worked for the enemy. If, however, he consented to work in any capacity which would embarrass his fellow countrymen, he would be considered a renegade; a cheat; a man unworthy to belong to the people of God. Therefore, we must seek elsewhere the evidence which might enable us to decide the true worth of this man's character.

The usual interpretation suggests Zacchaeus had been an extortioner; that he had unjustly taxed the people, and as a result, had become exceedingly wealthy. When he met the Saviour, his conscience was so stirred that spontaneously he confessed his sin and vowed to make restitution. There would be no difficulty in accepting this view but for the fact that the language used by the tax gatherer presents problems. He did not say, "I will give," neither did he add, "I will restore." He appeared to indicate that this was his general practice. Let it be remembered that in a busy customs post there would be numerous tax gatherers—Zacchaeus was their chief, but there were times when these other men might have deliberately swindled the travellers. The head official might not have known all that was being done by those in lesser positions of authority. The *false accusation* mentioned in the text might have originated with others on the staff at the customs post, and whenever such cases were brought to the overseer, he made restitution in a most generous way. Readers must decide for themselves which interpretation is to be preferred, but in any case, here is food for thought. Godet suggests the Greek word *statheins*, translated *standing*, "denotes a firm and dignified attitude, such as suits a man whose honour is attacked." "*He whom Thou hast thought good to choose as thy host, is not, as is alleged, a being unworthy of Thy choice.*" Bishop Ryle quoting Burgon says, "Zacchaeus imposed upon himself the severest measure enjoined by the law concerning anyone convicted of theft. 'It is written, he shall restore four sheep for a sheep' (Exodus 22: 1), but even this was exacted only of him who had made away with property he had stolen. 'If the theft be found in his hand alive, he was only to restore double' (Exodus 22: 4). But with respect to him who confessed his crime, it is only said, 'He shall recompense his trespass with the principal thereof, and add unto it the fifth part thereof, and give it unto him against whom he hath trespassed' (Numbers 5: 7). Zacchaeus therefore judged himself most severely." When he referred to the half of his goods, he probably meant one half of his yearly income, that is, in produce or cash. On the other hand, as gratitude filled his soul, he might have

voluntarily decided to give away to the poor one half of his considerable estate. The only thing that is beyond dispute in this story is the
impact which Jesus made upon this man. Zacchaeus was a dwarf who
became a giant in record time!

> **And Jesus said unto him, This day is salvation come to this house, for-**
> **asmuch as he also is a son of Abraham. For the Son of man is come to**
> **seek and save that which was lost (vv. 9–10).**

The term "son of Abraham" reminds us of Pauline doctrine. Abraham
had descendants who were known as the seed of Abraham; the Jews
called the patriarch their father, but each time Christ used the term,
He did so to reveal faith in a person's soul. Abraham had believed
God, and righteousness thereafter was imputed to him. His *true*
*children* also believed with similar results. The faith of Zacchaeus had
brought salvation—in the Person of Christ—to his home, and perhaps
to his family. Thus did the Lord reveal the true purpose of His mission
to earth. He came to seek and to save the lost—not only those who
might have been excommunicated from the realms of Jewry; those
who were considered lost to Israel: but those also who had wandered
from the fold of God; whose sin endangered their souls.

## HOMILIES

Study No. 59

### THE DWARF WHO BECAME A GIANT

This is a simple study in height. There are very tall men who are
unable to look over small disappointment; there are tiny Davids who
can look over the shoulder of Goliath to see God. This incident happened at the close of the Saviour's ministry, when His fame had been
spread abroad; when everyone in the land would have heard of the
great Carpenter. His amazing miracles could not have passed unnoticed. Yet suddenly, as though he had come from overseas, we find
a man who knew nothing about Jesus. "And behold, there came a man
named Zacchaeus, which was the chief among the publicans, and he
was rich. And he sought to see Jesus *who he was.*"

### Zacchaeus the Dwarf

We cannot possibly avoid a question. Where had this man been
during the three memorable years of the Saviour's ministry? It appears
that he had had no contact with the Lord. He had not even seen Him.
Such a condition seems hardly possible. At best we can only hazard

a guess, but it is significant that this man was the chief among the publicans. He had not only sold his services to the accursed Romans, he had attained to a place of official importance in the esteem of his employers. His duty was to stimulate the wavering tax-gatherers; to see they never faltered in the odious task of collecting money from unwilling taxpayers. He would be especially detested and isolated by his fellow countrymen. His friends would be few, and his social activities unimportant. He avoided Jewish feasts, and shunned crowds where his presence would lead to embarrassment. Thus the ministry of Jesus had never been able to reach him. Poor Zacchaeus was so small that his vision was limited to Jewry. He probably hated them.

### Zacchaeus the Desirous

After three years a most interesting thing occurred. One day he went forth into the street to become aware of the presence of a very great crowd. Naturally he wondered why so many people had gathered. When he heard about the coming of the Prophet, for once in a while, he ceased thinking about the Jews and refused to permit hypocrites to fill his horizons. He, the chief of the publicans, became so anxious to see the visiting Teacher, that he looked around for a vantage point for he was little of stature. Within a few moments he was safely seated in the branches of a tree, and the stage was set for his most thrilling experience. As long as he thought of Jews, he could only see Jews. Once he began to grow, wonderful things became possible. After all, *there was a Christ* somewhere. Yet many people still find difficulty in accepting this fact. They are aware only of the existence of hypocrites. Yes, this is definitely a study in height.

### Zacchaeus the Discoverer

Amazed and curiously interested, he watched as the Stranger came along the cobbled street. Then suddenly the Teacher came across to say, "Zacchaeus, make haste and come down; for today I must abide at thy house." And Zacchaeus came down, and received Him joyfully. Instantly it seemed as if the dwarf had explored unlimited continents. He realized that he was known by name to Jesus, and discovered that Christ had come seeking for sinners—even the chief of the publicans. He became aware that whether he liked it or not, he had to make a choice; that Christ was waiting for his response—a response that would mean an overwhelming welcome into the place called home. Then he discovered how little men can suddenly grow tall. He had climbed a tree because he was small; he came down because he had grown! All men increase their stature when they respond to the Saviour's call. And from that day forward the little-big man ceased looking at people. His eyes were focused on the Master. "And Zacchaeus stood, and said unto the Lord; Behold, Lord, the half of my goods I give to the poor; and if I have taken anything from any man by false accusation, I restore him fourfold. And Jesus said unto him, This day is salvation come to this house . . . For the Son of man is come to seek and to save that which was lost." God desires that all men should see Christ. Sometimes He even plants trees—*but man must decide to climb!*

## SECTION TWO

### *Expository Notes on the Parable of the Pounds*

**And as they heard these things, he added and spake a parable, because he was nigh to Jerusalem, and because they thought that the kingdom of God should immediately appear. He said therefore, A certain noble-man went into a far country to receive for himself a kingdom, and to return. And he called his ten servants, and delivered them ten pounds, and said unto them, Occupy till I come (vv. 11-13).**

This parable is of great interest because it appears to have been based upon a well-known historical event. When Herod the Great died, his kingdom was divided between Herod Antipas, Herod Philip, and Archelaus. The division of the inheritance was not legally valid until it had been ratified by the Romans who were the actual overlords of the country. Josephus, in his *Antiquities of the Jews,* xvii: 8: 11, describes how Archelaus, to whom Judea had been left, went to Rome in order to persuade Caesar to permit his entering into the inheritance. He was followed by a deputation of fifty men who opposed this act; they did not want him as ruler. Augustus Caesar refused their request, but compromised in that he did not grant to Archelaus the full powers of kingship. It will be remembered that this parable was uttered by the Lord somewhere near to Jericho, and the occasion was all the more suggestive for it was at this city that Archelaus had erected a most magnificent palace. This is just another piece of evidence to prove Christ was the Prince of Preachers. He used incidents which although simple, perfectly illustrated what He desired to teach.

As the disciples continued their journey to Jerusalem their excite-ment increased for the coming of the kingdom appeared to be very imminent. The Lord recognized the symptoms and tempered their optimism with caution. The word translated pounds is *minas,* which in present value equalled nearly twenty dollars. The servants were entrusted with this amount and told to trade on the Master's behalf during his absence. The spiritual implications of this story were obvious. Christ was about to receive a kingdom—but not in Jerusalem. He was to travel into a far country—Heaven, where the kingdom would be ratified by the Great Ruler of the Universe—God Himself.

During the Lord's absence on this special mission, the disciples were to be active on His behalf. They were instructed to trade with the talents with which He had endowed them.

> But his citizens hated him, and sent a message after him, saying, We will not have this man to reign over us. And it came to pass that when he was returned, having received the kingdom, then he commanded these servants to be called unto him, to whom he had given the money, that he might know how much every man had gained by trading (vv. 14-15).

It will be noticed that whilst there were different kinds of servants; there was also a great difference between the servants and the citizens. The former at least belonged to their Master; the latter were only related in that they belonged to the territory over which he was to rule. The dividing lines of demarcation are thus clearly drawn between the followers of Christ and the inhabitants of this world. The animosity of the latter cannot change the verdict of the Supreme Ruler, but at least, their protests indicate they are not in sympathy with the purposes of God. The Bible teaches that when the Lord returns, saints will be called before the judgment seat of Christ to give account of their stewardship. See I Corinthians 3: 12-15, II Corinthians 5: 10. Our *presence* in the kingdom is guaranteed by the promises of God; our *position* in the kingdom will be earned or lost by the quality of the service we render now. Salvation is a gift through faith in Christ. Honour is a reward for service to Christ.

> Then came the first saying, Lord, thy pound hath gained ten pounds. And he said unto him, Well, thou good servant: because thou hast been faithful in a very little, have thou authority over ten cities. And the second came saying, Lord, thy pound hath gained five pounds. And he said likewise to him, Be thou also over five cities. And another came, saying, Lord, behold, here is thy pound, which I have kept laid up in a napkin: For I feared thee, because thou art an austere man: thou takest up that thou layest not down, and reapest that thou didst not sow. And he said unto him, Out of thine own mouth will I judge thee, wicked servant. Thou knewest that I was an austere man, taking up that I laid not down, and reaping that I did not sow. Wherefore then gavest not thou my money into the bank, that at my coming I might have required mine own with usury? And he said unto them that stood by, Take from him the pound, and give it to him that hath ten pounds. And they said unto him, Lord, he hath ten pounds. (And Jesus answered) For I say unto you, That unto every one that hath shall be given; and from him that hath not, even that he hath, shall be taken away from him. But those mine enemies, which would not that I should reign over them, bring hither and slay them before me (vv. 16-27).

There are four kinds of people in this passage. (1) *The Faithful*. (2) *The Less Faithful*. (3) *The Unfaithful*. (4) *The Faithless*. Let us consider the first two together. Both started equal; both received one pound. How the one man succeeded in making twice as much profit as the other we are not told; maybe he was more diligent in his business associations. The possibility exists that the one man worked equally hard making five pounds as did the one who made twice that amount. Yet, of this we cannot be sure. The second man might have been perfectly content that he was doing a very fine job, and resting on his satisfaction, watched the bank balance increasing. The first man, energized by a great ambition, probably invested his money, withdrew it again at the opportune moment, and reinvested it where the dividends were higher. He, constantly watching the investment, saw his initial sum increasing by leaps and bounds. He worked hard making money. Faithful service is one thing, but enthusiasm breathing new life into that service is another thing. Faithfulness keeps the house clean; enthusiasm keeps the house clean but also places flowers in every room. Sometimes imagination can turn a hovel into a palace; a plain piece of canvas into an entrancing picture of loveliness. Within the Christian church are those whose loyalty can never be questioned; yet alongside those same members may be others whose enthusiasm turns the place upside down! It must be readily admitted that some would set the city on fire whilst others look for a match.

It will be remembered that there were ten servants, and that only three are now mentioned. Seven are not mentioned again. This is probably explained by the fact that Jesus was citing types or examples. There might have been more than one faithful servant; there might also have been more than one less faithful. The third type indicated in the text was a man who excused his indolence by criticizing his master. Some details are obvious. (1) *He was Cautious*. Probably he was either lazy or scared. The money in his hand might disappear! If he lost it, the lord would be angry. He therefore wrapped it in a napkin and stood guard over it until the day came when it was brought once more into the light. Some might find merit in the act, but sober reflection reveals the man was stupid. He might have placed the money in a bank; he might have emulated the example of his fellow servants; he might have used part of the pound, at least, to try to make money; in fact he might have done anything, and that would have been better than doing nothing. In most matters of industry it is better to try and fail than to sit still and go bankrupt! (2) *He was Critical*. Even when the day of reckoning arrived, there was no sense of regret; there was no apology for the obvious failure to please the master. The indolent servant indirectly blamed the nobleman for an example which had paralysed his own initiative. "It was not my fault,

Master. You are a hard man, and if I had failed, you would have criticized me. Because you are so clever reaping that which you never planted, you expect everybody else to be as ruthless and as clever. I do not have the brains that you possess, so it was your fault in the first place to give me the job." We seem to hear echoes from Eden. "Oh God, it was not my fault. The woman thou gavest me, she made me eat. If you had left me alone in the first place, that woman would not have upset me. I did not ask for her; you gave her to me, so it was your fault." Possibly this unfaithful servant was also a little jealous of the master's possessions, and bitterness poisoned his spirit. (3) *He was Condemned.* There is always danger when we permit ourselves to remain negative. Many people spend a lot of time talking about history but never make any. Each new task presents a fresh opportunity; every new battle affords the chance of gaining a new victory. Each time the sun rises, it reveals a new world, and that world should be captured for Christ. To fail in the hour of supreme need; to hide our talents in a napkin just because of the ugly thought of failure, is to miss the challenge that comes from a perishing world. The man in the text knew (1) all he possessed, had first been received from his master: (2) his master desired a certain course of action: (3) other servants were succeeding (4) there would come a reckoning day: (5) he knew beforehand what the results of inefficiency would be. At least *he could have tried* to please his lord. The fellow worked hard doing nothing. His descendants are still with us!

The closing statement in the section should fill us with awe. The citizens who had actively opposed the reign of the nobleman were called to account for their actions. The results may be summarised under three headings. Rejection—Retribution—Ruin. The Christ who is rejected by men will someday reject men. This truth is sometimes ignored; God is said to be too merciful to banish any sinner from His presence. This is not true. The Bible speaks of the possibility of becoming eternally lost, and if this is not true then Christ was to be blamed for misleading His listeners. They who risk their destiny on the strength of modern opinions play with fire.

# HOMILIES

Study No. 60

## MAKING MONEY FOR THE MASTER

The expository notes dealing with the Parable of the Pounds describe how this incident was based upon historical fact. Through death, a

man had inherited a kingdom, but that inheritance had to be ratified
by Caesar who was the overlord of the country. Archelaus therefore
went to Rome fully expecting his loyal subjects to be active on his
behalf throughout his absence. Ultimately this earthly ruler returned
to reward his faithful servants and to chastize his enemies. These
simple facts enabled the listeners to understand the meaning of Christ's
parable. Yet after many years of Christian history we are able to
review the parable and see in it things which the initial listeners could
hardly have understood.

## A Gracious Reception

Through death, the Lord Jesus had inherited a kingdom, but unfortunately His followers failed to realize the kingdom was infinitely
larger than anything confined within the boundaries of Palestine. He
who had loved the world and died for it, now longed to claim it, but
the right to rule had to be ratified in heaven. There, the great Ruler—
the Righteous Caesar of the entire Universe waited to receive the Lord
Jesus. Perhaps this explains other verses in the New Testament. "Jesus
said unto her, Touch me not; for I am not yet ascended to my Father:
but go to my brethren, and say unto them, I ascend unto my Father,
and your Father; and to my God, and your God" (John 20: 17). "But
this man, after he had offered one sacrifice for sins for ever, sat down on
the right hand of God; from henceforth expecting till his enemies be
made his footstool. For by one offering he hath perfected for ever
them that are sanctified" (Hebrews 10: 12–14). After His resurrection
Lord returned to Heaven, where in the presence of angelic hosts, God
received His Son; crowned Him with glory and honour, and ratified
eternally the right of the Man of Calvary to reign over His people. The
kingdom which had been offered by Satan, and refused by Christ;
See Luke 4: 5–8, had been won the hard way. It is only against this
setting that we are able to understand the parable of the pounds.

## A Great Responsibility

To every Christian has been given one or more talents. The commission of the Master was made quite clear—*"Occupy till I come."*
It is the responsibility of every follower of Jesus to do everything to
further the cause of Christ. We must not be jealous of the man who
has more talents; neither should we despise the man who appears to
have fewer than we possess. It is our duty to do what we can; to
prepare to the best of our ability for that day when we must give an
account of our stewardship. The expository notes outlined various
kinds of servants revealed in the text. Unfortunately there are men of
whom might be said, "They put not their necks to the work." During
the building of the walls of Jerusalem, there were many workers, but

unfortunately some had no love for overtime! Yet there was one man of whom it was said, "he *earnestly* repaired the other piece" (Nehemiah 3: 20). Whilst some of the builders were slackers, this delightful man worked until he nearly dropped. He obtained a place in God's "Hall of Fame." The Christian church today is made up of all kinds of people. Some, unfortunately are ecclesiastical ornaments adorning the sanctuary; others ease the burden on their conscience by doing a fair share of the work; but there are some whose hearts are aglow with love for the Master; they live and die to please Him. To which category do we belong?

## A *Glorious Return*

Some day the Master will return, for whilst His right to the kingdom was ratified in Heaven, the kingdom itself is to be here on this earth. If the work of the church is to prepare the ground for the establishing of that kingdom, it is the duty of the Lord to return to reward those who have earnestly worked in His Name. The Saviour's message drew a strange contrast between pounds and cities. The faithful and industrious servant not only retained what he had used; he was also given authority over cities. Thus did the Lord indicate that true service would bring rewards of infinite worth. To be faithful in small things means a chance to serve the Lord in a greater capacity. It is not possible to appreciate fully what it might mean to reign over ten cities in the kingdom of our Lord. That there will be an organization ruling the kingdom; that certain officials must have their appointed tasks is surely obvious. The Lord was striving to suggest to His listeners that faithful service can never pass unnoticed—that even a cup of cold water given in the Name of Christ would bring its own reward. But by the same token He also indicated the unfaithful people must give an account of their stewardship. Whether we like it or not, HE EXPECTS US TO WORK FOR HIM. And whether we believe it or not, some day certain Christians will be exceedingly embarrassed when the poor quality of their service is revealed. If certain businessmen worked as hard for the Lord as they work for themselves, the church would never need to appeal for money. If young people were controlled by a desire to serve the Saviour, the mission field would never be in need of recruits.

### SECTION THREE

### *Expository Notes on Christ's Entry into Jerusalem*

**And when he had thus spoken, he went before, ascending up to Jerusalem. And it came to pass when he was come nigh to Bethphage, and**

Bethany, at the mount called the mount of Olives, he sent two of his
disciples, Saying, Go ye into the village over against you; in the which
at your entering, ye shall find a colt tied, whereon yet never man sat:
loose him, and bring him hither. And if any man ask you, Why do ye
loose him? thus shall ye say unto him, Because the Lord hath need of
him (vv. 28–31).

For the complete record of this part of the story of Christ, it is
necessary to consider together the accounts in all the synoptic Gospels.
Matthew 21: 1–9; Mark 11: 1–12; and Luke 19: 28–40 supply details
both interesting and challenging. It would appear the Lord drew near
to the city; commissioned His disciples to obtain the colt, and finally
rode into the city. Later, He went back to Bethany, and the following
morning proceeded to the temple to drive out the money changers.
The site of Bethany is well known but the place and importance of
Bethphage are obscure. It has been said that Bethphage was a suburb
of Jerusalem; that it was a convenient extension to the sacred precincts
of the city; an extension made necessary by the ever increasing
numbers of pilgrims who came to the feasts. There were certain legalistic requirements which demanded that worshippers should be housed
within the camp—the city, and when this became an impossibility,
something had to be done to remedy the situation. The priests therefore—it is said—*sanctified* that portion of land which stretched out
from the city walls toward the Mount of Olives. This was known as
Bethphage. Bethany itself was only two miles from Jerusalem, and
therefore it is easily understood why these two places should appear
together in the sacred record.

The actual details of the commissioning of two disciples to go for
the colt seem to suggest supernatural knowledge, but probably this
was not essential. The Lord had often passed that way, and He had
many friends throughout the area. It is probable that the owner of the
colt knew, and perhaps believed in Jesus. The statement "THE LORD
hath need of him" would indicate this. Thus the man readily surrendered the young animal, and the scene was quickly set for the
triumphant entry. If the disciples entertained any doubt as to the
validity of the Master's claim to Messianic powers, this was instantly
removed when He sent for the colt. They knew that it had been
written, "Rejoice greatly, O daughter of Zion; shout, O daughter of
Jerusalem: behold, thy king cometh unto thee: he is just and having
salvation; lowly, and riding upon an ass, and upon a colt the foal of an
ass" (Zechariah 9: 9). Their hearts were singing when they brought
the little donkey to Jesus.

And they that were sent, went their way, and found even as he had
said unto them. And as they were loosing the colt, the owners thereof

said unto them, Why loose ye the colt? And they said, The Lord hath need of him. And they brought him to Jesus: and they cast their garments upon the colt, and they set Jesus thereon. And as he went, they spread their clothes in the way. And when he was come nigh, even now at the descent of the mount of Olives, the whole multitude of the disciples began to rejoice and praise God with a loud voice for all the mighty works which they had seen: Saying, Blessed be the King that cometh in the name of the Lord: peace in heaven, and glory in the highest (vv. 32–38).

The pathway to Jerusalem wound its way through the hills until suddenly at a turn in the road, the entire city lay before the gaze of the pilgrims. Godet says, "From this elevated point, three hundred feet above the terrace of the temple, which was itself raised about one hundred feet above the level of the valley of the Cedron, an extensive view was to be had of the city and the whole plain which it commands, especially of the temple, which rose opposite, immediately above the valley." This thrilling sight stirred the emotions of the disciples, and remembering the mighty exploits of their Leader, their cries of joy echoed from the plateau until the entire valley rang with the praises of God. Those were moments never to be forgotten. Luke omits the title, or exclamation, Hosannah; he was writing for Gentiles. Hosannah was a Jewish word which expressed sentiments such as "God save the Queen." Gentiles would not necessarily have appreciated this detail and therefore Luke omitted it from his manuscript. We should not under-estimate the importance of this tremendous occasion. There had been times when Jesus deliberately withdrew Himself to the quiet places; there had been occasions when the people would have made Christ king, but their efforts had been thwarted by the Lord's own actions. Now the outlook had changed. With courage, probably unsurpassed at any time, the Saviour deliberately mounted his donkey and rode toward the city. This was all the more remarkable for the High Priest had already issued an edict commanding any man who was aware of the presence of Christ to reveal the information. A price had been placed on the head of the Carpenter, and no stone was to be left unturned in the frenzied search for Him. Jesus was considered to be an outlaw; yet with tremendous courage, the Lord calmly rode toward the city.

And some of the Pharisees from among the multitude said unto him, Master, rebuke thy disciples. And he answered and said unto them, I tell you that, if these should hold their peace, the stones would immediately cry out (vv. 39–40).

Probably the Pharisees were frightened. The noise on the hill would be heard in the valley; the ascription of royalty now being given to

408 Luke's Thrilling Gospel

Christ might result in serious repercussions. Any man who made himself a king spake against Caesar. If the Governor heard this, and if his mood at the time were unfavourable, he might even send the soldiers to put down a suspected uprising. There might be bloodshed, and therefore the Pharisees urged the Lord to prevent the disciples from being imprudent. Jesus refused to yield to their desires.

And when he was come near, he beheld the city, and wept over it, Saying, If thou hadst known, even thou, at least in this thy day, the things which belong unto thy peace! but now they are hid from thine eyes. For the days shall come upon thee, that thine enemies shall cast a trench about thee, and compass thee round, and keep thee in on every side. And shall lay thee even with the ground, and thy children within thee; and they shall not leave in thee one stone upon another; because thou knewest not the time of thy visitation (vv. 41-44).

This was the most disappointing day the disciples ever knew; when the kingdom seemed to be within His grasp; when the crowds delirious with joy were ready to crown Him KING, the Master washed away His prospects with His tears. They could not believe their eyes; this was the tragedy supreme! The poignant feelings of their souls found expression when their eyes seemed to say, "Oh, Master, what a time to weep. The crowds have gone; it will take years to obtain another chance such as we have just lost. Oh Master!" See the following homily.

## HOMILIES

Study No. 61

### God in Tears

Across the valley of the Cedron lay the city of Jerusalem with its temple roof glistening in the light of the setting sun. The streets were moderately quiet for the hush of evening was settling upon the homesteads. Yet on the overlooking hill things were different. A crowd followed Jesus, but the cries of enthusiasm, which ten minutes earlier had echoed into the valley, were now hushed. The people were watching Him, and even the disciples were a little bewildered. They had commenced this journey to the city with eager expectation of great things to come, but now, they were apprehensive. Something had gone wrong with their plans; the Master was not co-operating, and the people were becoming suspicious. Men who would have gladly fought in His army were now sombre and silent; some were beginning to leave. Then suddenly the Lord commenced to weep. The Greek word used in the description of the event is strong, signifying bitter anguish as though one bewailed the dead. This was not silent grief welling up in a few tears; this was audible sobbing; the evidence of great sorrow. The disciples were bewildered. "Behold, God in tears!"

### The Tears of Perplexity

For once, the Lord was confronted by failure, for there were some things which even God could not accomplish. Continually throughout His ministry the Lord Jesus had endeavoured to reach the hearts of those Jewish people, but each time His efforts were rejected. The rulers did not like His interference; they did not believe His message; they resented what they considered to be the interference of an upstart. The Lord had healed their sick; cleansed their lepers, fed their hungry but alas, for the most part, had failed to win an abiding place in their affection. Now the time was getting short, and His ministry would soon terminate. They were in terrible danger, but what more could He do? They had spurned His warnings, and refused His help. As a hen gathered her chicks under her wings, so He had desired to gather these people under the shadow of the Almighty but His efforts had ended in failure. Now it was too late. He was helpless and completely frustrated, and as He considered these tragic facts, the tears ran down His face. Yes, there were things which even God could not do. He was able to place planets into orbit; He was able to make the light shine out of darkness, but when God faced the closed door of a human heart, He could only knock, and hope to gain admittance. Sometimes this was denied.

### The Tears of Pain

With the eye of a Seer, the Lord unerringly saw and described the horrors soon to fall upon the city He loved. "For the days shall come upon thee, that thine enemies shall cast a trench about thee, and compass thee round, and keep thee in on every side, And shall lay thee even with the ground, and thy children within thee; and they shall not leave in thee one stone upon another; because thou knewest not the time of thy visitation." All this, and very much more came to pass when the Romans overwhelmed the city of Jerusalem in A.D. 70. Josephus described the terrible sufferings of those days and indicated that as far as the eye could see in every direction, there was no sight other than crucified Jews. Rivers of blood flowed through the gates of the city, when a generation perished. Great trenches were dug; mounds of earth were raised to isolate the city. Unable to leave, thousands of people perished. Women were molested, children were slaughtered and finally the stones of the temple were taken down one by one. Unwilling that their sanctuary should fall into the hands of the enemy, a band of fanatical Jews fought to the end, and finally burned the temple to the ground. Days later, when the fierce heat had somewhat subsided, the soldiers in their frenzied search for molten gold, carefully demolished the walls, looking in every crack in the hope of finding treasures. The Saviour's prediction was literally fulfilled. When the Jews cried, "His blood be on us, *and on our children*," they signed their own death warrant. Christ saw this and broke His heart. He was hurt long before they were touched.

### The Tears of Pity

He loved them. This fact is inscrutable; it is bewildering; it is amazing, but when all the definitions have been exhausted, we can only repeat, Christ loved them. Had it been possible, He would have given all He possessed to ward off the coming disaster, but He was helpless. He wanted to save them but this was beyond His capability. And here is food for thought. The Bible teaches that another day of judgment is to come. "And I saw a great white throne, and him that sat on it, From whose face the earth and the heaven fled away; and there was found no place for them. And I saw the dead, small and great, stand before God, and the books were opened: and another book was opened, which is the book of life, and the dead were judged out of those things which were written in the books, according to their works . . . And whosoever was not found written in the book of life was cast into the lake of fire" (Revelation 20:11-15). Christ still loves the world; the Lord still yearns to save sinners, but unfortunately in spite of His great compassion, souls are to be found wanting in the day of judgment. *There is nothing He can do to prevent it.* There is a limit even to the capability of the Saviour. And thus the Lord Jesus looked at the city, and wept tears of pity. The disciples may be excused for their lack of understanding, but we should know better. Then slowly a tremendous resolve arose within His soul. If He could not save that generation, He might be able to do something for those who would come later. At least, He could open a door into everlasting happiness and thereby make it possible for others to succeed where these had failed. Slowly He went down into the city toward a lumber yard in which a cross was already waiting for a victim. He knew His course of action: He would take our sins, and in His own body, nail them to the tree.

> The Son of God in tears,
>   The wondering angels see.
> Be thou astonished, O my soul,
>   He shed those tears for thee.

*Expository Notes on the Cleansing of the Temple*

And he went into the temple, and began to cast out them that sold
therein, and them that bought; saying unto them, It is written, My house
is the house of prayer: but ye have made it a den of thieves. And he
taught daily in the temple. But the chief priests and the scribes, and
the chief of the people sought to destroy him. And could not find what
they might do: for all the people were very attentive to hear him
(vv. 45-48).

Mark indicates that the Lord entered into the temple late in the
afternoon; that he looked around the place, and then returned to
Bethany to spend the night in the home of His friends. The following
morning, He returned to the temple to cleanse it. This had been done
during an earlier part of His ministry, but the House of God had become filthy again. The Lord therefore proceeded to repeat the action
of earlier years. Very much has been written of this event, but perhaps
the most complete, the most thought-provoking account comes from
the pen of Barclay. He says: "Why did Jesus, Who was the very
incarnation of love, act with such violence to the money changers, and
the sellers of animals in the temple courts? First, let us look at the
money changers. Every male Jew had to pay a temple tax every year
of a half a shekel. That was equal to about 1s. 2d. or 17 cents, but in
evaluating this, it must be remembered that this was equal to two days'
pay for a working man. A month before the Passover, booths were set
up in all the towns and villages, and the money could be paid there.
But by far the greater part of the tax was actually paid by the pilgrims
in Jerusalem when they came to the Passover feast. In Palestine all
kinds of currencies were in circulation: Greek, Roman, Tyrian, Syrian,
Egyptian, and all were equally valid. But this special tax had to be
paid either in exact half-shekels of the Sanctuary or in ordinary
Galilaean shekels. This is where the money changers made their
fortune. To change a coin of exact value, they charged one *maan*,
which was equal to 2d. If a larger coin were tendered, a charge of one
*maan* was made for the requisite half-shekel, *and of another for the
giving of change*. It has been computed that these money changers
made a profit of between 8,000 and 9,000 pounds ($26,000) per year. . . .
Let us look at the sellers of animals. Sacrifices could be bought outside
at very reasonable prices, but the temple authorities had appointed
inspectors, for the law required that sacrificed animals should be without spot and blemish. It was therefore far safer to buy victims from
the booths officially set up in the Temple. (These had been already

certified as acceptable.) But there were times when a pair of doves cost as much as fifteen shillings ($2 : 20) inside the Temple, and considerably less than one shilling (15c) outside. . . . These Temple shops were known as *The Booths of Annas*, and were the property of the High Priest . . . Annas was delighted to gloat over Jesus who had struck such a blow at his evil monopoly. Jesus cleansed the temple with such violence because the Temple traffic was being used to exploit helpless men and women. . . . It was the passion for social justice which burned in Jesus' heart when He took this drastic step." (Barclay, *The Gospel of Luke*, pp. 251–252.)

Continuing the manifestation of His magnificent courage, the Lord taught daily in the Temple, and although the hierarchy persisted in their efforts to arrest and arraign Him, they were helpless. The crowds of pilgrims, now aware of His presence, flocked to His meetings, and their wrapt attention indicated to the rulers it would be unwise to interfere.

For the special homily dealing with the two cleansings of the Temple, see the Author's companion volume, *John's Wonderful Gospel*, pp. 63–65.

# The Twentieth Chapter of Luke

THEME: *Jesus Answers Questions in the Temple*

OUTLINE:

      I. The Saviour and His Preaching. Verses 1–18
     II. The Spies and their Penny. Verses 19–26
   III. The Sadducees and their Problem. Verses 27–38
   IV. The Scribes and their Pride. Verses 39–47

### SECTION ONE

*Expository Notes on Christ's Messages in the Temple*

**And it came to pass, on one of those days, as he taught the people in the temple, and preached the gospel, the chief priests and the scribes came to him with the elders, And spake unto him, saying, Tell us, by what authority doest thou these things? or who is he that gave thee this authority? (vv. 1–2).**

It is not surprising that the Jewish leaders asked this question. The Lord had deliberately ridden into the city, and had proceeded to throw out of the temple those who had the official sanction of the High Priest to sell their animals. They wanted to know who had given permission for this kind of action. The chief priests, and their scribes with the elders represented the aristocracy of the nation; the leading members of the ruling body known as the Sanhedrin. This would be the equivalent of the British *House of Lords* or the *American Senate*. If today, someone walked into the British Houses of Parliament, or into the American Senate Building to overturn the tables and drive out those who were working there, he would probably end the day either in prison or in a mental institution. The ancient rulers would have gladly placed Jesus under arrest, but at that particular time he was followed by many people who believed in His doctrines, and any arrest would have led to rioting in the sacred house. The rulers decided to be extremely careful; that is, they planned to find a less conspicuous way of capturing Him.

**And he answered and said unto them, I will also ask you one thing; and answer me: The baptism of John, was it from heaven, or of men?**

And they reasoned with themselves, saying, If we shall say, From heaven; he will say, Why then believed ye him not? But and if we say, Of men; all the people will stone us: for they be persuaded that John was a prophet. And they answered, that they could not tell whence it was. And Jesus said unto them, Neither tell I you by what authority I do these things (vv. 3-8).

Many people might be tempted to describe this as *A battle of wits*. Obviously the leaders had carefully planned their course of action; and equally as obvious was the Lord's determination not to be caught in their web. Had He stated clearly that He had been sent by God, they would have had grounds upon which to accuse Him; had He given any other answer, they would have found ways to discredit His claims. The Lord recognized their subtlety, and countered with a question of His own. The ministry of John the Baptist was known throughout the nation; yet the leaders had never committed themselves in regard to the validity of his teaching. Therefore Jesus deliberately asked this question concerning the slain prophet. Instantly the rulers became cautious, and debating the dangers of the question, recognized extreme care was necessary in formulating an answer. John had publicised the fact that *he believed* in Jesus. The wilderness preacher had affirmed that the Carpenter was *the Lamb of God*; if then the rulers admitted John's ministry was from heaven, Jesus would reply, "Why then ask me for the source of my authority—John told you." If on the other hand, they charged John with being an egoist—a self-appointed preacher, the multitude would rebel for they claimed John had been a prophet of God. Here then was great danger. The rulers replied that they did not know the answer to the Lord's question. The Lord sadly smiled and refused to answer their question. Jesus was wise; His answer proved that he who walks with God need not fear his enemies.

Then began he to speak to the people this parable; A certain man planted a vineyard, and let it forth to husbandmen, and went into a far country for a long time. And at the season, he sent a servant to the husbandmen, that they should give him of the fruit of the vineyard: but the husbandmen beat him, and sent him away empty. And again he sent another servant: and they beat him also, and entreated him shamefully, and sent him away empty. And again he sent a third: and they wounded him also and cast him out (vv. 9-12).

The Lord never refused to answer any honest question, and whilst the insincerity of the rulers was obvious to all, there might have been others in that crowd who would have asked a similar question for different reasons. Therefore, instead of evading the issue, the Saviour proceeded to tell a story which effectively supplied the information required. There were many landowners who rented their acres to tenants whilst they vacationed elsewhere. The rent was seldom paid in cash; the husbandmen preferred to give an agreed portion of the harvest to the land owner. At the proper season an emissary was dispatched to collect these dues, and for the most part, everybody was satisfied. Occasionally there was some trouble, and therefore this parable was easily understood by the Lord's audience. Nevertheless, even as they listened, they were able to discern deeper trends of truth. This was a story with an application; this was a parable with a very obvious meaning.

Throughout the Old Testament, Israel was likened to the vineyard of the Lord. "And now, O inhabitants of Jerusalem, and men of Judah, judge, I pray you, betwixt me and my vineyard. What can have been done more to my vineyard, that I have not done in it? . . . For the vineyard of the Lord of hosts is the house of Israel . . ." (Isaiah 5: 1-7). The owner of the vineyard was the Lord; the people who were supposed to manage the estate were the rulers of the Jews; they were in charge of the nation; the servants who were mistreated can only be the prophets sent by God to remind the tenants of their debt of gratitude. God was only asking for His own. However, let it be remembered the Lord had been asked for the source of His authority for His action. The answer was made perfectly clear in the verses to follow.

Then said the lord of the vineyard, What shall I do? I will send my beloved son: it may be they will reverence him when they see him. But when the husbandmen saw him, they reasoned among themselves saying, This is the heir: come, let us kill him, that the inheritance may be our's. So they cast him out of the vineyard and killed him. What therefore shall the lord of the vineyard do unto them? He shall come and destroy those husbandmen, and shall give the vineyard to others. And when they heard it, they said, God forbid (vv. 13-16).

*God* is not found in the original Greek, and therefore the closing sentence would be better rendered, "And when they heard it, they said, May it never be." *The Amplified New Testament.* The inference in the parable cannot be mistaken. After the mission of the old Testament prophets had apparently ended in failure, God sent His beloved Son. This was a deliberate claim by Jesus to be the Son of God; this was the answer to the question designed to trap Him. The Lord knew He was to be killed; He was also aware of the destruction which would "give the vineyard to others." The fact that the hearers said, "May it never be" is proof they also understood the implications of this parable.

And he beheld them and said, What is this then that is written. The stone which the builders rejected, the same is become the head of the corner? Whosoever shall fall upon that stone shall be broken; but on whomsoever it shall fall, it will grind him to powder (vv. 17–18).

The text quoted by Christ comes from Psalm 118: 22–23; there is also a veiled reference to Isaiah 8: 14–15. The fact that the Saviour used the verse impressed the disciples and thereafter they also used it as one of their favourite quotations. (See Acts 4: 11 and II Peter 2: 7–8.) The usual interpretation is that whether one falls on the stone, or whether the stone falls on the sinner, the result must be disastrous. This is the stone of judgment; the rejected stone destined to become the chief corner stone of an eternal kingdom (see Isaiah 8: 14–15). However, there is another interpretation. If one falls in penitence upon the Rock of Ages, it leads to a broken heart and a contrite spirit. Then the stone becomes a Sheltering Rock in the time of storm. If, however, the sinner remains arrogant, the day will come when that same Rock will fall in judgment upon the offender. The Greek word *likmeesei* which has been translated *will grind him* to powder, provides a word picture. Thayer says it means: (1) *to winnow, to cleanse away the chaff from the grain by winnowing;* (2) *to scatter;* (3) *to crush to pieces, to grind to powder.* The ideas therefore expressed in the text include: examination; separation; retribution, and finally oblivion. This is a frightening picture. The Lord of the vineyard intends to punish those who murdered His Son. He also plans to exalt that same Son—the stone which the builders rejected—until He has been acknowledged as King of kings and Lord of lords. Throughout the limitless ages of eternity, Jesus will be the headstone of the corner.

## HOMILIES

Study No. 62

### THE ROCK OF AGES

Many tourists who have known the privilege of travelling in Egypt are aware of the great stone lying in an ancient quarry. It has been symmetrically planned and chiselled from the solid rock; is of immense size, but unfortunately is still joined to its bed. The sides; the ends; the top, have all been fashioned with amazing skill, but at the last moment, so it is said, the sculptors or contractors discovered a hidden fault in the massive stone, and the work was abandoned immediately. Throughout the East many tales are told of a stone which although previously rejected, eventually was taken to occupy an important position in a magnificent structure. It is said that the earlier builders were too premature; too critical in their judgements; that the stone they rejected, was ultimately proved to be strong and reliable. Therefore, at a later date, it was cut from its foundations; transported to the building site, and carefully raised to occupy a place of importance in the elaborate palace under construction. It may well be that the ancient texts were the outcome of such events. Throughout the Old Testament the prophets spoke of the rejected stone, and their message was so understood that even Christ and His followers continued to use the illustration.

## The Stone of Stumbling

Schofield correctly says, "To Israel, Christ coming not as a splendid monarch, but in the form of a servant, is a stumbling stone, and rock of offence (Isaiah 8: 14–15; Romans 9: 32–33; I Corinthians 1: 23; I Peter 2: 8). The idea of a suffering servant was something completely opposed to anything they had been taught. They looked for a magnificent king whose power would sweep from the life of the nation every offending foreign element. They thought of the glory of Solomon's kingdom, and considered even that to be insignificant compared with the Glory of the Messianic kingdom. They thought only of what the King would do *for* them, and had no interest whatsoever in anything He might desire to do *within* them. Self-examination; self-condemnation were unknown. They had no conviction of sin; they considered themselves to be the children of Abraham, the chosen people of Jehovah. Other people might be wrong; but they were always right! Occasionally a prophet tried to tell them they were mistaken, but invariably those prophets died for interfering. When Jesus came to continue the ministry of the prophets; when He supported the teaching with miraculous powers of healing, the Jews suddenly considered this Nazarene to be a nuisance. He, as a boulder, stood in the centre of their planned highway of progress. They could not avoid Him, He was a nuisance; a hindrance; a stumbling block.

## The Stone of Strength

Yet, although Israel rejected Jesus, the Almighty elevated Him to a position of great honour. As the corner piece, He was destined to unite stones. Through Him, two separate walls would be united to form part of an immense structure. Jews and Gentiles; bond and free; would meet in Him to become part of One Building—the Church. As the Chief Corner Stone, He would exhibit His mighty strength for the roof; the walls; everything would be held fast by His ministry. A chief corner-stone is a stone of support. Massive pieces of timber rest upon its prepared surfaces; the storms would never beat into the sanctuary because all would be secured by the ministry of the head-stone.

When the apostles used this ancient illustration, they proclaimed their Master was Lord; He was indeed the Head of the Church.

## The Stone of Shelter

All travellers on a stormy night have known the value of the corner stone. When the biting winds of winter seem to freeze the blood within the veins; when every inch of progress along a gale-swept street has to be won against the onslaught of nature, the warmth, the calm, the shelter one finds behind the corner of a building are not to be forgotten. Isaiah probably had this thought in mind when he wrote: "*And he shall be for a sanctuary,* but for a stone of stumbling . . . to the houses of Israel . . ." (Isaiah 8: 14). Perhaps this same idea is expressed in Hebrews 6: 18–19: ". . . we might have strong consolation, *who have fled for refuge,* to lay hold upon the hope . . . which hope we have as an anchor of the soul . . ." God has always been known as a Refuge in the time of storm. Many and varied are the storms which threaten the believers, but throughout each one we may hide behind our Corner-Stone, and be safe.

## The Stone of Smiting

"Upon this rock I will build my church." So spake the Lord after Simon Peter had expressed eternal truth in his confession, "Thou art the Christ, the son of the Blessed." Yet, unfortunately, there are many people who resolutely resist every attempt to win their allegiance. They prefer sinful ways to the paths of righteousness. They build their own kingdom and ignore the claims of the King of Kings. This has always been the case, and this will continue to the end. Daniel described that in the end of the days, when the mighty image of world systems had been erected on the plains of time, "the God of heaven shall set up a kingdom, which shall never be destroyed." "Thou sawest till that a stone was cut out without hands, which smote the image . . . and the stone which smote the image became a great mountain, and filled the whole earth" (Daniel 2: 34–35). This age of grace will be followed by one of judgment, and the entire Bible tells the same message. "Upon whomsoever the stone shall fall, it will grind him to powder." In view of God's continuing testimony, it is hard to understand the stupidity of men who refuse to believe what has been spoken.

## The Stone of Splendour

"Jesus shall reign where'er the sun doth his successive journeys run; His kingdom spread from shore to shore, till moons shall wax and wane no more." He Who once was crowned with thorns will someday be proclaimed Lord of the Universe. Forever, united with His redeemed people, the Lord of Glory will be the headstone of the corner; eternally, the redeemed will see the wounds in His hands, and thrill to the song "Thou art worthy for thou hast redeemed us to God by thy blood out of every kindred, and tongue, and people, and nation. And hast made us unto our God kings and priests: and we shall reign on the earth." "And they shall see His face." From time immemorial it was considered impossible to see the face of God, for the Lord was said to dwell in light to which no man could approach and live. Once, Moses was permitted to see back parts of the Lord as Jehovah passed through an elevated canyon in the heights of Mount Sinai. Yet what the law could not permit, Grace has already promised—*we shall see His face,* and "know Him by the print of the nails in His hands."

## SECTION TWO

### *Expository Notes on the Tribute to Caesar*

And the chief priests and the scribes the same hour sought to lay hands on him; and they feared the people; for they perceived that he had spoken this parable against them. And they watched him and sent forth spies, which should feign themselves just men, that they might take hold of his words, that so they might deliver him unto the power and authority of the governor (vv. 19–20).

Enraged by the story which Christ had told, and resenting furiously its implications, the rulers now resorted to subterfuge. Spies were sent among the followers of Jesus commissioned to uncover evidence by which the Carpenter could be condemned. Alas, it is sad to admit that men could listen to the greatest sermons ever preached; see the greatest miracles ever performed; be near to the greatest Saviour the world ever knew, and yet remain blind to His grace. These men were within inches of Heaven, but worked for Hell. They smiled with their eyes whilst hate occupied their hearts.

And they asked him saying, Master, we know that thou sayest and teachest rightly, neither acceptest thou the person of any, but teachest the way of God truly: Is it lawful for us to give tribute unto Caesar, or not? But he perceived their craftiness, and said unto them, Why tempt ye me? Shew me a penny. Whose image and superscription hath it? They answered and said, Caesar's. And he said unto them, Render therefore unto Caesar the things which be Caesar's, and unto God the things which be God's. And they could not take hold of his words before the people: and they marvelled at his answer, and held their peace (vv. 21–26).

To appreciate fully the dangerous elements expressed in the question, it is necessary to understand conditions existing at that time. The poll-tax payable to Caesar was a denarius—a silver coin worth about ninepence. This did not impoverish the people but it did offend their consciences. When the tax was first imposed, certain people, led by Judas the Galilean, rebelled. There was some bloodshed but the rebellion was subdued. Seeds of discontent continued in the hearts of the people, and at the time of Christ's ministry, this payment of dues represented one of the greatest disputes in Israel. The archaeologists have unearthed coins from those times, and upon these may still be read the inscription—TI (BERIVS) CAESAR DIVI AUGUSTI F(ILIVS) AVGVSTVS. "Tiberius Caesar Augustus, son of the divine Augustus." This inscription represented blasphemy to every orthodox Jew. They had been strictly commanded to honour no God but Jehovah, and the idea that any man could elevate himself to deity was totally obnoxious. Therefore with increasing discontent in their hearts the militant elements in Israel continued to rebel against Caesar's imposition, and taking advantage of these facts, the spies sought to lead Jesus into a political maze.

Luce says, "The penny represented the Roman monetary unit. Herod had never had the right to strike silver coins. The Romans reserved this privilege for themselves. For current use they struck bronze coins, and, to spare the scruples of the Jews at seeing human portraits which had for them an idolatrous flavour, these little local coins had emblems imprinted on them from the world of nature, ears of corn, palms, vine-leaves, or other objects. But the denarii, Roman money, 'par excellence', bore the emperor's portrait." This is understandable for there was a principle at stake. A king's domain was recognized as far as his currency circulated. As long as a people accepted the coinage of a ruler, they tacitly admitted they were his subjects. Caesar undoubtedly wished to avoid trouble with Jewish zealots, but nevertheless he was Caesar, and there were some privileges he did not intend to surrender.

Mark 12: 13–17 should be read in conjunction with this passage. The Pharisees and the Herodians—usually bitter enemies, had united in this instance to put down a movement which threatened both. Their insincere compliment prefaced their real attack, and the danger in the question became apparent to all. If the Lord supported the national rebellion against the paying of tribute to a foreign ruler, then the authorities could accuse Him of treason. His arrest would take place almost immediately. If, on the other hand, he admitted the liability of the Jews to do as they were commanded, He would lose the support of many of those who followed Him. These men were hoping the Messiah would free them forever from the Roman yoke. If Jesus apparently accepted it, His claims to Messianic distinction would disappear. This was the insidious nature of the question. When the penny was brought to Him, the Lord pointed to the image of Caesar and asked to whom the coin belonged. When they answered "Caesar," He replied with a statement which has now passed into the language of all nations. Nevertheless, there is fine distinction in the text. The coin in the hand of Jesus bore the inscription which claimed deity for the Roman over-lord. When the Saviour placed Caesar in one class and God in the other, He cleverly drew the line of demarcation between the two. Every Jew would recognize this and appreciate the inherent wisdom of the Lord Jesus. Yet, even the Romans, when they heard this answer, would have no cause for complaint. Those who listened to this reply could only marvel and remain silent. Thus did Christ teach that Christians should become model citizens and uphold the highest prin-ciples of any government. If they use their roads; enjoy the amenities offered by the councils; desire the protection of its law officers, and take freely the blessings offered by the State, they should pay their taxes willingly. He who takes all and gives nothing can never be a good Christian nor a reliable citizen. Yet, even Christians must recog-nize the importance of having a higher court of appeal. Conscience controlled by the Spirit of God must ever be the final standard by which conduct is judged. We must render to Caesar the things that are Caesar's, and to God the things which belong to God. Good Christians will be ideal citizens; poor citizens will never be anything but un-reliable church members.

HOMILIES

Study No. 63

### WHOSE PENNY IS IT?

The problem of ownership is sometimes confusing. Can I own what I do not possess? Can I possess what is not mine? Some day these matters may become clear, but at the moment the issues are somewhat vague. I own a penny, but if I deface it, the Government has the right to prosecute me. The coin belongs to them, and has only been given to me on trust as a means of monetary communication. I possess a penny, but if I owe that to some other man, does the penny really belong to me? To keep what is not legally mine is to be a thief. Great moral issues appear to be at stake in the handling of all my money. The penny may be mine; but it may belong to the Government; and yet again, it may belong to anybody. Then whose penny is it? That answer can only be supplied after careful thought and conscientious examination. Probably these things were brought into bold relief when Jesus asked for a penny and pointing to the image upon its face, asked, "Whose image and superscription is this?" When the people replied stating it was that of Caesar, Christ replied, "Then give to Caesar that which is his, and render to God those things that belong to God." This was one of the wisest answers ever given by the Lord Jesus.

### God Never Desires More than His Own

It would be well if all men gave sober consideration to this simple fact. If we are asked to give anything to God, should we not first enquire if we have anything which we did not, directly or indirectly, receive from God? The coins used in a country must first be issued by that country. Even when we pay our taxes, we merely return to the Government that which they owned even before we saw it. Even if we appear to be extremely talented, whence came our talents? Even if we appear to have been most successful in business activities, from what source did we acquire the strength to perform our daily tasks? Long ago, the prophet Daniel calmly informed an arrogant king that "his very breath was in the hand of God." In the final analysis we cannot give to God more than He has first given to us, for without Him we should be nothing. Even life itself is the gift of God. We may train; educate; and develop life, but we cannot create it. Even radio, television and the marvels of modern science are but discoveries or applications of principles which have been existent in the universe for untold periods of time. Man is only justifiably great in that he is now discovering the amazing potentialities of the world in which he lives— but without his intellect, he would still be ignorant of these things.

### God Never Asks More than He Deserves

There is something exceedingly reasonable about all the requests of the Almighty. The problem of giving ceases to be a problem when it is viewed in its true perspective. The patriarchs were asked to contribute one tenth of their income; this was a tithe returned to the Lord as an expression of gratitude. Perhaps there were occasions when that tenth seemed an enormous amount, but the giver always remembered he was permitted to retain nine times as much for himself. Then experience taught that without the help of the Creator, probably there would have been no harvest whatsoever; there would have been nothing either for God or man. The God who had given so lavishly surely deserved a portion for Himself. If Jehovah had asked for nine-tenths, man might have accused Him of being selfish, but what was one-tenth, when God had given all ten-tenths? Furthermore, even God knows earthly rulers will make demands upon the purse of the believer, and wisely sanctions legal co-operation with them. How else can we bear witness to these men of the faith which thrills our hearts? We look at the Cross and confess we owe everything to God. We remember our fellow man, and realize that somehow we must impart to them the treasures of our knowledge. We cannot do this unless we win their confidence, and that will be impossible if we violate the accepted standards of law and order.

## God Never Takes More than He Gives

This may be closely allied to the first proposition, but investigation reveals there is a fine line of demarcation. It is true that God never desires more than His own, but the truth must be carried further. We cannot outgive the Lord. When we render our penny to Caesar, and our other treasures to God, immediately eternal machinery is set in motion which returns to us more than we ever gave to anybody. The sure way to become poor is to hold *in a closed hand* all we have; the only way to become eternally wealthy is to give away what we have. It is a law of life that in some miraculous way all we give to God is sent back to us with interest. God is a proud and a jealous God; He is no man's debtor. The Lord Jesus said, "Give, and it shall be given unto you, pressed down, shaken together, and running over." God has always been determined to prove the Saviour knew what He was talking about.

## God Never Promises More than He can Perform

This not only applies to money; possessions; materialistic things; this applies to events; to everything appertaining to life and conduct. When God promises to answer prayer; He is able to do so. When God promises to supply every need, we shall never want. When God promises never to leave us, loneliness should become a thing of the past. The only thing which should concern us is that we conscientiously render to Caesar the things which are his; to God the things that are God's. Those whom God can trust are surely destined for positions of even greater trust within the kingdom. Let us for a moment deliberately mix up the propositions and the following will emerge.

(1) *I owe it to God to be a good citizen.* It is the will of God that in some wonderful way other people should be brought into the divine family. As we were won, now we must be used to win others. We are to be evangelists in our own right, reaching out to our neighbours and friends; demonstrating to them the greatness of our salvation. Good Christians do not spend half their lives in liquor parlours; saints are not arrested for being drunk and disorderly. Young men and women whose hearts have been won for the Lord Jesus do not waste their lives in prostitution. Christians should be the best people in a com-

munity; in this way they win the respect of their neighbours; in this way they work and witness for God.

(2) *I owe it to myself to be a good steward.* I cannot afford to be mean with my money. God has given me brains to use! Christ said, "Occupy till I come," and I must therefore earnestly covet the best gifts so that my ministry will become increasingly effective. I cannot afford to give less than my best to God, for this is the sure way to reach higher heights of prosperity. This is the safe way of acquiring new tools to be used in the service of my Lord. If I wish to become wealthy, I must master the art of giving liberally to the work of God. If I desire greater happiness, then I must endeavour to make other people happy. If I want more liberty, I should try by all means within my power to become a bond-slave of Jesus Christ.

(3) *I owe it to my fellow man to be a faithful witness.* My testimony might bring a soul to Christ. Communities are made up of individuals, and whilst there may be disreputable and unpleasant characters, the fact remains that we are helped by many people. We sleep safely at night because police officers try to keep our streets safe. We enjoy a measure of national security because soldiers, whom we have never met, stand ready to resist aggression. We eat food because farmers grow it; trucks bring it to us; people process it, sell it, pack it. We read newspapers because somebody takes the time to gather news and print it. We listen to radio because someone supplies the programmes and makes the sets to bring them into our homes. We go to hospitals because doctors studied many years to help us in the realm of medicine; we send our children to schools because somebody has the patience to teach them. The world is made up of people inextricably woven together; we depend upon each other for so much, and thus it is the duty of every sincere man to help his neighbour. Christians have an even greater responsibility; they are able to share the riches of God in Christ; to be lights shining in the darkness. Jesus implied all this when He said, "Render to Caesar the things which are Caesar's and to God the things that are God's."

## SECTIONS THREE AND FOUR

### *Expository Notes on the Sadducees Question concerning the Resurrection*

**Then came to him certain of the Sadducees, which deny that there is any resurrection; and they asked him, Saying, Master, Moses wrote unto us, If any man's brother die, having a wife, and he die without children, that his brother should take his wife, and raise up seed unto his brother (vv. 27–28).**

The religious life of Israel was largely divided into two classes: the Pharisees and the Sadducees, but in many instances these groups were far removed from each other. For the most part the Pharisees were the theological element in the nation and remained content with any kind of government which upheld the ceremonial laws. The Sadducees were fewer in number but infinitely greater in political power. They were wealthy; they supplied the High Priestly rulers; they collaborated with Rome. It has been often said that whereas the Pharisees accepted the law and the prophets, the Sadducees refused to accept anything except the first five books of the Old Testament. Yet, when their pride or their pockets were touched, they refused to acknowledge some of the Mosaic law. The Pharisees were militant, and expressed their doctrines openly. They believed in the resurrection and also in the existence of angels. The Sadducees were sinister, ruthless, scheming. They denied both the resurrection and the existence of angels (Acts 23: 8).

Some of the Sadducees had probably been listening to the Lord's answers, and feeling they were quite capable of succeeding where others had failed, they awaited a suitable moment, and asked their question concerning the levirate marriage laws outlined by Moses. This title comes from the Latin *levir* which means *brother-in-law or husband's brother*. We do not know if this was being practised in New Testament times, but the law itself may be found in Deuteronomy 25: 5–10. "If brethren dwell together, and one of them die, and have no child, the wife of the dead shall not marry without unto a stranger: her husband's brother shall go in unto her, and take her to him to wife, and perform the duty of an husband's brother unto her . . . And if the man like not to take his brother's wife, then let his brother's wife go up to the gate unto the elders . . . Then the elders of his city shall call him, and speak unto him: and if he stand to it, and say, I like not to take her; Then shall his brother's wife come unto him in the presence of the elders, and loose his shoe from off his foot, and spit in his face, and shall answer and say, So shall it be done unto that man that will not build up his brother's house. And his name shall be called in Israel, the house of him that hath his shoe loosed." This was considered a great disgrace, and sometimes the offender was viewed with disdain and scorn. The Sadducees, who denied the resurrection, were aware of this old law, and had probably cited it in their speeches many times. This was a special argument; they were quite sure it would embarrass Jesus.

**There were therefore seven brethren: and the first took a wife and died without children. And the second took her to wife, and he died childless. And the third took her; and in like manner the seven also; and they**

left no children, and died. Last of all the woman died also. Therefore in the resurrection whose wife of them is she? for seven had her to wife (vv. 29-33).

It cannot be stated dogmatically that this never happened in Israel, but it is more probable the situation had been imagined to provide what appeared to be an insoluble problem. The Sadducees were capable of saying or doing anything to embarrass their enemies. They would probably smile and describe seven brothers fighting for possession of the one wife.

And Jesus answering said unto them, The children of this world marry, and are given in marriage: But they which shall be accounted worthy to obtain that world, and the resurrection from the dead, neither marry, nor are given in marriage: Neither shall they die any more: for they are equal unto the angels; and are the children of God, being the children of the resurrection (vv. 34-36).

The key statement in this passage is *"Neither shall they die* any more." To perpetuate the race, marriage was instituted as an honourable institution. Birth was the replacement of death. Unless babies were born to take the place of people who succumbed either to age or sickness, man would eventually disappear from the earth. Therefore marriage was a necessary ordinance commanded by God to meet a continuing need. There will be no death in the eternal state and therefore marriages and births will be unnecessary. There, the saints live for ever for they have become like the angels—that is they have become immortal. This cannot mean that they will be sexless. If saints are to have bodies like unto His glorious body; then as He retained His earthly body, and knew the tremendous change which had turned the mortal into the immortal, so also will Christians. The Lord's risen body was the same as that in which He was crucified, for it still retained the marks of the nails in His hands. Yet it had been changed; glorified; quickened; never to see death again. It follows that this procedure will be known in the resurrection. The ravages of time will be banished for ever, and mortal frames will be clothed with the radiant splendour of eternal youth. The disciples were able to recognise their Master; they had been able to recognize Moses and Elijah on the Mount of Transfiguration, therefore Christians will know each other in heaven. Nevertheless amidst conditions previously unknown, marriage and everything that goes with it will be unnecessary. There will be sources of happiness and deep fountains of satisfaction which were completely unexperienced during our earthly career. It is worthy of note that Jesus spoke about the necessity of being accounted worthy to attain to the resurrection. Obviously there must be some who will not be worthy; they remain in the grip of decay for ever. Here is wisdom; let him that hath ears, use them!

> Now that the dead are raised, even Moses shewed at the bush, when he called the Lord the God of Abraham, and the God of Isaac, and the God of Jacob. For he is not a God of the dead, but of the living: for all live unto him (vv. 37–38).

There may be those who consider this answer to be inadequate. They should remember that it completely silenced the questioners and gained the approbation of the scribes who had overheard the conversation. Even though we may not appreciate the full importance of this answer, at least, the people present at that time knew exactly what Christ meant to teach. A God who only rules over dead subjects might just as well be dead himself. A king whose kingdom only includes a graveyard can hardly be classed as a king—he is rather a lonely old man. To be a king, the ruler must have subjects over whom to reign. To be God, Jehovah must have living people to whom He can be a Father. Therefore when Moses declared God to be the God of the patriarchs, he affirmed they were still living. The final statement in this section is peculiar to Luke's narrative. Its meaning is somewhat obscure. Probably the Lord wished to state that in the sight of His Father all souls lived—cessation of existence was unknown. The Rev. C. H. Spurgeon was once asked if Christians would know each other in heaven. His answer deserves perpetuation. He replied, "Do you think we shall be greater fools up there than we are down here?"

> Then certain of the scribes answering said, Master, thou hast well said. And after that they durst not ask him any question at all. And he said unto them, How say they that Christ is David's son? And David himself saith in the book of Psalms, The Lord said unto my Lord, Sit thou on my right hand, Till I make thine enemies thy footstool. David therefore called him Lord, how is he then his son? (vv. 39–44).

These scribes in all probability belonged to the Pharisees. They were pleased that their opponents, the Sadducees, had been discomforted on the verbal field of battle. Yet as the Lord saw the complacent self-satisfaction spreading over their faces, He determined to address a question to them. It was the popular belief that some day, a mighty descendant of King David would establish an earthly kingdom of great power. The vision of world dominion was ever with some of the Jewish people, and each time they were subjected to a fresh indignity from the Romans, they fervently prayed that David's son would arrive soon. Quoting from Psalm 110: 1, the Lord asked how Messiah could be David's son when David himself addressed Him as Lord. Very much discussion has taken place around this statement, and often the most fantastic assertions have been made. There is no difficulty here, unless in our brilliant (!) stupidity we succeed in "straining at a gnat and swallowing a camel!" The Saviour was merely trying to impress upon His hearers that their conception of the Messiah was far too small; far too limited. The Messiah indisputably would be a descendant of David, *but He would be very much more.* If He were just a son of David, the great king of Israel would hardly have addressed him in terms ascribed to deity. Let us remember the earlier question asked by the rulers: "By what authority doest thou these things? or who is he that gave thee this authority?" The Lord was now supplying the answer. He was the Son of God; He had come from God. This was His authority, and this was the reason why David called him Lord. The Saviour claimed that David knew Him, and owned His Lordship. And if David had known this, they should also be willing to accept the truth.

**Then in the audience of all the people he said unto his disciples, Beware of the scribes, which desire to walk in long robes, and love greetings in the markets, and the highest seats in the synagogues, and the chief rooms at feasts; Which devour widows' houses, and for a shew make long prayers; the same shall receive greater damnation (vv. 45-47).**

Quoting from Hebrew literature, Barclay says, "Respect for a teacher should exceed respect for a father, for both father and son owe respect to a teacher. If a man's father and teacher have lost anything, the teacher's loss has the precedence, for a man's father only brought him into this world; his teacher, who taught him wisdom, brought him into the life of the world to come . . . If a man's father and teacher are carrying burdens, he must first help his teacher, and afterward his father. If his father and teacher are in captivity, he must first ransom his teacher, and afterward his father." These and many other fantastic claims were made by the leaders of whom Christ was speaking. They wore long flowing garments to advertise their piety; they expected to be greeted ostentatiously in the streets, and any seat short of the most prominent at feasts, they instantly rejected. They preyed upon susceptible women; they filled their purses with gifts which came from impressionable widows. They used their religion as a means by which to enjoy increasing comforts in life. They were hypocrites, and fully deserved the condemnatory words which Christ uttered in their presence. The Lord's final statement indicated degrees of punishment in the hereafter. (See also Matthew 10: 15; and Matthew 11: 22.)

HOMILIES

The Lord Jesus was the greatest Question Master of all time. It mattered not how difficult the problem, He supplied an answer, which confounded His critics; and displayed wisdom that could only have come from God.

## MEN WHO KNEW THE TRUTH

Study No. 64

*The men who read the truth and rejected it*

The Sadducees were known for their acceptance of the five books of Moses. They viewed other Old Testament writings with suspicion. Therefore whenever they read the Scripture, their meditations were based upon this special area of Mosaic law. It is said that men could read the sacred writings only to formulate questions to support their pet theories. They read, not to learn but to criticize, for in the final analysis they only believed what they wanted to believe. These men came to Christ to ask a question about the resurrection, but at the same time, they denied the fact which they mentioned. If there were no resurrection, why bother Christ with a hypothetical question? Unfortunately, some modern men emulate the example of the ancients. They recognize no law but that of self-will; they worship no God but one of their own creation. One wonders if anything could ever be done for such people. Surely this lends emphasis to the "greater damnation" mentioned in Luke 20: 47.

*The men who received the truth and rejoiced in it*

The Lord Jesus in replying to the statements of the Sadducees and the scribes mentioned two men; both of whom were held in high esteem by the nation: Moses, the great patriarch, and King David to whom Israel would always be indebted. It may be taken for granted that those who were listening to the Saviour were aware of the historical details pertaining to the lives of their two famous ancestors. Moses, the only authority acceptable to the Sadducees, had confessed that God was the God of the living. The strong underlying implications of the Lord's testimony suggested that either Moses had been mistaken, or the Sadducees were poor students! They who prided themselves most on their knowledge of the written law had failed to understand its message. Moses had seen the truth of survival and it had thrilled his soul. David, the great king of Israel; the composer of most of the immortal psalms, had also recognized the exalted nature of the Messiah. He had written sonnets about Him; had spoken about Him; and his testimony was clear and convincing. The coming One would be the Lord. How could the followers of David be so blind and stupid to reject what their honoured leader had so clearly revealed? Seeing the truth, he had rejoiced in it, and the melodies of his soul had been bequeathed to the world.

*The men who recognized the truth and renounced it*

"Master," said the scribes, "thou hast well said." They had singled out a part of the Lord's message, and because it did not offend them, admired it. The superficiality of their confession made it impossible for the Lord Jesus to accept their compliment. Their austerity garments did not condone the luxury of their living. Their humble demeanour did not adorn their demanding the highest seats at the feasts. Their embezzling of money which belonged to impressionable women did not enhance their claims to virtue. They liked to be thought good, but were unwilling to pay the price of virtue. They talked of the blessedness of the hereafter, but made sure they were enjoying the present. They urged women to give generously to God, but appointed themselves directors of God's bank. Probably these were the hardest of all men to reach with the Gospel. They had some knowledge of truth, could quote scripture, and even praise sermons. They attended the meetings and were very popular. They were expert fund-raisers but they seldom did anything without the plaudits of men. They never desired to be alone with God; they never offended any wealthy patron; they never occupied a prison cell with John the Baptist! They were expert at keeping out of trouble but somewhat reckless in their advance toward hell. This is precisely what Jesus meant when He said, "The same shall receive greater damnation."

# The Twenty-First Chapter of Luke

THEME: *The Signs of Christ's Return to Earth*

OUTLINE:
> I. The Lord's Pronouncement concerning Stewardship.
> Verses 1–4
> II. The Lord's Predictions concerning His Coming.
> Verses 5–36
> III. The Lord's Pattern concerning Service. Verses 37–38

SECTION ONE

*Expository Notes concerning the Widow's Mites*

And he looked up and saw the rich men casting their gifts into the treasury. And he saw also a certain poor widow casting in thither two mites. And he said, Of a truth I say unto you, that this poor widow hath cast in more than they all: For all these have of their abundance cast in unto the offerings of God; but she of her penury hath cast in all the living she had (vv. 1–4).

Major says, "In the second court of the temple, in the court of the women, were fixed thirteen chests, with inscriptions directing to what use the offerings in each were allotted. Into one of these the widow cast her two mites. This court was called 'The Treasury' (John 8: 20). These offerings were made at the three great feasts, to compound for tithes and dues, and to fulfil the precept, 'Thou shalt not appear empty before the Lord'" (Exodus 23: 15; Deuteronomy 16: 16). Furthermore, attached to these chests were chutes or devises into which the offerings were placed. These were fashioned in the shape of a trumpet; the narrow end was joined to the chest and the larger end with its open mouth pointed in the direction of worshippers. Something of the sort may be seen at American toll bridges, where automobile drivers, without leaving their cars, may throw their toll money into the chute which leads down into the chest, and from which the "go-ahead" signal is controlled. These containers in the temple were sometimes called "the Trumpets," the name being derived from the shape of the receptacles.

After His altercations with the Sadducees and scribes, the Lord was weary, and sitting near the treasury, placed His head into His hands. We do not know for what length of time He remained in this position, but ultimately, looking up, He saw the rich men casting gifts into the money chests. Then He became aware of the approach of a widow woman. Slowly she went to the nearest box and dropped two *lepta* —two small copper coins called mites, into the opening. Then quietly, she went away. The coins were the smallest in use at that time and represented a very meagre sum of money. Mark 12: 42 states the two mites were equal to one farthing, but in modern currency this would be worth about one-half of a farthing (British) or one-eighth of a cent (American). The observation of F. L. Godet is singularly beautiful: "This incident witnessed by Jesus at such a time, resembles a flower which He comes upon all at once in the desert of official devotion, the sight and perfume of which make Him leap for joy."

When the Lord declared she had cast in more than all the other donors, He indicated that gifts to God are assessed not by their monetary worth but by the sacrifice made by the worshipper. There are two Greek words which are very much alike. *Hustereesis* means *want* or *poverty; Hustereema* means *deficiency* or *that which is lacking*. It is the second word that is used in this account. Jesus said, ". . . she of her deficiency, hath cast in all the living she had." This means the poor woman did not have enough money to buy food for the day's meal. She was probably living "a hand to mouth" existence, gleaning a little here and there, and striving always to earn a few coins to purchase supplies. At the time of her gift, she probably had to choose between food for her body or satisfaction for her soul. She needed sustenance but she wanted peace. It was not difficult to make a choice; she took all she had and gladly gave it to the Lord. And the Saviour saw her, and loved her. We do not even begin to give to God, or to anyone else, unless the act of giving means sacrifice. Unless first of all we have to do without something we really want, then our gift is not a true gift.

Preachers might like to consider the following homiletical suggestions. (1) *He saw*. That widow woman might have had the shock of her life had she known she was being watched. She might have been ashamed for anyone to know how small her gift had been. She knew God would understand, but had no confidence others would. Perhaps she looked around to see if other people were busy elsewhere, and thinking no one was watching, made her contribution. But Jesus saw the sacrifice—He always does. (2) *He knew*. Maybe this suggests a problem. How did He know the value of the coins; how did He understand that she was giving everything she possessed? We answer with another question—Is there anything He does not know? (3) *He assessed.* "This poor widow has cast in more than they all." The financiers would have disputed His findings; the wealthy Pharisees would have argued fiercely that He was mistaken, nevertheless God has His own computors; He measures gifts by sacrifice, and sometimes the results are astonishing. (4) *He appreciated.* The Lord was never slow to recognize true worth, and since " . . . the eyes of the Lord run to and fro throughout the whole earth, to shew himself strong in the behalf of them whose heart is perfect toward him," there is reason to believe that later that day, somehow, somewhere, the Lord gave to her the best meal she had received all that week. See II Chronicles 16: 9.

## SECTION TWO

### *Expository Notes on Christ's Predictions of the Future*

**And as some spake of the temple, how it was adorned with goodly stones and gifts, he said, As for these things which ye behold, the days will come, in the which there shall not be left one stone upon another, that shall not be thrown down (vv. 5–6).**

It is not easy to appreciate fully the unsurpassed magnificence of the temple as it was at this time. Herod had beautified it with a great golden vine, and it has been said that some of the clusters of grapes hanging from the walls were as tall as a man. Throughout the centuries the pious in Israel had revered the sacred place and their gifts had helped to beautify the house of God. Josephus, the Jewish historian, to whom we owe so much, went to great lengths to describe the scintillating beauty of this sacred edifice. At section five, book five of *The Wars of the Jews*, he has written, "The outward face of the temple in its front wanted nothing that was likely to surprise either men's minds or their eyes, for it was covered all over with plates of gold of great weight, and, at the first rising of the sun, reflected back a very fiery splendour, and made those who forced themselves to look upon it to turn their eyes away, just as they would have done at the sun's own rays. But the temple appeared to strangers, when they were at a distance, like a mountain covered with snow, for as to those parts of it that were not gilt, they were exceeding white." The temple pillars were columns of white marble forty feet in height, and each one was made from a single block of stone. The wealth of the world had been brought to this great sanctuary; its jewels, treasures, and gold ornaments beggared description. Naturally the Jewish people were intensely proud of their temple, but when Jesus overheard their conversation regarding the place, He shocked them by predicting it would be levelled to the ground.

And they asked him, saying, Master, but when shall these things be? and what sign will there be when these things shall come to pass? And he said, Take heed that ye be not deceived; for many shall come in my name, saying, I am Christ; and the time draweth near: go ye not after them. But when ye shall hear of wars and commotions, be not terrified, for these things must first come to pass; but the end is not yet. Then said he unto them, Nation shall rise against nation, and kingdom against kingdom: And great earthquakes shall be in diverse places, and famines, and pestilences; and fearful sights and great signs shall there be from heaven. But before all these, they shall lay their hands on you, and persecute you, delivering you up to the synagogue, and into prisons, being brought before kings and rulers for my name's sake. And it shall turn to you for a testimony (vv. 7-13).

This is not an easy scripture to interpret. It should be remembered the Lord was able to scan the future; to see at a glance things which would take centuries to unfold. Some of His predictions have yet to be fulfilled, and this fact has caused confusion. The primary interpretation of these verses indisputably belongs to the period relating to the destruction of the temple in A.D. 70. The Lord was giving warning of the terrible times soon to come upon the land, and was preparing His followers for the greatest testing they would ever undergo. History makes no mention of false Messiahs prior to the fall of the temple, but that is not conclusive evidence there were no such men. Certain leaders attracted many people, and in later years it was necessary for John to utter stern warnings against men of that kind. As great political upheavals took place, rumours began to circulate, and when to all this were added the terrible famine which took place during the reign of Claudius, and the devastating earthquake which destroyed Laodicea, it is not difficult to understand why Christians might have been terrified.

It is possible that when the Lord referred to signs from heaven, He might have meant eclipses, falling meteors, or even devastating storms. Nevertheless these signs might have been the result of the supernatural. Ryle quoting Bishop Pearce says: "Josephus has given us a very particular account of the prodigies of this kind which preceded the destruction of Jerusalem. He speaks of a flaming sword seen over the city, and of a comet which appeared there for a twelve-month. He mentions a light, which for the space of half an hour, shone so bright in the night between the temple and the altar, that it seemed as if it were noonday. He takes notice also of what eyewitnesses had related to him, that chariots and armed troops were seen fighting in the sky upon a certain day. He adds, that on the day of Pentecost, when the priests entered into the inner temple, they heard a great noisé and voice as of a multitude, crying out, 'Let us depart hence.'

The substance of this account is also given by Tacitus the Roman historian." (*Ryle's Expository Thoughts on the Gospel. Luke*, p. 365.) Whether or not this account be authentic, to say the least, it is extremely interesting in view of the fact that Christ predicted strange sights in the heavens.

It is known that when the Christians were accused before the rulers, former friends and even members of their own families bore testimony against them. There is nothing surprising in this for under the Nazi regime, the family life of Germany was disrupted when misguided members of households helped to send their brothers and sisters to the concentration camps. The Lord urged that these heart-breaking conditions be met with fortitude, for even in their sorrow, the saints would be presented with the opportunity to witness to the Truth. The fulfilment of the Lord's predictions would be a testimony to their own souls; the patience with which they endured their tribulations would be a testimony to their oppressors.

> Settle it therefore in your hearts, not to meditate before what ye shall answer: For I will give you a mouth and wisdom, which all your adversaries shall not be able to gainsay nor resist. And ye shall be betrayed both by parents, and brethren, and kinsfolk, and friends; and some of you shall they cause to be put to death. And ye shall be hated of all men for my name's sake. But there shall not an hair of your head perish. In your patience, possess ye your souls (vv. 14–19).

Verses 16 and 18 appear to be at variance. If some of the disciples were to be slain, how could it be said that not one hair of their heads would perish? The Lord surely was indicating that whilst the outward man would perish, the inward man would be renewed day by day. Although Satan might win a temporary battle, the war would be won by God. Some Christian soldiers would die on the battlefield, but in a deeper sense none would suffer irreparable loss for they rested in the hand of God. With this assurance filling their souls they were not to be worried about anything. Throughout times of betrayal, God would be faithful; He would be their refuge and strength. When testimony was needed, the Holy Spirit would suggest the words to be uttered, and if they were called to pass through the valley of the shadow of death, they would not be alone, for God would lead them out of the shadows into the eternal sunlight of a new world.

> And when ye shall see Jerusalem compassed with armies, then know that the desolation thereof is nigh. Then let them which are in Judea flee to the mountains; and let them which are in the midst of it depart out; and let not them that are in the countries enter thereinto. For these be the days of vengeance, that all things which are written may be

fulfilled. But woe unto them that are with child, and to them that give suck in those days! for there shall be great distress in the land, and wrath upon the people. And they shall fall by the edge of the sword, and shall be led away captive into all nations: and Jerusalem shall be trodden down of the Gentiles, until the times of the Gentiles be fulfilled (vv. 20–24).

There is no need to expound this prediction; it is self-explanatory. It is a known fact that the majority of the Jerusalem Christians were spared the slaughter which fell upon their kinsmen. Remembering the Master's warning, and recognizing the signs He had mentioned, they left the city and fled across the Jordan to the city of Pella, where they found sanctuary. Later, when the horrible siege of Jerusalem came to an end, they obtained permission to live in some of the outlying parts of their ruined city. The Christian community continued there until the second century when once again a Jewish insurrection began. Since that time the city of Jerusalem, for the most part, has remained under Gentile domination, and today the Mosque of Omaar stands where once stood the magnificent temple. After the destruction of the sanctuary in A.D. 70, no living Jew was left in the city. The wounded, the sick, the aged that had survived the onslaught were mercilessly put to death; 97,000 young men who remained alive, were taken into captivity. Thus was the prediction of Jesus literally fulfilled; thus came to an end one of the darkest chapters in Israel's history. The reference to the "times of the Gentiles" deserves special consideration. Dark as the outlook appeared to be; bleak as was the threatening future, the Lord clearly indicated there would be a limit to the overlordship of the Gentiles; their times would terminate; Israel would be back in her own land. That closing detail in the remarkable prophecy has already been partially fulfilled.

And there shall be signs in the sun, and in the moon, and in the stars; and upon the earth distress of nations, with perplexity; the sea and the waves roaring. Men's hearts failing them for fear, and for looking after those things which are coming on the earth: for the powers of heaven shall be shaken. And then shall they see the Son of man coming in a cloud with power and great glory. And when these things begin to come to pass, then look up, and lift up your heads; for your redemption draweth nigh (vv. 25–28).

It will be recognized instantly that Christ has now extended His message. Whatever happened in A.D. 70, we know that Jesus did not come in a cloud with power and great glory. Having outlined the events to take place when Jersualem fell, the Saviour proceeded to describe others to take place at the end of this age. The distressing conditions known in the first century were to be foreshadowings of things to take place before the return of Christ in glory. Throughout the Bible, the seas are emblematical of the nations; the sun, moon, and stars are symbols describing rulers, but the teaching under consideration can hardly be allegorical. The things which Christ predicted were literally fulfilled; how then can we be justified in assuming this part of the prediction to be allegorical when the other was literal? The scripture suggests that at the end of the age, this planet will show signs of breaking up. "Like a ship creaking in every timber at the moment of its going to pieces, the globe which we inhabit, and our whole solar system, shall undergo unusual commotions" (Godet). Then, as if to rescue a planet from complete destruction, the Lord Jesus comes from heaven. His appearing will be preceded by recognizable signs. As the fall of Jerusalem was preceded by signs which warned the Christians to escape, so the latter day signs will warn of the imminent return of the Lord. When these become visible, Christians are enjoined to look up for their redemption will be drawing near. Redemption applies both to soul and body; we are not only saved from the guilt and penalty of sin; we are to be delivered eternally from its presence. Through faith in Christ, man's soul is delivered now; when Christ returns, even his body will be changed in a moment, in the twinkling of an eye. Then the last taint of sin will be banished from his being. Christians are therefore urged to lift up their heads, because the final phase of their redemption is about to be accomplished.

And he spake to them a parable; Behold the fig tree, and all the trees; When they now shoot forth, ye see and know of your own selves that summer is now nigh at hand. So likewise ye, when ye see these things come to pass, know ye that the kingdom of God is nigh at hand. Verily I say unto you, This generation shall not pass away, till all be fulfilled. Heaven and earth shall pass away: but my words shall not pass away (vv. 29-33).

Some teachers make the fig tree mean the Jewish nation, and the other trees the Gentile nations, but this interpretation is not acceptable. Christ was merely drawing attention to the fact that signs of spring are easily recognized. Similarly the signs of the approaching return of Christ should be discernible to all who look for the Master's appearing. There is, however, some difficulty in stating precisely the meaning of "this generation." Probably the Lord was thinking of the Jewish nation; and indicating that in spite of persecution, they would still be present to see the Lord's glory. It is interesting to notice that the Greek word here translated *generation* has been translated *nation* in Philippians 2: 15. There is something triumphant about the Saviour's final utterance. He does not speak of God's word—He speaks of His own word, and signifies that although the cosmic system would eventually pass away, His own statements would remain indestructible. This was a claim to deity, and how certain clerics say Jesus was only a man is something hard to understand.

> And take heed to yourselves, lest at any time your hearts be over-charged with surfeiting, and drunkenness, and cares of this life, and so that day come upon you unawares. For as a snare shall it come upon all them that dwell on the face of the whole earth. Watch ye therefore, and pray always, that ye may be accounted worthy to escape all these things that shall come to pass, and to stand before the Son of man (vv. 34–36).

Abruptly, the Lord changed His theme. The disciples were urged never to lose sight of the fact that He would return. It would not be enough to believe the doctrine; they should be ready to greet the Lord when He arrived. Strength of faith should formulate dependable character. The coming of Christ would bring disaster to many people throughout the earth, but Christians, waiting for their Lord, should be ready, and unashamed to stand in His presence. Verse 36 is thought-provoking, and to say the least, it is not difficult to understand why some teachers insist that unless Christians are found worthy; that is, unless they are truly consecrated, they will not escape the tribulation which must spread through the earth. This school of thought advocates a "partial rapture," insisting that only the truly sanctified among the church will attain unto the resurrection of the just (I Thessalonians 4: 16–18). This theme has been debated for decades, and sometimes the bitterness of the argument proved the contestants were in danger themselves! Why argue on an obscure point of doctrine. It is better to strive *to be worthy*; then at least we shall be certain we shall not be found wanting. See the homily at the end of the next section.

## SECTION THREE

### *Expository Notes on the Daily Custom of Jesus*

> And in the day time, he was teaching in the temple; and at night he went out, and abode in the mount that is called the mount of Olives. And all the people came early in the morning to him in the temple, for to hear him (vv. 37–38).

The climax to this chapter is most fitting. The Lord had previously warned His followers about the necessity for watching and praying; here, He sets the example. His days of tribulation were at hand; therefore, to meet them victoriously, He retired to Olivet where in communion with God, He found the strength which carried Him through the day to follow.

There has been discussion about the place of His nightly sojourn. Luke says, ". . . and at night he went out, and abode in the mount that is called the mount of Olives." Matthew 21: 17 says: "And he left them, and went out of the city into Bethany; and lodged there." There is no conclusive evidence that this refers to the same occasion, but J. C. Ryle, quoting Major, says: ". . . the expression, 'abode in the mount of Olives' means, 'at Bethany, because it was a town on the mount of Olives.' Comparison with the text in Matthew makes this highly probable. It is not necessary to suppose that our Lord lodged in the open air." Ryle may be correct, but on the other hand he may not. The Greek word translated *lodged* is *eelizeto*; it is derived from *aulizomai* and does not give that meaning. Thayer says it means: *to lodge in the courtyard, especially at night; of flocks and shepherds* (2) *to pass the night in the open air, bivouac.* If the Lord, as has been suggested, stayed in Bethany, He would doubtless have stayed with His friends, and would have found shelter within their home. This would not be in harmony with the text. Possibly, the Lord stayed alone on the hill, but when the dawn began to spread across the sky, He made His way to the well-known home to breakfast with those He loved. This would be in keeping with His custom, and to some degree at least, would illustrate the necessity of fleeing to the mountains when danger threatened to overwhelm the people of God. Beneath the stars, the Lord communed with His Father; amidst the solitude He drank of the eternal springs of divine fellowship, and refreshed, the following morning returned to teach in the temple. Thus did He set the example that all must follow. Satan does not mind how hard we work for God as long as that service is ineffective. The evil one will not even protest if we work ourselves to death proclaiming the Gospel as long as our words never remain in the minds of the audience. It is the quiet time in the hillside that Satan fears, for he knows that if we meet with God in the holy place, our service in the valley will be invincible.

## HOMILIES

Study No. 65

### MEN THAT WAIT FOR THEIR LORD

"Let your loins be girded about, and your lights burning; And ye yourselves like unto men that wait for their Lord, when he will return from the wedding, that when he cometh and knocketh, they may open unto him immediately. Blessed are those servants, whom the Lord when he cometh shall find watching . . ." (Luke 12: 35–37.) The greater part of the twenty-first chapter of Luke's gospel is filled with startling predictions of the Lord's return. The account makes exciting, and occasionally even frightening reading, for the author has gone into great detail to describe the things to take place in the heavens and upon the earth. There is danger that in reading these sensational predictions, we might fail to see the unfolding of progressive truth concerning the people of God. Of equal importance with the coming of Christ is the effort that Christians must make to be ready to welcome Him. Viewed from this angle, Luke's narrative divides into four sections.

## My Testimony of Christ

Jesus said, "Settle it therefore in your hearts, not to meditate before what ye shall answer; For I will give you a mouth and wisdom, which all your adversaries shall not be able to gainsay nor resist" (Luke 21: 14–15). The Saviour warned His followers they would be brought before magistrates; that even members of their families would testify against them. There would be suffering, and in some instances even death for the Christian. Charges and counter-charges would be made against them, and if the saint permitted these things to harass his mind, there would be many sleepless nights. Therefore Christ urged His follower not to worry; not to plan ceaselessly what defence to offer; what things to say. They were told to remain in a state of receptivity; to listen carefully for the unmistakable whispers which would come from God. They would be given instructions; they would know when to give their testimony. They should be ready to speak as soon as the Lord gave such guidance. How else could their captors hear the matchless story of Grace? Each prisoner would become a preacher; each cell a challenge. History was made in some of the Roman court-rooms. There were times when the accused became exceedingly eloquent; when even hired lawyers failed to refute the amazing testimony of the prisoners. And as it was, so must it be. We wait for the coming of our Lord; the future might bring trials to many members of the family of God. We must remain calm and be ready whenever the Lord directs, to give testimony to the faithfulness of God. We must never be ashamed; we should never be afraid.

## My Confidence In Christ

"And ye shall be hated of all men for my name's sake. But there shall not an hair of your head perish. In your patience possess ye your souls" (Luke 21: 17–19). There is a limit to what the enemy can do. Three young Hebrews discovered this for they looked at King Nebuchadnezzar and said, ". . . we are not careful to answer thee . . . If it be so, our God whom we serve is able to deliver us from the burning fiery furnace, *AND HE WILL DELIVER US OUT OF THINE HAND, O KING.* But if not, be it known unto thee . . . we will not serve thy gods, nor worship the golden image which thou hast set up" (Daniel 3: 16–18). Those young men obviously differentiated between their souls and bodies. They believed God could actually deliver them from the fire, but in any case, even though they died in the furnace, they would at least be delivered from the power of the king. The great fire would only sever the fleshly bonds which tied them to earth. Those Hebrews were a fitting type of the faithful who will bear testimony during the closing days of this age. We journey to mansions in the sky; our confidence is in God. Even though our outward man perish, the inner will be renewed day by day, and in that sense, not one hair of our heads can be hurt. Such confidence remains unshaken, for "perfect love casteth out fear."

## My Desire for Christ

"And then shall they see the Son of man coming in a cloud with power and great glory. And when these things begin to come to pass, then look up; for your redemption draweth nigh" (Luke 21: 27–28). The saints look for their Lord, not only because His coming promises deliverance from a ruthless enemy, but because they desire to be for ever with the Lord. Then the dreams of a lifetime will be realized; then all that was purchased through the precious blood of Christ will become a reality. Salvation lifts the sinner from the depths of sin to the heights of unprecedented glory. "Beloved," said John, "now are we the sons of God, and it doth not yet appear what we shall be, but we know that when he shall appear, we shall be like him, for we shall see him as he is" (I John 3: 2). The cross brought to us pardon; the indwelling Holy Spirit brings to us *power,* but the coming of the Saviour will deliver from the very *presence* of sin. Then in the fullest possible sense, our redemption will reach absolute perfection. It is hardly possible to understand all this will mean, but when the signs of Christ's appearing become visible, we can lift up our heads with eager anticipation knowing God's plans will be nearing fulfilment.

## My Likeness to Christ

John was correct when he said, "And every man that hath this hope in him purifieth himself, even as he is pure" (I John 3: 3). Luke records that Jesus said, "And take heed to yourselves, lest at any time your hearts be overcharged with surfeiting, and drunkenness, and cares of this life, and so that day come upon you unawares . . . Watch ye therefore, and pray always, that ye may be accounted worthy to escape all these things that shall come upon the earth, and to stand before the Son of man" (Luke 21 : 34–36). Sound doctrine is nothing unless it leads to sound living. The man who proclaims one thing and practises the other is a sham, a humbug, a hypocrite. All Christians must stand before the judgment seat of Christ, but Paul speaks of some who will be ashamed before Him at His coming. There has been much disputing as to whether or not the saints will go through the tribulation. Some affirm the church, or part of the church will be caught away to meet the Lord in the air; others state this is conditional; that the unfaithful must reap the reward of carnality, and will be judged as unworthy. Perhaps there is immature thinking on both sides of the argument. We should strive to be worthy NOT BECAUSE WE DESIRE TO ESCAPE ANYTHING, but because we yearn to be like Christ. If it were necessary, we should prefer to be in tremendous pain AND BE LIKE CHRIST, than to escape the pain and remain unlike Him. It is all a matter of love. If we adore Him truly, everything else falls into its proper place.

# The Twenty-Second Chapter of Luke

THEME: *The Events Leading to the Condemnation of Jesus*

OUTLINE:

SECTION ONE

*Expository Notes on the Treachery of Judas*

**Now the feast of unleavened bread drew nigh, which is called the Passover. And the chief priests and scribes sought how they might kill him; for they feared the people. Then entered Satan into Judas surnamed Iscariot, being of the number of the twelve. And he went his way and communed with the chief priests and captains, how he might betray him unto them. And they were glad, and covenanted to give him money. And he promised, and sought opportunity to betray him unto them in the absence of the multitude (vv. 1-6).**

Strictly speaking the Passover and the Feast of Unleavened Bread were not one and the same thing. The Passover, the time when the lamb was slain to commemorate the deliverance of the nation from the bondage of Egypt, began on the 15th day of Nisan. The second feast followed immediately afterward and lasted for one week. Because of their close proximity to each other, in the thinking of Israel they were classed as one, for any man attending the one feast would be able to observe the other which followed immediately. This time of the year was always regarded with awe and reverence, and very elaborate preparations were made for the Passover. Multitudes of visitors from near and far would be making their way toward Jerusalem, and the entire country would feel the impact of the great event to take place in the city of God. Pilgrims, rich and poor, walking along the roads would create the atmosphere of excitement and expectation, but weeks before these began to arrive, intense activity throughout the land announced the Feast of the Lord was soon to take place. Signposts were erected; and graves were painted white so that no traveller would be defiled through accidental contact with a tomb. Such were the requirements of the Mosaic law.

Barclay has a thought-provoking paragraph in his delightful little book, *The Daily Study Bible*. At page 274, he says:" . . . To this day, when Jews keep the Passover, in every land they pray that they may keep it next year in Jerusalem. Because of this, vast numbers came to Jerusalem at the Passover time. Cestius was governor of Palestine in the time of Nero, and Nero tended to belittle the importance of the Jewish faith. To convince Nero of it, Cestius took a census of the lambs slain at one particular Passover time. Josephus tells us that the number was 256,500. Now the law laid it down that the minimum number for a Passover celebration was 10. And that means that on that occasion, if these figures are correct, there must have been more than *two million, seven hundred thousand* pilgrims to the Passover . . ."

When the comparatively small size of the country is considered; and the limitations of the city borne in mind, these figures are astonishing. The city must have been crammed with people; the accommodation taxed to the limit, and thousands of people were forced to seek lodgings in the nearby villages. Many probably camped along the hills of Olivet. The presence of Jesus would fan to fever heat the excitement of the crowd, and as the religious feelings of the congregations were stirred, any attempt to arrest Him could easily have resulted in rioting. It was this fact which made the rulers of the nation exercise extreme caution. When one of the disciples offered to assist, the chief priests could hardly believe their eyes and ears. This was too good to be true; their problems were solved, for if one of the disciples would bear testimony against the Carpenter, defence would be impossible. John 13: 2 suggests Satan first made the suggestion to Judas, and that afterward (John 13: 27), when Judas had yielded, Satan entered into him. It seems clear from the text that Satan cannot control anyone until that individual indicates a willingness to co-operate. The Devil can only make the suggestion that we do certain things; but when we yield, he takes possession and drives us to destruction. Calvin said, "Though Satan drives us every day to crime, and feigns in us, when he hurries us into a course of extraordinary wickedness; yet he is said to enter into the reprobate when he takes possession of all his senses, overthrows the fear of God, extinguishes the light of reason, and destroys every feeling of shame."

The agreed price of betrayal was thirty pieces of silver; the price of a slave. Our finite minds cannot comprehend this act of stupidity. He

Who had dispensed healing to the nation; He Who had turned night to day and storms to calm, was valued at the price of a slave in the market place. Why did Judas do this awful thing? It has been suggested that this was the despairing act of a patriot who firmly believed in the Messianic authority of Jesus; that Judas was trying to force his Messiah to take action. The New Testament does not support this interpretation. Judas was a man who hoped for pre-eminence in the Messianic kingdom; he followed Jesus because by so doing he hoped to realize his greatest ambitions. Then when the Lord failed to live up to his expectations, Judas decided it was time he cut his losses! Even thirty pieces of silver would be better than nothing—and probably reasoning that if Jesus were not to be the Messiah, His death would not be a loss anyhow, he went to the priests to offer assistance. "And they were delighted and pledged to give him money." (*The Amplified New Testament.*)

## HOMILIES

Study No. 66

### JUDAS THE GAMBLER

The account of the treachery of Judas Iscariot is the most tragic story in history. It is beyond comprehension that a man who had occupied a position of trust and friendship in the disciple band, should ultimately betray his Leader. Many questions have been asked concerning this pathetic episode; but one thing has become evident. It is that the complete story of Judas is summed up in the opening statement of Luke 22: 4, "And he went *his* way." It is indeed most doubtful whether he ever went any other way.

### The Way of Glory

"And Jesus ordained twelve, that they should be with him, and that he might send them forth to preach. Simon . . . James . . . and Judas Iscariot" (Mark 3: 14–19). The foreknowledge of God does not change the responsibility of man. Even though Christ knew what would take place, Judas of his own volition deliberately betrayed the Master. To him the call of Christ had been irresistible. It opened vistas of unprecedented possibilities. If this new leader were to be the Messiah, then the kingdom was at hand, and every man in the nation would have welcomed a place at the side of the King. Eagerly anticipating the splendour of a glorious future, Judas left his friends and followed the Saviour. There is reason to believe he worked as hard as anyone else in the days of preaching that followed. This was indeed *his own way*, and it is easy to imagine how fervently he proclaimed his message to all who would stop and listen.

## The Way of Greed

Many years later, when the apostle John described the criticisms made by Judas concerning Mary's gift of ointment, he wrote, "Then saith one of his disciples, Judas Iscariot, Simon's son, which should betray him; Why was not this ointment sold for three hundred pence, and given to the poor? This he said, not that he cared for the poor; but because he was a thief, and had the bag, and bare what was put therein" (John 12: 4–6). There had been times when the disciples were puzzled by the shortage of money. It was inconceivable that one of their number should steal from the common fund; and yet . . . ? Long afterward they remembered, and understood. "Judas went *his* way." It was a way of self-pleasing. Probably he argued with himself that his position as treasurer deserved remuneration. He therefore helped himself to money which was not his. Ultimately it was this love of gain which wrecked his soul. As the end of Christ's pilgrimage approached, Judas became increasingly suspicious that something had gone wrong. The promised kingdom seemed to be receding; the Master had grown sad and thoughtful; the enemies were becoming jubilant. Judas noted all these things, and realized Christ's way and his own were not identical paths. When the Lord failed to take advantage of the delirious welcome afforded by the crowd as He rode into Jerusalem, Judas knew that tragedy loomed on the horizon.

## The Way of Guilt

At an eastern feast, the offering of a sop by the host is recognized as a mark of esteem. Almost the last thing Jesus did for Judas was to offer friendship. Judas replied with the traitor-kiss. When the betrayer felt the coins in his hand, he smiled. They were better than nothing! Yes, he was getting out whilst he was able! He went *his own way*. Poor man! With remorse playing havoc with his conscience; with the coins rudely scattered over the floor; with his hopes and plans completely broken, a poor tormented man, he went out to commit suicide. And of his final destiny there can be no doubt. Jesus prayed and said, ". . . those that thou gavest me I have kept, and none of them is lost, but the son of perdition; that the scripture might be fulfilled" (John 17: 12). Certain teachers have declared that Judas was Satan's imitation of the Son of God. They have drawn attention to the fact that the same title—"The son of perdition" is also used of the antichrist (II Thessalonians 2: 3). Mention has also been made that of Judas alone it is said, ". . . from which Judas by transgression fell, *that he might go to his own place"* (Acts 1: 25). Here are great mysteries; but one thing is certainly clear. Judas had staked his all; he was a reckless gambler. He lost because he had not the ability to see God's way was better than his own. (Taken from the Author's book, *Bible Pinnacles*, pp. 113–114.)

SECTION TWO

*Expository Notes on the Commission given to Peter and John*

> Then came the day of unleavened bread, when the passover must be killed. And he sent Peter and John, saying, Go and prepare us the passover, that we may eat. And they said unto him, Where wilt thou that we prepare? And he said unto them, Behold when ye are entered into the city, there shall a man meet you, bearing a pitcher of water; follow him into the house where he entereth in (vv. 7–10).

This is a passage of scripture about which many questions have been asked. Was it through His amazing foreknowledge that Jesus was able to predict there would be a man carrying a pitcher of water, or was this the result of very careful planning? Was the man in whose home the passover was celebrated a follower of Jesus, or was he an ordinary citizen willing to accommodate pilgrims at the feast? Throughout the centuries, these and other questions have engaged the minds of the theologians. Perhaps there is room for such questions, but after careful thought, it surely becomes clear this episode was not something that happened by chance. Judas had already promised to find a suitable time and place for the act of betrayal. The rulers considered it would be necessary to avoid publicity, and if they could have taken Jesus within the confines of some home, the arrest might have taken place even before the neighbours were aware of it. Judas was determined to find a quiet place in which to do his dastardly work, but equally as determined was the Lord that this should not take place until He had eaten the passover. It would not be easy to find a home, for there were great numbers of people seeking accommodation. Probably every home in and near the city had been engaged for that same purpose. Furthermore, it must be remembered that each householder also wished to celebrate passover. Therefore a suitable house would be almost impossible to obtain.

It seems probable then that Jesus arranged with one of His friends that the feast should be celebrated at his home. Furthermore, since men do not carry pitchers in the East—when they carry water, they invariably carry it in water skins—for pitchers are only carried by women, this must have been a pre-arranged signal by which the man could be recognized in a crowd of people. Probably he had been instructed to be at a certain place at a specific time when the disciples would be looking for their guide. Thus even Judas would be unaware of the home in which the passover was to be celebrated. He would therefore be unable to carry information to the rulers. Thus did Jesus make sure that the last hours with His disciples would remain undisturbed. There has been much speculation concerning the identity of the stranger. That he knew the Master, none can doubt; that he responded with enthusiasm is also obvious. It has been suggested he was probably the father of John Mark; that his home was destined to become famous as a place where Christians congregated. See Acts 12: 12. This may well be true.

> And ye shall say unto the good man of the house, The Master saith unto thee, Where is the guest-chamber, where I shall eat the passover with my disciples? And he shall shew you a large upper room furnished; there make ready. And they went, and found as he had said unto them: and they made ready the passover (vv. 11-13).

Eastern homes in the days of Jesus were for the most part divided into two sections. There were two rooms, one larger than the other, and standing as it were above it. As one entered into the larger, lower room, one would see at the one end an elevated room, entrance to which was gained by climbing a few steps. Sometimes, this was so constructed that it was almost as another dwelling; the entrance was gained from an external door. On the other hand, the archaeologists have uncovered the remains of ancient dwellings which stood around an open court. Above, on what we would call *a terrace* or *landing*, were second-storey rooms. Some of these may still be seen in the ruins of Pompeii. The house into which the disciples were led was one of these two types. Following the host into the lower room, Peter and John delivered their message, and were thereupon taken to the large upper room, which according to previous instructions was already furnished with the necessary articles to enable a company of men to observe the passover.

We do not know if any specific instructions regarding details had been given to the disciples; this after all was the passover, and there is reason to believe the owner of the house, helped by his visitors, prepared according to custom. Concerning the necessary preparation and order of service used at such times, Godet says: *"First Step.* After prayer, the father of the house sent round a cup full of wine (according to others, each one had his own cup) with this invocation, 'Blessed be thou, O Lord our God, King of the world, who hast created the fruit of the vine.' Next there were passed from one to the other the bitter herbs (a kind of salad) which recalled to mind the sufferings of the Egyptian bondage. These were eaten after being dipped in a reddish sauce (charoseth), made of almonds, nuts, figs, and other fruits; commemorating, it is said, by its colour the hard labour of brick making, imposed on the Israelites, and by its taste, the divine alleviations which Jehovah mingles with the miseries of His people. *Second Step.* The father circulates a second cup, and then explains, probably in a more or less liturgical form, the meaning of the feast, and of the rites by which it is distinguished. *Third Step.* The father takes two unleavened loaves (cakes), breaks one of them, and places the pieces of it on the other. Then uttering a thanksgiving, he takes one of the pieces, dips it in the sauce, and eats it, taking with it a piece of the Paschal lamb, along with bitter herbs. Each one follows his example. This is the feast properly so called. The lamb forms the principal dish. The conversation is free. It closes with the distribution of a third cup, called the cup of blessing, because it was accompanied with the giving of thanks by the father of the house. *Fourth Step.* The father distributes a fourth cup; then the *Hallel* is sung (Psalm 113—Psalm 118). Sometimes the father added a fifth cup, which was accompanied with the singing of the *Great Hallel*" (Psalms 120–127. F. L. Godet's *Commentary on Luke,* pp. 286–287).

If the disciples prepared to meet these requirements, then they would need cups; wine; bitter herbs; unleavened bread, and above all else, a slain lamb.

## HOMILIES

Study No. 67

### FULL SURRENDER

The passage of scripture which has just been considered is only a very brief one, for as students must realize, it is only the introduction to the keeping of the Passover. Peter and John were commissioned to go into the city; to look for the man with the pitcher of water; to follow him, and within his home, prepare for the forthcoming feast. Throughout the centuries preachers have concentrated on expounding the great truths of the communion, but just in case some readers may be attracted to this introductory story, let us consider very briefly, the details of full surrender.

*He gave his home*
This is obvious for when two disciples pushed their way through the passover throngs; when they actually followed him into his home, he was in no way surprised. Probably he could have made a nice sum of money by letting that large room to any number of people.

Thousands of pilgrims—some very wealthy, would gladly have paid a great sum for the exclusive use of that place. The man was not even tempted; it was enough for him to know the Master wanted it. Therefore when the disciples came on their appointed errand, the home was ready; the room awaited the guests.

### He gave his heart

This surely is obvious. There were no questions asked; no conditions laid down; no payment demanded. Let it be carefully considered that this was the large upper room; *the guest-chamber.* This was the choice part of the building. The man was giving to the Lord the best place he possessed. An innkeeper at Bethlehem once stayed in his own hotel and offered to the parents of Jesus a stable! Now things were reversed. This man gave the best to Jesus, and remained content with anything that happened to be left.

### He gave his head

Sometimes the most sincere motives are ruined by stupidity. As the expository notes explained there was great danger that Judas might lead enemies to that home. The Master wished to celebrate the passover feast, but it was necessary to keep His place of meeting a secret. That man might have become the centre of great attraction; he could have broadcast the fact that he was to be honoured by the presence of the great Teacher. Indeed that is precisely what some would have done. They would have boasted to all and sundry about the identity of their special guest. And this publicity would have ruined the Master's plans. Happy is the man who can be trusted to keep the Lord's secrets.

### He gave his hands

The room was already furnished! the coming of thirteen men would necessitate extra furniture; this had been obtained and unostentatiously placed in position. Water would be needed for the celebration of the feast; the man therefore went to the well so that the Master would not have to interrupt proceedings to obtain supplies. A lamb would need to be prepared; bitter herbs would be desired; the wine and the cups would all have to be provided. He did what he could, and then waited for the two men who would recognize the pitcher. When they arrived, he stood respectfully in the corner of the room. "Peter and John. I know you are busy, but if you want anything else, just tell me. I'm ready to do anything or go anywhere. It is an honour to do anything for the Master." When I get to heaven, I would like to meet that man. He was a wonderful fellow.

*Expository Notes on the Institution of the Lord's Supper*

**And when the hour was come, he sat down, and the twelve apostles with him. And he said unto them, With desire I have desired to eat this passover with you before I suffer. For I say unto you, I will not any more eat thereof, until it be fulfilled in the kingdom of God (vv. 14-16).**

The appointed hour had come; all was in readiness. Calmly, solemnly the Lord took His place at the head of the table—He was the Father of the house—and with His disciples seated around Him, prepared to celebrate the feast. It must be remembered that the Lord was faithfully observing the commandment as commanded in Exodus 12, but during this feast, He intended to institute a new one. With the Lord presiding at the table, old things were to pass away. This was a momentous occasion, and the fact that Luke mentions more than one cup, or at least, that he states the cup was used more than once, only supports the assertion now being made. This primarily was the observance of the Passover; however, the disciples were destined to remember it as the first Lord's Supper. Deep satisfaction shone in the Saviour's eyes as He took His place; He had yearned with deep desire to preside at this table; to instruct the disciples in the things which lay on His heart. Furthermore, for Him this was finality; it would be His last passover feast, for He knew that within a matter of hours He would die on a tree.

**And he took the cup, and gave thanks, and said, Take this and divide it among yourselves: For I say unto you, I will not drink of the fruit of the vine, until the kingdom of God shall come (vv. 17-18).**

This surely corresponded to the first step outlined by Godet, the passing around of the cup of wine so that all might drink of its contents. There has been debating as to whether or not the Saviour drank of the cup. Some think He did, but the text implies that He refrained.

**And he took bread and gave thanks and brake it, and gave unto them, saying, This is my body which is given for you: this do in remembrance of me. Likewise also the cup after supper, saying, This cup is the new testament in my blood which is shed for you (vv. 19-20).**

At the place in the ceremony when the head of the feast was expected to take the unleavened bread, break it, dip it in the sauce, and eat it, Jesus introduced a new feature. Where the father of the family would be expected to explain the meaning of the observances, the Lord introduced the teaching of the communion. Earlier, Peter and John surely prepared the Paschal lamb, for a passover feast without a lamb would have been unthinkable. When Christ reminded His listeners that the flesh of the slain animal was meant to remind of the night of terror in Egypt, He paused, and deliberately added words to the effect that He would be another lamb—God's Lamb which would take away the sins of the world. Holding the broken piece of unleavened bread in His hand, He said, "This is my body, which is given for you. As you have always taken the elements of passover and remembered the deliverance from Egypt, take this, and when you eat, think of me."

Then, following the custom of the passover feast, He allowed them to talk; at least there was an interval of time, until suddenly, it became apparent to all, the feast was to continue. After supper, He again took the cup, and indicated that forever it was to remain the symbol of His precious blood about to be shed for their redemption. The doctrine of transubstantiation which is supposed to rest upon these statements of Christ is illogical. Christ's body was still intact, so how could they eat it? Furthermore, in view of the strict requirements of the law, if the Saviour had been urging them to eat His flesh and drink His blood, He would have been violating one of the commandments of God. Leviticus 3: 17 clearly states: "It shall be a perpetual statue for your generations throughout all your dwellings that ye eat neither fat nor blood." The disciples were not surprised when He uttered His words; they obviously understood these were emblems destined to deepen their devotion.

**But behold the hand of him that betrayeth me is with me on the table. And truly the Son of man goeth, as it was determined: but woe unto that man by whom he is betrayed! And they began to enquire among themselves, which of them it was who should do this thing (vv. 21–23).**

This verse is pregnant with meaning. Judas was with Him at the table; it is strange how close a man may get to Heaven and still be lost! "As it was determined." This can hardly mean as it was determined by the Jewish leaders. Christ was the Lamb slain before the foundation of the world. Within the eternal councils of the divine family it was pre-arranged that through the sacrifice of the Son, redemption would be brought to a guilty world. The part played by humans in bringing this to fruition was secondary. The guilt of man is unquestionable, but neither Jew nor Gentile crucified the Son of the Highest. ". . . it pleased the Lord to bruise Him . . ." (Isaiah 53: 10). Not all the armies of all the continents could have nailed Christ to the tree without divine sanction. Our sins were stronger than the spikes used by the soldiers. It was the determinate counsel of God that led Jesus to Calvary.

Finally it must always remain a conundrum why the disciples were ignorant of the identity of the betrayer. Even John had no idea who the traitor would be. When the disciples began to ask their questions it became clear that during His entire ministry, although the Lord had lived with a snake in His bosom, never by word nor deed had He betrayed to the other disciples that Judas would be the transgressor. The love He offered to Judas equalled the love He showed toward John. Unfortunately whilst John responded by leaning on the Master's breast, Judas retaliated with treachery.

And there was also a strife among them, which of them should be accounted the greatest. And he said unto them, The kings of the Gentiles exercise lordship over them: and they that exercise authority upon them are called benefactors. But ye shall not be so: but he that is greatest among you, let him be as the younger; and he that is chief, as he that doth serve. For whether is greater, he that sitteth at meat, or he that serveth? is not he that sitteth at meat? But I am among you as he that serveth (vv. 24–27).

This was the second time this kind of trouble had broken out among the disciples. Luke 9: 46 describes the first instance when Christ placed a child in the midst of the quarrelsome men. In spite of the lesson given at that time, the disciples were slow to learn. The strife now mentioned was probably occasioned when they began to seat themselves at the Lord's table. At a feast, the chief guest was seated to the immediate right of the host. The second in importance occupied the seat to the immediate left of the host. Thereafter the guests in order of importance sat second to the right, second to the left, third to the right, third to the left, and so on until all were in place. Some of the disciples probably thought they should have been honoured by a more ostentatious place at the table. It must forever be a shame that when the shadow of the cross was falling across the soul of the Master, His followers could only think of self and even go to the lengths of quarrelling because their pride had not been satisfied.

Against such a setting, and in such an atmosphere the Lord repeated the lesson of earlier days. "The kings of the earth exercise dominion; authority over their subjects. They take to themselves the name *Benefactor*, because they are proud to claim that all subjects benefit through their reign. Within my kingdom, things are different. All men are helped, but the greatest are not those who occupy any particular place at any table or banquet; the greatest are those who serve faithfully. My favourite disciple—if I had one, might just as well be helping in the kitchen as sitting at my side. Throughout Israel, the unpleasant tasks are often given to the youngest son because it would be beneath the dignity of the oldest to attend to menial tasks. I say unto you, that even the oldest of my disciples must be ready to do anything—even the tasks allotted to the insignificant. Only these people are *great*. I came to serve, are you greater than your Master?"

> Ye are they which have continued with me in my temptations, And I appoint unto you a kingdom, as my Father hath appointed unto me. That ye may eat and drink at my table in my kingdom, and sit on thrones judging the twelve tribes of Israel (vv. 28-30).

Each testing has its own reward; each trial its recompense. No one works for Christ without adequate compensation, and often those who are faithful in the small things are rewarded in ways which exceed their greatest imagination. These words of the Saviour probably implied that He was appointing to them a special place of honour within the kingdom. They would have kingdoms of their own. Probably light may be shed on this when we consider the King of Babylon in releasing Jehoiachin from prison, ". . . spake kindly to him, and set his throne above the throne of the kings that were with him in Babylon" (II Kings 25: 28). Similarly, the great King will be the Saviour Himself, but around Him will be the apostles who will reign as kings within the great domain of the Lord. There has been continuing discussion about the interpretation to be placed on the judging on twelve thrones of Israel. The consensus of opinion seems to be that since the Lord Jesus will return to earth to establish His kingdom; and since that earthly reign will continue for a millennium, the Lord will need an organization to administer His righteous laws throughout the earth. None would be better fitted to execute this authority than the twelve men who at the beginning helped to propagate the Gospel and found the Christian church.

> And the Lord said, Simon, Simon, behold, Satan hath desired to have you, that he may sift you as wheat; but I have prayed for thee, that thy faith fail not; and when thou art converted, strengthen thy brethren. And he said unto him, Lord, I am ready to go with thee, both into prison, and to death. And he said, I tell thee, Peter, the cock shall not crow this day, before that thou shalt thrice deny that thou knowest me (vv. 31-34).

Some think this warning was given to Simon Peter because he had been one of the disciples who argued fiercely about the seats of importance at the supper table. "Satan *HATH DESIRED*" suggests this conflict had been taking place in the spiritual realm whilst Peter remained unaware of what was transpiring. This is thought-provoking for the same thing might be happening with any of us. Simon's reaction was typical of the man. Impulsive, blustering, often speaking before he considered what he was about to say; but always sincere, Peter gained an abiding place in the heart of every Christian. The Lord's foreknowledge is once again revealed for He not only knew that Peter would deny his Lord, He knew also how many times this would take place and precisely the time the third denial would terminate. See the homily at the end of this section.

> And he said unto them, When I sent you without purse, and scrip, and shoes, lacked ye anything? And they said, Nothing. Then said he unto them, But now, he that hath a purse, let him take it, and likewise his scrip: and he that hath no sword, let him sell his garment and buy one. For I say unto you, that this that is written must yet be accomplished in me, And he was reckoned among the transgressors: for the things concerning me have an end. And they said, Lord, behold, here are two swords. And he said unto them, It is enough (vv. 35-38).

This is a difficult passage of scripture, and every commentator since the inception of the church has been obliged to admit it. Things were changing fast for the disciples and the commandments of yesterday were not to be necessarily the commandments of tomorrow. They recalled how the Master had sent them to preach; that His promise on that occasion had been gloriously fulfilled; they had lacked nothing. Now, however, they were urged to give more attention to their financial support; God would not do for them what they should be doing for themselves. However the point at issue is whether or not the command concerning the sword should be taken literally. Were the disciples to sell their garments; purchase a sword, and when occasion demanded use it to defend themselves and their families? Many interpretations have been given of this intriguing commandment, but through the centuries, the thinkers of the church have divided into two camps. Doubtless, students will join one of these, but meanwhile, all that is necessary is to set forth the viewpoints of both schools of thought.

1. Until the time of this pronouncement, the Lord had been with His servants; their problems, their needs had been brought to Him and solved instantly. His power had healed their sick; His provision had fed their hungry; His instruction had banished their doubts, and His graciousness had been to them as the balm of Gilead. Now things were to change. The Saviour would be with His Father; the disciples would need to face their problems without Him. It would be true that the Holy Spirit would be with them, but discerning His mind, interpreting His unspoken guidance would demand much more than had been necessary when they poured their complaints into the listening

ears of their Lord. The demands of the future necessitated a new out-look; a new approach. Instead of relying implicitly upon their Lord's provision, they would need to think and act for themselves. Until this moment they had been as little children walking with their father; enjoying the experience and realizing there was no need to worry for father was there to attend to all those things. Now the children have grown up; they are to go out into the big world to make their own decisions; earn their own money; manage their affairs, and to know both failure and success. Thus the Lord tried to teach them the necessity of paying more attention to the mundane matters of every day living. "Take a purse and be careful how you handle your money; buy a sword—that is, think for yourselves and take those measures which will guarantee some measure of protection." This was not meant to be taken literally, it was a part of the overall way in which Jesus urged them to be more practical. When the disciples immediately misunderstood His remark, He answered. "It is enough." This would be the equivalent of our saying, "Oh, forget it!" He knew that the day would come when their ignorances would be succeeded by knowledge; when their immaturity would be replaced by wisdom. In support of this interpretation the incident in the garden of Gethsemane is con-stantly quoted. When Simon Peter actually used his sword to wound the servant of the High Priest, he was instantly rebuked by the Lord.

2. The former interpretation seems logical, pleasing, and in keeping with the spirit of the Gospels. Yet, when one looks at the text care-fully, one has to admit there are flaws in the argument. If Christ meant to teach what has been suggested, could He not have done so without speaking of the necessity to buy a sword? No one knew the minds of the disciples as He did; He was aware of their intellectual limitations, and probably understood perfectly the reactions which would follow His utterance. Could He not therefore have chosen other language to say the same things, and at the same time avoid a great difficulty? All pacifists love this text for it is a great argument in the case against aggression. The outlook had certainly changed for the disciples; the days were at hand when thousands would die for their faith. Some would be burned in the gardens of the emperor; others would be fed to hungry lions in the arena. There would be times when innocent children would be molested. Were responsible fathers to stand idly by when irresponsible heathens ravaged their families? Christ was urging His followers to take precautions against such days; to be prepared to fight for their faith when that was necessary. Naturally, He rebuked Simon Peter for the misuse of the sword in the garden; Christians are not to be savages, and whilst Malchus was there with the enemies, he was only a servant who suffered because of his curiosity. Therefore the Lord rebuked the over-eager Peter. Such

things should never be done. However, if Peter had been standing by whilst an innocent child was being tortured, the Lord's reactions might have been different. It is with such thoughts in mind that the exponents of the second interpretation express their opinions. My own thoughts are that the best interpretation of this difficult text would be something to combine both suggestions. The hand that holds the sword needs to be strong but gentle; the mind that makes the decision to use it must be under the control of the Spirit of God. There may—and I stress, there MAY be a time to fight; there may be a time to surrender. Happy is the man who has the courage to fight and if needs be, die; blessed is the man who is wise enough to submit when God and conscience lead in that direction. Foolish and stupid is the man who criticizes others because their decisions are not in harmony with his own. In matters such as these, every man must be persuaded by his own conscience.

## HOMILIES

Study No. 68

### Christ's Prayer for Peter

The atmosphere in the upper room was tense. Incredulity had given place to indignation, and Peter's eyes were expressing the rising feelings of his heart. The other disciples were listening, and Peter resented this statement of his Lord. It was preposterous that He should suggest such a thing. Had He no confidence in His followers? Peter's eyes swept around the little gathering. Almost imperceptibly his chin was pushed out, and his hands became fists. "Lord, what are you saying?" "And the Lord said, Simon, Simon, behold, Satan hath desired to have you, that he may sift you as wheat: But I have prayed for thee, that thy faith fail not: and when thou art converted, strengthen thy brethren." Peter's eyes became pin-points of anger; his lips pursed, then, "Lord, I am ready to go with thee, both into prison, and to death." His statement was an outburst and a challenge. The other disciples might be unreliable, but he would never disown his Lord! And Jesus quietly answered, "Peter, the cock shall not crow this day, before that thou shalt thrice deny that thou knowest me ". . . *But I have prayed for thee.*"

### The Vision of His Prayer

The Lord Jesus was never taken by surprise, and consequently was never rash in words nor actions. Every major decision in His ministry was preceded by a period of communion, when God gave the guidance so necessary to Christ's inspired ministry. Probably, during one of these times of prayer, the conviction deepened that all was not well with Simon. It became so clear to the Lord. Peter would slip into the shadows; his hold upon eternal realities would weaken; his future would be in jeopardy! Then the Lord's face revealed the holy determination in His heart. His lips moved and He prayed, and that unrecorded prayer proved to be Peter's lifeline when the coming storm swirled around his soul.

### The Virtue of His Prayer

It is noteworthy that the Lord never mentioned the matter to his self-confident disciple until the secret battle had been fought and won. Perhaps other people acquainted with such knowledge would have uttered loud and persistent condemnation of the unreliable Simon. Within seconds a fiery argument could have filled the little sanctuary with strife. So often, one hasty word has been a match to start a devastating fire, and before the conflagration has been extinguished, blackened scars have appeared on the souls of men and women. This never happened with the Lord Jesus for His times of prayer were constant safeguards against the activities of evil. He won the battle for Peter's soul even before the disciple heard there would be a battle.

### The Value of His Prayer

"When thou art converted, strengthen thy brethren." The Lord not only saw the approaching tragedy, He looked beyond to see the new Peter resplendent in the power of a new life. Christ was certain that His prayer would be answered. He had wrestled in the secret place, and the issue was no longer in doubt. Possibly He had no wish to prevent the coming of the time of testing. He preferred that Simon should undergo the trial, for afterward, the disciple would emerge a better and a stronger man. We are persuaded that since the ultimate triumph was won in prayer, it was not possible for Simon to be lost. Each time the waves of remorse and guilt threatened to sweep the despairing man to oblivion, the strong arms of redeeming love brought him closer to safety.

### The Victory of His Prayer

It was all over. A sickening silence had fallen upon the people around the fire; their questionings had ceased. Yet within the mind of a haunted man, a deafening clamour had broken loose. The searing sword of conscience was playing havoc with his peace of mind. Sweeping aside the onlookers, Peter ran into the night—he had failed; he had disowned his Lord, he was a disgrace! And within the court-house, the Lord was calm. There was no need to worry, for already poor tormented Peter was safe in the arms of a Father's kindness. Later, when the Lord looked down from heaven to see a new man telling forth the word of life on the day of Pentecost, surely His great heart throbbed with thanksgiving; He was so glad He had prayed for Peter. The denial had become a stepping stone to unprecedented triumphs. And because the Lord loves to do things of this nature, He prays for all His followers. There are times when He says, "Father, remember Ivor Powell. Things are becoming difficult and dangerous in his experience." Reader, there are times when He prays for YOU. I'm thrilled—are you?

## SECTIONS FOUR AND FIVE

### Expository Notes on the Events in the Garden of Gethsemane

**And he came out, and went, as he was wont, to the mount of Olives; and his disciples also followed him. And when he was at the place, he said unto them, Pray that ye enter not into temptation. And he was withdrawn from them about a stone's cast, and kneeled down, and prayed, Saying, Father, if thou be willing, remove this cup from me: nevertheless not my will, but thine, be done. And there appeared an angel unto him from heaven, strengthening him (vv. 39-43).**

Barclay thinks that because gardens within the city of Jerusalem were almost unknown, many wealthy citizens had their own private gardens on the side of the mount of Olives. He thinks that some unknown friend of the Saviour had given the Lord permission to use that private garden any time He desired. This may be true. We only know that there was such a place to which the Master loved to retire, and now on the eve of the most distressing experience of His life, the Lord sought sanctuary in the customary spot. Certain other details supplied by the other evangelists are missing from Luke's document; probably this is explained by the fact that Luke was writing for Gentiles.

Elsewhere we are told that some of the disciples did not accompany the Lord into the garden. Perhaps they followed for some distance, but eventually, recognising His intentions, went elsewhere. Peter, James, and John accompanied their Leader into the garden, but when He knelt to pray, respectfully, they stayed about a stone's cast away. It is also said that they went to sleep; however, this could not have taken place immediately. For a little while they continued to watch and wait, and thus heard enough to furnish details for the story yet to be written.

Here we kneel upon holy ground. Ryle says, "Our Lord was a man exactly like ourselves in all things, sin only excepted. His bodily constitution, His nervous system, His capability of suffering, were all precisely like our own. Therefore it is that He says, 'Remove this cup from me' and yet adds, 'Not my will, but thine, be done'." Probably there is very much more in the text than would at first appear. What was this cup to which the Lord referred? It was unthinkable that He should be seeking a way to avoid the death of the Cross. It was for that specific cause He came into the world, and Hebrews 12: 1–2 makes it perfectly clear that when He contemplated going to the Cross, He did so with great joy. He never shirked His responsibilities; He never tried to avoid what He had helped plan in the earliest of all ages. Therefore *the cup* could not have meant the cross.

Hebrews 5: 7 makes an important contribution to our consideration. "Who in the days of his flesh, when he had offered up prayers and supplications with strong crying and tears unto him that was ABLE TO SAVE HIM FROM DEATH, and was heard in *that he feared.*" First, let it be clearly understood that Christ's prayer *was answered.* The cup DID pass from Him. This is something we need to comprehend. The Lord never prayed any prayer but what it was answered; He always prayed in the will of God. This is the first thing we must remember. The Saviour's petition *was granted* whilst a deadly fear gripped His soul. It was not the fear of death—but rather the fear that *He might die too soon.* Reconciliation was to be made through the blood of the Cross; there, the forces of evil would be put to flight. Even Satan believed this, and knowing the time was short, the hosts of evil attacked the Son of God. This was the greatest attempt ever made upon the Lord's life. The onslaught was so intense that blood began to ooze from the Saviour's temples. When His life seemed to be in jeopardy, the thought occurred—"Am I to die within sight of my goal?" The cup was the experience of physical weakness, and the Lord's desperate cry for help was answered when the angel came to assist Him. The imparted strength enables Jesus to vanquish the forces besieging his soul and to proceed calmly toward the realization of His greatest ambition. The Saviour's submissiveness was never in doubt. Although He desired to redeem sinners, His yieldedness to His Father was obvious when He said, "Not my will, but thine, be done." He yearned to save a lost world, but longed even more to please His Father. Only thus could He prove His fitness to become our Redeemer. It *was* the will of God to save Him; and in answer to the Son's prayer, the angel came to do what was necessary.

And being in an agony he prayed more earnestly: and his sweat was as it were great drops of blood falling down to the ground. And when he rose up from prayer, and was come to his disciples, he found them sleeping for sorrow, And said unto them, Why sleep ye? rise and pray, lest ye enter into temptation (vv. 44–46).

Medical experts attest the fact that the conditions described here indicate mental strain of the most intense type. It is noteworthy that Luke alone describes these details; he was a doctor. The disciples had continued to watch until grief, and weariness overcame them, and their eyes closed in slumber. It is not for us to criticise them; we only regret that during the saddest moments of His life, the Lord was deprived of every vestige of comfort except that which came from heaven. Not even John who had leaned upon the Lord's bosom was close enough to hold His hand. The Master's question might well be directed toward us all.

And while he yet spake, behold a multitude, and he that was called Judas, one of the twelve, went before them, and drew near unto Jesus to kiss him. But Jesus said unto him, Judas, betrayest thou the Son of man with a kiss? When they which were about him saw what would follow, they said unto him, Lord, shall we smite with the sword? And one of them smote the servant of the high priest, and cut off his right ear. And Jesus answered and said, Suffer ye thus far. And he touched his ear, and healed him (vv. 47–51).

This was not a casual arrest by a few police officers; this was a military operation. The Greek word translated *band* in John 18: 3 is *speiran* and means one tenth of a legion; six hundred men. Their marching through the streets would have attracted attention and upwards of one thousand people were in that multitude. Peter's impetuous action could easily have cost the lives of all the disciples. Thus even the evangelizing of the world was in jeopardy. How foolish to permit a false enthusiasm to beget impetuosity.

Students greeted their beloved rabbi by placing hands on the teacher's shoulders and then kissing him. Judas feigned devotion when he attempted to kiss the Lord. It is interesting to remember that this was the only *fresh* wound that Jesus ever healed; the miracle was unasked, undeserved, and performed for one who apparently had no faith and who forgot to say "Thank You." Stranger still is the fact that this mighty manifestation of God's power had no effect upon the crowd. Either the night was too dark for most of the people to be aware of what had happened, or their minds were filled with a prejudice even darker than the surrounding night. The "Suffer ye thus far" appears to indicate that the Lord was making a request to the arresting officers —"Before you take me, allow me to do this one charitable act."

Then Jesus said unto the chief priests, and captains of the temple, and the elders, which were come to him, Be ye come out as against a thief, with swords and staves? When I was daily with vou in the temple, ye stretched forth no hands against me: but this is your hour, and the power of darkness (vv. 52–53).

The captains of the temple were the temple police who received their orders from the Jewish hierarchy. As the Lord remarked, these men could have arrested Him on innumerable occasions; they had not done so because they feared an uprising among His supporters. Things had changed; the crowds were now absent; day had been followed by night; this was indeed their hour, and that of the powers of darkness. The rulers of the darkness of this world were about to do battle with the Son of God.

HOMILIES

Study No. 69

### The World's Greatest Battle

The life of the Lord Jesus was a time of constant watchfulness against the wiles of Satan. One mistake would have been sufficient to wreck the entire plan of God's salvation; and both Christ and His enemy knew it. Through direct methods, when Jesus was promised the kingdoms of the world; and through indirect methods, when the spite and bitterness of men endeavoured to irritate and annoy Him, Satan continually tried to overcome the Son of God. "He was in all points tempted like as we are, yet without sin" (Hebrews 4: 15). And the nearer Christ went to His cross and victory, the more desperate became the enemy. It would appear that Satan finally abandoned any attempt to make Christ fall into sin, realizing that in this matter the Lord Jesus was invincible. There remained but one possibility. The garden of Gethsemane became the scene of the world's greatest conflict, when Satan tried to kill the Saviour before the triumph of the cross could be won.

*THE GREAT CONFLICT . . . How great Christ's subservience to the will of God*

"And he was withdrawn from them about a stone's cast, and kneeled down, and prayed, saying, Father, if thou be willing, remove this cup from me: nevertheless not my will, but thine, be done." Probably this was the greatest prayer ever offered. The writer to the Hebrews adds a few poignant details: "Who in the days of his flesh, when he had offered up prayers and supplications with strong crying and tears *unto him that was able to save him from death,* and was heard in that he feared" (Hebrews 5: 7). Obviously Christ dreaded death; but that could not have been the death of the cross. Calvary, and what lay beyond, brought great joy to the Lord's heart, for we read in Hebrews

12: 2, ". . . *who for the joy that was set before him* endured the cross, despising the shame, and is set down at the right hand of the throne of God." The death dreaded by the Saviour was the premature death planned by the evil one. If the Lord had died in the garden of Gethsemane, the triumph of the cross would have been unknown. Therefore Satan directed against the physical resistance of the Lord Jesus every power at his command. In His moments of agonizing strain and weakness, the Lord realized His need, and "the strong crying and tears" brought instant relief.

*THE GREAT CRY . . . How great Christ's supplication to the heart of God*

Language is inadequate to describe the spiritual stature of the Lord when, in spite of His intense longing to reach Calvary, He cried, "Not my will, but thine, be done." Yet, *IT WAS THE WILL OF GOD TO SAVE HIM,* for the mind of the Son was in perfect alignment with the mind of the Father. Prayer was not a new exercise to the Lord Jesus. Day after day He had communed with God; yet these prayers in Gethsemane were unique. "And being in an agony he prayed *more earnestly*: and his sweat was as it were great drops of blood falling down to the ground." It would appear that this was a desperate cry for assistance. His life blood was being shed too soon. The appeal reached the heart of God, and the prayer was answered. "And there appeared an angel unto him from heaven, strengthening him" (Luke 22: 43). This is probably the Bible's greatest portrait of prayer. If only the followers of Jesus would emulate the Master's example, revival would begin immediately.

*THE GREAT CONQUEST . . . How great Christ's succour through the help of God*

True prayer is always answered; but if we ask according to the will of God, the answer is always in the affirmative. The coming of the angel provided Jesus with the much needed strength which enabled Him to overcome the fierce assault of Satan, and ultimately to proceed triumphantly to Calvary. Satan's last great attempt to frustrate the purposes of God in Christ failed completely. Exultantly Paul was able to write: "And having spoiled principalities and powers, he made a show over them openly, triumphing over them in it" (Colossians 2: 15). The foundation of Calvary's victory was laid in the prayers of Gethsemane. Thus, in a remarkable fashion, God would teach us life's greatest achievements are only made possible as we seek the place of prayer. A man is never as great as when he kneels before his Maker.

## Sections Six and Seven

*Expository Notes on the events which followed the Arrest of Jesus*

Then took they him, and led him, and brought him into the high priest's house. And Peter followed afar off. And when they had kindled a fire in the midst of the hall, and were set down together, Peter sat down among them. But a certain maid beheld him as he sat by the fire, and earnestly looked upon him, and said, This man was also with him. And he denied him, saying, I know him not. And after a little while another saw him, and said, Thou art also of them. And Peter said, Man, I am not. And about the space of one hour after another confidently affirmed, saying, Of a truth this fellow also was with him: for he is a Galilean. And Peter said, Man, I know not what thou sayest. And immediately, while he yet spake, the cock crew (vv. 54–60).

Possibly the place mentioned was an enclosed courtyard, and since at Passover time the nights would be cold, it became necessary to light a fire. The maid who was on duty at the door and who yielded to John's request to admit Simon Peter, had her suspicions concerning the newcomer and, at the first opportunity, expressed what was in her mind. That Simon Peter succumbed is now known to all; he had been so self-confident, so boastful that he would never fail. Alas, "let him that thinketh he standeth take heed lest he fall." "It is a curious fact that the Greek word here rendered *fire*, is a totally different word from the one rendered *fire* in the preceding verse (verses 55–56). Here it means literally *the light*. The word is found sixty-nine times in the New Testament, and in sixty-seven places is translated *light*. The two exceptions when it is rendered *fire*, are the passage before us, and the parallel passage in Mark, describing the same transaction. It is evident that the word was used intentionally by St. Luke in order to show us that it was by *the light of the fire* that Peter was recognized and charged with being a disciple. Had he kept in the background, and been content with a darker position, he might have escaped notice." (*Ryle's Expository Thoughts on the Gospels*. Luke, p. 440. See the homily at the end of this section.)

And the Lord turned, and looked upon Peter. And Peter remembered the word of the Lord, how he had said unto him, Before the cock crow, thou shalt deny me thrice. And Peter went out and wept bitterly (vv. 61–62).

This look broke Peter's heart. The disciple gazed into the eyes of his Lord and saw the heart of God. Had the Saviour been angry, Peter might have rebelled; but the intense pity of the Saviour's eyes was more than he could bear. Barclay has a striking verse which expresses all that needs to be said.

> I think I'd sooner frizzle up,
> In the flames of a burning Hell,
> Than stand and look into His face,
> And hear His voice say—Well?

See the homily at the end of this section.

**And the men that held Jesus, mocked him, and smote him. And when they had blindfolded him, they struck him on the face, and asked him saying, Prophesy, who is it that smote thee? And many other things blasphemously spake they against him. (vv. 63–65).**

Throughout the night the Saviour was made to suffer, but His captors were waiting for the dawn. The Sanhedrin, the supreme Jewish council, so it has been said, was not permitted to meet during the hours of darkness, and therefore, the temple police had to hold their Prisoner until He could be brought before the assembly. The force of some of the Greek words used by the various evangelists suggest that their blows were not slight taps on the face, but solid punches. It is not possible to understand all that the Lord Jesus suffered in that night of horror, but probably Peter's lapse hurt more than the blows.

**And as soon as it was day, the elders of the people, and the chief priests, and the scribes came together, and led him into their council, saying, Art thou the Christ? tell us. And he said unto them, If I tell you, ye will not believe. And if I ask you, ye will not answer me, nor let me go. Hereafter shall the Son of man sit on the right hand of the power of God. Then said they all, Art thou then the Son of God? And he said unto them, Ye say that I am. And they said, What need we any further witnesses? for we ourselves have heard of his own mouth (vv. 66–71).**

The charge brought against the Saviour was one of blasphemy, and this appeared to be substantiated when the Lord predicted His exaltation. Daniel 7 : 13–14 had foretold the greatness of Him who would be called the Son of man. That this title had been used by Christ everyone was aware. Now Jesus claimed the Son of man was indeed the Son of God, and it was with this thought in mind the Jewish leaders asked their questions. *The Amplified New Testament* renders Christ's final answer: *"It is just as you say; I am."* The Lord never lost His confidence; in spite of all that man could do to Him, He knew that in the end the purposes of God would triumph.

HOMILIES

Study No. 70

## SIMON PETER ... Who Sat at Two Fires
### (Luke 22 : 55; John 21 : 9)

During the night in which our Lord was betrayed, two men passed through a doorway into the darkness of the city. One man turned and walked into the bitterness of eternal remorse; the other walked into the arms of God. At that doorway Judas and Simon Peter parted forever. The Lord has set forth in detail the account of Peter's great tragedy, and since his path of sorrow is so clearly defined, let us consider it.

### The Downward Path to Calamity

Peter should have known better, for the Lord had said unto him, "Simon, Simon, Satan hath desired to have you that he might sift you as wheat," but in self-confidence the disciple replied, "Lord, I am ready to go with thee, both into prison, and to death." Almost immediately he began to drift from Christ. (1) *And Peter followed afar off.* This was his first mistake. When a Christian backslides the commencement of the trouble can always be traced to this cause. The loss of intimate communion leads to disaster. (2) *And Peter warmed himself at the fire* (Mark 14: 67). This was his second mistake. Following in the distance, he became cold, and was thereafter attracted to the fire—the enemies' fire. There appeared to be little danger in his actions, but the real menace was to be found in the company gathered around the fireplace. And this danger is still obvious for people of our modern age. When devotion begins to die within the Christian's heart, worldliness will always be a source of attraction. (3) *And Peter sat down among them* (Luke 22: 55). Any plan concerning an early departure was forgotten. He intended to stay and enjoy the fellowship around the blazing coals. This was his greatest mistake. Something was surely wrong when a disciple of Jesus felt at home among the Master's enemies. (4) *And Peter denied his Lord—"I know HIM not."* We are told that Simon Peter denied thrice, yet strange to relate, the details were not identical. The first denial concerned his allegiance to Christ. It is always thus. (5) *And Peter denied his association with the disciples—the Church.* To the accusation, "Thou art also of THEM," he replied, "Man, I am not." Satan is never satisfied with a first denial. He endeavours to bring the backslider away from the fellowship of the saints, for otherwise the falling Christian might recover. (6) *And Peter began to curse and swear* (Mark 14: 71). When he was accused of speaking with a different dialect, he used their type of expression, and so overcame their final objections. His sin appeared to sever all his connections with Christ, and he seemed completely lost. He stumbled through the doorway into the darkness of the street, *but took the right turn.*

## The Upward Path to Conquest

"And the Lord turned, and looked upon Peter, and Peter remembered the word of the Lord . . . and he went out and wept bitterly." Somewhere in the city, he broke his heart. (1) *The risen Lord sent a special invitation asking Peter to return.* When Mary came to the tomb she was met by an angel who said, "Go your way, tell his disciples *AND PETER* that he goeth before you into Galilee: There shall ye see him, as he said" (Mark 16: 7). We must remember that in spite of his great mistakes, Peter was still a disciple. Special mention was made of his name, for this was a great effort to bring back a wanderer. (2) *The risen Lord personally sought for Simon.* When the Emmaus travellers returned to announce the resurrection of Christ, they heard the disciples saying, "The Lord is risen indeed, *and hath appeared unto Simon.*" Paul also mentioned this great appearance for it was known to all the church (I Corinthians 15: 5). The Lord knew of Peter's shame, and understanding his reluctance to accept the invitation, went in search of him. What they said to each other has remained a great secret. It is better that way. (3) *The Lord publicly gave a new commission to His restored follower.* The scene which took place at the edge of the sea of Galilee has now become famous. At the Lord's fire, Peter made his threefold confession, and received his thrilling commission. His service on the day of Pentecost, and throughout the following years, demonstrated how complete had been his recovery. We are able to understand why he wrote: "Unto you therefore which believe, He is precious" (I Peter 2: 7).

(Taken from the Author's book, *Bible Cameos,* pp. 121–122.)

# The Twenty-Third Chapter of Luke

THEME: *The Death of Jesus*

OUTLINE:

      I. Jesus is Condemned ... by the Judge. Verses 1–25
     II. Jesus is Crucified ... by the Jews. Verses 26–49
    III. Jesus is Claimed ... by Joseph. Verses 50–56

## SECTION ONE

*Expository Notes on the Interrogation before Pilate and
King Herod*

**And the whole multitude of them arose, and led him unto Pilate. And
they began to accuse him, saying, We found this fellow perverting the
nation, and forbidding to give tribute to Caesar, saying that he himself
is Christ a king. And Pilate asked him, saying, Art thou the king of the
Jews? And he answered him and said, Thou sayest. Then said Pilate
to the chief priests and people, I find no fault in this man. And they
were the more fierce, saying, He stirreth up the people, teaching
throughout all Jewry, beginning from Galilee to this place (vv. 1-5).**

Godet says, "There is a tradition, quoted in the Talmud, that, 'forty
years before the destruction of the temple (and so about the year 30
of our era), the right of pronouncing capital sentences was taken from
Israel ...'" This would explain why the leaders of the nation thought
it necessary to take their Prisoner before the Roman governor. Some
writers state they wished to implicate the Gentile ruler in their affairs,
so that in the event of any repercussions, they could blame him for
what was essentially their crime. The charge brought against Jesus
was notoriously false, for in answer to the question whether or not
tribute should be paid to Caesar, the Saviour had answered, "Render
unto Caesar the things which belong unto Caesar, and to God the
things which belong unto God." Probably aware that the Roman
would dismiss a religious charge, the Jews cited political matters knowing this was their only chance of gaining a verdict. Luke does not
supply all the details of the interrogation conducted by Pilate, but
these can be obtained from a comparison of the synoptic records. After
cross-examining the Prisoner, Pilate pronounced Him innocent, and

it was at this juncture the lawyers made their insidious suggestion. They knew that any man found guilty of plotting against Caesar, was commanded to commit suicide in his bath. When he failed to obey that order, he was taken to Rome and executed in the streets. When the Jewish lawyers threatened to accuse Pilate of supporting insurrection, the Governor trembled, knowing their accusations might rob him of everything he possessed.

**When Pilate heard of Galilee, he asked whether the man were a Galilean. And as soon as he knew that he belonged unto Herod's jurisdiction, he sent him to Herod, who himself also was at Jerusalem at that time. And when Herod saw Jesus, he was exceeding glad: for he was desirous to see him of a long season, because he had heard many things of him; and he hoped to have seen some miracle done by him (vv. 6–8).**

We have not been told the cause of the dispute between Pilate and King Herod; possibly the trouble arose over some matter of jurisdiction for the Roman overlords where always encroaching upon the civil rights of Israel, and every move was fiercely resented. Tension had existed in the relations between these two men, and suddenly, the thought occurred to Pilate that this was a chance to kill two birds with one stone. His conciliatory move toward Herod would satisfy the pride of the Galilean ruler, and at the same time, the responsibility of sentencing Jesus would pass to another judge. It seemed a wonderful idea, but sometimes these things can become a boomerang to return whence it came with devastating results. Each man must remain responsible for his relationship with the Son of God. Herod had come to Jerusalem to attend the feast. When the opportunity presented itself to receive the Carpenter, he was delighted for the performance of any miracle would provide excellent entertainment for his men. It should be noticed carefully that Herod was the only man to whom Christ refused to speak. Within a matter of weeks, the king was destined to fall from his throne. He already had one foot in the grave, nevertheless the Lord Jesus refused to speak to him. It is a sober thought that although Christ knew the man was dying in his sin, the Saviour never even tried to save him. When Herod ordered the execution of John the Baptist, he slammed the door on his own chances of forgiveness. Thereafter, the Spirit of God ceased to strive with him.

**Then he questioned with him in many words; but he answered him nothing. And the chief priests and scribes stood and vehemently accused him. And Herod with his men of war set him at nought (treated him with contempt—Amplified New Testament), and mocked him, and arrayed him in a gorgeous robe, and sent him again to Pilate, And the same day, Pilate and Herod were made friends together: for before they were at enmity between themselves (vv. 9–12).**

The word translated gorgeous is the Greek word *lampran*. This is an interesting term meaning *splendid, shining, brilliant, magnificent.* Thayer also concedes that it means *glistening whiteness.* Some think Herod was trying to make the Prisoner appear as a spurious high priest; others see in the action an unwitting testimony to the innocence of the Saviour. In the light of the vehement accusation hurled against the Saviour's name, we can only marvel at His dignified bearing. His enemies would have been elated by any infuriating outburst of anger, for then they would have added more to the list of things brought against the Lord. His calm and dignified manner repudiated their evil suggestions. Finally, Herod sent the Prisoner back to Pilate. It is strange to relate that some people are never happier than they are in the presence of the Master; others are never happy in His presence or away from it.

> And Pilate, when he had called together the chief priests, and the rulers and the people, Said unto them, Ye have brought this man unto me, as one that perverteth the people: and, behold, I, having examined him before you, have found no fault in this man touching those things whereof ye accuse him: No, nor yet Herod: for I sent you to him; and, lo, nothing worthy of death is done unto him. I will therefore chastise him, and release him. (For of necessity he must release one unto them at the feast.) And they cried out all at once, saying, Away with this man, and release unto us Barabbas: (Who for a certain sedition made in the city, and for murder, was cast into prison.) (vv. 13-19).

Norval Geldenhuys in his *Commentary on Luke's Gospel* says on page 600: "Pontius Pilate was the fifth Roman governor who, after the deposition of Archelaus in A.D. 6, ruled over Judea (A.D. 26-36). According to the description of Pilate by the Jewish-Hellenistic writer Philo . . . he was a man of unyielding character, but nevertheless corruptible; he was notorious for his cruelty and unbearable coarseness; he often ill-treated and executed persons without a preceding judicial sentence. He was an arbitrary tyrant and respected no one's feelings, *except when his own interests were imperilled.*" It was at this point that Pilate's worries began. The earlier historical details concerning Pilate's altercations with the Jews are well known, for Josephus described in detail the unpleasant experiences through which he and the nation had passed. Jewish law condemned idolatry, and thus the Roman soldiers formerly had removed from their weapons the small image of Caesar. The emperor was considered to be divine, and thus the soldiers carried a small bust of their leader every time they went into battle. The Jews denounced this as idolatry, and to conciliate them, the earlier governors had ordered a compromise. The soldiers removed these small images from their weapons, and peace had been maintained. Pilate refused to do this, and the result was disastrous. There was another occasion when he attempted, or at least threatened, to use temple funds in order to meet the cost of bringing much needed water supplies into the city. Once again, there was danger of insurrection. Had the Jews appealed to Caesar for a judgment, Pilate might have been replaced. This he knew, and when the threat was made to report his indiscretions to the Emperor, Pilate knew he was standing upon very dangerous ground. He made at least four attempts to avoid the responsibility of passing sentence, but in the end, as Haman of old, he was hung upon his own gallows. We do not know when the custom of releasing a prisoner at the feast began; possibly this had been another way of appeasing the people whose hearts had become embittered. As a last desperate measure to avoid the death of Jesus, Pilate suggested He be released according to custom. His effort ended in failure when the people chose Barabbas. This man had committed murder; we do not know whom he had killed, but in any case the spirit of rebellion had been evident in his action. He might have killed a Roman soldier, and if that were the case, it was thought-provoking when the multitude asked for his pardon. The thought has been expressed that the crowds now turned against Jesus because they had become disappointed in Him. They had believed Him to be the Messiah, but when He refused to fight for His kingdom, their admiration turned to anger. This may or may not be the truth. When men reject the light they make it obvious that they prefer the darkness.

Pilate therefore, willing to release Jesus, spake again unto them. But they cried, saying, Crucify him, crucify him. And he said unto them the third time, Why, what evil hath he done? I have found no cause of death in him: I will therefore chastise him, and let him go. And they were instant with loud voices, requiring that he might be crucified. And the voices of them and the chief priests prevailed. And Pilate gave sentence that it should be as they required. And he released unto them him that for sedition and murder was cast into prison, whom they had desired; but he delivered Jesus to their will (vv. 20–25).

Poor Pilate! He began the day as the appointed judge; he ended it standing in the dock accused before God of being a worthless coward. This is a paragraph of choices. The crowd chose between Barabbas and Jesus; Pilate chose between justice and self-preservation; the soldiers chose between lifting the cross themselves and forcing a stranger to do it for them. All people make some kind of a choice the moment the Saviour approaches. He is the unavoidable Carpenter.

HOMILIES

Study No. 71

## Pilate's Last Chance!

The scene was set for the greatest drama in history. At the gates of the Governor's palace, an insistent mob clamoured for attention. The feast day was at hand, and before it commenced dirty work had to be done—and done quickly. As the sun arose to send its silvery beams across the darkened sky, the shouts of the people echoed along the cobbled streets. Awakened thus from his sleep, Pilate went forth to the trial of Jesus ignorant of the fact that his own soul would be on trial that day. Losing his balance on the slippery slope of indecision and compromise, the judge began to fall, and every passing hour brought him closer to disaster. How wonderful it is to recall that in those moments God sufficiently loved this sinner to plan a final attempt to save him. In common with all other aspects of redeeming love, this is beyond comprehension.

### How Great was the Grace of God

Pilate's wife lay deep in slumber; she had not yet arisen from her bed. Outside, her husband endeavoured to outwit the bigoted people who were beginning to blackmail him, and silently Christ stood listening. The woman stirred uneasily; she was restless. God had touched her slumbering eyes, and as she slept, she dreamed—of Jesus. Suddenly, awaking with a start, she remembered that Pilate had gone to be the judge of the prophet. Trembling with premonitions of disaster, she wrote her urgent message, "Have thou nothing to do with that just man: for I have suffered many things this day in a dream because of him." If Pilate had taken her advice, his soul might have been saved. Had he not been so devoid of true understanding he would have recognized this dream to be a medium of grace. God never ceases His attempt at rescue while there is still a chance to succeed.

### How Great was the Goodness of a Woman

Possibly the Governor dismissed this appeal as an intrusion into his own affairs. His wife should mind her own business. How could she understand the intricacies of this difficult case? These Jews had threatened to tell Caesar, and if a charge of treason should be brought against him, his future would be ruined. He had nothing to lose in crucifying the Prisoner; he had nothing to gain in resisting these arrogant Jews. Let her mind her own affairs! She did not understand.

Ah, but she did. If misfortune overtook her husband, she could not escape; irrevocably her life was linked with his. She knew more. She knew that death was not the greatest of all tragedies. It was far better to die in honour than to live in shame. "Husband," she would have cried, "do that which is right. This Man is just, therefore, stand by Him whatever the cost." Pilate should have been very proud of this noble partner. A good woman is the greatest jewel outside of heaven; a bad woman is the vilest creature outside of hell.

### How Great was the Guilt of a Man

Rudely brushing aside both the grace of God and the entreaties of his charming lady, Pilate washed his hands before the multitude, saying, "I am innocent of the blood of this just person." Then, in contradiction of his verdict, he sent Jesus forth to be scourged and crucified. He had washed his hands, but had never touched the soiled places of his soul. To save himself, he had sacrificed his Prisoner and his honour. Yet we are told that within seven years of his deed, a broken and destitute man removed from high office by the Governor of Syria; alone and unwanted by Caesar, Pilate went out into the darkness of the night to commit suicide. His body was found by a workman. Poor, guilty man, I feel sorry for him. He met the Saviour and refused to love Him. And now it is dark—awfully dark.

### SECTION TWO

### Expository Notes on the Crucifixion of Jesus

**And as they led him away, they laid hold upon one Simon, a Cyrenian, coming out of the country, and on him they laid the cross, that he might bear it after Jesus (v. 26).**

When a man was sentenced to be crucified, he was taken into the streets, surrounded by soldiers, who in turn placed the cross upon the shoulders of the condemned. The route of the procession was deliberately planned to take in as many streets as possible so that the greatest number of citizens could see the spectacle. This was supposed to be a warning to any person tempted to commit the same crimes. It should be remembered that after the Lord's scourging, his body would be covered with evidence of His sufferings. He had been spread-eagled on a rough frame; His body had been drawn taut, and upon that defenceless back, the cruel lash had fallen. Cicero, the historian, stated that the practice and even the name itself should be abolished from the life and language of the Romans. The scourge was made of thongs of leather into which small pieces of metal had been inserted to rip the flesh from the body of the victim. Many prisoners died under the lash. During the preceding night the Lord had been tortured; sleep had been denied, and now utterly weary, He was trying to pull a heavy cross through the streets. The task was too great, and fearing that He might succumb before the procession could reach its destination, the Romans conscripted help. All that was necessary in order to make a bystander assist was to pat him on the shoulder with the broad, flat end of a spear. At the right moment, a visitor from Cyrene, a man who had come to worship at the feast, reached the place of conscription, and before he knew what was taking place, he was being compelled to carry the cross of Jesus. Every angel would have changed places with him. See the homily at the end of this section.

And there followed him a great company of people, and of women, which also bewailed and lamented him. But Jesus turning unto them said, Daughters of Jerusalem, weep not for me, but weep for yourselves, and for your children. For, behold, the days are coming, in the which they shall say, Blessed are the barren, and the wombs that never bare, and the paps that never gave suck. Then shall they begin to say to the mountains, Fall on us; and to the hills, Cover us. For if they do these things in a green tree, what shall be done in the dry? (vv. 27-31).

The procession was suddenly halted when the Lord saw the weeping women. We are not told why they were crying. Possibly they were overwhelmed by His indescribable anguish, and sympathy filled their eyes with tears. They might have been some of His disciples, but this hardly seems likely for His message did not suggest they had been among His followers. To bear children was the greatest desire of Hebrew women, and to remain childless was considered a disgrace. Childlessness was a valid ground for divorce in the days of Jesus, and therefore the words of Christ on this occasion were, to say the least, startling. He saw once again the downfall of the nation He had tried to win; He regretted His inability to save them. His words on this occasion suggested that even though He could do nothing else, at least, He could warn them. The message concerning the green tree was probably proverbial. It would mean, "If these things can be done when the tree is green; when the sap is flowing through the branches; and when all is well, what will be done when things are not well?" "If they do this with a Saviour, what will they do in times of judgment?"

And there were also two other, malefactors, led with him to be put to death. And when they were come to the place, which is called Calvary, there they crucified him, and the malefactors, one on the right hand, and the other on the left. Then said Jesus, Father, forgive them; for they know not what they do. And they parted his raiment and cast lots. And the people stood beholding. And the rulers also with them deriding him, saying, He saved others; let him save himself, if he be Christ, the chosen of God. And the soldiers also mocked him, coming to him, and offering him vinegar. And saying, If thou be the king of the Jews, save thyself. And a superscription also was written over him in letters of Greek, and Latin, and Hebrew, THIS IS THE KING OF THE JEWS (vv. 32–38).

Crucifixion was a form of punishment reserved by the Romans for criminals of the worst type; it was exceptionally shameful and painful, and represented the most ignominious death anyone could die. "The crucified usually lived twelve hours, sometimes even until the second or third day. The fever which soon set in produced a burning thirst. The increasing inflammation of the wounds in the back, hands, and feet; the congestion of the blood in the head, lungs, and heart; the swelling of every vein, an indescribable oppression, racking pains in the head; the stiffening of the limbs, caused by the unnatural position of the body—these all united to make the punishment" (Godet).

It is incomprehensible that after Christ had ministered unceasingly for three wonderful years; when the sick had been healed; the dead had been raised; the hopeless had found a new incentive for living; when a matchless new era of spiritual potential had opened as a refreshing vista before the eyes of the faithful, the people should respond by crucifying their greatest Benefactor. Surely there is no height to which the redeemed cannot climb; there is no depth to which villainy cannot sink.

The cross was composed of two pieces of wood formed as a letter T. There has been much debate as to the method of crucifixion. Some say the cross was placed flat on the ground; that the prisoner was nailed before it was dropped into the hole prepared to receive it. The sudden jarring to every nerve and sinew in the body made it necessary for a small footrest to be attached to the main step of the cross. When the excruciating agony of a body tearing on the nails made the pain unbearable, the crucified could ease the strain momentarily by pressing, as best he could, on the small ledge beneath his feet. This gives credence to the other text which speaks of the soldiers finding it necessary to break the limbs of the dying prisoners. They came with an iron bar to smash the legs of the crucified, and thereby making it impossible for any alleviation of agony. Thus death was hastened, and the removal of the bodies before sunset made possible. Yet, on the other hand there are writers who affirm that the cross was first erected, then the body was raised by means of ropes to the required height, and nailed in position by the officials waiting to finish their unpleasant task. Some historians claim that only the hands were nailed; that the feet were left free to use the ledge just mentioned. Others contradict this, stating one foot was placed above the other; that one spike was driven through both. Does it really matter? There appears to be a great tendency to argue over the machinery of the crucifixion, when we might be spending the time worshipping at the Lord's feet.

Perhaps the most heart-searching prayer ever uttered by the Lord was the one asking pardon for the people responsible for His death. If Christ could forgive His enemies, can we ever permit bitterness to occupy our hearts? For a while, the watching crowd was kept at a distance, for there was always the possibility that ardent followers of the Nazarene might attempt a last minute rescue of their Leader. When this became impossible, the people were allowed to draw nearer to shout at him. Even the Gentiles enjoyed the spectacle, for they also urged Him to manifest His Messianic powers. Early historians speak of the presence in Jerusalem of certain women who made a practice of trying to help the condemned. They prepared a stupifying drink to dull the senses of criminals. This was offered to the Lord, but His refusal to accept the drink suggested He was determined to remain in charge of all His faculties until the moment He dismissed His spirit.

The title nailed to the cross was written in three languages: Greek, the language of the scholastic world; Latin, the language of the Empire, and Hebrew the language of the Jews. These tongues covered the known world of those days, and thus by one simple inscription, the unknown scribe suggested this was a matter of such importance that the entire world should know and understand what was taking place.

> And one of the malefactors which were hanged railed on him, saying, If thou be Christ, save thyself and us. But the other answering rebuked him, saying, Dost not thou fear God, seeing thou art in the same condemnation? And we indeed justly; for we receive the due reward of our deeds: but this man hath done nothing amiss. And he said unto Jesus, Lord, remember me when thou comest into thy kingdom. And Jesus said unto him, Verily, I say unto thee, Today shalt thou be with me in paradise (vv. 39-43).

Matthew 27 : 44 declares the two thieves cursed the Lord. It therefore follows that in some marvellous way, the Spirit of God brought conviction to the one guilty man, and that ultimately he ceased his ravings. Then, as he looked at the Lord more closely, the eyes of his spiritual perception began to open, and suddenly the greatest of all miracles was performed. Seven centuries earlier, the prophet Isaiah had predicted: "Yet it pleased the Lord to bruise him; he hath put him to grief; when thou shalt make his soul an offering for sin, he shall see his seed . . . He shall see of the travail of his soul . . ." (Isaiah 53: 10-11). The word *travail* throughout the Bible is used to describe child-birth. It is a feminine word closely related to labour-pains. The prophet uttered words which at first surely sounded fantastic—A man would bring forth a child; a man would be in labour; a man would see of the travail of his soul. Furthermore, the exact time of this event was accurately foretold: WHEN THOU SHALT MAKE HIS SOUL AN OFFERING FOR SIN. It was at such a moment the thief was born into the kingdom of God. Isaiah predicted that Christ would die in childbirth!

Various explanations of Paradise have been offered to the church. It has been argued that the term describes a section of Hades. See the notes on Luke 16: 19–31. Christ was promising the penitent thief that he would accompany Him as He went to proclaim deliverance to the captives. Others affirm this term describes the very presence of God; that the thief was promised a welcome by God at the end of that particular day. Paul, in II Corinthians 12: 3–4, says: "And I knew such a man . . . how that he was caught up into paradise, and heard unspeakable words, which is not lawful for a man to utter." The Saviour also used the term in His message to the church at Ephesus. ". . . To him that overcometh will I give to eat of the tree of life, which is in the midst of the paradise of God" (Revelation 2: 7). Doubtless there will be more discussion on this point, but the only thing of which we can be reasonably sure is that the word Paradise came from an old Persian vocabulary and was used to describe a royal garden. The exact geographical location of Paradise is a matter of secondary importance. Christ was telling the thief that they would share fellowship in that place. There is reason to believe that ANY PLACE would have been heaven for the sinner as long as he could remain close to his Redeemer. See the homilies at the end of this section.

**And it was about the sixth hour, and there was a darkness over all the earth until the ninth hour. And the sun was darkened, and the veil of the temple was rent in the midst. And when Jesus had cried with a loud voice, he said, Father, into thy hands I commend my spirit: and having said thus, he expired (Amplified New Testament.) (vv. 44–46).**

For the testimony of God as it was expressed in the realm of nature, see the homily at the end of this section. "Into thy hand I commit my spirit" was a very much used quotation from Psalm 31: 5. We are told that Jewish mothers taught this as a prayer to their small children so that it might be said before they retired to bed at night. Many mothers today teach their children to say:

> Now I lay me down to sleep:
> I pray the Lord my soul to keep.
> If I should die before I wake;
> I pray the Lord my soul to take.

In much the same way, but with added meaning, the Lord placed Himself into the hands of His Father, when He uttered the immortal words: "Father, into thy hands I commend my spirit."

> Now when the centurion saw what was done, he glorified God, saying, Certainly this was a righteous man. And all the people that came together to that sight, beholding the things which were done, smote their breasts and returned. And all his acquaintance, and the women that followed him from Galilee, stood afar off, beholding these things.

The first man to respond to the death of Jesus was in all probability a dying Jew—the thief; the next was a Gentile, the centurion in charge of the men who had nailed Christ to the tree. This is the divine order; the gospel is first to the Jew and then to the Gentile. The phenomenal events taking place around the greenhill destroyed the confidence of the bystanders, and as fear seized their minds, they smote their chests and hurried home. Yet neither their tears nor their confessions could undo the dastardly work which had been done. Had that been the prelude to the day of judgment, they would have been calling for the rocks and the hills to fall upon them to hide them from the wrath of the Lamb. However, it was the forerunner of the age of grace. The Saviour's prayer, "Father, forgive them . . ." was to be gloriously answered, for on the day of Pentecost three thousand souls were won for Christ. Probably some of those converts had been present when the Lord was crucified.

The Saviour's intimate friends had watched the proceedings from a distance. Alas, their sun had been eclipsed; their day had ended in the darkness of sorrow. They turned and went away, not knowing that soon the Son of Righteousness would arise with healing in His wings.

## HOMILIES

## Study No. 72

### THE MAN WHO CARRIED THE CROSS

The entire Gospel story may be described as an account of God's giving to man. At Bethlehem He gave His Son to the world; in the ministry of Jesus He gave His message to the world; at Calvary He gave His life for the world. Human indebtedness increased daily, yet when the disciples had their greatest opportunity to express real gratitude, they miserably failed. There came a day when Christ urgently needed help; when a cruel cross had crushed Him to the ground. In those moments of supreme opportunity, the disciples refused to respond, and it was "a stranger coming out of the country" who carried the cross after Jesus.

## Carrying the Cross

Simon the Cyrenian lived in North Africa, but in common with all other people of his race he loved to attend the feasts at Jerusalem. This he was able to do because he had two sons who were capable of managing family affairs while he was away. Greatly excited, Simon completed the long journey and drew near to the city of his fathers. The temple roof glistening in the sunshine, the surging crowds, and the city itself, made sacred by the ministry of all the prophets, increased the thrill of his soul. He pressed along the street and came to the soldiers who at that moment were seeking the services of a strong man. "And as they came out, they found a man of Cyrene, Simon by name: him they *compelled* to bear his cross" (Matthew 27 : 32). There was no court of appeal against the injustice of the soldiers' request. These men were a law unto themselves, and even the other Jews laughed at the stranger's embarrassment. Simon was probably angry. It seemed inexcusable that they should inflict upon him the indignity of carrying a cross for a malefactor. His arguments were useless—"They compelled him to carry the cross." Perhaps God looked down and smiled! Such service would be amply rewarded. When the cross was lifted, the Saviour slowly arose, and with quiet dignity gazed upon His helper. Sullenly Simon returned the look, and in seeing the face of Jesus, he looked into the heart of God.

## Avoiding the Cross

We can understand the reluctance of the Cyrenian; but another problem arises. Where were the disciples in this hour of crisis? They had promised to be true to their Master; they had vowed to go with Him to prison and to death—where were they now? Probably they stood in the crowd watching the unfolding of the sad drama, but when conscience suggested their going to aid the Lord, fear made them cowards. They were ashamed and afraid. To make a public confession of loyalty would invite the scorn of the entire multitude; they therefore left Him to suffer alone. Had any disciple rushed forward to lift the cross, he would have won eternal honours. Alas, they were all ashamed to respond, and the task was left to a man from Africa. He listened to the words addressed to the sorrowful women (Luke 23 : 28) and then followed to Calvary. He heard the request of the thief, and the response of Jesus; he listened as the Lord prayed, "Father, forgive them, for they know not what they do," and finally marvelled at the confession of the centurion, who said, "Certainly, this was the Son of God." And by this time, Simon's anger had disappeared.

## Proclaiming the Cross

Was it true? Had he carried a cross for the Son of God? What did it all mean? And perhaps God smiled again. He knows how to reward His workmen, and is never in debt to any man. The work commenced at Calvary was completed in the garden tomb. The news of the resurrection brought great excitement to the city, and more particularly to Simon. Soon he heard another message: "If any man will come after me, let him deny himself, and take up his cross daily, and follow me." When Simon lifted the second cross, he was more than compensated for his work in carrying the first one. Alexander and Rufus are mentioned in the New Testament, and Bible Teachers are agreed they were the sons of the man who carried the cross. Mark 15: 21 tells us Simon had sons by these names. As Barclay says, "You do not identify a man by the names of his sons, unless these sons are well known members of a community to which you write. There is general agreement that Mark wrote his Gospel to the Church at Rome. Now turn to Paul's letter to the Romans. Amongst the greetings at the end, he writes: 'Salute Rufus, chosen in the Lord, and his mother and mine' (Romans 16: 13). So in the Roman church there is Rufus, so choice a Christian that he can be called one of God's chosen ones, with a mother so dear to Paul that he can call her his mother in the faith. It may well be that this Rufus is the same Rufus who was the son of Simon of Cyrene . . . " Who brought this boy to the Saviour? Why, father of course. God not only paid His debt, He gave "good measure, pressed down, and running over." He always does.

Study No. 73

## THE THIEF WHO FOUND MORE THAN HE EVER STOLE
(Luke 23: 42–43)

John Wesley once said, "Conversion is a work of God's grace in the heart," and nothing short of this can be conversion. It is a supernatural event resulting from a new vision. This is perfectly represented in the account of the thief's conversion. Against the sombre background of excruciating pain, this poor man had cursed the figure on the central cross. Then an indefinable charm emanated from the Lord. It seemed a balm from heaven, and before its soothing power, the fever cleared from the brain of the sinner.

## He Saw Royalty in Jesus

"Lord," he cried, "remember me when thou comest *into thy kingdom*," and at that precise moment no other person in the world believed in the kingship of Christ. Thirty-three years earlier the wise men had thrilled all Jewry with their announcement of the Messiah's birth. Much had happened since that memorable night. The wise men were no longer present. Later, the rugged disciples had gone forth boldly to proclaim the coming of the Kingdom; but Calvary had ruined their faith. Then, Pilate either in mockery or to annoy his Jewish opponents, had written a title: "This is Jesus of Nazareth, the King of the Jews," and had nailed it to the cross. Yet, apparently, he had no real faith whatsoever. No one believed Jesus to be the King—except the thief, *and he was sure*. How did he find out?

### He Saw Resurrection in Jesus

"Lord, remember me when *thou comest* into thy kingdom." Dead men do not have kingdoms, and it is well for us to remember that the thief saw a dying Jesus who seemed far more likely to inherit a tomb. "No," cried the sinner, "this is not the end of you. Somewhere, sometime, you will rise again and enter into your kingdom. When it happens will you think of me?" This is most remarkable, since no other was so rich in knowledge. The Lord Jesus had often foretold both His death and resurrection but His words were remembered only by His enemies. "This deceiver said he would rise again," and to protect the body, they arranged for a guard to watch the tomb. Many of the people of the nation did not even think of an after-life, for the Sadducees believed death to be the termination of all existence. How then could anybody rise from the dead? The dying thief scorned such views. He knew Jesus would rise again to inherit a great kingdom. How could he be so sure?

### He Saw Redemption in Jesus

"Lord, remember me—ME. I am but a poor despicable sinner, and am unable to take any lamb to the priest. I cannot obey the commands of the law, but it matters not. O Lord, Thou canst be to me both lamb and priest. Thou art able to get me into the kingdom. My sins will not be an insurmountable barrier if Thou wilt be my offering; the law will never sentence me if Thou wilt be my advocate. O Lord, remember me." What vision! We learned these things from the sacred Gospel record; but the thief had no Testament, and yet he knew. Whence came such knowledge? Surely God revealed it to him. Later Simon Peter preached this marvellous message on the day of Pentecost, but the thief saw and understood these things when Peter was running for his life. John had leaned upon the Master's bosom, but the thief discovered more in a few minutes than John learned in three years. How can these things be explained? His triple confession of guilt, need, and faith, prepared the way for the Holy Spirit to illumine his soul.

The sinner opened his heart, and the Saviour opened the door into the Kingdom. "Today, shalt thou be with me, in paradise." "O grave, where is thy victory? O death where is thy sting? Thanks be unto God who giveth us the victory through our Lord Jesus Christ." That day, the thief found more than he had ever stolen. Happy man—and happy shall we be if we make a similar discovery.

> There is a fountain filled with blood,
>     Drawn from Immanuel's veins;
> And sinners plunged beneath that flood
>     Lose all their guilty stains.
>
> The dying thief rejoiced to see
>     That fountain in his day;
> And there may I, though vile as he,
>     Wash all my sins away.

Study No. 74

## THE THIEF WHO LOST MORE THAN HE EVER REGAINED
### (Luke 23 : 41)

I fear that our interpretation of the conversion of the dying thief is a little one-sided. Far be it that we should ever under-estimate the marvel of forgiving grace, but the fact remains that some things are impossible even to the grace of God. We adore the Master, and gratefully remember how His wonderful words brought hope to the heart of this guilty man, but we must recognize that some sad features of the man's record remained unchanged. He had gained immeasurably —he had lost even more.

### He had Lost his Life

We do not know the complete details of the man's life-story. His boyhood days had been spent in some home, but from that place of memory he had drifted on the currents of sin. Vice and folly had been characteristic of his actions, and in company with others of his type, he went from bad to worse. His evil life was destined to lead to his downfall. He was captured, brought to trial, and led to the place of execution. Then, when all seemed lost, the arms of God lifted him from the depths of depression, and the promise of Christ offered eternal assurance. Yet even God could not restore the years he had wasted. The man's life had vanished forever. We have only one life to live, and when it is terminated we shall surely look in retrospect and mourn our failures. A life lost, cannot be regained.

## He had Lost his Opportunities

Perhaps it will not be inexcusable if we imagine for a moment what might have happened had the thief been granted a last-minute stay of execution. He might have become one of the greatest evangelists ever to tell the story of Jesus. Of course, this is mere speculation, but the sincerity of his pardoned soul would yearn for an opportunity of serving the Saviour. If only he could have returned to his former associates in crime, in order to preach the Gospel. Would his ministry have been successful? Who can tell? The truth remains that with his life had gone all his opportunities—except one. He desperately seized what remained, and thus became the only man to speak in defence of the Saviour. He looked across at his brother thief and cried, "Dost not thou fear God, seeing thou art in the same condemnation? and we indeed justly, for we receive the due reward of our deeds: *but this man hath done nothing amiss.*" Well done, thief, we are proud of you! "Ah," he whispers, "if only I had the chance to do more." But there were no further opportunities. Alas, he was too late, and went into eternity empty-handed—except for his Saviour's handclasp.

## He had Lost his Eternal Rewards

We are not given many facts concerning the life hereafter, but among those revealed is one great truth. We shall not all be on the same level of importance in heaven. Our works will be tried in the fires of divine scrutiny. "Every man's work shall be made manifest: for the day shall declare it, because it shall be revealed by fire, and the fire shall try every man's work of what sort it is. If a man's work abide . . . he shall receive a reward. If any man's work shall be burned, he shall suffer loss, but he himself shall be saved, yet so as by fire" (I Corinthians 3: 13–50; Luke 14: 14; Daniel 12: 2–3). Our eternal destiny is settled by faith. Our eternal status is to be determined by the quality of service we render in this life. The thief went home to heaven with nothing but his faith. He had postponed his decision until time for service was non-existent. He gained much when Christ said, "Today, shalt thou be with me," but he had also lost far more than tongue can tell. And let this be a warning to us. Paul urged his fellow-Christians so to live that they would be unashamed at Christ's coming. *Now is the time to remember his words.*

> Must I go—and empty-handed?
> Must I meet my Saviour so?
> Not one soul with which to greet Him?
> Must I empty-handed go?

Oh, ye saints, arouse, be earnest!
Up and work while yet 'tis day;
Ere the night of death o'ertake you,
Strive for souls while yet you may.

## SECTION THREE

### Expository Notes on the Burial of Jesus

**And, behold, there was a man named Joseph, a counsellor; and he was a good man and a just. (The same had not consented to the counsel and deed of them;) he was of Arimathaea, a city of the Jews: who also himself waited for the kingdom of God. This man went unto Pilate, and begged the body of Jesus. And he took it down, and wrapped it in linen, and laid it in a sepulchre that was hewn in stone, wherein never man before was laid (vv. 50-53).**

The small village of Arimathaea was situated about six or seven miles from the city of Jerusalem, and at some time in his life, Joseph, the honourable counsellor lived there. We cannot be sure why, if indeed at all, he had decided to leave the place and to reside in the capital. We know that he was a member of the Sanhedrin, and perhaps his duties in this respect necessitated his living nearer the place of meetings. The fact that he had arranged for his tomb to be hewn out of the rock in or near the city is quoted by most writers as evidence that he was at this time a citizen of Jerusalem.

John 19: 38 says he was a secret disciple of Jesus, but just how this began we have no knowledge. Possibly he had stood on the outskirts of a meeting one day; had heard the Master preaching, and from that moment expectancy filled his soul. He was sure that this Carpenter was the Messiah, and earnestly awaited the time when Jesus would declare Himself to be the king of Israel. He refrained from making public his allegiance to the cause of the Saviour for he feared the repercussions among his colleagues. We do not know all that is implied by the statement: "the same had not consented to the counsel and deed of them." It is certain that this good man did not agree with the other rulers, but whether or not he voted against the motion to crucify the Lord, has not been revealed. Possibly his opposition was only an attitude of his soul, for had he openly opposed the council on this important matter, it could hardly have been said he was a secret disciple of Jesus. It was only after the death of the Lord, that he became ashamed of his cowardice. Then as remorse overwhelmed him, he threw caution to the winds and asked Pilate's permission to bury the Carpenter. John states that in this project he was helped by another counsellor, Nicodemus, who first came to Jesus by night. To their everlasting credit it should be remembered they buried a dead Christ, and had no idea that within a matter of hours, the tombs would be empty again. Believing their action would bring a storm of abuse on their heads, they did what they could for the Lord. Details concerning the embalming of the body are supplied in the other Gospels. With loving care, this man took the body from the cross, wound it in the grave clothes, and gently placed it where, one day, he had planned his own body would rest in peace. Students interested in this great man of a bygone age might find interest in the following suggestions. (1) *His Startling Discovery*. There was a day when for the very first time, he heard the Saviour. Probably that was the most exciting discovery he ever made. The logic of the Preacher's utterances: His amazing miracles; the charm of His personality exceeded anything Joseph had ever known. That night he probably lay awake for hours; he had found the Messiah! (2) His Secret Discipleship. He would need to be very careful. Enemies abounded everywhere, and even some of his colleagues would not hesitate to criticize him if they suspected his allegiance to this Carpenter. He would bide his time, and be ready if ever the Teacher declared Himself, to give whatever support might be possible in the high council meetings of Israel. Then, on the other hand, if anything went wrong, his precautions would safeguard his own future. (3) *His Sincere Devotion*. The Lord was dead! The tragic news was devastating; for now Joseph would never be able to kneel at the Master's feet. Cowardice had deprived him of the greatest privilege ever afforded to man. Then there arose from the depths of this troubled soul a noble resolve to give his tomb to the Lord. Crucified prisoners were seldom, if ever, buried; their bodies were devoured by vultures or dogs. This could never be permitted with the body of the Master. Joseph thought of the tomb which he had prepared against the day of his own decease, and with love filling his heart, knew what he had to do. (4) *His Stubborn Determination*. The Sanhedrin members would hear of his action; their lips would register scorn; their tongues would be vindictive. He could not care less! His Master was dead; but at least, he himself was very much alive. The shame of the silent years would be partially, at least, blotted out by a somewhat belated confession of faith. He went to Pilate; then he found a new friend in Nicodemus, and together, they carried the precious burden from Calvary, and gently laid it in the new tomb. That was the best piece of work they ever did. (5) *His Supreme Delight*. The Lord was alive! It could not be true; it was impossible! Surely, as the rumours began to circulate, the thrill increased in his soul; ultimately he ran to the tomb to see for himself what had transpired. The grave clothes were meticulously in order; they had fallen flat; the folds of linen were still in their original convolutions. It would be impossible to place clothes in that position unless they were wound around a body; and quite impossible to remove the body without disarranging the coverings. This was a miracle. The moment came when with 500 brethren he too saw the Lord. It was a great day. He smiled! Jesus knew now that finally, he had taken his stand; the whole world would know his heart belonged to his Master.

# The Twenty-Fourth Chapter of Luke

THEME: *The Resurrection of the Lord Jesus.*

OUTLINE:

      I. A Glad Announcement. Verses 1–12
      II. A Gracious Appearance. Verses 13–35
      III. A Great Astonishment. Verses 36–48
      IV. A Glorious Ascension. Verses 49–53

### SECTION ONE

*Expository Notes on the Lord's Appearance to the Women at the
Tomb*

> Now upon the first day of the week, very early in the morning, they
> came unto the sepulchre, bringing the spices which they had prepared,
> and certain others with them. And they found the stone rolled away
> from the sepulchre. And they entered in, and found not the body of
> the Lord Jesus. And it came to pass, as they were much perplexed
> thereabout, behold, two men stood by them in shining garments (vv.
> 1–4).

Students know that all four Gospels describe the resurrection of
the Lord, and that they differ in their accounts. There are more
apparent discrepancies at this point of the Gospel story than at any
other. Matthew 28:2 says: "And behold, there was a great earthquake: for *the Angel of the Lord* descended from heaven, and came
and rolled back the stone, and sat upon it. His countenance was like
lightning, and his garment white as snow." Mark 16:5 says: "And
entering into the sepulchre, they saw *a young man* sitting on the right
side, clothed in a long white garment, and they were affrighted".
Luke 24:4 says: ". . . *two men* stood by them in shining garments."
John 20:11–12 says: "But Mary . . . seeth *two angels* in white, one
at the head, and the other at the feet, where the body of Jesus had
lain." At first glance this appears to be confusing, and authors in all
ages have had difficulty in solving the problems supplied by these
versions. Probably the wisest thing to be said is that it would take
all four accounts to provide the complete story of the events which
happened on that memorable morning. It must be remembered that

none of the Gospel writers was an eye-witness; all their accounts were second-hand. These men wrote what they had been told, and four or five people can describe the same event and mention details undetected by others. The difference in the number of angels is not really a problem for one might have been remembered as the spokesman. Some of the other details can be explained by the fact that all the women did not arrive at the tomb together. We know for example, that Mary came; that she ran to tell her story to the apostles; that Peter and John ran to the sepulchre; that later, Mary, who would have been unable to keep stride with the running men, came herself to stand there. The accounts described by the writers of the Gospels might have been the descriptions of a sequence of events. The only thing of superb and thrilling importance is the fact that the tomb was empty. God had presented the world with a diamond of incalculable worth. Who cares whether the jewel box was lined with black velvet, blue velvet, or any other kind? Must we argue about the length and thickness of the ribbon around the box? When we examine this great treasure, when we look more closely, the wrappings fade into insignificance.

> And as they were afraid, and bowed down their faces to the earth, they said unto them, Why seek ye the living among the dead? He is not here, but is risen: remember how he spake unto you when he was yet in Galilee, Saying, The Son of man must be delivered into the hands of sinful men, and be crucified, and the third day rise again. And they remembered his words, And returned from the sepulchre, and told all these things unto the eleven, and to all the rest (vv. 5-9).

According to Luke 23: 55-56, certain women from Galilee had ascertained where the body of the Lord had been placed; then because of the Jewish restrictions regarding defilement, they stayed away from the tomb during the Sabbath. They used the time to prepare the necessary spices with which to embalm His body. The Jewish Sabbath, it will be remembered began at six o'clock in the evening, and therefore for all practical purposes, the day had virtually ended when the first signs of dawn began to spread across the sky. Bringing their spices with them, the women hurried to the tomb only to discover that something had gone wrong! Tombs were sealed by a large round stone rolled into a prepared groove across the mouth of the cave-like opening. This heavy stone had been rolled back; someone apparently had desecrated the tomb! As dread, misgivings, and a little anger filled their souls, suddenly they were aware of the shining ones. When the frightened women tried to hide their faces, the reassuring words of the angels dispelled their fears. They were told to remember what the Lord had often told them.

There is danger that in seeking new revelations of truth, we neglect what we have already received. If we remembered all the Lord Jesus promised, we would never be surprised by anything. Remembering the Master's words, the women hurried to tell the disciples what had happened. We do not know how many were in their audience. The eleven disciples were there, but others were also present to hear the glad tidings. It will be remembered that later, five hundred people saw the risen Lord at one time, and although this number had decreased by the day of Pentecost, there were still one hundred and twenty people awaiting the fulfilment of the Lord's promise.

**It was Mary Magdalene, and Joanna, and Mary the mother of James, and other women that were with them, which told these things unto the apostles. And their words seemed to them as idle tales, and they believed them not. Then arose Peter, and ran unto the sepulchre; and stooping down, he beheld the linen clothes laid by themselves, and departed, wondering in himself at that which was come to pass (vv. 10–12).**

The women whose names are mentioned were among the most faithful of the Lord's followers; the unnamed women were probably others who had followed the Master throughout His travels. Perhaps, Luke was never told all the names of these people, but if he were, he considered the inclusion of their names unnecessary. The word translated *idle tales* is *leeros*. This according to Thayer means *nonsense*. Plummer states: ". . . *the word is applied in medical language to the wild talk of the sick in delirium.*" The idea is therefore suggested that momentarily at least, the disciples considered these women to be emotionally unbalanced; a little sick in the mind; speaking words unsupported by fact. The fourth Gospel relates how two disciples ran to the sepulchre; Luke is content to speak only of Simon Peter. That Simon was there at all is something which deserves consideration. He had denied his Lord, and was very much ashamed of his own cowardice. It was difficult to face his brethren, but face them he did, and this proved his sincerity. When he arrived at the sepulchre to see the graveclothes lying in meticulous order, the sight filled him with amazement. John saw and believed; Peter could only see and wonder. When Peter had been somewhat arrogant, John had leaned on the Master's bosom; when Peter cursed; John had been keeping vigil. Dedication begat perception; self-assurance placed cataracts on the eyes of Peter's understanding.

## HOMILIES

Study No. 75

### The Women Who Remembered

It was really on the morning of the first Christian Sunday, when a few women left their homes and sorrowfully walked toward the tomb of Jesus. Their Master had been crucified, but when His body had been laid to rest, their expectations were buried with Him. They had been so sure that God had sent Him; so certain that it was only a matter of time before God would rend the heavens to come to His assistance. They had prayed in vain; they had wasted their time; everything had been disastrous for their cause and their Christ. Yet they loved His memory, and because love never dies, they planned to embalm His body. The story of the events which took place on that memorable day has been preserved immortally in Luke's Gospel. The sequence of their thrilling experience is set forth in order. *They came*—verse one; *they found*—verse two; *they entered*—verse three; *they were much perplexed*—verse four; *they were afraid*—verse five; *they remembered*—verse eight; *they returned*—verse nine; *they testified*—verse nine. The account seems to revolve around one outstanding statement—*"And they remembered!"*

### THEY REMEMBERED THEIR PROBLEM—*but forgot His promise*

The angels said unto them, "Why seek ye the living among the dead? He is not here, but is risen: remember how he spake unto you, when he was yet in Galilee . . ." Yes, it was true. Often during the eventful years of Christ's ministry, He emphasized the fact He would be delivered into the hands of sinful men and be crucified. Yet never did He announce His impending death, unless at the same time He predicted the glorious fact that He would rise again. Unfortunately, His followers had poor memories. They saw evil men; the cross; the nails; they heard the blasphemous sneers, and knew the frustration of disappointment within their hearts. Things had gone wrong; their prayers had not been answered; their future was bleak and uninviting. They had no idea why God had permitted these wretched things to happen. Probably He knew what He was doing, but nobody else did! The Master's body needed to be embalmed, and the requisite materials had to be obtained. With meticulous care the women attended to these details; they remembered, too, the restrictions imposed upon them by the laws of Moses. Yes, everything was in readiness; they had remembered all the details—except the most important. He had promised to rise again. Their fears; their preparation; their coming would be in vain. Throughout their time of sorrow, the sun had been shining; but forgetfulness had placed shutters over their windows.

## THEY REMEMBERED HIS WORDS—*but lacked His wisdom*

Suddenly, as the angels revived their memories, these delightful women recalled what the Lord had said. Yes, it was true that away in Galilee, Jesus had spoken about tragedy and triumph. He had certainly uttered these things, but even now the promise seemed fantastic. It sounded wonderful, but surely, those promises could not have been fulfilled. "And they went out quickly and fled from the sepulchre; for they trembled and were amazed; neither said they anything to any man; for they were afraid" (Mark 16: 8). We cannot tell how long unbelief was permitted to fill their hearts; ultimately, it was banished for ever. They remembered the Master's words, but failed to believe them. They might have believed anything else, but this matter was personal. Could God have been forgetful during the hours of their greatest sorrow? Could order be begotten by chaos? Could God make all things—even these things—work together for their good? It sounded wonderful, but wishful-thinking might fill their hearts with false expectancy! They were foolish but we can hardly blame them, for we have made the same mistake. We are sure our way is best; that God should endorse all we decide. Sometimes when this does not happen, our hopes are buried; our God has failed!

## THEY REMEMBERED THEIR TASK—*and proclaimed His triumph*

The first human preachers of the resurrection were women! The first person aware of the coming of Christ was the woman to whom the promise was given; the first one with whom she shared her secret was her cousin Elizabeth. Throughout the Gospel story there is no place where any woman either said or did anything evil in regard to Jesus. They loved Him; served Him; listened to Him, followed Him, but they never criticized Him, opposed Him; nor did anything afterward, to be regretted. If men had emulated the example set by the women, they would have been infinitely wiser than they were. Recovering from their initial dread, ". . . they departed quickly from the sepulchre with fear and great joy; and did run to bring his disciples word" (Matthew 28: 8). They had news to announce, but as the testimony echoed through the room, ". . . their words seemed to the men as idle tales, and they believed them not" (Luke 24: 11). Those women were gloriously insistent; they seemed to have known

the slogan: "If at first you don't succeed, try, try again." When a
woman believes she should be heard, *she will be heard!* Slowly the
doubts began to disappear; tragedy was followed by triumph; sadness by songs; despair by glorious deliverance. Their Master was
alive! God had surely known what He was doing. If only they had
remembered earlier, their burdens would have been lighter. When
we are confronted by a Calvary, it is better to proclaim Christ's
triumph than to prolong our tears.

## SECTION TWO

### *Expository Notes on the Disciples' Walk to Emmaus*

**And behold, two of them went that same day to a village called
Emmaus which was from Jerusalem about threescore furlongs. And
they talked together of all these things which had happened (vv. 13-14).**

Probably this verse has caused more discussion than any other
verse in the Gospel of Luke for since the inception of the church,
religious leaders have speculated regarding the identity of these
travellers. Luke, as we shall see, discloses the fact that one of the
two disciples was named *Cleopas,* but the name of the second traveller remained a mystery throughout the centuries. Some writers suggest that as John refused to name himself as the disciple who leaned
upon the Lord's bosom, Luke declined to admit he was the companion of Cleopas. Yet, however interesting the suggestion appears
to be, writers agree there is no conclusive evidence to support the
idea. From time to time other authors suggested that Simon Peter,
or certain of the apostles accompanied Cleopas, but always, after
lengthy and animated discussions, the problem returned whence it
came, into obscurity. There is another possibility which seems more
logical than most of the ideas expressed by the commentators. John
19: 25 says: "Now there stood by the cross of Jesus his mother, and
his mother's sister, Mary the wife of Cleophas, and Mary Magdalene."
Luke says that one of the two travellers to Emmaus was named
Cleopas. Godet suggests that these two names are different; that the
one comes from a Jewish background; the other from a Greek. Thus,
on what appears a very flimsy foundation, he makes the suggestion
that the second traveller might have been a Gentile; a proselyte who
had attended the feast. Yet when we remember that Luke, a Gentile
himself, was writing his Gospel for Gentile readers; that to make
his message intelligible he would spell names in a way his readers
could understand and appreciate, it is difficult to avoid the conclusion
that the woman present at the cross might have been the wife of the

Emmaus traveller. Obviously, now that the feast had ended, these people were returning home, and it is extremely unlikely—if they were men—that they would occupy a house without their wives. Certain writers therefore believe Cleophas and his wife were returning to their home in Emmaus when the Lord joined them on the road. Doubtless, readers will consider the evidence and form their own conclusions. The exact location of the village of Emmaus has always been in dispute; we only know it was a place about seven or eight miles from Jerusalem.

And it came to pass, that, while they communed together and reasoned, Jesus himself drew near, and went with them. But their eyes were holden that they should not know him. And he said unto them, What manner of communications are these that ye have one to another, as ye walk, and are sad. And the one of them, whose name was Cleopas, answering said unto him, Art thou only a stranger in Jerusalem, and hast not known the things which are come to pass there in these days? And he said unto them, What things? And they said unto him, Concerning Jesus of Nazareth, which was a prophet mighty in deed and word before God and all the people: And how the chief priests and our rulers delivered him to be condemned to death, and have crucified him. But we trusted that it had been he which should have redeemed Israel: and beside all this, today is the third day since these things were done (vv. 15–21).

Mark 16: 22 adds the significant detail that *"He appeared in another form unto two of them as they went into the country."* He came in disguise, and this surely indicates a change in His physical capabilities. Prior to His death the Lord would have been unable to disguise Himself so easily; now the mortal had put on immortality, and what before might have been difficult, could now be performed with ease. The Lord deliberately hid His identity when He joined the travellers. Their faces were sad and strained, therefore the Lord enquired concerning the cause of their troubles. The fact that He appeared to be ignorant of current events nonplussed them. Alford translates the question in verse 18 as follows: "Dost thou lodge alone at Jerusalem?" Major translates: "Are thou that one individual who sojournest at Jerusalem—that one person who does not know?" These disciples could not believe that any man present in the city could have remained unaware of what had transpired. This Stranger surely either had a very long sleep, or had been a recluse. To be unaware of what had taken place, was beyond comprehension.

Yea, and certain women also of our company made us astonished, which were early at the sepulchre; And when they found not his body, they came, saying, that they had also seen a vision of angels, which said that he was alive. And certain of them which were with us went to the sepulchre, and found it even so as the women had said: but him they saw not (vv. 22-24).

We are reminded again that the first witnesses of the resurrection were women. Sometimes, women had more discernment than men; often they had more brains! Behind His disguise the Lord smiled as He listened to this outburst from the two whom He loved so much. Yet how wise were His methods. Had He revealed His identity immediately, they would have rejoiced in His presence but their problem would have remained. They would have continued asking, Why did God allow Him to die? Why this and why that? They were sick in their souls, and whilst the Lord had been able to heal the body instantly, it took more time and different methods to heal souls.

Then he said unto them, O fools, and slow of heart to believe all that the prophets have spoken: Ought not Christ to have suffered these things, and to enter into his glory? And beginning at Moses and all the prophets, he expounded unto them in all the scriptures the things concerning himself (vv. 25-27).

Obviously the Lord was well acquainted with His own word; the two disciples going to Emmaus were privileged to hear the greatest sermon ever preached. (1) It was *expository* for it was based on the law and the prophets. (2) It was *explanatory* for the preacher explained how it was all fulfilled in Jesus. (3) It was *emancipatory* for it completely lifted them from the depths of depression. The Lord probably spoke of the sacrifices as commanded by God, and in the course of His exposition explained the predictions of Isaiah (Isaiah 53). If that sermon had been reported in detail, the document would be of incalculable worth.

And they drew nigh unto the village whither they went; and he made as though he would have gone further. But they constrained him, saying, Abide with us: for it is toward evening, and the day is far spent. And he went in to tarry with them. And it came to pass as he sat at meat with them, he took bread, and blessed it, and brake, and gave to them. And their eyes were opened, and they knew him; and he vanished out of their sight. And they said one to another, Did not our heart burn within us, while he talked with us by the way, and while he opened to us the scriptures? (vv. 28-32).

The Emmaus travellers had never known the time to pass so quickly; they had never considered the journey so short. When the lights of the village began to appear across the fields, they were amazed, but when the Stranger wished them good night and continued His journey, their amazement turned to disappointment. They were glad to be home, but they could have walked all night to listen to the unfolding of the Word of God. Then one of the two suggested they invite the Stranger to supper, and the events which followed the acceptance of that invitation made history. As they sat at the table, the Visitor took the loaf of bread and, breaking it before their eyes, blessed it. Probably they had seen Another breaking bread in just the same manner; possibly they saw also the wounds in His hands, and in the moments which followed, they recognized their Master. When their problems had been solved, and their spiritual ailments cured, nothing remained to prevent the Master revealing His identity. "He was known unto them in the breaking of the bread." Then they remembered the thrill of listening to His exposition of truth; they recalled how their hearts responded to His message and knew they had been stupid in not knowing earlier that only the Lord could have talked as He had talked. Then they jumped to their feet; they had news to tell; and furthermore the telling of it could not wait until the morning.

And they rose up the same hour, and returned to Jerusalem, and found the eleven gathered together, and them that were with them, Saying, The Lord is risen indeed, and hath appeared to Simon. And they told what things were done in the way, and how he was known of them in breaking of bread (vv. 33-35).

They hurried along the darkened roads to the city and although they arrived late at night, they found the disciples gathered together. What they expected to be news, was already known to the followers of the Lord; He had been seen by Simon Peter. (See also I Corinthians 15: 5.) Mary, by this time, would have informed Peter that Jesus desired to meet him, but whether or not Peter was willing to respond is open to debate. He probably felt ashamed of himself, and Jesus found it necessary to search for him. This fact was being discussed when the Emmaus travellers walked into the room. When they related the events that had taken place that evening, and how the risen Lord had been at their dinner table, the amazement of the disciples beggared description. Could all this be true or were their imaginations beginning to run riot? And then, suddenly, their conversation ceased; a strange new experience hushed their spirits. Behold, the Master was there.

HOMILIES

Study No. 76

### The Lord Jesus in Disguise!

The Emmaus story is among the best-known of the Scriptures, but our familiarity with its details is apt to interfere with our understanding of its more serious teaching. Four questions are suggested by this stimulating account. (1) Why were the disciples going to Emmaus? It is worthy of note that apart from their contact with the Saviour, the journey was a waste of time. Their purpose in visiting Emmaus was unfulfilled, for they returned almost immediately. (2) Why did they fail to recognize the Lord Jesus? (3) Why did they enjoy the Stranger's sermon when its opening statements charged them with great folly? (4) Why did they return at such a late hour of the night, and thus prove the inadvisability of their walk to Emmaus?

### The Strange Road

Calvary had completely ruined the hopes of the disciples. These delightful people had followed Christ because they honestly believed He would establish the Messianic kingdom. Every day they witnessed new manifestations of power, and never questioned the imminence of His coronation. When He surrendered to His enemies and was led forth to be nailed to a cross, their hearts turned to stone. Weary and despondent, they began making plans for the future, and ultimately two of the company decided to return home. Their walk into the country took them away from the cross; their backs were toward the sanctuary, and every step was one taken in the wrong direction. The Emmaus road has had many travellers, for embittered men have often made a contemporary Judas an excuse for backsliding. In the greater issues of life, the Emmaus road is a cul-de-sac and not a highway.

### The Strange Redeemer

"And it came to pass, that, while they communed together and reasoned, Jesus himself drew near, and went with them. But their eyes were holden that they should not know him" (Luke 24: 15–16). Had Christ revealed Himself immediately, and commanded their return to Jerusalem, they would have obeyed instantly; but their intimate difficulties would have remained. There was very much more at stake than their return to the holy city. Recurring problems had ruined their peace of mind, and a strange unrest had conquered their hearts. In order to deal with these hidden troubles, the Lord Jesus disguised Himself and drew near. "He appeared in another form" (Mark 16: 12). And thus He was able to handle the difficult task of revealing to two headstrong disciples the fact that they were capable of making mistakes.

### The Strange Reaction

His sermon had an inauspicious beginning, and could never be a pattern for ministerial students. He began by calling His audience "fools". Yet in some mysterious fashion His message was delivered in a delightful way that made their hearts burn. We believe literature would have been enriched immeasurably had Christ's sermon been preserved for posterity. He systematically expounded in all the Scriptures, the things concerning Himself, and His utterances cheered their drooping spirits. They had never heard such a message, for it suggested the cross would became a beacon from which radiant happiness would shine out to a world. They had been wrong in all their conclusions. The Lord Jesus touched the trouble-spot in their agitated souls; but without His disguise, this would have been impossible.

### The Strange Return

When Christ accepted their invitation to supper, the scene was set for their greatest surprise. As He broke the bread, "they knew Him by the print of the nails in His hands." Then their plans were instantly changed; they desired to rejoin the brethren. The loneliness of the road, and the dangers of the night, were unable to keep them in Emmaus, for "they rose up the same hour and returned to Jerusalem." The darkness of their night of sorrow had given place to a dawn, and they desired to spend the new day in fellowship with the people of God. And as it was, so it is. Man is never so stupid as when he journeys away from the cross. A tent at Calvary is better than a palace in Emmaus.

## SECTIONS THREE AND FOUR

### Expository Notes on Christ's Evidence of His own Resurrection

And as they thus spake, Jesus himself stood in the midst of them, and saith unto them, Peace be unto you. But they were terrified and affrighted, and supposed that they had seen a spirit. And he said unto them, Why are ye troubled? and why do thoughts arise in your hearts? Behold my hands and my feet, that it is I myself: handle me and see; for a spirit hath not flesh and bones, as ye see me have. And

**when he had thus spoken, he shewed them his hands and his feet (vv. 36-40).**

There is nothing startling nor contradictory about the reaction of the disciples to the sudden appearance of the Lord in their midst. It is true they had just related the fact of His appearance to Simon, but His sudden and totally unexpected coming to stand before their eyes, frightened them and momentarily at least, they were exceedingly troubled. Even this testifies to the reality of the resurrection; this was no figment of the imagination; no hallucination. Whatever the critics may say concerning this event, one thing is certainly evident—*Christ was there*. Faith is exceedingly excellent, but within the kingdom of God, blind faith is not always expected of believers. The claims of God in Christ stand the test of the closest scrutiny, and this in all probability accounts for the continuing progress of the glorious Gospel. There are people and movements that suggest the resurrection of Jesus was only spiritual; that the body of the Lord either was transported to some unknown realm or that it suffered the decomposition that always follows death. How they harmonize their teachings with the scripture now under consideration, remains an insoluble problem. This was no mirage; these men were not invited to handle a sunbeam! There was substance; there was tissue in that form. The body of the Master had become resplendent with the garments of immortality. If only men would sincerely examine the claims of Jesus, most of them would exclaim, "My Lord and my God."

**And while they yet believed not for joy, and wondered, he said unto them, Have ye here any meat? And they gave him a piece of a broiled fish, and of an honeycomb. And he took it, and did eat before them (vv. 41-43).**

While the disciples still struggled with their astonishment and fear, the Lord took the necessary measures to remove for all time every vestige of doubt from their minds. He asked for food and ate, not because His new body needed sustenance, but because their faith needed stimulation. He ate food in order to feed those who watched. But, and this is important, *He did eat*, and that food passed into the organs of His body. We have not been told all the details connected with the immortality which must become the eternal inheritance of the saints, but this passage of Scripture proves we are not thinking about theoretical principles. As Job long ago said, "For I know that my redeemer liveth, and that he shall stand at the latter day upon the earth. And though after my skin, worms destroy this body, *yet in my flesh shall I see God*" (Job 19: 25-26).

> And he said unto them, These are the words which I spake unto you, while I was yet with you, that all things must be fulfilled, which were written in the law of Moses, and in the prophets, and in the Psalms, concerning me. Then opened he their understanding, that they might understand the scriptures. And said unto them, Thus it is written, and thus it behoved Christ to suffer, and to rise from the dead the third day: And that repentance and remission of sins should be preached in his name among all nations, beginning at Jerusalem. And ye are witnesses of these things (vv. 44–48).

It is significant that once again the Lord directs the attention of His followers to the scriptures. His claim to have been the subject of the writings of the prophets; the fulfilment of all their predictions; was the corroboration of things He had expressed many times earlier: He knew also that soon He would be returning to Heaven; the importance therefore which He placed on the written word was meant to make an indelible impression upon their minds. All they needed to know had been expressed in the Scriptures. The Holy Spirit would become their Teacher; He would guide them into the truth and recall to their minds the things they had heard from His lips. They were to announce their message throughout the world; they would become prophets in their own right.

> And behold, I send the promise of my Father upon you: but tarry ye in the city of Jerusalem, until ye be endued with power from on high (v. 49).

The evangelizing of a lost world demanded more than willing men with a knowledge of the written word. Soundness of doctrine would be nothing unless the Gospel were proclaimed with living power from a clean heart. Even the soundest of fundamental teachings could become expressions of dogma; even the most sincere preachers might only be heresy hunters. Unless the sermon first stirred the heart of the preacher, the audience would remain unmoved; unless the doctrines of grace first bore the fruits of the Spirit in the heart of the messenger, his hearers would probably consider him to be a hypocrite. The divine order appears to be: First—*the promise,* secondly—*the power,* thirdly—*the preaching.* The preacher should first learn to kneel in his upper room, and only then to stand in his pulpit.

> And he led them out as far as to Bethany, and he lifted up his hands, and blessed them. And it came to pass, while he blessed them, he was parted from them, and carried up into heaven. And they worshipped him, and returned to Jerusalem with great joy: And were continually in the temple praising and blessing God. Amen (vv. 50–53).

His earthly mission accomplished, the Lord led His faithful followers toward the oft-visited Mount of Olives, and there, overlooking the home He loved, He lifted His hands to impart His farewell blessing. He was about to begin his work as the great High Priest of His people. His followers were to launch a crusade against the world-wide citadels of evil. Some of His disciples would lay down their lives; others would press toward distant continents, but some day all would see the realization of their dreams. Therefore, with confidence, He blessed them, and as His benediction rested upon their souls, defying the laws of gravity, He slowly went home. It was fitting He should go in this way. Yet the end of the story was not a climax; it was a new beginning; it was a thrilling challenge; a soul-stirring commission. Instead of the sadness which might have been expected to overwhelm their souls, a fierce joy surged through their beings, and with dancing feet and singing hearts they almost ran toward the city. The future was bright with prospect and hope; their Master would still be with them; anything could be possible. Luke's Gospel began in the temple; it ended in the same place. It began with one priest in the Sanctuary; it ended with a lot of people standing or kneeling in the presence of God. It began with one old man who lost his voice because of his unbelief; it ended with people crying aloud for joy because they had found a faith which thrilled their souls. *Luke's Thrilling Gospel* supplied the story which joined the beginning and the end. We are indebted to the beloved physician; he did a great job both as a doctor and an author.

## HOMILIES

Study No. 77

### THE END OF THE STORY

Some of the most popular books are those which never end! The author weaves his web of enchantment around the readers by unfolding his tale in such a way that when one episode ends, another begins. The readers thrilled by what they have just read, thereafter anticipate the author's next book, for they are anxious to read again of the character whose image and exploits can never be forgotten. If this be the standard of greatness; if this be the hallmark of success, then Luke was one of the first writers to master the art. His thrilling story of the Christ enchants us. We follow him through the countryside of Galilee; we visit the greenhill, we stand amazed before the risen Lord, but when Luke writes his final chapter, we are left with the stimulating feeling that this is not the end. Our glorious Lord has finished one exploit; but He will be back. Soon, there will be another book; soon our author will have more news about the Hero. This end is but a beginning; there is much more to tell.

### Great Peace

"And as they thus spake, Jesus himself stood in the midst of them, and saith unto them, Peace be unto you" (Luke 24: 36).

*Luke's Thrilling Gospel* is nearing completion; the tension has been increasing, but when the cause of God appeared to be in jeopardy, Jesus rose again triumphantly to say, "Peace be unto you." Thus the sad, and almost terrifying end of a story was transformed into a gloriously thrilling beginning. New vistas of possibility spread out into the future, the disciples were to go forth with a new message. Instead of being overwhelmed with shame, they would lift their heads high with a justifiable pride; their achievements would astonish the world. Instead of sorrow they had peace; their hitherto storm-tossed hearts were now filled with matchless tranquillity. They had to tell their story to a waiting world so that what had happened to them could happen to millions of others. How could this be done? They had no academic degrees; the time was short; how could they succeed? To preach when their Master was with them, was one thing; to preach when He was far away would be quite another. How could they succeed?

### Great Preaching

"Then opened he their understanding, that they might understand the scriptures, and said unto them, Thus it is written, and thus it behoved Christ to suffer, and to rise from the dead the third day: and that repentance and remission of sins should be preached in his name among all nations, beginning at Jerusalem" (Luke 24: 45–47). Thus did He demonstrate for all to know that preaching is quite useless unless it is based upon the written word of God. "He expounded unto them in all the scriptures the things concerning himself" (Luke 24: 27). Twice therefore within the scope of his final chapter Luke explained how Christ expounded the truth. First He *Comforted* them; then he *Challenged* them, and finally He *Commissioned* them. "And ye are witnesses of these things." They could not succeed in their mission until they were impregnated with the word of God. Academic experience would be of great worth to the preachers of the new message; a knowledge of human nature would be of invaluable assistance as they grappled with the crushing problems of life, but above all else, they would need to use the sword of the Spirit if they were to do valiantly on spiritual battle fields.

## Great Power

"And behold I send the promise of my Father upon you: but tarry ye in the city of Jerusalem, until ye be endued with power from on high" (Luke 24: 49). The church and the Trinity were thus linked together in the thrilling cause of evangelism. The Father's promise; the Son's plans; the holy Spirit's power were to unite in making unlearned disciples the most invincible weapons ever to be held by the hand of God. Even increasing knowledge of the Scriptures would be inadequate to undermine the citadels of evil. Thrilling powers of oratory would excite great appreciation in the minds of listening audiences, but when oratory and a knowledge of the Word of God combined, then the preacher would become a prophet. However, even then, he would fall short of what would be required to overcome the powers of wickedness. There never had been, and there never would be any effective substitute for the power of the Holy Spirit. It was true that the world was waiting for the sunrise; it was true that millions of people were dying in their sin, nevertheless it was essential that the disciples return to the city and wait for the enduement which alone could make them invincible. A very sincere enthusiasm might have suggested immediate services in the streets; a compelling desire to preach might have suggested lengthy revival meetings, but those services would have ended in frustration and failure. They needed the power of the Holy Spirit; and the Holy Spirit needed them. And as it was, so it is today. Preaching without prayer is vain babbling; yet preaching in the power of the Holy Spirit is God's weapon against evil; it has always pleased the Lord, by the foolishness of preaching to save them that believe.

## Great Praise

"And they worshipped him, and returned to Jerusalem with great joy: and were continually in the temple, praising and blessing God. Amen" (Luke 24: 52-53). Yes, it was the end of the story, but only the beginning of the author's series. This was the end of volume one; volume two was already in production. Their Lord was alive; their Master was wonderful. (1) *They worshipped Him.* (2) *They witnessed for Him.* (3) *They worked for Him.* (4) *They would wait for Him until He returned.* They watched as He ascended into the sky, and then hurried back to the city to share their news with others. It was natural that they should congregate in the temple for it was there they had often listened to Him during those momentous days prior to the Cross. They looked into each other's faces, they gripped each other's hands; their testimonies stirred the souls of all who listened. Everything had changed; their Lord was alive. He had promised to send the Holy Spirit to control their actions; He had promised to accompany them as they went forth to preach the everlasting Gospel. Yes, every-thing had changed. What had already happened was but the first episode in a great drama; future chapters promised excitement; thrills, triumphs, blessing. When they thought about it, they praised the Lord. Life was just beginning.

# INDEX OF HOMILIES

# *Books by Ivor Powell*

**BIBLE CAMEOS**
Vivid biographies of 80 Bible characters graphically portrayed. Full of helps and hints for sermon preparation.
ISBN 0-8254-3515-3                  192 pp.                  paperback

**BIBLE GEMS**
Preachers will enjoy an ample supply of sermon starters, teachers will find many illustrations, and laymen will be led to the deep truths of God's Word as Powell traces 80 various Bible themes.
ISBN 0-8254-3527-7                  176 pp.                  paperback

**BIBLE HIGHWAYS**
This volume transports the reader through a variety of over 40 themes found in the Scriptures and then provides over 90 rich illustrations to communicate the message effectively. *Bible Highways* contains valuable material for the pastor for the pastor or teacher.
ISBN 0-8254-3521-8                  176 pp.                  paperback

**BIBLE NAMES OF CHRIST**
A unique presentation of 80 short studies on the names and titles of Jesus Christ. The simplicity and freshness of these mini-messages will provide enlightening devotional studies for believers and many outlines and illustrations for teachers and preachers.
ISBN 0-8254-3530-7                  176 pp.                  paperback

**BIBLE PINNACLES**
Over 80 graphic character sketches, pivotal incidents, miracles, and parables. Excellent homiletical helps.
ISBN 0-8254-3516-1                  192 pp.                  paperback

## BIBLE TREASURES

The author uses 80 Bible character studies to provide for us treasures of truest worth from the world's richest storehouse.

ISBN 0-8254-3518-8          182 pp.          paperback

## BIBLE WINDOWS

A rich collection of over 80 carefully chosen illustrations to better communicate the gospel message. These stories will bring to life the key points of any gospel message, enhancing the ministry of the faithful pastor and teacher.

ISBN 0-8254-3522-6          180 pp.          paperback

## DAVID: His Life and Times

David, the "sweet psalmist of Israel," comes alive in the unique and refreshing manner typical of Ivor Powell's writings. The author provides a biographical commentary on David's life and times as well as devotional studies, outlines, and illustrations for teachers and preachers.

ISBN 0-8254-3532-3          448 pp.          paperback

## WHAT IN THE WORLD WILL HAPPEN NEXT?

A scripturally sound work which effectively describes the important prophetic events yet to be fulfilled. The book offers a wealth of material in the author's popular style on this fascinating and increasingly studied subject.

ISBN 0-8254-3524-2          .176 pp.          paperback

## DISTINCTIVELY DIFFERENT COMMENTARIES SERIES

In an exciting, different style, Powell presents vivid illustrations, and alliterated outlines which blend exposition and rich spiritual insight. To read and study his writings is to embark on a thrilling journey. Full of practical teaching and preaching helps.

### MATTHEW'S MAJESTIC GOSPEL

ISBN 0-8254-3525-0          526 pp.          hardcover

### MARK'S SUPERB GOSPEL

ISBN 0-8254-3523-4          432 pp.          hardcover

**LUKE'S THRILLING GOSPEL**

ISBN 0-8254-3513-7          508 pp.                    hardcover

**JOHN'S WONDERFUL GOSPEL**

ISBN 0-8254-3514-5          446 pp.                    hardcover

**THE AMAZING ACTS**

ISBN 0-8254-3526-9          478 pp.                    hardcover

**THE EXCITING EPISTLE TO THE EPHESIANS**

ISBN 0-8254-3537-4          304 pp.                    hardcover

Available at your local Christian bookseller, or:

**KREGEL** Publications
P. O. Box 2607, Grand Rapids, MI 49501